INTEGRITY, RISK AND ACCOU

The global economy is yet to recover from
(GFC). In particular many national econon
grams that are a direct result of the toxic e   ....cnts, regulatory
agencies, international organisations, media commentators, finance industry organisations and professionals, academics and affected citizens have offered partial explanations
for what has occurred. Some of these actors have sought to introduce legislative and other
regulatory initiatives to improve operational standards in capital markets. However, the
exposure post-GFC of the scandal surrounding the manipulation over many years of the
London Interbank Offered Rate (Libor) highlighted that the most important obstacles to
counter the destructive potential of our global finance system are normative not technical.
Regulating the culture of the finance sector is one of the greatest challenges facing contemporary society.

This edited volume brings together leading professionals, regulators and academics with
knowledge of how cultural forces shape integrity, risk and accountability in capital markets.
The book will be of benefit not only to industry, regulatory and academic communities
whose focus is upon financial markets and professionals. It is of value to any person or
organisation interested in how the cultural underpinnings of the finance sector shape how
capital markets actually operate and are regulated. It is a stark lesson of history that financial crises will occur. As national economies become ever more inter-connected and interdependent under conditions of global financial capitalism, it becomes ever more important
to know how cultural and other normative forces might be adjusted to militate against the
effects of future disasters.

Integrity, Risk and Accountability in Capital Markets

Regulating Culture

Edited by

Justin O'Brien

and

George Gilligan

·HART·
PUBLISHING
OXFORD AND PORTLAND, OREGON
2013

Published in the United Kingdom by Hart Publishing Ltd
16C Worcester Place, Oxford, OX1 2JW
Telephone: +44 (0)1865 517530
Fax: +44 (0)1865 510710
E-mail: mail@hartpub.co.uk
Website: http://www.hartpub.co.uk

Published in North America (US and Canada) by
Hart Publishing
c/o International Specialized Book Services
920 NE 58th Avenue, Suite 300
Portland, OR 97213-3786
USA
Tel: +1 503 287 3093 or toll-free: (1) 800 944 6190
Fax: +1 503 280 8832
E-mail: orders@isbs.com
Website: http://www.isbs.com

British Library Cataloguing in Publication Data

Data Available

ISBN: 978-1-84946-567-0

Typeset by MPS Limited, Chennai, India
Printed and bound by CPI Group (UK) Ltd, Croydon, CR0 4YY

Dedicated to the Memory of James M Landis

One grasps for shadows, the better to comprehend sunlight. One reaches into the past, more clearly to know today and tomorrow. It is the privilege of all who care about education to test the depth and quality of that shadow for there, perhaps more than anywhere, one must try to pierce the brilliance of continuing dawns.

James M Landis
Chairman of the Securities and Exchange Commission,
Washington, DC,
20 March 1937

Preface

The Global Financial Crisis has demonstrated in startling detail the externalities caused by emasculated conceptions of corporate responsibility. Corporate executives and their professional advisors conspired to push through deals and strategies informed by legal technicalities and accounting conventions. If not in direct violation of the letter of the law, these strategies led to sub-optimal results for both the sustainability of specific corporate models and the professional standing of their advisors. The fact that the statute of limitations has against the most senior executives run in most jurisdictions without the bringing of criminal charges for wilful blindness poses a series of fundamental and unresolved questions. Has the panoply of reform initiatives at national, regional and global level addressed the core normative problem? Alternatively, have we privileged the politics of symbolism, creating the illusion of a robust architecture incapable of withstanding a crisis of similar magnitude? The scandal involving the manipulation of the London Interbank Offered Rate (Libor) offers a perfect case study to explore these questions.

There can be no doubting the magnitude of the scandal. The allegations of misconduct span the globe. Critically, the evidence proffered in settlement agreements to date, involving $2.6 billion in fines, points to the operation of a cartel, an aspect currently under investigation by the European Commission. Of equal significance, the willful misconduct continued long after the onset of the GFC, making future criminal prosecution a distinct possibility. What the investigation contained within this book demonstrates is that Libor and its administration have been carried out within codes of conduct incapable of addressing hubris, myopia and the decoupling of ethical considerations from core business.

As the book was going to press the Parliamentary Banking Standards Commission released its final report. The Approved Person regime that lies at the heart of the Wheatley Review on Libor has been dismissed by the Commission on Banking Standards as a mechanism that created 'a largely illusory impression of regulatory control over individuals, while meaningful responsibilities were not in practice attributed to anyone.'[1] The lack of accountability for past failings is seen as critical in bringing the banking sector into disrepute. Incremental change, it concludes, 'will no longer suffice.'[2] In a damning assessment of prior regulatory design, compliance is dismissed as the key architectural innovation in the building of Potemkin villages that give 'the appearance of effective control and oversight without the reality.'[3] The fact that 'prolonged and blatant misconduct' as evidenced in the Libor and associated scandals occurred without comment, suggest to the Commission a degree of systemic institutional corruption, allied to a 'dismal' and 'striking limitation on the sense

---

[1] Parliamentary Banking Standards Commission, *Changing Banking for Good* (HM Parliament, Westminster, June 2013), Vol 1, 9.

[2] Parliamentary Banking Standards Commission, *Changing Banking for Good* (HM Parliament, Westminster, June 2013), Vol 2, para 566.

[3] Ibid, para 684.

of personal responsibility and accountability' of banking leaders.[4] The Commission advocates scrapping the Approved Person framework and introducing instead a Senior Persons Regime. This is designed to assign specific roles to specific individuals. It is proposed to combine this with a licensing regime and replace general principles and codes of conduct with 'a single set of rules to be drawn up by the regulators.'[5] Breach of these formal rules would provide grounds for enforcement action. The Commission maintains that while the existing principles are not

> intrinsically wrong…they do not constitute a sufficiently robust foundation for improving banking standards…The rules should explicitly encapsulate expectations about behavior which are currently absent from the statements of principle for individuals, such as treating customers fairly and managing conflicts of interest and a requirement to draw to the attention of senior management and regulators conduct which falls below the standards set out.[6]

This will, argues the Commission, deal with a critical failure of the current regime, the fact that 'regulators have rarely been able to penetrate the accountability firewall of collective responsibility in firms that prevents actions against individuals.'[7] The approach is also designed to simultaneously provide enforcement action against staff senior enough to satisfy public outrage and broad enough to capture those not currently on the Approved Person register. The introduction of a criminal offence for reckless behaviour adds significant teeth to the proposals but only if exercised. Jail or the prospect of it is, as the Commission acknowledges, a critical deterrent. Whether the regulatory authorities have the stomach for such enforcement strategies is however another matter entirely. But for the fact that the United Kingdom has already gone through a radical redesign of its regulatory architecture, the Commission would advocate creating a specific statutory enforcement agency.[8]

Throughout the report there is evidence of continued suspicion of both banks and their regulators. The emphasis on better governance and the lack of confidence in the ability of boards of directors to recognise their responsibilities is manifest in the suggestion that the Companies Act should be amended 'to prioritise financial safety over shareholder interests in the case of banks.'[9] As the Commission makes clear 'it is essential that the risks posed by having a large financial centre do not mean that taxpayers or the wider economy are held to ransom.'[10] Unless the lessons of history are learnt, however, banks will inevitably fail, hence the need for stringent oversight as 'many banks remain too big and too complex to manage effectively.'[11] By extension, it infers, they are too complex to regulate. In a critical passage, the Commission warns against the myth that the problem in British banking is the result of individual failure or that banking has indeed learnt form its mistakes, thus requiring no further action. Specifically, it rejects any suggestion that robust intervention could threaten the future of the industry. 'If the arguments for complacency and inaction are heeded now,

---

[4]   Ibid, para 105.
[5]   Parliamentary Banking Standards Commission, above n1, 9.
[6]   Parliamentary Banking Standards Commission, *Changing Banking for Good*, above n2, para 634.
[7]   Parliamentary Banking Standards Commission, above n1, 10.
[8]   Parliamentary Banking Standards Commission, above n2, para 1200.
[9]   Parliamentary Banking Standards Commission, above n1, 11.
[10]   Parliamentary Banking Standards Commission, above n2, para 8.
[11]   Ibid, para 86.

when the crisis in banking standards has been laid bare, they are yet more certain to be heeded when memories have faded. If politicians allow the necessary reforms to fall at one of the first hurdles, then the next crisis in banking standards and culture may come sooner, and be more severe,' it warns.[12] It is this fear that animates the Commission's discussion of professional standards in the industry and whether codes of conduct can have any restraining value.

The Commission is exceptionally cautious about the stated ambition of the banking industry to develop a professional standards body. While seeing potential value, it is exceptionally concerned that this too could become an exercise in regulatory gaming. 'There are also very substantial risks of duplication between the powers and role of a professional standards body and those of regulators as well as risk that the creation of such a body could become a focus of public policy, diverting attention from the changes that are urgently needed within the existing regulatory framework,' it warns.[13] The proposals for a professional body run the additional risk that power is stripped away from regulators at the very point it is most needed. It is a risk that the Commission is not prepared to countenance. 'On the basis of our assessment of the nature of the banking industry, we believe that the creation of an effective professional body is a long way off and may take at least a generation,' it concludes.[14] The reform of British banking remains, therefore a work in progress. The Potemkin facade has been pierced not yet demolished.

Building a sustainable framework necessitates warranted belief in the underpinning rationale. For the process to be effective necessitates commitment in the end itself–that of market integrity–rather than a mechanism to forestall external oversight. Critically, therefore, there is a need to separate 'purpose' from 'ends.'[15] No practice can lead to the sustainable achievements of desired 'ends' if the 'purpose' for holding the beliefs that animates practice differs in substance from the primary goal. The ultimate end of the physician, for example, is to heal. If, however, the purpose of believing in or seeking to achieve that goal is to make money, for example, risks subverting that end. Unnecessary tests or procedures may be prescribed that increase the financial burden on the patient, insurance company or taxpayer. The patient may not necessarily be harmed; she may in fact be healed. The conduct, however, if replicated across a given market, is undesirable. It can impose additional costs, financial and emotional. It also threatens the corruption of the primary end: the protection of life through the application of the do no harm thesis. The imposition of unnecessary costs clearly violates the individual. It also risks bringing the wider institutional system into disrepute. This critical distinction between ultimate 'ends' and 'purpose' has deep resonance for participants involved in the governance of financial markets. The failure to articulate and integrate purpose, values and principles within a functioning ethical framework has created toxic and socially harmful corporate cultures in urgent need of reform, which an emphasis on technical measures alone will be incapable of addressing.

---

[12] Ibid, para 273.

[13] Ibid, para 598.

[14] Ibid, para 601.

[15] A MacIntyre, 'Ends and Endings' (Speech delivered at the Catholic University of America, Washington, DC, 25 September 2009); see also D Rose, *The Moral Foundations of Economic Behaviour* (Oxford University Press, 2011) 188 ('There is no escaping the fact that why one holds the required moral tastes matters as much as having the right kind of moral tastes.').

The work presented here is the result of a major project conducted by the Centre for Law Markets and Regulation at UNSW Law in conjunction with academic partners at the University of Melbourne Law School and the School of Law at the University of Leeds. The funding provided by the Australian Research Council though Justin O'Brien's Future Fellowship ('Measuring and Evaluating Performance in Securities Market Regulation,' FT120100104) is gratefully acknowledged along with the invaluable assistance provided by the Office of the Legal Services Commissioner, New South Wales through its co-financing of an ARC Linkage Grant. The Centre for Corporate Law and Securities Regulation at Melbourne Law School kindly hosted one of the three workshops that informed this project we are very grateful for the support of its Director, Professor Ian Ramsay. We are also immensely grateful to Professor John Braithwaite at the ANU for his erudite conclusion, which emphasises, correctly in our view, the critical importance of narratives and the need to reframe conceptions of blameworthiness. Effective academic research is predicated on capacity to inform and influence the trajectory of policy and this necessitates the involvement of practitioners and regulators. We would like to acknowledge the engagement of Allens-Linklaters, which hosted the initial workshop in Sydney and Allen & Overy for staging the final workshop in London. In addition, Justin O'Brien would like to acknowledge the support of Harvard Law School in facilitating the excavation of the university archives in relation to James M Landis, in the memory of whom this book is dedicated.

Justin O'Brien and George Gilligan, Sydney, June 2013

Contents

Contributors

John Braithwaite is Distinguished Professor and founder of the Regulatory Institutions Network, Australian National University

Andrew Campbell is Professor of International Banking and Finance Law at the School of Law, University of Leeds

David Campbell is Professor in the School of Law, Lancaster University

Judith Dahlgreen is a Lecturer at the School of Law, University of Leeds

Olivia Dixon is a Lecturer at Sydney Law School, University of Sydney

Bob Ferguson is a Head of Department at the Financial Conduct Authority in London and a former Visiting Professor at the Centre for Law, Markets and Regulation, UNSW Law, Sydney

George Gilligan is a Senior Research Fellow at the Centre for Law, Markets and Regulation, UNSW Law, Sydney

Tahlia Gordon is the Research and Projects Manager at the Office of the Legal Services Commissioner of New South Wales

Pamela F Hanrahan is an Associate Professor at the Melbourne Law School, University of Melbourne and former regional commissioner for the Australian Securities and Investments Commission

Joan Loughrey is Professor of Law and Director of the Centre for Business Law and Practice at School of Law, University of Leeds

Michael Legg is an Associate Professor of Law at UNSW Law, Sydney

Steve Mark is the inaugural Legal Services Commissioner of New South Wales

Seumas Miller holds a joint Professorial Research Fellowship at the Centre for Applied Philosophy, Charles Sturt University (Canberra) and the for Fellow 3TU Centre for Ethics and Technology, Delft University of Technology (The Hague).

Justin O'Brien is Professor of Law and Director of the Centre for Law, Markets and Regulation at UNSW Law, Sydney and holder of an Australian Research Council Future Fellowship

Samantha Strimling is a graduate student at Boalt Law, University of California at Berkeley

Eric Talley is the Rosalinde and Arthur Gilbert Foundation Professor of Law and Director, Berkeley Center for Law, Business, and the Economy, University of California at Berkeley

David A Westbrook is Professor of Law, Director of Strategic Initiative and Floyd H and Hilda Hurst Faculty Scholar at the Law School, State University of New York, Buffalo

Introduction

Regulating Culture: Problems and Perspectives

Justin O'Brien and George Gilligan

I CULTURE, TRUST AND THE FINANCE SECTOR

Trust in our corporations and in our institutions, both secular and religious, is at an all-time low. Across myriad domains and jurisdictions, from policing to the media, faith-based schooling to banking, governance failures have blighted individual lives, ruined reputations and, in the case of the global financial crisis, social cohesion.[1] Irrespective of domain, corporate culpability for individual ethical failures is invariably and inevitably informed by the relative strength or weakness of organizational culture (ie, the degree to which egregious conduct is informed by a disconnect between stated and lived values).[2] The disjunction can lie along a continuum. It ranges from willful neglect, through reliance on formal but transacted around compliance programs, to misaligned incentives.[3] It is equally dispiriting but nonetheless inescapable that neither commitments to enhanced self-regulation nor strengthened external oversight have proved capable of arresting a decline in the trustworthiness of the financial sector.[4] This is the case irrespective of whether rules or principles-based approaches to regulatory design have been privileged.[5] Indeed, recent legislative

---

[1] See MD Higgins, 'President's Remarks at the Launch of Up The Republic,' (Speech delivered at the Royal Irish Academy, Dublin, 14 November 2012).

[2] J Sorensen, 'The Strength of Corporate Culture and the Reliability of Firm Performance' (2002) 47 *Administrative Science Quarterly* 70, 72 (defining culture narrowly as a system of shared values (that define what is important)) and norms that define appropriate attitudes and behaviors for organizational members (how to feel and behave); see also L Smircich, 'Concepts of Culture and Organizational Analysis' (1983) 28 *Administrative Science Quarterly* 339 (noting that research into corporate culture is an inquiry into the social order: at 341).

[3] G Rossouw and L van Vuuren, 'Modes of Managing Morality: A Descriptive Model of Strategies for Managing Ethics' (2003) 46 *Journal of Business Ethics* 389 (noting a five-stage process in which corporate activity moves from '(1) immorality; (2) reactivity; (3) compliance; (4) integrity; (5) total alignment: at 391).

[4] J O'Brien, 'Re-Regulating Wall Street: Substantive Change or the Politics of Symbolism Revisited,' in I. MacNeil and J. O'Brien (eds.), *The Future of Financial Regulation* (Oxford, Hart Publishing, 2010).

[5] K Keasey, H Short and M Wright, 'The Development of Corporate Governance Codes in the United Kingdom,' in K Keasey, S Thompson and M Wright (eds), *Corporate Governance: Accountability, Enterprise and International Comparisons* (2005) 21 (noting that reform impulses are driven by scandal).

innovations have resulted in the design of suboptimal regulatory structures; suboptimal, that is, to society if not the financial sector itself, ostensibly the target but ultimately the beneficiary of flawed implementation.[6] This is particularly apparent in the United States.[7] The *Public Company Accounting Reform and Investor Protection Act* (2002), better known as Sarbanes-Oxley, designed to enhance audit standards in the aftermath of the Enron and associated scandals, for example, transmogrified into an enormous rent-seeking opportunity for the accounting profession.[8] Equally, the *Wall Street Reform and Consumer Protection Act* (2010), or Dodd-Frank, has facilitated ongoing trench warfare between the Securities and Exchange Commission (SEC) and regulated entities over its nature, scope and legislative intent.

These conflicts and tensions are unsurprising consequences of the cultural realities of the financial sector, both past and present. More generally societies, firms, professional associations, specific industries and other groups (including regulatory actors), develop modes of preserving and transmitting through time and generations the mental programming that constitute routines, or *the ways that things are done* in processes that may be difficult to discern specifically, but which nonetheless are well understood, not only by those who may be involved directly but also by those who are not.[9] These mental programs interact with individual and collective value systems, which simultaneously are reflexively interacting with prevailing cultural influences, and thus inevitably shape behaviours. So, the City of London or Wall Street for example, develop patterned modes and mechanisms for evaluating issues and events that are transmitted within their core groups as well as to the broader populations at home, and abroad, as the routine and legitimate ways of doing business – in short, the operational culture of an industry.[10]

Culture can be simultaneously local and general. A universal hermetic definition of what constitutes culture is perhaps impossible. It is, therefore, perhaps more fruitful to accept the conceptual imprecision that permeates debates about culture and understand it as a complex

---

[6]   See, for example, A Haldane, 'The Dog and the Frisbee,' (Speech delivered at Federal Reserve Bank of Kansas Annual Symposium, Jackson's Hole, 31 August 2012), available at www.bankofengland.co.uk/publications/Documents/speeches/2012/speech596.pdf.

[7]   D Mitchell, 'The End of Corporate Law' (2009) 44 *Wake Forest Law Review* 703 ('In the course of the past century corporate law has been used first to legitimate corporate power and then to exempt those exercising it from liability': at 703); see more generally H Collins, *Regulating Contracts* (Oxford, Oxford University Press, 1999) 59 (describing private law as 'the index finger of the invisible hand that guides the markets'); for the importance of political framing, see E Orts, 'The Complexity and Legitimacy of Corporate Law' (1993) 50 *Washington & Lee Law Review* 1565 (noting 'corporate law involves the simultaneous pursuit and coexistence of a number of ends or purposes, with the mix a preponderance of different values depending on particular legal context': at 1565).

[8]   J O'Brien, *Redesigning Financial Regulation: The Politics of Enforcement* (Chichester, John Wiley & Sons, 2007); for discussion of the role of politicians as active rent extractors, see F McChesney, *Money for Nothing* (New York, Oxford University Press, 1987) 157 (characterizing politicians 'not as mere brokers redistributing wealth in response to competing private demands but as independent actors making their own demands to which private actors respond.').

[9]   The residual, seemingly perennial relative regulatory autonomy (especially in the Anglo-American context), of the financial sector to shape its own regulatory discourse and infrastructures over many centuries is testimony to this power. For a detailed analysis of these forces at work in the UK context, see: G Gilligan, *Regulating the Financial Services Sector* (London, Kluwer Law International, 1999).

[10]   G Hofstede, *Culture's Consequences: International Differences in Work-Related Values*, (Beverley Hills, CA, Sage, 1980) 25 (Culture could be defined as 'the interactive aggregate of common characteristics that influence a human group's response to its environment. Culture determines the identity of a human group in the same way as personality determines the identity of an individual.').

interaction between networks of specific epistemic communities that aggregate interweaving dimensions. For example, Becker views culture as a set of shared understandings that permit a group of people to act in concert with each other.[11] Cotterrell sees culture as having four general components: beliefs/values; traditions; instrumental (economic/technological) matters; and matters of effect (emotion).[12] These elements can be especially mutually reinforcing amongst professional communities that have a history of shared customs and business practices. So, when one analyses how a regulatory culture evolves within any given industry, numerous sources of regulatory culture are apparent. Significant amongst these are: general culture (especially in a national context); social structures; law (particularly statutes and court decisions); regulatory traditions; and the practice of regulatory work itself.[13] It is important to remember that as these regulatory sources emerge and grow, the groups that comprise *the regulated* are almost invariably much larger than the regulatory agencies charged with regulating them. Moreover, the former may well have far greater resources available to shape the discourses and evolutionary pathways of ostensibly more powerful regulatory sources.

The financial sector is one of the areas in which these regulatory source imbalances have been most pronounced over the years. Professional, structural and cultural embeddedness condition the interplay of regulatory authority and regulatory responses. These coalitions of embeddedness allow those players or firms with the requisite resources and inter-organisational alliances to build up and legitimate their image of regulatory authority.[14] If their regulatory authority is strong, then they can subsequently challenge and/or negotiate the rules of regulation. Contemporary regulatory conditions shape future regulatory structures. It is clearly in the self-interest of powerful actors within an industry like financial services to be as reflexively influential as possible on current regulatory practice, so as to maintain or increase future levels of influence.

Historically, more aggressive enforcement has proved problematic in changing corporate culture, with the imposition of ever increasing fines written off as part of the cost of doing business.[15] Paradoxically, in the contemporary crisis accusations of 'overreach'[16] frequently accompany judicial complaints that a façade of enforcement is being privileged.[17] In cases in which insiders have been brought to trial, juries have been reluctant to

---

[11] H S Becker, 'Culture: A Sociological View' (1982) 71 *The Yale Review* 513.

[12] R Cotterrell, 'Law and Culture–Inside and Beyond the Nation State' (2008) 31 *Retfærd: Nordisk Juridisk Tidsskrift* 23.

[13] E Meidinger, 'Regulatory Culture: A Theoretical Outline' (1989) 9 *Law & Society* 355.

[14] The term regulatory authority is being used advisedly. It refers to those situations in which it is deemed legitimate for the regulated to have power and this legitimacy is recognised by regulators. The larger and more influential a firm is within the financial services sector, the more likely it is that it can legitimately build up its image of regulatory authority.

[15] H Rockness and J Rockness, 'Legislated Ethics: From Enron to Sarbanes-Oxley, the Impact on Corporate America' (2005) 57 *Journal of Business Ethics* 21 (noting the need for meaningful sanctions, increased investigatory capacity and external fines that exceed expected gains).

[16] JB Stewart, 'Another Fumble By the SEC on Fraud,' *New York Times*, 16 November 2012, available at www.nytimes.com/2012/11/17/business/another-fumble-by-the-sec.html?_r=0.

[17] T Hemphill and F Cullari, 'Corporate Governance Practices: A Proposed Policy Incentive Regime to Facilitate Internal Investigations and Self-Reporting of Criminal Activities' (2009) 87 *Journal of Business Ethics* 333, 335–342 (noting the increased prosecutorial arsenal); for critiques of its application, see J Hasnas, 'Ethics and the Problem of White Collar Crime' (2005) 54 *American University Law Review* 579; M Koehler, 'Revisiting a Foreign Corrupt Practices Act Compliance Defense' (2012) *Wisconsin Law Review* 609; M Koehler, 'The Façade of FCPA Enforcement' (2010) 41 *Georgetown Journal of International Law* 907.

convict.[18] At a broader strategic level, judicial skepticism over the agency's use (or misuse) of cost-benefit analysis has significantly curtailed the efficacy of its discretionary ability to introduce enhanced standards.[19] Despite the long-standing antagonism between the DC circuit in particular and the SEC, deference to agency discretion remains intact. The unresolved question is how that discretion is applied, a question to be explored more fully below. The point to underscore at this stage, however, is the abject failure of moral exhortation alone as a regulatory strategy. For example, huge bonuses in the banking industry, even when firms are reporting massive losses or are being rescued by taxpayers, is an issue that highlights the seemingly willful blindness and deafness of finance industry professionals towards strident criticism from the media, community, governments and regulators alike.[20] In far too many instances, boards remain impervious to exhortations from the SEC that 'those who act on behalf of a company give life to the corporate conscience.'[21] There is, of course, an inherent tension between monitoring and the provision of strategic advice.[22] The failure of the 'conscience' metaphor calls into question the extent to which self-regulation is possible, a fact acknowledged by the SEC.[23] If exhortations from regulatory agencies are viewed with derision, so too are common law precedents. Guidance to corporations and their advisors as to what should constitute minimal compliance standards has served little better.[24] Transactions have been carried out around codes of conduct through a combination of hubris, myopia and the decoupling of ethical considerations from core business.[25] Taken together, the failure to articulate and integrate purpose, values and principles within a functioning ethical framework has created toxic and socially harmful corporate cultures.

It is equally dispiriting that policymakers have conflated the essential function provided by banking with the security of individual banks, a compromise that because of the

---

[18] See P Henning, 'Mixed Results for SEC in Financial Crisis Cases,' *New York Times*, 19 November 2012, available at dealbook.nytimes.com/2012/11/19/mixed-results-for-s-e-c-in-financial-crisis-cases.

[19] See J Fisch, 'The Long Road Back: Business Roundtable and the Future of SEC Rulemaking' (2012) *Seattle University Law Review*, forthcoming.

[20] See A Cuomo, *No Rhyme or Reason: The Heads I Win, Tails You Lose, Bank Bonus Culture*, (New York, State Attorney General Office, 2009).

[21] C Glassman, 'Sarbanes-Oxley and the Idea of "Good" Governance' (Speech delivered at the American Society of Corporate Secretaries, 27 September 2002). The belief in common purpose animates SEC policy formulation; see M Shapiro, 'Address to the Practising Law Institute' (Speech delivered at PLI Securities Regulation Seminar, New York, 4 November 2009): 'We might sit on opposite sides of the table in any given matter, but I believe that all of us—regulators, attorneys, and business people alike—all share the common goal of ensuring that our capital markets work—and work fairly and effectively.'

[22] J Fisch, 'The New Federal Regulation of Corporate Governance' (2004) 28 *Harvard Journal of Law and Public Policy* 39.

[23] See 'Securities and Exchange Commission's Chairman Cox Announces End of Consolidated Supervised Entities Program' (Press Release, Washington, DC, 26 September 2008), noting that 'self-regulation does not work,' available at www.sec.gov/news/press/2008/2008-230.htm.

[24] *In Re Caremark International Inc Derivative Litigation*, 698 A.2d 959 (Delaware Chancery Court) at 970 (holding that directors can be held liable and this can be easier to prove in the absence of an effective compliance program).

[25] J O'Brien, 'Managing Conflicts: The Sisyphean Tragedy (and Absurdity) of Corporate Governance and Financial Regulation Reform' (2007) 20 *Australian Journal of Corporate Law* 317.

maintenance of an explicit 'too big to fail' subsidy facilitates risk-taking.[26] Ingrained cultural forces can distort perceptions within organisations about risk and incentives, especially in the hyper-competitive environment of international finance which may adapt ever-increasing matrices of risk as the norm.[27] Moreover, the complexity of modern finance and globalized, fragmented chains of command governing the production and dissemination of specialized knowledge increases the information asymmetry risk. As a consequence, the risk that the unscrupulous will take advantage of what the economist David C. Rose has termed the 'golden opportunities' of deception is increasing.[28] Recent survey evidence from the corruption and anti-money-laundering domain confirms this insight. The annual Ernst & Young global fraud survey, for example, is one of the most detailed snapshots of the bribery and corruption challenges facing multinational corporations.[29] One of its most 'troubling' findings is what Ernst & Young terms a growing widespread acceptance of unethical business practices (eg, 64 per cent of respondents believe that the incidence of compliance failure has increased because of the downturn).[30] The trend is particularly apparent in East Asia (eg, 60 per cent of respondents in Indonesia deemed it acceptable to make cash payments to secure new contracts; 36 per cent of respondents in Vietnam suggested it was permissible to misstate financial accounts).[31] The decline in ethical commitment is traced to a lack of training, and, more significantly, to mixed messages from senior management as to the importance of compliance with Anti-Bribery and Corruption Policies (ABACP). As Ernst & Young concludes, if action is not taken to hold offenders to account, stated commitment to high standards remains an exercise in symbolism. While many reported the existence of sophisticated compliance systems, these were not subject to ongoing external testing. Only 33 per cent reported using external law firms or consultants to provide assurance.[32] In a significant finding, 54 per cent of CFOs surveyed had not taken ABACP training,[33] while 52 per cent of all respondents reported that the board was not sufficiently aware of operating risk.[34] The report concludes, somewhat bleakly, that hard times stretch ethical boundaries.[35]

---

[26] See R Whelan, 'Misunderstanding the Banking Industry,' Rethinking Financial Markets Online Conference, World Economics Association, 1–30 November 2012, available at rfconference2012.worldeconomicsassociation. org/wp-content/uploads/WEA-RFMConference2012-Whelan.pdf.

[27] DC Langevoort, 'Chasing the Greased Pig Down Wall Street: A Gatekeeper's Guide to the Psychology, Culture and Ethics of Financial Risk Taking' (2011) 96 *Cornell Law Review*, 1209.

[28] DC Rose, *The Moral Foundations of Economic Behavior* (New York, Oxford University Press, 2011) 16; see also P Pettit, 'Republican Reflections on the Occupy Movements,' in F O'Toole (ed), *Up the Republic* (Dublin, Faber & Faber, 2012) 169–81 (noting 'it is a sad fact of human nature that while not many of us might be corrupt, not many are incorruptible; when opportunity offers not many are capable of resisting the temptation to make a quick buck. The timber may not be rotten but it is crooked:' at 177).

[29] Ernst & Young, *Growing Beyond, A Place for Integrity* (New York, EYGM Limited, 2012), hereinafter *Ernst & Young Survey*. The survey is drawn from a sample of 1700 senior executives. It includes respondents drawn from incumbent Chief Financial Officers (CFO) and senior executives charged with running the legal, compliance and internal audit functions of major corporations across 43 different countries

[30] ibid, Figure 1, 4.

[31] ibid, Figure 2, 5.

[32] ibid, Figure 4, 7.

[33] ibid, 3.

[34] ibid, 3.

[35] ibid, 5.

The critical importance of trust in lowering agency and transaction costs, building cooperation and innovation and creating more efficient exchanges has, of course, long been recognized.[36] Absent ongoing substantial institutionalized commitment to ethical behavior, however, credible *ex ante* detection of unthinking, blinkered or compartmentalized ethical consideration remains implausible.[37] The critical question, therefore, is how to strengthen the restraining forces and whether this effectiveness can be monitored and evaluated. As Weaver, Revino and Cochran have nicely phrased it, 'how does one ensure integrated rather than decoupled corporate social performance?'[38] Resolution of this conundrum cannot take place without critical reflection on the corporation and its place in society.[39]

Corporate cultures do not exist in a vacuum; nor are they mere reactive responses to externally mandated rules. Instead they reflect the values of the organization. The emphasis on culture underpins an influential definition of corporate governance provided by the Australian jurist Justice Neville Owen. In his investigation into the collapse of HIH Insurance, Justice Owen maintained that he was "not so much concerned with the content of a corporate governance model as with the culture of the organization to which it attaches." For Justice Owen, "the key to good corporate governance lies in substance, not form. It is about the way the directors of a company create and develop a model to fit the circumstances of the company and then test it periodically for its practical effectiveness. It is about the directors taking control of a regime they have established and for which they

---

[36] S Banerjee, N Bowie and C Pavone, 'An Ethical Analysis of the Trust Relationship,' in R Bachman and A Zaheer (eds), *Handbook of Trust Research* (Cheltenham, Edward Elgar, 2006) 303; more broadly see D North, 'Economic Performance Through Time' (1994) 84 *American Economic Review* 359 (noting 'societies that get "stuck" embody belief systems and institutions that fail to confront and solve new problems of societal complexity': at 364. For origins of the administrative process and its legitimation, see JM Landis, *The Administrative Process* (New Haven, Yale University Press, 1938) 4 (noting that increased complexity calls 'for greater surveillance by government of the appropriate use of these resources to further the admittedly dim but recognizable aims of our society.'). See more generally, R Frank, *Passions Within Reason: The Strategic Role of the Emotions* (New York, Norton, 1988) 19 (noting that indoctrination and practice are essential building blocks of character formation).

[37] D Murphy, 'The Federal Sentencing Guidelines for Organizations: A Decade of Promoting Compliance and Ethics' (2002) 87 *Iowa Law Review* 697 (noting that compliance programs without an explicit framework for assessing ethical dilemmas are unlikely to work: at 716–17); for the danger of compartmentalization, see A MacIntyre, 'Social Structures and their Threats to Moral Agency' (1999) 74 *Philosophy* 311 (Compartmentalization occurs when a distinct sphere of social activity comes to have its own role structure governed by its own specific norms in relative independence of other such spheres. Within each sphere, those norms dictate which kinds of consideration are to be treated as relevant to decision-making and which are to be excluded:' at 322); for discussion of the application of virtue ethics to the problem of sustainable financial reform, see J O'Brien, 'The Future of Financial Regulation, Enhancing Integrity Through Design' (2010) 32 *Sydney Law Review* 39.

[38] G Weaver, LK Trevino and P Cochran, 'Integrated and Decoupled Corporate Social Performance: Management Commitments, External Pressures and Corporate Ethics Practices' (1999) 42 *Academy of Management Journal* 539; see also LS Paine, 'Managing for Organizational Integrity' (1994) 3 *Harvard Business Review* 106 (noting that ethics has everything to do with management: at 106).

[39] E Mason, 'Introduction,' in E Mason (ed), *The Corporation in Modern Society* (Cambridge, Harvard University Press, 1960) 19. ('[T]he fact seems to be that the rise of the large corporation and attending circumstances have confronted us with a long series of questions concerning rights and duties, privileges and immunities, responsibility and authority, that political and legal philosophy have not yet assimilated').

are responsible.'[40] Warranted commitment to moral restraint necessitates ongoing critical reflection on what constitutes obligation—to whom and for what purpose.[41] It is in this context that corporate culture plays an essential disseminating role. It informs employees of what the company stands for.[42] To be effective, it must be informed by belief not prudence (ie, the fear of detection) precisely because the risk of detection can be quite low and fines written off as part of the price of doing business.[43] As Rose puts it, 'there is no escaping the fact that why one holds the required moral tastes matters as much as having the right kind of moral tastes.'[44] This, in turn, suggests it is essential to build the governance of the financial sector on an explicit normative foundation, a fact recognized, for example, but not implemented by senior regulators.[45] Notwithstanding plausible demands for a return to

[40] Report of the HIH Royal Commission, *The Failure of HIH Insurance* (Canberra, Commonwealth of Australia, 2003) xxxii, available at www.hihroyalcom.gov.au/finalreport/index.htm. For rare recognition of failure to internalize responsibility from former head of compliance at British Bank HBOS, see Paul Moore, 'Memo to Treasury Select Committee,' Westminster, London, 10 February 2009 ('My personal experience of being on the inside as a risk and compliance manager has shown me is that, whatever the very specific, final and direct causes of the financial crisis, I strongly believe that the real underlying cause of all the problems was simply this—a total failure of all key aspects of governance. In my view and from my personal experience at HBOS, all the other specific failures stem from this one primary cause.')

[41] See J Kay, *The Kay Review of Equity Markets* (London, HM Government, July 2012) 9. (According to Professor Kay, sustainable reform must be predicated on capability to 'restore relationships of trust and confidence in the investment chain, underpinned by the application of fiduciary standards of care by all those who manage or advise on the investments of others.' This necessitates a move away from short-termism, as 'trust and confidence are the product of long-term commercial and personal relationships: trust and confidence are not generally created by trading between anonymous agents attempting to make short term gains at each other's expense': at 5), available at bis.gov.uk/assets/biscore/business-law/docs/k/12-917-kay-review-of-equity-markets-final-report.pdf.

[42] See also Paine, above n38 (noting that the task of ethics management is to define and give life to an organization's guiding values, to create an environment that supports ethically sound behavior, and to instill a sense of shared accountability among employees.' As such, 'organizational ethics helps define what a company is and what it stands for: a 111).

[43] See O'Brien above, n4. The rise of class actions, however, may change this dynamic, see J Harris and M Legg, 'What Price Investor Protection: Class Actions vs Corporate Rescue' (2009) 17 *Insolvency Law Journal* 185. Recent litigation success (through settlements) in Australia has underscored the monetary pain; see for example, the $200m settlement reached by Centro and its auditors PwC to end a class action, N Lenaghan and B Wilmont, 'Centro, PwC to Take Record $200m Hit,' *Australian Financial Review*, 9 May 2012, available at afr.com/p/national/centro_pwc_take_record_legal_hit_6CaSTKu6K1w7nJFFIZOxWL.

[44] Rose, above n28, 188.

[45] See H Sants, '*Annual Lubbock Lecture in Management Studies*' (Speech delivered at Said Business School, University of Oxford, March 12, 2010) ('We need to answer the question of whether a regulator has a legitimate focus to intervene on the question of culture. This arguably requires both a view on the right culture and a mechanism for intervention. Answering yes to this question would undoubtedly significantly extend the FSA's engagement with industry. My personal view is that if we really do wish to learn lessons from the past, we need to change not just the regulatory rules and supervisory approach, but also the culture and attitudes of both society as a whole, and the management of major financial firms. This will not be easy. A cultural trend can be very widespread and resilient—as has been seen by a return to a 'business as usual'. mentality. Nevertheless, no culture is inevitable'); see more generally D North, *Structure and Change in Economic History* (New York, Norton, 1981) 47 (suggesting that ethical standards are the 'cement of social stability'); see also O Williamson, 'The New Institutional Economics: Taking Stock, Looking Ahead' (2000) 38 *Journal of Economic Literature* 595. (Williamson notes that analysis of the 'non-calculative social contract' or 'level one' component of social theory is conspicuous by its absence within regulatory studies: at 597). The other three levels comprise institutional arrangements viewed primarily through property rights and positive political theory, governance mechanisms through transaction cost economics and resource allocation frameworks generally examined through agency theory.

simplicity in regulatory design,[46] this cannot be achieved without an agonistic dialogue in which the principles underpinning obligation and the rationale for external intervention in the event of circumvented, are negotiated and accepted.[47] The advantages of associational governance, such as flexible design attuned to the interests of institutional actors, cannot be sustainable in the event that the negotiations are entered into in bad faith. It is only by returning to first principles that the relationship between law, regulatory rulemaking and society can be ascertained and evaluated.[48] Absent a theory of society it is impossible to build a theory of the corporation or the capital markets in which it is nested.[49] Writers as diverse as Hayek,[50] Schumpeter,[51] Polanyi[52] and, more recently, Granovetter,[53] have long noted the political calculation required to construct the economically rational. The interaction between market norms and economic and regulatory policy served an essential legitimating purpose.[54] The problem facing regulatory authorities is that that model has lost its legitimacy. The privileging of innovation over security and emaciated conception of responsibility and accountability has led to a profound authority crisis that can only be resolved by reconstituting the social contract governing the operation of global finance.

---

[46] Haldane, above n6; see also Editorial, 'Speech of the Year,' *Wall Street Journal*, 12 September 2012, A14 (noting 'a belief among regulators that models can capture all necessary information and then accurately predict future risk. This belief is new, and not helpful.')

[47] J Seligman, 'The SEC at a Time of Discontinuity' (2009) 95 *Virginia Law Review* 667, 678–79 ('Core principles are an inspiring aspiration. All of us would like to make regulation simpler and more efficient.... Core principles may be helpful, they are inadequate without an enabling statute, often detailed regulation, case law, and agency interpretative guidance. What, for example, is manipulation? It is not a self-defining term.').

[48] A Turner, 'Reforming Finance: Are We Being Radical Enough' (Speech delivered at Clare College, University of Cambridge, 18 February 2011) 3 (noting 'we must understand' the crisis as one of markets and systems rather than of specific institutions. Lord Turner continued that 'today's regulators are, in a sense, the inheritors of a half-century long policy error, in which we have allowed private sector banks to pursue their private interest in maximizing bank leverage, at times influenced by a deep intellectual confusion between private cost and social optimality:' at 6).

[49] See Mason, above n39, ('to suggest a drastic change in the scope or character of corporate activity is to suggest a drastic alteration in the structure of society.... All of this is to suggest not that the corporation cannot be touched but that to touch the corporation deeply is to touch much else beside:' at 1).

[50] F Hayek, *The Road to Serfdom* (New York, Routledge, 1944) 29 ('To create conditions in which competition will be as effective as possible, to supplement it where it cannot be made effective. . . . provide indeed a wide and unquestioning field for state activity. In no system that could be rationally defended would the state just do nothing. An effective competitive system needs an intelligently designed and continuously adjusted legal framework as much as any other').

[51] J Schumpeter, *Capitalism, Socialism and Democracy* (New York, Allen and Unwin, 1942) 137. ('No social system can work in which everyone is supposed to be guided by nothing except his short-term utilitarian ends.... [T]he stock market is a poor substitute for the Holy Grail').

[52] K Polanyi, *The Great Transformation* (Boston, Beacon Press, 1944) 171 ('The principle of freedom to contract... is... merely the expression of an ingrained prejudice in favour of a definite kind of interference, namely such as would destroy non-contractual relations').

[53] M Granovetter, 'Economic Action and Social Structure: The Problem of Embeddedness' (1985) 91 *American Journal of Sociology* 481 ('Idealized markets of perfect competition have survived intellectual attack in part because self-regulating economic structures are politically attractive to many. Another reason for survival, less clearly understood, is that the elimination of social relations from economic analysis removes the problem of order for the intellectual agenda, at least in the economic sphere': at 484).

[54] A Giddens, *The Constitution of Society: Outline of the Theory of Structuration* (Berkeley, The University of California Press, 1985) 25 ('The constitution of agents and structures are not two independent given sets of phenomena, a dualism but represent a duality. . . . [T]he structural properties of social systems are both the medium and the outcome of the practices they recursively organize').

II   THE MORALITY OF CONTEMPORARY BANKING

We are living at a moment of potential paradigmatic change. The dominant conception of corporate governance and financial regulation, based on rational actors operating within efficient markets, is losing coherence, legitimacy and authority.[55] Effective governmental control through dominant shareholdings in major banks has forced unresolved reflection on what constitutes or should constitute optimal corporate governance and regulatory oversight. The Global Financial Crisis (GFC) has unleashed an avalanche of reform initiatives.[56] It is unclear, however, not only to what extent this will lead to convergence or facilitate ongoing arbitrage, but also how well-equipped national regulators are.[57] Implementation carries real risks that national systems will develop frameworks that may preserve short-term competitiveness but do little to improve either the quality of oversight or shift the dynamics of financial regulation. More problematically, they may not reduce the transmission of cross-border contagion. Undoubtedly, any successful proposal to extend responsibility and accountability to those involved in product design rather than clarifying the enabling conditions governing marketing and sale would constitute a seismic shift in the structure of the financial services industry. Specifically, it would breach the self-referential logic of private law. The initial fracture could lead to unintended consequences, including what Hugh Collins has vividly termed its 'productive disintegration.'[58] The integration of more interventionist normative objectives with enabling ones may also significantly change the ethical boundaries of global finance. In doing so it would render the bifurcation between investor classes conceptually incoherent.

Three intersecting trends have contributed to the embedding of narrow terms of reference within political and academic debate: liberalisation, globalisation and financialisation. Each was vital in generating and legitimating the contours of the debate on the limits

---

[55] Turner, above, n48; see also A Sen, 'Introduction', in A Smith, *The Theory of Moral Sentiments* (first published 1759; London, The Penguin Press, 2009 ed) vii–xxiv (noting that neglect of Smith's opus has led to stunted appreciation of the complexity and 'plurality of human motivations, the connections between ethics and economics and the co-dependent—rather than free-standing—role of institutions in general and free markets in particular in the functioning of the economy': at viii); see also John Cassidy, *How Markets Fail* (New York, The Penguin Press, 2009) 337 ('Between the collapse of communism and the outbreak of the subprime crisis, an understandable and justified respect for market forces mutated into a rigid and unquestioning devotion to a particular, and blatantly unrealistic, adaptation of Adam Smith's invisible hand').

[56] The Financial Stability Board has provided a critical coordinating role in implementing the architectural design mandated by the G20. This has buttressed the work of pre-existing sector-specific supranational regulatory groupings, including the Basel Committee on Banking Supervision, the International Organization of Securities Commissions (IOSCO) and the International Association of Insurance Superintendents (IAIS). Global trends and the domestic regulatory responses have, in turn, been tracked by the Organization for Economic Cooperation and Development (OECD) and the International Monetary Fund (IMF).

[57] Financial Stability Board, *Overview of Progress in the Implementation of the G20 Recommendations for Strengthening Financial Stability* (Basel, 19 June 2012) 2 (noting 'Many jurisdictions still need to address weaknesses in their supervisors' mandates, to ensure sufficient independence to act, appropriate resources, and a full suite of powers to proactively identify and address risks'.)

[58] H Collins, *Regulating Contracts* (Oxford, Oxford University Press, 1999). Collins' point is not that that private law has lost vitality. Indeed he goes as far as to suggest that it 'is the index finger of the invisible hand that guides the markets' (at 59). Rather, continued relevance requires the discipline to interdict with changed realities about how standards, monitoring and sanctions can, or should, be best applied.

of regulatory intervention.[59] The combination of mechanisms, processes and principles governing corporate governance and financial regulatory reform agendas generated what political scientists term a Structured Action Field (SAF).[60] Power within a SAF is determined by the salience of the ideational terms of reference, the coherence of the underpinning vision, values and norms and the degree to which the interaction between both appear to provide beneficial outcomes. Once established, such a field is remarkably resilient, particularly if framed by the inculcation of a Shared Mental Model.[61] Inefficiencies (or indeed illegalities) can be—and often are—ignored, downplayed or addressed by the application of what appears to be more stringent rules or the more granular articulation of overarching principles. This dynamic is particularly apparent in corporate governance and financial regulation reform.[62] More often that not, however, these same initiatives tend to privilege the politics of symbolism.[63] By 2007 the ideational structure had not only become merely embedded but almost impervious to challenge. Two accounts from notable insiders highlight the extent of the groupthink. The first comes from Claudio Borio, the chief economist at the Bank for International Settlements. He used a G20 forum in Mumbai to explain why policymakers were incapable of exercising *ext-ante* restraint.

> To varying degrees, policymakers, just like everyone else, underestimated the threat. They were caught up in what, in retrospect, has partly turned out to be a Great Illusion. And even had the threat been fully recognized–and some no doubt did–the political economy pressures not to change policies would have been enormous. On the face of it, the regimes in place had proved to be extremely successful. A lot of reputational capital was at stake. And not even the often more critical academic community provided any support for change. Indeed, as regards macroeconomic policy, that community turned out to be part of the problem, not of the solution.[64]

[59] For socio-legal exploration of this process, see S Picciotto, *Regulating Global Corporate Capitalism* (Cambridge, Cambridge University Press, 2011); see more generally, T Porter and K Ronit, 'Self-Regulation as Policy Process: The Multiple and Criss-Crossing Stages of Private Rule Making' (2006) 39 *Policy Sciences* 41.

[60] N Fligstein and L Dauter, 'The Sociology of Markets' (2007) 33 *Annual Review of Sociology* 21; see more generally P Bourdieu, *The Logic of Practice* (Cambridge, Polity Press, 1990). Bourdieu refers to the importance of mapping the *habitus*–the complex social and physical institutional geography in which communities of practice assimilate and constantly adjust practice,

[61] A Denzau and D North, 'Shared Mental Models: Ideologies and Institutions' (1994) 47 *Kyklos* 3.

[62] See O'Brien, above n25; for global perspective, see J Hill, 'Evolving "Rules of the Game" in Corporate Governance Reform' in J O'Brien (ed), *Private Equity, Corporate Governance and the Dynamics of Capital Market Regulation* (London, Imperial College Press, 2007) 29–54.

[63] A case in point is Sarbanes-Oxley, the *Public Company Accounting and Investor Protection Act* (2002). Introduced in the aftermath of Enron and conflicts of interest in analyst research scandals, it privileged a rules-based approach to regulation. Rather than being seen as an early warning sign, the travails facing the US system were themselves arbitraged. The City of London exploited the unease of business, additional audit costs and litigation risk costs by suggesting an alternative framework based on the articulation of principles. Both practitioners and regulatory officials argued that the model could provide and did offer alternative and better oversight. The primary supporting evidence proffered for this derived from positive testing but the absence of an accounting scandal in the United Kingdom, see D Kershaw, 'Evading Enron: Taking Principles Too Seriously in Accounting Regulation' (2005) 68 *Modern Law Review* 594.

[64] C Borio, 'The Financial Crisis of 2007? Macroeconomic and Policy Lessons' (Speech delivered to the *G20 Workshop on the Global Economy*, Mumbai, 24–26 May 2009) 13, available www.g20.org/Documents/g20_workshop_causes_of_the_crisis.pdf.

The second comes from Raghuram Rajan. Professor Rajan gave a paper at the influential Jackson Hole retreat organized by the Federal Reserve Bank of Kansas in August 2005 at which he warned of the inevitability of collapse. In a book published in 2010, he recounted the audience reaction to the presentation he had made at Jackson Hole with the prescient title 'Has Financial Development Made the World Riskier?'.

> I exaggerate only a bit when I say I felt like an early Christian who had wandered into a con-vention of half-starved lions. As I walked away from the podium after being roundly criti-cized by a number of luminaries (with a few notable exceptions), I felt some unease. It was not caused by the criticism itself, for one develops a thick skin after years of lively debate in faculty seminars: if you took everything the audience said to heart, you would never publish anything. Rather it was because the critics seemed to be ignoring what was going on before their eyes.[65]

The material and ideational certainties associated with the privileging of this model finan-cial capitalism have eroded. The testimony provided by Alan Greenspan in 2008 of a flaw in his 'ideological reasoning' punctured the self-referential belief in the power of free-mar-kets to self-correct.[66] The externalities associated with introducing the austerity agenda to bail out large swathes of the financial sector in many developed countries demonstrate the bankruptcy of belief in the market's capacity to self-correct. It also demonstrates the need to resolve the existential conflict between enabling and communitarian approaches to cor-porate law.[67]

The claim by the Goldman Sachs chief executive Lloyd Blankfein in 2009, for example, that the bank was doing 'God's work' is a carefully circumscribed one.[68] Apparent suc-cess was measured by short-term *efficiency* criteria (eg, lower transaction costs, expan-sion of corporate profits, increased shareholder returns). These retrospectively justified and legitimated the innovation. The potential negative externalities were glossed over or ignored.[69] In much the same way, the 'asset-lite' strategy pioneered by Enron at the turn of the millennium suggested a new paradigm for financial reporting and the rise of private equity in the period 2004–2007 reprised claims that the leveraged-buyout governance

---

[65] R Rajan, *Faultines: How Hidden Fractures Still Threaten the World Economy* (Princeton, Princeton University Press, 2010) 3; see also E Dash and J Creswell, 'Citigroup Saw No Red Flags Even As It Made Bolder Bets,' *New York Times*, 23 November 2008 A1 (quoting an April 2008 interview in which Rubin argued: 'In hindsight, there are a lot of things we'd do differently. But in the context of the facts as I knew them and my role, I'm inclined to think probably not'). This reprised an argument made in his autobiography on the financial reporting scandals at the turn of the millennium; see R Rubin, *In an Uncertain World* (New York, Random House, 2003) 337 ('The great bull market masked many sins, or created powerful incentives not to dwell on problems when all seemed to be going well—a natural human inclination').

[66] Evidence to the House Committee on Oversight and Government Reform, Washington, DC, 23 October 2008 (A Greenspan).

[67] See D Millon, 'Communitarianism in Corporate Law: Foundations and Law Reform Strategies' in Mitchell, above n7, 1–34.

[68] J Arlidge, '"I'm Doing God's Work." Meet Mr. Goldman Sachs,' *The Sunday Times*, 8 November 2009 4.

[69] C Borio, above n64, 13; see also Rajan, above n65, 1 ('The problem was not that no one warned about the dangers; it was that those who benefited from an overheated economy—which included a lot of people—had little incentive to listen.').

model heralded the demise of the public corporation. Following the implosion of the securitisation market, the individual corporate and societal consequences of this myopia became clear.

The fallout impacted negatively the *responsibility* and *legitimacy* as well as long-termer *efficiency* dimensions. Investment losses triggered an enormous erosion of private wealth. Housing and capital markets went into a downward spiral and credit stopped flowing. Emergency funding to the banking and financial services sector solved neither the underlying liquidity nor solvency problems. It merely transferred the risk. Sloganeering about the inherent unfairness of 'privatized profits and socialized losses' became more than a worn-out cliché. Throughout the crisis and beyond, as we moved from the great moderation to the institutionalization of the politics of austerity, senior bankers expressed carefully couched regret. At no stage did they accept responsibility.[70] Instead a narrow technical defense was proffered. As the immediate crisis facing the banks receded, the strategies were framed even more aggressively. To preserve the sanctity of contract, there was a stated need to uphold terms entered into freely (if misguidedly). Moreover, a similar rationale justified the payments of market-determined bonuses to executives then working in de facto nationalized institutions. Second, the privileging of caveat emptor facilitated the transference of responsibility. Equally understandably, both sets of strategies fuelled public resentment. This prompted, in turn, political recognition of the need for substantive reform to safeguard legitimacy. It is in this toxic environment that the London Interbank Offered Rate (Libor) scandal emerged. To date, the still burgeoning investigation has resulted in two multi-million dollar settlements against UBS, Barclays and the Royal Bank of Scotland. The latter is rendered more embarassing precisely because the institution is under effective taxpayer control.

The regulatory fine is just the beginning for Barclays, for example, which is a defendant in some of the 24 interrelated Libor lawsuits that have been aggregated before a Manhattan federal court.[71] US liabilities may be higher because US plaintiffs are permitted to request punitive damages, while UK plaintiffs are limited to compensatory awards.[72] Criminal liability could be added to those regulatory fines and civil lawsuits. Further, the Barclays settlement is just the first in the joint trans-Atlantic investigation. For example, it has been followed in December 2012 by the announcement from the US Department of Justice (DOJ) that due to UBS's role in the manipulation of the Libor, UBS Japan not only had signed a plea agreement admitting its criminal conduct and would pay a fine of US$100 million, but also that two UBS former traders would face criminal charges. In addition, UBS AG (the Swiss parent company of UBS Japan), had entered into an Non-Prosecution Agreement (NPA) under which it would: admit and accept responsibility for its misconduct; pay a DOJ penalty of US$400 million; US$700 million due to Commodity Futures Trading Commission (CFTC) action; US$259.2 million due to the UK Financial Services Authority (FSA) action; and $64.3 million due to the Swiss Financial Markets Authority

---

[70] See, for example, A Hornby, 'Memo to Treasury Select Committee' Westminster, London, 10 February 2009, 38 (in a joint statement the CEO and Chairman of HBOS stated they were 'profoundly sorry' but claimed unprecedented global circumstances affected virtually all the top banks in the world but HBOS specifically').

[71] A Harris, C Harper and L Fortado, 'Wall Street Bank Investors in Dark on Libor Liability,' *Bloomberg*, 5 July 2012.

[72] ibid.

(FINMA) action for a combined total of more than US$1.5 billion.[73] While the method by which Libor is set contributed to such widespread collusion, it could not have persisted without negligent oversight and the failure to enforce by regulators. In the aftermath of the scandal, the New York Federal Reserve has played defense, stating that although in 2008 it was aware of the structural flaws in setting Libor, it lacked the jurisdictional power[74] to effect any meaningful change other than provide written recommendations to the Bank of England.[75] However, the limits of jurisdictional authority have rarely been an issue for US regulators when national interest issues have been privileged in the past and it is far from clear that this state of affairs has changed. For its part, the Bank of England claimed that the recommendations lacked the granularity to either start an investigation or set off alarm bells. The tortured justifications provided at corporate and regulatory level, while self-serving and deeply problematic, could also equally apply to regulators in the US who are faced with equally serious questions of competence. In the United Kingdom itself, the Libor scandal has had a deep impact on regulatory authority. The Treasury Select Committee stated in its report that it was 'concerned that the FSA was two years behind the US regulatory authorities in initiating its formal LIBOR investigations and that this delay has contributed to the perceived weakness of London in regulating financial markets.'[76] The strongly worded report notes that 'the standards and culture of Barclays, and banking more widely, are in a poor state. Urgent reform, by both regulators and banks, is needed to prevent such misconduct flourishing.'[77] The Committee provides a devastating critique of past, current and future trajectories. The FSA is accused of privileging a myopic approach that blinded it to the initial and ongoing systemic failure of compliance at Barclays. 'The FSA has concentrated too much on ensuring narrow rule-based compliance, often leading to the collection of data of little value and to box ticking, and too little on making judgments about what will cause serious problems for consumers and the financial system,' it finds.[78] In sharp contrast to the claims of sophistication and prudence that informed discussions of the risk-based approach of the British regulatory system prior to the Global Financial Crisis invalidating their assumptions, such as the Paulsen Review in the United States, the Committee now finds that 'naivety' and inaction underscored the 'the dysfunctional relationship between the Bank of England and the FSA which existed at that time to the detriment of the public interest.'[79] It would appear from the trenchant views expressed by the Treasury Select Committee that not much has changed. The erroneous calculation by the bank and the FSA as well as the Bank of England was that early cooperation would pay dividends. The Barclays settlement did not place the blame on any individual executive; nor was there initially any expectation from the regulatory authorities in the UK or the US that resignations

---

[73] Department of Justice, 'UBS Securities Japan Co. Ltd. to Plead Guilty to Felony Wire Fraud for Long-running Manipulation of LIBOR Benchmark Interest Rates' (Press Release, Washington, DC, 19 December 2012), available at www.justice.gov/opa/pr/2012/December/12-ag-1522.html

[74] S Nasiripour, 'Fed "Lacked Jurisdiction" on Libor,' *Financial Times*, 17 July 2012, 1.

[75] T Geithner, 'Libor Email from Timothy Geithner to Bank of England,' *The Guardian*, 1 June 2012, available at www.guardian.co.uk/business/interactive/2012/jul/13/libor-email-timothy-geithner-bank-england (last visited 5 February 2013).

[76] House of Commons Treasury Committee, *Fixing LIBOR: Some Preliminary Findings* (London, HM Government, 18 August 2012).

[77] ibid.

[78] ibid, 112.

[79] ibid, 107.

were required or appropriate. Each was taken aback by the ferocity of political criticism of the deal and the perceived lack of accountability for infractions that point to widespread collusion, a fact belatedly acknowledged by the chairman of the FSA, Lord Adair Turner, who claimed that the activities of Barclays revealed 'a degree of cynicism and greed which is really quite shocking…and that does suggest that there are some very wide cultural issues that need to be strongly addressed.'[80]

III   THE STRUCTURE AND PURPOSE OF THIS BOOK

The contributions to this book are motivated as a response to this prevailing climate of shocking cynicism and greed, entrenched for so long under Anglo-American models of finance capitalism.[81] In 2012 corrosive manipulation, deception and *poor* culture have been highlighted in scandals and prosecutions featuring names such as Barclays, Goldman Sachs, Lehman Brothers, Standard Chartered and UBS to name but a few. A decade earlier, there was widespread public outrage surrounding similar entrenched poor corporate practices at Enron, HIH and WorldCom. A decade or so before that, BCCI and Polly Peck were mired in eerily similar scandals. Indeed, if one tracks back through most decades, it is relatively easy to find many examples of poor corporate behaviour and scandal. Just like the tide, crises, especially in the financial sector, just seem to keep coming in and their impacts seem to be growing in their capacity for social and economic pollution. The carnage wrought by the GFC is yet to play out fully as seen in recent mass public demonstrations of protest in Europe against forced austerity programs and falling living standards. The GFC has illustrated dramatically that poor operational culture in business organisations, especially banks, can have devastating impacts beyond business bottom lines and across social and political structures. It is questionable just how robust the contemporary global economy would be if faced with another GFC any time soon and that possibility is by no means a far-fetched scenario. So, what potential is there to re-cast operational cultures in business, especially in the financial sector? Together the authors seek to make a contribution to a policy discourse that prioritises the need to address industry cultural deficiencies in initiatives to reconfigure financial regulatory infrastructures.

Part 1 explores the structural and historical dimensions that have shaped the evolution of financial regulation. In chapter 1, David Westbrook emphasises the utility of a conversational ethnography perspective, first in providing analytical purchase on how culture shapes contemporary market practice; and second in identifying what changes have to be made in institutional design to facilitate more convergence between the goals of finance organisations and the societies in which they exist. In chapter 2, George Gilligan first examines the political, economic and cultural imperatives that established and delivered high levels of regulatory autonomy to the City of London, thereby producing a model and culture of financial regulation which have been influential in other jurisdictions, most importantly

---

[80] P Jenkins, J Gapper and B Masters, 'The Gathering Storm: Flaws in Banking Fuel the Case for Structural and Cultural Reform,' *Financial Times* 29 June 2012, available at www.ft.com/intl/cms/s/0/26d8a33c-c1e0-11e1-8e7c-00144feabdc0.html (last visited 5 February 2013).

[81] Obviously cynicism and greed are as well rooted in other models of finance capitalism operating around the world, but the focus of this book is on the Anglo-American model.

the US; and second discusses national and international tensions regarding regulatory standard setting that affect prevailing cultures in national financial sectors. In chapter 3, Justin O'Brien argues that the Libor scandal has exposed as never before the deleterious effect of piecemeal erosion of purpose through ad hoc reframing of regulatory instruments in response to scandal. Consequently credible, sustainable reform necessitates revisiting the initial framing of capital market regulation. This in turn requires re-examining the normative impulses that informed the key architects of the administrative state, most notably the political thought of James M Landis, the driving force behind state involvement in capital market governance.

Part 2 continues the exploration of cultural influences in financial regulation with particular emphasis on the effects of incentives and integrity. In chapter 4, David Campbell and Joan Loughrey examine how self-interest in financial markets could be regulated, in particular the limits of the rules and principles approach. They use the lens of Adam Smith's writings on self-interest and market exchange and how they have been interpreted by prominent welfare economist Amartya Sen. In chapter 5, Bob Ferguson details the long history of divergence between popular conceptions of decency and the operating culture of sales-oriented financial institutions, demonstrating that what is different in recent times is not so much the behaviour of bankers as the public outrage it has prompted as man-in-the-street and inside-player conceptions of acceptable behaviour collide in the aftermath of the financial crisis. As a result, the key to change for the better lies not just in the sphere of ethics and culture but in the material incentive structures that condition the behaviour of institutions and individuals. In Chapter Six, Seumas Miller highlights the micro and macro-institutional structural problems that lead to recurring scandals such as Libor in the financial sector. He considers the Libor scandal as an example of a collective action problem which needs to be countered by processes of professionalisation and ethical acculturation.

Part 3 uses the Libor scandal as a specific lens through which to consider how culture might be regulated in the financial sector in a post-Libor environment. In chapter 7, Eric Talley and Samantha Strimling explain how distorted incentive systems and widespread flouting of compliance protocols within financial organisations involved with Libor became normal elements of operational practices surrounding the setting of Libor rates, thus creating the cultural context for sustained manipulation of the system. In chapter 8, Andrew Campbell and Judith Dahlgreen examine the new governance model of the financial sector in the United Kingdom, in particular the role of the Bank of England following the major reforms brought by the Financial Services Act 2012. In chapter 9, Justin O'Brien examines how the Libor scandal has accelerated the increased use by US regulatory actors of deferred prosecution and imposition of an external monitor as mechanisms that seek to embed increased and improved levels of integrity within the organisational frameworks of firms. In chapter 10, Steve Mark and Tahlia Gordon discuss the model of regulating lawyers that is used by the Office of the Legal Services Commissioner (OSLC) in New South Wales, an approach which integrates the positive potential of ongoing regulatory conversations between the regulator and regulated that emphasises a commitment to high ethical standards and which has the potential to be applied in the financial sector.

Part 4 evaluates the realities and limitations associated with regulating culture in the financial sector. In chapter 11, Pamela Hanrahan examines how the 'fiduciary idea' is often invoked to explain what the relationship is, or ought to be, between financial intermediaries (including broker-dealers, advisers and investment managers) and their clients. But is the fiduciary idea the right conceptual model for this relationship? If it is, why does fiduciary law struggle to deliver a culture in financial services firms in which the clients' interests are at the centre of the endeavour? Thus her chapter explores the limits, and limitations, of the fiduciary idea in financial services law in the context of the Future of Financial Advice (FoFA) reforms to chapter 7 of the *Corporations Act 2001 (Cth)* in Australia. In chapter 12, Michael Legg analyses whether class actions commenced by shareholders against financial organisations can regulate culture through the lens of the Bank of America Corporation class action arising from the acquisition of Merrill Lynch & Co in the United States and the National Australia Bank Limited class action arising from the increase in provisions for losses from its portfolio of collateralised debt obligations in Australia. The link with culture is explored by examining the following questions: who sues, who gets sued and what are the outcomes? In chapter 13, Olivia Dixon discusses the *Criminal Code Act 1995* (Cth) which is regarded as one of the most sophisticated models of corporate criminal liability in the world. However, despite repeated instances of corporate misconduct linked to a toxic culture, prosecution based on cultural culpability has been noticeably absent. The chapter considers to what extent definitional, pragmatic and ethical issues explain this. In the concluding chapter, eminent regulatory theorist John Braithwaite remarks on the various contributions to the book and ponders the prospects for situating cultural change within the financial regulatory reform paradigm. His argument that the integration of rules, principles and norms interact and are disseminated through storytelling is both erudite and intuitive. It is inescapable that credible reform necessitates a refashioning of the narrative governing the place of capital markets in society.

The extension of the role of the state through legal and other mechanisms cannot be considered in a vacuum, nor too can the role played by crisis and contingency in facilitating ideational change. As with the current crisis afflicting the Anglo-American model of capitalism, the debate in the 1930s on whether and how the government should intervene was based on a social as well as economic catastrophe in which the gullible and the unwary were beguiled by the lure of instant gratification. The resulting New Deal legislation and regulatory infrastructure in the US was a profound recalibration in which private interests were rendered subservient to societal obligation. Not for the first time in regulatory design, the contemporary search for credible reform necessitates going back to the future and re-absorbing the lessons of regulatory history, and this is a recurring theme in this book.

Part One

Regulating Culture in the Financial Sector – Structural and Historical Dimensions

CHAPTER 1

The Culture of Financial Institutions: The Institution of Political Economy

David A Westbrook

An expert's questions tend to be bounded by the expert's claim to special knowledge, ie, expertise, and usually institutional accreditation. So it is not surprising that when experts who think about the regulation of financial institutions are asked to think about 'culture,' the issue tends to be framed in their terms (what we know, or at least think we learned in graduate school or in the course of our professional careers). For example, how should regulators confront the culture within a financial institution so that the institution performs in accordance with societal norms, even when the law is unclear? This is a good question (the answer is seven), and as Justin O'Brien's and George Gilligan's excellent introduction to this book makes clear, variations on the question have been heard in recent years across the financial world.

As with all ordinary science, much is assumed, as the introduction also demonstrates.[1] The model question posed above assumes that we know what financial industries are, and what purposes their regulation serves. Not so long ago, for example, it seemed pretty clear what a bank is, and what the central bank's responsibilities are toward such institutions. This is no longer the case; we now speak not only of shadow banking, but the central bank as dealer of last resort,[2] and we observe a pronounced unwillingness to follow Baghehot's advice and let insolvent banks fail.[3] Nor can it be said that we are clear on just what 'societal norms' financial institutions are to serve. Sticking with central banking (and by extension, the banking industry in operation) do we think that monetary policy ought to be conducted in accordance with real economic, as opposed to monetary, goals?[4] For another set of examples, it is easy enough (tautological) to say that fraud is bad, but when we get down to brass tacks—what disclosure is required under what circumstances, or else the transaction be deemed fraudulent, with financial and even criminal consequences?—little agreement exists.

---

[1] See generally Thomas Kuhn, *The Structure of Scientific Revolutions* (Chicago, University of Chicago Press, 1996).

[2] See Perry Mehrling, *The New Lombard Street: How the Fed Became the Dealer of Last Resort* (Princeton, Princeton University Press, 2011).

[3] Walter Bagehot, *Lombard Street: A Description of the Money Market* (London, Henry S. King and Co., 1873) 101–103.

[4] See Charles Goodhart, '*Central Banks Walk Inflation's Razor,*' *Financial Times,* 30 January 2013, available at http://www.ft.com/cms/s/0/744e4a96-661c-11e2-b967-00144feab49a.html.

To a large extent, such mindlessness must be forgiven under the flag of Neurath's boat, which must be rebuilt even while it is at sea.[5] We cannot pay attention to everything at once, and if we seek to address something as nebulous as 'culture' in financial regulation, assumptions are going to have to be made. But it should also be acknowledged that our assumptions also may be convenient, or otherwise intellectually dubious. So before we stride off into the rough of financial institution regulation, and what has or has not been learned from the global financial crisis, and what 'culture' might mean, at least for the purposes of preventing or at least containing the fire next time, it is worth pausing to reflect on the fact that financial culture is not only, or even most importantly, the culture within financial industries, including of course their customers and regulators. That is, the most important part of financial culture may have very little to do with that on which we, as experts of one sort or another, are authorized to speak. 'I'm sorry about the cancer, ma'am, but I'm a podiatrist.'

Financial culture also is the product of financial industries; it is the heart of contemporary political economy, what I have elsewhere called the City of Gold.[6] The GFC matters in a way that, for example, the Silicon Valley bubble did not, not merely because of the former's scale, but because the mismanagement of financial institutions led to the disruption of so many human relationships, most obviously employment relationships. Unemployment—or lack of employment opportunities—blights a generation. Unemployment correlates with suicide, divorce, and addiction rates.[7] With massive unemployment (or worse, little employment prospects for the young, energetic, and sometimes violent) we may see a loss of faith in social institutions, a rise in ethnic animosity and virulent nationalism, an anarchist moment. 'The best lack all conviction, while the worst/Are full of passionate intensity,' as Yeats has it.[8] This year, 2013, does not appear to be 1913, nor even 1933, though the situation in Southern Europe remains particularly dismaying. But to say that history teaches that things can be worse is a pathetic excuse. Members of the financial community (or at least its talking heads) tend to be all too blithe about recent colossal failures, and the harm that has been inflicted not only on 'the little people,' but also on the structures that sustain the lives of the privileged.

Understanding financial culture and the failings of the global financial crisis in social terms does more than to remind us of the human significance of events, significance that is perhaps easy to forget in technical discourses on institutional regulation. Indeed part of the point of this or any other expert discourse (consider here medicine, or the military) is to be able to discuss fraught questions, such as cancers, bombs, or indeed insolvencies, as if they were merely objective. And in recent years, the discipline of economics has struggled to

---

[5] Otto Neurath, *Logical Positivism* (Glencoe, IL, The Free Press, 1959) 201. The image was later taken up by the Harvard philosopher WVO Quine. See WVO Quine, *Word and Object* (Cambridge, MA, MIT Press, 1960) 3–4. My thanks to Vitor Gaspar.

[6] See DA Westbrook, *City of Gold: An Apology for Global Capitalism in a Time of Discontent* (New York, Routledge, 2004).

[7] See D Baker and K Hassett, 'The Human Disaster of Unemployment,' (12 May 2012) *The New York Times*, available at www.nytimes.com/2012/05/13/opinion/sunday/the-human-disaster-of-unemployment.html?pagewanted=all; L Sayer, P England, P Allison and N Kangas, 'She Left He Left: How Unemployment and Satisfaction Affect Women's and Men's Decisions to Leave Marriage' (2011) 6 *American Journal of Sociology* 116, 1982–2018; D Henkel, 'Unemployment and Substance Use: A Review of the Literature' (2011) *1 Current Drug Reviews 4*, 4–11.

[8] WB Yeats, 'The Second Coming' (1921).

define itself in scientific terms, understood to be concerned with objects, and thus in some sense outside of culture and by extension politics. So, from an economic perspective, one may speak of, for familiar examples, the independence of central banking, or a 'technical' government, or make the claim that while it is clear what reforms need to be made, the problems are political.

But from the more traditional and perhaps defensible perspective of political economy, finance is social in the structural sense used by sociologists and anthropologists. Our financial institutions are absolutely central to the way we as people conduct ourselves and understand our lives. This may be most obvious in the United States, where so many social goods—including much education, health care, and retirement—are provided through institutions directly dependent on portfolio investment. But as the European debt crisis makes clear, in countries where social obligations are met by the state, governments are quite dependent on healthy financial markets, in turn dependent on healthy 'private' (!) financial institutions. Other examples abound. We securitize fixed assets. We pay for daily operations through credit arrangements, both as individuals (credit cards) and businesses (commercial lending and paper). As both individuals and especially institutions, we are comfortable with leverage, exchange rate risk, and all sorts of other dangers, in large part because we have developed derivative markets intended to hedge our risks. One could go on, but in short, we have capitalized our worlds; this is what it means to have a 'social capitalism.'[9] To put the matter differently: if the GFC represents a colossal failure of finance, it also demonstrates just how successful finance has been in monetizing contemporary economies, so that it seems rather quaint to talk about the distribution of goods and services and the problem of scarcity.

Thus while we still tend to teach finance in entrepreneurial terms (finance is progressive, because it allows people to do what they cannot do out of retained earnings), credit—sweet liquidity—is absolutely central to daily operations of leveraged (and interconnected, and vulnerable) governments, institutions and individuals. All of this makes the spectacle of young bucks at Barclays promising one another bottles of champagne in exchange for modest market manipulation[10] seem like a farce, but symptomatic—Marie Antoinette dressing up as a shepherd. And this makes financial regulation an essentially custodial, or as is said in the banking context (now including the securities context)[11] 'prudential,' enterprise, like the provision of electricity or water.

At this point, the expert debate on the regulation of financial institutions does not seem so harmless. Without being sentimental, at issue is not merely how banks and other financial institutions are to be run, but our political economy, ie, little questions like whether kids in Spain will ever get a job, or just how many people in the US will be on food stamps. It would be intellectually convenient to say, with Foucault, that our claims to expert knowledge are also assertions of authority, power.[12] While there is a truth here, this point is easily overdone: bureaucrats want to live comfortably, which requires a modicum of authority, but not power in the sheer rushing sense of being Alexander. Few

---

[9] DA Westbrook, 'Dinner Parties During "Lost Decades": On the Difficulties of Rethinking Financial Markets, Fostering Elite Consensus, and Renewing Political Economy', (2013) 36 Seattle University Law Review 1187.

[10] Report From The Treasury Committee of Parliament, *Fixing Libor: Some Preliminary Findings* (London, HM Parliament, 2012).

[11] See Mehrling, *The New Lombard Street* (2011).

[12] M Foucault, *Discipline and Punish* (New York, Pantheon, 1977) 184.

bureaucrats, including bankers, seek to conquer India or even be the big swinging dicks legend has it stalk Wall Street.[13] More modestly, in bureaucratic fashion, we might ask, if social capitalism is the 'culture' of which financial institutions are the mainspring, then what sort of social capitalism may be hoped? That is, if we ask about the culture of our political economy, then what does that teach us about the culture we seek to foster in our financial institutions?

Regulators have turned to 'culture' in frustration.[14] Through the GFC and now again with the Libor scandal, we observe market participants who simply do not abide by the spirit of the rules.[15] They are, in a word, bad sports. So how do we as a society—and in particular regulators, charged with refereeing the markets—get financiers to be good sports? Or as a recent conference given by the law firm of Allens and the University of New South Wales Center on Law, Markets and Regulation phrased it, how do we regulate culture?[16]

In policy discourse, culture is commonly approached in two basic ways, both centered on the notion of assessing the significance of an action vis-à-vis a social frame of reference, the 'culture'.

Lawyers tend to think of culture on the model of law, conceived of as a rule. So, cultures establish rules. Big general rules are expressed as laws (statutes, judicial decisions, constitutions); technical administrative rules are usually called regulations; the softest and most 'cultural' rules are deemed norms, eg, best practices, which may be important even in the absence of an official sanction. In this view, law is often understood to bound otherwise free behavior, much as a fence bounds movement. The law determines a 'line,' it is often said, which is not to be crossed. As with borders, the metes and bounds of real estate and mining claims, the claims of patents—the imaginary of the 'line' is ubiquitous in the law—the lines of financial regulation are themselves invisible. They are products of statute, regulation, and best guesses as to, as Holmes wrote, 'what the judge will do in fact'—and as such are subject to professional divination (funny how Holmes's emphasis on 'fact' so quickly requires 'divination'—faith and a gift).[17] In consequence, entrepreneurs often seek legal advice, and lawyers themselves may turn to regulators, eg, by seeking a no-action letter at the SEC, for some sense of where the law's lines are. If, however, a transaction is deemed to be within the fence, then the actor is free to take the action. This imaginary is familiar, useful, indeed inescapable—but it must be recognized as only one way of imagining the law.

Economists tend to begin with rational actors who are incessantly attempting to better their situations. When contemplating an action, such actors evaluate the benefits (incentives) and harms (disincentives) they are likely to receive from taking, or not taking, the action. Many incentives are determined by other people. For example, a bank might not want to be known to take unreasonable risks, because a reputation for recklessness might dissuade people from depositing money or otherwise investing in the bank. In extreme

---

[13] See eg, T Wolfe, *The Bonfire of the Vanities* (New York, Picador, 1987).

[14] See 'Regulating Culture: Compliance, Risk and Accountability in the Aftermath of Libor,' (Workshop co-sponsored by Allens-Linklaters and the Centre for Law, Markets and Regulation, UNSW Law, 26 October, 2012).

[15] See RM Abrantes-Metz, M Kraten, AD Metz, and GS Seow, 'Libor Manipulation?' (2011) 36 *Journal of Banking & Finance* 1, 136–50; see also F Laurens, 'UK Banking Regulatory and Market Framework: Post-Crisis Reform,' (July 2012) Swiss Management Centre (SMC) University.

[16] D Westbrook, 'Regulating Culture: Navigating economies,' CLMR Portal, UNSW Law (October 2012), available at http://www.clmr.unsw.edu.au/article/ethics/regulating-culture-navigating-economies

[17] See OW Holmes Jr, 'The Path of the Law' (1897) *10 Harvard Law Review 457.*

cases, a bank could lose its licence. So, for the bank, the immediate expected profit (return on investment) must be balanced against somewhat more nebulous reputational risk if the investment goes bad, and people find out.

If lawyers unsurprisingly imagine culture to be like law, and imagine law as drawing lines that constrain otherwise free behavior, economists unsurprisingly imagine culture as a market, presenting opportunities and imposing costs on rational actors. Both approaches fundamentally externalize culture as something to be confronted by actors, as outside the actors, like weather. Neither approach understands culture to constitute market actors, or more especially the institutions that empower people to operate at all. (One cannot do a merger in the state of nature.) To be blunt, financial policy discourse tends to have a very shallow understanding of culture. There are exceptions, of course, and not to be unkind, but people with profound understandings of the significance of things tend to occupy themselves with endeavors other than the manipulation of money. And it was precisely the shallow understanding of financial culture regnant in financial discourse—culture reduced to the black letter rules of endless yet ineffectual financial regulation, and the undue faith that self-interest, including reputational cost, would serve to discipline risk-taking—that, we were told by Greenspan and others, would ensure the soundness of our financial markets.[18] Suffice it to say, such weak thinking has been of little help in recent years. Clearly, if financial culture is to be a part of the solution, then a more serious understanding of financial culture is required.

So how might we begin to think about financial culture? We might begin by thinking not about 'culture' in the abstract, but as found in specific situations. Indeed, not only does 'culture' resist final definition, as O'Brien and Gilligan note in the introduction, but much anthropology of the contemporary does not even try[19] None of the cultural anthropologists with whom I speak make any attempt to define 'culture' objectively and externally. Instead, one attempts to understand this or that 'present situation'[20] (other frequently heard words are 'assemblage' and 'constellation')—my friend Doug Holmes' forthcoming work on central bankers is exemplary.[21] In this view, culture is a placeholder for a web of understandings in which both anthropologists and their interlocutors are implicated. So for example, we might look at actors surrounding Libor: the various reporting banks (including investment bankers, traders, and directors, to say nothing of shareholders, depositors and other investors, as well as counterparties); the British Bankers Association, Thompson Reuters, the regulators broadly construed, including not just the Financial Services Authority (FSA) and the Bank of England, but ultimately Parliament itself; and perhaps most importantly, those who use Libor, and those who study it, including the ethnographer herself, with her capacities, limitations, and interests.

To put it differently, Libor may be understood not as an objective fact (that is self-evidently naive, or should be by now), but as a collective narrative about the expected cost of various forms of capital. Contemporary economies evidently need a collective narrative

---

[18] See A Greenspan, *Remarks before the 31st Annual Conference on Bank Structure and Competition* (11 May 1995).
[19] O'Brien & Gilligan, Introduction at 2.
[20] DA Westbrook, *Navigators of the Contemporary, Why Ethnography Matters* (The University of Chicago Press, Chicago, 2008) 27–28.
[21] See DR Holmes, *Economy of Words: Communicative Imperatives in Central Banks* (Chicago, University of Chicago Press, 2013).

about the future cost of capital, more prosaically known as a benchmark.[22] A serious ethnographic inquiry into how such a tale is told could be useful. Such an inquiry might even help legislators in their task of encouraging more reliable tellings.

As suggested above, however, we also could begin our inquiry into financial culture from the outside, rather than the inside, of financial institutions. We might begin by thinking about financial culture in terms of their artifacts, the products of financial institutions that we use every day, and that shape the way we live. In other words, we might think about financial culture in terms of political economy writ large, as that which financial institutions institute, make: our commercial society.

So how does finance work in the social world? For purposes of discussion, entertain the following proposition: the Occupy Wall Street movement considered (perhaps generously) as argument, was descriptively correct and normatively incorrect. That is, Occupy Wall Street was right to complain about the one per cent (or better, less); substantial material inequality in fact inheres in contemporary market societies. Consider further the possibility that, despite regnant ideologies of autonomy and equality, our fundamental social structures cannot plausibly be discussed in those terms. To be blunt, Occupy Wall Street was normatively wrong to believe that our society—that any financial society, including proudly egalitarian Nordic ones—is fundamentally about equality and autonomy.

Progress, as Henry Sumner Maine famously wrote, consisted in the historical movement from societies in which order was defined by status or birth, to societies in which order was defined by contract.[23] This is as succinct a definition of liberal modernity as one might wish, and its connections to commercial ideology are both visible to this day and well documented.[24] But suppose that finance does not work that way. Suppose that in moving from an economy of goods and services to an economy of money, and from the antithesis of capital and labor familiar since Marx to social capitalism, we have also moved from contract to status as the foundation of social order. Suppose we are neo-feudal, and have not yet awoken to our lives?

A full account, much less a defense, of this idea would require a book that I may not write. Among other things, I find the idea unappealing, and the days are short. So the rest of this essay may be considered maliciously suggestive, an ideological ghost story, at the very least a provocation. But if our society is inherently unequal, and that inequality is realized and enforced through financial institutions, surely the regulation of financial institutions ought to reflect that reality? More broadly, how might we think about political economy writ large after republican pieties have been washed away in a sea of liquidity, or, to put it more bluntly and in European terms, after austerity has made it clear what matters?

In hesitantly entertaining such politically incorrect (for heirs of the French Revolution, blasphemous) thoughts, let us begin innocently enough, with the example of travel. One sets out armed with a piece of plastic and sometimes a little book (for Americans, the book is blue). The traveler exhibits her tokens to people, generally 'agents' of governments or corporations. If the tokens are found valid, the traveller is given airplane rides, hotel rooms, refreshments, and so forth. The traveler retains the plastic and the book, indeed, need not give anybody anything. Instead of actual exchange, various accounts on various computers are changed; ie, by 'payment' we usually mean a communication and a promise to account.

---

[22] See M Wheatley, 'The Wheatley Review of Libor,' (London, Financial Services Authority, 2012).

[23] HS Maine, Ancient Law (London, JM Dent & Sons, 1861) 170.

[24] G Binder, 'Legal Metaphors for Self in Twentieth Century Social Thought,' in Looking Back at Law's Century (New York, Cornell University Press, 2002).

Thus travel, and for that matter economic activities generally, take place in 'economies of money.'[25] Virtually all of what is 'exchanged' does not exist in any material sense. 'Exchange' has itself become a metaphor for essentially legal communication about the terms of financial instruments, promises to alter numbers which, like sports statistics, express relative standing. All that is solid melts into air, as it were.[26]

One cannot think of communication (one cannot speak) outside of a culture. Financial culture is the water in which we all swim, regulators and regulated and just plain folks. Finance itself is an expression and constitutive of culture; payment (contract, property, and so forth) is always already cultural. Thus the recent discovery of 'culture' in financial discourse—as an afterthought, what to do when the rules fail to keep up with developments in the market—is wrongheaded. In the same vein, the imaginary of the lawyers and economists, for whom culture is understood is something to be confronted by actors, as rule or incentive, is misleading. Culture was always the question, and culture was always also internal to the individuals, institutions, modes of interaction that constitute financial markets.

If culture was always the question, then why has culture come to the fore just now? What has changed in recent years? For a long time, before the GFC, the culture of financial elites was both workable and tacit, went without saying (*comme il faut*), and so 'culture' was not something that required worrying. Business communities, like all communities, have their virtues and of course their vices. It is important to remember, however, that such arrangements are not stable over time (virtues and vices have histories). So, for example, by the 1930s, New York had been a financial center for generations; surely business could not have been done for so long and on such scale if everyone were a cheat and there were no trust. But the Peccora Commission, or in our time, Eliot Spitzer, were not wrong in their aspirations to clean up Wall Street, asserting that norms had faded and needed to be enforced.[27] Not even crime is constant. So with regard to British banking, as with regard to investment banking on Wall Street, knowledgeable commentators report their sense that social norms have frayed, that business is not what it used to be. (Corporate lawyers universally do so.) That is, when a commercial culture is working, and especially when money is being made, the question of culture fades into the background. When a community's norms lead it to harm itself, culture comes into question.

So it is because these are hard times—because our financial thinking or at least policy failed to prevent disaster—that we must think anew about financial culture. We must reconsider whether we still believe what we long thought we know about financial culture, viz, is it really sensible to think about finance in terms of the trade of scarce resources, ie, the exchange of goods, among equals? To shift examples slightly, assume that you 'order' dinner, or better still, 'command' it in French, and your credit card is accepted, that is, the waiter (or 'server') and the kitchen obey your wishes. The restaurant and its staff accept that you are the sort of person to whom dinner should be brought. Unless you leave a tip in cash on the table, you do not actually pay for the meal. You send (or sign) a message authorizing your institutions to credit their institutions. Various back offices handle looking out for the restaurant, which looks after its suppliers, its staff, and so forth. From this perspective the

---

[25] DA Westbrook, *Problematique* in *Rethinking Financial Markets*, The World Economics Association, available http://rfconference2012.worldeconomicsassociation.org/problematique/.

[26] K Marx and F Engels, *The Communist Manifesto*, J Katz edn (New York, Pocket Books, 1998).

[27] See e.g., The United States Committee On Banking and Currency, *The Pecora Report: The 1934 Report On the Practices of Stock Exchanges From the "Pecora Commission,"* available at www.archives.gov; see also A Ignatius, 'Eliot Spitzer: Wall Street's Top Cop,' *Time Magazine*, 30 December 2002.

credit card establishes the diner's social standing. Credit transactions are rather feudal, in the fairly literal sense of a web of obligations and obedience built upon trust.

There are, of course, other accounts to give of what it means to order dinner. Those on the left would like to maintain that people get things, or should get things, because they have done some work. That would be nice, but let me be honest: I do not work much, and therefore do not assume that wealth is the artifact of labor. More to the point, I do not work for the waiter, and what work I have done, he does not know. All he knows is I have plastic, and that is more than enough. Or, to turn the problem around, feudal lords 'worked' too: they fought their kings' wars, struggled with rivals, ran manors, and sired heirs. But it would be foolish to say that they were obeyed in exchange for their labors.

Those on the right sometimes maintain that capital markets, great engines of progress and security, require investors. Even though investors do not work, they bear risk, for which they should be paid. As a professor of finance, I teach this story, but again, I really do not risk much. I have tenure, and I hope I am not being let onto a plane to bear risk. In short, neither the ideology of the left nor the ideology of the right does a very good job of articulating what is happening in an ordinary financial transaction: on the basis of messages—in this case, swiping credit cards—agents are authorized, or not authorized to act.

As already suggested, this does not sit well with the liberal mind. Conventionally, we imagine transactions as exchanges among contracting parties who are legally presumed to be equals. That is, we see economic activity as the expression of liberty, choice: one chooses to buy or sell. We speak of 'free markets' instead of 'command economies' much less 'neo-feudal obligation.' We conceive of liberty in opposition to status. So the wife, child or slave under the Roman law (*patria potestas*) are unfree—their social position is determined not by their choice, but by action of law, generally referring to the circumstances of birth or battle. That is, liberal political economy has often defined itself in opposition to other ways of social ordering. Maine himself was a scholar of Roman law, and intimately familiar with the Indian caste system. But to say that nineteenth century England or the twenty-first century US is unlike the Rome of the Twelve Tables does not mean that our own self-understanding is sufficiently deep, that we have our ideology right enough. The fact that a world of difference exists between being a 'server' today and chattel slavery in the US in the early nineteenth century does not mean we should understand restaurant service in terms of autonomous exchange rather than, literally, service.

As noted, in economies of money, we see webs of obligation without direct exchange. We see service, indeed, obedience, even if not the right to physical coercion or outright alienation, as with chattel slavery. In 'The Theory of the Firm,' Ronald Coase was disturbed by the fact that so much economic activity was governed by hierarchies of command rather than by bargain, a price mechanism.[28] He argued that a system of contractual subservience saved transaction costs. Perhaps, but this led Coase to the uneasy recognition that any economic system—including slavery—might be justified on the basis of efficiency demonstrated by its existence.[29] Coase took refuge in, of all things, the law. Agency law, in twentieth century Anglo-American systems, simply did not allow employment agreements for indentured servitude, and slavery was illegal, so its practice could not be taken as evidence of a saving

---

[28] See RH Coase, 'The Nature of the Firm,' (1937) 4 *Economica*, 386.
[29] See ibid. at 403–404.

of transaction costs.[30] But if the question is what should the law be, ie, how should we begin thinking about the regulation of financial institutions, and in particular, their hierarchical exercises of power, 'the law' is hardly an answer. What law?

Much more may be said about the use of 'transaction costs' to rescue the economic imaginary of autonomous and presumptively equal contracting parties, but more old fashioned and honest words are 'privilege,' 'status,' and even 'class,' understood as a relation to authoritative institutions and especially the social capital they command. It should go without saying that corporations, including banks, are—as the church and the military have always been—such authoritative institutions.

Currently polite words for economic status are title, meaning institutional affiliation, and brand. So an individual may be invited to teach in a university, or run a large bank, and exercise the authority of that office, because that individual has achieved a certain reputation among those with the power to appoint, what the Middle Ages meant by the word 'invest.' There is an amusing moment, at policy and academic conferences, when speakers publicly proclaim that they are not speaking in their institutional capacity. True enough, of course, in the sense that the presenter is not formally authorized to speak for the institution understood as a corporate body. But the vast majority of speakers must be legitimated through a chain of institutional affiliations, or they would not be asked to speak at all. Nobody besides perhaps great artists speaks purely on his or her own authority. Titles matter, hence nametags.

A business attracts custom—depositors and other investors in a bank—based on a differentiated reputation, secured by the sorts of intellectual property that make up a brand. But investors generally do not 'know' what 'their' banks do. As Jamie Dimon will admit, even bankers are pretty hazy on what their institutions are doing.[31] Investment is usually highly social, based on reputation and commonly held (hence publicly defensible) belief, and hence the need for credit rating agencies.

From this perspective, handing over a credit card is like showing a letter from the king, or wearing a uniform that displays an officer's rank. The credit card establishes a position vis-à-vis a chain of financial institutions, and by extension, the governments that attempt to back them up, not always successfully. None of this is very democratic, and in that sense not very modern, and therefore difficult to think, but so it goes. Unsurprisingly, financial discourse typically treats payment in terms of an Arcadian quid pro quo, in spite of the fact that financial activities (collectively, culture) consists largely of communications about relative social standing defined in terms of accounting. And, after Enron and Worldcom, the implosion of various intensively managed financial institutions during the GFC, the Greek scandal, and now Libor, accounting seems to be a rather dubious enterprise.

At this point in the discussion, we have sketched a political economy (social capitalism) founded primarily on economies of money (the exchange of tokens, rather than goods or services) in which 'trade' consists largely of communications about relative social standing defined in terms of a rather dubious system of accounting.[32] In this context, how might we think about regulating financial culture?

---

[30] DA Westbrook, 'A Shallow Harbor and a Cold Horizon: The Deceptive Promise of Modern Agency Law for the Theory of the Firm,' (2012) 35 *Seattle University Law Review* 1369, 1373–75.

[31] See US Senate Committee on Banking, Housing, and Urban Affairs, *Hearing: A Breakdown in Risk Management: What Went Wrong at JPMorgan Chase?* (Wednesday, June 13, 2012) Testimony of James Dimon.

[32] It is worth noting in passing that the supply of tokens is in principle infinite—limited by the willingness to participate (promise, bet, extend credit). But if supply is indefinitely large, is indeed positively associated with

At least four differences between the regulatory demands of the social capitalism we in fact have and the orthodoxies of contemporary regulatory discourse (what both regulators and regulated say) are salient.

First, insofar as economic activity consists of communications that affect relative standing ('positions') among authoritative institutions, the public–private distinction is largely effaced. From the bottom up: webs of speech form the public sphere. The fact that speech is transactional does not somehow make it private. (The agora is a public space.) From the top down, all of the actors are licensed, regulated, and generally insured by the government. To quip, all finance is more or less public, a lesson from the recent wave of bailouts, and once again being demonstrated in Europe.[33]

Second, almost all actors at issue in finance are officials, whose authorities and obligations are defined by law. Banks are institutions authorized to conduct certain kinds of intermediation. Bankers act not in their own capacity, but as officers of the bank. The legal capacity to dispose of assets depends on institutional status and authority, almost never on personal ownership—even in the case of so-called proprietary trading. Shareholders simply have no legal power to dispose of corporate assets. Thus the imagination that suffuses financial policy discourse, of the sheriff attempting to constrain yeoman traders, is silly. Financial policy asks, or should ask, after the proper relationships among different sorts of bureaucrats, whose powers are legally defined, whose collective actions allocate assets. The fact that an economy is neither a command economy nor even socialistic (the state does not have substantial ownership of key enterprises), does not mean that markets are not institutionally and legally comprised, and therefore only understood in social terms.

Third, and by extension from the first two points, the regulator and the object of regulation need to be understood in terms of one another, reciprocally rather than antagonistically. Here again the metaphor of sports is instructive. The referee does not exist without the game. Conversely, games cannot be won without a set of conventions to determine the bounds of the field, what counts as a point, and the like. To understand rules—and regulators, and ultimately law—as essentially external to marketplace activity is a common error, but an error nonetheless. It is legal instruments that are being traded, all the way down.

Fourth, regulators and policy makers and even academics are conceptually 'within' the culture they seek to regulate. To some extent, this is a matter of biography–one must know a lot of finance even to follow the conversation. Cultural bias is also a matter of interest. The Wheatley Report is quite candid about the government's wish to preserve the preeminence of London as a financial center[34] More profoundly, financial market participants have difficulty thinking about finance in ways other than 'like what we've done, only somewhat better.' And, as noted above, financiers, like practitioners of most any art, are good at thinking about how to do what it is they do—they are far less good at thinking about what it means.[35]

---

demand, then distribution under conditions of scarcity is hardly what financial markets, at least, are doing. This essay, therefore, could have focused not on the absence of exchange, but on the political character of both supply and demand, and by extension, the social (cultural) qualities of price, none of which can easily be squared with liberal theology. As financial markets, especially derivative markets, become more important to how society operates, political economy should be revised accordingly.

[33]   Incidentally, it is not entirely clear what is meant, in the Libor context, by 'unsecured' lending. Who needs collateral if obligations are backed by the taxing power of the state?

[34]   *See* Wheatley above n 22

[35]   A point that runs back at least to Plato.

To sketch the image of financial culture that is emerging: contemporary social capitalism uses more or less competitive markets, operated and overseen by corporate and governmental officials (bureaucrats) in reciprocal relationships, within shared webs of understanding, to determine the flow of goods, services, and most importantly the financial assets (social capital) that largely determine the power of institutions, including governments, the provision of social services, and much of the status of individuals (who is rich). If this—rather than some sort of fence, within which private actors legally deemed to be equal seek personal gain through trade, perhaps in the faith that the invisible hand will direct the sum of their actions to the common weal—is a plausible description of our capitalism, then what might be said about financial culture? Financial culture is far more social, bureaucratic, hierarchical, and intellectually conservative than is commonly admitted in, for example, the pages of the *Wall Street Journal*. (One recalls Schumpeter's thoughts about the end of capitalism, ie, the entrepreneur giving way to the manager.)[36]

What might be said about regulation in such a society? The general impulse of the law is conservative. In ordinary times, the king wishes to see good order in his kingdom, whenever and wherever he might reign. Even in times of revolution, the authority of the law is almost always understood as prior—the ancien régime has strayed from the true law, and therefore must be overthrown, so that society may return to the path of righteousness (hence 'revolution,' a wheel returning to whence it began).[37] So we may assume that the financial regulation required by social capitalism will be, or should be, custodial in character.

As noted above, the social order has largely been capitalized—we rely on portfolio management to ensure the operation of our governments, our payment systems, the way institutions and individuals operate daily. We rely on endowments to provide social services, ranging from education to health care to retirement. In such a deeply capitalistic society, financial markets are essentially like utilities or weapons systems: disruption of operations cannot be tolerated for any length of time. From this perspective, the purpose of financial regulation is to ensure smooth functioning, even at the cost of liquidity and capital formation, of financial markets in which positions are taken, and by extension, portfolios are constructed. In short, the shift from entrepreneurial capitalism to social capitalism implies a corresponding shift, admittedly not yet taken, from permissive regulation to custodial regulation.

How might one begin to think about custodial regulation? While it is difficult to think about the context of one's own thought, it is not quite impossible. Much contemporary anthropology is marked by the acknowledgment that it fundamentally is 'reflexive' rather than objective—the account of a culture is always also the account of the writer of the culture. Hence the transformation of anthropology in the 80's has been called 'writing culture.'[38] The difficulty in the anthropological enterprise is acknowledging the self-referential character of the inquiry, and proceeding nonetheless.[39] Something similar might be said—is being said—about the need for financial market regulators to think about

---

[36] See generally J Schumpeter, *Capitalism, Socialism, and Democracy* (New York, George Allen & Unwin Publishers 1943).

[37] HJ Berman, *Law and Revolution: The Formation of Western Legal Tradition* (Massachusetts, Harvard University Press, 1983) 20.

[38] See generally G Marcus and J Clifford, *Writing Culture: The Poetics and Politics of Ethnography* (Berkeley, University of California Press, California, 1986).

[39] As another aside, economics and so finance has not yet really taken the turn to interpretation that marks the rest of the social sciences and also the humanities.

the culture that they are trying to regulate, yet which forms their own understanding of what it is that they regulate.

Libor itself is reflexive. The respondents are asked at what rate would your important bank be able to borrow a reasonable sum in a given currency for a specific tenor at 11:00 am?[40] In constructing Libor, the BBA, through Thompson Reuters, asks bankers for their view of their place in the world, asks them to enact Keynes's beauty pageant on themselves.[41] In speculating on the price at which a bank would be able to borrow a reasonable sum, the Libor respondent is forced to ask himself how (un)desirable is my credit in the context of this currency market?

My friends the anthropologists Doug Holmes and George Marcus have termed such insider/outsider views of a present situation, like participating in a Libor survey, 'paraethnographic.'[42] Actors in complex contexts like large banks must articulate their own culture and their standing within it to themselves as a condition of their functioning in the culture, doing their jobs. Although global finance is an impossibly complex context, those who would act within it must in fact imagine it somehow, tell themselves some story about it, in order to be able to navigate—much as ancient sailors had to have some picture, however incomplete, of their seas. To rephrase, participants in complex contemporary sites stand in much the same relationship to their own cultures as traditional anthropologists stood in relation to native cultures.

Not only do actors describe their contexts to themselves; in so doing, they help constitute the context. For the present example, Libor is traded upon. The beauty contest establishes standards of beauty. Nor is Libor the only place where we observe financial conversation operating to create the conditions under which finance is done. Consider inflation targeting: central banks announce not only their objectives, but the means by which they hope those objectives will be achieved, in a self-conscious effort to have those objectives priced in and traded upon, in a communicative circle.[43]

A para-ethnographic perspective, ie, a conversational style of anthropology, could provide some grasp on contemporary contexts, and especially on how complicated bureaucracies like banking generate social, economic, and inevitably political realities.[44] The opportunity for anthropologists, and perchance bankers and their regulators, is to make critical use of para-ethnographic perspectives to accomplish not the interests of their interlocutors, but their own objectives, whether it be complex evaluation or the maintenance of sound markets. If regulators were to approach their jobs through a para-ethnographic

---

[40]   See Wheatley at 22.

[41]   See JM Keynes, *The General Theory of Employment, Interest and Money* (Orlando, Harcourt, 1953) 156.

[42]   See DR Holmes and G Marcus, 'Collaborative Imperatives: A Manifesto, of Sorts, for the Re-Imagination of the Classic Scene of Fieldwork Encounter,' in M Konard (ed) *Collaborators Collaborating: Counterparts in Anthropological Knowledge and International Research Relations*, (New York, Berghahn, 2012) 126–43; DR Holmes and G Marcus, 'Cultures of Expertise and the Management of Globalization: Toward the Re-functioning of Ethnography,' in A Ong and S Collier(eds) *Global Assemblages: Technology, Politics, and Ethics as Anthropological Problems* (Hoboken, John wiley @ sons, 2005) 235–52; DR Holmes and G Marcus, 'Fast Capitalism: Para-Ethnography and the Rise of the Symbolic Analyst,' in M Fisher and G Downey (eds) *Frontiers of Capital, Ethnographic Reflections on the New Economy*, (Durham, Duke University Press, 2006) 33–57; DR Holmes and G Marcus, 'Collaboration Today and the Re-Imagination of the Classic Scene of Fieldwork Encounter,' (2008) 1 *Collaborative Anthropologies* 136, 170.

[43]   See Holmes, n 17.

[44]   See eg, Westbrook, n 20.

understanding of financial institutions, then the regulatory relationship, especially with regard to prudential regulation, would be subtly but pretty profoundly reconfigured.

The Bank of England's Andrew Haldane recently gave a very fine speech at the Federal Reserve's annual meeting in Jackson Hole.[45] In it, Haldane argued that financial regulation, and specifically the Basel process, had grown far too complex—and that such complexity was counterproductive. So Haldane argued that compliance with norms should rely less on elaborate articulation of rules, and rely more on the judgement of experienced officials. In terms of the common law tradition, Haldane argued that it was time for regulators to shift their approach from law toward equity. One might also make an analogy to perennial argument between rule-based and principle-based approaches to accounting. Haldane was not too explicit about what bank regulation would look like under such circumstances, but it seems fair to imagine that there would be many discussions in which regulators asked actors to convince them why their practices were safe, and their portfolios sound. Another analogy might be drawn to a start-up business, perhaps a technology company, which seeks early stage investment. The onus is on the leaders of the young business to explain to potential investors why theirs is a good idea, worthy of realization. The regulator of an important financial operation should be considered invested, under the motto, 'If you fail, I fail.'

The argument here is not nearly as abstract as it may appear. To recapitulate: as the GFC has demonstrated, vast numbers of tax dollars may be spent, unemployment may rise, growth falter, and the host of institutions that rely on pools of assets, from family retirement and education funds to sovereign debt, may be shaken. Relationships may fray and individual human possibilities may be diminished. Contemporary societies depend on well functioning financial markets much as they depend on electricity, hence 'social capitalism.'[46] To be blunt, the (orthodox) understanding of financial markets as the bounded interaction of essentially private actors (the understanding with which discussions of culture generally begin) is both intellectually primitive and politically impoverished. Understanding finance in human terms—social capitalism—should cause one to understand regulation in explicitly custodial terms, in which bankers and their regulators come to mutually agreed understanding on how to manage assets. Thus, the relationship between regulator and regulated could be transformed from one of opposition to mutually reinforcing and interdependent participation in the custody of social assets.[47]

A custodial approach to regulation should engender, within regulatory relationships, the sensitivity and tough mindedness traditionally associated with trust obligations.[48] From this perspective, regulators might think of what happened at Barclays and many of the shenanigans of the last years not just as actions of a few 'bad apples,' or even as more general expressions of a corrupt institutional culture, but as a kind of personal and professional betrayal for which the appropriate response is anger. If management deceived key equity

[45] See AG Haldane, Executive Director, Financial Stability and member of the Financial Policy Committee, Bank of England, address at the Federal Reserve Bank of Kansas City's 36th economic policy symposium, The Changing Policy Landscape (12 August 2012).

[46] See Westbrook, n 25.

[47] The elegant exchange of letters between Barclays Chairman Marcus Agius and the FSA's Adair Turner is exactly what I'm NOT talking about. See the exchange of letters between Lord Turner, Chairman of the FSA, and Marcus Agius, Chairman of Barclays, available at www.publications.parliament.uk/pa/cm201213/cmselect/cmtreasy/481/48111.htm.

[48] See eg, *Meinhard v. Salmon*, 249 N.Y. 458 (1928) (A trustee is held to something stricter than the morals of the market place. . .).

investors in a company, would we not expect to see such managers replaced, and in the extreme case, the company merged out of existence? It would have been completely understandable had the radical interventions of 2008 and since resulted in the dissolution of the corporations involved: the discharge of management, the forfeit of equity, and the abolition of the brands. While some banks were resolved—especially smaller banks and especially in the US—over and over again and in jurisdiction after jurisdiction, banking, which is necessary, was confused with specific banks, which are replaceable. And banks, as Bagehot taught a long time ago, should conduct themselves with the understanding that they are replaceable.[49] And even if a society does not have the stomach to replace its banks, it should at least have the will to replace its bankers.

From a para-ethnographic perspective, however, there is a structural reason to dissolve banks or at least discharge management: if management is no longer trustworthy, then the para-ethnographic regulation, founded on trust, is not possible, and the institution cannot be licensed or backed by the state. Society should replace its bankers with more trustworthy, careful, or at least blameless, mandarins.

Turning to specifics, and the immediate occasion for this essay: what does a custodial understanding of regulation mean for the efforts to 'fix' Libor? Most proposals for reform, including Wheatley, treat Libor as if it were a device like a thermometer that directly measured an aspect of the natural world, and Barclays and others tampered with the instrument so that it gave an inaccurate reading. But Libor doesn't measure anything outside the social context of its formation. As every teacher knows, at the end of the day, performance on a test is always about the test and maybe the class, but only tangentially about the truth. Similarly, Libor is a ritual for expressing sentiment about the cost of capital and therefore the relative standing of financial institutions in the present environment. But nothing is measured. Libor estimates are provided even in the absence of trades, that is, on a speculative basis.[50]

Thus Libor wasn't untrue in the way that a faulty thermometer is inaccurate. The ritual was performed, and the BBA did generate a very important number on a daily basis. Libor was untrue in the sense of dishonest. Asked 'what do you believe,' players lied. That is, the virtue at issue is not the mechanical one of accuracy, but the moral virtue of honesty. The question is not how to 'regulate' the culture from somewhere outside the culture; the question is how do we collectively construct contexts in which we wish to participate, that is, a social capitalism of which we're happy to be members.

Various proposals for Libor reform may go some way toward 'cleaning up' the Libor process, either by reputational cost and the threat of criminal prosecution,[51] by automatic market mechanisms,[52] or by enhanced transparency coupled with ex post sanctions.[53] And it may well be that such mechanisms would be morally instructive, that is, would cause bank officials to make good faith efforts to conform. At the same time, any reform that seeks more conformity to elite consensus is also by definition conservative. Moreover, as nicely outlined by the Wheatley Review, any alternatives, comprised by different inputs, would

---

[49] See Bagehot, n 3
[50] See *Wheatley* at 6–7.
[51] Ibid at n 22, 74.
[52] See F Partnoy, *Make Banks Pay if They Cheat on Libor* (London, July 2012) *The Financial Times*.
[53] RM Abrantes-Metz and DS Evans, *Replacing the Libor with a Transparent and Reliable Index of Interbank Borrowing*, (Sept. 2012) Comments on the Wheatley Review of Libor Initial Discussion Paper.

entail a somewhat different perspective on the cost of money. And the British banking industry thinks that its perspective is best. Moreover, market participants use this number, so that shows that Libor must be fulfilling a demand, right? And besides, these expectations are now wired into countless contracts, with more being made regularly, and radical change might disrupt the markets. Unsurprisingly, the Wheatley Review urges caution. Too much change would not be prudent. So what started out as a first mover advantage and was then buttressed by path dependency has become legitimated, and even needs to be protected. Or, in another language, an innovation has become a habit, which became a custom and eventually a norm attended by the lawgiver, here the British Parliament. Unsurprisingly and as noted above, the lawgiver is disinclined to change.

More than the usual interests of immediate stakeholders are at issue. The global order that allows the operation of credit cards and so much else seems to require Libor or something very much like it. Financial institutions need to be able to contractually account for the cost of money, and for this, they require a benchmark. So what is needed is a Libor that can be believed, so that confidence in banking will be restored. Banking needs to reform its culture; we must become good sports. It is not at all clear that conservative responses will suffice; the GFC was largely due to the triumph of economic orthodoxies, and so reaffirmation of such orthodoxies is unlikely to be enough.[54]

For this reason, it makes sense to base financial regulation on the acknowledgment of hierarchy and in particular the power of financial institutions, rather than a spurious claim that financial officials are merely private actors who are to act within bounds arguably set by lawyers, and in rational accordance with the disincentives of reputational cost, as the economists unconvincingly have it. Instead, through a para-ethnographic encounter with their regulators, leaders of financial institutions could assist in the design of their own constraints, could shape the terms of their service. And financial leaders, like leaders in other realms, must stand or fall by their success. We may yet imagine Libor reform, and what we have learned from the financial crisis more generally, in happy terms. Bankers and their regulators could come to recognize that they are profoundly privileged, and as such, have great obligations. The current culture of disingenuous reporting, pro forma compliance with byzantine and contested rules, and perennially insufficient oversight could be replaced by a more reciprocal relationship in which those who act and those who authorize and ultimately insure speak earnestly and candidly about their worlds. Together these elites could exercise their power wisely, navigate a prudent course forward. Honest conversations about worlds dimly imaginable could lead to good policy in spite of unavoidable uncertainty. The people would be grateful for the custody of their institutions. The ship of state would make good, but not rash, progress.

Even in such a well-governed financial order, sometimes an institution would fail, and the taxing power of the state would have to be used to sustain the viability of the order. At issue, then, would also be the nature of the failure. Was management unworthy? As we have seen, sometimes an institution or an entire industry may lose sight of its own virtues, a story of decadence and decline easily told in London and New York. When the privileged abuse their trust, they would be removed from office, and their responsibility (and attendant wealth and social standing) transferred to more worthy mandarins.

---

[54] See generally DA Westbrook, *Out of Crisis: Rethinking Our Financial Markets* (Boulder, Paradigm Publishers, 2009).

But the privileged would not often abuse their trust. People rarely willingly leave their class for a lower one. Thus a para-ethnographic, conversational, and reciprocal understanding of the regulatory relationship could go a long way toward making banking a more virtuous enterprise. Presently empty promises to reform could be made serious by establishing contexts in which elites were answerable to other elites, at pain of losing their offices and so their status, and thenceforth having to live small.

Perhaps, but insofar as this provocation is also a ghost story, let us consider two darker courses of regulatory development. In the GFC and lately the Libor scandal, the fact that key financial institutions strayed from the commercial virtues traditional in their business (monitoring risk, honesty, and so forth) has led to a concern for culture, meaning the reassertion of traditional norms. That is, the overwhelming response to recent financial crises has been conceptually conservative. But perhaps a conservative response is insufficient. Suppose the world has changed enough that calls for transparency, for obvious instance, will do little to avert the fire next time?

In *Macbeth*, Macbeth says
I dare do all that may become a man
He who does more, is none.[55]

Macbeth of course begs the question: what becomes a man? What are the virtues appropriate to a Scottish nobleman? So it is with banking. If we think of banking as a business, and our imaginary of 'business' is fundamentally based on sole proprietorship, then the purpose of banking is to make money within the bounds of the law. But if we acknowledge that our capitalism is deeply social and banking in particular is custodial and the economy of money is in important respects new, such simple answers will not suffice.

Surely financial markets are in need of reform. But the financial world is necessarily somewhat blind to itself. The Delphic injunction, know thyself, has not gotten any easier. So it is hard for the financial policy community to think deeply about what kind of financial markets we as a society want, for student debt or housing or anything else.

These are essentially aesthetic, in the philosophical sense of the word, questions. *Out of Crisis* used the metaphor of games to talk about market regulation.[56] In both markets and games, different kinds of rules favor different kinds of competition, and foster different kinds of outcomes. So what kind of rule sets, informing what sorts of participation, do we want banking to have? In what kind of game do we want Barclays and its kin to be good sports?

As suggested above, we can imagine a world in which bankers and their regulators have long, honest conversations about how different kinds of financial games—institutions and their markets—should be played, and what were the advantages and risks attendant upon this or that way of doing things. That would not be our current situation. There is reason to be skeptical about the capacity of elites in advanced markets to have the sort of publicly minded conversation suggested here. It is worth remembering that *Macbeth* is a tragedy. Macbeth overreaches, and there has been a lot of that in recent years, at Barclays and elsewhere. So although we may imagine what custodial regulation would look like, it may be

---

[55] William Shakespeare, *Macbeth* (London, McMillan & Co., 1871) 17.
[56] See Westbrook, n 54, Chapter 7 ('Metaphors for Thinking Socially about Capitalism').

difficult, if not impossible, to achieve in fact. The imagination of banks as 'private' actors who are monitored by 'the government' is simply too deeply embedded. And in due course, we will again watch 'private' actors do in principle unnecessary harm to their, and our, communities.

Our situation may be tragic in another sense. Cultures and institutions may themselves be wrong in the very exercise of their virtues. Americans like to believe that if one does the right thing, things will go well. But the tragic perspective is that one may do the right thing, or what is honestly believed to be right, and things may go very badly. It is not difficult for an American Southerner of German descent to recall that nations may march off to misguided wars. As already noted, a great deal of the GFC was due not to misfeasance but the enthusiastic use of the substantial accomplishments of post-war finance. Just suppose, contra the Introduction, that we need not enforce or return to the virtues of finance, but that the virtues of finance are just the danger we should fear?

More specifically, let us assume that, through considerable collective efforts, Libor is reformed (and we agree on global accounting standards and an international insolvency regime) and, as a result of such policy diligence, faith in global banking is renewed. Presumably this will strengthen and extend our financial culture. Would this be a good thing?

In the US, banks are concentrated, inequality is stratospheric by our own historical standards, and unemployment is high while growth is slow. Perhaps worst of all, especially after *Citizens United*, political outcomes are openly discussed as assets.[57] In Europe, Martin Wolfe reports that banked assets are equal to 350 per cent of GDP.[58] Due to demographics and otherwise, prospects for growth are dim. Wolfgang Munchau speculates that banking union, and ultimately the institutional apparatus required to secure European financial institutions and national budgets, will supersede both the member states and European institutions.[59] This would amount to a Europe 2.0, explicitly enacted to preserve finance. That is, finance will have become constitutional.

The reemergence of naked privilege—defined in terms of bureaucratic standing rather than noble birth—may be a change of the *longue durée*. Perhaps we are watching Marx backwards, the slow motion and technocratic victory of a new sort of financial class, rather than the revolutionary violence of the proletariat. It is not at all clear how desirable the society under construction is, even if recent experience in airports ('Our platinum, diamond and gold passengers may now board through the priority boarding lane') suggests it may be an inevitable corollary of doing business on a global scale. But surely nobody with democratic republican sentiments can welcome such developments. In this much, at least, the Occupy Wall Street protesters were correct.

Nor is it clear how stable a global economy of money might be. The number of financial crises in recent years gives one pause. Surely there must be practical limits to the level

---

[57] *Citizens United v. Federal Election Commission (2010)*. My thoughts on the decision are available in, 'If Not a Commercial Republic? Political Economy in the United States after Citizens United.' See David A Westbrook, 'If Not a Commercial Republic? Political Economy in the United States after Citizens United,' (2011) 1 *U. Louisville L. Rev. 50*.

[58] See M Wolf, 'You Can't Measure An Economy's Performance on Recovery Alone', *Financial Times*, 30 October 2012, available at http://blogs.ft.com/martin-wolf-exchange/2012/10/29/you-cant-measure-an-economy-on-recovery-alone/

[59] See W Munchau, 'The Eurozone Crisis is Not Finished,' *Financial Times*, 3 February 2013.

of abstraction, the scale, interconnection, and general complexity of our institutions. And would not Libor reform, indeed would not almost any successful financial reform, only increase the scale and complexity of our institutions, with the attendant alienation and danger of catastrophe? From this perspective, financial policy may well be a noble enterprise; tragedy requires nobility. So perhaps the regulation of financial institutions is like worrying about the steering gear on the *Titanic*. Either we fail to fix it, and remain adrift, or we succeed in fixing it, and hasten on.

Even then, one should try to remember, some folks always survive.

CHAPTER 2

'Bad' Behaviour in International Financial Markets: National and Multilateral Perspectives

George Gilligan

I INTRODUCTION

This chapter examines the issue of harmful behaviour in financial markets by first exploring operational cultures in contemporary financial markets through the lens of the recent London InterBank Offered Rate (Libor) financial scandal.[1] Second, the chapter analyses the history of the English model of financial regulation and its influence in how international financial markets developed and continue to function. Third, in an era of globalisation with increasingly inter-locked and interdependent markets and national economies, national and international tensions regarding regulatory standard setting are discussed. The chapter concludes by considering the implications of these issues for the operational cultures of financial professionals and firms.

Financial professionals rank fairly low in public esteem these days,[2] but are they any worse than their predecessors and are operational cultures in modern financial markets really as rotten as some media reports might have us believe?[3] Scandals are a recurring feature of financial services on a global scale, including the UK, but they were probably more common in the 1840s than they are now. There is no overwhelming evidence that general financial practice is less ethical than it was and it appears more likely that ethical

---

[1] This chapter was completed in early March 2013 and seeks to take account of developments up until that time.

[2] For example, a November 2012 poll of more than 1,000 adults by US pollster Gallup found that stockbrokers ranked 18 across a range of 22 professions in terms of perceived honesty and ethical conduct. This placed them above advertising practitioners, Members of Congress and car salespeople, but below many others including insurance salespeople, lawyers and business executives. Obviously, this is not conclusive in any way, but it is an indicator of low public esteem. See: Gallup Politics, 'Congress Retains Low Honesty Rating' (2 December 2012), available at www.gallup.com/poll/159035/congress-retains-low-honesty-rating.aspx.

[3] See for example: A Hill, 'Corporate Culture: Lofty Aspirations' *Financial Times* (15 July 2012), available at www.ft.com/cms/s/0/d1b4b71a-ccde-11e1-9960-00144feabdc0.html#axzz2L9E8ENao; 'The Rotten Heart of Finance' *The Economist* (7 July 2012), available at www.economist.com/node/21558281.

standards have risen over time.[4] They are certainly higher than in the Victorian era in the UK. For example during the period of *The Railway Mania* of 1845–46, hundreds of railway schemes were launched as a source of enormous fees for promoters, lawyers, engineers and surveyors. Many were never intended to be built, with some promoters, (once they had accumulated substantial funds from investors) actively lobbying for their Railway Bills to be rejected by Parliament.[5] However, any relative rise in the ethical standards of contemporary general financial practice would be, for example, of little comfort to the hundreds of thousands of angry investors who have been mis-sold payment protection insurance by UK banks in just one of the recent scandals to swamp UK financial services in 2012 and 2013.[6] Their anger is understandable because modern society expects increasing levels of security from its industries and institutions, and regulation is the medium for achieving this. The state does not guarantee the stability of individual financial organisations, but ultimately it takes on the role of guaranteeing the systemic security of the system within which those relationships exist.[7] It is this guarantor role of the state which ensures that when scandals happen, the anger of victims is not merely directed at the financial services professionals and organisations, but also at the regulatory system and the government which is responsible for that system.

Contemporary financial markets, like those in the past, are based on sociologies of trust whose historical influences and operational cultures developed in relatively insular financial centres such as the City of London (hereafter the City) and Wall Street. However, these sociologies of trust are increasingly being extenuated across time and space, as not only the number of actors involved in financial markets increases dramatically, but also the number, scale and complexity of the products brought to market seem to increase exponentially, especially through an ever-growing range of derivative products. There are literally thousands of financial derivative products with most having a swap, forward or option character, and they may be traded on exchanges or as over the counter (OTC) derivatives which are negotiated and traded directly between two contracting parties—'the financial weapons of mass destruction at the heart of the economic system' to use superstar investor Mr Warren Buffet's famous phrase.[8] The Bank for International Settlements (BIS) estimated that by June 2012, the global notional outstanding amount of OTC derivatives stood at

---

[4] J Welby, 'Do Business Ethics Matter?' (1992) 3 *International Company and Commercial Law Review* 45.

[5] G Robb, *White-Collar Crime in Modern England, Financial Fraud and Business Morality, 1845–1929* (Cambridge, Cambridge University Press, 1992), 11.

[6] The total number of customers mis-sold payment protection insurance is not yet finalised but is likely to be more than 1,000,000, and the total costs of compensation payment costs set aside by UK banks already exceeds £12 billion. See for example: S Read, 'Insurance Scandal Leads to 20,000 Complaints a Day' *The Independent* 28 September 2012, available at www.independent.co.uk/news/business/news/insurance-scandal-leads-to-20000-complaints-a-day-to-britains-banks-8182603.html; and J Treanor, 'PPI mis-selling charge reaches £5.5bn at Lloyds' *The Guardian* (1 November 2012), available at www.guardian.co.uk/business/2012/nov/01/lloyds-ppi-mis-selling-5bn.

[7] M Clarke, *Business Crime: Its Nature and Control* (Cambridge, Polity Press, 1990) 242.

[8] Mr Buffet made this famous analogy in 2003 but it still has substantive traction in contemporary markets. See eg, L Story, 'A Secretive Banking Elite Rules Trading in Derivatives' *The New York Times* (11 December 2010), available at www.nytimes.com/2010/12/12/business/12advantage.html?_r=0; and F Burks, 'Financial time bomb: Five megabanks monopolize $700 trillion derivatives market' *examiner.com* (14 March 2012), available at www.examiner.com/article/financial-time-bomb-five-megabanks-monopolize-700-trillion-derivatives-market.

US$639 trillion, which is a massive figure.[9] This evolution of financial services and markets, especially derivative trading products, carries with it increasing difficulties of verification and measurement of the scale of operational and cultural problems that may exist in the sector. Debates on these issues are affected significantly by what empirical data exists. The problem of a dearth of empirical data regarding exposure to systemic financial risk is not simply a result of the evolution of derivative products. An example from the 1980s is the savings and loans scandal in the US in which most failures were initially assessed as careless management practices, but later reports produced by the US Government: '. . .strongly suggest that criminal activity in the form of fraud was a central factor in 70 to 80 per cent of these failures'.[10]

That such a gross and widespread miscalculation as this could occur is partially explained by the political reality that scandals in the financial services sector are portrayed mostly as exceptional rather than structural features of the industry. The *bad apple* metaphor,[11] and other types of imagery are applied in all types of legal discourse, but they perform a particular camouflage role regarding white collar crime. The culture of the industry itself is a crucial factor regarding these issues, because tolerance of business misconduct is a question of moral legitimacy and standards can vary between different industries, and as discussed below the finance industry seems especially prone.[12] Despite such variance, in all industries there is a myriad of *plausible* grounds for non-compliance or partial compliance with regulation. Consequently, regulators must tread a tricky path between the sometimes competing claims of state regulation and free enterprise.[13] However, this dilemma is acute in financial services where innovation and outperformance are essential for commercial success, making standardisation extremely difficult and helping to create ambiguity in regulation. Regulators must decide how they operationalise the statutes and guidelines of their industry, so they may have to choose between conflicting goals. It is against this backdrop that the Libor scandal should be viewed because it highlights some of the harmful core features of prevailing operating cultures in contemporary financial markets.

The enormous scale of the Libor scandal was acknowledged by Assistant Attorney General of the US Department of Justice (DOJ) Lanny A. Breuer in January 2013: 'Libor will prove to be one of the largest, if not the largest white-collar case in history'.[14] Despite the proclivity of codes of conduct across various occupational groups, sectors and jurisdictions to promote good behaviour and practice, as the Libor debacle illustrates, there seem to be structural forces at work within the financial industry that limit transparency.

---

[9] Bank for International Settlements, *Semiannual OTC Derivatives Statistics at End-June 2012* (November 2012), available at www.bis.org/statistics/derstats.htm.

[10] HN Pontell and K Calavita, 'Bilking Bankers and Bad Debts, White-Collar Crime and the Savings and Loans Crisis' in K Schlegel and D Weisburd (eds), *White Collar Crime Reconsidered* (Boston, Northeastern Press, 1992), 196.

[11] See: G Gilligan, 'Jérôme Kerviel the "Rogue Trader" of Société Générale: Bad Luck, Bad Apple, Bad Tree or Bad Orchard?' (2011) *The Company Lawyer* 32, 355.

[12] See: BW Heinemann, 'Why Are Some Sectors (Ahem, Finance) So Scandal-Plagued?' (2013) *The Harvard Law School Forum on Corporate Governance and Financial Regulation*, available at blogs.law.harvard.edu/corpgov/2013/01/10/why-are-some-sectors-ahem-finance-so-scandal-plagued/#more-38557.

[13] K Hawkins, *Environment and Enforcement: Regulation and the Social Definition of Pollution* (Oxford: Clarendon Press, 1984), 12.

[14] *PBS Frontline*, 'Lanny Breuer: Financial Fraud Has Not Gone Unpunished' (22 January 2013), available at www.pbs.org/wgbh/pages/frontline/business-economy-financial-crisis/untouchables/lanny-breuer-financial-fraud-has-not-gone-unpunished/.

The enormous international strategic significance of Libor was emphasised at the announcement of the establishment of the International Organisation of Securities Commissions (IOSCO) Task Force on Financial Market Benchmarks (The IOSCO Task Force), when its Co-chair, Mr Gary Gensler, Chairman of the US Commodity Futures Trading Commission (CFTC) stated: 'When people save money in a money market fund or short term bond fund, or take out a mortgage for a home or a small business loan, the rate they receive or pay is often based, directly, or indirectly, on Libor'.[15] So, it should be clear that reliance on the veracity of the Libor benchmarks is one of the integral fulcra of the contemporary global financial system, as it is perhaps the primary benchmark for short term interest rates globally. As the *Wheatley Review*, (an official response by the UK Chancellor of the Exchequer to the Libor scandal) notes, Libor '. . .was established in the 1980s in order to provide a fair and standardised interest rate benchmark for loans, thereby facilitating the growth of the syndicated loans market'.[16]

Perhaps the most important word used in the last quote is *fair*, because it is this assumption of fairness regarding Libor which explains why there has been so much outrage about manipulation of Libor, including one of the UK's most significant banks, Barclays. In its high profile Order of 27 June 2012 which filed and settled charges against Barclays, the CFTC found that since at least 2005, Barclays PLC, Barclays Bank and Barclays Capital: '. . .repeatedly attempted to manipulate and made false, misleading or knowingly inaccurate submissions concerning two global benchmark interest rates. . .Libor. . .and the Euro Interbank Offered Rate (Euribor)'. The CFTC Order required Barclays to pay a $200 million civil penalty, cease and desist from further violations, improve its internal controls and ensure the integrity and reliability of its future Libor and Euribor submissions.[17] Also on 27 June 2012, after agreeing with the DOJ that manipulation of submissions affected the Libor rates on some occasions, Barclays agreed to pay a DOJ penalty of $160 million.[18] Again on 27 June, but this time in the UK, the Financial Services Authority (FSA) fined Barclays £59.5 million for its misconduct relating to Libor.[19]

These are substantial amounts, but they are unlikely to seriously hamper Barclays, because despite the damage wrought to its balance sheet by the Global Financial Crisis (GFC) and the fallout from sovereign debt crises in Europe, for the year 2011 Barclays was still able to report a profit of almost £6 billion.[20] These figures prompt public anger, especially when combined with earlier headlines such as the one that revealed that in 2009 when it made record annual profits of £11.6 billion, (and of course was manipulating the Libor),

---

[15] IOSCO, *IOSCO Creates Board Level Task Force on Financial Market Benchmarks*, *IOSCO/MR/22/2012*, (14 September 2012), available at www.iosco.org/news/pdf/IOSCONEWS250.pdf.

[16] HM Treasury, *The Wheatley Review of LIBOR: Initial Discussion Paper* (3 August 2012), available at www.hm-treasury.gov.uk/d/condoc_Wheatley_review.pdf, 9.

[17] Commodity Futures Trading Commission, Release pr6289-12, *CFTC Orders Barclays to pay $200 Million Penalty for Attempted Manipulation of and False reporting concerning LIBOR and Euribor Benchmark Interest Rates* (27 June 2012), available at www.cftc.gov/PressRoom/PressReleases/pr6289-12.

[18] Department of Justice, *Barclays Bank PLC Admits Misconduct Related to Submissions for the London Interbank Offered rate and Agrees to Pay $160 Million Penalty* (27 June 2012), available at www.justice.gov/opa/pr/2012/June/12-crm-815.html.

[19] Financial Services Authority, *Barclays fined £59.5 million for significant failings in relation to LIBOR and EURIBOR* (27 June 2012), available at www.fsa.gov.uk/library/communications/pr/2012/070.shtml.

[20] 'Barclays Bank profits fall 3% to £5.9bn' *BBC News* (10 February 2012), available at www.bbc.co.uk/news/business-16977865.

Barclays only paid £113 million in corporation tax in the UK.[21] Currently banks are largely held in low public esteem globally, and so when a scandal such as Libor emerges, a bank such as Barclays has a very shallow reservoir of public goodwill on which to draw.

There have been a multitude of critical media headlines in the UK, the US and elsewhere castigating Barclays over its manipulation of Libor, but in terms of regulatory or government actor criticism, perhaps the most damning and virulent has come from the House of Commons Treasury Select Committee (Select Committee). The Select Committee is withering in its critique of how the FSA and the Bank of England were largely ineffectual over a prolonged period in terms of Barclays' Libor activities.[22] That the Select Committee should be so critical of regulatory actors such as the FSA and the Bank of England and their relationship with a prominent City finance institution like Barclays, as well as actively canvassing the possibility of increased criminal prosecution of poor behaviour in the finance sector, shows that it is much more on the front foot than some of its predecessors. A revealing historical insight into the hegemony, power and relative autonomy of the City was provided with the passage of *Leeman's Act 1867* which sought to stop the widespread practice of not recording transactions individually but instead recording them as house transactions, and which also aimed to reduce speculative dealing in banking securities, (sound familiar?). The disregard of the City even for existing statutory controls, was clear in the evidence given in 1875 by Mr. Samuel Herman de Zoete, the then chairman of the London Stock Exchange to a parliamentary committee: 'Sirs, we disregarded for years Sir John Barnard's Act and we are now disregarding in the same measure Mr. Leeman's Act'.[23]

It is difficult to imagine any other business interest group openly defying a parliamentary committee and statutory instruments in such a manner, but it indicates the confidence of a disparate arrangement of groups and individuals in the City with shared economic interests in being able to tailor the discourse that constructs the regulation of their activities. A key explanatory factor for this is that the City has been tremendously successful in having its own interests widely identified as converging with the *public interest* on matters of financial regulation. This ability to shape perceptions of what entails the public interest has interacted with broader legal developments to influence significantly the City's financial markets and their regulation, and these traditions have been exported to a significant degree to other finance centres such as New York. Like other powerful actors, the City has been able to set goals for the general interests of society. The utility that its regulatory authority has held for the diverse interests that constitute the City is the fact that its cultural norms and values were for many years adopted as conventional working practice in the UK financial sector. Constellations of interests in the City have been successful in projecting their preferred model of financial regulation and routinised social and business practices as the *natural* social and economic order, thereby ensuring its hegemony.[24]

Similar processes are at work today in London, and in other finance centres around the world, in the management of conflicts and with regard to many other issues. We should not be too surprised by this because regulation can be viewed as a commodity, a raw material

---

[21] J Treanor, 'Barclays bank forced to admit it paid just £113 million in corporation tax in 2009' *The Guardian Business* (18 February 2012), available at www.guardian.co.uk/business/2011/feb18/barclays-bank-113m-corporation-tax.

[22] House of Commons Treasury Committee, *Fixing LIBOR: some preliminary findings*, (18 August 2012), available at www.publications.parliament.uk/pa/cm201213/cmselect/cmtreasy/481/48102.html. 102.

[23] *House of Commons Journals*, (1875), London.

[24] See: G Gilligan, *Regulating the Financial Services Sector* (London, Kluwer Law International, 1999).

which is subject to market forces and may be facilitative, inherently contradictory, manipulative and complex. The twin pressures of special interest groups and market forces remain extremely influential in shaping contemporary regulatory praxis in financial services in the UK and elsewhere, just as they have done for centuries. In a market society, much power lies with capital resources and those involved with the raising, organising and marketing of capital have great influence. Also, the complexity of the financial services industry excludes most people from being able to evaluate specifically its processes, and it is within this paradigm that the Libor scandal should be understood.

Notions and practices of recurring routinisation and neutralisation of deviance are well-entrenched in the finance sector, as they are in some other industries, for example real estate, with its seemingly perennial problems of transparency and accountability in pricing and sales campaigns. Barclays' role in the manipulation of Libor is likely to be an example of routinised and normalised deviance in the industry and in July 2012 the Executive Committee of Barclays flagged that they were not the only bank manipulating Libor. They distributed a memo entitled 'Restoring our Reputation, Building our Business' to all Barclays employees. In that memo, which was co-signed by outgoing Barclays Chairman Marcus Agius, the Committee stated: 'As other banks settle with authorities, and their details become public, and various governments' inquiries shed more light, our situation will eventually be put into perspective'.[25] Barclays has declined to make public comment on the memo but time has proven that manipulation of Libor was a practice that was routinised and neutralised within the financial services sector. For example, RBS, which following the GFC, was bailed out by the UK Government using more than £40 billion of taxpayer funds and is now effectively 81 per cent owned by the British taxpayer. Following US and UK investigations of its manipulation of Libor, RBS was fined £90 million by the FSA and £300 million by the CFTC and the DOJ.[26] Similarly UBS, in December 2012 as part of its agreement with the DOJ, agreed that UBS Japan not only had signed a plea agreement admitting its criminal conduct and would pay a fine of US$100 million, but also that two UBS former traders would face criminal charges. In addition, UBS AG (the Swiss parent company of UBS Japan), had entered into a non-prosecution agreement under which it would admit and accept responsibility for its misconduct, and pay: a DOJ penalty of US$400 million; US$700 million due to CFTC action; US$259.2 million due to the FSA action; and $64.3 million due to the Swiss Financial Markets Authority (FINMA) action for a combined total of more than US$1.5 billion.[27]

The scale of the pecuniary damage wrought by Libor has yet to be calculated. Massive legal claims against relevant banks for damages as a result of manipulation of Libor are likely and some are already in train. For example, the US city of Baltimore is already a litigant and class action lawyers have described the potential pool of losers from the manipulation of Libor as vast, although proving the relevant counterfactual case is likely to be difficult, protracted and expensive.[28] If successful, these claims will generate enormous sums,

---

[25] 'Barclays Implicates Libor Rivals' *orange news* (16 July 2012), available at web.orange.co.uk/article/news/exclusive_barclays_implicates_libor_rivals.

[26] J Treanor, 'RBS Fined £390 Million for "Widespread Manipulation" in Libor-Rigging Scandal' *The Guardian* (6 February 2013), available at www.guardian.co.uk/business/2013/feb/06/rbs-fined-libor-rigging-scandal.

[27] Department of Justice, Office of Public Affairs, *UBS Securities Japan Co. Ltd. to Plead Guilty to Felony Wire Fraud for Long-running Manipulation of LIBOR Benchmark Interest Rates* (December 19 2012), available at www.justice.gov/opa/pr/2012/December/12-ag-1522.html.

[28] T Harford and R Knight, 'Libor: Who Lost Out When the Rate was Fixed?' *BBC News Magazine* (14 July 2012), available at www.bbc.co.uk/news/magazine-18826396.

but perhaps the greatest damage wrought by the Libor scandal has been the further erosion of public trust in the finance sector. It further contributes to the depressing reality that many people, both inside and outside the financial sector, in the UK, the US and elsewhere, have endured so many financial scandals over the years that they see deviant behaviours such as the Libor manipulation as entrenched and normalised within the finance industry's culture and operational practices.

II   THE HISTORY OF THE ANGLO MODEL AND ITS INFLUENCE
IN INTERNATIONAL FINANCIAL MARKETS

The Libor scandal is just one of the many contemporary examples of widespread *bad* behaviours within today's financial sector that present such intractable problems to regulators. To understand why this is so, it is necessary to examine the historical traditions of financial markets and in particular, the pre-eminent influence of the Anglo model on how not only the UK, but also international financial markets have developed. Also, it is important to consider the development of financial services regulation in tandem with the development of the market because the two are inextricably entwined. Financial services regulation and law in general are products of, and subsequently respond to, social, political and economic phenomena. Law is not an autonomous entity; it may be ambiguous and indeed contradictory at times. It needs to be studied in terms of both its function and its form; its function in how law came to be given its tasks and whose interests it serves; its effect in how law does what it is supposed to, and its mode of operation and appearance.

In the eighth century BC, the Greeks began to develop their *polis*, the social and political organisation which responded to market conditions and simultaneously aimed to limit the effects of the market. The Greek polis had a clearly defined social order and the economic development of their society also brought political conflict and transformation. Redfield comments on the tension of the polis/market relationship arguing that:

'..., The Greeks looked upon the market as a threat to the political order. The function of the state, to a large extent, was to correct the effects of the market – not by regulation, but by creating a superordinate structure of social regulations.'[29]

Many Greeks today might empathise with the collective belief of their ancestors of the market as a threat to the political order as violent protests against post-GFC austerity programs become a commonplace occurrence in contemporary Greek society.[30] Nevertheless, this model of social organisation with its inherent ambiguities is still dominant in Western society and the largely self-regulatory nature of the financial services industry is an unsurprising legacy of such a tradition. The evolution of financial services regulation has a long history; for example, forgery and counterfeiting posed regulatory problems for the Roman and the Byzantine states.[31] The regulation of securities in Britain derives from the theories

---

[29] JM Redfield, 'The Development of the Market in Archaic Greece' in BL Anderson and AJH. Latham (eds), *The Market In History* (London, Croom Helm, 1986), 52.

[30] See for example: 'Chaos in Athens: Greece in New Round of Austerity as Protests Rage' *RT.com* (7 November 2012), available at rt.com/news/greece-austerity-bill-protests-144/; and 'Thousands across Greece Protest Austerity' *DW News*, (20 February 2013), available at www.dw.de/thousands-across-greece-protest-austerity/a-16612903.

[31] M Levi, *Regulating Fraud: White Collar Crime and the Criminal Process* (London, Tavistock, 1987) 1.

of markets, with the concept of barter markets being the earliest authority. In England from 1,000 A.D. a sophisticated form of market regulation begins to emerge. Its central purpose was to introduce more certainty into economic exchange by impacting upon the processes of supply and demand. The ancient common law offences of engrossing, (buying in quantity corn, etcetera, to sell again at a high price), forestalling, (raising the price of certain goods by holding up supplies etcetera), and regrating, (buying corn or other grains in any market so as to raise the price, and then selling it again in the same place), were all rendered statutory offences in the fourteenth century.[32] Thus market manipulations such as the rigging of the Libor rates are not exclusively modern phenomena and neither are regulatory efforts to counter their effects. Financial services regulation is mainly concerned with capital resources and how those resources are raised, organised and marketed. Trade is the major motivation for capital exchange and banking is the industry that facilitates these processes. As noted at the start of this chapter, according to contemporary opinion polls, bankers are not widely admired or respected and Bridbury comments that in the Middle Ages, financiers were considered to be usurers and, '. . .universally deprecated and formally anathematised'.[33] Many today who have antipathy for modern bankers might say plus ça change? but the merchant and banking classes managed to endure medieval moral opprobrium and between the eleventh and seventeenth centuries began to assume greater influence in society.[34]

That greater influence was fuelled by a long history of mutual self-interest, (partly driven by the traditional weakness of the central state in England), between the financial markets of the City and not only the monarchy, but also elected governments after the English Civil War, which was crucial in developing the relative autonomy of the City. This political significance gave City professional groups and markets enormous influence with the Crown and central government. Britain is no longer a dominant world power, but the colonial expansion of the British Empire and the international character of the City transported the City's traditions and routinised financial services praxis around the globe. These forces not only have allowed the City to retain its status as one of the world's key financial centres, but also have shaped how Wall Street has evolved. Wall Street, physically, is an even smaller area than the City but it has become the world's dominant finance centre as a reflection of the economic and political supremacy of the US. Thus the Anglo model of financial services regulation became the most influential in shaping global financial markets.

The City is in fact a village, both in terms of its physical confines and its social mores. For many centuries, those who worked in its financial markets operated under a moral code that was unwritten, but which reflected their standing as gentlemen. Transgressors of that code rarely faced criminal proceedings; instead they were merely shut out of the City's social and professional life by the actions of a remarkably effective peer network. This *social ostracism* proved over centuries to be the most enduring and powerful sanction in the regulation of the City.[35] The substructure of this largely intangible edifice of self-regulation was the ethos–*dictum meum pactum,* my word is my bond, between members of the London Stock Exchange. This system of honour was crucial in providing certainty for trading conditions because many common trading practices were not legal for prolonged periods, for

---

[32] *Statutes of the Realm,* (1363), 37 Edw. III c8.

[33] AR Bridbury, 'Markets and Freedom in the Middle Ages', in Anderson & Latham, above n.29 at 83.

[34] ME Tigar and MR Levy, *Law and the Rise of Capitalism* (New York, Monthly Review Press, 1977).

[35] A Sampson, *The Changing Anatomy of Britain* (London, Hodder & Stoughton, 1982).

example, the widespread acceptance of the non-recording of all individual transactions. Recourse to legal processes to settle disputes would have led to commercial chaos, so the City developed internal arbitration procedures. This *my word is my bond* approach to self-regulation delivered a stable if monopolistic trading environment and its success is well-documented, ensuring its central importance to the British economy and sustaining its political influence.[36]

The key relationship that established, nurtured and maintained the City's pre-eminence in the British economy has been its connection with the Crown and central government. It is an example of a core driver in the construction of regulatory space[37] and the deployment of resources therein, as relative sets of power relations facilitate key actors in shaping regulatory discourse, and the subsequent production of regulatory structures and processes. For example, during the sixteenth and seventeenth centuries, the costs of government rose dramatically as the Crown's borrowing requirement soared and it was the City that funded that borrowing.[38] Direct taxation was unpopular and the lack of a strong central bureaucracy depleted the Crown's tax-gathering potential. As a result, collection of tax revenue was extremely difficult and the Crown became heavily dependent upon loans from City merchants and financiers to cover expenditure. The Crown's need for loans was instrumental in the creation of the City's most important financial institutions:

'. . .Both the Bank of England and the Stock Exchange were the products of England's "second revolution" in the late seventeenth century which ended Charles II's attempts to restore arbitrary royal powers in financial matters. . . . Over 1000 subscribers, including London's leading merchants, were incorporated as the Governor and the Bank of England in 1694. The Charter was granted in return for an initial loan of £1.2 million, and in 1708 the Bank was extended by Act of Parliament the privileged status of the country's only joint-stock bank. This early monopoly which lasted for over a century, meant that other banks could only be partnerships, which were limited in number to six persons. This legislation was the direct result of the City's power and effectively retarded the development of provincial branch banking on any scale.'[39]

The private nature of both the Bank of England and the Stock Exchange helped shape the self-regulatory system of the UK financial services sector for centuries. The privileged market positions of the Stock Exchange and the Bank of England, and the evolution of the UK's system of financial self-regulation were a direct result of the post-medieval financial dependence of the Crown upon the City. It is an example of the structuration theory of Anthony Giddens at work,[40] as individual London merchants combine the human agency effects of their political and economic strength with the structural leverage of the financial and commercial markets, in order to prise a privileged trading and regulatory position from the central state. The privileged position of the financial sector and its associated culture in the contemporary global economy is a legacy of this interactive tradition, a legacy that

---

[36] See generally: H McRae and F Cairncross, *Capital City, London as a Financial Centre* (Methuen: London, 1985).

[37] For a discussion of the concept of regulatory space, see L Hancher and M Moran, 'Organizing Regulatory Space' in L Hancher and M Moran (eds), *Capitalism, Culture, and Economic Regulation* (Oxford, Clarendon Press, 1989) 271.

[38] EV Morgan and WA Thomas, *The Stock Exchange: Its History and Functions* (London, Elek Books, 1962) 17.

[39] G Ingham, *Capitalism Divided? The City and Industry in British Social Development* (London, Macmillan, 1984) 17.

[40] A Giddens, *The Constitution of Society, Outline of the Theory of Structuration* (Cambridge, Polity Press, 1984).

has been able to prevail despite the many financial scandals and crises that have occurred over the years.

The irrational exuberance and great bull market run of the 2000s with the subsequent GFC has many parallels in financial history, including the boom of 1693–95 and the crisis that followed. When financial crises hit, they magnify hostile public attitudes towards financial services professionals and the culture within which they operate. For example, the famous author Daniel Defoe was vitriolic in his assessment of the stock-jobbing profession of the late seventeenth and early eighteenth centuries:

'. . .there is not a man but will own 'tis a complete System of Knavery; that 'tis a Trade in Fraud, born of Deceit and nourished by Trick, Cheat, Wheedle, Forgeries, Falsehoods and all sorts of Delusions'.[41]

Defoe reflected broader community views about finance professionals and a parliamentary inquiry was appointed in November 1696, '. . .to look after the Trade of England. . .', as a response to this widespread public disquiet about the rapacious nature of England's early capital markets. The Royal Commissioners were alarmed by the promotion of frauds and manipulation of the market. They complained that:

'The pernicious Art of Stock-jobbing hath, of late,. . .wholly perverted the End and Design of Companies and Corporations, erected for the introducing, or carrying on of Manufactures,. . .by selling their shares for much more than they are really worth. . . . Thus. . .the Management of that Trade and Stock comes to fall into unskilful Hands, whereby the Manufactures. . .dwindle away to nothing'.[42]

The damning report of the Royal Commissioners prompted Parliament in 1697 to pass an *Act to Restrain the Number and Practice of Brokers and Stock-Jobbers*. It marks the first reference point of a regulatory cycle that has been a recurring feature of the financial services sector—a depressingly repetitive pattern of economic boom accompanied by deregulation, followed by recession and attendant social regulation. The 1693–95 boom and the 1697 Act, the South Sea Bubble boom and the Bubble Act 1720. In the United States, the bull market of the 1920s and the Wall Street Crash of 1929 that led to the New Deal legislation of the 1930s, embodied in the Securities Act 1933 and Securities Exchange Act 1934; and more recently the GFC and the Wall Street Reform and Consumer Protection Act 2010. The complexity of the financial services industry excludes most people from being able to evaluate specifically its processes and operational cultures. Occasionally an insider will leave a firm or the industry and shed light on these cultural processes. For example, US Law Professor and former derivatives salesman Frank Partnoy's account of the working culture and attitudes of his contemporaries on Wall Street in the early 1990s highlights the operational culture of the firm and the industry at the time and contains some graphic examples of the callous indifference of some traders to the well-being of their clients. For example in April 1994, the instructions of Morgan Stanley's leader John Mack to the increasing derivatives losses of some of Morgan Stanley's clients was allegedly: 'There's blood in the water. Let's go kill someone'.[43] Partnoy writes how a fellow salesman described his sale of a Principal Exchange Rate Linked Security (PERLS)

---

[41]   BAK Rider, C Abrams, and E Ferran, *Guide to the Financial Services Act 1986*, 2nd edn (Bicester, CCH, 1989) 2.

[42]   *House of Commons Journals*, 25 November 1696, London.

[43]   F Partnoy, *F.I.A.S.C.O.—Blood in the Water on Wall Street* (New York, W.W. Norton & Co., 1997), 15.

derivatives trade to a treasury officer of an insurance company who did not understand the trade as: '. . .ripping his face off'.[44] The latitude that derivatives traders received
from their controllers was largely explained by the enormous profits that they generated
for their firm:

> 'From 1993 to 1995. . .the seventy or so people. . .in the derivatives group at Morgan Stanley in
> New York, London, and Tokyo generated total fees of about $1 billion—an average of almost
> $15 million. . .arguably the most profitable group of people in the world.'[45]

This observation goes to the core issue that drives the culture of financial firms—the
generation of fees and profits for the firm and the incentive regimes for individuals within
firms that are designed to generate those fees and profits. The short-termism orientation
of incentive systems is a major determinant of the culture of the finance industry. Over the
years, it has been a crucial factor stimulating tolerance of business misconduct as many
financial professionals such as Partnoy and his colleagues at Morgan Stanley normalise
these activities as being relatively unexceptional. This is achieved through the same techniques of neutralisation used by the juvenile delinquents studied by Sykes and Matza in the
1960's: i) denial of responsibility; ii) denial of injury; iii) denial of the victim; iv) condemnation of the condemners; v) appeal to higher loyalties.[46] These neutralisation processes
were apparent in the behaviours of many of those involved in the manipulation of Libor
and many other financial scandals over the years. If the prevailing rapacious culture of
the finance industry is to improve for the better, then these neutralisation tendencies and
short-termism incentive structures need to be rolled back. These are big challenges in a
global industry such as finance, and international standard-setting mechanisms may have
the potential to have an impact in a positive way, but they are likely to be affected by issues
of national self-interest and regulatory competition.

III   REGULATORY COMPETITION, NATIONAL INTEREST, AND STANDARD SETTING IN INTERNATIONAL FINANCIAL MARKETS

One of the substantive implications of globalisation is that information, knowledge and
normative behaviours—in particular business norms and protocols and their attendant regulatory standards—may be transmitted and dispersed across national, sectoral and cultural
boundaries. There are a number of international organisations that have regulatory impact
upon the financial sector. Among them are: the Basel Committee on Banking Supervision
(BCBS); the G20 and its mechanism for impacting upon finance markets and financial
actors—the Financial Stability Board (FSB); the International Organisation of Securities
Commissions (IOSCO); the International Association of Insurance Supervisors (IAIS);
the International Monetary Fund (IMF), the Organisation for Economic Cooperation and
Development (OECD), the World Bank and the World Trade Organisation (WTO). All
of these organisations act as conduits for national-based actors to influence multi-lateral
trading environments, especially their regulatory character. These normative transmissions

---

[44] ibid at 61.
[45] ibid at 13.
[46] GM Sykes and D Matza, 'Techniques of Delinquency' in M Wolfgang, L Savitz, and M Johnston (eds),
The Sociology of Crime and Delinquency (New York: John Wiley, 1970) 295.

and dispersals can become constituent factors in the *game* between jurisdictions as they seek to attract and/or retain capital investment. These processes of regulatory competition are more pronounced in this current era of globalisation, when economic and political ties between many jurisdictions are deepening and jurisdictions increasingly are playing a mediating role regarding the interests of much business that may be conducted within, and around, their spheres of influence.

It is within such pragmatic parameters that financial regulators must function both in the good economic times and in times of crisis. This realpolitik of international financial regulation should always be borne in mind when considering how prevailing cultures in national and international financial markets might be improved because some multilateral regulatory bodies are more likely to have impact than others because they are underpinned by powerful national actors, for example, the G20[47] via the FSB.[48] G20 members account for: 90 per cent of global GDP; 80 per cent of international global trade; and 64 per cent of the world's population. So the attendant assumption is that the G20's policy statements, declarations and initiatives will gain more traction and application in the global economy, especially in international financial markets, than their equivalents that emanated from the G7 or the G8. At their first Summit in Washington DC in November 2008, G20 leaders agreed an action plan to counter the worst effects of the GFC.[49] That ongoing action plan has three main objectives: 1) restoring global growth; 2) strengthening the international financial system; and 3) reforming international financial institutions. That action plan is at the heart of ongoing multilateral attempts to regulate global financial markets and since 2008, the FSB and other multilateral regulatory actors such as IOSCO have been engaging in research and constructive dialogue with key public and private sector actors in both national and international financial environments. This regulatory space can become hotly contested at times as defined interest groups, including both national and international regulatory organisations, flex their influence and it is in this political reality that regulatory initiatives must evolve. Examples of these strategic and cultural tensions in recent times are regulatory initiatives regarding money market funds (MMFs) and OTC derivatives.

The Technical Committee of the IOSCO's report of 27 April 2012 *Money Market Fund Systemic Risk Analysis and Reform Options* (the IOSCO Report),[50] is an exercise in regulatory realpolitik, as the public interest priorities of a multilateral actor such as IOSCO meet the hard surface of economic self-interest, in this case the commercial interests of MMFs in the US. MMFs are investment funds that invest in high-quality low-duration fixed-income instruments such as US Treasuries. They comprise a systemically important element of

---

[47]   Following a number of financial crises in the 1990s that were especially damaging to emerging economies, most notably in Asia, the Finance Ministers and Central Bank Governors of emerging and advanced economies deemed to be of *systemic importance*, (a key term in contemporary multilateral financial regulation discourse), met in December 1999 in Berlin to discuss key issues for global economic stability. Since then, the G20 Finance Ministers and Central Bank Governors have met annually in various member locations. The G20 constitutes the European Union (EU) and 19 countries: Argentina, Australia, Brazil, Canada, China, France, Germany, India, Indonesia, Italy, Japan, Mexico, Republic of Korea, Russia, Saudi Arabia, South Africa, Turkey, United Kingdom and the United States. See www.g20.org.

[48]   See www.financialstabilityboard.org.

[49]   See: 'Group of Twenty Finance Ministers and Central Bank Governors', *The G20 Washington Summit Leaders' Declaration* (14 November 2008), available at www.g20.org/load/780988448.

[50]   IOSCO, *Money Market Fund Systemic Risk Analysis and Reform Options, Consultation Report*, CR7/12 (27 April 2012), available at www.iosco.org/library/pubdocs/pdf/IOSCOPD379.pdf.

the financial sector. For example, in the third quarter of 2011 the IOSCO Report notes that MMFs totalled US$4.7 trillion in funds under management, approximately 20 per cent of the assets of Collective Investment Schemes (CIS) globally. This issue of the MMFs as part of the broader cash management industry is important, especially regarding the decision (discussed in more detail below), by SEC Commissioner Luis Aguilar and his fellow Commissioners, Troy Paredes and Daniel Gallagher, to oppose then SEC Chairman Mary Schapiro's[51] efforts to persuade the SEC to raise the regulatory requirements for MMFs as suggested by IOSCO. The strategic importance of MMFs was highlighted dramatically during the GFC of 2008, when the collapse of Lehman Brothers was a trigger for a run on the oldest MMF in the US, the Reserve Primary Fund, which owned $785 million in Lehman Brothers commercial paper. The contagion spread to other MMFs and was the catalyst for the GFC to impact significantly on Main Street America, not just Wall Street, because it meant that many US corporations were unable to issue new securities and so the US Treasury and Federal Reserve intervened to back the assets of the MMFs. Their actions averted the collapse of the financial system but made US taxpayers potentially liable for more than US$3 trillion, the assets held by MMFs at that time.

This episode demonstrated clearly the global systemic risk posed by the cash management industry in general and MMFs in particular. So as part of its broader mandate from the G20 leaders to strengthen the oversight and regulation of the shadow banking system, the FSB asked IOSCO to undertake a review of potential regulatory reforms for MMFs that would mitigate the systemic risk that they posed. In its October 2011 Report (the FSB Report), the FSB estimated the size of the global shadow banking industry to be US$60 trillion, of which MMFs at US$4.7 trillion are clearly a significant segment.[52] The IOSCO report was in response to this FSB mandate, but nevertheless it is important to remember that the report, as acknowledged by the Technical Committee of IOSCO, is for public consultation only and that IOSCO has no substantive enforcement processes, relying essentially on peer pressure and a consensual approach. However, in this instance that limited and essentially voluntary character still stirred up significant opposition and controversy.

That opposition centred on two issues, both of which the FSB specifically mandated IOSCO to investigate. The first surrounds the practice of variable net asset value (VNAV) which ordinarily in market practice means that the value of bonds held by funds fluctuates as funds comply with mark-to-markets valuations. However, for more than thirty years, MMFs in the US under the SEC exemption rule 2a-7 have not had to operate with a VNAV. Instead they have maintained a steady $1 stable net asset value (SNAV) by using amortised cost accounting and penny rounding. The IOSCO Report urged its member organisations to consider moving to a VNAV approach. The second major point of contention concerned liquidity management and the prospect that MMFs should be required to increase their capital buffers and hold back a small percentage of funds that had been deposited for a fixed period of time to help reverse the dynamics of any future run on funds.

---

[51] Ms Schapiro left the SEC in December 2012. President Obama has announced that she will be replaced by Mary Jo White. Currently Ms Elisse B Walter is Acting Chairman. See: Securities and Exchanges Commission, 'Current SEC Commissioners', available at www.sec.gov/about/commissioner.shtml.

[52] Financial Stability Board, *Shadow Banking: Strengthening Oversight and Regulation, Recommendations of the Financial Stability Board* (27 October 2011), available at www.financialstabilityboard.org/publications/r_111027a.pdf.

Then SEC Chairman Mary Schapiro thought that both of these options had merit.[53] Nevertheless, furious lobbying efforts from the MMF industry in the US viewed them '. . .as detrimental and severely flawed'.[54] Subsequently three of the five member SEC, Commissioners Aguilar, Paredes and Gallagher, announced that IOSCO should: '. . .withdraw the report for further consideration and revision.'[55] Additionally, Chairman Schapiro faced hostile questioning from both Democrats and Republicans when she appeared before the US Senate Banking Committee in June 2012 where she told the Panel that IOSCO normally waits for the SEC's full input and prematurely released the IOSCO Report in a timing mismatch, which was in Chairman Schapiro's own words 'a genuine screw-up'.[56] Nevertheless, Chairman Schapiro continued to champion the proposals declaring: '. . .these proposals have merit, address the two structural issues identified, and deserved to see the light of day so that we could receive public feedback'.[57] Three days later Masamichi Kono, Chairman of IOSCO issued his own statement taking 'careful note' of Chairman Schapiro's statement.[58] Within the US, Press reports in *The Wall Street Journal* and other media forums stated that the proposed reforms had widespread public agency support, including within the Obama Administration, the US Treasury and the Federal Reserve.[59]

Nevertheless Commissioners Aguilar, Paredes and Gallagher argued that neither the Commission, nor its staff, had undertaken a comprehensive study and reported on the effects of the SEC's 2010 Money Market Amendments which increased the obligations of MMFs in a number of ways, these included: improving credit quality, mandating stress testing, raising the transparency of fund holdings, raising liquidity requirements and reducing maturity periods.[60] The Commissioners felt that such a review should precede any further reform proposals for MMFs and/or the cash management industry in general.[61] On 30 November 2012, SEC staff delivered the requested report to the Commission and it is still under consideration.[62]

---

[53]   Securities Exchange Commission, *Remarks at SIFMA's 2011 Annual Meeting by Chairman Mary L. Schapiro* (7 November 2011), available at www.sec.gov/news/speech/2011/spch110711mls.htm.

[54]   Investment Company Institute, *IOSCO Money Market Fund Systemic Risk Analysis and Reform Options, ICI Comment Letter* (25 May 2012), available at www.ici.org/pdf/12_iosco_mmf_com_itr.pdf.

[55]   Securities Exchange Commission, *Statement Concerning Publication by IOSCO on April 27, 2012 of the 'Consultation Report of the IOSCO Standing Committee 5 on Money Market Funds: Money Market Fund Systemic Risk Analysis and Reform Options'* (11 May 2012), available at www.sec.gov/news/speech/2012/spcho51112laatapdmg.pdf.

[56]   United States Senate Committee on Banking, Housing, Urban Affairs, *Perspectives on Money Market Mutual Fund Reforms* (21 June 2012), available at banking.senate.gov/public/index.cfm?FuseAction=Hearings. Hearing&Hearing_ID=bba4146c-6b7f-47d0-93bc-ebc73189c9c0.

[57]   Securities and Exchange Commission, 'Statement of SEC Chairman Mary L. Schapiro on Money Market Fund Reform' (22 August 2012), available at sec.gov/news/press/2012/2012-166htm.

[58]   IOSCO, 'Statement of the Chairman of the IOSCO Board on IOSCO's work on MMFs' (25 August 2012), available at www.iosco.org/news/pdf/IOSCONEWS248.pdf.

[59]   P Eavis, 'A Third Option for regulators in the Money Market Fund Fight' *The New York Times, Dealbook* (30 August 2012), available at dealbook.nytimes.com/2012/08/30/a-third-option-for-regulators-in-the-money-market-fund-fight.

[60]   Securities and Exchange Commission, Rules, *Money Market Fund Reform*, Release No. IC-29132, File Nos. S7-1-09, S7-20-09, 2010, available at www.sec.gov/rules/final/2010/ic-29132.pdf.

[61]   LA Aguilar, 'Money Market Funds Need Further Study' *The Harvard Law School Forum on Corporate Governance and Financial Regulation* (30 August 2012), available at blogs.law.harvard.edu/corpgov/2012/08/30/money-market-funds-need-further-study/#more-32363.

[62]   LA Aguilar, 'Recent Developments in Money Market Funds' *The Harvard Law School Forum on Corporate Governance and Financial Regulation* (21 December 2012), available at blogs.law.harvard.edu/corpgov/2012/12/21/recent-developments-in-money-market-funds/#more-37542.

So the MMF regulation argument rumbles on and will continue to produce tensions both nationally and internationally because in essence MMFs are uninsured investments whose value can alter on a daily basis and so they can carry a high degree of risk. It will be interesting to see whether there will be more alleged screw-ups involving how IOSCO reports on other international regulatory issues are coordinated and published in the future, as part of the contestation that almost inevitably accompanies the realpolitik that is the development of financial regulation in both public and private domains.

National: international regulatory tension also emanated from the CFTC's Proposed Guidance on Cross-Border Application of Certain Swap Provisions of the Commodity Exchange Act (CFTC Proposed Guidance).[63] The major effects of the CFTC's Proposed Guidance are that US registration and regulatory obligations will apply to non-US institutions carrying out derivatives transactions with US persons, (or in specific situations where US persons are acting as guarantors for non-US clients), although in certain contexts the CFTC will allow 'substituted compliance' via home jurisdiction regulatory obligations in place of the US requirements. Some Asia-Pacific financial regulatory actors reacted with alarm issuing public letters of concern to the CFTC about the extra-territorial implications of the CFTC's Proposed Guidance. First came a joint letter from Japan's Financial Service Agency (JFSA) and the Bank of Japan.[64] Second a joint letter came from: the Australian Securities and Investments Commission (ASIC); the Reserve Bank of Australia; the Hong King Monetary Authority; the Securities and Futures Commission, Hong Kong; and the Monetary Authority of Singapore.[65] It is highly unusual for national regulators to go public in this concerted way, especially to criticise, (albeit implicitly), a US regulator.

The CFTC Proposed Guidance had both internal and external critics. For example the CFTC Commissioner Scott D O'Malia: 'Moreover, the Commission's interpretation of CEA section 2(i) is overly broad to the point where the extent of the Commission's jurisdiction is virtually endless'. Commissioner O'Malia went on to criticise not only what he saw as: '. . .the CFTC's loose consideration of the principles of international comity. . .' arguing that: '. . .the CFTC should engage in real and meaningful cooperation with foreign and domestic regulators that honours these principles in order to respect the legitimate interests of other sovereign nations'; but also that the CFTC was : '. . .engaging in what amounts to high-frequency regulation. I am very critical of this regulatory approach because it generally results in regulatory uncertainty and unintended, adverse consequences'.[66] Some of Commissioner O'Malia's opinions resonate with the observations expressed by the

---

[63] Commodity Futures Trading Commission, Release pr6293-12, June 29 2012, *CFTC Approves Proposed Interpretive Guidance on Cross-Border Application of the Swaps Provisions of the Dodd-Frank Act*, available at www.cftc.gov/PressRoom/PressReleases/pr6293-12.

[64] M Kono and H Hayakawa, *Re: Proposed CFTC Cross-Border Releases on Swap Regulation* (August 13, 2012), available at www.fsa.go.jp/en/news/2012/20120820-1/01.pdf.

[65] B Gibson, M Edey, A Yuen, K Lui, and TS Lian, CFTC's *Proposed Guidance on Cross-Border Application of Certain Swap Provisions of the Commodity Exchange Act* ("Proposed Guidance") (27 August 2012), available at docs.google.com/viewer?a=v&q=cache:gB2AAnNMyq4J:comments.cftc.gov/Handlers/PdfHandler .ashx%3Fid%3D24604+&hl=en&gl=au&pid=bl&srcid=ADGEESh59A2Kyy6kDIryvZOvwPlV3j7PXcZYQ6n4n Qug_FGe1a73G4qxePhhphiid5VDEqovNO73ln-Dgx_CkLo3FEDyAjoP8qL8kPBtWkLObYZyWifSCH9HDAjUz mvCX87uV3TjIxjO&sig=AHIEtbQtv1AT6cxXsINf9DCLc4ixdGiuLA.

[66] SD O'Malia, *CFTC Speeches and Testimony, Statement of Concurrence: (1) Proposed Interpretive Guidance and Policy Statement Regarding Section 2(i) of the Commodity Exchange Act; and (2) Notice of Proposed Exemptive Order* (29 June 2012), available at www.cftc.gov/PressRoom/SpeechesTestimony/omaliastatement062912.

Asia-Pacific regulators in their letters to CFTC Chairman Gensler discussed above. An external commentator Breteau was even more strident in his criticism:

> 'The CFTC's disregard of non-US regulators and regulations smacks of imperialism at a time when international co-ordination is ever more necessary. . . . Just as there is no longer a place in the world for economic colonialism by nations, there is no longer a place in the world for colonialism by regulators'.[67]

Labelling the CFTC as a regulatory imperialist is perhaps unfair, but it is almost inevitable that the economic and political reality of the US being the largest and most significant global finance centre imbues its key regulators such as the CFTC with more influence than other national regulators. Whether, how and when, regulators such as the CFTC choose to flex that greater influence in the rough and tumble of multi-lateral regulatory praxis is a moot point. It is not insignificant that so many Asian regulatory actors combined in attempts to counter the greater influence and reach of the CFTC. They politely elected to challenge some of the propositions of 'The Proposed Guidance', by requesting the CFTC to delay and reconsider the potential consequences of such unilateral action. In February 2013, the CFTC Chairman Gary Gensler, in testimony to the US Senate, confirmed that a compromise of sorts had been reached through a CFTC Final Order that applies until mid-July 2013 which: '. . .provides time for the Commission to continue working with foreign regulators as they implement comparable swaps reforms and as the Commission considers substituted compliance determinations for the various foreign jurisdictions with entities that have registered as swap dealers under Dodd-Frank'.[68] The levels of consensus and international cooperation that can be generated, especially regarding the thorny issue of extraterritoriality always will be crucial in determining how cohesive, confused or colonial regulatory innovation on swaps provisions will be.

Nevertheless, it is ironic that whereas regarding increasing multilateral supervisory requirements for MMFs, some US regulatory figures bemoaned the lack of regulatory consultation before a proposed guidance that has implications within the US was issued by an international regulatory actor (i.e. IOSCO), in the case of 'The CFTC Proposed Guidance' we have international regulatory actors criticising the extraterritorial implications of a US proposal and clamouring for increased international regulatory consultation with the aim of modifying its implications outside the US. Such ironies are seemingly inevitable in the push-me pull-you environment that constitutes regulation of international finance.

IV   CONCLUSION

The IOSCO and CFTC case studies discussed above are indicative of the regulatory realpolitik that competition between finance centres to attract capital will inevitably impact upon national and international regulatory infrastructures and the attendant operational

---

[67] N Breteau, 'US rules challenge global regulatory reform' *efinancial news* (10 September 2012), available atwww.efinancialnews.com/story/2012-09-10/us-rules-challenge-global-regulatory-reform.

[68] Commodities and Futures Trading Commission, 'Testimony of Gary Gensler, Chairman, Commodity Futures Trading Commission before the U.S. Senate Banking, Housing and Urban Affairs Committee, Washington, DC' *US Commodities and Futures Trading Commission, Speeches and Testimony*, (14 February 2013), available at www.cftc.gov/PressRoom/SpeechesTestimony/opagensler-131.

cultures of financial actors subject to those infrastructures. Similarly, the regulatory traditions of a finance centre will also shape the prevailing operational cultures of financial actors and financial markets, whether centuries ago in the City or Wall Street, or in contemporary interconnected but disintermediated financial trading zones. Generally, firms and individuals are evaluated in terms of economic performance and in some situations regulatory compliance may inhibit their economic success. Consequently, as was made clear as the GFC unwound, there can be organisational tendencies towards regulatory deviance. However, it is extremely difficult to evaluate exactly how much avoidance is systemic, calculated, or due to individual self-interest. Intensive analysis of the sociology of compliance can help build a picture of the relative influence of these factors and assist regulators in their work and assist financial organisations in strengthening their operational cultures.

Normative issues are crucial in understanding the sociology of compliance and there is strong empirical evidence of '. . .a linear relationship between legitimacy and compliance, as legitimacy increases, so does compliance'.[69] There is every reason to believe that similar forces operate in the financial services sector and could be even more influential given the symbiotic nature of its regulation, and the less secure mandate that its regulatory agencies possess in comparison to the police and courts. Most people believe that laws should be obeyed and it this broader normative commitment to compliance as a general principle amongst those regulated which is perhaps the greatest asset that regulators can access. Harnessing this broader normative commitment should be a primary objective for regulation, compliance, risk management and crime prevention strategies in this area, in combination with integrating appropriate incentive regimes that are less short-term and align finance sector priorities more closely with civic society goals.

However, the operational reality of financial services is that ignoring or abusing regulatory standards can be common practice[70] and regulators have limited flexibility in instrumental approaches to sanction. For more conventional offences like burglary and theft, it is easier to take an instrumental view because the law is fairly clear and rarely challenged on a moral basis. However, it is harder to do this in the financial services sector because ambiguity and moral contestation may be features of a range of market behaviours. A significant explanatory variable of widespread rule violations in the financial services sector is that many offenders feel relatively immune from conviction and imprisonment. Generally conventional offenders such as burglars and shoplifters are dealt with more arduously by the criminal justice system. Over the years, white collar offenders have tended to receive

---

[69] TR Tyler, *Why People Obey The Law* (New Haven: Yale University Press, 1990) 57.

[70] For example, the mis-selling of pensions scandal in the UK in the 1980s and early 1990s. UK regulatory authorities have acknowledged that as many as 1.5 million people may have been wrongly advised to withdraw from company pension schemes by insurance companies and financial advisers. See: Financial Services Authority, 'The FSA Launch Final Reminder to Consumers Mis-sold a Pension' (7 February 2000), available at www.fsa.gov. uk/library/communication/pr/2000/022.shtml. In eerily similar contexts, through 2012 and 2013 it has become increasingly clear that systematic payment protection insurance mis-selling has been undertaken by UK banks for many years, showing how little they have learnt (cared?) about the lessons of the pensions mis-selling scandal twenty years earlier. Since the latest mis-selling scandal was exposed, UK banks have set aside more than £12 billion to cover compensation to their customers for mis-selling them payment protection insurance; Lloyds Banking Group alone has set aside £5.3 billion. See: D Schafer and J Thompson, 'Lloyds Fined £4.3m for PPI Delays' *Financial Times* (19 February 2013), available at www.ft.com/intl/cms/s/0/506ce648-7a88-11e2-9c88-00144feabdc0.html#axzz2M9rextmf; and Financial Services Authority, *Payment Protection Insurance*, (2013), available at www.fsa.gov.uk/consumerinformation/product_news/insurance/payment_protection_insurance_.

more lenient treatment from the criminal justice system than lower status lawbreakers.[71] However, ambiguous regulation of the financial sector reflects to some extent society's general tolerance of deviance in commercial matters, which in turn can nurture ambivalent attitudes towards white collar crime. By way of analogy, in other economic sectors large numbers of people may trade in the black economy by paying tradesmen cash to avoid goods and services taxes, or deliberately understating their assets to reduce their tax responsibilities. Criteria of legitimacy and normative codes of conduct fluctuate as social, economic and political conditions change, and inevitably this affects law enforcement. Nevertheless, although its constituent elements may vary, the importance of moral issues in regulatory compliance remains central.

In many situations, normative considerations are more influential than potential instrumental sanctions and: 'It seems that a firm's cultural and economic climates exert more influence toward reoffending than the legal environment exerts against reoffending'.[72] Law breaking and deviant behaviour can become socially normative within any company or industry, especially if industry leaders, board members or senior managers set moral codes which promote regulatory deviance.[73] The most significant element in regulatory compliance is the choice by people to comply. This occurs as part of their reflexive theoretical understanding of their own personal standing within an organisation or industry, and/or in response to their own sets of normative values. This is perhaps the area of greatest potential for crime prevention programmes in business, especially in finance—impacting upon individuals within organisations and activating their own value systems to work towards crime prevention, reducing and/or eliminating bad behaviour in organisations, re-aligning incentive structures, improving organisational cultures and prioritisation of the public interest.

Moral evaluations are inherent in the exercise of choice and discretion is the essence of the law. This means that regulators and those whom they regulate are engaged constantly in a moral balancing process about regulation. Statutes, case law, and a host of regulatory mechanisms can be shells that have to be filled out by moral principles and decisions. Often these decisions are guided by moral judgements on levels of harm and fault involved. This interactive relationship between law and morality is especially pronounced within financial services because much definition and enforcement of legal norms can be a social process of negotiation. Practical concerns shape the operational morality of regulation, both in a practical, and in a philosophical sense. Political factors are crucial in these processes, for example as discussed earlier at a national level as different jurisdictions compete against each other in their efforts to be attractive to inward capital investment and be the preferred centre of exchange of financial services and products. As a result, the effectiveness of regulating the financial sector becomes in reality inseparable from its political legitimation and this means that whatever may be the best methods of controlling behaviour in financial

---

[71] For a compelling analysis of the structural inequalities associated with the implementation of legal processes see: D Cook, *Rich Law, Poor Law, Different Responses to Tax and Supplementary Benefit Fraud* (Milton Keynes, Open University Press, 1989).

[72] S Simpson and CS Koper, 'Deterring Corporate Crime' (1992) 3 *Criminology* 347, 367. Simpson and Koper studied the recidivism patterns of a sample of 38 US corporations charged with one or more serious anti-trust violations between 1928 and 1981.

[73] There have been a large number of scandals which illustrate these processes at work, some with tragic consequences. Notorious examples include: *Dalkon Shield, Ford Pinto, Thalidomide* and the *Heavy Electrical Equipment Anti-trust Cases* in the US. For an analysis of several case studies of deviant corporate managerial practice and business culture see: M Punch, *Dirty Business: Exploring Corporate Misconduct* (London, Sage, 1996).

markets, whether those methods are pursued is shaped by the political effects produced by regulatory norms and interventions.

Nevertheless, for many organisations there can be a rational symbiosis between sensible commercial strategies, notions of individual and corporate ethical responsibility, and statutory legal obligations. Many firms strive to be good corporate citizens and act as agents for positive change in the community.[74] However, this is not always the case and the situational nature of individual morality can be moulded to meet less positive organisational objectives,[75] as exhibited in the manipulation of Libor, for example. An important issue is that corporate managers frequently perceive regulatory violations as organisational problems rather than issues of individual accountability and:

'...distinguish between peers who are deserving of severe sanctions from those who need treatment or rehabilitation. The former–the personal gain profiteers–deserve swift and certain punishment. Every company, no matter how ethical, will be vulnerable to these offenders. ... Conversely, those who offend for "the good of the company" are viewed less harshly. The behaviour may be unacceptable, but its causes are understandable. And, depending on who is perceived as being at fault (that is, the individual or the organisation), non-punitive remedies are more likely to be promoted'.[76]

The influence of this organisational approach to ethical responsibility is important and has ramifications for financial services regulation. For example, on a macro level there is the issue of moral hazard and organisational, even industry-wide, abdication of responsibility. Moral hazard can be prominent in a financial crisis, for example the GFC, when a financial bailout, (usually funded from the public coffers), may mean that banks and other financial actors, especially those considered too big to fail, avoid the negative consequences of economic decisions that they have taken. On a micro level, employees in large organisations can be ethically numb due to their institutional organisational responsibilities which may '...strongly discourage independent ethical judgements...' and '...the relative isolation of corporate managers from significant interactions with those outside their own social world'.[77] There is a need to impact upon these individual and collective perceptions, so that organisations develop a more holistic approach to crime prevention and harm reduction. Such an approach would emphasise public interest concerns and stimulate organisations to integrate economic goals with attendant civic society responsibilities.

The financial services sector is underpinned by sociologies of trust that are intrinsically vulnerable to abuse. Its social organisation can confound systems of social control, allowing wrongdoers to elude investigators and escape the justice system.[78] The world of business in the twenty-first century sees relationships of trust being extended continually across time, space, information systems and anonymous commercial networks, which enlarge significantly the zones of risk. This expansion of risk places the trust networks of the financial

---

[74] RB Taub, DG Taylor, and JD Dunham, *Paths of Neighbourhood Change* (Chicago, University of Chicago Press, 1984).

[75] R Jackall, *Moral Mazes: The World of Corporate Managers* (New York, Oxford University Press, 1988).

[76] S Simpson, 'Corporate-Crime Deterrence and Corporate-Control Policies' in Schlegel and Weisburd above n10 at 295.

[77] JW Coleman 'The Theory of White Collar Crime, From Sutherland to the 1990s' in Schlegel and Weisburd, above n10 at 69.

[78] SP Shapiro, 'Collaring the Crime, Not the Criminal: Reconsidering the Concept of White-Collar Crime' (1990) 3 *American Sociological Review* 346, 353.

services sector under increasing strain and makes it harder to allocate trust or responsibility in the vast inter-organisational matrix of the securities industry.

If public interest goals and higher standards of regulatory compliance are to be achieved in the financial services sector, then individuals and organisations whose interests and ambitions are largely commercial have to be sufficiently motivated to mount meaningful regulatory compliance and crime prevention strategies. Instrumental deterrence will play a part in these processes. However, it is the promotion of normative commitment to public interest goals which represents the best hope of countering bad behaviour within business, and this is the challenge which must be met by both national and international regulatory organisations as the twenty first century progresses. In many ways, this moral element is the master card for the promotion of positive cultures and meaningful crime prevention strategies within business organisations.

The activities of organisations such as the FSB, IOSCO and the EU will be influential in setting the required standards in financial markets, but these standards must align with the commercial realities that financial professionals and financial organisations face. That balance is only likely to be achieved if incentives regimes within those organisations are calibrated appropriately. What is appropriate can mean different things to different people, especially industry insiders who were weaned on a culture of large annual bonuses, but external actors are increasing the pressure on financial institutions to rein in the bonus culture so endemic within the industry and at the heart of so many financial crises and scandals. For example, in February 2013 the European Parliament announced that it had provisionally agreed a deal to impose a cap on the remuneration that financial institutions in the EU can pay. The proposed basic salary: bonus ratio would be 1:1, which could rise to a maximum of 1:2 with shareholder approval. Also, the risk posed by banks of over-leveraging would be reduced by requiring them to hold a minimum of 8 per cent Tier 1 high quality capital and the proposed legislation would require banks to reveal profits made, taxes paid and subsidies received country by country. These provisions would have to be implemented in the remuneration structures of banks headquartered in the EU and in the EU operations of non-EU headquartered banks. The EU has announced that these provisions must be approved by member states and the European Parliament, which it expects to occur in the April 2013 session. Assuming that the legislation is approved, and the EU expects that it will be, member states would have to include these rules in their national laws by 1 January 2014.[79] The proposed legislation may be the long-awaited game-changer in terms of incentive structures in finance, time will tell on that issue. However as the previous discussion of both the historical traditions and the standard-setting case studies illustrate, there have been powerful interest groups at work for many centuries in the finance sector. It is likely that there will be fierce lobbying efforts in the political economy space of multilateral regulation of finance on this core issue of alignment of incentives. Nevertheless, the tide does seem to be moving towards financial organisations being pressured to provide more substantive support to fostering operational cultures within their firms that more legitimately meld public and private interest goals.

---

[79] 'MEPs Cap Bankers' Bonuses and Step Up Capital Requirements', *European Parliament/News* (28 February 2013), available at www.europarl.europa.eu/news/en/pressroom/content/20130225IPR06048/html/MEPs-cap-bankers%27-bonuses-and-step-up-bank-capital-requirements.

CHAPTER 3

Back to the Future: James M. Landis, Regulatory Purpose and the Rationale for Intervention in Capital Markets

Justin O'Brien[*]

I INTRODUCTION

On Wednesday 29 September 2010, the *Financial Times* published a radical pledge. Seventeen senior financiers in the City of London committed to subjugating the profit motive of trading floors and financial advisors to what was termed 'a larger social and moral purpose which governs and limits how they behave.'[1] Corporate responsibility to society, it was argued, could not be shirked nor delegated by the board and senior management:

> Ultimately, it is the responsibility of the leaders of financial institutions–not their regulators, shareholders or other stakeholders–to create, oversee and imbue their organizations with an enlightened culture based on professionalism and integrity. As leaders of financial institutions we recognize and accept this personal responsibility.[2]

The pledge, coming in the aftermath of the global financial crisis, provided what appeared to be a demonstrable commitment to higher ethical standards. The public commitment was underscored by a major conference the following week at the Mansion House, the official residence of the Lord Mayor of the City of London. The incumbent, Nick Anstee, termed the pledge a 'manifesto.' It had, he claimed, the capacity to 'silence the cynics and the pessimists who doubt the ability of the City to put its house in order.'[3] The symbolic power of both the pledge and the conference framing derived from the articulation of a tangible corporate responsibility to society. Both were predicated on an acknowledgement that external oversight, no matter how invasive, could not vouchsafe societal protection.

[*] I acknowledge the financial support of the Australian Research Council for the award of a Future Fellowship to conduct a five year program of research on market conduct regulation.
[1] M Agius et al, 'Financial Leaders Pledge Excellence and Integrity' *Financial Times* (29 September 2010) available at: www.ft.com/intl/cms/s/0/eb26484e-cb2d-11df-95c0-00144feab49a.html#axzz2C8HKL1jb.
[2] ibid.
[3] N Anstee, 'Ethics and Values' (Speech delivered at the Mansion House, 5 October 2010) available at 217.154.230.218/NR/rdonlyres/2C29CDB2-C8FF-45D8-9068-070040EF999F/0/EthicsandValueshd.pdf.

This could only be secured through 'the culture of organizations, and what they see themselves as existing to do, and how they ensure this culture is promoted and strengthened.'[4] The formulation appeared to transcend narrow legal obligation. It repositioned the corporation as an agent of societal preferences. This, the signatories agreed, was the foundation stone of trust, without which no sustainable market could function. Nick Anstee warned with prescience, however, that failure would lead, inevitably and necessarily, to external monitoring. Three years later, the initiative lies in tatters.

It is both ironic and (perhaps) fitting that the originator of the pledge should have been Marcus Agius, the chairman of Barclays. He was forced to resign in August 2012 because of the bank's complicity in the still burgeoning London Interbank Offered Rate (Libor) price manipulation scandal.[5] The implications of the reputational demise of the Barclays chairman extend far beyond personal humiliation. As the influential United Kingdom Treasury Select Committee reported in August 2012, 'the standards and culture of Barclays, and banking more widely, are in a poor state. Urgent reform, by both regulators and banks, is needed to prevent such misconduct flourishing.'[6] The societal cost of the bifurcation between stated and lived values exposed in the Libor scandal poses a series of fundamental questions. Can corporate culture be regulated? If so, should it be? Thirdly, how does one ensure the ongoing accountability of regulatory intervention? This chapter explores these questions by revisiting the debates that accompanied the passage of the New Deal architecture in the United States.

The New Deal remains the paradigmatic and most sophisticated holistic attempt to shift cultural mores by imposing external restraints on capital market governance. As with the contemporary manifestation of financial crisis, the designers of the New Deal were forced to confront questions associated with opacity and complexity in the design and marketing of financial products: how to embed restraint and how to define and limit systemic risk. Despite the similarities in terms of scale and societal impact, there is one fundamental difference. In sharp contrast to the piecemeal reforms of today, the architectural design of the New Deal was based on a fundamental rethinking of corporate and regulatory purpose. Disentangling the ideational roots of these disputes, then and now, provides critical evidence as to why the New Deal was so transformational and why current attempts to manage the aftermath of conflict have proved so ineffective. The review conducted here of the aims and objectives of the framing of the administrative process draws on a series of interviews provided to the Columbia University Oral History Project by James M Landis.[7] It is also

---

[4] Agius et al, above n 1.

[5] See J O'Brien, 'Where the Buck Stops' *Australian Financial Review* (27 July 2012) R1, 10–11. In evidence before the Treasury Select Committee on 9 January 2013, Andrea Arcel, the head of investment banking at UBS, conceded 'these are industry-wide problems. We all got probably too arrogant, too self-convinced that things were correct the way they were. I think the industry needs to change.' See M Scott, 'UBS Executives Questioned By Parliament Over Rate-Rigging Case' *New York Times* (9 January 2013) available at dealbook.nytimes.com/2013/01/09/british-parliament-questions-ubs-executives-in-wake-of-1-5-billion-fine/?src=dlbksb.

[6] Treasury Select Committee, *Fixing Libor: Some Preliminary Findings* (London, HM Parliament, 22 August 2012). Another pressure for change is likely to come from litigation, with Lanny Breur, Assistant Attorney General of the Department of Justice, noting that 'Libor will prove to be one of the largest if not the largest white-collar case in history. It goes after financial institutions, and it goes after the most major players in Wall Street.' See J O'Brien, 'Mary Jo White and the SEC,' CLMR Online Portal (25 January 2013) available at www.clmr.unsw.edu.au/article/compliance/market-conduct-regulation/prosecutors-return-mary-jo-white-and-sec.

[7] JM Landis, *The Reminiscences of James M. Landis* (New York, Oral History Collection, Columbia University, 1964).

informed by a review of additional personal papers Landis had deposited with the Harvard Law School that were made available to scholars for the first time in January 2013.

The mercurial Landis had a stellar record at Harvard, becoming the first tenured professor of legislation after serving as a clerk to Justice Louis Brandeis and academic collaborator with Felix Frankfurter, who was himself to be elevated to the Supreme Court in 1940. An appreciation in the *Harvard Law Review* on his death in 1964 noted that Landis was 'on fire' as a student. This may well be taken to epitomize his public career.'[8] At Frankfurter's request, Landis was to become a critical architect of the Securities Act (1933), governing new issuance and the Securities Exchange Act (1934), which extended regulatory oversight to existing securities and mandated associational governance with the exchanges through the establishment of the Securities and Exchange Commission (SEC).[9] He served on the inaugural board of the SEC, becoming its chair following the departure of Joseph Kennedy in 1934, with the public endorsement of his predecessor.[10] As Joseph Kennedy left the SEC headquarters, he interrupted the first Landis press conference by calling out 'Good-bye Jim. Good luck to you. Knock 'em over.'[11] The author of an influential treatise on regulatory rule-making, legitimacy and authority that retrospectively provided theoretical justification for the proposition that law is made, not found,[12] Landis, two decades later, prepared a seminal study for the president-elect, John F. Kennedy, on how and why the regulatory apparatus he was so instrumental in designing, predicated on rule by experts, had failed.[13]

---

[8] E Griswold, 'James McCauley Landis 1899–1964' 78 *Harvard Law Review* 313, 316 ('Surely a man who has done so much should be judged by the best that he can do; and Landis at his best was a great lawyer and legal scholar.').

[9] For biographies of Landis, see D Ritchie, *James M. Landis, Dean of Regulators* (Cambridge, Harvard University Press, 1980); T McCraw, *Prophets of Regulation* (Cambridge, Harvard University Press, 1984); see also J Braithwaite and P Drahos, 'Globalisation of Corporate Regulation and Corporate Citizenship' in F. MacMillan (ed), *International Corporate Law Annual* (Oxford, Hart Publishing, 2003) 26 (describing Landis as a seminal scholar of regulatory strategy). On his death in July 1964, the *New York Times* noted that he 'achieved the rare distinction of being regarded as a conservative by liberals and as an extreme liberal by conservatives.' See 'James M. Landis Found Dead in Swimming Pool of Home,' *New York Times* (31 July 1964) 1, 21. For institutional history of the SEC, see Joel Seligman, *The Transformation of Wall Street* (New York, Aspen Publishers, 3rd Edition, 2003).

[10] 'Landis Heads SEC; Succeeds Kennedy' *New York Times* (24 September 1935) 1, 37 (quoting Kennedy saying 'I see no reason in the world why any business interests need have the slightest misgiving that he will not give them the fairest and squarest deal a man can get. I would deem it an honor to have him as a trustee of anything I owned. He is thoroughly cognizant of the important of the successful administration of these acts in helping to revive the business of the country:' at 1). It was to be a life-long association; see D Nasaw, *The Patriarch: The Remarkable Life and Turbulent Times of Joseph P. Kennedy* (New York, The Penguin Press, 2012), 769 (noting appointment of Landis as special advisor to John F. Kennedy, the president-elect, in 1960 and articulating that next to family, Joseph Kennedy 'trusted no one to watch out for his son as he did Jim Landis').

[11] *New York Times*, above n10 at 37. The position allowed Landis to experiment with a regulatory design he had first articulated in 1931. Critical in this context was the decision on which 'device for enforcement' is to be used; see also JM Landis, 'The Study of Legislation at Law Schools: An Imaginary Inaugural Lecture' (1931) 39 *Harvard Graduates Magazine* 433, 437. ('The criminal penalty, the civil penalty, the resort to the injunctive side of equity, the tripling of damage claims, the informers share, the penalizing force of pure publicity, the licence as a condition of pursuing certain conduct, the confiscation of offending property–these are the samples of the thousand and one devices that the ingenuity of many legislatures has produced. Their effectiveness to control one field and their ineffectiveness to control others, remains yet to be explored.').

[12] JM Landis, *The Administrative Process* (New Haven, Yale University Press, 1938).

[13] JM Landis, *Report on Regulatory Agencies to the President-Elect* (21 December 1960) available at: c0403731. cdn.cloudfiles.rackspacecloud.com/collection/papers/1960/1960_1221_Landis_report.pdf; See also Landis, above n 7 at 638 (noting that 'routine business before these administrative agencies was much too heavy to permit

Notwithstanding the personal tragedy of Landis' subsequent suspension for failing to file income tax returns,[14] the Columbia interviews—read in conjunction with the recently released Harvard material, contemporary scholarly debates and media interventions[15]—make clear that in design and application, the normative question of why one regulates trumps the technical considerations of how one regulates, which is a second-order consideration. As such, these sources in combination provide a particularly illuminating lens through which to explore the contemporary problem of whether and how to change the incentives governing capital market governance.[16]

The privileging of innovation over security and an emaciated conception of responsibility and accountability has led to a profound authority crisis that can only be resolved by reconstituting the social contract governing the operation of global finance. This is a difficult but not insurmountable task, as witnessed by the initial power of the New Deal architecture to transform the governance of Wall Street. As with the current crisis afflicting the Anglo-American model of capitalism,[17] the debate in the 1930s on whether and how the government should intervene was based on a social as well as economic catastrophe. The result was a profound recalibration in which private interests were rendered subservient—if only temporarily—to societal obligation. Moreover, it was to be the progressive erosion of that compact, with the explicit support of political agency, which has, in large part, brought us to the current crisis. Seen in this context, the crisis is a result not of a failure of culture but what happens when the needs and cultural framing of specific communities of practice gain ideational support for what purports to be communal virtues but more accurately reflects unsustainable (and ultimately failed) commercial virtues. Not for the first time in regulatory design, the search for credible reform necessitates going back to the future. The chapter is structured as follows. Section II examines the critical importance of James M. Landis in providing practical and theoretical justification for state intervention in the regulation of securities markets. Section III sets out concrete steps capable of changing the incentives culture of contemporary markets by revisiting the strategies initially used by Landis as both a practitioner and theoretician of regulatory policy. Section IV provides the conclusion.

them to do the broad kind of policymaking that was essential. They didn't have the power to delegate enough of their duties, so that they could keep, in a sense, their desks clean and their minds free to think about the major problems they faced.'). The arguments foreshadowed many made by regulatory capture theorists, see G Stigler, 'Public Regulation of the Securities Markets' (1964) 37 *Journal of Business* 117.

[14] Following an investigation by the Department of Justice, he was charged and sentenced to one month in prison, commuted to house arrest. He was subsequently suspended. It was an ignominious end to an illustrious career. A month later he was found dead in his swimming pool; see *New York Times*, above n 9.

[15] See 'Landis Retiring, Reviews SEC Acts' *New York Times* (10 September 1937) 1.

[16] This is particularly apparent in the United States itself, where structural problems combined with intra-agency regulatory turf-wars impede progress; see J Eisinger, 'For Obama No Easy Fix for Convoluted Regulatory System' *New York Times* (14 November 2012) available at: dealbook.nytimes.com/2012/11/14/in-obamas-second-term-regulation-is-not-likely-to-be-simplified/.

[17] B Obama, 'Remarks on Financial Regulatory Reform' (Press Conference, White House, Washington DC, 17 June 2009) 2 ('In many ways, our financial system reflects us. In the aggregate of countless independent decisions, we see the potential for creativity—and the potential for abuse. We see the capacity for innovations that make our economy stronger—and for innovations that exploit our economy's weaknesses. We are called upon to put in place those reforms that allow our best qualities to flourish—while keeping those worst traits in check. We're called upon to recognize that the free market is the most powerful generative force for our prosperity—but it is not a free license to ignore the consequences of our actions').

II JAMES M. LANDIS AND THE RATIONALE FOR SECURITIES REGULATION

For the progenitors of the original administrative state, the aim was not to operate within accepted paradigms—legal, institutional and theoretical—but to destabilize them by creating an alternative reality, one that legitimated state intervention.[18] Extending far beyond the narrow realm of banking and securities regulation, the New Deal was designed to recalibrate society itself through the guidance of neutral experts. The scale of the ambition, as outlined in Franklin D. Roosevelt's speech accepting the Democratic nomination for the presidency, remains as breathtaking in its audacity as eerily apposite to contemporary problems:

> Out of every crisis, every tribulation, every disaster, mankind rises with some share of greater knowledge, of higher decency, of purer purpose. Today we shall have come through a period of loose thinking, descending morals, an era of selfishness, among individual men and women and among Nations. Blame not Governments alone for this. Blame ourselves in equal share. Let us be frank in acknowledgment of the truth that many amongst us have made obeisance to Mammon, that the profits of speculation, the easy road without toil, have lured us from the old barricades. To return to higher standards we must abandon the false prophets and seek new leaders of our own choosing.[19]

The debates that the New Deal engendered were as much political as judicial, practical as theoretical. They took place in the context of domestic industrial and financial failure and looming conflagration in Europe—the rise of the Soviet Union, and the emergence of Fascism in Italy and Nazism in Germany. Although it was conducted well in advance of the exposure of the faults of centralized planning, there can be no mistaking the extent to which concern over centralized planning cut against valorization of individual enterprise, later articulated in Ayn Rand's cataclysmic *Atlas Shrugged* (1957). Re-reading the primary sources from the 1930s evokes a sense of fin de siècle, with the old order buckling under the strain of its internal contradictions.[20] The interventionist imperative reflected what

---

[18] J Fisch, 'The New Federal Regulation of Corporate Governance' (2004) 28 *Harvard Journal of Law and Public Policy* 39, (39) (noting that securities regulation is a species of public law. . . . [A]lthough securities transactions are private contracts, they take place in public markets and have effects extending far beyond the specific parties involved') at 39.

[19] FD Roosevelt, 'The New Deal' (Speech delivered at the Democratic National Convention, 2 July 1932). The rhetoric intensified by the time of the inauguration; see FD Roosevelt, 'Inaugural Address' (Speech delivered at Washington, D.C., 7 March 1933 ('The moneychangers have fled from their high seats in the temple of our civilization. We may now restore that temple to the ancient truths. The measure of the restoration lies in the extent to which we apply social values more noble than mere monetary profit. . . . There must be an end to a conduct in banking and in business, which too often has given to a sacred trust the likeness of callous and selfish wrongdoing. Small wonder that confidence languishes, for it thrives only on honesty, on honor, on the sacredness of obligations, on faithful protection, on unselfish performance; without them it cannot live. Restoration calls, however, not for changes in ethics alone. This Nation asks for action, and action now.').

[20] For review, see W Bratton and M Wachter, 'Shareholder Primacy's Corporatist Origins' (2008) 34 *Journal of Corporation Law* 99 (noting a corporatist consensus that 'the calculus of corporate rights and duties must adjust and recognize a public interest constraint:' at 103. As a consequence, the debates tell 'a story about corporate law at a time of regime change; in which 'directors could not only address and comply with a broad, new set of government-specified rules, but also be cooperative participants in a common enterprise with the regulators' at 104); see generally M Horwitz, *The Transformation of American Law 1870–1960* (New York, Oxford University Press, 1992) 213–46 (noting 'disputes over questions of administrative law became thoroughly intertwined with raging political struggles over the legitimacy of the regulatory state itself.' at 231).

Thomas Kuhn famously termed 'the structure of scientific revolution,' in which the under-pinning assumptions of normal science were progressively destabilized through practice and political agency.[21] Experience, experiment and avowed faith in the rule of experts to solve the complexity of modern society underpinned a powerful inter-disciplinary intel-lectual movement. Given the opportunity to simultaneously translate theory into practice and generate theory from practice, the crisis also revealed significant conceptual short-comings in prior policy design, the power of which was exponentially increased by the temporary fracturing of previously powerful electoral and ideational coalitions.[22]   In the legal realm, it was informed by Justice Oliver Wendell Holmes' pithy comment that 'the life of law is not logic but experience.'[23] As with their economic counterparts, legal realists and pragmatists used the institutions created by the New Deal as a laboratory to explore how an alliance between government and business could best institutionalize restraint. The critical objective was not, however, the overthrow of capitalism or the financial system but rather credible ongoing sustainable reform in which the regulatory authority could guide a given industry as a whole towards socially beneficial outcomes. The self-proclaimed cru-sade brought the Roosevelt administration into immediate and repeated conflict with the Supreme Court over what constituted or should constitute the appropriate balance between individual rights and public duties.[24] The critical normative move was the institutionaliza-tion of partnership, forced if necessary.

The subsequent judicial battle was played out in the context of rising unemployment, an increasingly disputatious labor environment and a deepening recession. In ruling flagship programs, such as the National Recovery Authority and Agricultural Adjustment Act,

---

[21] In a legendary debate with Thomas Kuhn at the LSE, Karl Popper famously argued that theory remains relevant only insofar as it is not falsified. Kuhn, by contrast, argued that most academics work within the confines of normal science (ie, the prevailing fashions of the time and the prejudices of conventional academic wisdom). There are, of course, many reasons for this. Comprehensive rejection of a deeply embedded thesis is difficult to achieve. The power of underlying terms of reference to color academic debate through measures such as citation indexing is a powerful incentive to work within accepted boundaries. See S Fuller, *Kuhn v Popper: The Struggle for the Soul of Science* (New York, Columbia University Press, 2004).

[22] Academics played a critical role in this process, most notably Adolf A. Berle at Columbia; see J Schwarz, *Liberal: Adolf A. Berle and the Vision of an American Era* (New York, Free Press, 1987) 70–75 (noting the recruitment of Berle as a founding member in 1931 of then Governor Franklin D. Roosevelt's Brains Trust.). Harvard was also a critical source of ideas on the shaping of regulatory purpose, in particular Felix Frankfurter, who was irritated by the degree to which Berle influenced economic policy; see J Srodes, *On Dupont Circle: Franklin and Eleanor Roosevelt and the Progressives Who Shaped Our World* (Berkeley, CA, Counterpoint, 2012) 198. It is indicative of Frankfurter's standing that his elevation to the Supreme Court could be deemed a demotion; see 'Profile: Felix Frankfurter' *The New Yorker* (30 November 1940); for Landis' criticism of Berle as too cautious, see Landis above n 7 at 237 (noting Berle's caution in relation to the establishment of the Securities and Exchange Commission, Landis recalled that 'it was perfectly honest on the part of Berle, no question about that. It would not be fair to accuse him of trying to favor the other side. That would be the wrong way of looking at it. But the approach was that of gradualism, not jumping in headlong.').

[23] OW Holmes, *The Common Law* (Boston, Little, Brown and Co, 1881) 1 (for Holmes 'state interference is an evil, where it cannot be shown to be a good,' at 89).

[24] The most radical of these innovations, the National Recovery Administration, imposed a series of production codes. The enabling legislation, the National Industrial Recovery Act (1933) was deemed unconstitutional in 1935, see *A.L.R. Schechler Poultry v. U.S.*, 295 U.S. 495 (1935); for background to the NRA and its notoriously erratic first director, General Hugh Johnson, see J Whitman, 'Of Corporatism, Fascism and the First New Deal' (1991) 39 *American Journal of Comparative Law* 749, 751–752. The Supreme Court also invalidated the Agricultural Adjustment Act (1933) in *United States v. Butler*, 297 U.S. 1 (1936); for balanced review of the literature, see GE White, *The Constitution and the New Deal* (2000) 16–32.

unconstitutional the Supreme Court sharpened an existential dispute about the relative authority of the federal government and business elites that dated back to its infamous 1905 decision to strike down state-based working hour restrictions in New York bakeries on the basis that it was 'unreasonable, unnecessary and arbitrary interference with the right and liberty of the individual to contract.' [25] By 1937 it was clear that an emboldened Roosevelt had had enough of this debate and what he perceived to be the recalcitrant justices who fanned its flames. In the 1936 presidential campaign, he had hinted that something must be done to deal with Court activism and the threat he deemed it to pose to the functioning of democratic order. In his second 'fireside chat" following re-inauguration, broadcast on 7 March 1937, he reiterated the campaign promise and announced a plan to dilute the poison by expanding the number of federal judges up to and including the Supreme Court:

> If these problems cannot be effectively solved within the Constitution, we shall seek such clarifying amendments as will assure the power to enact those laws, adequately to regulate commerce, protect public health and safety, and safeguard economic security. . . . I [have come] by a process of elimination to the conclusion that, short of amendments, the only method which was clearly constitutional, and would at the same time carry out other much needed reforms, was to infuse new blood into all our courts. We must have men worthy and equipped to carry out impartial justice. But, at the same time, we must have judges who will bring to the courts a present-day sense of the Constitution–judges who will retain in the courts the judicial functions of a court, and reject the legislative powers which the courts have today assumed.[26]

It is no surprise that to generate support for this goal, Roosevelt turned to James M. Landis. Landis was the critical figure in the academic and policy debates over the rise of and justification for the administrative state.[27] He was steeped in the administrative process as both an academic and policymaker. As early as 1930, he had dismissed any restrictions on

---

[25] *Lochner vs. New York*, 198 US 45 (1905). Leading progressives saw such an approach both unsustainable and unworkable, see F Frankfurter, *The Public and its Government* (1930) 45 (noting that "members of the Supreme Court continued to reflect the social and economic order in which they grew up and "sought to stereotype ephemeral facts into legal absolutes" turning "abstract conceptions concerning 'liberty of contract' . . . into constitutional dogmas."). See also, D Bernstein, *Rehabilitating Lochner: Rediscovering a Lost Constitutional Right* (Chicago, University of Chicago Press, 2011) 3 (noting that 'the bakers' maximum-hours law invalidated in *Lochner*, like much of the other legislation the Court condemned as violations of liberty of contract, favored entrenched special interests at the expense of competitors with less political power.').

[26] FD Roosevelt, 'Fireside Chat on the Reorganization of the Judiciary' (Public Radio Address, 7 March 1937), available at www.wyzant.com/Help/History/HPOL/fdr/chat/. ('In the last four years the sound rule of giving statutes the benefit of all reasonable doubt has been cast aside. The Court has been acting not as a judicial body, but as a policymaking body. When the Congress has sought to stabilize national agriculture, to improve the conditions of labor, to safeguard business against unfair competition, to protect our national resources, and in many other ways, to serve our clearly national needs, the majority of the Court has been assuming the power to pass on the wisdom of these acts of the Congress–and to approve or disapprove the public policy written into these laws. . . . We have, therefore, reached the point as a nation where we must take action to save the Constitution from the Court and the Court from itself. We must find a way to take an appeal from the Supreme Court to the Constitution itself. We want a Supreme Court which will do justice under the Constitution and not over it. In our courts we want a government of laws and not of men.')

[27] See McCraw, above n 9 at 172 (noting that Landis 'persistently emphasized the necessity of using all the incentives potentially inherent in the industry to give every person involved – executive, accountant, broker, banker–a stake in helping to enforce the law.') For explicit justification of associational endeavor, see Landis, above n 12 (noting that increased complexity calls 'for greater surveillance by government of the appropriate use of these resources to further the admittedly dim but recognizable aims of our society:' at 4). See also Braithwaite and Drahos, above n 9 (noting the 'regulatory brilliance' of the partnership model).

agency discretion as little more than an attempt to curtail the legitimate exercise of public power for the public good.[28] Asked by his long-term confident Professor Felix Frankfurter to help the Roosevelt administration transform an initial election pledge to regulate securities in 1932 into credible legislation, Landis began a commute from Cambridge to Washington that was to transform the governance of Wall Street and American society through the auspices and example of the Securities and Exchange Commission. Putting into practice the ideas developed in his innovative course on legislation at Harvard, he became one of the most significant policy actors of his generation (and arguably in the history of regulatory design).

Landis had stewarded the agency through early legitimacy and accountability firefights with the financial sector, showing as much acumen in navigating the complexity of political contingency and judicial gamesmanship as in legislative drafting.[29] Although the enforcement methods used by the SEC had come under attack from a Supreme Court and a legal profession deeply troubled by the expansion of the administrative state, it had been deemed constitutional, if potentially dangerous. In *Jones v SEC*, a case that ostensibly centered on subpoena power over withdrawn securities offerings, the Supreme Court had publicly questioned the methods used by the SEC. Justice Sutherland noted that its demands were both wholly arbitrary and unreasonable, invoking by analogy the notorious Star Chamber.

> Arbitrary power and the rule of the Constitution cannot coexist. They are antagonistic and incompatible forces; and one or the other must of necessity perish whenever they are brought into conflict.... Our institutions must be kept free from the appropriation of unauthorized power by lesser agencies as well. If the various administrative bureaus and commissions, necessarily called and being called into existence by the increasing complexities of our modern business and political affairs, are permitted gradually to extend their powers by encroachments–even petty encroachments–upon the fundamental rights, privileges and immunities of the people, we shall in the end, while avoiding the fatal consequences of a supreme autocracy, become submerged by a multitude of minor invasions of personal rights, less destructive but no less violative of constitutional guarantees.[30]

Notwithstanding the rhetorical flourishes, the Court, however, did not find the underpinning legislation flawed. The SEC and its rationale for intervention, a creature of Landis' ambition and commitment to the duties as well as the rights provided by associational governance, had survived initial challenge. Landis was sanguine about the efficacy of the Securities and Exchange Commission's approach, in part because of the cautious nature of

---

[28] JM Landis, 'A Note on Statutory Interpretation' (1930) 43 *Harvard Law Review* 886; for a critique of Landis' approach, see R Pestritto, 'The Progressive Origins of the Administrative State: Wilson, Goodnow and Landis' (2007) 24 *Social Philosophy and Policy* 16, 26–37.

[29] J Burk, *Values in the Marketplace: The American Stock Market Under Federal Securities Law* (New York, Walter de Gruyter Books, 1988) 43.

[30] *Jones v Securities and Exchange Commission*, 298 US 1, 24–25 (1936). Dissenting, Justice Cardozo noted that 'a commission which is without coercive powers, which cannot arrest or amerce or imprison though a crime has been uncovered, or even punish for contempt, but can only inquire and report, the propriety of every question in the course of the inquiry being subject to the supervision of the ordinary course of justice, is likened with denunciatory fervor to the Star Chamber of the Stuarts. Historians may find hyperbole in this sanguinary simile.' Correspondence between Felix Frankfurther and Supreme Court Justice Harlan Stone revealed profound skepticism with the reasoning. According to Frankfurter, 'Sutherland writes as though he were still a United States senator making partisan speech.' Stone was even more caustic in reply; the judgment, he maintained, 'was written for morons and such will no doubt take comfort from it,' cited in M Tushnet, 'Administrative Law in the 1930s: The Supreme Court's Accommodation of Progressive Legal Theory' (2011) 60 *Duke Law Journal* 1565, 1608 (quoting an exchange of letters dated 7 April 1936, on file with Harvard Law School Special Collections Library).

his initial stewardship. He was much less certain about the future of the New Deal itself. By the time that he had decided to retire from the SEC, much broader questions of regulatory authority were at stake. This was most apparent in the debate over the fate of the Public Utility Holding Company Act (1935). The legislation dealt with the vexed question of 'too big to fail,' by mandating the SEC to dissolve entities that that served no clear competitive purpose. The constitutionality of the Act was in play in the 1937 docket. A negative ruling would have severely curtailed the SEC.[31] When Roosevelt broadcast the fireside warning to the Supreme Court, Landis was, therefore, in a unique position to provide intellectual as well as practical help in justifying the threat of judicial reorganization. He was about to return to Cambridge in triumph as Dean of the Harvard Law School, taking over from Roscoe Pound, his nemesis as critic of the administrative state.[32] It was a task that Landis was more than willing to engage in—an opportunity to both settle old scores and present a theoretical justification for the administrative state just as conflict between the forces of capitalism, socialism and democracy was reaching an unavoidable denouement.[33] The aim was not, as critics such as Pound had alleged, to centralize unaccountable power, but to render it more accountable through impartial analysis and review.

Dispatched to Chicago, Landis enwrapped himself in the language of Roosevelt. He then put forward an argument for agency discretion that was to form the basis for his influential Storrs Lectures at Yale, subsequently published as *The Administrative Process* (1938) the following year. Landis argued that the 'real issue we face today is not a new one. It is the old issue of the degree to which this nation shall be a government of laws or men'.[34] Noting that the 1787 Constitutional Convention had twice rejected amendments put forward by James Wilson to give the Supreme Court power to strike down legislation, 'more than one hundred years later, in 1905, as though James Wilson had himself inspired it, the Supreme Court had aggregated to itself the immense super-legislative power that the Constitutional Convention had so deliberately denied it.'[35] Quoting Justice Holmes' famous dissent in *Lochner*,[36] Landis argued that the conflict

arises out of the disregard of constitutional limitations by a majority of the members of the Supreme Court who insist upon writing their own individual economic prejudices and predilections into the fabric of constitutional law. . . . It means today an attitude towards constitutional

---

[31] The constitutionality of the Act was subsequently upheld in *Electric Bond and Share v SEC*, 303 US 409 (1938).

[32] Pound played a pivotal role in writing the ABA Report of the Special Committee on Administrative Law; see *Annual Report of the American Bar Association* (1938) 331–68 (referring to the rise of administrative absolutism).

[33] Landis, above n 7 at 300 ('The National Labor Relations Act, the Holding Company Act, Social Security, Minimum Wage–all these things were pending and if they went down as unconstitutional , the whole effort of the New Deal would fail. . . . I was scared and I think the President was scared of the potentiality of what could happen here.').

[34] JM Landis, 'The Power the Court has Appropriated' (Speech delivered at Fourth Annual Woman Conference, Chicago, 10 March 1937, Reprinted in *Vital Speech of the Day* (1 April 1937)) 358 available at web.ebscohost.com/ ehost/pdfviewer/pdfviewer?sid=ea9e0eb3-63db-41a9-bfdd-2960ba8ffd95%40sessionmgr4&vid=2&hid=.

[35] ibid.

[36] *Lochner v New York*, 198 U.S. 45 at 75 ('This case is decided upon an economic theory which a large part of this country does not entertain. If it were a question whether I agreed with that theory, I should desire to study it further and long before I made up my mind. But I do not conceive that to be my duty, because I strongly believe that my agreement or disagreement has nothing to do with the right of the majority to embody their opinions in law.').

law which incites to litigation, incites to defiance of government, and too frequently leads to the paralysis of a program before it even has a chance of initiation.[37]

Landis endorsed wholeheartedly the president's proposal to inject new blood into the court, dispensing with any pretence that the move was designed to enhance the efficiency of court business. Instead, the unalloyed political reality was presented in forceful terms: 'the issue is not one of the Constitution but an issue of men whose interpretations of that document makes it a straitjacket upon our national life.'[38]

The plan to stack the court marked a defining moment in New Deal politics. It sparked enormous opposition and created new coalitions that challenged Roosevelt's hold on power. Crucially, however, the plan coincided with a remarkable volte-face in the Court's jurisprudence. It marked the point that the court (if not coalitions of the disaffected, mainly comprised of industry participants) finally recognized the legitimacy of administrative power.[39] It was this legacy that Landis was most concerned with protecting, hence his willingness to debate the issue in Chicago as a protagonist. Landis' belief in the supremacy of democratic will linked to the capacity of expert agencies, isolated from the travails of politics and with the resources to enforce mandate, lies at the heart of the New Deal experiment in regulating the capital markets. It could only achieve its dominance because of the extraordinary political circumstances of the time. The unresolved question was what to do with this power. Here too, we see evidence of a coordinated approach built on gaining consensus rather than the imposition of externally generated dictates.

Tracing the rationale from initial framing to the publication of *The Administrative Process* (1938) provides an indication of the centrality of specifying regulatory purpose in legitimating this process. It provided a dual function. First, it limited the grounds for judicial challenge on constitutionality. Second, it limited the grounds for suspicion of the exercise of arbitrary power. Within this framework, disclosure was designed to inform the investing public of actual practice, thereby incrementally changing the boundaries of what could be constituted as acceptable. It is in this context that the abiding strength (and limitations) of the Landis approach to governance, which combines elite wisdom and capacity to both capture and use populist sentiment, becomes clear. At the heart of the compromise lies an uneasy compact on how to evaluate expertise. In the initial framing, this was conceived as the remit of impartial career-driven bureaucrats, prepared to forgo personal material advancement in exchange for societal improvement. The critical flaw pivots on what happens when claims to expertise are evaluated according to different criteria, which is explored more fully in section 3. First, however, it is essential to highlight the ingenuity of the design.

Primary responsibility for the 1932 electoral promise to introduce securities regulation had initially been provided to Houston Thompson, a former Federal Trade Commissioner,

---

[37]   Landis, above n 34 at 360.

[38]   ibid, 361.

[39]   Landis, above n 7 at 302 ('I made a series of speeches after that, but the most important speech I made was the Chicago speech. That one, in fact, I made at the request–I don't think it was the direct request of the President but someone near him. . . . It was a trial balloon. Not that the fight in the end was successful, but it was successful in getting away from the false ideas that were current, or had been made current. . . . A lot of people opposed this. Frankfurter for instance. He opposed it.

Q: He said so to you?

Landis: Oh yes. Yes. He had no use for it at all. Of course he is a traditionalist in many ways'); see also P Irons, *The New Deal Lawyers* (Princeton, Princeton University Press, 1982) 280–89.

whose carriage of it was, according to Landis, 'a complete debacle.'[40] The problem was that rather than implementing 'what Mr. Roosevelt had set forth in his message [his electoral pledge, Thompson] sought to introduce a standard of qualification.' As Landis observed, 'by qualification I mean that some federal agency would determine whether securities themselves, no matter how truthfully they might be described, could nevertheless not be sold on the basis that they didn't meet certain standards of qualification. These standards were never well described.'[41] For Landis, such an approach—based on the very predilections and bias he identified in the decisions of the Supreme Court from *Lochner* onwards—was doomed to fail. Poor drafting and excessive deference combined to make the approach unworkable. 'It was a terribly poorly drafted piece of legislation. In the first place it didn't carry out the President's ideas. In the second place, it introduced sanctions and responsibilities on the federal government for the quality of securities that were being sold, which even today [1963] I don't believe the federal government and I don't believe even a state agency ought to exercise,' he reasoned.[42]

This reasoning represented a clear limit to what the administrative state should do. As Landis explained, 'my fundamental belief is that if the truth is told about these things, then it is up to the parties to decide whether they want to buy them or not. If they want to buy them, and speculate, well, let them go ahead and speculate. I've always felt that the furthest that practical administration could go was to call for a statement of the truth about any enterprise; but that some governmental agency should say you shouldn't but stock in ABC company—I don't know who can decide a thing like that.'[43] None of this is to suggest that Landis was in any way either enamored by or trustful of Wall Street; rather, his strategy was based on explicit enrolment and sustained attempt to leverage the restraining power of reputation, a commodity devalued because of how sections of the industry had operated. Reliance on truth and reputation were narrower and more easily communicable frameworks. In conjunction with Benjamin Cohen, another Frankfurter connection, and assisted by Tommy Corcoran, a Wall Street veteran, the trio 'knocked this thing out in two days.'[44] This thing was to be the initial draft for the Securities Act (1933), which Cohen and Landis were to serve as consultants on, under the direction of the legislative draftsman of the House, Middleton Beaman. Landis' taped interviews provide a revealing insight into how the process unfolded:

> For two days, Beaman wouldn't allow you to put a pencil to paper. He wanted you to know just exactly what you wanted to do, before you started writing. I know that both Cohen and I were a

---

[40] Landis, above n 7 at 158.

[41] ibid, 157 (Brandeis said to me, "Houston Thompson has every great quality that makes a great lawyer, except one. He's got a great bearing, he's got a good presence." I said, "What quality does he lack, Mr. Justice?" Brandeis replied, "Brains.").

[42] ibid, 157.

[43] ibid, 158. It was a formulation that was to stand the test of time; see *Securities and Exchange Commission v Capital Gains Research Bureau*, 375 US 180 (1963) (Goldberg J) ('A fundamental purpose common to these statues, was to substitute a philosophy of full disclosure for the philosophy of caveat emptor and thus to achieve a high standard of business ethics in the securities industry': at 186). This necessitates, however, balancing valid and spurious claims; see J O'Brien, *Redesigning Financial Regulation: The Politics of Enforcement* (Chichester, John Wiley & Sons, 2007) 66–67 (citing Judge Milton Pollack's argument that the federal securities laws are not meant 'to underwrite, subsidize and encourage . . . rash speculation in joining a free-wheeling casino that lured thousands obsessed with the fantasy of Olympian riches but which delivered such riches to only a scant handful of lucky winners').

[44] Landis, above n 7 at 160.

little suspicious of him, as to whether he didn't want to kill this whole thing, with all these dilatory tactics. But within four or five days, we began to appreciate his work and his method of approach. I guess we worked for three or four weeks perfecting the draft, and with his help . . . we put this thing together. In my opinion and the opinions of a great many other people, it's about as good a piece of legislative draftsmanship as you can find in federal legislation.[45]

Once the legislation was enacted, Landis was soon called upon to return to Washington as a consultant to the Federal Trade Commission, where he found the agency 'had no conception about how to administer this act. . . . They had no sympathy with this legislation. It was pretty much damned by Wall Street and regarded as one of these crackpot New Deal measures.'[46] Subsequently promoted to commissioner, Landis recalled an early meeting with Roosevelt in which the president recounted 'the Republicans never want to do anything, so they're always united. But we Democrats want to do things, and we get disunited in wanting to do things.'[47] Thereafter, according to Landis, he assumed leadership. 'I didn't bother him. I mean I assumed the responsibility of deciding things that I felt I had the right to decide.'[48] As Landis recounts the history of the passage of the Securities Exchange Act (1934), the extent of that delegation becomes clear. Along with Ferdinand Pecora, whose congressional investigations had created the contingency for fulfilling electoral pledges in relation to regulating securities, separating investment and commercial banking and replacing caveat emptor with a disclosure philosophy,[49] Landis was invited to the White House:

> Roosevelt met us–well he was in bed when he interviewed us, gave us an interview. He had stacks of papers around him, I know. I recall that. Well Ferdi didn't know anything about the Boss. Great investigator the guy was, really a great investigator, but from the standpoint of a creative artist, he just didn't have that quality. Of course, we built on his work. We built completely on his work. But he just doesn't have that quality of putting together the work in the form of draft legislation. But we both went up to you him, to see the President and the President asked a few questions about the bill. I don't think we spent more than 20 or 30 minutes. We covered this, we covered that–quite intelligent questions–and he hadn't read the bill. The he said, "All right. Go ahead."[50]

Landis was always alert to the possibility that congressional amendments were in fact traps for the unwary. Proposed amendments in the Senate to the corporate 'death sentence' provision of the Public Utility Holding Company legislation, for example, were ostensibly designed to provide SEC additional discretion on whether to exercise that power. For Landis, however, the reforms would have made it 'completely impossible for any commission to administer a statute of that nature because the pressures on the commission should

---

[45] ibid, 162–63.

[46] ibid, 173.

[47] ibid, 178.

[48] ibid, 187. For Landis it was only through experimentation that effective policy could be implemented. In a 1937 speech in Philadelphia, he argued that 'broadly speaking the problems of legislation and administration divide themselves into two phases. The first relates to the determination of what policies to pursue; the second to the discovery of how to make the chosen policies effective.' Quoted in McCraw, above n 9 at 202.

[49] M Perino, *The Hellhound of Wall Street: How Ferdinand Pecora's Investigation of the Great Crash Forever Changed American Finance* (New York, The Penguin Press, 2011) 292–94 (noting how the Securities Exchange Act had finally put a cop on Wall Street).

[50] Landis, above n 7 at 199. This freedom to act is a constant refrain in the reminiscences. Recalling another meeting, Landis noted 'he might not have helped you at all. He might have just thrown the problem right back at you. The feeling of joviality that he gave you, the stimulation and what not–then you'd go back and solve the damn problem yourself, without too much advice from the President' at 244.

be insufferable. Physical standards such as were proposed–that was capable of administration. But to draw a distinction between good and bad holding companies seemed an impossible thing.'[51] Again, here is evidence of good regulatory design: clearly enunciated legislative power, linked to equally clear objectives and discretion only applied after careful and intensive scrutiny that was capable of surviving legal challenge.

Throughout his career, Landis was determined to ensure flexibility without subjecting the agency to accusations of economic or ideological bias, a leitmotif that underpins *The Administrative Process* (1938), a retrospective theoretical justification for what amounted to a new form of government. It remains the defining text of administrative rule. As with the classic Berle and Means treatise on the implications of the separation of ownership and control in major corporations, *The Modern Corporation and Private Property* (1932), Landis' book was designed to inform an increasingly polarized debate over corporate purpose and responsibility. Its central premise and critical thrust was to position regulatory lawmaking as an essential pre-condition for democracy.[52] In a critical passage, Landis argued that 'if the doctrine of the separation of power implies division, it also implies balance, and balance calls for equality. The creation of administrative power may be the means for that balance, so that paradoxically enough, though it may seem in theoretic violation of the doctrine of the separation of power, it may in matter of fact be the means for the preservation of the content of that doctrine.'[53] For Landis, therefore, the rise of the administrative state was an exercise in modernization, legitimated by 'the inadequacy of a simply tripartite form of government to deal with modern problems.'[54]

Legitimacy originated for Landis on how the initial granting of authority was framed. This must 'specify not only the subject matter of the regulation but also the end which the regulation seeks to attain.'[55] Once delegated, regulatory rulemaking, like law itself, was merely 'an instrument, or a social institution, if you will for the advancement of the health of society as a whole.'[56] According to the legal historian Jessica Wang, the formulation 'reflected legal pragmatism's view of law as a process and ongoing experiment, rather than a set body of rules.'[57] For Landis, however, it was a much more complete agenda. 'The expansion of regulatory activity is, of course, the most outstanding characteristic of the nature

---

[51] Landis, above n 7 at 217.

[52] For his critics, foremost among them his predecessor as Dean at Harvard, Roscoe Pound, the rise of the administrative state was something to be feared, Horwitz, above n 20 at 219. The political disagreements were matched by personal rivalries; see Landis, above n 7 at 150–51 (noting 'faculty politics is about as dirty politics as can evolve.').

[53] Landis, above n 12 at 46; for contemporary review, see C Rorhlich, 'Business Administration and the Law,' *New York Times* (16 October 1938) 3, 29 (noting support for Landis' admonition that 'governmental administration should be determined by needs rather than numerology:' at 29).

[54] Landis, above n 12 at 1; see also E Glaeser and A Shleifer, 'The Rise of the Regulatory State' (2003) 41 *Journal of Economic Literature* 401 (noting 'the regulation of markets was a response to the dissatisfaction with litigation as a mechanism of social control of business': at 402).

[55] Landis, above n 12 at 51.

[56] J Wang, 'Imagining the Administrative State: Legal Pragmatism, Securities Regulation and New Deal Liberalism' (2005) *The Journal of Policy History* 257, 264 (citing a letter sent by Landis to Harvard colleague Sidney Simpson, 27 May 1936).

[57] ibid, 265. The following two chairmen of the SEC, William O. Douglas and Jerome Frank—both of whom were academic lawyers—mirrored this approach, taking a much more aggressive view of enforcement. Wang underplays the extent to which Landis was constrained by initial legitimacy battles. Without clearing the space, it is unlikely that Douglas could have adopted his more aggressive approach.

of twentieth century governmental development,' which is founded on the 'creation rather than the restriction of liberties,' he wrote in 1939.[58] This framing was a critical response to a concerted campaign led by the American Bar Association to defenestrate the commissions.[59] This campaign ended only with the passage of the Administrative Procedure Act (1946), which opened regulatory decision-making to extensive judicial review.[60]

What becomes clear from this necessarily truncated review is that the battle over the authority to intervene was fought and won as early as 1937. Moreover, ongoing deference to agency power has been recognized in cases that date back to the 1940s and where definitively ruled upon in 1984 in the landmark Chevron ruling. Prior to the Supreme Court's decision in *Chevron U.S.A. Inc. v. Natural Resources Defense Council, Inc.*,[61] judicial deference to agency interpretations was based on pragmatism. Courts would give deference to agency interpretations depending upon 'the thoroughness evident in [the agency's] consideration, the validity of its reasoning, its consistency with earlier and later pronouncements, and all those factors which give it power to persuade, if lacking power to control.'[62] Additionally, courts looked to see if the agency, opinion had 'warrant in the record and a reasonable basis in law.'[63] Accordingly, while some deference was accorded to agencies, the amount of deference varied considerably, based on the facts surrounding the interpretation.[64] *Chevron* changed the basis for deference. It laid out a two-step process for determining the validity of an agency's statutory construction.[65] First, if the intent of Congress in enacting a statute is clear, then the court must ensure that the agency has given effect to the unambiguously expressed intent of Congress.[66] If, however, a statute is silent or ambiguous with respect to the specific issue, then a court must apply a second step, which is to ask whether the agency's interpretation is based on a permissible construction of the statute.[67]

In developing its two-step framework, the Court articulated three reasons to justify its decision to defer to the agency: implicit delegation,[68] agency expertise,[69] and political accountability.[70] First, with respect to the 'implicit delegation' rationale, the Court reasoned that with the power to administer a congressionally created program comes the power to formulate policy and make 'rules to fill any gap left, whether implicitly or explicitly, by Congress.'[71] When Congress explicitly leaves a gap for an agency to fill, the agency's inter-

---

[58] JM Landis, 'Law and the New Liberties' (1939) 4 *Missouri Law Review* 105, 106.

[59] 'The ABA Report of the Special Committee on Administrative Law' *Annual Report of the American Bar Association* (1938) 331–68.

[60] See G Shephard, 'Fierce Compromise: The Administrative Procedure Act Emerges from New Deal Politics' (1996) 90 *Northwestern University Law Review* 1557; see also Horwitz, above n 20 at 230–33.

[61] *Chevron U.S.A. Inc. v. Natural Resources Defense Council, Inc.*, 467 U.S. 837 (1984).

[62] *Skidmore v. Swift & Co.*, 323 U.S. 134 (1944) at 140.

[63] *NLRB v. Hearst Publ'ns, Inc.*, 322 U.S. I1, 131 (1944) (citing to *Rochester Tel. Corp. v. United States*, 307 U.S. 125, 146 (1939)).

[64] CS Diver, 'Statutory Interpretation in the Administrative State' (1985) 133 *University of Pennsylvania Law Review 549* ('The decision whether to grant deference depends on various attributes of the agency's legal authority and functions and of the administrative interpretation at issue:' at 562).

[65] *Chevron*, above n 61 at 842–43.

[66] ibid, 342–43.

[67] ibid, 843.

[68] ibid, 844.

[69] ibid, 865.

[70] ibid.

[71] ibid, 843.

pretation controls, so long as it is not arbitrary, capricious, or manifestly contrary to the statute.[72] And when delegation is implicit, 'a court may not substitute its own construction of a statutory provision for a reasonable interpretation made by the administrator of an agency.'[73] This interpretation effectively expanded the powers of legitimate agency lawmaking. Second, while the Court had previously alluded to 'agency expertise' in the decisions of *Skidmore* and *Hearst*,[74] in *Chevron* it clarified that '[j]udges are not experts,' at least not in these technical areas.[75] Agency personnel are highly qualified to make technical determinations and are charged with making these determinations.[76] Regardless of whether Congress actually intended to delegate to the agency, it simply makes sense to defer to such expertise.[77] Third, the Court was of the view that the Executive, unlike the judicial branch of government, is accountable to the public.[78] It is therefore more appropriate for the political branch of the government to resolve conflicting policies 'in light of everyday realities.'[79] In a pointed reference, the Court held that 'Federal judges, who have no constituency, have a duty to respect legitimate policy choices made by those who do.'[80] The reasoning and logic mirrors the rationale first outlined by Landis in the maelstrom of the battle over the constitutionality of the administrative process.

Deference, however, is only half of the story. The other half focuses on how that deference is deployed. This has a large impact on the extent to which the regulatory agency enjoys bipartisan political or broader community support, which in part is determined by the performance of the market. The travails facing the contemporary SEC were well noted by its official biographer, Joel Seligman, in a 2009 symposium marking the agency's 75th anniversary.

> The challenge is to strike the right balance between expertise, which is a consequential virtue of a well-run regulatory agency, and political effectiveness, which often can be better achieved by reducing the number of responsible agencies and increasing resources for each.[81]

Here again, revisiting the thought of Landis on regulatory design pays dividends. In 1960, in what was to be his last public intervention in regulatory politics, Landis provided an extraordinary report to the president-elect, John F. Kennedy.[82] The report highlighted both the ambition and the intrinsic flaws associated with the delegation of discretion. The delegation he still maintained was necessary and rendered even more persuasive given the increased complexity of modern society, the incapacity of Congress to devote the time or the resources to deal with them and a conviction that 'the issues involved were different

---

[72] ibid, 843–44.

[73] ibid, 844.

[74] *Skidmore*, above n 62 (opining that the agency administrator had "accumulated a considerable experience in the problems" that the agency faced, at 137–38); *NLRB v. Hearst Publ'ns., Inc.,* 322 U.S. 111 (1944) (commenting that administrators had the benefit of "[e]veryday experience in the administration of the statute" which "gives it familiarity with the circumstances and backgrounds of employment relationships" at 130–31).

[75] *Chevron U.S.A. Inc. v. Natural Resources Defense Council, Inc.* 467 U.S. 837, 865 (1984).

[76] ibid.

[77] ibid.

[78] ibid.

[79] ibid, 865–66.

[80] ibid, 866.

[81] Seligman, above n 9 at 676.

[82] Landis, above n 13 at 4.

from those that theretofore had been traditionally handled by courts and thus were not suited for judicial determination.'[83] The policy problem was that once ceded, it had become impossible to limit or retract authority. Indeed 'on the contrary, the tendency is to expand them as more and more complex problems arise. The legislative standards under which the delegations are made are similarly increasingly loosened so that not infrequently the guide in the determination of problems that faces the agencies in not much more than their conception of the public interest.'[84] He warned that in sharp distinction to the optimism that accompanied the New Deal, the 'fires that then fed a passion for public service have burned low.'[85] This, he attributed to rising cynicism, unacceptable delays, increased costs and a deterioration in the quality of staffing. The 'prevalence is threatening to thwart hope so bravely held some two decades ago by those who believed that the administrative agency, particularly the "independent" agency, held within it the seeds for the wise and efficient solution of the many new problems posed by a growingly complex society and a growingly benevolent government.'[86] Urgent action was required because 'the spark, the desire of public service, has failed of re-ignition.'[87] Complaining of sinecures and the power of practitioners to gain privileged off-the-record access to senior commission staff, he foreshadowed many of the recurrent problems associated with the regulatory capture literature.[88] He also complained bitterly about the failure to address 'foreseeable problems. Absent such planning the need for ad hoc solutions to the particular manifestations of the problem precede and, indeed, may preclude any basic policy formulation.'[89] As Landis puts it, 'where, however, the greatest gaps exist are in the planning for foreseeable problems. Absent such planning the need for *ad hoc* solutions to the particular manifestations of the problem precede and, indeed, may preclude any basic policy formulation.'[90]

Resolving these foreseeable problems are, ultimately, questions of political design, a fact Landis always recognized.[91] By 1960, however, the unease that was to transmogrify into outright opposition in the Reagan era and beyond was already apparent. The problem intensified because the definition of what constituted expertise and where the repository of knowledge lay moved geographically from Washington, DC to Wall Street itself. It is in this broader political context that the Global Financial Crisis of 2008 and its aftermath have such potential transformative programmatic power. This, in turn, has profound implications for the conceptual frameworks that underpin contemporary regulatory practice; practice that is informed by timidity rather than audacity, inaction, and the maintained faith in what Roosevelt would have termed false prophets. It is a response that would—justifiably—have horrified both the president and his chief regulatory architect, James M. Landis.

---

[83] ibid.

[84] ibid, 4.

[85] ibid, 9.

[86] ibid, 6.

[87] ibid, 10.

[88] The concern about moral rectitude of regulatory authorities pre-dated the passage of the Exchange Act; see Seligman, above n 9 at 100 (quoting Ferdinand Pecora, who ran the hearings into Wall Street abuse, saying the legislation to create a specialist agency to monitor the securities market would 'be a good or bad law depending upon the men who administer it.').

[89] Landis, above n 12 at 16.

[90] ibid, 16.

[91] It is more than a little ironic that Landis was to fall foul of a foreseeable problem in the non-payment of his income tax. It meant his effective retirement from public life; see McCraw, above n 9 at 207.

III   REGULATING CULTURE

The disjuncture between stated and lived values, linked to the failure of internal compliance or disclosure to counteract it, underpins variable political demands for an oversight design that better institutionalises restraint.[92] The emphasis on intervention transcends the hoary bifurcation of whether prescriptive 'rules' or more granular articulation of 'principles' are more effective in guiding market behavior. Each had failed to address what is now widely acknowledged to be a systemic ethical deficit.[93] The moral deficit revealed most recently in the Libor scandal underscores how ineffective the normative capacity of compliance is in embedding cultural change if perceived to be little more than a necessary minimum legal and mechanistic response to (unwarranted) external restraints. The crisis and its aftermath demonstrate, therefore, that much more holistic approaches to risk management are required that link private rights to public duties. It is this more holistic approach that informed the early (and now partially lost) agenda of both the Federal Trade Commission and the Securities and Exchange Commission under James M. Landis.

What also becomes clear from the recently released archive is that across a whole swathe of industries, there was early recognition at the FTC that far from weakening power, the codes provided industry with an opportunity to retain it, a factor that must be taken into consideration given the fact that the British Banking Association has canvassed the idea of developing a code of conduct underpinned with statutory authority. The archives suggest that such an approach is exceptionally problematic. The notoriously erratic General Hugh Johnson, the head of the National Recovery Administration (NRA), ignored the possibility of regulatory capture. For Johnson, the new agency, unrestrained from past restrictions on coordinated responses, marked an innovative 'sociological experiment.' As he told a meeting of the National Retail Dry Goods Association in New York in January 1934, the NRA was not only more nimble but it could become a vital partner, something he deemed the FTC incapable of.[94] The speech was a rearguard action against the FTC, which had increasingly come to see the NRA itself as a failed experiment. Critically, the resiling coincided with the promulgation of the Code of Fair Competition for Investment Bankers, which was endorsed on 27 November 1933. It had ensured that power to determine the extent of compliance would remain with the banks themselves. It mandated that the management committee administering the code would contain 21 voting members, 15 appointed by the president of the Investment Banking Association of America, 6 through a 'fair method to represent employers not members of the IBA and a representative appointed without vote by the President of the United States of America.'

Landis, by then heavily embroiled in disputes over the operation of the Securities Act, was horrified by the way in which industry was behaving. 'How truly despicable some

---

[92]   See Obama, above n 17.

[93]   H Sants, 'Delivering Intensive Supervision and Credible Deterrence' (Speech delivered at the Reuters Newsmaker Event, London, 12 March, 2009) 2 ('The limitation of a pure principles-based regime have to be recognized. I continue to believe the majority of market participants are decent people; however a principles-based approach does not work with people who have no principles.').

[94]   H Johnson, Speech delivered at the National Retail Dry Goods Association, New York City, 24 January 1934 ('There was – and there is about as much cooperation between the Federal Trade Commission and the Industry as there is between a lion tamer with a black-snake whip a revolver and a strong-backed chair, standing in a cage with six great jungle cats snapping and snarling on six star-spangled hassocks–that is their version of economic planning and industrial self-government.').

of their tactics are. I really thought they were essentially decent though somewhat misguided people, but I have my doubts now,' he wrote Frankfurter on 13 December 1933. Those doubts were in part informed by unease about the willingness of industry to engage in meaningful partnership. This unease was captured by an internal report prepared for Landis and the other members of the FTC on the workings of the NRA. Assigned to be the chief legal liaison to the General Johnson's NRA, Millard Hudson was flabbergasted by what he termed the 'chaotic conditions' at the agency. 'There is hardly an important form of monopolistic practices which the Federal Trade Commission and the courts have endeavored to prevent in the past, that is not authorized and more or less explicitly provided for in these codes; not of course by individuals, but what is a great deal worse, by the cooperative activities of whole industries. It would be an exaggeration to say that any remonstrances against these things have resulted in any substantial improvement,' he reported on 6 December 1933.[*]

Two weeks later, Hudson provided a more in-depth account of regulatory failure. 'The industries, having got the bit in their teeth, are running amok, and are bent upon destroying the good work accomplished by the Commission in the past and to prevent its doing any more in the future,' he reported on 22 December.[**] Four principal reasons were attributed. No representative of the Commission had power to draw up and enforce a model code. Second, legal representatives were 'practically all young, inexperienced men, many of whom knew nothing whatever about the Commission's work. It was easy for the industries to put things over on them.' Third, 'having given the industries in the early codes practically everything they asked for, it was difficult to refuse those which came later. But the most alarming development is the unwillingness of the Administrator to set up any effective form of control over the administration of the codes. He is leaving it, by his own statement, as far as possible to the boards set up within the industries themselves. This means that matters in which they are interested will receive attention and probably little else will.'[***]

The internal report was forwarded to Roosevelt who, in turn, turned over responsibility for evaluation of code operation to the FTC, effectively limiting the power of the NRA long before the Supreme Court deemed it unconstitutional the following year. The release of the new material suggests that the administration had come to the conclusion that the partnership approach was a failure long before then, although for very different reasons. Critically, notwithstanding this failure, the initial success of the New Deal experiment can be traced to the combination of five ideational and political economy factors. First, the policy imperatives of the initial Roosevelt administration (1932–36) advanced the necessity and legitimacy of state intervention. Second, the policy imperatives were predicated on a rebalancing of private rights and public duties, a strategy that was subsequently overwhelmingly endorsed at the ballot box in 1936. Third, initial judicial skepticism that rendered legislative action unconstitutional was overcome by a progressive whittling away of the influential freedom of contract model, the growing institutionalization of judicial restraint and, in part, through an unconsummated but nevertheless real threat in 1937 following Roosevelt's comprehensive electoral victory to 'pack the court' unless the judiciary accepted political will. Fourth, the nascent administrative agencies, in particular the Securities and Exchange Commission, placed a 'cop on the beat,' doing much to restore public confidence. Fifth,

---

[*] Memorandum for the Federal Trade Commission: Work at the NRA, Millard E Hudson, December 6, 1933, Papers of JM Landis. Harvard Law School, Box 18-8.

[**] Memorandum for the Federal Trade Commission provided by Millard F Hudson, 22 December 1933, Papers of JM Landis. Harvard Law School, Box 18-8.

[***] ibid.

however, the initial emphasis was not on direct enforcement but changing industry practice through an associational model of governance. It clearly specified purpose and sought to enroll market actors within a regulatory paradigm that replaced caveat emptor with a disclosure philosophy. At its core was a belief that sustainable reform could only be achieved at an industry-wide level, with the administrative agency operating at one stage removed from the sector it regulated, rather than having a role to secure its survival and growth.

For Landis, 'the art of regulating an industry requires knowledge of the details of its operations [and the] ability to shift requirements as the condition of the industry may dictate.'[95] Landis' early faith in governance by experts had already eroded by the time of the election of John F Kennedy in 1960. In part this derived from what he saw as the failure of the agencies to remain focused on narrow regulatory purpose, a process that intensified because of patronage appointments at the level of the commission and declining commitments to the public service as a career.[96] For Landis, the power of the disclosure model, first set out in the Securities Act (1933) and reinforced by the Securities Exchange Act the following year, was the capacity to set, evolve and frame broader discourse. The aim was not to mandate organizational change as some early commentators—including William O. Douglas—advocated,[97] but to present disclosure as a necessary response to societal obligation. In 1937 Landis told the *New York Times*, somewhat optimistically, that brokers 'are beginning to realize more clearly that their interest is tied up with the public interest. They are beginning more often to subordinate their own interest to the larger interest. People are beginning also to look upon the exchanges not so much as private institutions as public utilities.'[98] The real tragedy here is not the misplaced optimism of Landis but the misplaced trust in financial services sector statements that through their disclosures they had recognized their obligations.

If defective disclosure was not the cause of the myopia in the Global Financial Crisis and the primary problems operated in the sophisticated sector a more granular ex ante articulation of risk is unlikely, in itself, to be effective in fashioning change. Satisfactory answers require an evaluation of how a reform agenda addresses not just objective *efficiency* (ie, lower transaction costs). Three additional distinct but overlapping subjective normative criteria must be applied. First, *permissibility* (ie, whether a particular product can be sold and if so to whom

---

[95] Quoted in Seligman, above n 9 at 62.

[96] See Landis, above n 13.

[97] WO Douglas and G Bates, 'The Federal Securities Act of 1933' (1933) 43 *Yale Law Journal* 171. Douglas viewed the disclosure paradigm as insufficient. What was required, he argued, was a much more substantive reordering of relations between market participants. This essentially corporatist approach, advocated mainly by the Columbia-based members of the original Roosevelt 'brains trust' was always regarded as suspect by Landis and his colleagues at Harvard, most notably Felix Frankfurter. The personal nature of these disputes becomes clear with the release in January 2013 by Harvard Law School of additional personal papers of James M Landis, the driving force behind the creation and management of the Securities and Exchange Commission. The papers include correspondence between Landis and Frankfurter, arguably the most influential academic advisor to the Roosevelt administration. The correspondence reflects a growing frustration by both men towards industry opposition to and academic misunderstanding of the paradigm shift associated with the passage of the Securities Act and its corollary, the Securities Exchange Act (1934). Most notably, this derision is directed towards Douglas himself, whom, it is clear, neither man entirely trusted from the very beginning. On 6 March 1934, Landis noted to Frankfurter that 'Douglas seems to me to lack a tremendous sense of the realities that are involved in this problem and how the relentless drive for profits leads men to do things and then defend them.' On 17 March 1934, Frankfurter replied that 'Douglas is trying to reflect too much the people in the big offices and the business schools, among whom he likes to appear as a sound and knowing fellow.' Frankfurter goes on to comment that Douglas had privately opined to him that 'his public articles against us are a form of high strategy. Well its [sic] too high for my eyes to scale.'

[98] *New York Times*, above n 15.

and on what basis); second, *responsibility* (ie, who carries the risk if the investment sours and on what terms); and third, *legitimacy* (ie, does the product serve a legitimate purpose and who should determine it). This, in turn, suggests the need for the dynamic integration of rules, principles and social norms within an interlocking responsive framework. As John Kay has persuasively argued, sustainable reform must be predicated on capability to 'restore relationships of trust and confidence in the investment chain, underpinned by the application of fiduciary standards of care by all those who manage or advise on the investments of others.'[99]

The Kay formulation builds on an insight first advanced by the recently retired managing director of the Financial Services Authority, Hector Sants. Sants had famously complained that it was impossible for principles-based regulation to work when those charged with informal authority to maintain the integrity of the system had no principles.[100] This was not simply a particularly memorable aside. It reflected belated cognizance of the importance of what Oliver Williamson has termed the 'non-calculative social contract.'[101] Sustainable reform must also be consistent with principles of good regulation. It must be proportionate, consistent in application, transparent and targeted. The danger is that an ill thought out structure will exacerbate rather than resolve conflicts within the industry.[102] It risks creating another layer of formal restraint that does little to change either corporate practice or facilitate voluntary progression towards higher ethical standards. It is also clear, however, that the construction of accountability mechanisms cannot rely on self-certification alone. It demands external validation. The recent history of financial regulation has demonstrated conclusively the dangers of past self-referential framing.

Ironically, the framework to measure and evaluate culture was outlined at the same 2010 Mansion House conference by the then chief executive of the Financial Services Authority, Hector Sants. The regulatory executive, who now runs compliance and government and regulatory relations at Barclays, argued for triadic calculation: 'Even if you believe the regulator should and could judge culture, how would the regulator facilitate or enforce the adoption of its judgments by firms?' Starting from the premise that society has the right to expect ethical behavior and warranted commitment to stated values, he maintained that regulators cannot avoid judging culture, a term he judged less problematic and more amenable to measurement than ethics.

> What should matter to the regulator are the outcomes that the culture delivers and that the firm can demonstrate it has a framework for assessing and maintaining it. The regulator must focus on the actions a firm takes and whether the board has a compelling story to tell about how it ensures it has the right culture that rings true and is consistent with what the firm does.[103]

---

[99]   See John Kay, *The Kay Review of Equity Markets* (HM Government, London, July, 2012).

[100]   Sants, above n 93.

[101]   O Williamson, 'The New Institutional Economics: Taking Stock, Looking Ahead' (2000) 38 *Journal of Economic Literature* 595, 597. Williamson notes that analysis of this 'level one' component of social theory is conspicuous by its absence with regulatory studies. The other three levels comprise institutional arrangements viewed primarily through property rights and positive political theory, governance mechanisms through transaction cost economics and resource allocation frameworks generally examined through agency theory.

[102]   Critically, it must also be based on a re-conceptualization of the regulatory architecture, see Kay, above n 99 at 10 ('Bad policy and bad decisions often have their origins in bad ideas. . . . Regulatory philosophy influenced by the efficient market hypothesis has placed undue reliance on information disclosure as a response to divergences in knowledge and incentives across the equity investment chain. This approach has led to the provision of large quantities of data, much of which is of little value to users.').

[103]   H Sants, 'Regulating Culture' (Speech delivered at the Ethics and Values Conference, Mansion House, London, 5 October 2010).

The tragedy for both the banking industry and the Financial Services Authority has that neither internal nor external oversight was pursued until it was too late. Accountability and integrity, as Sants pointed out however, are, in essence, design issues. It is time to get to work. A necessary starting point would be virtual attendance at the imaginary inaugural lecture James M. Landis offered in 1931. It is time to go back to the seminar room.

IV   CONCLUSION

As I write this conclusion, the news emanating out of both London and New York is unremittingly bleak.[104] Attempts by business today to limit the remit of the Securities and Exchange Commission over the granularity of regulation covering internal control mechanisms mirror the charged atmosphere pertaining as Landis was drawing up the legislation that established the agency. Writing in 1934, just before the bill was debated in Congress, Landis complained: 'The Stock Exchange Bill is receiving a terrific beating. All the corporate wealth of this country has gone into the attack and carried it all the way to the White House.'[105] Although the bill was passed and the SEC established, its remit and authority waned incrementally at first and dramatically in the 1990s. The reduction in power has consistently failed to ignite public controversy. In the absence of the kind of catastrophic crisis witnessed in the Great Crash of 1929 or the extent of corporate scandal revisited at the cusp of the millennium, again in 2008 and most recently the exposure of the Libor scandal, battles over financial regulation take piecemeal form through refinements to individual legislative clauses.

Just as prevalent, however, are disputes between executive agencies and associational groups with differing degrees of enfranchisement over the design and implementation of specific regulatory instruments. The fragmented and technical nature of this glacial process masks the cumulative effect of technical change. It can leave an outer shell of protection lacking the structural substance to withstand systemic shocks. Unfortunately until the exposure of the Libor scandal, we were stuck in this dispiriting rut. In this sense the failure to deliver on the pledge for restraint by the erstwhile chairman of Barclays to the *Financial Times* is talismanic of the sector's bad faith. Society has a right to expect better. Regulators have a duty to ensure protection is offered and political actors an obligation to ensure the lessons of history are learnt.

---

[104] See H Sender, 'It's 2007 Again, Thanks to the US Fed' *Financial Times* (1 December 2012) available at www.ft.com/intl/cms/s/0/818517a6-3a4a-11e2-a32f-00144feabdc0.html#axzz2DviqSchm (noting 'the world is much more frightening today than it was in 2008. Growth in most parts of the world is far slower, while Europe looks to be in recession. Joblessness is a challenge in many parts of the globe. The geopolitical situation is far less stable. Governments are cash strapped and have far less room to support either their economies or their banks.').

[105] McCraw, above n 9 at 178.

Part Two

Regulating Culture in the Financial Sector–Incentives and Integrity

CHAPTER 4

The Regulation of Self-interest in Financial Markets

*David Campbell and Joan Loughrey**

I INTRODUCTION

An increasingly prominent theme of the search for a form of financial market regulation superior to that which so blatantly failed in 2007 is that, behind the shortcomings of the specific rules and techniques of regulation, lies a defective culture. Those working in the financial services industry are believed to have become possessed by a self-interest that knows no quantitative limit, and so degenerates into greed, and has no regard for the propriety of the means by which it may be pursued, and so degenerates into rapacity. Perhaps conscious of the way that the financial services industry itself now seems to wish to return to business as usual but little troubled by the way that what appears to be such business is possible only because it is backed by free life support from the taxpayer, those charged with financial market regulation argue that regulatory reform will be impossible without a changed culture. In 2010, in his then capacity as Chief Executive of the Financial Services Authority (FSA), Sir Hector (then Mr) Sants told us that it was his 'personal view ... that if we really do wish to learn lessons from the past, we need to change not just the regulatory rules and supervisory approach, but also the culture and attitudes of both society as a whole, and the management of major financial firms'.[1] Sir Hector added that '[T]his will not be easy'.[2]

* We are grateful to Joanna Gray for her comments.

[1] H Sants, 'UK Financial Regulation: After the Crisis' (12 March 2010) at www.fsa.gov.uk/pages/Library/Communication/Speeches/2010/0312_hs.shtml.

[2] Mr Sants has himself decided to approach the problem from a different direction. In December 2012, he joined Barclays, surely a pathological case as he himself had previously said, as Head of Compliance and Government and Regulatory Relations [*sic*], after six months gardening leave following his resignation from the FSA. Had he remained at the FSA, he would have been the Chief Executive of the new Prudential Regulation Authority he had done much to set up: P Aldrick, 'Hector Sants Departure from FSA Leaves Regulators in Disarray' (16 March 2012) *Daily Telegraph*. Mr Sants' new post is not at Board level, and Barclays is not obliged to disclose his salary (Anon, 'Hector Sants Joins Barclays to Improve Its Reputation' *BBC News* (18 December 2012) at www.bbc.co.uk/news/business-20695316), but it is known to be in the order of £3 million per annum, much the largest

We are in agreement with Sir Hector about the necessity of a change in the culture of the financial services industry if financial markets are in future to be welfare-enhancing to a greater degree, and even more about the difficulty of bringing about that change. For, at a general level, the points are hardly worth making. The culture of the financial services industry must be changed. But the question is whether concrete regulation can be directly addressed to so vague a task. One cannot but suspect that the regulatory retreat to a critique of something so amorphous as culture follows from an acknowledgement that previous regulation was a deplorable failure, upon which the regulator does not now know how to improve in any concrete way: '[w]hen policy debates are dominated by the c-word, you know we are out of practical ideas'.[3] We ourselves are of the opinion that it was structural defects in the organisation of the financial services industry and in its regulation that generated the defective culture.[4] But, insofar as the issue can be addressed as one of the motivation of financial market participants, then in this chapter we wish to engage with the conceptualisation of the regulatory task at a somewhat more precise level in order to caution against a common misunderstanding about what should be involved in this change of culture.

In much criticism of the culture of the financial services industry, what is being criticised is, not a debased version of self-interest, but self-interest per se. The target of this criticism is a failure to constrain what are believed to the normal outcomes of 'financialisation', 'competition', 'capitalism', etc; in a word, of markets. In a very authoritative recent review of the issues involved in the proposal that regulation should seek to promote a change of culture, Dan Awrey, William Blair and David Kershaw have argued that the crash has exposed '[t]he limits of *markets* as mechanisms for constraining socially suboptimal behaviour', and that the turn to culture (and ethics) is necessary to deal with this market failure, to which conventional regulation itself is a most inadequate response.[5] The basic sense that emerges from the idea of changing culture is that market failure may be addressed by the inculcation

---

part of which will be bonus! P Jenkins, 'Sants Secures £3m Package at Barclays' (18 December 2012) *Financial Times*. Despite Mr Sants' appointment, Barclays has awarded £39 million in shares to nine senior executives, including the head of its investment banking arm, representing accumulated remuneration dating, in some cases, back to 2007. This gives every sign of business proceeding as usual and of the financial crisis, LIBOR and mis-selling scandals being disregarded: 'Barclays Awards Shares Worth £39 million to Nine Executives' (20 March 2013) *BBC News* at www.bbc.co.uk/news/business-21867735.

[3] S Mallaby, 'Woodrow Wilson Knew How to Beard Behemoth' (6 July 2012) *Financial Times*. As this chapter was being drafted, this retreat into rhetoric by the regulator was taken to an even more absurd extreme. The Commission on Banking Standards gave it as its opinion that, not only should investment banking be 'ring-fenced' from retail banking, but, so that the fence would work, it should be 'electrified'! H Wilson. 'Electrify Ring Fences to End Bank Gaming' (21 December 2012) *Daily Telegraph (Business Section)*.

[4] In addition to issues specific to the 1980s reorganisation of the financial sector, the limited personal liability of those principally causing the risk, the drastic shortcomings of shareholder monitoring, and the creation of derivative instruments which did not need to pass any form of product testing, about which one of the current authors has written elsewhere (D Campbell and S Griffin, 'Enron and the End of Corporate Governance, in S MacLeod (ed), *Global Governance and the Quest for Justice*, vol 2, *Corporate Governance*, Oxford, Hart, 2006; D Campbell, 'Adam Smith, *Farrar on Company Law* and the Economics of the Corporation' (1990) 19 *Anglo-American Law Review* 185; D Campbell and S Picciotto, 'The Justification of Financial Futures Exchanges' in A Hudson (ed) *Modern Financial Techniques, Derivatives and Law* (London, Kluwer, 2000)), call into question whether the financial markets which crashed can usefully be regarded as displaying the structural properties of markets at all.

[5] D Awrey et al, *Between Law and Markets: Is There a Role for Culture and Ethics in Financial Regulation?* LSE Law, Society and Economy Working Papers 14/2012 (2012) 1; forthcoming in (2013) 1 *Delaware Journal of Corporate Law*.

of a more ethical form of economic action than that of the self-interested individual utility maximiser of 'the complete and perfectly competitive markets' of neo-classical economic theory.[6] What is needed, as Awry et al tell us, is a culture of 'other-regarding action'.[7]

Though, as will become evident, we have drawn heavily on this excellent paper, and though we are in complete agreement with many of Awrey et al's specific diagnoses and prescriptions, their basic criticism of market failure, important because it is now so widely shared, involves, in our opinion, a most serious mistake. It is our belief not, only that rational economic action analytically is based on self-interest, but that, of its nature, the self-interest that generates rational economic action and is the basis of the market economy cannot be self-interest of the sort that led to financial markets dominated by greed and rapacity, for market self-interest is a self-interest that is based on respect for the legitimate interests of others.

The form of regulation in place at the time of the crash was itself by no means unconcerned with culture. An earlier form of regulatory technique based on the extremely detailed stipulation of outcomes by the application of a proliferation of rules had been substantially replaced by a more sophisticated mixture of rules and principles, and the very aim of this principles-based regulation was to generate a responsible financial services culture. By close examination of examples of this more sophisticated structure of regulation in place at the time of the crash, we will show that it was, precisely, a failure to ensure that financial market participants' action was oriented to the self-interest that is necessary to the operation of markets that was the fundamental regulatory problem. The significance of this is, of course, that welfare-enhancing regulatory reform of financial markets must now look to inculcate a culture of self-interest, rather than a culture in some way opposed to self-interest.

The criticism of self-interest in financial markets has received very influential support from the enormously distinguished welfare economist and political philosopher Amartya Sen, who has argued, not merely that self-interest in financial markets must be modified in such a way as to really amount to its elimination, but that, in saying this, he is essentially restating the views of Adam Smith. If Sen's interpretation of Smith's views was right, his argument against self-interest would, of course, be extremely powerful. But it is not right. It is a very serious distortion of those views. This is worth dwelling upon because Sen is right to say that Smith would have had no truck with the greed and rapacity of the financial markets. But this tells us that those markets were very inadequate markets, not, as Sen believes, that they tell us that our use of markets should be much more highly restricted.

Though we shall refer to all of Sen's substantial contributions to the interpretation of Smith, which one may trace back to works published in the 1980s, the works on which we will focus intimately couple the exposition of Smith to a response to the crash. These are the 'Introduction' which Sen wrote for a 2009 Penguin edition of *The Theory of Moral Sentiments*,[8] brought out on the occasion of *The Theory*'s 250th anniversary, and two related articles which he published in *The Financial Times*[9] and *The New York Review of Books*.[10]

---

[6] ibid 5.

[7] ibid 4.

[8] A Sen, 'Introduction' in A Smith, *The Theory of Moral Sentiments* (London, Penguin Books, 2009). This edition was not intended to and, of course, does not supplant the *variorum* edition published as a volume of The Glasgow Edition in 1976: A Smith, *The Theory of Moral Sentiments*, corrected edn (Oxford, Clarendon Press, 1979). Liberty Press has made the Glasgow edition available in print at a lower price than the Penguin edition, and available without charge on-line at oll.libertyfund.org/?option=com_staticxt&staticfile=show.php%3Ftitle=192.

[9] A Sen, 'Adam Smith's Market Never Stood Alone' *Financial Times* (11 March 2009).

[10] A Sen, 'Capitalism Beyond the Crisis' (15 February 2009) *New York Review of Books*.

Much of the argument of the 'Introduction' is to be found, quite often identically expressed, in Sen's two most important works of more recent vintage, *Development and Freedom*[11] and *The Idea of Justice*,[12] in which he restates the philosophical underpinnings of his development economics and his welfare economics more generally in a way which repeatedly engages with *The Theory of Moral Sentiments*.

Of course, comparison of Smith's views with those of any other modern writer rarely shows to the advantage of the latter. But the contrast between what Smith said about the conditions for a welfare-enhancing market economy and what Sen believes Smith to have said about this is symptomatic of the way that much current thinking about the market economy is so far out of sympathy with market values that it thinks those values can be realised only by the implementation of policies that, if carried through, would certainly destroy them. Welfare-enhancing reregulation of the financial markets must, we will argue, take a completely different line, one which encourages self-interest as the core value of all markets, including the financial markets, but a Smithian self-interest which is intrinsically opposed to the conduct of financial markets participants that led to the crash.

II   THE USE OF RULES AND PRINCIPLES IN THE ATTEMPT TO CURB SELF-INTEREST

The Limits of Rules

The particular difficulty for recent criticism of a financial services culture of self-interest is that examination of the extensive regulation in place at the time of the crash shows that it was itself intended to inculcate a superior culture. The form of financial services regulation that, in the UK, was introduced by the Big Bang, was an excessively detailed attempt to provide rules and codes which (inevitably inadequately) prescribed the conduct to be followed in all circumstances, but which emptied financial services regulation of moral content. These detailed rules of behaviour were substituted for the trust accumulated in the financial services industry, the value of which was inadequately understood and appreciated, following the Big Bang's move away from the complex of relationship-based dealings to ideal–typically anonymous, one-off, transactional dealings. Instead of having a proper regard for the legitimate interests of the client, those selling financial services were able to substitute a claim that they were following the rules and codes. As Kay amongst many has argued, a system of financial services built around the proposition that most people cannot be trusted creates the risk that 'such a system will stimulate the very behaviour it seeks to constrain, as people come to believe that appropriate standards of behaviour are defined by rules rather than by the integrity of the participants'.[13]

We must be clear about the nature of the error committed here. The diversity and complexity of the factual situations which will arise in the selling of financial products makes the ex ante specification of acceptable courses of conduct by detailed rules a practical

---

[11] A Sen, *Development as Freedom* (Oxford, Oxford University Press, 1999).
[12] A Sen, *The Idea of Justice* (London, Penguin, 2010).
[13] J Kay, *The Kay Review of UK Equity Markets and Long-Term Decision Making Final Report* (July 2012) 45.

impossibility. However, this is not the fundamental problem. If one ignored the insuperable practical difficulty, one might allow that a sufficiently detailed set of rules could in theory be devised. But it is *in principle* impossible to ex ante specify these rules because such specification must create the possibility of gaming those rules, as the process of rule-following is reflexive. This is the problem for regulation which economists generally call moral hazard. When not informed by a proper regard for the client, the attitude to obeying the rules and codes could and did lead to the opportunistic pursuit of unrestrained self-interest.

R (on the application of the British Bankers Association) v Financial Services Authority,[14] which arose out of the payment protection insurance (PPI) mis-selling scandal, clearly illustrates the problem. This was an unsuccessful application by the British Bankers Association (BBA) for judicial review of a policy statement issued by the Financial Services Authority (FSA)[15] and an online resource issued by the Financial Services Ombudsman. The policy statement set out how PPI complaints should be handled and listed a series of 'common failings' identifying types of conduct that could constitute mis-selling.[16] The FSA indicated that these common failings potentially breached several of the over-arching, high-level principles contained in the FSA *Handbook*, such as Principle 6, which requires firms to pay due regard to customer interests and to treat customers fairly, and Principle 7, which requires firms to pay due regard to clients' information needs by communicating information in a way which is clear, fair and not misleading,

The BBA's argument about the relationship between the principles and the more detailed Insurance Conduct of Business Rules is highly pertinent. The BBA accepted that the principles could impose obligations in relation to activities not covered by a rule. However, when an activity was covered by detailed rules which were intended to give effect to particular principles, then, as a matter of statutory construction, a firm's only obligation was to comply with those rules, and the FSA could not look to the relevant principles to augment the specific rules.[17]

The BBA's primary objective was to challenge the FSA's position that firms should pay compensation to customers when principles alone were breached.[18] However, the effect of its argument was that, provided firms did not breach any of the specific rules governing a particular area of conduct, then those firms effectively could treat customers unfairly contrary to Principle 6, or mislead them contrary to Principle 7, by, for example, failing to orally explain the limitations and exclusions in a PPI policy while emphasising the policy's benefits.[19]

J Ouseley rejected these arguments, holding that the principles were mandatory overarching standards, and that firms' obligations went beyond mere compliance with rules as these did not exhaustively state the types of conduct that could be required to comply with

---

[14] *R (on the application of the British Bankers Association) v Financial Services Authority* [2011] EWHC 999 (Admin); [2011] Bus LR 1531.

[15] FSA, *The Assessment and Redress of Payment Protection Insurance Complaints*, PS10/12 (August 2010) at www.fsa.gov.uk/pubs/policy/ps10_12.pdf.

[16] ibid Appendix 4.

[17] *R v FSA*, above n 14, 98. The arguments reflect long-standing industry anxiety that the Principles were too uncertain to be fairly justiciable.

[18] ibid at [7]–[8].

[19] ibid at [120]–[121]. For further examples of this attitude, see the industry responses collected in FSA, *The Assessment and Redress of Payment Protection Insurance Complaints: Feedback on CP09/23 and Further Consultation*, CP10/6 (March 2010) 10–11, 13–14.

the principles. Moreover, a regulatory system based on rules alone would be inflexible and could be circumvented unfairly.[20]

The BBA's position demonstrates how detailed rules can lead to claims that anything that is not prohibited is permitted, despite the FSA long making it clear that adherence to rules alone would not exhaust a firm's regulatory obligations.[21] Detailed, rule-based regulation annihilates responsibility, and without acceptance of responsibility, economic action will be self-interested in the wrong way, and inevitably will be suboptimal.

The Limits of Principles

Due to the weaknesses of rules-based regulation, financial services regulation has long used principles, at least in conduct regulation. In 1992, as part of the New Settlement, the Securities and Investment Board issued ten principles (as well as forty 'Core Rules') with the intention that these would prevent the regulated from pleading technical compliance with the letter of the rules and from exploiting technical gaps in those rules.[22] Although the FSA initially focused on creating the vast accumulation of rules that became the FSA *Handbook*,[23] from the beginning the *Handbook* also contained high-level principles stating general behavioural standards, and firms were required to interpret the rules in the light of these. Since 2005, the FSA has determinedly sought to rebalance regulation by reducing the detail of its rules and increasingly emphasising a principles-based approach.[24] Even when more rules have been introduced, such as those governing oral disclosure in PPI sales, they set outcomes to be achieved, rather than prescribing compliance with rigid processes.[25] Since the FSA adopted the policy of credible deterrence in 2008, the number of actions taken for breach of the principles alone has increased.[26] So, at least in the sphere of conduct of business, regulation at the time of the crash had, for some time, involved a mixture of principles and rules, with the former appealing to the regulated to curb their pursuit of their self-interest.[27] The conduct issues which have plagued the financial sector are therefore a challenge to principles-based regulation and demonstrate the limits of regulating for a superior culture.

This is most apparent when one considers the FSA's Treating Customers Fairly Initiative (TCF), launched in 2001.[28] The TCF set six outcomes for firms to achieve, including

---

[20]   *R v FSA* (n 14) at [161]–[66].

[21]   eg FSA, *Treating Customers Fairly: Progress and Next Steps* (July 2004) 9–12 at www.fsa.gov.uk/pubs/other/tcf_27072004.pdf.

[22]   J Black, '"Which Arrow?": Rule Type and Regulatory Policy' [1995] *Public Law* 94, 103–106.

[23]   FSA, *Designing the FSA Handbook of Rules and Guidance*, CP8 (April 1998) at www.fsa.gov.uk/static/pubs/cp/cp08.pdf.

[24]   FSA, *Better Regulation Action Plan: What We Have Done and What We Are Doing* (December 2005) at www.fsa.gov.uk/pubs/other/better_regulation.pdf; see also FSA, *Principles-based Regulation: Focusing on the Outcomes That Matter* (April 2007) at www.fsa.gov.uk/pubs/other/principles.pdf.

[25]   E Ferran, 'Regulatory Lessons from the Payment Protection Insurance Mis-selling Scandal in the UK' (2012) *European Business Organization Review* 248, 258.

[26]   M Cole, 'Delivering Credible Deterrence', speech to the FSA Annual Financial Crime Conference (27 April 2009).

[27]   eg see SIB Principle 1 (firms must observe high standards of integrity and fair dealing); Principle 5 (firms to take reasonable steps to give customers, in a comprehensible, timely way, information customers needed to make balanced informed decisions); Principle 6 (firms must not unfairly place their interests above those of customers); FSA Principles 6 and 7 (see text at n 16 above) Principle 8 (conflicts of interest must be managed fairly) and Principle 9 (obligation to provide suitable advice).

[28]   FSA, *Treating Customers Fairly After the Point of Sale*, DP7 (June 2001) at www.fsa.gov.uk/pubs/discussion/dp7.pdf.

ensuring that consumers could be confident that they were dealing with firms that had made fair treatment of customers central to their corporate culture, and that consumers were provided with clear and appropriate information before, during and after the point of sale. Firms were assigned responsibility for designing internal processes to realise these outcomes.[29] In theory, this transfer of the ownership of regulatory responsibility to firms should have encouraged firms to 'buy-in' to regulatory objectives, resulted in more effective internal compliance systems, and, given the influence of firm culture and organizational structure on individual behaviour, made the formation of norms of acceptable behaviour, more likely.[30]

TCF appeared to place acceptable limits on the pursuit of self-interest, sought to make a business case for fair treatment of customers, and suggested measures to promote retail customers' autonomy. In early documentation the FSA defined fairness as requiring, inter alia, firms to act honestly, openly and in good faith; to honour representations, assurances, and guarantees where these created legitimate expectations in the minds of customers; to act in accordance with the manifest intention of the parties or the spirit of the contract, even when this conflicted with the 'small print'; and to refrain from exploiting customers by, for example, imposing manifestly harsh and disadvantageous terms upon them, or by otherwise taking advantage of their poverty, ignorance or need; or by generally writing contracts which created a significant imbalance in the parties' contractual rights and obligations to the detriment of the customer.[31]

Awrey et al argue that, within sensible limits of what might be expected, TCF provided a sound basis for the promotion of a more ethical culture within firms.[32] Current calls for reform typically emphasise the importance of the 'tone from the top', that good conduct is a business and not just a compliance issue, and that senior managers must signal that their firms take regulatory objectives seriously, inter alia by ensuring that infractions will be internally sanctioned.[33] TCF looked to senior management to lead a change in their firms' culture so as to ensure that customers were treated fairly.[34] Drawing on Gilad's empirical findings that TCF did succeed in engaging senior management and firms were responding positively,[35] Awrey et al concluded that a regulatory strategy such as TCF could make a 'notable contribution to ethical cultural formation in financial firms', and, in particular, to the promotion of 'other-regarding' values.[36]

The TCF model is likely to play a significant role in the new regulatory regime for conduct. The Financial Conduct Authority (FCA) has stated that it will look to firms to 'base

---

[29] FSA, *Treating Customers Fairly: Building on Progress* (July 2005) 11 at www.fsa.gov.uk/pubs/other/tcf_06072005.pdf.

[30] Awrey et al above n5, 25-26.

[31] FSA above n28, Annex A, 3-4.

[32] Awrey et al (n 5) 23–24.

[33] ibid 8.

[34] FSA above n21, 11-12.

[35] S Gilad, 'Overcoming Resistance to Regulation via Reframing and Delegation': law.huji.ac.il/upload/Sharon. Gilad.pdf. Awrey et al cite this earlier version of Gilad's empirical study, which does not contain the caveats she enters in her later article: S Gilad, 'Institutionalizing Fairness in Financial Markets: Mission Impossible?' (2011) 5 *Regulation and Governance* 309, although she makes a similar point about senior management at 323. For a contrary view see C Adamson, 'Delivering Fair Treatment for Consumers of Financial Services', speech by FSA Director of Supervision (6 December 2011).

[36] Awrey et al above n5, 21, 26

their business model, their culture, and how they run their business, on a foundation of fair treatment of customers as set out in [TCF]'.[37] It has warned that fair treatment of customers will not be sacrificed in the interests of financial success.[38]

The problem, however, is that there is little evidence that TCF resulted in more ethical conduct by firms and there is significant evidence that it did not. As Gilad states, her empirical study was *not* directed at assessing the impact of regulated firms' greater engagement with TCF, and, in particular, whether this had led to the 'successful institutionalization of the FSA's regulatory goals'.[39] Rather, she tells us that:

> given the vague requirements of TCF, and the absence of absolute criteria for compliance, it was practically impossible for me to assess whether or not firms have successfully implemented TCF. It is nonetheless imperative to clarify that *there is nothing in [my research] to suggest that TCF was a success from the regulator's point of view.*[40]

While Gilad found that the FSA's enforcement activity had caused firms to overcome their resistance to TCF and to change internal systems in order to implement it, this had resulted in 'incremental improvement to firms' performance *against those indicators that firms set for themselves*'.[41] But this occurred whilst banks continued to mis-sell PPI and deal with PPI complaints unfairly,[42] and to mis-sell interest rate hedging products to small and medium-sized enterprises![43] The FSA's own research found that firms were measuring processes, rather than ensuring fair outcomes.[44]

The fact that TCF may not have worked raises serious questions. TCF *should* have worked. Although principles-based regulation and the manner in which the FSA applied it has come under fire, TCF avoided weaknesses that were seen elsewhere.[45] A large amount of resource was poured into it.[46] It was not light touch.[47] It focused on outcomes and not just processes, which was not the case with all aspects of the FSA's regulatory system, such as, for example, the regulation of the wholesale markets.[48] A regulator must engage to some degree sceptically with the regulated community (or else what is the rationale of regulation?),[49] and, at least in respect of TCF, the FSA did not unquestioningly accept what firms told them and thus was

---

[37]   FSA, *Journey to the FCA* (October 2012) 25 at www.fsa.gov.uk/about/what/reg_reform/fca.

[38]   ibid.

[39]   Gilad, 'Institutionalizing Fairness in Financial Markets: Mission Impossible?' (n 35) 312.

[40]   ibid 323 (emphasis added).

[41]   ibid (emphasis added).

[42]   FSA, *Payment Protection Insurance: A Thematic Update* (September 2008) at www.fsa.gov.uk/library/other_ publications/miscellaneous/2008/ppi_update.shtml; FSA (n 15).

[43]   FSA, *Interest Rate Hedging Products: Pilot Findings* (March 2013) at www.fsa.gov.uk/pubs/other/interest-rate-swaps-2013.pdf.

[44]   FSA, *Treating Customers Fairly: Progress Update* (June 2008) 13 at www.fsa.gov.uk/pubs/other/tcf_progress.pdf.

[45]   C Ford, 'Principles-Based Securities Regulation in the Wake of the Global Financial Crisis' (2010) 55 *McGill Law Journal* 257, 280–86 and also FSA, *The Turner Review: A Regulatory Response to the Global Banking Crisis* (March 2009) 86–88.

[46]   Until the crisis, the FSA focused its regulatory energy on consumer protection matters rather than on prudential regulation: ibid 87–88.

[47]   Thus, although in 2002 the FSA did not explicitly refer to Principle 6 (the duty to treat customers fairly) in enforcement actions, it was one of the grounds for enforcement in 10% of cases in 2003, 13% in 2004, 20% in 2005, 58% in 2006, and 67% in 2007: Gilad 'Institutionalizing Fairness in Financial Markets: Mission Impossible?' (n 35) 317. However, Ferran (n 25) 261 found that enforcement actions in respect of PPI sales tailed off after 2008.

[48]   J Black, 'The Rise, Fall and Fate of Principles-based Regulation', *LSE Law, Society and Economy Working Papers* 17/2010 (2010) 14, 17–19.

[49]   Ford, above n45, 261

able to detect ongoing problems. Nevertheless, TCF was based on trusting the regulated community to establish and apply to itself 'basic moral norms' in day-to-day business.[50] And as trust is not argued, only to be central to principles-based regulation,[51] but also to be essential for encouraging the regulated to exercise their moral judgment, this was a laudable feature.

Why, then, is there no firm evidence of TCF's success but, on the contrary, indications that it failed? Gilad suggests that it met with initial resistance as a result of an emotional reaction to its moral connotations. By identifying firms' conduct as unfair, TCF challenged individuals' and firms' identities.[52] But this does not explain firms' later behaviour. It may be that TCF was beginning to work but that, as the financial crisis continued, resources were diverted away from it. However, it may be more significant that TCF depended on firms to determine whether their internal practices and systems met the regulatory outcomes. Regulatory goals may be defeated if the regulator's (representing society's) understanding of what those goals mean diverges from the understanding of the regulated. Given the vagueness of the term, might this not be the case in respect of the FSA's concept of 'unfairness'? Black points out how firms had argued that customer satisfaction was an indication that they were treating customers fairly, while the FSA argued that consumers were not well placed to assess the suitability of products that firms sold to them, and could be satisfied even though they had been treated unfairly.[53] Gilad meanwhile found her interviewees asserting that their firms did treat customers fairly even whilst those firms were mis-selling PPI![54]

It would be difficult to assert that firms did not know what fairness meant to the FSA. We agree with Awrey et al that TCF 'articulates a relatively intelligible and non-arbitragable standard of other-regarding behaviour'.[55] Even if this is contested, the FSA engaged in a regulatory conversation with firms through its supervision process and, by producing an extensive range of documentation which was aimed at establishing a shared understanding of what fairness required, certainly set out what its expectations of TCF were.[56]

The amount of FSA guidance may itself have caused problems as it constituted a drift from broad principles to more detailed rules, and so suffered from the inherent weaknesses of a rules-based approach.[57] However, the guidance often took the form of examples of good and bad practice which demonstrated fairness or unfairness, or risks to the former. While there was a great deal of guidance, much was perforce repetitive, having to highlight the same problems arising year after year. So, for example, from 2004 the FSA voiced concern that the manner in which sales advisors were remunerated, in particular when sales volume was the main factor determining staff-bonuses, created the risk of mis-selling.[58] The FSA repeated its warnings over several years.[59] In 2005 and 2006, these

[50] A Georgosouli, 'The FSA's "Treating Customers Fairly" (TCF) Initiative: What Is So Good About It and Why It May Not Work' (2011) 3 *Journal of Law and Society* 405, 412.

[51] J Black , 'Forms and Paradoxes of Principles-Based Regulation' (2008) 3 *Capital Markets Law Journal* 425, 456.

[52] Gilad, 'Institutionalizing Fairness in Financial Markets: Mission Impossible?' above n55, 324.

[53] Black above n48, 17.

[54] Gilad, 'Institutionalizing Fairness in Financial Markets: Mission Impossible?' above n35, 314-16.

[55] Awrey et al above n5, 25.

[56] On the nature and function of regulatory conversation see J Black, *Rules and Regulators* (Oxford: Clarendon Press, 1997) 30–37; J Black, 'Talking About Regulation' [1998] *Public Law* 77; Ford above n45, 277-78.

[57] Georgosouli above n50, 421.

[58] FSA above n21, 17.

[59] FSA above n21, 12, 16-17; FSA, *Treating Customers Fairly: Culture* (July 2007) 19–20 at www.fsa.gov.uk/pubs/other/tcf_culture.pdf.

problems were linked to PPI sales, with the FSA pointing out that a commission-based remuneration system in which commission rates varied between different products created a powerful incentive to mis-sell products that generated higher commission, such as single premium PPI.[60] From 2005, the FSA also pointed out that PPI salespeople were providing an unbalanced account of their product, talking up its benefits whilst relying on written information to outline the limitations and exclusions, and that there were particular problems around single premium PPI.[61] Nevertheless, the industry failed to engage seriously with these issues.[62] PPI continued to be mis-sold and, as late as 2012, incentive structures which were designed to maximise firm profits, but created the risks of mis-selling, remained common.[63]

It is therefore difficult to concede that there was some form of misunderstanding which meant that firms did not realise that their conduct was problematic. Rather, according to Gilad, it appears likely that they knew that, in relation to PPI, they were acting contrary to TCF, but their boards decided that they could not afford to desist when competitors were engaging in similar practices.[64] TCF may have succeeded in educating firms about what the regulator considered fair or unfair, but it did not prevent them from engaging in unrestrainedly selfish behaviour.

The Limits of Rules and Principles

Where does this leave us? Financial regulation arguably still involves too many rules[65] and there has been a move towards more prescriptive regulation in response to the financial crisis. The FSA has proposed converting some TCF guidance into rules,[66] whilst the FCA has been given the power to make product intervention rules.[67] Black has argued that when the regulated are ill-intentioned, such rules-based regulation works best,[68] and there is evidence that rules are sometimes necessary to promote ethical decision-making.[69] But

---

[60] FSA, *The Sale of Payment Protection Insurance: The Results of Thematic Work* (November 2005) 18–19 at www.fsa.gov.uk/pubs/other/ppi_thematic_report.pdf; FSA, *Treating Customers Fairly: Towards Fair Outcomes for Consumers* (July 2006) 30–31 at www.fsa.gov.uk/pubs/other/tcf_towards.pdf. This risk was also highlighted in the Retail Distribution Review (RDR) which led to the ban on paying commission to retail financial advisors: see the RDR Library at www.fsa.gov.uk/about/what/rdr/rdr-library.

[61] FSA, *The Sale of Payment Protection Insurance: The Results of Thematic Work* (n 60) 21–25; FSA, *Treating Customers Fairly: Towards Fair Outcomes for Consumers* above n60, 33-34; FSA (n 42); FSA (n 44) Annex 3, 6.

[62] FSA, *Treating Customers Fairly: Measuring Outcomes* (November 2007) 9, 12 at www.fsa.gov.uk/pubs/other/tcf_outcomes.pdf.

[63] FSA, *Guidance Consultation: Risks to Customers from Financial Incentives* (September 2012) 5–6 at www.fsa.gov.uk/static/pubs/guidance/gc12-11.pdf.

[64] Gilad, 'Institutionalizing Fairness in Financial Markets: Mission Impossible?' above n35, 323. Firms ignored even precise rules relating to oral disclosures in PPI sales about which there could have been no confusion: FSA, *Insurance Conduct of Business Sourcebook(ICOBS) Post-Implementation Review: Statement of Findings* (June 2010) 14–21 at www.fsa.gov.uk/pubs/other/icobs_review.pdf.

[65] A Haldane, Executive Director, Financial Stability and Financial Policy Committee, Bank of England 'The Dog and the Frisbee', speech given at the Federal Reserve Bank of Kansas City's 36th Economic Policy Symposium on *The Changing Policy Landscape* (31 August 2012).

[66] FSA, *Product Intervention*, DP11/1 (January 2011) 45–46 at www.fsa.gov.uk/pubs/discussion/dp11_01.pdf; FSA, *Product Intervention Feedback on DP 11/1*, FS11/3 (June 2011) 34–39 at www.fsa.gov.uk/pubs/discussion/fs11_03.pdf. See further Ferran, above n25, 259.

[67] Financial Services and Markets Act 2000, s137D.

[68] Black (n 48) 7.

although financial institutions abused the trust that was reposed in them, and although this was the cause of the failure of principles-based regulation,[70] and therefore a proximate cause of the crash, we would not advocate a return to a system that is based primarily on prescriptive rules. It will not work, for the reasons we have discussed.

That *R v FSA* sought to put the enforceability of Principles beyond doubt is welcome, as is the FCA's indication that it will continue with the FSA's policy of credible deterrence, seeking higher penalties, pursuing more senior staff, and intervening earlier when it detects problems.[71] Although sanctioning should only be used as a last resort, after persuasion and warnings have been ineffective,[72] or in response to serious misconduct, TCF's limited impact demonstrates that the regulated community have been particularly recalcitrant and their actions highly damaging. This would suggest that frequent and punitive sanctioning may be required to encourage compliance. Yet to take this line may undermine a positive culture, because it is now a truism of regulatory theory[73] that if norms are obeyed solely because of fear of external sanctions, the force of the norms will be weakened and may eventually collapse, unless the possibility of effective sanctioning is very high.[74] While enforcement may be necessary to encourage compliance, it may reduce the likelihood that the norm of enlightened self-interest will be internalised and so entrench selfishness.

In the end, far from TCF altering culture, culture may well have defeated TCF, and one has to question whether regulation which sets itself squarely against the prevailing culture of financial market participants can possibly work. In the remainder of this paper, we hope to show that it both possible and necessary to sidestep this conflict by giving an account of the proper relationship of financial market culture and its regulation in which the core of the former–self-interest–is the positive goal of the latter.

III   THE MARKET PARTICIPANT'S VIEW OF SELF-INTEREST

The bleak picture of regulatory failure that we have painted involves, at one level, a perfectly accurate description of the culture of the financial services sector, and, in particular, of market participants' view of their self-interest. Awrey et al are right to argue that a dysfunctional culture of self-interest, reinforced by incentive structures which generated 'pressure to exploit counterparties' interests and ignore the societal impact of . . . risk-taking',[75] were

---

[69]   T Herron and D Gilbertson, 'Ethical Principles v Ethical Rules: The Moderating of Moral Development on Audit Independence Judgments' (2004) 14 *Business Ethics Quarterly* 499. Rules have other uses, eg, when promoting consistency is important so that consumers can accurately compare disclosures from different providers: J Black et al, 'Making a Success of Principles Based Regulation' (2007) *Law and Financial Markets Review* 191, 201; FSA, *Principles-based Regulation* (n 24) 7.

[70]   Black above n51, 456.

[71]   FSA, *The Financial Conduct Authority: Approach to Regulation* (June 2011) 7 at www.fsa.gov.uk/pubs/events/fca_approach.pdf; FSA, *Journey to the FCA* above n37, 37.

[72]   I Ayres and J Braithwaite, *Responsive Regulation: Transcending the Deregulation Debate* (Oxford, Oxford University Press, 1992) 35.

[73]   Though one which may be traced to Bentham's distinction between political and moral sanctions and the significance of the distinction for the proportioning of punishment: J Bentham, *An Introduction to the Principles of Morals and Legislation* (London, Methuen, 1982) 35.

[74]   M Eisenberg, 'Corporate Law and Social Norms' (1999) 99 *Columbia Law Review* 1253, 1260–61, 1291–92.

[75]   Awrey et al above n5, 20.

highly significant causes of the crash. But we have seen that Awrey et al claim that this culture is evidence of a serious limitation of markets. However, we do not believe that market self-interest was the problem, but rather that it was an absence of market discipline which allowed selfishness to be pursued without restraint.

So deplorable has been the conduct of many market participants that it is legitimate to wonder whether they really formed their judgements in what it is sensible to call a moral fashion at all. Any reader of the confessions of repentant former insiders is perfectly well aware that intentionally exploitative and even outright criminal conduct was common. And, as Sir Hector Sants put it in his justly famous phrase: 'a principles-based approach does not work with individuals who have no principles'.[76] But if we accept that market participants predominantly did form their judgements in a moral fashion, then the principal problem is that their morality was based on such a distorted view of market action that they identified that action with a self-interest which, when taken to its logical end-point, naturally allowed of greed and rapacity.[77] A culture of excessive selfishness was fostered, not just by internal structures within firms, but externally through a particular political and economic perspective that viewed unrestrained selfishness as legitimate market behaviour, and, believing an unregulated market to be a natural state of affairs, saw regulation as constituting a generally illegitimate interference in this state of affairs.[78] This is evident in the criticism the industry levied at the FSA's proposals for handling PPI complaints, which, if a genuine indication of market participants' attitudes, emphatically demonstrates that they have wholly failed to grasp the unacceptability of their conduct.[79]

That leading market participants considered their appalling behaviour legitimate was strikingly demonstrated in the BBC Today Programme's inaugural Business Lecture given by Mr Bob Diamond, then Chief Executive of Barclays, in November 2011.[80] In a way which stretched the credulity of the listener, this lecture, to the limited extent it focused on private financial sector failure at all, lamented a previously defective culture, which Mr Diamond told us was in the process of thoroughgoing reform. PPI was one of the things Mr Diamond had in mind when he declared that '[w]e have to try to make sure that things like that don't happen again'. He went on to say:

> In part that comes down to culture. It's a very personal thing, but throughout my career–from my time as a teacher, to my time as a banker–I have seen just how important culture is to successful organisations. Culture is difficult to define, I think it's even more difficult to mandate–but for me the evidence of culture is how people behave when no-one is watching. Our culture must be one where the interests of customers and clients are at the very heart of every decision we make; where we all act with trust and integrity.

At this time, it would seem that Barclays was playing a major role in the outright manipulation of crucial market information, such as LIBOR, and the facts about this which are

---

[76]   H Sants, 'Delivering Intensive Supervision and Credible Deterrence' (12 March 2009).

[77]   The fundamental philosophical issues as examined by Kant, which turn on an appreciation of the possibility of pure individualism wrongly but plausibly serving as a maxim of moral conduct, are discussed in D Campbell, 'Individualism, Equality and the Possibility of Rights' (1991) 6 *The Connecticut Journal of International Law* 507.

[78]   H McVea, 'Financial Services Regulation under the Financial Services Authority: a Reassertion of the Market Failure Thesis?' (2005) 64 *Cambridge Law Journal* 413, 416. For an illustration of these attitudes, see S Breyer, 'Analysing Regulatory Failure: Mismatches, Less Restrictive Alternatives, and Reform' (1979) 92 *Harvard Law Review* 549, 552.

[79]   FSA above n19.

[80]   At news.bbc.co.uk/today/hi/today/newsid_9630000/9630673.stm.

emerging have done what one would have thought was impossible by lowering one's opinion of financial services culture. Only the perennial weaknesses of the SFO prosecutorial process can possibly prevent this manipulation being found to be a criminal fraud which should attract substantial terms of imprisonment. A *Financial Times* editorial called this an episode which exposed the 'rotten heart of the financial system' and the 'rotten culture at Barclays'. As for Mr Diamond's striking statement that 'the evidence of culture is how people behave when no-one is watching', the Editor remarked: 'Well, now we know'.[81] But Mr Diamond felt no qualms giving this lecture despite this background and, more generally, despite the concerns about the application of an investment bank mentality to retail banking which had been raised by his own appointment as Barclays' Chief Executive.

We do not want to suggest that Mr Diamond did not mean what he was saying about banking culture, although he would not have been the first not to have done so.[82] The significance of his views is that they were sincerely held. He did not see banking, even his type of banking, as playing anything other than a vital, beneficial economic and social role, but, unfortunately, banks 'had done a very poor job of explaining how we contribute to society'. But Mr Diamond displayed a complete misunderstanding of the nature of legitimate market behaviour. He focused only on the necessity of his bank making tremendous profits and simply equated this with general economic success. This is an utterly tendentious view of the nature of economic action which extols the unlimited pursuit of self-interest as the driver of economic growth because such self-interest is believed to be market action, to which ethics, business ethics, financial regulation, company law, corporate social responsibility, and consumer protection generally, are thought to be mere external restraints.

It is our aim in the remainder of this chapter to argue that, when the regulated purport to defend their excessive self-interest, they should not be able to seek legitimacy for doing so by claiming that they are acting in the name of the market, for their action is not market action. Any such argument cannot remain at the crude level of the self-understanding of the financial services sector but will have to trace the issues back to the most profound discussion of economic action and self-interest ever made, that of Adam Smith. The way we think it most advantageous to make this approach is, not through a discussion of the views of market participants such as Mr Diamond, but by, as it were, reversing the focus and looking at the call for a better culture by a representative and influential critic of (financial) markets, specifically Amartya Sen's criticism of the self-interest that he believes brought about the crash.

IV   SEN ON SMITH ON SELF-INTEREST

The principal contribution which Amartya Sen has made to welfare economics and to the political philosophy of equality has turned on the concept of 'capability'. Whereas other forms of welfare economics have addressed themselves to the distribution of resources

---

[81] Editorial, 'Shaming the Banks Into Better Ways', *Financial Times* (28 June 2012) 12. That the financial system was rotten to its core was a rhetoric almost universally adopted in the media in the immediate wake of the exposure of the LIBOR scandal.

[82] For example Goldman Sachs' *Code of Business Conduct and Ethics* states at 7 that 'Our clients' interests always come first' and at 6 that 'integrity and honesty are at the heart of our business'. However, the bank subsequently argued that these principles were mere opinions and puffery: *Richman v Goldman Sachs Inc*, 10 Civ. 3461 US District Court, Southern District of New York (21 June 2012).

amongst economic actors, Sen has purported to directly address what unarguably is the point of ultimate importance, which is the advantage an actor can derive from the resources at her disposal. In Sen's conception, the focus of welfare economics and the assessment of equality shifts from the size of resource endowment to the actor's capability to convert that endowment to advantage, which is a function of personal and social conversion factors. An example of the former is acuity, as opposed to fecklessness, in making expenditure choices; and an example of the latter is access to an education which effectively inculcates acuity in the adult economic actor. In this way, this 'capabilities approach' targets, not equality of endowment, but equality of realised advantage, and brings to the foreground the vital role of the social conversion factors in giving effect to the possibility of realising advantage.

The claim on which the capabilities approach is based is that, to use Sen's excellent coinage in this connection,[83] 'opulence' is not necessarily an accurate measure of welfare.[84] Save in exceptional cases which themselves are mostly indicative of a pathology, there undeniably is a significant correlation between opulence and welfare such that a certain degree of the former is essential to well-being.[85] Nevertheless, to regard the correlation between opulence and well-being as perfect or very close to perfect is to take 'an alienated, commodity fetishist view', which is, 'ultimately, a confusion of "well-being" with being well off", and 'a confounding of the state of a person with the extent of his or her possessions'.[86] In calling this mistaken view 'commodity fetishism', Sen is not, as he seems to claim he is, using this term in at all the way Marx intended, but one can see what he is trying to say. The extent of 'commodity command' is only a partial measure of well-being. Save again in exceptional, typically pathological, cases, an economic actor should not value wealth as such: '[c]ommodity command is a means to the end of well-being, but can scarcely be an end in itself'.[87]

But, of course, some actors do regard opulence in itself as the end of economic action, or at least, if they regard it as one of a number of ends, they place far too high an importance on it in their assessment of their well-being. In Sen's view, a very important class of such actors is the senior owners and managers of the financial institutions the failure of which produced the crash, whose motivation was greed:

> The nature of the present economic crisis illustrates very clearly the need for departures from unmitigated and unrestrained self-seeking in order to have a decent society. Even John McCain, the 2008 Republican Presidential candidate, complained constantly in his campaign speeches of "the greed of Wall Street". Smith had a diagnosis for this: he called promoters of excessive risk in search of profits "prodigals and projectors", which, by the way, is quite a good description of many of the entrepreneurs of credit swaps insurances and subprime mortgages of the recent past. The term "projector" is used by Smith not in the neutral sense of "one who forms a project", but in the pejorative sense, apparently common from 1616 (or so I gather from *The Shorter Oxford English Dictionary*), meaning, among other things, "a promoter of bubble companies, a speculator, a cheat". . . . Relying entirely on an unregulated market economy can result in a dire predicament

---

[83] With Rothschild, Sen has discussed the more conventional usage of opulence in Smith's thinking in E Rothschild and A Sen, 'Adam Smith's Economics' in K Haakonssen (ed), *The Cambridge Companion to Adam Smith* (Cambridge, Cambridge University Press, 2006) 319.

[84] A Sen, *Commodities and Capabilities* (Oxford, Oxford University Press, 1999) 19.

[85] A Sen, 'Well-being, Agency and Freedom' (1985) 82 *Journal of Philosophy* 169, 199.

[86] Sen above n84, 16.

[87] ibid 19.

in which, as Smith writes, "a great part of the capital of the country" is "kept out of the hands which were most likely to make a profitable and advantageous use of it, and thrown into those which were most likely to waste and destroy it".[88]

Sen is lending his great authority, and claiming to lend Smith's immense authority, to what we have noted is the predominant analysis and proposed response to the crash, which is that it was the product of 'unmitigated and unrestrained self-seeking' in 'an unregulated market economy'. Two policy recommendations are taken to follow from this: to regulate more, and, through such regulation, to curb self-interest.

The Quantity Metaphor of Regulation

The first recommendation is based on what we might call the quantity metaphor of regulation. Deregulation, based on 'a huge overestimation of the wisdom of market processes', led to 'the insufficient regulation of financial activities',[89] and we now need to reverse this. Changes in the financial services industry 'in recent years' have meant that:

> the need for supervision and regulation has become much stronger. And yet the supervisory role of government in the United States in particular has been, over the same period, sharply curtailed, fed by an increasing belief in the self-regulatory nature of the market economy. Precisely as the need for state surveillance grew, the needed supervision shrank. There was, as a result, a disaster waiting to happen, which did eventually happen . . . and [which] has certainly contributed a great deal to the financial crisis that is plaguing the world. . . . The implicit faith in the ability of the market economy to correct itself, which is largely responsible for the removal of established regulations in the United States, tended to ignore the activities of prodigals and projects in a way that would have shocked Adam Smith.[90]

In light of what has been argued earlier,[91] we can be brief about this quantity metaphor. A belief in deregulation certainly played a very substantial part in causing the crisis, but to concede that deregulation adequately describes what happened is a most serious mistake. The Big Bang, to consider only this, was a major exercise in reregulation[92] by a UK government very markedly in thrall to City interests,[93] after which financial markets were far more highly formally regulated by numerous agencies.[94] But those agencies, in line with the government policy that created them, essentially saw their role as the expansion of the volume of financial trading in order to increase the profitability of, and therefore the taxable revenue of, the financial sector. Putting to one side the facilitation by nation states of the globalisation of sophisticated financial dealing, this was seen as a matter of increasing the rewards of, and therefore the inducement towards, the expansion of, financial dealing. The creation of a regulatory environment which privileged this expansion over other concerns

---

[88] Sen above n8, xii. In the Glasgow Edition, the quotation is to be found in A Smith, *The Wealth of Nations* (Oxford, Clarendon Press, 1976) 357.

[89] Sen above n10.

[90] ibid.

[91] And in light of criticism of by one of the current authors of the concept of deregulation more generally, most recently of Richard Posner's version of the concept: D Campbell, 'The End of Posnerian Law and Economics (Review of RA Posner, *A Failure of Capitalism*)' (2010) 73 *Modern Law Review* 302; D Campbell, 'Welfare Economics for Capitalists: The Economic Consequences of Judge Posner' (2012) 33 *Cardozo Law Review* 2233.

[92] D Gowland, *The Regulation of Financial Markets in the 1990s* (Aldershot, Edward Elgar, 1990) 3.

[93] M Moran, *The Politics of the Financial Services Revolution* (New York NY, St Martin's Press, 1991).

[94] S Vogel, *Freer Markets, More Rules* (Ithaca NY, Cornell University Press, 1996) ch 5.

allowed, inter alia, the introduction of selling techniques which generated very large sub-prime mortgage assets that were actually liabilities;[95] the repackaging and trading of those assets in ways about which little or nothing was understood save that the trading was the source of immense revenues;[96] and the creation of the febrile macro-economic climate in which all this took place.[97] Though brought about by private actors, these outcomes were all direct products of a particular, detailed channelling of private action by government policy.[98] The deregulation of financial markets is a myth which merits no further comment here, and we intend to focus on what does merit discussion, which is the form of reregulation of the failed financial markets that is needed now, consideration of which takes us to what we wish to discuss, Sen's second policy recommendation, of curbing self-interest.

Curbing Self-interest

Seeing that what was perceived as financial deregulation rested on an 'implicit faith in the ability of the market economy to correct itself', Sen turns to the source of that faith, which is the concept of the generally competitive market in mainstream economics, a concept that, in many hands, including the hands of those most responsible for the financial economics that underlay the trading that proved disastrous, is indeed often linked to Smith:

> There is a strong tradition in the economic literature that has tended to assume—indeed assert—that Smith believed 'self-interest dominates the majority of men', to quote the distinguished economist George Stigler, who took this belief, which he championed, to be 'on Smithian lines'. A great majority of economists were—and some still are—evidently quite enchanted by something that has come to be called 'rational choice theory', in which rationality is identified with intelligently pursuing self-interest. Further, following that fashion in modern economics, a whole generation of rational choice political analysts and of experts in so-called 'law and economics' have been cheerfully practising the same narrow art. And they have been citing Smith in alleged support of their cramped and simplistic theory of human rationality.[99]

The problem, in sum, is the impoverished view of human motivation maintained in mainstream economics:

> a very large part of modern economics has increasingly fallen for the simplicity of ignoring all motivations other than the pursuit of self-interest, and the brand named 'rational choice theory' has even elevated this falsely alleged uniformity in human behaviour into the basic principle of rationality.[100]

It is Sen's argument that the attempt by mainstream economists to associate their views with those of Smith is quite wrong. This is a criticism he had made of Stigler on a number of previous occasions,[101] and, as the formal statement of neoclassical equilibrium does

---

[95] M Zandi, *Financial Shock: A 360 Degree Look at the Sub-prime Mortgage Implosion, and How to Avoid the Next Financial Crisis* (Saddle River NJ, Financial Times Press, 2008).

[96] ST Omarova, 'The Quiet Metamorphosis: How Derivatives Changed the "Business of Banking"' (2009) 63 *University of Miami Law Review* 1041.

[97] J Taylor, *Getting Off Track: How Government Actions Caused, Prolonged and Worsened the Financial Crisis* (Stanford CA, Hoover Institution Press, 2009).

[98] LJ Kotlikoff, *Jimmy Stewart is Dead* (Hoboken NJ, Wiley, 2011) chs 1–4.

[99] A Sen above n8, x. The quotation is from GJ Stigler, 'Smith's Travel on the Ship of State' in AS Skinner and T Wilson (eds), *Essays on Adam Smith* (Oxford, Clarendon Press, 1975) 237.

[100] Sen above n12, 187.

[101] A Sen, 'Adam Smith's Prudence' in S Lall and F Stewart (eds), *Theory and Reality in Development* (Basingstoke, Macmillan, 1986) and A Sen, *On Ethics and Economics* (Oxford, Basil Blackwell, 1986) 22–28.

involve assumptions of individual rational utility maximisation which cannot possibly empirically obtain, it is a criticism which does point to a major shortcoming of mainstream economics as a guide to policy formulation. But the way that Sen conceives of this criticism is wrong, both in itself and as an interpretation of Smith. Smith would have disapproved of the actions and motivations of the 'projectors' of 'Wall Street', but Sen misunderstands why Smith would have disapproved. Sen has a negative view of self-interest and his regulatory policy recommendation is to minimise the role it plays, and with it the role markets play, in economic action, and to do this he misleadingly minimises the role of self-interest in Smith.

For Sen, the crash is evidence of a radical inadequacy in 'capitalism':

> What exactly is capitalism? The standard definition seems to take reliance on markets for economic transactions as a necessary qualification for an economy to be seen as capitalist. In a similar way, dependence on the profit motive, and on individual entitlements based on private ownership, are seen as archetypical features of capitalism.[102]

Sen maintains that the 'usefulness' of this idea of capitalism 'may well be fairly exhausted' because, as a cursory examination of the general economies of '[a]ll affluent countries in the world' readily shows, such affluence has:

> for quite some time now, depended partly on transactions and other payments that occur largely outside markets [such as] unemployment benefits, public pensions, other features of social security, and the provision of health care, and a variety of other services distributed through non-market arrangements. The economic entitlements connected with such services are not based on private ownership and property rights. . .the market economy has depended for its own working not only on maximising profits but also on many other activities, such as maintaining public security and supplying public services. The creditable performance of the so-called capitalist system. . .drew on a combination of institutions–publicly funded education, medical care, and mass transportation are just a few of many–that went much beyond relying only on a profit-maximising economy and on personal entitlements confined to private ownership.[103]

At one level, this obviously is true, as is Sen's claim that Smith did not argue 'against the importance of economic institutions other than markets'.[104] Sen is right to say[105] that Smith had a strong perception of some of what would now be called the social costs of capitalism,[106] for criticism of certain brutalising effects of the division of labour on the working class was central to the Scottish Enlightenment understanding of commercial society. Sen rather misses a trick by not pointing to Smith's clear anticipation of what would now be called the market failure argument for the provision of public goods.[107] Nevertheless, Sen also is right that, overall Smith did see one of the two tasks of political economy as supplying 'the state or commonwealth with a revenue sufficient for the public services',[108] of which Sen gives as examples 'free education and poverty relief'. Smith's views of the legitimate range of public services was, of course, much narrower than Sen's, but Smith did envisage a 'market-including' general economy in which 'interventions aimed at doing those important things that the market may leave undone' could be made,[109] and Sen is right that

---

[102] Sen above n9.
[103] Sen above n10.
[104] Sen above n8, xiii.
[105] ibid xiii–xiv.
[106] Eg, Smith above n88, 781-82.
[107] ibid 723.
[108] ibid 428, quoted in Sen above n8, xiii.
[109] ibid.

any 'attempt to see Smith as an advocate of pure capitalism, with complete reliance on the market mechanism guided by pure profit motive, is altogether misconceived'.[110]

Of course, one immediately asks what this has to do with the financial markets. Does Sen conceive of extending the amount of regulation of financial markets in such a way as to ensure that they are run as public services rather than private markets? As a matter of fact, Sen actually *is* arguing for further extension of the range and extent of public provision based on 'an understanding of how a variety of organisations–from the market to the institutions of the state–can together contribute towards a more decent economic world'.[111] Sen subscribes to what is something of a current vogue for Pigou's case for intervention on what is rightly believed to be a far wider range of grounds than Keynes,[112] who was dismissive of Pigou's belief that there were many cases of what we would now call externalities.[113] We do believe that Sen would be prepared in principle to subordinate any market to some form of government intervention based on second-guessing market outcomes on all the occasions this is felt necessary. This is the general principle of welfare economics, and Sen is a particularly consistent adherent of that principle.

Sen seems to be possessed of a degree of confidence in the operation of public, rather than private, institutions that betrays a lack of familiarity with the development of a concept of government failure to complement the concept of market failure that has been at the centre of regulatory theory since 'The Problem of Social Cost' was published.[114] Sen's views anachronistically evidence the mere assumption that public institutions will work well that Anthony Downs showed to be central to policy formulation in the period prior to Coase's paper.[115] Always naive, this assumption can be offensive, as current scandals in the public provision of medical services in the UK, which that assumption seems to place beyond criticism and accountability,[116] manifestly demonstrate. But all this can be put to one side here, for, as it happens, Sen advances no concrete proposals to do away with private financial markets, and it seems that he would leave those markets within the reduced market sphere he envisages. We do not pretend to think Sen's views coherent here. What is the right proportion of self-interest and other-regarding values? How does one describe the admixture? The point cannot fruitfully be pursued as Sen appears to have nothing

---

[110] ibid.

[111] Sen above n9.

[112] Sen above n10.

[113] Though Pigou is not mentioned by name at this point of *The General Theory*, in one of the final chapter's 'Concluding Notes' Keynes maintained that his own views were 'moderately conservative' because he sought to alter the volume but not, save as was necessary to alter volume, the direction of private investment. There was 'no reason to assume that the existing system seriously misemploys the factors of production which are in use', and an attempt to alter the direction of investment would threaten the 'efficiency and freedom' of 'the classical system': JM Keynes,*The General Theory of Employment, Interest and Money* (London, Macmillan, 1973) 377, 379. A correction of such misemployment is, of course, Pigou's entire case for 'social' intervention.

[114] RH Coase, 'The Problem of Social Cost' (1960) 3 *Journal of Law and Economics* 1.

[115] A Downs, *An Economic Theory of Democracy* (Boston MA, Addison Wesley, 1957) ch 15.

[116] *Report of the Mid Staffordshire NHS Foundation Trust Public Inquiry* HC 898 (2012–13): www. midstaffspublicinquiry.com/report. No person has been held responsible for the Mid Staffordshire Trust killing over a thousand patients in its care by unspeakably cruel neglect, and Sir David Nicholson, Chief Executive of the relevant supervisory(!) Strategic Health Authority at the time, has since been promoted to become Chief Executive of the entire health service for England, and will retain this position after the latest major rearrangement of the deckchairs, which currently is in progress: B Cash, 'Sir David Nicholson Must Resign Over the NHS Scandal' (14 March 2013) *Daily Telegraph*.

to say on what should, in any concrete sense, be done about the regulation of financial markets.

But this absence of concrete proposals is significant, for what Sen is driving at is, indeed, a change of culture making concrete regulation in an important sense otiose, and it is to this that he attempts to marshal Smith. He, of course, has much work to do. Sen has called *The Wealth of Nations* 'the greatest book ever written about economic life'.[117] This may be so, but it is a point not worth disputing that it is even more clearly the case that it is the greatest paean to self-interest written in modern times. Smith had an extremely positive view of self-interest, which he perceived as an intrinsically moral motivation of action, and his conception of the 'system of natural liberty',[118] the understanding of market organisation on which all subsequent general economics and sociology of any value rests, turns on this moral conception.

Nevertheless, Sen's argument is far from groundless, and he is right that Smith 'extensively investigated the strong need for actions based on values that go well beyond profit-seeking'[119] and that Smith 'discussed how the functioning of the economic systems in general and of the markets in particular can be helped enormously by other motives'.[120] In his more recent work of which *The Idea of Justice* is the centrepiece, Sen has given an account of Smith's analysis of the motivations of human action which emphasises motivations other than self-interest. Sen rightly says that to regard Smith's view of human nature as based entirely on the pursuit of self-interest is quite wrong, and attributes the narrowing of mainstream economics of which we have seen him complain to such a belief. Sen rightly points to the much more comprehensive analysis of the motivations of human action in *The Theory of Moral Sentiments* as counter-evidence to the view that Smith was concerned exclusively with self-interest. In his *Introduction* he says the same things and quotes the famous lines at the beginning of *The Theory of Moral Sentiments*:

> 'How selfish so ever man may be supposed, there are evidently some principles in his nature, which interest him in the fortune of others, and render their happiness necessary to him, though he derives nothing from it except the pleasure of seeing it'.[121]

The narrowing of mainstream economics involves a narrow interpretation of Smith: 'While some men are born small and some achieve smallness, it is clear enough that Smith has had much smallness thrust upon him'.[122]

But all this is very familiar to those with more than a superficial knowledge of Smith. Sen is essentially recapping the exposure of the 'Adam Smith problem',[123] an episode in the history of the interpretation of Smith which may be traced to what has been regarded as HT Buckle's postulating, in 1861, of a strong disjunction between a focus on sympathy in *The Theory of Moral Sentiments* and a focus on self-interest in *The Wealth of Nations*,[124] as a

---

[117] Rothschild and Sen, above n83, 365.
[118] Smith, above n88, 687.
[119] Sen, above n10.
[120] Sen, above n8, xi.
[121] Smith, above n8, 9.
[122] Sen, above n12, 186; Sen, above n8, xi.
[123] ibid viii–ix.
[124] HT Buckle, *History of Civilisation in England*, vol 2 (London, Parker, Son and Bourn, 1861) 449. We believe Buckle's overall account, ibid 432–57, to be much more subtle than it is generally taken to be. Our interpretation of Smith is heavily indebted to A Oncken, 'The Consistency of Adam Smith' (1897) 7 *Economic Journal* 443, in which it is argued, ibid 444, that Buckle 'emphatically upheld the homogeneity of Smith's two works'.

false problem. Self-interest took its place in Smith's general account of the various motivations of human action, which include benevolence, and surely there is no longer any need to argue that there is no change of fundamental position between Smith's two great books, though, of course, the exact understanding of their true relationship remains of great interest.[125] When Sen tells us that '[t]he role of self-love in explaining particular economic phenomena does nothing to reduce the relevance of different motivations in the understanding of economic regularities',[126] this is such a commonplace in the interpretation of Smith that one is at first put at a loss to see what he means. What, really rather amazingly, it seems to mean, is that Sen actually does not appreciate the proper solution of the Adam Smith problem. He does see self-interest as an amoral motivation of action to be distinguished from the moral, other-regarding motivations. The actually live problem, especially in connection with our concerns here, is to understand self-interest within Smith's undoubtedly larger conception of the range of human motivations based on sympathy.

V   SMITH'S CONCEPTS OF SELF-INTEREST AND MARKET EXCHANGE

In the way he addresses this much more subtle issue, Sen provides a very clear illustration of the distance between welfare economics and market economics, or, at a more general level, between the typical criticism of markets and the nature of their actual operation. For although Sen has made what unarguably is one of the most theoretically provocative contributions to welfare economics, a contribution analytically based, as is all welfare economics, on claiming that intervention can produce a superior welfare outcome than the market, there is, extremely reluctant as we are to put it this way, little evidence that he has any real sympathy with the way the market works.

Though there are numerous brief statements about the great value of market freedom to be found in Sen's writings,[127] we are unaware of any substantial engagement with how the market constituted of exchanges legally institutionalised in contract actually works to produce that freedom.[128] It is necessary to say something about some important aspects of this.[129]

---

[125] It is our opinion that the most valuable modern account, though it is itself now approaching its centenary, of the relationship of *The Theory of Moral Sentiments* and *The Wealth of Nations*, and in particular of the role of self-interest in all of Smith's thought, remains that of Jacob Viner: 'Adam Smith and *Laissez Faire*' (1927) 35 *Journal of Political Economy* 198. Sen's interpretation of Smith is heavily indebted to the work of the distinguished economic historian Emma Rothschild, whose work on Smith has from the outset been very concerned to stress the positive role of sympathy and public expenditure in his thought: E Rothschild, 'Adam Smith and Conservative Economics' (1992) 45 *Economic History Review* 74. It is highly regrettable that Rothschild nowhere properly engages with Viner, not even in her full length account of Smith: E Rothschild, *Economic Sentiments* (Cambridge MA, Harvard University Press, 2001). Her references to Viner convey an unbalanced impression of his views by always marshalling them in support of her own stress on the 'social' side of Smith's views: eg Rothschild and Sen (n 83) 363.

[126] Sen, above n8, ix.

[127] eg Sen, above n11, 6,112. The entire section of *Development and Freedom* headed 'Markets and Freedoms', ibid 25–31, is vacuous.

[128] His most sustained effort in this regard of which we are aware is A Sen, 'The Concept of Efficiency', in M Parkin and AR Nobay (eds), *Contemporary Issues in Economics* (Manchester, Manchester University Press, 1975) 196. But even this paper treats questions of optimisation as neoclassical allocation problems and shows no real appreciation of the value of private, voluntary choice which no planning authority can in principle reproduce.

[129] PH Wicksteed, *The Commonsense of Political Economy*, rev edn (London, Routledge and Kegan Paul, 1933) ch 5.

Ideal-typically, market exchange is a system of mutual advantage. In order for a seller to persuade a buyer to buy, the seller must be able to convince the buyer that she will increase her well-being by exchanging her goods at a ratio which the seller also believes will increase her well-being. This is simultaneously an intrinsically private and an intrinsically social process. What properties of the seller's goods are relevant to the buyer's choice to buy and what the buyer will do with those goods are private matters for the buyer.[130] The seller might attempt to persuade the buyer to choose differently, but the autonomy of the buyer entirely rests on the privacy of her choice, which the seller must socially recognise by confining herself to persuasion as the means of obtaining the buyer's consent to the exchange. A fortiori, the state must normally enforce the voluntary contractual agreement that legally expresses that exchange, not second-guess it, and the core value of the law of contract, expressed in all its principal doctrines, is neutrality about the intentions of the contracting parties.

Much criticism of the market economy turns on a criticism of the selfishness of market actors. Sen's variant, the criticism of the fetishisation of opulence, is a criticism of selfishness as a degrading narrowness of focus. But selfishness does not really capture the essential property of market action, which is autonomy. A market actor may buy goods to increase her well-being by, say, gratifying a desire to smoke, or to read Homer, or to feed her family, or to equip a foundlings' hospital. Why the actor wants to buy the goods is irrelevant to the process of exchange. What is essential is her autonomous choice to do so. When one says a market actor is selfish, all one is really saying if one is speaking of what is analytically essential to market action is that the actor makes up her own mind about the choice she will make. Of course, that may be a selfish choice in the commonly understood, pejorative way; or it may not.

If one identifies freedom with an absence of constraint, then the market is not a system of freedom. But given the existential condition of scarcity, no economic order is a system of freedom in this sense. Freedom viewed in this way is bliss, and this is not vouchsafed to human beings. Once one acknowledges this, not only is criticism of the market for transmitting information about scarcity absurd,[131] but the ideal typical market may properly be regarded as a system of perfect freedom, for in contractual exchange economic actors must mutually recognise the autonomy of each, and therefore of all, to make their choices within the ineluctable constraint of scarcity. The satisfaction of the economic actor is mediated by the voluntary alienation of private property in material resources, but it is this very mediation which posits the existential relationship with nature in such a way as to allow private choice which produces a social order. Market exchange is a social system which allows economic order to be the product of voluntary choice. No other form of economic order humanity has devised reproduces the autonomy of economic actors in this way. This is the basic claim to legitimacy of the market economy.

All this may be found in what Sen rightly says is the 'most famous and widely quoted passage from *The Wealth of Nations*',[132] which we will quote again:

---

[130] We cannot go into the issue here as it would take us further into the problem of identifying a 'commodity' in the theory of general competitive equilibrium than would be of interest to the readership of this book, but the entire capabilities approach may be said to rest on a use of the concept of commodity characteristics diametrically opposed to the sense in which it is used in that theory: Sen, above n84, 6.

[131] D Campbell, 'The Critique of Bourgeois Justice After the Failure of Marxism' in A Kerner et al (eds), *Current Legal Issues in the Czech Republic and the United Kingdom* (Prague, Charles University Press, 2003) 9; D Campbell, 'How Sensible is the Left-Wing Criticism of Money, Exchange and Contract' (2011) 20 *Social and Legal Studies* 528.

[132] Sen, above n12, 186.

> It is not from the benevolence of the butcher, the brewer, or the baker that we expect our dinner, but from their regard to their own interest. We address ourselves, not to their humanity but to their self-love [and never talk to them of our own necessities but of their advantages].[133]

It is surely highly significant that when Sen quotes this passage, he ends it, in the middle of a sentence, at 'self-love', for the remaining clause of that sentence, which we have placed in square brackets in the quotation, makes it clear that Smith's market self-interest is intrinsically directed at the satisfaction of others as the means of satisfying oneself. It may be as well also to bring to the reader's attention the lines which precede those quoted by Sen:

> man has almost constant occasion for the help of his brethren, and it is in vain for him to expect it from their benevolence only.[134] He will be more likely to prevail if he can interest their self-love in his favour, and shew them that it is to their advantage to do for him what he requires of them. Whoever offers to another a bargain of any kind proposes to do this. Give me that which I want, and you shall have this that you want, is the meaning of every such offer.[135]

The treatment of self-interest in *The Theory of Moral Sentiments* is based on, first, an approval of it as a legitimate, indeed divinely ordained, motivation of action; and, secondly, an account of it which does not remotely approximate to a sanctioning of license but a framing of it within the discipline of 'self-command.'[136] One important aspect of self-command is the refinement it allows of the pursuit of self-interest, which Smith commonly calls prudence, to which we shall shortly return. But the genius of Smith's Scottish Enlightenment conception of self-command is that it intimately involves recognition of the legitimate interests of others, particularly recognition of their property. It is, to use Hegel's expression on which it is impossible to improve, a system of 'mutual recognition'.[137] Sen makes some accurate observations about Smith's analysis of judgment that are relevant to the understanding of self-command,[138] but, because he does not appreciate the intrinsic morality of self-interest, he simply cannot see that the limit of legitimate self-interest in market relationships is that it recognises the autonomy of other economic actors. Smith perceived the simultaneous privacy and sociality of exchange, and his account of self-interest is in these terms. It is an account of the motivation that allows the ideal typical market exchange to take place. One who is legitimately self-interested must:

> humble the arrogance of his self-love, and bring it down to something which other men can go along with. They will indulge it so far as to allow him to be more anxious about, and to pursue with more earnest assiduity, his own happiness rather than that of any other person. . . . In the race for wealth, and honours, and preferments, he may run as hard as he can, and strain every nerve and muscle, in order to outstrip all his competitors. But if he should justle, or throw down any of them, the indulgence of the spectators is entirely at an end. It is a violation of fair play,

---

[133]   Smith, above n88, 26-27.

[134]   This is not entirely a statement about the inefficacy of depending upon charity. Self-worth normally requires one to avoid such dependence: 'Nobody but a beggar chuses to depend chiefly upon the benevolence of his fellow citizens': ibid 27.

[135]   ibid 26.

[136]   Smith, above n 8, 189.

[137]   GWF Hegel, *Phenomenology of Spirit* (Oxford, Oxford University Press, 1977) 111–19. Marx describes exchange in this way in K Marx, *Capital*, vol 1, in K Marx and F Engels, *Collected Works*, vol 35 (London, Lawrence and Wishart, 1996) 95. See further n 144.

[138]   Sen, above n8, xvii-xxi.

which they cannot admit of . . . they do not enter into that self-love by which he prefers himself so much to this other.[139]

Sen quotes a very famous passage in *The Theory of Moral Sentiments* which distinguishes 'prudence', ie, a competent regard for one's self-interest, as 'of all the virtues that which is most helpful to the individual', from 'humanity, justice, generosity, and public spirit', which 'are the qualities most useful to others'.[140] Now, that economic goods by no means exhaust the range of goods that a legitimate modern society will provide for its citizens, and that the public and charitable provision of goods cannot be motivated by self-interest in the same way that economic exchange is, does demonstrate that a range of principles of allocation, and a range of corollary motivations of action, is necessary to such a society. But Sen takes this to indicate a gap between immoral or amoral self-interest, prudence being merely a matter of, as it were, technical competence, and the morality of the other-regarding virtues. This is quite wrong. Legitimate self-interest and the other-regarding virtues are both moral, albeit in a different way. It is, of course, undeniable that unrestrained self-interest played a major part in causing the crash, but that unrestrained self-interest likely will and did lead to a grave diminution of welfare does not mean one should abandon legitimate self-interest. Should one abandon the public virtues because, as has been the principal lesson of the history of the twentieth century,[141] when these virtues are unrestrained, they lead to authoritarianism or even totalitarianism? The point is that all welfare-enhancing action involves what Durkheim called constraint,[142] the public institutionalisation of which is regulation.

The issue in regulating for welfare enhancing market economic action is not the replacement of self-interest with other motivations of action but the constitution of self-interest in a legitimate form, and this is the core of Smith's thought. As the reader no doubt will be aware, Smith ultimately rested his commitment to markets on the existence of 'a certain propensity in human nature. . .to truck, barter, and exchange',[143] and much of our difficulty in the sociological understanding of rational economic action must still be traced to the way Smith's perception of the necessity of a public legal framework for such action is undermined by the limits of his understanding of the historical specificity of the orientation towards rational economic action which was criticised by Marx.[144] But this does not alter the fact that Smith's view is that self-interest has a legitimate place among human motivations, and that, if there certainly is a space for other motivations, then those motivations must leave a space for self-interest, and this space is by far the most important space

---

[139] Smith, above n8, 83.

[140] ibid 189, 190; quoted in Sen, above n8, xi.

[141] A MacIntyre, *After Virtue*, 2nd edn (London, Duckworth, 1985).

[142] E Durkheim, *The Rules of Sociological Method* (Basingstoke, Macmillan, 1982) 50–54. Skinner has used 'constraint' in its normal sense to describe this aspect of Smith: AS Skinner, in 'Moral Philosophy and Civil Society: Ethics and Self-love' in AS Skinner, *A System of Social Science*, 2nd edn (Oxford, Clarendon Press, 1996) 65–69.

[143] Smith (n 88) 25.

[144] We have argued that Smith's conception of exchange is a form of Hegelian mutual recognition. But the form of ethical life based on a system of needs or wants that Hegel called 'civil society', which is a conception of capitalism based on the views of, inter alia, Smith, was, in Hegel's view, inadequate because it lacked social self-consciousness: GWF Hegel, *Elements of the Philosophy of Right* (Cambridge, Cambridge University Press, 1991) 227–39. **It is this lack of self-consciousness that Marx addressed in his critique of the alienation of labour under capitalism: Marx, above 137, 81–94.**

for the allocation of economic goods: 'it is by...purchase that we obtain from one another those mutual good offices we stand in need of'.[145]

It will be recalled that Sen's account of Smith's criticism of projectors represented it as an argument that, in 'an unregulated market economy', their unbridled self-interest would, quoting Smith, lead to 'a dire predicament' in which 'a great part of the capital of the country' is placed in the hands of those who 'were most likely to waste and destroy it', and that the response to this is to place greater reliance on institutions other than the market and on motivations of action other than self-interest. But the warning about waste of capital which Sen quotes is taken from a passage in *The Wealth of Nations* that could not be less suitable for Sen's purposes. This passage is concerned with setting rates of interest so as to discourage speculation, and in particular with setting the legal rate of interest, by which Smith means a maximum rate set by the government in order to prevent usury. In the UK, it is no longer sought to regulate even consumer, not to speak of commercial, credit in this way, though such legal rates are set in, for example, numerous US states.[146] But the principle behind what Smith is saying is that, when the government considers what legal rate it should set, it should bear in mind that it is when rates of interest are too high that capital is thrown into hands which are most likely to waste and destroy it, because only prodigals and projectors, not '[s]ober people',[147] will borrow at those rates. When this is understood, then it is clear that nothing could show less respect to Smith's basic idea than the expansionary monetary and fiscal policies the UK and the US followed that played an enormous part in causing the crash; indeed, the results of these policies are a textbook illustration of Smith's point. But, of course, this is a criticism, not of the 'unregulated market', but of government policy.

The most substantial thing Smith ever wrote on projectors of which we are aware is not to be found in *The Wealth of Nations* nor in *The Theory of Moral Sentiments* but in a paper, probably ultimately from what are now known as Smith's *Lectures on Rhetoric and Belles Lettres* of 1748–50,[148] the original of which has not survived but of which we have a brief report. The problem which Smith actually finds with projectors, a generalisation of the remarks above, is that they:

> disturb nature in the course of her operations on human affairs, and it requires no more than to leave her alone and give her fair play in the pursuit of her own ends that she may establish her own designs.... Little else is required to carry a state to the highest degree of affluence from the lowest barbarism but peace, easy taxes and a tolerable administration of justice; all the rest being brought about by the natural course of things.[149]

Now, proper understanding of what Smith means here by nature does depend on seeing that he had in mind, as Pigou put it, 'the actual world as he knew it, with an organised system of civilised government and contract law',[150] a system which fosters the human motivations

---

[145] Smith, above n88, 27.

[146] Sen, above n8, xii, notes that Smith was criticised by Bentham for arguing that the government should set rates of interest in this way as it contradicted freedom of contract: J Bentham, *Defence of Usury* in J Bentham, *Works* (Edinburgh, William Tait, 1843) letter 13.

[147] Smith, above n88, 357.

[148] A Smith, *Lectures on Rhetoric and Belles Lettres* (Oxford, Clarendon Press, 1983).

[149] D Stewart, 'Account of the Life and Writings of Adam Smith LLD' in A Smith, *Essays on Philosophical Subjects* (Oxford, Clarendon Press, 1980) 322.

[150] AC Pigou, *Economics of Welfare*, 5th edn (New Brunswick NJ, Transaction Books, 2002) 128.

appropriate to market exchange. But that Sen takes the criticism of projectors to be some sanction for in principle unlimited intervention when the very criticism of projectors on which Sen bases his argument is actually entirely dependent on Smith's own conception of laissez faire shows how incapable Sen's welfare economics are of understanding liberal market freedoms based on legitimate self-interest.

The lesson of the current crisis is not that the other-regarding virtues need to be taken onboard to ground greater regulation of financial markets. We do not want trading to be informed by 'humanity, justice, generosity, and public spirit'. We want trading to be informed by self-interest. It cannot be rational economic action otherwise. The point is that the current crisis was not caused by what Smith would regard as self-interest. It was caused by the debased, unrestrained form of self-interest which on occasion he did call selfishness and was prepared to associate with rapacity, [151] the precise defect of which, in respect of market action, is that it does not respect the autonomy of the other party to an exchange.

VI   CONCLUSION

The turn in the theory of financial regulation towards a critique of the culture of the financial services industry is, at one level, welcome. At the time of the 2007 crash, that culture was, in truth, in substantial part disgusting, and it is manifest that, even after that crash, the financial services industry remains incapable of self-regulation. But to direct regulatory effort at a change of culture has at least three debilitating shortcomings. First, it leaves the nature of the regulatory effort to be mounted extremely vague. What concrete steps can a regulator take to change a firm's or a business sector's culture? Such a change can be produced only by, as it were, indirect measures. This leads to the second shortcoming, for it is not as if attempts to indirectly produce a change of culture have not been made; it is that they did not work. The recognition of the inevitable failure of detailed, rules-based regulation has led to an attempt to base regulation on a mixture of rules and principles, the form of the latter representing, in the examples we have examined, an attempt to place responsibility on the financial services industry to ensure that trade in financial services was welfare-optimising.

And it is here that we would seek to identify the third and most important regulatory shortcoming that led to the crash. The culture that is being criticised undoubtedly is a culture of self-interest, but the principal rationalisation of the resistance of those criticised to the regulation intended to improve their culture is that they believe self-interest is legitimate because it is market action. All the arguments for market organisation are taken to support resistance of the regulation. In the end, the strength of this rationalisation is that it is based on a fundamental truth. If regulation required the relinquishment of market action, then the regulatory solution would be worse than the problem caused by those to be regulated. But it isn't, because the self-interest of those who caused the crash was, not merely not market self-interest, but very substantially its opposite.

Policy prescriptions that require those in the financial services sector to pursue other-regarding virtues at the expense of enlightened self-interest are misconceived, and even the

---

[151] Smith, above n8, 184.

more co-operative amongst the regulated community will rightly resist them. Regulation of the financial services sector that proceeds on the basis that self-interest should be curbed and public regarding values promoted must fail regardless of whether it is principles- or rules-based. We believe that a regulatory framework predicated on the legitimacy of market self-interest is essential, once one recognises that a dimension which we might borrow the term other-regarding to describe is analytically essential to market action, the legitimacy of which inheres in its being a system of self-interest and of mutual recognition.

CHAPTER 5

Sanctions, Incentives and Better Behaved Banks

Bob Ferguson[1]

I   INTRODUCTION

For several global banks headquartered in the UK and Switzerland, 2012 was a year of public torment, mainly at the hands of American prosecutors and regulators, but also of their domestic supervisors. Condemnation poured down on Barclays when it became the first to settle its account for involvement in Libor manipulation.[2] HSBC was lashed by the US Senate Permanent Subcommittee on Investigations, and later entered into a deferred prosecution agreement with the US Department of Justice, in which it admitted wilful failure to maintain anti-money-laundering controls and contraventions of sanctions laws.[3] Standard Chartered's share price briefly fell 22 per cent when it was accused of sanctions contraventions by the New York State Department of Financial Services, and was summoned to show cause why its banking licence should not be revoked; it settled first with the Department of Financial Services and subsequently with a group of federal prosecutors and regulators.[4] And for its bankers' heavy involvement in Libor manipulation, UBS settled simultaneously in the US, UK and Switzerland at a total cost of CHF 1.4 billion.[5]

---

[1] The views expressed here are my own and are not to be attributed to the FCA. Much of the research for this chapter was undertaken while a Visiting Professor at the Centre for Law, Markets and Regulation (CLMR) University of New South Wales, October–December 2012. I am grateful to the CLMR for that opportunity.

[2] US Department of Justice [DoJ], *Barclays Bank PLC* (26 June 2012); Financial Services Authority [FSA], Final Notice, *Barclays Bank Plc* (27 June 2012); House of Commons Treasury Committee, *Fixing LIBOR: Some Preliminary Findings,* HC 481-1 (18 August 2012).

[3] Senate Permanent Sub-Committee on Investigations, *US Vulnerabilities to Money Laundering, Drugs and Terrorist Financing: HSBC Case History,* (Washington DC, US Congress, 2012); *USA v HSBC Bank USA, N.A. and HSBC Holdings PLC,* Deferred Prosecution Agreement (US District Court, Eastern District of New York, 11 December 2012).

[4] '*Standard Chartered v New York*', *The Economist* (18 August 2012), available at www.economist.com/node/21560583; New York State Department of Financial Services [DFS], *Standard Chartered Bank, New York Branch,* Order Pursuant to Banking Law § 39(6 August 2012), available at www.dfs.ny.gov/banking/ea120806.pdf; DFS, *Standard Chartered Bank, New York Branch,* Consent Order under New York Banking Law § 44 (21 September 2012); DoJ, 'Standard Chartered Bank Agrees to Forfeit $227 Million for Illegal Transactions with Iran, Sudan, Libya, and Burma' (10 December 2012), available at www.justice.gov/opa/pr/2012/December/12-crm-1467.html.

[5] UBS, 'UBS Board of Directors Authorizes Settlements of LIBOR-Related Claims with US and UK Authorities; Swiss Regulator to Issue Order' (19 December 2012), available at www.ubs.com/global/en/about_ubs/media/

These settlements and the accounts of protracted and widespread lawbreaking that emerged with them imparted fresh impetus to critical debate and exasperated polemic about the culture of the banking sector, the business morality and motivations of bankers, and the proportionality and effectiveness of legal and regulatory sanctions in this context. The chairman of the UK Financial Services Authority (FSA) spoke of 'a dealing room culture of cynical greed'.[6] The chief executive-designate of the UK Financial Conduct Authority talked of the culture of viewing financial consumers 'simply as sales targets'.[7] An executive director of the Bank of England spoke of banking having become 'a transactional business, underpinned by a sales-driven, commission-focussed culture'.[8] Politicians and journalists uttered withering denunciations:

> The business model of modern finance–banks trading on their own account in rigged derivatives markets, skimming investment funds and manipulating interbank lending. . . is not the result of a mistake. It represents a series of choices made over 30 years in which finance has progressively resisted any sense it has a duty of custodianship to its clients or wider responsibilities to the economy. It was capitalism allegedly at its purest. We now understand it was capitalism at its most rotten.[9]

While there was near unanimity on the moral wasteland of the banking sector and the need for a new, ethical culture, the penalties exacted from the delinquent banks prompted divergent assessments of their proportionality and impact. One view was that: 'Banks must now manage regulatory risks as rigorously as market exposures. Fines are getting too big to write off as acceptable costs of doing business.'[10] For others, though, the penalties were a 'rap on the knuckles', greeted by 'investor insouciance'.[11] 'Representing less than three weeks' operating income', the UBS settlement was 'no more punitive than the docking of a miscreant footballer's wages–and arguably as effective in deterring amoral behaviour'.[12] Some urged that the managers and executives who preside over such practices should be exposed to loss of bonuses and employment.[13] Others were outraged by the absence, in the case of

---

switzerland/releases/news-display-media-switzerland.html/en/2012/12/19/20121219a.html ; *USA v UBS Securities Japan Co. Ltd.,* Plea Agreement (US District Court, District of Connecticut, 19 December 2012); Financial Services Authority, Final Notice, *UBS AG* (19 December 2012), available at www.fsa.gov.uk/static/pubs/final/ubs.pdf; Swiss Financial Market Supervisory Authority, *FINMA Summary Report UBS LIBOR* (19 December 2012), available at www.finma.ch/d/aktuell/Documents/summary-report-ubs-libor-20121219-e.pdf.

   [6] A Turner, 'Banking at The Cross-Roads: Where Do We Go from Here?' (Speech delivered on 24 July 2012), available at www.fsa.gov.uk/library/communication/speeches/2012/0724-at.shtml.

   [7] M Wheatley, 'The Incentivisation of Sales Staff–Are Consumers Getting a Fair Deal?' (Speech delivered on 5 September 2012), available at www.fsa.gov.uk/library/communication/speeches/2012/0905-mw.shtml.

   [8] AG Haldane, 'A Leaf Being Turned' (Speech delivered to Occupy Economics, 'Socially Useful Banking' London, 29 October 2012), available at www.bis.org/review/r121031f.pdf.

   [9] W Hutton, 'Bank Rate-Fixing Scandals Reveal the Rotten Heart of Capitalism', *The Observer* (23 December 2012), available at www.guardian.co.uk/commentisfree/2012/dec/23/banking-reform-ubs.

   [10] J Guthrie, 'Big Banks Must Find Their Moral Mojos', *Financial Times* (19 December 2012), available at www.ft.com/intl/cms/s/0/f3156d44-49c7-11e2-a7b1-00144feab49a.html#axzz2QE5DUCiL.

   [11] 'HSBC / StanChart–Rap on the Knuckles', *Financial Times* (11 December 2012), available at www.ft.com/intl/cms/s/0/f3156d44-49c7-11e2-a7b1-00144feab49a.html#axzz2QE5DUCiL.

   [12] M Vincent, 'Fines are About More than Deterrence', *Financial Times* (22 December 2012), available at www.ft.com/intl/cms/s/0/f3156d44-49c7-11e2-a7b1-00144feab49a.html#axzz2QE5DUCiL.

   [13] 'Paying the Price for Banks' Mistakes', *Financial Times* (11 December 2012), available at www.ft.com/intl/cms/s/0/7e97873a-43a1-11e2-a48c-00144feabdc0.html; J Guthrie, 'Bank Fines Fail to Reflect Wrong-Doing', *Financial Times* (13 December 2012), available at www.ft.com/intl/cms/s/0/1f84ec64-451e-11e2-838f-00144feabdc0.html.

HSBC, of criminal prosecution and by indications from the US prosecutors that they had taken prudential and systemic considerations into account. On this view, the HSBC settlement formalises a double standard in the American criminal justice system:

> if you're not an important cog in the global financial system, you can't get away with anything, not even simple possession [of drugs]. You will be jailed and whatever cash they find on you they'll seize on the spot.... . On the other hand, if you are an important person, and you work for a big international bank, you won't be prosecuted even if you launder nine billion dollars.[14]

Against that background, the central purpose of this paper is to highlight and explore the key role of sanctions and incentives as a means of bringing about behavioural and cultural change in the banking sector. The next section focuses on the dimensions of the problem. The one after examines its interplay with the financial crisis. We then turn to the motivational potential of sanctions, both regulatory and criminal, upon financial institutions and individuals employed in them, and after that to the motivational potential of remuneration structures.

II   THE DIMENSIONS OF THE PROBLEM

Dysfunctional behaviour by and in banks is not a one-dimensional problem. Three analytically and historically distinct strands can be discerned. Each bears its own relationship to the global financial crisis, and each interplays with sanctions and incentives in somewhat different ways, as we shall see. Nevertheless, it is right to view the three strands separated out below as facets, in the final analysis, of one and the same phenomenon–the evolution of banking into a business where high risks would be run for high returns, where individual bankers' remuneration hinged to a substantial extent on a narrow, profit-oriented conception of performance, and where the pursuit of corporate profit and personal gain trumped customer welfare and in some areas the law of the land.[15]

(i) Prudential recklessness

It is not contentious that many commercial strategies, judgements and actions in the wholesale and credit markets in the lead-up to the global financial crisis were, at least in retrospect, imprudent and ill-founded. In the US:

> There was a view that instincts for self-preservation inside major financial firms would shield them from fatal risk-taking without the need for a steady regulatory hand, which, the firms argued,

---

[14] M Taibbi, 'Outrageous HSBC Settlement Proves the Drug War is a Joke', *Rolling Stone* (11 December 2012), available at www.rollingstone.com/politics/blogs/taibblog/outrageous-hsbc-settlement-proves-the-drug-war-is-a-joke-20121213; see also G Greenwald, 'HSBC, Too Big to Jail, is the New Poster Child for US Two-Tiered Justice System', *The Guardian* (13 December 2012), available at www.guardian.co.uk/commentisfree/2012/dec/12/hsbc-prosecution-fine-money-laundering.

[15] For an overview of the failings of one bank—Barclays—see A Salz, *Salz Review: An Independent Review of Barclays' Business Practices* (April 2013), available at group.barclays.com/about-barclays/citizenship/salz-review-report.

would stifle innovation. Too many of these institutions acted recklessly, taking on too much risk, with too little capital, and with too much dependence on short-term funding.[16]

This is not a story confined to the US. Haldane's UK-centred summary, for example, is that

> the stewardship of many financial institutions was reckless, fuelled by a cocktail of leverage and a culture which put short-term transactions ahead of long-term relationships. Among especially the bigger banks, there was a quest for size over safety, for quantity over quality.[17]

If a headstrong propensity to run big risks, or to misjudge them, is one side of the coin of recklessness, the other is weakness and laxity in systems and controls over the business. The free and easy approach to mortgage lending in the US became a 'crime-facilitative environment'.[18] Before the crash in Ireland, 'lending guidelines and processes seem to have been quite widely short-circuited'.[19] The Royal Bank of Scotland's ruinous acquisition of ABN AMRO was made on the basis of due diligence that was 'inadequate in scope and depth'.[20]

At its most extreme, weakness and laxity in systems and controls can combine with the deviousness of an individual trader to give rise to major or even catastrophic losses for the bank concerned. Nick Leeson famously brought Barings down in 1995.[21] More recently both Société Générale and UBS have suffered heavy losses at the hands of rogue traders.[22]

It is important to distinguish, though, between recklessness as a term used in a broad, expansive sense and its sharper, narrower meaning in the context of analyses of legal and regulatory liability. In this latter context, judgements and behaviour cannot normally be characterised as reckless unless there was either conscious running of excessive risks, or something amounting to serious or gross negligence (in other words, judgements or behaviour falling substantially short of generally accepted standards of care). As we shall see, this narrower concept of recklessness is a major constraint upon the potential of sanctions as a means of circumscribing prudentially significant risk-taking.

(ii) Abuse of customers

While the market failures underlying prudential recklessness culminated in a sudden and catastrophic tipping point, chronic asymmetries of information and conflicts of interest have long provided fertile ground for mis-selling financial products (for example, through

---

[16] Financial Crisis Inquiry Commission, *Final Report of the National Commission on the Causes of the Financial and Economic Crisis in the United States* (January 2011), xviii.

[17] Haldane, above n 8.

[18] Financial Crisis Inquiry Commission, above n 16 at 160–64, 187.

[19] K Regling and M Watson, *A Preliminary Report on the Sources of Ireland's Banking Crisis* (Dublin, Government Publications, 2010), 35. In January 2013, an English judge sentencing two men for £740 million property frauds committed in the years before the financial crisis against Allied Irish Bank and Bank of Scotland described the banks' lending checks as 'superficial and cursory': 'Judge Criticises Banks at Fraud Trial', *Financial Times* (18 January 2013), available at www.ft.com/cms/s/0/398b9714-60b4-11e2-a353-00144feab49a.html.

[20] Financial Services Authority, *The Failure of the Royal Bank of Scotland* (2011), 39, 55.

[21] And for the responsibilities of some of Barings' senior executives, see *Re Barings plc (No 5)* [1999] 1 BCLC 433.

[22] For Société Générale's control failings, see *Décisions juridictionelles publiées par la Commission bancaire au cours de mois de juillet 2008, No 1, Société Générale*, in *Bulletin officiel. . .de la Commission bancaire* (July 2008). For UBS's control failings, see FSA, above n 5.

unsuitable recommendations or one-sided depictions of prospects relative to risks) and more generally for the sale of 'rip-off' products. The UK in particular has been beset by a number of major retail mis-selling scandals:[23]

- *Pension transfers and opt-outs.* The introduction of personal pension products in the late 1980s gave commission-remunerated sales forces and advisers the opportunity to persuade hundreds of thousands of beneficiaries of generous defined-benefit employer-sponsored pension schemes to switch to less favourable defined-contribution personal schemes with market exposure, and in some cases to forgo employer contributions. In most cases, the sales were effected by means of unsuitable recommendations and defective explanations of risk.[24]
- *Endowment mortgages.* Throughout the 1990s, many mortgage borrowers were persuaded to take out interest-only loans on the footing that repayment would be made from the proceeds of a collateral investment vehicle, the endowment policy. Borrowers were frequently misled about the status of projections of returns and the risks involved.[25]
- *Payment protection insurance.* It became normal practice in the 2000s among banks lending to retail consumers to tie in a 'payment protection' policy as part of the sale of the loan and to add its cost to the repayment schedule. Borrowers were often given to understand that they had no choice, or even left unaware of the tie-in. In some cases the policy was sold even when the circumstances of the borrower ruled out any prospect of a valid claim upon it.[26]

Nor has mis-selling been confined to the retail sector: it has become increasingly clear that the way in which interest rate derivatives were sold to small businesses and municipal authorities not only in the UK but also in Spain, Italy, Australia and the US is highly dubious.[27]

(iii) Non-Observance of Public-Interest Laws

A growing trend of the last decade has been for banks to be found out breaking laws and regulations laid down, not for the purposes of prudential soundness or financial consumer protection, but to serve some separate public policy purpose. In addition to market integrity (in particular, Libor manipulation), the key areas are tax, trade sanction regimes, and anti-money-laundering (AML):

---

[23] For Australia, see Parliamentary Joint Committee on Corporations and Financial Services, *Inquiry into Financial Products and Services in Australia* (Canberra, 2009).

[24] J Black and R Nobles, 'Personal Pensions Misselling: The Causes and Lessons of Regulatory Failure' (1998) *Modern Law Review* 789.

[25] J Gray, 'The Legislative Basis of Systematic Review and Compensation for the Mis-Selling of Retail Financial Services and Products' (2004) 25 *Statute Law Review* 196.

[26] P McConnell and K Blacker, 'Systemic Operational Risk: The UK Payment Protection Insurance Scandal' (2012) 7 *Journal of Operational Risk* 79; E Ferran, 'Regulatory Lessons from the Payment Protection Insurance Mis-selling Scandal in the UK' (2012) 13 *European Business Organization Law Review* 247.

[27] FSA update, 'Interest Rate Hedging Products' (July 2012), available at www.fsa.gov.uk/static/pubs/other/interest-rate-hedging-products.pdf; JD Finnerty and K Pathak, 'A Review of Recent Derivatives Litigation' (2011) 16 *Fordham Journal of Corporation and Financial Law* 73; Allen & Overy, 'Recent Interest Rate Swap Litigation' (17 March 2011), available at www.allenovery.com/publications/en-gb/Pages/Recent-interest-rate-swap-litigation.aspx; *Wingecarribee Shire Council v Lehman Brothers Australia Ltd (in liq)* [2012] FCA 1028.

- *Tax evasion.* In 2009 the Swiss bank UBS entered into a deferred prosecution agreement with the US in which it admitted that UBS private bankers had colluded with US citizens to evade US tax.[28] The UBS case illustrates a more widespread and long-standing private-banking business model. In the words of an expert opinion written for UBS in 2010:

> It would be. . .wrong to see the errors committed by UBS in its cross-border business with US clients as an isolated or unique case. It was certainly more aggressive and less careful than others in the way it went about things. In essence, however, it was all about a business practice that had a tradition established over decades.[29]

Or as another Swiss bank, Wegelin, put it in pleading guilty to conspiracy to defraud the US in January 2013, 'such conduct was common in the Swiss banking industry'.[30]

- *Circumvention of trade sanctions.* Until the US crackdown against it, it was normal business practice, too, for European banks to manipulate wire transfer data in order to circumvent filters designed to pick up wire transfers with a connection to Iran. The Standard Chartered case which caused outrage in the summer of 2012 was in fact just the latest in a series where the delinquent banks entered into deferred prosecution agreements and paid substantial fines.[31]

- *Defective AML arrangements.* Even if HSBC's failings in the US and Mexico were particularly egregious, there is ample reason to believe that AML compliance problems, too, are multi-jurisdictional. The FSA's 2011 thematic examination of UK banks' handling of situations with high money-laundering risk led to the conclusion that:

> Serious weaknesses identified in banks' systems and controls, as well as indications that some banks are willing to enter into very high-risk business relationships without adequate controls when there are potentially large profits to be made, mean that it is likely that some banks are handling the proceeds of corruption or other financial crime.[32]

In 2011 the Swiss federal AML authority identified issues comparable to those described in the FSA report.[33] In Australia, telling doubts have been raised about the quality of Australian banks' AML compliance in relation to customers who are Papua New Guinea 'politically exposed persons'.[34]

---

[28] *United States v UBS AG,* Deferred Prosecution Agreement (US District Court, Southern District of Florida, February 2009).

[29] T Straumann, 'The UBS Crisis in Historical Perspective' (2010), available at www.ubs.com/transparency report, 20.

[30] *United States v Wegelin & Co.,* Plea Agreement, 3 December 2012 [Wegelin signatures dated 3 January 2013], Exhibit A. A number of Swiss banks (or banks with Swiss operations) remain under criminal investigation in the US, Germany and France.

[31] G Dunn, '2012 Year-End Update on Corporate Deferred Prosecution Agreements (DPAs) and Non-Prosecution Agreements' (3 January 2013), available at www.gibsondunn.com/publications/pages/2012YearEnd Update-CorporateDeferredProsecution-NonProsecutionAgreements.aspx.

[32] FSA, *Banks' Management of High Money-Laundering Risk Situations* (2011), [24]. The FSA subsequently fined Coutts, the private-banking subsidiary of the Royal Bank of Scotland, £8.75 million: FSA, Final Notice, *Coutts & Company* (23 March 2012), available at www.fsa.gov.uk/static/pubs/final/coutts-mar12.pdf. Also sanctioned were Habib Bank AG Zurich: Financial Services Authority, Final Notice, *Habib Bank AG Zurich* (15 May 2012), available at www.fsa.gov.uk/static/pubs/final/habib-bank.pdf; and Turkish Bank (UK) Ltd: Financial Services Authority, Final Notice, *Turkish Bank (UK) Ltd* (2 August 2012), available at www.fsa.gov.uk/static/pubs/final/turkish-bank.pdf.

[33] Swiss Financial Market Supervisory Authority, *Due Diligence Obligations of Swiss Banks When Handling Assets of "Politically Exposed Persons"* (Bern, 2011), 7–9.

[34] JSharman, 'SubmissiontotheNationalAnti-CorruptionPlan' availableatwww.ag.gov.au/CrimeAndCorruption/ AntiCorruption/Documents/ProfJasonSharman.pdf. See also Sam Koim, speech to AUSTRAC Major Reporters

Left to their own devices, banks have little material interest in improving the quality of their compliance with public-interest laws which effectively require them to turn business away. In the event of non-compliance, there is no aggrieved customer, and no heightened risk to the balance sheet other than the risk of investigation by law-enforcement or regulatory agencies. This is germane to our discussion below of the potential role of sanctions and remuneration structures as disciplines which may have traction on corporate behaviour.

III   DYSFUNCTIONAL BEHAVIOUR AND THE FINANCIAL CRISIS

The threefold distinction above will help us see that the relationship between behavioural scandals in the banking sector and the global financial crisis is one of both cause and effect.

Category (i)

Everyone can agree that prudentially reckless risk-taking, 'reckless' being understood in a broad sense, was a major factor in the crisis. What is more difficult to assess is the contribution of behaviour *culpable* in a legal or regulatory sense, and not just causative. Drawing mainly on evidence of mortgage fraud and Ponzi schemes, Freeman argues that the US financial system experienced a 'financial crime wave' in the years preceding the financial crisis, and that 'while the epidemic of criminal and near criminal behaviour and chicanery were not the main cause of the 2007–2008 financial implosion and ensuing "great recession" they contributed more to the disaster than economists appreciate'.[35] In part, though, Freeman's argument depends on a (deliberate) conflation of outright criminality with near crime and sharp practice. Moreover, mortgage fraud is a pro-cyclical crime, and its prevalence in the years before the crisis broke should be seen as symptomatic of loose credit conditions more than as significantly causative.

Overall (and perhaps frustratingly), legal and regulatory authorities in the US and UK have generally been able to find little of the kind of material that would found viable actions to attribute criminal or regulatory liability for negligence in connection with the notable bank failures of the crisis.[36] The stumbling block is the pre-crisis prevalence of the beliefs, assumptions, business style, and misconceptions which proved to be so disastrous. In Ireland, whose banks foundered in the property market, there was

> an uncritical enthusiasm for property acquisition that became something of a national blind-spot. It was in this sense at least a wide political and social phenomenon, and some of the underlying misjudgements about debt and property were so embedded in collective psychology that this . . . [may] mitigate institutional failures to some degree.[37]

, Meeting (Sydney, 4 October 2012), available at http://files.pngperspective.com/200000454-b99d7bb91e/Speech%20 by%20Sam%20Koim%20at%20Austrac%20Meeting%20in%20Sydney.pdf.

[35] RB Freeman, 'Financial Crime, Near Crime, and Chicanery in the Wall Street Meltdown' (2010) 32 *Journal of Policy Modeling* 690, 692. See also Financial Crisis Inquiry Commission, *Final Report,* xxii: 'we witnessed an erosion of standards of responsibility and ethics that exacerbated the financial crisis'.

[36] An isolated UK exception is FSA, Final Notice, *Peter Cummings,* 12 September 2012.

[37] Regling and Watson, *Sources of Ireland's Banking Crisis,* 34–35.

The case of Ireland is just one example of the 'self-reinforcing cycle of falling risk aversion and rising irrational exuberance', whose objective precondition was the glut of credit that preceded its implosion.[38] In general, it was not so much a matter of conscious recklessness as of systematic miscalculation or misjudgement of risks, reflecting the illusions and standards of the era. As Haldane puts it: 'the financial crisis was in the main not a story of *individual* fallibility, greed or hubris. . . . The crisis was instead the story of a *system* with built-in incentives for self-harm'.[39]

Against this background, the difficulty of attributing negligence of the kind that is a basis for legal or regulatory liability to any particular individual or institution is obvious: the yardstick by which the recklessness of one is to be judged is the recklessness of countless others. The pervasiveness of the illusions and ill-founded assumptions that fostered the crisis thus critically undermines any suggestion that recklessness *in a legal or regulatory sense* was a major factor in the crisis. The problem was indeed the culture of the sector as a whole.

Categories (ii) and (iii)

Turning to categories (ii) and (iii) above, the financial crisis itself has played some part in prompting, or heightening consciousness of, bad behaviour in banking. The credit squeeze prompted the later phase of misconduct in the Libor scandal—systematic attempts to window-dress perceived creditworthiness. (But this would have been much more difficult if manipulation had not already been culturally acceptable.) Likewise the post-crisis persistence of low interest rates prompted the perception among municipal and small-business customers that they had been mis-sold interest rate derivatives. The laxity (or even complicity) that aids tax evasion, money laundering and sanctions circumvention has nothing to do with the financial crisis: but in the aftermath of the crisis, when public finances are squeezed and austerity is demanded of taxpayers, bearing down on tax evasion has obvious practical and symbolic attractions.

Above all, current popular and political outrage over banks' bad behaviour must be seen as the combined and cumulative effect of all the problematic behaviour noted above. To understand the extent of the furore over Libor manipulation, we must view it in the context of 'consumer experience of exploitative product sales'[40] and the frustration of seeing banks and bankers emerging with virtual impunity from the fiascos of 2008. There is an element of displaced anger in all this.

IV   THE ROLE OF SANCTIONS

This section explores the potential and limitations of sanctions, regulatory and criminal, as a means of shaping banking behaviour. The US deferred prosecution agreement (DPA) does not fit comfortably into this dichotomy: On the one hand it is regulatory in the sense that the matter is settled by means of a financial penalty and a commitment (sometimes

---

[38] Financial Services Authority, *The Turner Review: A Regulatory Response to the Banking Crisis* (London, 2009) 25.
[39] Haldane, above n 8.
[40] Turner, above n 6.

monitored) to operate proper systems and controls in future; on the other, it is an agree-ment with a criminal prosecutor (often the Department of Justice), criminal behaviour is acknowledged, and the threat of prosecution remains should the bank not implement the DPA in full. Here the DPA will be regarded primarily as a regulatory mechanism on the ground that the criminal aspect is the bargaining counter which enables the prosecutor to proceed as a regulator.[41]

Corporations

A useful starting point is the economic deterrence model classically put forward by Gary Becker.[42] That model was of course formulated in the context of criminal sanctions, but it is arguably even more relevant in the context of regulatory sanctions where the costs of the sanction are more straightforwardly economic, and symbolic costs, such as the stigma of conviction, are less important. The economic model posits that the sanction should (a) exceed the profitability of the wrongdoing, and (b) be multiplied by a factor derived from the (im)probability of being both caught *and* selected for enforcement proceedings. This latter step in the calculation is necessary because a purely rational economic actor will discount for the risk of being sanctioned for non-compliance in relation to the size of the penalty. So, for example, if the profitability is $100 million and the chance of being caught and proceeded against is 5 per cent, the penalty should be more than $2 billion. Few financial regulatory authorities operate on this basis, and there is little sign of engagement with step (b), in particular, of the calculation above. The US comes closer than most, as the recent DPA with HSBC illustrates, and the UK comes second; in most other jurisdictions regulatory fines are modest by comparison. The Libor manipulation fines on Barclays and UBS afford indicative jurisdictional comparisons. Barclays paid $160 million in the US, and £59.5 million in the UK.[43] UBS paid $1.2 billion in the US, £160 million in the UK, and disgorged CHF 59 million of estimated profits to FINMA in Switzerland.[44]

There are significant correctives that must be applied to the crude economic deter-rence model but, as we shall see, none that fundamentally derogate from its value.

Ethical tendencies

The model postulates that each bank is nothing more than an amoral calculator of risk and reward. A more realistic model would recognise that within a large bank there are mutually contradictory tendencies at work—on the one hand control (and sometimes leadership) functions which represent the 'conscience' of the bank (and the internalised requirements of the legal and regulatory systems) and, on the other hand, trading, business acquisition and relationship management functions which (on the evidence of recent cases) approxi-mate more closely to the amoral calculator model. To the extent that there are forces for integrity and compliance at work within banks, it is reasonable to suppose that lower levels

---

[41] AS Barkow and RE Barkow (eds) *Prosecutors in the Boardroom* (New York, New York University Press, 2011), Introduction, 2–4.
[42] GS Becker, 'Crime and Punishment: An Economic Approach' (1968) 76 *Journal of Political Economy* 169.
[43] Above, n 2.
[44] Above, n 5.

of potential penalty may be capable of achieving deterrence by tipping the balance between those forces and the 'just do the business' side of the bank. Clearly, this does not solve the cultural question—how to arrive at a culture of integrity which *permeates* the bank and does not merely reside in specialised functions such as compliance—but, at this juncture, we are concerned with deterrence rather than conversion to virtue.

Reputational harm

It might be argued that the real penalty for wrongdoing by banks is the reputational harm they suffer when 'named and shamed' in enforcement proceedings. In this view, the main function of the enforcement outcome is to send a signal to the market, so that the discipline of the market can come into play; there is no need for the regulatory penalty itself to be heavy-handed. We need to appreciate, however, that reputational harm has nuances. Thinking ill of a bank does not necessarily translate into practical harm from that bank's point of view. Retail banking customers, in particular, show little propensity to vote with their feet, however much they might lament the AML performance of their bank, or even its history of mis-selling to its retail customer base.[45] And paradoxically, when an entire business sector has fallen into disrepute, the reputational impact of regulatory penalties on particular institutions may be dissipated, while they reinforce the low opinion in which the whole sector is held.

Reputationally adverse regulatory adjudications can, moreover, be expected to operate differentially depending on the category of dysfunctional behaviour in question. From a self-interested perspective, creditors, counterparties and customers generally are more likely to change their behaviour in response to an enforcement decision indicating that a bank is careless in relation to its own financial standing or predatory in relation to its customers (categories (i) and (ii) above) than one indicating a propensity to engage in socially harmful behaviour (category (iii)).[46] A recent econometric test in relation to UK FSA enforcement decisions (measuring their impact on share prices) displayed results strongly supportive of the proposition that reputational harm is felt differentially:

> [R]eputational sanctions are very real: their stock price impact is on average nine times larger than the financial penalties imposed by the FSA. Still more strikingly, reputational losses are confined to misconduct that directly affects parties who trade with the firm (such as customers and investors). The announcement of a fine for wrongdoing that harms third parties has, if anything, a weakly positive effect on stock price.[47]

If the general proposition is right, it follows that there should be no 'reputational harm' discounting of sanctions for breaking public-interest laws and regulations: 'The practical

---

[45]   Though they may be becoming less inert than they used to be: see eg www.moveyourmoney.org.uk.

[46]   CR Alexander and MA Cohen, 'The Causes of Economic Crime: An Economic Perspective' in Barkow and Barkow (eds), *Prosecutors in the Boardroom* above n 41, 23–24, 26–27.

[47]   J Armour, C Mayer and A Polo, 'Regulatory Sanctions and Reputational Damage in Financial Markets' (2012) Oxford Legal Studies Research Paper No. 62/2010 3, available at ssrn.com/abstract=1678028. The possibility remains open for the effects of reputational harm to be swamped by other factors affecting share price, or dissipated over time. UK banks outperformed the market in 2012, at the height of their reputational troubles: 'In several cases 2012 share prices were seemingly driven by some bizarre inverse correlation with lenders' misdeeds': P Jenkins, 'Bank Shares Buoyed on a Sea Of Scandal', *Financial Times* (8 January 2013), available at www.ft.com/intl/cms/s/0/d4751006-58c7-11e2-99e6-00144feab49a.html.

implication is that for a given harm, sanctions should be higher for firms engaged in misconduct that harms the public in general than for firms engaged in misconduct that harms specific customers, creditors, or others with whom the corporation has ongoing business dealings. . . .'[48]

Redress

The cost imposed by regulatory sanctions—and hence their deterrent power—also needs to be viewed alongside the costs of redress, when the misbehaviour falls into category (ii) above and attracts individual claims before courts or ombudsmen or, more compellingly, class actions or UK-style systematic redress programmes. In principle, the prospect of being compelled to make redress to mistreated customers might be expected to exert some restraining influence on banks' predatory impulses, or at least to operate in conjunction with deterrent penalties so that those penalties could be lower than otherwise necessary. In other words, the prospective costs of making redress, it might be argued, also have deterrent value and should therefore be factored into the mix.

However the very nature of redress (unless it comes with a punitive multiplier such as triple damages) militates against attaching much weight to it in this context. Redress is merely restitutive: by definition it is satisfied by step (a) of the economic deterrence model, and takes no account of step (b). The 'worst that can happen', from the point of view of the bank, is to make good the loss to which the customer has been subjected (admittedly incurring some administration costs in so doing). At most, therefore, the prospect of having to make redress is broadly neutral in terms of deterrence. And of course the worst may not happen.[49]

The absence of long-term deterrent impact from systematic consumer redress programmes mandated by UK financial regulators is a dispiriting illustration of this abstract point. In the mid-1990s, the UK regulators required firms that had recommended unsuitable transfers of pension entitlements, and opt-outs from employer-funded occupational pension schemes, to undertake a proactive, across-the-board review of their sales, and to make redress for all mis-sales. That exercise ultimately cost the bank/life insurance sector about £11.5 billion in redress, and a further £2 billion in administration costs.[50] Notwithstanding the scale of the costs, however, subsequent mis-selling episodes were not averted. From its formation in the late 1990s, the FSA found itself dealing successively with problems relating to the selling of split-level investment trusts,[51] endowment mortgages[52] and, above all, payment protection insurance (PPI) which has necessitated a redress programme which by late 2012 had already cost the banking sector some £8 billion; the cost still to come was a

---

[48] Alexander and Cohen, above n 46 at 24. See also Armour, Mayer and Polo, above n 47 at 29.

[49] A Salz, above n 15, at 6.18: ('Overall, between 2002 and 2012, Barclays' total revenues from. . .[payment protection insurance], net of claims and provisions for alleged mis-selling, amounted to an estimated £940 million'.

[50] Financial Services Authority, '11.8 Billion Compensation for Pensions and FSAVC Reviews' (June 2002), available at www.fsa.gov.uk/library/communication/pr/2002/070.shtml.

[51] AA Adams (ed), *The Split Capital Investment Trust Crisis* (Chichester, John Wiley and Sons, 2004).

[52] Financial Services Authority, 'Endowments: FSA letter to Consumers Association' (2002), available at www.fsa.gov.uk/library/communication/pr/2002/062.shtml.

matter of conjecture.[53] There is no evidence that earlier redress exercises exerted any lasting deterrent influence on the sales behaviour of the banking sector. Indeed the cumulative experience of these episodes led the FSA (soon to be succeeded by the Financial Conduct Authority) to commit its successor to a new focus on early intervention as a means of tipping the balance in favour of preventing consumer detriment as opposed to after-the-event remedial exercises.[54]

Prudential constraints

A different kind of argument is that the punitive thrust of the economic deterrence model needs to be constrained by prudential considerations, especially in relation to systemically significant institutions. In particular, it would be self-defeating to impose a fine of prudentially damaging magnitude upon a bank in order to sanction it for prudentially reckless behaviour. Accepting the validity of this point leaves open the question of where the limit lies, a question that can only be answered by reference to the circumstances of the individual institution. Overall, however, there is no evidence that current levels of fine have approached that limit. As it announced its CHF 1.4 billion fine, UBS could say: 'Despite the . . . payments announced today, UBS remains one of the best capitalized banks in the world'.[55] HSBC's fine of $1.9 billion did not amount to more than one sixth of earnings in the first half of the year.[56] If even US fines have not reached the prudential barrier, fines in the rest of the world must generally fall well short of it.

Nevertheless there may be occasions, especially in the case of category (i) behaviour, when regulators could avoid a self-defeating outcome by combining a prudentially tolerable financial penalty with the imposition of heavier capital requirements through the exercise of supervisory powers. That said, prudential intervention is not satisfactory as a general substitute for enforcement proceedings for misconduct, because it lacks the transparency and demonstration effects of the latter.

Criminal sanctions

Corporations cannot be jailed. In principle, therefore, criminal and regulatory monetary sanctions should be susceptible to broadly the same analysis in terms of their deterrent effect upon financial corporations. However there are also significant differences. The stigma of criminal conviction (or even of criminal indictment) must be seen as a particularly severe form of reputational risk. And criminal conviction may engender automatic consequences, such as loss of banking licence.

The classic example of the potentially 'nuclear' character of criminal prosecution is the demise and dismemberment of Arthur Andersen, triggered by an indictment whose 'collateral

---

[53] Financial Services Authority, 'Monthly PPI Refunds and Compensation' (January 2013), available at www.fsa.gov.uk/consumerinformation/product_news/insurance/payment_protection_insurance_/latest/monthly-ppi-payouts; Bank of England, *Financial Stability Report* (November 2012), available at www.bankofengland.co.uk/publications/Pages/fsr/2012/fsr32.aspx, 20-21; S Coates, 'The Bill for Mis-Selling PPI is Getting Higher . . . and Higher . . . and Higher' [speculating that the total cost might be £25 billion], *The Times* (7 January 2013).

[54] Financial Services Authority, *The Financial Conduct Authority: Approach to Regulation* (London, June 2011), 4.3-4.5, 5.13-5.16.

[55] UBS, above n 5.

[56] 'HSBC/StanChart–Rap on the Knuckles', above n 11.

consequences. . .none of which depended on a conviction, were vastly in excess of the puny fine sought for the violation'.[57] More recently Wegelin (the oldest Swiss private bank) anticipated the consequences of indictment for conspiracy to defraud by selling off its business and effectively becoming a shell.[58] HSBC is said to have escaped indictment partly because of concerns about the manageability of the chain of consequences that might follow.[59] UBS, on the other hand, pled guilty to a single count of felony wire fraud in connection with Libor.[60]

There may well be good reasons for pursuing regulatory rather than criminal sanctions upon banks in many cases even where there is prima facie evidence of criminality—for example, the difficulty in some jurisdictions of imputing to the corporation itself criminal liability for the conduct of junior staff or middle managers. But it is important that the example of Arthur Andersen should not be allowed to found a 'law' to the effect that it is impossible to prosecute a financial institution without bringing it down, and to foster de facto immunity from prosecution. In reality the effect of criminal charges will depend upon a number of factors, including the gravity of the charges, the reputational impact of the underlying misconduct unmediated by the charges, whether ulterior consequences such as loss or restriction of licence depend on a separate regulatory judgement or are in some sense automatic, and the jurisdiction in which the charges are brought. A criminal indictment in the US is more likely to entail dramatic consequences than one brought in most other jurisdictions. On the same day that UBS settled over Libor, it (along with other banks) was convicted in Milan of *truffa* (that is, fraud) in connection with the sale of interest rate derivatives to the municipality of Milan.[61] The world received this news with equanimity, as seemingly did the banks concerned.

To sum up: in this section we have reviewed a number of factors (the presence of good intentions within banks, the costs of redress, the potential for reputational harm and the capacity of the criminal justice system in certain circumstances to aggravate that harm exponentially), all of which might to a greater or lesser extent mitigate the scale of fine otherwise warranted by the deterrence model. Overall, though, none has enough weight to dispel the impression that save in one or two jurisdictions financial penalties (if applied at all) fall materially short of the level needed to optimise deterrence of bad behaviour by banks.

Individuals

It is not surprising that there has been a renewed appetite in recent years for coupling corporate liability with liability for key senior individuals in banks. This has several

---

[57] RA Epstein, 'Deferred Prosecution Agreements on Trial: Lessons from the Law of Unconstitutional Conditions' in Barkow and Barkow, above n 41 at 38, 48. The firm was ultimately acquitted: *Arthur Andersen LLP v United States* 544 US 696 (2005).

[58] K Scannell, 'Wegelin to close after US guilty plea', *Financial Times* (4 January 2013), available at www.ft.com/cms/s/0/fe22179e-55e0-11e2-9aa1-00144feab49a.html.

[59] B Protess and J Silver-Greenberg, 'Bank Said to Avoid Charges Over Laundering', *New York Times* (11 December 2012), available at query.nytimes.com/gst/fullpage.html?res=940DEFDE1F3DF932A25751C1A9649D8B63.

[60] *USA v UBS Securities Japan Co. Ltd.*, above n 5.

[61] So were three other banks—Deutsche Bank, JP Morgan Chase and Depfa Bank: E Martinuzzi, 'Deutsche Bank, UBS Convicted by Milan Judge for Fraud Role', *Bloomberg* (19 December 2012), available at www.bloomberg.com/news/2012-12-19/deutsche-bank-ubs-convicted-by-milan-judge-for-role-in-fraud.html. All four banks are appealing.

sources—concern that fines against institutions may not be able to attain deterrent level without adverse prudential and macroeconomic side effects;[62] the disagreeable spectacle of senior individuals who presided over debacles emerging unscathed in legal terms; and the need to strengthen deterrents against individual irresponsibility and moral hazard. In principle, moreover, individuals might well be easier to deter than corporations: they have smaller pockets, most are susceptible to embarrassment, shame and career jeopardy (perhaps more uncomfortable than 'reputational harm'), and they can be put in jail. And hitherto respectable business people will feel the force of these factors more keenly than professional criminals. By the same token, when a case is indeed brought, these factors often prompt the accused individual to fight the case strenuously, whereas corporations are usu-ally more disposed to reach a settlement. The heavy resource implications of pursuing cases against individuals are therefore a serious constraint.

By and large, though, this appetite for reckonings with senior individuals has gone unsatisfied. On the regulatory side, this reflects the considerable difficulty of successfully formulating and pursuing cases based on allegations of negligent management, as opposed to hands-on fraud or active personal misconduct. Cases against 'doers' are appreciably eas-ier to mount.[63] In the UK at least, the difficulty with negligent management cases does not flow from any lack of applicable rules: negligence in the conduct of business is prohibited as much as behaviour which displays a lack of integrity.[64] Rather the problem is one of evidence and proof—how to demonstrate that a senior manager's leadership, supervision and (non)interventions fell so far short of the standard reasonably to be expected as to amount to a failure of due skill, care and diligence. When the conduct in question was in line with the prevailing wisdom before the global financial crisis, a demonstration of this kind becomes all the more difficult, as the FSA's report on the downfall of the Royal Bank of Scotland showed.[65]

The outcome of the less well known *Pottage* case also illustrates the difficulty of for-mulating and successfully concluding 'leadership' cases even when the illusions of an era are not in play.[66] John Pottage was the chief executive of UBS's UK wealth management division during a time when various compliance problems came to light and it eventually became apparent that there were serious flaws in the operational effectiveness of UBS's risk management arrangements. Initially he dealt with the problems ad hoc as they came to his attention; eventually he set in train a systematic review and overhaul. The FSA's case against him was, in essence, that he should have conducted a more systematic review of the

[62] 'The more capital the state takes from banks, the less they can lend': J Guthrie, above n 13.

[63] For example, the Financial Services Authority has successfully brought over 100 regulatory cases for mortgage fraud: 'FSA Bans Four More Brokers for Mortgage Fraud. . .', (19 April 2011), available at www.fsa. gov.uk/portal/site/fsa/menuitem.10673aa85f4624c78853e132e11c01ca/?vgnextoid=5dabf937a3ef2310VgnVCM 10000013c110acRCRD&vgnextchannel=02db208a6d8f2310VgnVCM10000013c110acRCRD&vgnextfmt= default. In Iceland the former chief executive of Glitnir bank has been convicted of fraud: R Milne, 'Ex-Iceland Bank Chief Convicted of Fraud', *Financial Times* (30 December 2012), available at www.ft.com/cms/s/0/76ff5a36-525e-11e2-aff0-00144feab49a.html. Other prosecutions for fraud/breach of trust will follow. See H Gunnlaugsson, 'Economic Crisis, Explanations, and Impact on Crime' (2012), available at www.escnewsletter.org; and for the basis of prosecutions, *Report of the Special Investigation Commission (SIC)*, ch 2 (Executive Summary, English language version), available at www.rna.is.

[64] Financial Services Authority, 'Statements of Principle for Approved Persons' 1,2 (APER 2.1.2).

[65] Financial Services Authority, above n 20.

[66] *John Pottage v FSA* (2012) FS/2010/33, Upper Tribunal (Tax and Chancery Chamber) Financial Services.

business upon his appointment as chief executive, displayed more scepticism in relation to assurances he was given, and recognised sooner than he did that a general overhaul was needed; he had therefore failed to take reasonable steps to secure the overall compliance of the business for which he was responsible, as required by the FSA's Principles for approved persons. The tribunal found otherwise. In its view, Pottage had been proactive enough in getting to grips with the business and had reacted reasonably to the evidence and warning signals available to him. The mere fact that compliance failure occurred in the business for which he was responsible did not put him in breach; there had to be personal culpability on his part.

Pottage is of course fact and circumstance-specific. Nevertheless it graphically illustrates the problems of attribution which can be expected to arise whenever an attempt is made to inculpate senior executives who have multifaceted responsibilities and much on their minds, not for active misconduct, but for the quality of their overall management and supervision. The outcome of *Pottage* stands in contrast to the FSA's successful pursuit of UBS employees who were actual perpetrators of misconduct in the relevant business area.[67]

Not only are these problems replicated when we turn to the possibility of pursuing serious leadership and management failures through the criminal justice system, but there is a further stumbling block. This is the mismatch between the popular impulse to criminalise bankers whose stewardship of major institutions has ended in scandal or fiasco[68] and the legal definitions of criminal offences. Leaving aside cases of outright fraud, most of the dereliction of leadership associated with the financial crisis and other scandals seems to defy categorisation in criminal terms, however much we might wish otherwise. Short-sightedness and weak judgment are far removed from the criminal law's preoccupation with dishonesty, intention and conscious recklessness.

In the UK, the government has reacted to this mismatch by floating the idea of a new criminal offence–'reckless misconduct in bank management'. An air of defeatism, however, hangs over the government's discussion of the practicalities:

> Assembling evidence to use as part of the case would be a huge undertaking. . .and the task of analysing it to a proper standard would be formidable. This could make such investigations extremely costly, and result in prosecutions which could run into years rather than months. In the circumstances, the decisions whether to investigate and prosecute would be extremely complex.[69]

There seems to be little scope, then, for the criminal law to transcend its customary role of being mobilised from time to time against individuals in the financial sector who have been actively engaged or complicit in serious wrongdoing. Even here there are important

---

[67] FSA, Final Notice, *Andrew Johnson Cumming* (13 November 2009); *Sachin Karpe v FSA* (2012) FS/2010/0019, Upper Tribunal (Tax and Chancery Chamber) Financial Services.

[68] eg 'Criminal Bankers Should Be Jailed, According to Survey' (9 October 2012), available at www.huffingtonpost.co.uk/2012/10/09/should-we-jail-bankers-avaaz-yougov-germany-france_n_1950085.html.

[69] HM Treasury, *Sanctions for the Directors of Failed Banks* (July 2012), available at http://www.hm-treasury.gov.uk/d/consult_sanctions_directors_banks.pdf, 4.17. The idea of criminalising reckless misconduct by senior bankers was, nevertheless, taken up by the Parliamentary Commission on Banking Standards, and it has now been adopted by the UK government: *Changing banking for good: Report of the Parliamentary commission on Banking Standards* (June 2013), HL paper 27-I, HC 175-I; *The Government's response to the Parliamentary Commision on Banking Standards (July 2013),* Cm 8661. This will be a classic example of symbolic legislation.

limiting factors: criminal justice is a costly commodity, prosecution agencies are stretched in terms of resources,[70] and cases against bankers are likely to be keenly contested.

Overall, it is inevitable that there will be an undersupply of enforcement proceedings, whether against corporations or individuals, whether regulatory or criminal, relative to the number of situations in which they would be warranted. This makes it all the more important that when proceedings actually are brought and successfully concluded, the sanctions imposed should not only outweigh any profit that accrued to the wrongdoer, but should also be heavy enough to be deterrent to others even in situations where the probability of their being subjected to enforcement proceedings is relatively small.

V   THE ROLE OF INCENTIVES

There is no doubt that remuneration structures have been and are a major driver of dysfunctional behaviour in the banking sector. In the words of the Financial Stability Board:

> Compensation practices at large financial institutions are one factor among many that contributed to the financial crisis that began in 2007. High short-term profits led to generous bonus payments to employees without adequate regard to the long-term risks they imposed on their firms. These perverse incentives amplified the excessive risk-taking that severely threatened the global financial system and left firms with fewer resources to absorb losses as risks materialised.[71]

The role of incentives in the abuse of customers is as well understood as its role in prudentially reckless behaviour. The UK regulatory system has wrestled with mis-selling motivated by commission payments and bonus-sweetened sales targets since its inception in 1988. In the words of Vander Weyer:

> [I]n the hollowed-out, systems-driven branch networks, lower-paid staff demanded their share of the spoils. . . .So they were offered commissions for flogging savings, mortgage and insurance deals–whether or not they were good for the customer. Service standards slipped from bad to worse, and the whole business model, from top to bottom, focused on product-pushing rather than 'relationship banking'.[72]

The part played by motivation and incentive can also be glimpsed where public-interest laws have been broken. In the UBS tax evasion case, it emerged that UBS had introduced a new system of incentives in 2004 that made bonuses conditional on 'new net money':

> This created a conflict for many US client advisors. On the one hand, they were expected to comply strictly with [UBS's agreement with the US tax authorities] while, at the same time, their superiors expected them to rapidly acquire new client assets. Some client advisors concluded that

---

[70] In the UK, the Serious Fraud Office had to obtain additional funding of £3 million from the government so as to be able to mount its Libor investigation: C Binham, 'SFO Bows to Calls for Libor Probe', *Financial Times* (7 July 2012), available at www.ft.com/intl/cms/s/0/39675a66-c76c-11e1-85fc-00144feab49a.html#axzz2QQ5dArcm.

[71] Financial Stability Board, *FSF Principles for Sound Compensation Practices* (April 2009), 1.

[72] M Vander Weyer, 'Banking Crisis: Why Bob Diamond is Not the Only One to Blame', *Daily Telegraph* (1 July 2012), available at www.telegraph.co.uk/finance/newsbysector/banksandfinance/9367364/Banking-crisis-why-Bob-Diamond-is-not-the-only-one-to-blame.html; see also *Which?* 'Bank Staff Under More Pressure Than Ever to Sell' (7 December 2012), available at www.which.co.uk/news/2012/12/bank-staff-under-more-pressure-than-ever-to-sell-305256/.

the Bank's management was not, in fact, serious about the literal application of the new US regulations, and no longer had any hesitation in the conduct of illicit advisory activities.[73]

As UBS itself admitted, client advisers were led to 'misconceive that a certain degree of non-compliance was tolerated by their line managers, which actually in part turned out to be the case'.[74] The imperative to generate profit and thus bonus is also the tacit premise behind many of the exchanges documented in the Libor decision notices.[75]

That profit (for the firm) and bonus and commission (for the individual) are overriding motivators of behaviour in banking is a commonplace observation. Nevertheless, it has powerful implications for regulatory design, for it points to the potential of regulatory intervention to restructure incentives as a means of reorienting the behaviour of banks and their people. If regulators can reshape the incentives at work in the banking environment, they will be speaking to bankers in their own language—in other words, harnessing their motivation and mobilising it to achieve a more socially acceptable end. Thus regulation of the incentives that motivate business behaviour in the first place (and not just the controls that aim to constrain them) becomes a critical task.[76]

The most advanced development in this connection is the Financial Stability Board's *Principles & Standards on Sound Compensation Practices*, which fall to be implemented throughout the G20.[77] The FSB explicitly characterises its principles and standards as designed to achieve 'lasting change in behaviour and culture within firms'.[78] The focus is on aligning the material incentives of key individuals in the firm—the 'material risk takers'— with the prudent long-term interests of the firm itself. A key device to accomplish this the requirement that payment of a substantial proportion of variable remuneration—crudely put, bonus—should be deferred for at least three years, and that a substantial proportion of bonus should take the form of equity, to give the executive more of a stake in the long-term performance of the firm. Coupled with these deferral arrangements are clawback provisions, so that vesting of deferred bonus is contingent on how major risks play out.[79]

---

[73] Straumann, above n 29 at 20.

[74] UBS, *Transparency report to the shareholders of UBS AG* (2010), available at www.ubs.com/transparency report, 37.

[75] eg Financial Services Authority, above n 5 at [101a]; Swiss Financial Market Supervisory Authority, UBS summary, para 2.4.2. A similar concern can be seen in the FSA's thematic AML report: *Banks' management of high money-laundering risk situations*: Financial Services Authority, above n 32 at [124].

[76] J Kay, *The Kay Review of UK Equity Markets and Long-Term Decision Making: Final Report* (London, July 2012), 11 ('Regulation should focus on the establishment of market structures which provide appropriate incentives, rather than the fruitless attempt to control behaviour in the face of inappropriate commercial incentives').

[77] Financial Stability Forum, *FSF Principles for Sound Compensation Practices* (2 April 2009), available at www.financialstabilityboard.org/publications/r_0904b.pdf; Financial Stability Board, *FSB Principles for Sound Compensation Practices: Implementation Standards* (25 September 2009), available at www.financialstabilityboard .org/publications/r_090925c.pdf.

[78] Financial Standards Board, *Implementing the FSB Principles for Sound Compensation Practices and their Implementation Standards: Progress Report* (June 2012), 3, 16.

[79] From 2014 an EU regime will operate alongside the FSB regime. It will apply to EU financial institutions within the scope of the Fourth Capital Requirements Directive and impose a "bonus cap" by virtue of which an individual's bonus must not exceed the amount of his or her salary, unless a substantial majority of shareholders resolve to raise the cap to twice salary. For obvious reasons this measure has enjoyed much political and popular support across the EU, except for the City of London and the UK government. Its value as a risk-management measure is more problematic. It remains to be seen whether the EU measure will put EU banks at a disadvantage in the competition for talent with non-EU competitors, and provoke a shift to higher fixed salaries and lower

It must be stressed that the FSB regime has a strongly *prudential* purpose, and this conditions its scope: the main focus is on systemically significant institutions, and on risks to their capital and liquidity. This has two important implications. First, at least in principle, the goals of the regulators and the long-term interests of the banks concerned—to avoid excessive prudential risk-taking—are mutually aligned. There is, therefore, substantial scope for a relatively consensual dialogue between the two. Secondly, however, the FSB regime has no automatic purchase on dysfunctional behaviour in categories (ii) and (iii) above, which does not always cross the threshold of prudential significance, and many firms and individuals with opportunities to mistreat customers or break public-interest laws fall outside the relatively small population encompassed by the FSB regime.

Remuneration at the interface between the bank and its customers therefore requires separate regulatory attention, at any rate in countries where it is pervaded by the sales culture and the distorting and detrimental effects of commission and bonus bias on advice and the choice of which products to 'push'. In the UK and Australia, radical regulatory experiments are getting under way: the Australian Securities & Investments Commission's prohibition of 'conflicted remuneration' came into force on 1 July 2013, and in the UK a ban on paying commission to financial advisers came into force at the beginning of 2013.

The FSA is also now paying more attention to the incentive environment around in-house customer-facing staff, signalling its expectation that firms will so structure their incentive schemes that they will not increase the risk of mis-selling.[80] These interventions will require intensive supervision and enforcement to succeed because they will (or should) interfere with product manufacturers' ability to retail high-margin products whose distribution has hitherto been incentivised by high commissions or other incentives.

By contrast, the motivational effect of incentives on behaviour in relation to money laundering and other financial-crime risks has yet to attract much direct regulatory attention.[81] After the Libor scandal, the string of settlements for US sanctions regime contraventions, and the UBS and HSBC settlements, there is every reason to believe that the issue of incentives, and the impulse to 'do the business', is as critical here as it is in relation to the customer interface generally.

This brief review suggests that there is scope for the regulation of incentives to be made more 'joined-up' and comprehensive. A more thoroughgoing approach would need to take full account of the potential for incentive-motivated violation of public-interest requirements (category (iii) above). But regulation of incentives operative at the customer interface will be a difficult undertaking. The relevant populations of firms are large, and therefore hard to monitor. Compared to the prudential sphere, banks, their staff and

bonuses which might impair the deterrent effect of the FSB bonus clawback provisions: A Barker and J Fontanella-Khan, 'UK overruled on financial services law', *Financial Times* (27 March 2013), available at www.ft.com/intl/cms/s/0/bd8c3926-9703-11e2-8950-00144feabdc0.html#axzz2QQ5dArcm.

[80] Financial Services Authority, *Risks to Customers from Financial Incentives* (2012), available at www.fsa.gov.uk/library/policy/guidance_consultations/2012/1211; Financial Services Authority, Final Guidance, *Risks to Customers from Financial Incentives* (January 2013) FG13/01.

[81] But see T McDermott, 'Strengthening Defences: Tackling Financial Crime from the Regulator's Perspective' (speech delivered at the 10th Annual British Bankers' Association Financial Crime Conference, 26 September 2012), available at www.fsa.gov.uk/library/communication/speeches/2012/0926-tm.shtml.

financial advisers will be less likely to identify their own long-term interests with the goals of the regulator. There will be a constant search for avoidance and circumvention devices. The need for profit will still actuate banks, and motivational devices other than commissions and bonuses can be found to sustain the pressure on staff to bring in business and make sales: these include social pressures and fear of job loss.[82]

To make headway, therefore, regulation of incentive structures must be characterised by sensitivity to industry developments and by flexible responsiveness. Regulators will have to be alert to the latest industry 'workarounds' and to operate within a framework of rules that allows them to counter them quickly. There will also need to be co-optation of senior management through corporate governance mechanisms[83] such as board-level remuneration committees whose operation is transparent to the regulator, and through regulatory obligations upon directors and senior managers to deliver compliant remuneration structures in their firms. Finally, regulators will need to practise active surveillance and to be prepared to bring enforcement proceedings for breaches of their incentive requirements per se—which brings us back full circle to the role of sanctions.

VI   CONCLUSION

It would not be enough to see the socially dysfunctional culture of the banking sector as a shared mindset that can be transformed by discrediting a handful of former leaders, setting a fresh 'tone from the top', and 'professionalising' banking along the lines of the legal or medical professions.[84] Rather the culture of banking needs to be understood as both cause and effect—as being in dialectical interplay with the structures that sustain it and that carriers of the culture will replicate as they move around. The Libor crisis is indeed a cultural crisis, but that culture 'must be addressed via structural and organisational reforms which get to the heart of banking business models'.[85]

It is of course important to address the right structural features. In relation to retail banking, Haldane offers us a story of contamination: the culture and practices of investment banking, he tells us, 'infiltrated' retail banking, a development which 'culminated in harmful cross-selling and unlawful mis-selling'. In this view, the kind of ring-fencing proposed by Vickers and the UK government will reverse the pattern, and restore relationship retail banking to its pristine state.[86] This narrative was echoed by a number of witnesses before the UK Parliamentary Commission on Banking Standards, and moved the commission

---

[82] See eg references to fear, bullying and humiliation in the comments appended to 'Revealed: The Bonus List That Encourages Hard Sell Culture Among "Advisers" in the Branches of Britain's Biggest Bank' (11 September 2012), available at www.thisismoney.co.uk/money/saving/article-2201063/Revealed-The-bonus-list-encourages-pressure-cooker-sales-culture-Lloyds.html.

[83] See eg, D Awrey, W Blair and D Kershaw, 'Between Law and Markets: Is There a Role for Culture and Ethics in Financial Regulation?' (2013) 38 *Delaware Journal of Corporate Law*, focusing on 'process-oriented regulation' as well as core governance arrangements.

[84] cf K Burgess and C Binham, 'BBA Details Plans for Checking Standards', *Financial Times* (15 January 2013), available at www.ft.com/intl/cms/s/0/8c5cbc58-5f0a-11e2-9f18-00144feab49a.html.

[85] A Bowman and others, 'Scapegoats Aren't Enough: A Leveson for the Banks ?' CRESC Discussion Paper (July 2012), available at www.cresc.ac.uk/publications/scapegoats-arent-enough-a-leveson-for-the-banks.

[86] Haldane, above n 8.

itself to claim that separation of investment banking and retail banking 'has the potential to change the culture of banks for the better'.[87] A policy originally put forward for its prudential benefits felicitously turns out to offer the prospect of a cultural reformation as well.

The historical accuracy of this contamination thesis is, however, highly dubious. Pushing and mis-selling of poor-value life and pensions products in the UK can be traced at least as far back as the market entry of hard-selling unit-linked life insurance companies in the 1960s, whose products were characterised by opaque charging structures and commissions designed to capture business from brokers and sales forces.[88] Arguably it was the mutual consolidation of the life/pensions and banking sectors in the 1990s which encouraged the hard-selling practices of the former to be adopted by the latter. The ethical decline of investment banking, on the other hand, is generally ascribed to 'Big Bang' in the 1980s and the supersession of the more gentlemanly ethos of merchant banking, or even to a later time.[89] And even if we supposed that the direction of travel was from investment banking to retail, there is no credible reason to look forward to a spontaneous recovery of virtue in retail banking, and every reason to suppose that bad behaviour will persist as long as incentive structures make it attractive for individuals and corporations.

Incentivising other-regarding behaviour and seriously penalising behavioural manifestations of amoral and predatory subcultures are key components of a credible strategy for the development of a more socially acceptable banking sector. But they are only part of the story. They need to be set in an overall context of prudential measures that foster circumspection, corporate governance arrangements focused on substance as well as process, cultural change programmes, and a regulatory style that probes beneath facades of ostensible compliance and does not shy away from tension—and in the last resort, conflict—between supervisor and corporation.

[87] Parliamentary Commission on Banking Standards, *First Report* (December 2012), HL Paper 98, HC 848, [45]. In its later report on the failure of HBOS, however, the Commission observes: 'HBOS had no culture of investment banking; if anything, its dominant culture was that of retail banking and retail financial services more widely.... Whatever may explain the problems of other banks, the downfall of HBOS was not the result of cultural contamination by investment banking': Parliamentary Commission on Banking Standards, *Fourth Report* (March 2013), HL Paper 144, HC 705, [138].

[88] Securities and Investments Board/Marketing of Investments Board Organising Committee, *Life Assurance and Unit Trusts and the Investor* (1986), para 9; J Walford, 'The big interview: Sir Mark Weinberg', *FT Adviser* (23 March 2012), available at www.ftadviser.com/2012/03/23/ifa-industry/people/the-big-interview-sir-mark-weinberg-Y95xAFibOKjxLlT8Uj6iqL/article.html.

[89] Vander Weyer, above n 72. Computerisation has also been implicated in the shift to a transactional business model in investment banking: SM Davidoff, AD Morrison and WJ Wilhelm, '*The SEC v. Goldman Sachs*: Reputation, Trust, and Fiduciary Duties in Investment Banking' (2011–12) 37 *Journal of Corporation Law* 529.

CHAPTER 6

The Libor Scandal:
Culture, Corruption and
Collective Action Problems in
the Global Banking Sector

Seumas Miller

I   INTRODUCTION

Perhaps the most prominent recent inflection of the Global Financial Crisis (GFC), at least in its moral aspect, is the Libor (London Interbank Offered Rate) scandal in the international banking sector.[1] Libor is a globally important benchmark calculated for ten major currencies, administered by the British Bankers' Association (BBA) and published daily. The Libor is the average short-term—eg daily (shortest term), yearly (longest term)— interest rate that leading international banks estimate they would have to pay if borrowing from other banks. The most important Libor is the three-month interest rate for US dollars. The average interest rate calculations are based on submissions to the BBA by the leading banks in question; these submissions ought to be the bona fide estimations by the leading banks of the interest rates they would have to pay.

Libor is used as an interest-rate benchmark by many financial institutions, mortgage lenders and credit card agencies; ie they use Libor as the reference point for setting their own interest rates. According to Martin Wheatley (of the 'Wheatley Review of Libor')[2] 'Libor is used in a vast number of financial transactions; with at value of at least $300 trillion'.[3] Indeed, according to *The Economist*, Libor is the most important figure in finance.[4]

The Libor scandal involves the rigging of Libor, either by pushing rates up or pushing them down. The leading banks in question rigged Libor by means of fraudulent and

---

[1] The scandal also involves rigging the Euribor (Euro Interbank Offered Rate).

[2] HM Treasury, 'The Wheatley Review of Libor (Final Report)' (London, September 2012), available at www.hm-treasury.gov.uk/wheatley_review.htm.

[3] M Wheatley, 'Pushing the Reset Button on Libor' (speech to FSA, London, 26 September 2012), available at www.fsa.gov.uk/library/communication/speeches/2012/0928-mw.shtml.

[4] 'Libor Scandal: The Rotten Heart of Finance' *The Economist* (19 February 2003), available at www.economist.com/node/21558281?%22%22.

collusive submissions to the BBA. For example, at the height of the GFC, Barclays' management caused their staff to falsify the bank's Libor submissions; on numerous occasions,
the interest rate submitted was lower than the actual estimation of the interest rate at
which the bank could borrow in order to give the appearance that the bank was in better
financial health than was in fact the case.[5] In addition, their bank traders made huge profits for the bank (and increased bonuses for themselves) by manipulating Libor. They did
so by causing their colleagues making the Libor submissions to adjust those interest rate
submissions (upwards or downwards). For even very small changes in Libor enable traders to make huge profits, if they can predict those changes in advance. On occasion, Libor
manipulation involved interbank collusion; the UK Financial Services Authority (FSA)
found this to be the case in its investigation of Libor manipulation in the Royal Bank of
Scotland (RBS).[6]

Thus far, investigations by the FSA, the US Department of Justice (USDJ) and other
regulatory authorities have resulted in massive fines being imposed on major banks such
as Barclays, UBS and the Royal Bank of Scotland. For example, UBS has been fined $1.5
billion[7] However, investigations continue and it is likely that more banks will be implicated
and fined. Clearly the problem is systemic.

In addition to the institutional and reputational damage and the massive fines, there
is the matter of (actual and potential) lawsuits filed on behalf of those who have been
adversely affected by the manipulation of Libor, eg, investors who earned a lower rate of
interest than otherwise would have been the case, mortgage holders whose interest payments were higher than otherwise would have been the case. The financial impact of these
lawsuits (including class actions) may ultimately dwarf the fines being imposed on banks
by the regulators.

The unfolding Libor scandal comes hot on the heels of money-laundering scandals, (eg
HSBC),[8] facilitating tax evasion through offshore accounts (eg, UBS)[9], an ongoing series
of rogue traders who have wreaked havoc (eg, the so-called 'London Whale' at JP Morgan
Chase),[10] reckless and predatory lending by numerous banks in the US (eg, Countrywide
Financial)[11] and elsewhere prior to the GFC, senior bank management reversing or, at the
very least, ignoring due diligence judgments of credit-unworthiness made by their own
underwriters (eg, at Countrywide Financial), creating and selling so-called toxic financial

---

[5] US Commodity Futures Trading Commission, 'CFTC Orders Barclays to Pay $200 Million Penalty for
Attempted Manipulation of and False Reporting Concerning Libor and Euribor Benchmark Interest Rates' (June
27 2012), available at www.cftc.gov/PressRoom/PressReleases/pr6289-12.

[6] Financial Services Authority, 'Final Notice: Imposing Financial Penalty' (6 February 2013), available at
www.fsa.gov.uk/static/pubs/final/rbs.pdf.

[7] BBC News, 'UBS Fined $1.5bn for Libor Rigging' BBC (19 December 2012), available at www.bbc.co.uk/
news/business-20767984.

[8] J Treanor and D Rushe, 'HSBC to Pay £1.2bn over Mexico Scandal' The Guardian (11 December 2012),
available at www.guardian.co.uk/business/2012/dec/10/standard-chartered-settle-iran-sanctions.

[9] L Browning, 'Former UBS Client in Florida Pleads Guilty to Tax Evasion' Reuters (8 January 2013), available
at www.reuters.com/article/2013/01/09/us-bc-swissbanks-ubs-idUSBRE90804820130109.

[10] S Neville and J Treanor, 'JP Morgan Trader "London Whale" Blows $13bn Hole in Bank's Value' The Guardian
(11 May 2012), available at www.guardian.co.uk/business/2012/may/11/jp-morgan-trader-london-whale.

[11] M Smith, 'The Untouchables' (2013) Four Corners (18 March 2013), available at www.abc.net.au/4corners/
stories/2013/03/18/3715426.htm.

products by leading international investment banks (eg, synthetic CDOs),[12] fraud (eg, Bernie Madoff's ponzi scheme) and, of course, major banking collapses and (in many cases) bailouts by taxpayers, eg, Northern Rock, Lehmann Brothers, Freddie Mac and Fannie Mae.

It seems that large-scale corporate collapses and corruption scandals in the global financial sector in general, and the global banking sector in particular, are a recurring phenomenon, and a phenomenon with massively harmful, economic and social impact on mortgage holders, shareholders, investors, employees, retirees, the list goes on.[13]

Evidently the magnitude of the problem is due in large part to global interdependence. However, interdependence in and of itself does not explain the underlying cause(s) of the problem, although it surely greatly exacerbates it. Wheatley argues that in the case of the Libor scandal, 'The key flaw was the inability in the system to manage conflicts of interest'.[14] The BBA, for example, was simultaneously the administrator of the Libor system and the association representing the interests of the banking industry; as such, the BBA was hardly an independent administrator of Libor. Accordingly, Wheatley has proposed an independent administrator of Libor (along with various other micro-institutional reforms).

However, given that the scandal involved, on many occasions, corrupt collaboration between interest-rate derivatives traders and Libor submitters within the same bank, it is not self-evident that a central conflict of interest that enabled and spawned much of the interest rate rigging has been adequately addressed by the Wheatley Review. Here, as elsewhere, removal of this conflict of interest by returning to the division between investment banks and retail banks—or, at the very least, imposing some form of iron-clad segregation—would be a more convincing response than establishing an independent administrator to, in effect, try to manage the conflict of interest.[15]

This point is amplified given, as we have just seen, that the Libor scandal is merely the latest in a series of banking scandals and, for that matter, collapses. So evidently there is a need for a holistic approach and a need to look not simply at micro-institutional mechanisms, such as Libor, but also at some of the macro-institutional aspects of the banking sector that might bear on this and related ethical problems. Central among these is surely the phenomenon of global financial institutions that are 'too big to fail'. Thus there were a number of bailouts of major banks and other financial institutions following the decision in 2008 to allow Lehman Brothers to fail, a decision which is thought to have virtually brought the international financial system to its knees. Importantly, for our concerns here, the phenomenon of banks that are 'too big to fail' has morphed into the phenomenon of banks that are 'too big to manage'

---

[12] Synthetic collateralised debt obligations did not actually contain any real assets: low quality (sub-prime) or high quality mortgage bonds. Rather they consisted of a promise to pay the investor whatever return the specified actual CDO paid. If abused, synthetic CDOs (at least) were the investment banker equivalent of a pyramid scheme. See R Garnaut, *The Great Crash of 2008*, (Melbourne, Melbourne University Press, 2009), 47–49.

[13] See, eg, Financial Services Authority *The Turner Review: A Regulatory Response to the Global Banking Crisis*, (London, Financial Services Authority, 2009). Some recent book collections offering discussions of many of these problems are: N Dobos, C Barry and T Pogge (eds) *The Global Financial Crisis: Ethical Issues* (Basingstoke, Palgrave, 2011); I MacNeil, and J O'Brien (eds) *The Future of Financial Regulation* (Portland, Hart Publishing, 2010); and J O'Brien (ed) *Private Equity, Corporate Governance and the Dynamics of Capital Market Regulation* (London, Imperial College of London Press, 2007).

[14] Wheatley, above n 3.

[15] J Kay, *Narrow Banking: The Reform of Banking Regulation* (London, Centre for the Study of Financial Innovation, 2009).

and, indeed, 'too big to jail'[16] or, less colloquially, 'too big to regulate'. For example, there is the recent case of the multinational bank, HSBC, and international money-laundering activities of criminal organisations, such as Mexican-based drug cartels.[17] The latter were found to have used HSBC for this purpose over a 10-year period resulting in a US$1.9 billion fine for HSBC for failing to have in place effective anti-money-laundering measures and for failing to conduct due diligence on some of its account holders. Criminal negligence notwithstanding, HSBC retained its licence to operate, having in effect been deemed by the regulators 'too big to fail'. However, the inference that is being drawn from HSBC's retention of its licence in these circumstances is that it is, in effect, too big to regulate.[18]

And there is a further point to be made here. If individual banks are too big to regulate and if, as seems to be the case, there has been collusion between banks in the systemic corrupting of Libor—'the most important figure in finance'—do not these banks constitute a de facto cartel that is too powerful to regulate effectively?

The general proposition that the banks are beyond the reach of regulators, whether because they are too big to regulate and/or for other reasons, (eg, regulatory capture), is further evidenced by the paucity of criminal convictions of senior bank personnel in this context of widespread and ongoing malfeasance in the global banking sector. For example, evidently the US Department of Justice has yet to successfully prosecute any bank personnel at the most senior levels for criminal behaviour, eg, fraud.[19] It simply beggars belief that senior Wall Street executives, including CEO's and board members, have not personally been engaged in various forms of criminal behaviour including, at the very least, criminal negligence.

In addition to structural reform, at both micro and macro levels, there is a need to address issues of culture, albeit these are closely related. For example, evidently is there a culture within the sector, or large parts of it, which is conducive to interest-rigging and, for that matter, other unethical practices. If so, structural redesign, no doubt including Libor at the micro-institutional level in accordance with some, if not all, of Wheatley's recommendations, needs to go hand in glove with the reformation of banking culture. Such reformation may well involve a process of professionalization, or at least of occupational ethical acculturation (of which more below).

In this paper, the focus is on the ethico-normative aspects of the Libor issue. I take it that the problem is, at least to a significant degree, a problem of institutional corruption and corruption is quintessentially a moral or ethical problem. While the concern is with the ethical, as opposed to the legal, regulatory, economic or political dimensions of the problem, nevertheless, the ethical dimension is intertwined with the others, not the least because serious ethical problems in the institutional sphere typically require legal, regulatory and so on redress. Accordingly, in the course of such ethical analysis of institutions, aspects of these other dimensions frequently come into view.

In the first section I introduce theoretical accounts of the notions required for an understanding of key normative aspects of the Libor scandal, and I apply these notions to relevant aspects of that scandal. The notions in question are ones I have developed in detail

---

[16] See eg, US Attorney-General Eric Holder's answers to the Senate Judiciary Committee as reported in AR Sorkin, 'Realities Behind Prosecuting Big Banks' *New York Times* (12 March 2013) B1.

[17] See: Senate Permanent Sub-Committee on Investigations, *US Vulnerabilities to Money Laundering, Drugs and Terrorist Financing: HSBC Case History*, (Washington D C, US Congress, 2012).

[18] A Viswanatha and B Wolf, 'HSBC to Pay $1.9 Billion US Fine in Money Laundering Case' *Reuters* (11 December 2012), available at www.reuters.com/article/2012/12/11/us-hsbc-probe-idUSBRE8BA05M20121211.

[19] Smith, above n 11.

elsewhere.[20] They are: social institutions and mechanisms, institutional corruption, and collective moral responsibility. As already mentioned, I take it that a fundamental problem that needs to be addressed in relation to the above described ongoing cycle of banking scandals is institutional corruption and, therefore, we require normative (theoretical) accounts of social institutions and (relatedly) of institutional corruption. Since a principal remedy for institutional corruption consists, I suggest, in embedding (both structurally and culturally) collective moral responsibility, I also offer a theoretical account of that notion.

In the second section, I frame the problem of institutional corruption in question as a collective action problem(s), and I provide a novel theoretical account of how collection action problems of this kind are to be understood, an account at odds with standard rational choice models. In doing so, I don't mean to rule out other ways of framing the problem. Rather I suggest that this way of framing it might be illuminating in itself and also potentially useful to those seeking to implement practical measures to combat institutional corruption in this and other areas.

II   NORMATIVE THEORY: SOCIAL INSTITUTIONS AND MECHANISMS, INSTITUTIONAL CORRUPTION AND COLLECTIVE MORAL RESPONSIBILITY

Social Institutions and Joint Institutional Mechanisms

Social institutions are often organisations. Moreover, many institutions are systems of organisations. For example, capitalism is a particular kind of economic institution, and in modern times capitalism consists in large part in specific organisational forms–including multi-national banking corporations–organised into a system. Further, some institutions are meta-institutions; they are institutions (organisations) that organise other institutions (including systems of organisations). For example, governments are meta-institutions. The institutional end or function of a government consists in large part in organising other institutions (both individually and collectively); thus governments regulate and coordinate economic systems largely by way of (enforceable) legislation.

Social institutions can be thought of as having three constitutive dimensions, namely, structure, function and culture.[21] Roughly speaking, an institution that is an organisation or system of organisations consists of an embodied (occupied by human persons) structure of differentiated roles. These roles are defined in terms of tasks, and rules regulating the performance of those tasks. Moreover, there is a degree of interdependence between these roles, such that the performance of the constitutive tasks of one role cannot be undertaken, or cannot be undertaken except with great difficulty, unless the tasks constitutive of some other role or roles in the structure have been undertaken or are being undertaken. Further, these roles are often related to one another hierarchically, and hence involve different levels of status and degrees of authority. Importantly, these roles are related to one another in part in virtue of their contribution to (respectively) the end(s) or function(s) of the institution; and the realisation of these ends or functions normally involves interaction between the institutional actors in question and external actors.

---

[20] S Miller, *The Moral Foundations of Social Institutions: A Philosophical Study* (New York, Cambridge University Press, 2010).

[21] S Miller, 'Social Institutions' *Stanford Encyclopaedia of Philosophy* (online journal), 2007 Winter Edition; Miller *The Moral Foundations of Social Institutions*, (2010), ch 1.

On my favoured teleological normative theory of social institutions,[22] the function of any given institution is a collective end which is also a human good[23], ie, the end is something jointly produced by the institutional actors in question and it is an item or service worth having. Arguably, many of the so-called innovative financial products of recent times, eg, synthetic CDOs, are not worth having since they are principally devices for redistributing producers' and investors' funds; as such, they are not products which generate a net value for market participants taken in aggregate. An important point to be made here about markets and business organisations is that, normatively speaking, they have both proximate ends and ultimate ends. The proximate end of market actors might be to maximize their financial self-interest or the firm's profits or shareholder value. However, such proximate goals are not the ultimate ends of markets or of the social institution of the modern corporation. Rather, the ultimate ends are the economic benefits of the goods produced and consumed, benefits that accrue to market participants and beyond by way of the so-called invisible hand. To claim that the ultimate purpose of the institution of the modern corporation—a product, if ever there was one, of institutional design—is, for example, simply and only to maximize profits or shareholder value is, on this ends-based, ie teleological, account of social institutions, to confuse proximate with ultimate purposes.[24]

Thus the proximate end of (retail) banks might be to maximize shareholder value, but the ultimate purpose is something beyond this, eg, to provide a safe and secure place for depositor's savings and (relatedly) to loan funds to enable families to buy homes, businesses to expand, long- term infrastructure investment needs to be met, and so on. Aside from the formal and usually explicitly stated or defined tasks and rules, there is an important implicit and informal dimension of an institution roughly describable as institutional culture. This notion comprises the informal attitudes, values, norms, and the ethos or 'spirit' that pervades an institution. Culture in this sense determines much of the activity of the members of that institution, or at least the manner in which that activity is undertaken. So while the explicitly determined rules and tasks might say nothing about bending or breaking the rules—or even forbid such activity—or about being driven by the need to win bonuses and generate profits, these attitudes and practices might in fact be pervasive; they might be part of the culture (as appears in fact to have been the case at many modern corporations, notably Enron,[25] but also throughout the banking sector).[26]

An important sub-element of most, if not all, institutions is what I have referred to elsewhere as a joint institutional mechanism.[27] Benchmarks, such as Libor, are instances of such mechanisms. Other examples are voting to elect a candidate to political office, use of money as a medium of exchange and, more generally, exchange systems such as markets for goods and services. Joint institutional mechanisms[28] consist of: (a) a complex of differentiated but interlocking actions (the input to the mechanism); (b) the result of the performance of those

---

[22] Miller, above n 20; S Miller, *Social Action: A Teleological Account*, (New York, Cambridge University Press, 2001).

[23] Miller, above n 20 at ch 2; and on collective ends, 41–45.

[24] Miller, above n 20 at ch 2. For a detailed critique of the shareholder value theory, see LA Stout, *The Shareholder Value Myth: How Putting Shareholders First Harms Investors, Corporations and the Public* (San Francisco, Berrett Keohler Publications, 2012).

[25] P Fusaro and R Miller, *What Went Wrong at Enron?* (Hoboken, NJ, John Wiley and Sons, 2002).

[26] J Kay 'Unfettered Finance Has Been the Cause of All Our Crises' *Financial Times* (6 January 2010).

[27] Miller, above n 20 at 50–52.

[28] Miller, above n 23; Miller, above n 20.

actions (the output of the mechanism); and (c) the mechanism itself. In the case of Libor, the inputs are the interest rate estimates submitted by the banks. So there is interlocking and differentiated action (the various inputs of the submitters). Further, there is the process applied to the inputs (the mechanism). This mechanism consists of averaging the various submissions.[29] The application of the mechanism (the averaging process) to the input (the submissions) yields an output, namely, the Libor interest rate for some currency over some period.

Note the following important points regarding this joint institutional mechanism, assuming it is working as it should and realising its normative institutional purposes, that is, if it is not malfunctioning or corrupted. Firstly, that there is a result is (in part) constitutive of the mechanism. The result, ie, the particular interest rate arrived at (Libor), is not aimed at by each or any of the banks; after all, none of the banks can predict the result, let alone bring it about by aiming at it. Nevertheless, each of the banks has a common end (more precisely, a collective epistemic end)[30] namely that the average interest rate— whatever that is—will be produced by this mechanism

Secondly, the generation of an interest rate by this mechanism serves a further institutional purpose which is the raison d'être of the mechanism (and, as such, in part constitutive of it), namely, that of providing a benchmark interest rate upon which various institutions and individuals can rely. So at one level of description, the result of the application of the mechanism is simply an interest rate arrived at by averaging, but at another level of description this interest rate is a benchmark. This ultimate benchmarking purpose is itself a collective end of the joint institutional mechanism, but one aimed at not just by the bankers but also by those who use Libor to set their own interest rates. That any one of the interest rates in question serves as a benchmark is an end which is realised not simply by the banks generating it via their submissions, but also by other institutions and individuals using it as such. Absent the participation of both parties (or categories of party), Libor would cease to exist.

Thirdly, and needless to say, providing false submissions or otherwise seeking to manipulate the results of the mechanism is a matter of moral obligation, given its important institutional purpose and the consequent trust placed in it by so many. This point has been reinforced by the Wheatley Review's recommendation that non-compliance, eg, by intentionally making false submissions, be a criminal offence. So much for the normative theory of institutions and institutional mechanisms; what of institutional corruption?

Institutional Corruption

Providing an acceptable definition of institutional corruption[31] has proven to be an elusive goal in part because the forms of corruption are many and diverse, eg, bribery, nepotism,

---

[29] The averaging process is somewhat more complex than simple averaging since some of the highest and lowest submitted rates are excluded from it. However, this is a sufficient description for our purposes here.

[30] More precisely, there is a two-stage process, the first stage of which is the production of Libor, and the second stage of which is its communication and acceptance by numerous institutions and individuals as a credible benchmark. The collective end is an epistemic one since it consists of an item of knowledge (ideally). For more on this see Miller, above n 20 at ch 11.

[31] See AJ Heidenheimer and M Johnston (eds) *Political Corruption: Concepts and Contexts,* 3rd edn (London, Transaction Publishers, 2002); S Miller 'Corruption' *Stanford Encyclopaedia of Philosophy* (online journal) 2005 Fall Edition; and Miller, above n 20 at ch 5.

fabricating evidence, perjury, abuse of authority, fraudulent use of travel funds, plagiarism. This problem is compounded when corruption is identified as simply a species of unlawful activity. What do legal offences listed have in common? In point of fact, corruption is fundamentally a moral, as opposed to a legal, phenomenon. While many corrupt acts are unlawful—or ought to be unlawful—this is not necessarily the case. For example, historically in many jurisdictions bribery has not been unlawful. Moreover, corruption is also a causal phenomenon. Institutional corruption—whether it is bribery, abuse of authority, fabrication of evidence or some other species of corruption—typically does institutional damage by undermining an institutional process or purpose. Because persons who perform corrupt actions do so intentionally or knowingly—or at least such persons should have known the corrupting effect that their actions would have—these persons are blameworthy, generally speaking.

It might be held that those who are corrupted have to some extent, or in some sense, allowed themselves to be corrupted; they are participants in the process of their corruption. Specifically, they have chosen to perform, or to refrain from performing, the actions or omissions that ultimately had the corrupting effects in question on them, and they could have chosen otherwise. The paradigm here is those who habitually engage in acts of corruption gradually corrupt themselves in the process.

Nevertheless, those who are corrupted need not be the ones who corrupt them, ie, the corruptors. Corruptors can corrupt persons other than themselves, and often do so intentionally, eg, organised criminals attempting to corrupt administrative officials or market actors.

Those who become corrupted, whether as a result of their own corrupt actions or at the hands of others, do not necessarily intend to become or foresee that they will be corrupted. Indeed, it might be the case that they could not reasonably have been expected to foresee that they would become corrupted. This is especially the case with the young and inexperienced. However, this claim needs to be distinguished from the earlier one to the effect that those who are corrupted could have chosen otherwise. It is one thing to have the capacity to choose otherwise; it is another thing to intend to choose otherwise or even think of doing so. More generally, one can have a capacity to choose to do what is right without necessarily being blameworthy for failing to do so; or at least one's blameworthiness might be mitigated in various ways. This is perhaps especially the case for those who occupy lower-level positions in hierarchical organisations run by corrupt cliques who have engendered corrupt workplace cultures and established remuneration systems which encourage the self-interested pursuit of huge monetary and status rewards at the expense of compliance with ethical principles. Arguably, many young bank traders exemplify this phenomenon. This does not necessarily excuse their behaviour, but it may well facilitate understanding of it.[32]

I suggest that acts of institutional corruption necessarily involve a corruptor and/or someone who is corrupted such that the corruptor performs the corrupt action qua occupant of an institutional role, and/or the person corrupted suffers the process of corruption qua occupant of an institutional role.

---

[32] The problem is compounded by the process often referred to as 'neutralization' by which a person sees his or her own behaviour as morally neutral, while seeing the same set of behaviour in others as morally problematic. For a recent discussion on the processes of neutralization in white-collar crime, see: WA Stadler and ML Benson, 'Revisiting the Guilty Mind: The Neutralization of White-Collar Crime' (2012) 37 *Criminal Justice Review*, 494–511.

If this is correct, then we can distinguish acts of corruption from moral (and legal) offences that undermine institutions—specifically, institutional processes and purposes—but which are nevertheless not acts of corruption. The latter are not acts of corruption because no person in his or her capacity as institutional role occupant either performs an act of corruption or suffers a diminution in his or her character. There are many legal and moral offences in this latter category. Consider individuals not employed by or otherwise institutionally connected to a large corporation who steal from or defraud the corporation. These offences may undermine the institutional processes and purposes of the corporation, but given the non-involvement of any officer, manager or employee of the corporation, these acts are not acts of corruption.

Acts of corruption bring it about that an institution (or sub-element thereof) is in a corrupt condition, eg, some institutional process has been undermined. But arguably this condition of corruption exists only relative to: (a) an uncorrupted condition, which condition is (b) the condition of being a morally legitimate institution (or sub-element thereof). Aside from specific institutional processes and purposes, such sub-elements also include institutional roles and the morally worthy character traits that are necessary for the discharging of these institutional roles.

Consider the uncorrupted Libor process. It consists of truthful, well-founded submissions being made by various banks and a correct calculation being made in accordance with the averaging procedure. This otherwise morally legitimate institutional process is corrupted, if one or more of its constitutive actions are not performed in accordance with the process as it is rightly intended to be. Thus to under- or overstate one's estimations in the service of influencing the result of the process so as to enable one's traders to make profits is a corrupt action. In relation to moral character, consider an honest submitter who begins to make false Libor submissions under the pressure of a corrupt senior management or a corrupt culture among the bank's traders. By engaging in such a practice, he risks the erosion of his moral character; he is undermining his disposition to act honestly.

In the view under discussion here, the corrupt condition of the institution or institutional mechanism corrupted exists only relative to some moral standards that are definitional of the uncorrupted condition of that institution, including the moral character of the persons in institutional roles.

Let us now turn to the notion of collective moral responsibility. I note that Wheatley himself stressed the centrality of collective responsibility to the integrity of the Libor process.[33] I suggest that the Libor corruption scandal can be viewed principally as a failure of collective moral responsibility at a number of levels and not, therefore, as simply an aggregate of failures of individual moral responsibility as the 'rotten apple' theory would have it.

Collective Moral Responsibility

Collective moral responsibility is a species of moral responsibility. Here we need to distinguish moral responsibility (including collective moral responsibility) from causal responsibility. A person or persons can inadvertently cause a bad outcome without necessarily being morally responsible for so doing. Moral responsibility typically requires not only causal

---

[33] Wheatley, above n 3.

responsibility but also an intention to cause harm or the knowledge that one's action will or may well cause harm, whether harm to persons or institutions or (more likely in the kinds of cases under consideration here) to both.

Collective moral responsibility is the moral responsibility that attaches to structured and unstructured groups for their morally significant actions and omissions. Thus an organised gang of thieves who carry out a million-dollar bank heist or a gang of bank employees who carry out a multi-million-dollar interest-rigging fraud is said to be collectively morally (and, one might have expected, legally) responsible for the theft and fraud (respectively) and also for the resulting harm to those affected, eg, depositors, investors.

Elsewhere I have elaborated and defended a relational account of collective moral responsibility; specifically, that of collective responsibility as joint responsibility.[34] In this view, at least one of the central senses of collective responsibility is responsibility arising from joint actions and omissions. Roughly speaking, a joint action can be understood thus: two or more individuals perform a joint action if each of them intentionally performs an individual action, but does so with the (true) belief that in so doing they will jointly realise an end which each of them has. On this view of collective responsibility as joint responsibility, collective responsibility is ascribed to individuals. Each member of the group is individually morally responsible for the outcome of the joint action. However, each is individually responsible, jointly with the others; hence the conception is relational in character. Thus in our million-dollar bank heist example, each member of the gang is responsible jointly with the others for the theft of the million dollars because each performed his contributory action in the service of that collective end (the theft of the million dollars).

On this kind of relational view, the various relevant bank submitters, traders and/or managers involved in some particular episode of Libor interest-rigging can be ascribed collective moral responsibility for this particular corrupt action and for any (personal and/or institutional) harm that might result from it. As we have seen in relation to the unfolding Libor scandal, the network of joint actions and omissions can be quite wide and complex without necessarily involving all, or even most, bank personnel. Moreover, some joint actions or omissions might be of greater moral significance than others, and some individual contributions, eg, those of senior bank managers, of greater importance than others. Further, the cumulative damage done by an ongoing series of such episodes of corrupt action by numerous bank personnel from different institutions and on multiple occasions might conceivably also be sheeted home to the entire large group, albeit there are various barriers to the ascription of collective moral responsibility in large groups in which each member only makes a small causal contribution.

Importantly, and as noted by the Wheatley Review, there is a collective institutional responsibility on the part of Libor submitters to provide well-founded, truthful submission and, thereby, arrive at correct Libor rates. It was this collective *institutional* responsibility—and, given the moral significance in terms of the resulting harm, breach of trust etc., collective *moral* responsibility—which those who engaged in false submissions failed to discharge and, in so failing, corrupted the Libor process. What is remarkable is that pre-Wheatley, it was probably not a legal offence to engage in Libor interest-rate rigging; evidently, bank robbery was regarded as one thing, but robbery by bankers quite another.

---

[34] S Miller, 'Collective Moral Responsibility: An Individualist Account' (2006) 30 *Midwest Studies in Philosophy* 176; and Miller, above n 20 at ch 4.

III COLLECTIVE ACTION PROBLEMS, LIBOR AND
THE GLOBAL BANKING SECTOR

Thus far we have characterized Libor as an essentially cooperative undertaking, ie, as a joint institutional mechanism defined in terms of the desirable collective end of serving as a benchmark interest rate. However, the ongoing processes of this joint institutional mechanism have been undermined by the corrupt acts of manipulation described above. What is the nature and what are the causes of this corruption? As noted above, the Wheatley Review identified the structural conflict of interest that the BBA had in its role as the administrator of Libor as the source of the problem. Moreover, I also noted the structural conflict of interest within Barclays and other banks as a consequence of their role as Libor submitters and their interest-based derivatives trading activities.

Arguably, this picture of multiple structural conflicts of interest as the source of the problem, while acceptable as far as it goes, is an oversimplification. Specifically, it ignores the competitive context in which banks operate and, in particular, various collective action problems arising from such competition, albeit especially in circumstances in which there are structural conflicts of interest of the kind in question. Note that my reference to a competitive institutional context is not meant to imply that the competitive contexts in question are necessarily ones involving fierce, free and fair, competition between institutional actors who are relatively equal; far from it. The attempt to frame recent Libor interest rigging as a collective action problem(s) is important for our purposes here, not the least because it casts the Libor corruption issue in a somewhat different light than the Wheatley Review and other influential analyses, including ones that rightly stress the importance of institutional culture in addition to structural features.[35] But what is a collective action problem in the sense in question?

A paradigmatic collective action problem is the so-called 'tragedy of the commons' scenario in which it is in the individual interest of each to continue to use some common resource, but it is not in the collective interest, at least in the long term. Thus it is in the interest of each fishing boat to continue to catch fish, irrespective of whether others do so since it provides a livelihood. Indeed, the fisherman are in de facto competition with one another in that each is seeking over time to get a larger share of the total fish stock than his competitors. Unfortunately this behaviour, whether explicitly competitive or not, is not in the collective interest, at least in the long term, since eventually the stock of fish will be depleted to the point where no one can make a living from fishing in the area in question.

As a response to this kind of problem, the fishermen might agree to a quota system, whereby each restricts his catch to a certain amount, thereby ensuring the long-term sustainability of fishing in the area. However, such cooperative schemes give rise to the so-called 'free-rider' problem. It is in the individual interest of each to ignore his quota, if he can get away with it. But, of course, if it is simply a matter of an unenforced quota system, then each can get away with non-compliance and so the system collapses. Accordingly, there is a need for someone to enforce the quota system. Unfortunately, enforcement is probably not a sufficient condition for compliance, although it is a necessary one. Notoriously, a population that does not for the most part want to comply cannot in the long term be

---

[35] For a recent general discussion of these issues, see J O'Brien and G Gilligan 'Introduction: Regulating Culture, Problems and Perspectives' (introduction to this volume).

forced to do so; this is the Achilles heel of one-dimensional regulatory-enforcement models. Let us refer to this problem as the 'insufficiency of enforcement mechanisms' problem.

Moreover, the enforcement 'solution' simply elevates the initial problem to a different level. Specifically, why should the enforcer adequately enforce the quota system when it is not in his individual rational self-interest to do so, eg, when he is bribed to look the other way or when he has a financial interest in specific fishing boats or when he simply doesn't feel like making the effort? Why does the enforcer necessarily pursue the collective self-interest embodied in the quota system when it is not in his individual rational self-interest to do so? The answer can only be that the enforcer's compliance with the requirements of his role is itself enforced; that is, a meta-enforcer is invoked. But irrespective of whether this meta-enforcer is an individual or a collective, the same problem will recur: Who enforces the compliance of the meta-enforcer? Let us refer to this infinite regress problem as the 'Who guards the guards?' problem

Collective action problems are, I suggest, endemic in the global banking sector. At the micro-level, there is the problem of excessive remuneration. Executives receive huge remuneration packages consisting in large part of bonuses. However, empirical studies[36] have consistently demonstrated that there is no significant correlation between large executive remuneration packages and executive performance as measured in terms of medium- to long-term profitability and/or share price (the favoured, if flawed, measure of performance.)(See discussion of normative theory of institutions above.) However, in the absence of external regulatory or other intervention, competition among corporations for senior executives has driven up executive remuneration packages to extraordinarily high, and completely unjustified, levels. However, the competitive arrangement in question does not remotely approach the pure competition market model beloved by economists in which neither buyers nor sellers can individually or collectively unduly influence the price at which goods are exchanged. Rather it takes place in the context of increased management power relative to shareholder—and board control—due in large part to a shift in share ownership from direct individual ownership to indirect share ownership and to share ownership in the hands of institutional share funds and (relatedly) in corporate power structures (dominated by managers).[37]

Accordingly, the sellers (the managers) can collectively and over time unduly influence (upwardly) the price at which their labour is sold to the buyers (the shareholders via their boards). Specifically, executive managers compete with one another for financial rewards within a competitive framework in which there is insufficient downward pressure on the overall level of those rewards from those who ultimately have to provide them (the shareholders). This is a collective action problem in which increased competition produces the perverse outcome of grossly inflated executive remuneration. And there is an additional perverse outcome. To the extent that there is a relationship between high executive remuneration and corporate performance, it is purely a relationship between remuneration and short-term profits and share price and, to that extent, part of the problem rather than the solution.

---

[36] For an overview and analysis of empirical studies, see S Elaurant 'Corporate Executive Salaries: The Argument from Economic Efficiency' (2008) 13 *Electronic Journal of Business Ethics and Organisation Studies*, available at ejbo.jyu.fi/pdf/ejbo_vol13_no2_pages_35-43.pdf.

[37] S Elaurant, 'A Philosophical and Economic Inquiry into Corporate Executive Salaries' (PhD thesis, University of Queensland 2011).

At the macro-institutional level, there are various collective action problems. For example, in the 'good' times, the banks engage in fierce competition for depositors' funds and as lenders to homebuyers, investors and so on. This contributes to housing bubbles, speculative investor bubbles, over-leveraged banks and so on. Eventually, indeed predictably, the bubble bursts. Investors, 'sensing' the bubble is about to burst, begin to sell en masse to a diminishing pool of buyers; stock prices collapse. Overleveraged investment banks, in particular, are at great risk from those who have borrowed heavily from them but are now unable to pay them back. In addition, depositors become increasingly nervous and banks fear a run on their deposits. Accordingly, in these 'bad times' it now becomes of critical importance to each bank that it is regarded as safe and secure, especially relative to other banks. The banks are no longer competing with one another in what might be referred to as the 'profligacy stakes', but rather in what might be referred to as the 'probity stakes'.

Note that the pursuit of individual self-interest in the 'profligacy stakes' is to some extent unavoidable by virtue of the fact that those banks who do not 'play the game' may well find themselves uncompetitive profit-wise and, hence, out of business. Note further that the pursuit of individual self-interest in the 'probity stakes' is also to some extent unavoidable by virtue of the fact that those banks who do not 'play the game' may well find themselves uncompetitive safety and security-wise and, hence, out of business.

The general form of the collective action problem is that each bank, in pursuing its own rational self-interest, initially in the 'profligacy stakes' and latterly in the 'probity stakes', threatens the collective self-interest of the banking sector (not to speak of the economic system, more generally). How is this so? Why does the market mechanism not simply come into play? Why don't the weaker banks fail and the stronger banks pick up their residual business, as outlined in Economics 1? Part of the problem is that a run on one bank can lead to contagion, even if the damage arising from the failure of any one bank on its own would be containable. But the problem is far greater than this in the global banking sector. For it turns out that pretty much all of the leading banks in the global banking sector are 'too big to fail'; for example, according to the respected international body, the Financial Stability Board, there are no less than 29 banks that are 'systemically important financial institutions (SIFIs)'.[38] It follows that while the banks are in competition with one another at one level, at another level each requires every other *not* to fail on pain of systemic collapse. Hence, there is a collective action problem: the pursuit of individual self-interest is ultimately at odds with collective self-interest.

The existence of this collective action problem as a problem for the banks, in particular, is obscured by the fact that governments have been prepared to step in and save those banks 'too big to fail'. But this does not demonstrate that there is no collective action problem but, at best, that there is a solution at hand. In fact, of course, this 'solution' is unacceptable. In the first place, it constitutes an abandonment of the market mechanism whenever it suits the banks: the so-called 'privatisation of profit' but 'socialisation of debt'. In the second place, it may not actually be a solution, however attractive it might be to the banks in the short term; it might simply be a way of hand-balling the problem onto reserve banks and, thereby, generating a sovereign debt crisis from which everyone, including the banks, may ultimately suffer.

---

[38] Financial Stability Board, Press Release, (Basel, 4 November 2011), available at www.financialstabilityboard.org/press/pr_111104ff.pdf.

The actual solution to this kind of collective action problem and, for that matter, to the executive remuneration collective action problems, is at least in part, an enforced cooperative scheme, as we saw with the tragedy of the commons over-fishing example. In relation to the micro-institutional problem of executive salaries, presumably the cooperative scheme in question could be the enforced removal of bonuses or at least an enforced cap on bonuses, eg, the recent EU proposal of an imposed salary to bonus ratio of a maximum of one to one.[39] As far as the macro-institutional problems are concerned, the cooperative scheme(s) in question would consist of enforceable measures such as capital to lending ratios, disclosure requirements, the segregation of retail from investment functions, and so on. However, enforced cooperative schemes cannot be the whole of the solution because of the above-mentioned problem of the insufficiency of enforcement mechanisms and that of guarding the guards.

The problem of guarding the guards has a specific form in the global banking sector and there is a problem not only with the regulators ('the guards') per se, eg, in respect of the intensity and effectiveness of their enforcement activities, but also with the regulations themselves, and hence with the governments who frame the regulations (the legislatures). It is one of the principal tasks of those who design and oversee the market system, including governments and—under the direction of governments—regulators, to ensure that the ultimate purposes of banks are in fact achieved. However, if one looks, for example, at the objectives of many regulators one typically finds only limited aims, eg, to reduce crime and protect consumers, and procedural concerns, eg, to promote competition and efficiency. There is little or no reference to what I referred to above as the ultimate ends of markets in general, ie, the outcome the invisible hand is supposed to bring about, and of the banking sector in particular. Rather the image of regulation of a free market is one in which regulators are umpires whose sole job is to impartially enforce the rules of the game. But in games, the pleasure of playing aside, there is only one end, namely, winning, and this is an end pursued by the players, not the umpires. But here the analogy between markets and games breaks down; markets, unlike games, have an end beyond 'winning'; they have ultimate, as opposed to proximate, ends. In the case of markets, 'winning', eg, making a profit, is only a proximate end and, as such, a means to a further and larger purpose.

Further, there is the problem of the ambiguous role of national governments and regulators when it comes to global markets, including global financial markets. National governments and their regulators are to some extent partisan, and (understandably) seek to look after the economic interests of their own industries and businesses, including their own financial and banking sector (eg, the 'City' in the case of UK regulators). Moreover, in the absence of a uniform set of global regulations and a single global regulator with real authority, regulators operating at a national level can be played off against one another by multinational corporations.

In the case of the global banking sector, regulation and integrity assurance are ultimately in the hands of national governments. However, national governments—and their regulatory authorities—are not simply umpires, they are also players in the financial—and, more generally, corporate— 'game'. For example, the UK government—and its financial regulator

---

[39] This proposal may be approved in April in the European Parliament; moreover, the ratio can go 2:1. See G Gilligan, 'Drawn to the Light: Will the EU Plan for Capping Bonuses Work?', CLMR Online Portal (14 March 2013), available at www.clmr.unsw.edu.au/article/compliance/internal-risk-management/drawn-light-will-eu-plan-capping-bonuses-work.

(formerly the FSA)[40]—cannot be expected to regulate entirely impartially in the interests of ethical ends and principles, given the substantial interest the UK government has in ensuring that the London-based UK corporate and financial sector retains and increases the benefits accruing to it from global financial markets.

What of Libor manipulation? How is it implicated in all this?

Libor is, as we saw above, itself a cooperative scheme to provide interest rate benchmarks. Evidently, Libor manipulation and, hence, corruption, is implicated both in the 'profligacy stakes' and the 'probity stakes'. In the 'profligacy stakes', the bank traders and Libor submitters are, as we saw above, engaged in corrupt collaboration for the purposes of enriching both individual traders via their increased bonuses and the bank itself in its competition with other banks and, in particular, by way of exploitation of the trust of those who use the Libor benchmarks. In the 'probity stakes' the senior management of the bank in question, eg, Barclays, submitted lower rates than their actual estimates in order to appear to be more safe and secure than was actually the case. Interestingly, here there was a mix of both individual self-interest and collective self-interest in play. On the one hand, it was in Barclays' individual self-interest that its own submissions not be in the upper end of the interest rate submissions scale, since this would signal that it was less safe and secure than other banks. On the other hand, it was in the collective self-interest of all the leading banks, including Barclays, that the Libor rates be low rather than high. As already mentioned, and as the Wheatley Review makes abundantly clear, the Libor cooperative scheme was woefully inadequate in respect of its structure, processes and enforcement mechanism; the administrator (BBA) was conflicted, the submissions were not audited or even systematically based on actual rates, and so on.

Having framed the Libor corruption scandal—and the global banking structure in which it took place—as involving a series of interconnected collective action problems, I now need to turn to the question of the adequacy of the rational choice model standardly used to explicate such problems. I suggest that this model is deficient in principle and to this extent it is an impediment to devising an appropriate institutional response to the Libor corruption scandal and like collective action problems.

The rational choice model assumes rational self-interested individuals in competition with one another. This is fine as far as it goes. However, as Amartya Sen and others have argued, it is far from being the whole of the story.[41] Specifically, it does not leave room for rational individual action performed in the collective self-interest and/or in accordance with socially engendered moral principles and purposes;[42] yet the latter are ubiquitous features of human collective life, including in the economic sphere. Importantly, this one-sided fixation with individually rational self-interested action eliminates the possibility, in

---

[40] At the time of writing, the FSA was in the process of being split into two complementary bodies, the Prudential Regulation Authority, (PRA) and the Financial Conduct Authority (FCA), with their mandates stated as: 'The Prudential Regulation Authority (the PRA), which will be a subsidiary of the Bank of England, will be responsible for promoting the stable and prudent operation of the financial system through regulation of all deposit-taking institutions, insurers and investment banks.... The Financial Conduct Authority (the FCA) will be responsible for regulation of conduct in retail, as well as wholesale, financial markets and the infrastructure that supports those markets. The FCA will also have responsibility for the prudential regulation of firms that do not fall under the PRA's scope.' Financial Services Authority, 'Regulatory Reform: Background', available at www.fsa.gov.uk/about/what/reg_reform/background.

[41] A Sen, *Rationality and Freedom* (Cambridge, Harvard University Press, 2002).

[42] See J Elster 'Rationality and Social Norms' (1989) 8 *Logic, Methodology and Philosophy of Science* 531.

effect, of finding a solution to collective action problems of the kind in question. This can be seen in the failure to find solutions to the problems described above of the 'insufficiency of enforcements mechanisms' and of 'who guards the guards'. As Elinor Ostrum, the Nobel laureate in economics, quipped[43] in relation to the title of Mancur Olsen's famous rational choice monograph, *The Logic of Collective Action*: "It should have been called, '*The Logic of Collective* In*action*,'".

What is needed at this point is the acceptance that individual human agents can, and often do, engage in action-determining reasoning from collective goals and interests to individual actions: collective goals and interests to which members of social groups and organisations are strongly committed. It is important that such acceptance does not imply any commitment to an irreducibly collective agent (or reasoner). Indeed, any such commitment would simply be the application of the rational choice model at the collective rather than the individual level and, as such, would not provide a solution to the problem at hand but simply elevate it to the higher level. Nor does it necessarily imply some ultimate individually rational self-interested reason which motivates the possession of the collective goals and interests in question; rather collective goals and interests may well in many cases function as ground-level explanations of behaviour.

On this view of individual reasoning from common goals and collective interests to their own individual action, what is called for is a conception of an individual human agent qua member of a social group or organisation, eg, qua banker. In short, individuals internalise the collective goals and interests of the social group or organisation to which they belong. It is crucial that these collective goals and interests can, and often do, transcend the role occupant's prior and limited, individually rational self-interested, goals and interests; moreover, the collective goals and interests in question can be, and often are, embraced by the individuals in question on the grounds that they are desirable from an impartial or, at least, collective standpoint. This capacity of individuals to reason from, and act in accordance with, collective goals and interests is not without its problems. For example, the collective goals in question might be inherently morally problematic (eg, those of the Third Reich), or the collective interest of the members of an organisation in question might be at variance with the interests of the wider society (eg, the members of an investment bank with a business model based on constructing and on selling toxic financial products).

Whether or not the members of some organisation internalise the *desirable* ends and principles of an organisation—as opposed to undesirable ones—is in part a matter of institutional culture. Institutional culture is in turn dependent on the extent to which the collective moral responsibility to achieve desirable ends and eschew corrupt practices is embedded in the organisation by way of explicit institutional mechanisms (eg, formal continuing education programs in professional ethics, whistleblower protection schemes, remuneration systems that do not encourage excessive risk taking) and implicit practices (e.g. managers who acknowledge their mistakes, employees who are unafraid to voice their concerns).

If, on the other hand, the prevailing ethos or culture of an organization, and perhaps even ideology of central elements of a sector, downplays desirable institutional goals and other ethical considerations in favour of the pursuit of individual self-interest, then it should hardly surprise when individual self-interest overrides compliance with ethical principles, even ones enshrined in the law. This is no doubt especially the case in a context of high

---

[43] At a presentation she gave at Delft University of Technology in June 2010 at which I was present.

temptation and opportunity, on the one hand, and low risk of detection and conviction, on the other, eg, Libor manipulation by bank traders motivated by large bonuses in a context of an oversight body with a structural conflict of interest.

The point here is not necessarily that the majority of individuals themselves engage in corrupt or unethical practices, but rather that in certain cultural or ideological contexts, they may well refrain from reporting them or otherwise preventing a minority from doing so. Many key elements of integrity systems such as ethics codes, codes of practice, education programs and the like, do not exist, for the most part, to directly prevent or deter the few people who are wrongdoers from doing wrong, but rather to ensure that the many are intolerant of the wrongdoing of the few. In this context, it is perhaps worth pointing out that most fraudsters are detected and convicted as a consequence of the disclosures of their colleagues.

An important potential engine of ethico-cultural education in the context of large, hierarchical organisations driven by commercial interest is the 'professionalization' process at the occupational level.[44] (This is, of course, not to exclude other relevant measures, such as flatter, more democratic, management structures.) Here we need to bear in mind that many occupations are not, and ought not to become, professions in the traditional sense of that term. In such cases the analogue of full-blown professionalisation is, what might be termed, occupational ethical acculturation: a process involving many of the elements of professionalization but stopping short of, in particular, the conferring of professional independence (and corresponding liability) characteristic of the traditional professions.

The process of occupational ethical acculturation in large banking organisations would consist of such things as the establishing an independent occupational association for the occupational group in question, the creation and use of codes of ethics, ongoing professional ethics education, reward and remuneration systems designed to realise the ultimate institutional purposes of the organisation rather than to maximise short-term profits and share prices (or line the pockets of executive managers), establishing of complaints processes conducted by the association, independent (of management) and well-resourced anti-corruption units within the banking organisation itself, appropriate whistle-blowing legislation (including legal protections) and the like. Such measures can assist in the generation and maintenance of a culture of collective moral responsibility and, not the least, one that is intolerant of corruption.

A marked feature of the GFC is the extent to which traditional 'gatekeeper' professions such as lawyers and auditors have been implicated in corruption scandals. Evidently, there is a need to reinvigorate these professions and strengthen their independence of management and commitment to their core professional values. Elsewhere[45] I have set forth a range of measures in this regard, eg, the establishment and use of reputational indices. Another area that might be looked at is the full professionalization of occupations that have not traditionally been professions. Given the nature of some of the problems identified in the banking sector, eg, conflation of lending and de facto selling roles, perhaps there is a need to establish the profession of banker (or at least extend the range of ethical and legal duties). Such a process of professionalization might include, crucially, attaching to (relevant categories of) bankers a fiduciary duty grounded in the vulnerability of the needy, eg, home buyers, and so on.

---

[44] See A Alexandra and S Miller, *Integrity Systems for Occupations*, (Aldershot, Ashgate, 2010).
[45] *ibid*

IV   CONCLUSION

In the first section of this paper I suggested that the Libor scandal, as one among many recent scandals in the global banking sector, is indicative of a problem of systemic institutional corruption. In so doing I have not only analysed the Libor scandal, but proffered analyses of key theoretical notions involved, namely, those of social institutions and mechanisms, institutional corruption and collective moral responsibility, and applied them to the Libor scandal. In the second section I framed the problem of institutional corruption in question as a collective action problem (or set of interconnected such problems) and set forth a novel theoretical conception of how such problems are best understood—a conception at odds with standard rational choice accounts. Further, I argued that the problem of corrupt cultures generated and maintained in large part by such collective action problems needs to be addressed to some extent on its own terms and, in the case of the banking sector by, in particular, processes of professionalization and occupational ethical acculturation.

However, as was made clear in the introduction and first section, addressing the problem of culture will not in and of itself deal with the larger problem of institutional corruption. The micro- and macro-institutional structural problems also need to be addressed if the collective moral responsibility for combating institutional corruption is to be adequately discharged. These problems include the specific micro-institutional conflicts of interest confronting Libor, but also macro-structural aspects of the various collective action problems in play. Evidently, the corruption-inducing collective action problems arising from commercial competition between the investment arms of banks in a market context in which there is an overriding imperative to maximise profit and in which many of these banks are 'too big to fail' looks to be too great to be overcome, other than by substantial institutional redesign. The redesign in question would involve splitting the investment from the retail arm of banks to form two separate institutions[46]—or, at the very least, iron-clad segregation within one institution, if that is possible—and 'downsizing' banks 'too big to fail' and, therefore, 'too big to regulate'.

---

[46] Perhaps in accordance with the so-called Volcker Rule originally within the Dodd-Frank Wall Street Reform and Consumer Protection Act, but subsequently watered down.

Part Three

Regulating Culture in the Financial Sector post-Libor

CHAPTER 7

The World's Most Important Number: How a Web of Skewed Incentives, Broken Hierarchies, and Compliance Cultures Conspired to Undermine Libor

Eric Talley and Samantha Strimling[1]

I INTRODUCTION

To many observers, the recent scandal involving the widespread and recurrent manipulation the London Interbank Offering Rate (Libor) may go down as one of the most significant of and far reaching events associated with the global financial crisis. And for good reason: by most estimates, approximately 350 trillion dollars' worth of global financial contracts—ranging from mortgages to credit cards to corporate debt securities to countless financial derivatives—hinge critically upon Libor to govern the cash flow positions and other obligations of contractual counterparties. Indeed, nearly immediately after its inception a quarter century ago, explosive network externalities allowed Libor quickly to realize the aspirations originally articulated by its creator, the British Bankers Association: To become the 'world's most important number'—the central navigating point for financial markets worldwide.

But with big stakes come big problems. In mid-2012, the British Financial Services Authority (FSA)—the regulatory overseer of first instance for Libor—joined with the Commodity Futures Trading Commission (CFTC) and the US Department of Justice to impose a half-billion dollars' worth of penalties on Barclays plc (one of Libor's core reporting banks) for a systematic and longstanding practice of manipulating its Libor submissions. It has now become clear that that Barclays' detected missteps were but the tip of an immense iceberg. Regulatory penalties of similar magnitudes have since been levied against

[1] Many thanks to participants at the University of British Columbia and UNSW Roundtable Conference on Regulating Culture: Compliance, Risk Management and Accountability in the Aftermath of LIBOR, Sydney Australia, for helpful comments and suggestions. All errors are ours.

two other significant participants, UBS and Royal Bank of Scotland,[2] and more are expected within months. In all, over twenty participant banks are now alleged to be caught up in the scandal, subject either to regulatory enforcement, criminal investigations, civil litigations, or some combination thereof. The scandal is now thought to have been so broad as to involve a set of coordinated practices between banks (not just within them), resulting in additional allegations of racketeering and/or antitrust violations.[3]

And in many ways, the longstanding and widespread nature of the Libor scandal is one of the most perplexing and intriguing things about it: for the June 2012 Barclays revelation surprised virtually no one even remotely familiar with the topic. Libor misreporting was— in effect—an open secret, hiding in plain sight. As far back as April of 2008, more than four years before the Barclays notice (and fully six months before the world's financial markets and economies were thrown into a global tailspin), the *Wall Street Journal* published a prescient investigative study of Libor's informational integrity.[4] In it, authors Carrick Mollencamp and Mark Whitehouse summarized research suggesting that many—and perhaps most—of the then sixteen reporting banks responsible for the North American Libor rate were regularly and systematically misreporting information to the Reuters, the agent charged with fixing the daily benchmark rate on the BBA's behalf. In particular, Mollencamp and Whitehouse noted that throughout early 2008, the spread between the reports that member banks submitted to the BBA on the one hand, and the rate that credit insurance markets implied for the banks on the other, was large and growing larger.

The *Journal* found that the evident degree of misreporting was far from uniform, and varied widely by bank.[5] For some banks, it appeared significant (led by Citibank, at nearly 90 bps). For others, it was relatively modest to non-existent. (Royal Bank of Canada's implied rate, for example, was statistically identical to its Libor reports.)

As can be seen from Figure 1, the reporting behaviour of Barclays, UBS and RBS fit comfortably into the middle of the pack (between 25 and 39 basis points [bps]). Moreover, although one could certainly quibble with the *Journal*'s methodology (such as its reliance on CDS market as a reliable external metric for banks' borrowing costs), most observers understood the *Journal* report, at core, to represent at face value persuasive critique of the integrity of Libor at least as far back as 2008 (if not almost two decades earlier still).[6] Consequently, much of the 'shock' now manifest among commentators and regulators

---

[2] See Financial Services Authority, Final Notice, *Barclays Bank Plc*; FSA Ref. Number: 122702 (London, FSA, 27 June 2012), available at www.fsa.gov.uk/static/pubs/final/barclays-jun12.pdf. In late December 2012, Swiss banking giant UBS became the second entity to be caught up in the scandal, incurring a regulatory penalty of approximately $1.5 billion for a record of Libor and Euribor manipulations similar to Barclays', see Financial Services Authority, Final Notice, *UBS AG*; FSA Ref. Number: 186958 (London, FSA, 19 December 2012), available at www.fsa.gov.uk/static/pubs/final/ubs.pdf. In February 2013, yet a third regulatory penalty of approximately $600 million was levied against the Royal Bank of Scotland; see Financial Services Authority, Final Notice, *Royal Bank of Scotland*; FSA Ref. Number: 121882 (London, FSA, 6 February 2013), available at www.fsa.gov.uk/static/pubs/final/rbs.pdf.

[3] *US v. Alexander et al.*, 12 MAG 3229 (Magistrate Court for SDNY), available at www.justice.gov/iso/opa/resources/7302012121911824496076.pdf.www.justice.gov/ag/Hayes-Tom-and-Darin-Roger-Complaint.pdf.

[4] C Mollencamp and M Whitehouse, 'Study Casts Doubt on Key Rate' *Wall Street Journal* 16 April 2008, WSJ Professional.

[5] 'See figure 1'.

[6] This date itself is arguably a vast underestimate. Some with knowledge of alleged manipulation claim it to be widespread as far back as 1991, see D Keenan, "My thwarted attempt to tell of Libor shenanigans" *Financial Times*, 27 July 2012, available at www.informath.org/media/a72/b1.pdf.

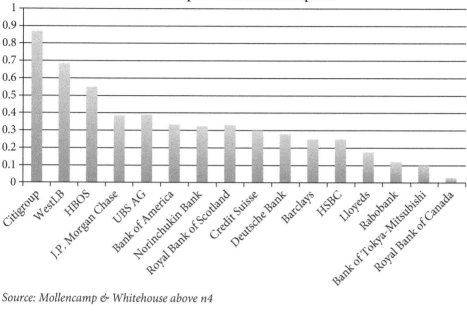

Source: *Mollencamp & Whitehouse above n4*

rings hollow and performative, akin to Captain Renault's professed shock in *Casablanca* that gambling was going on in Rick's Café.

A more intriguing (and somewhat more foreboding) question is why this largely open secret remained uncorrected and unaddressed by banks, regulators and NGOs for such a long period of time, particularly given Libor's critical centrality in financial markets. The ultimate answer to this question is certain to prove complex and multifaceted, and many of the facts needed to answer it are still not known. In this essay, however, we conjecture that at least a portion of the answer lies in a dangerous combination of incentives, hierarchies and organizational cultures among the various players involved. In particular, we consider three communities where these organizational cultures plausibly played a critical role: the BBA, as the monopoly supplier to the 'benchmark' market; the regulatory communities charged with bank oversight; and finally the cultures within the reporting banks and bank holding companies themselves. We close our discussion by floating some hypotheses about how Libor may be most effectively reformed in light of these factors.

II   THE MARKET FOR LIBOR AND THE BBA CULTURE

The most logical starting point of our inquiry is almost certainly at the BBA itself, and the critical role it has played in promulgating, developing and expanding the market demand for benchmark rates. On 13 September 2012, top executives from the 25 BBA member banks—who together compose the BBA's council—voted overwhelmingly to cede control of Libor, for which they have been the official coordinator since the benchmark's inception.

Significantly, this vote was taken one day following the release of the Wheatley Review, which suggested just such an independent spinoff as one of a number of major institutional and technical reforms to Libor.[7] A *Wall Street Journal* article recounting the decision dubbed it 'the biggest change in Libor's 26-year history.'[8] This characterization is almost certainly correct. Until recently, Libor's was a history marked by tremendous consistency, success, and growth. In the mid-1980s, financial contracts generally lacked a unified benchmark rate to govern variable-rate and contingent debt, as well as new financial 'derivatives'—products that had begun to explode in the wake of significant tax and regulatory reforms. As had become clear at the time, the viability of such financial innovations turned critically on the existence of a trustworthy common denominator upon which to frame and peg terms between contract counterparties. Dominant floating rates at the time (such as the US prime rate) were set too sporadically and were too geographically limited to buttress a global market in financial contracting. Thus, the BBA's more organized and systematic daily survey of banks' borrowing costs filled a niche that pre-existing measures could not. Libor's popularity skyrocketed as newer financial products—including interest rate swaps, collateralized assets, credit derivative and risk management contracts—increasingly incorporated the benchmark. The scale and heterogeneity of these new financial contracts strongly incentivized the BBA to expand its array of Libor rates across currencies and tenors (ie, borrowing periods). By the mid-1990s, the BBA began to publish daily Libor rates for ten currencies and for any monthly tenor up to one year.

The increased global popularity of Libor necessitated a number of important but piecemeal changes in response to new market demands globally. Currencies were added and subtracted (especially following the implementation of the euro); banks were added to or removed from each panel as they gained or lost market influence; and, in 1998, the official definition of Libor changed such that each member bank would now be asked explicitly to report its own cost of borrowing rather than that of a hypothetical 'prime' bank.[9]

Nevertheless, by the turn of the century, it had become clear that Libor was far more than a technocratic bookkeeping device: through its popularity, it had become a commoditized 'product'—one that could be bought, sold, purchased and licensed through the BBA. In the mid-2000s, the BBA began to seize on this potential, hiring John Ewan to serve as Libor Manager, to 'put BBA Libor on a secure commercial footing.' Ewan's charge was to develop and enhance appropriable revenue streams from Libor, introducing new products, securing intellectual property rights, and licensing the rights to Libor's use. In a short time Ewan increased the BBA's licensing revenue by an order of magnitude, and he was promoted in 2007 from Libor manager to BBA Director. With the increasing commoditization of Libor, however, came a significant cost: a growing commitment within the BBA organizational culture to refrain from casting doubt (at least in the public eye) on the integrity of the measure, since the exposure of reporting problems could potentially undercut Libor's (and the BBA's) market dominance. One such problem was a persistent lack of depth and liquidity in a number of Libor rates.

---

[7] HM Treasury, 'The Wheatley Review of Libor (Final Report)' (London, September 2012), available at www.hm-treasury.gov.uk/wheatley_review.htm. We discuss the Wheatley Review later in this essay.

[8] D Enrich, 'Banks Warned Not to Leave Libor: U.K. Regulator Seeks to Protect Benchmark Rate as Lenders Threaten to Quit Panel After Scandal' *Wall Street Journal* 13 February 2013, available at online.wsj.com/article/SB10001424127887324432004578302164058534372.html.

[9] BBA LIBOR Ltd, 'Historical Perspective', available at www.bbalibor.com/

Chart C.2: Unsecured deposit transaction by LIBOR contributing banks, per bank in 2011
Inter-bank deposit transaction

	O/N	1w	2w	1m	2m	3m	4m	5m	6m	7m	8m	9m	10m	11m	12m	No. of banks
USD																12
GBP																9
EUR																10
JPY																10
CHF																8
CAD																<7
AUD																<7
NZD																<7
SEK																<7
DKK																<7

low activity   medium-low activity   medium activity   high activity

Notr: This is based on data from a subset of contributing banks, may not be include all relevant transations or be entirely representative for all currencies.

Source: Oliver Wyman, Bank of England and Wheatley Review calculations

As seen in Figure 2 even though Libor rate reports are harvested across 150 different currencies/tenor combinations, the modal pattern of unsecured deposit transactions among banks has been much narrower, concentrating heavily on less than a dozen (involving US dollar, pound sterling and euro transactions of three months' duration or less). As a result, contracts pegged against the less focal Libor products regularly depended on a much thinner and more volatile set of underlying data. Though these problems were flagged repeatedly by external observers, little was done within the BBA to address them.

The protective concern BBA had over the public perception of Libor is apparent from more than circumstantial evidence, however. Shortly after the *Wall Street Journal*'s investigative 2008 report was published, the BBA convened a meeting of its Foreign Exchange & Money Markets Committee, whose principal task is to make policy decisions about Libor. The press accounts of their meeting suggest an organization that was as concerned as much (or more) with the measure's prospective vitality as it was with its accuracy:

> The committee is made up of banking-industry officials whose names and affiliations the BBA won't disclose. The meeting's agenda was how to improve Libor. 'We need to adopt a minimal approach,' said one executive, identified in a transcript as Representative 2 of 'Bank B.' 'Too big a change would cause an explosive reaction.' Another bank representative argued that the BBA should deal with banks that report artificially low data 'by just picking up the phone. . .and have a conversation behind closed doors.' The transcript indicates that other bank representatives agreed.[10]

Some months later, Angela Knight, then the BBA's chief executive, approached both the Bank of England and the Federal Reserve Bank of New York to solicit their assistance with oversight of Libor. Both demurred (for reasons we explore in greater depth below).

---

[10] D Enrich and M Colchester, 'Before Scandal, Clash Over Control of Libor' *Wall Street Journal* 11 September 2012, C1.

Nevertheless, the BBA chose to maintain its oversight and support of the rate even after its flaws were noted both by its chief executive and two significant World Bank regulators, as well as the business press.[11] Many involved in the discussions have implied that the BBA made this choice largely to retain control of the revenue streams it was earning (and continues to earn) through Libor.[12] While perhaps a rational short-term strategic calculation for the BBA itself, this decision had major implications for many others not at the table, and arguably catalysed a compliance environment at the BBA that grew increasingly tolerant of the rate's flagging credibility.

III   REGULATORY CULTURE

A second important potential contributor to the culture of non-compliance concerns the nature and evolution of bank regulation itself. Two important aspects of the regulatory landscape began to shift dramatically at the turn of the twenty-first century. The first was meta-regulatory: as a result of the mega-merger between Citibank and Travelers Insurance in 1998 (and the facilitating repeal of the Glass-Steagall Act months later), the 65-year-old regulatory boundaries that had long separated commercial banks, investment banks, and insurance companies substantially disappeared. For the first time since the Great Depression, commercial bank holding companies (BHCs) could (through their subsidiaries) explore new activities in proprietary securities trading, underwriting, financial derivatives, and securities distribution, largely free from the regulatory firewalls that had once constrained them. This event set into motion a series of deregulatory movements within the US—changes that had global implications as well.

From this meta-regulatory shift emanated a micro-regulatory shift: the increased scope of BHC operations led to a problem of coordinating 'multiple monitors' within jurisdictions. With commercial BHCs becoming heterogeneous in scope, the activities of their subsidiaries began to fall increasingly under a patchwork of regulatory overseers, ranging (within the US) from the Fed, to the Federal Deposit Insurance Corporation (FDIC), to the Securities and Exchange Commission (SEC), to the CFTC, to various state and national insurance and market regulators. Although the domains and duties of each of these regulators were distinct (at least in theory), the point where each domain left off and picked up was—at best—an opaque matter for speculation. Until the Dodd-Frank Act of 2010, virtually no US regulatory entity exercised broad oversight of how different regulatory domains interact within a particular BHC (eg, between the depository accounts and the trading desk). This regulatory oversight problem was especially pronounced where the various arenas of BHC activity intersected: and at the core of this intersection was fixing of benchmark

---

[11]   Ibid.

[12]   As the fortunes of Libor began to falter, in 2009 the BBA conveyed its activities into a new legal entity, BBA LIBOR, Ltd. According to at least one person involved in the decision, the BBA had the dual goals of shielding itself from prospective liability, as well as the (arguably) more altruistic goal of improving Libor's governance through an independent board. While the first goal may well have succeeded (though that remains to be seen), the second likely did not: a majority of the nine 'independent' Board of Directors were BBA executives, including Ewan and Knight. Marcus Agius, the chair of the Barclays board, also had a dual role as chairman of the BBA board. See Enrich and Colchester, above n10.

rates. (As we shall see, this regulatory lacuna opened up significant returns for the BHC that can coordinate the efforts of these divisions).

In the years preceding the financial crisis, regulators in the US offloaded much of their oversight onto others, especially as their oversight targets became larger, more sophisticated, and more complex. This trend was perhaps most publicly visible at the SEC, where then-Commissioner Cox occupied most of the first half of the 2000s pushing for increased 'self-regulation' of reporting firms. However, a qualitatively similar trend took hold elsewhere, such as in commodities/derivatives regulation and bank supervision (where capital adequacy requirements and risk weighting took on new dimensions that were unfamiliar to traditional forms of supervisory oversight).

To be sure, the 'multiple monitors' problem was likely the most prevalent within the United States. Through much of this same period of time, the Financial Services Authority (FSA) was charged with overseeing the entire British financial system. And, while less centralized than the British system, the Australian regulatory framework is divided into only two agencies with clearly defined domains: the Australian Securities and Investments Commission (ASIC) and the Reserve Bank of Australia (RBA), which assess real-time trading and licensed clearing and settlement facilities, respectively.[13] However, the multinational character of many major banks—eg, Barclays, a British bank, had sufficiently strong market presence to submit rates for every Libor currency calculated—appears to have left many BHCs susceptible to US regulatory frameworks, notwithstanding the regulatory structures of their home countries.

In the months and years following the advent of the crisis, a different type of regulatory collective action problem arguably took hold: one of practical damage control, self-preservation and sporadic finger-pointing through litigation. In addition to the recent action against Barclays, the total number of banks issued a subpoena related to the Libor investigation has since grown to nearly twenty.[14] One reason for action directed at individual banks may be the simple practical difficulty of ex ante regulation versus ex post litigation, particularly in an environment that is a state of near-continuous flux. Relatedly, even within the realm of ex post litigation, actions against individual banks are mechanistically far more feasible than are broad indictments or ex ante regulatory pronouncements affecting an entire industry (even if the industry is in some way jointly 'culpable'). Virtually all of the compelling probative evidence against Barclays, for example, consists (as described below) of inculpating emails, office memoranda, and other correspondence. Finally, many types of enforcement action are also plausibly motivated (at least in part) by careerist norms among enforcement regulators. It is reasonable to assume that enforcement officials aspire to participate in high profile cases, either to ascend internal promotion ladders or to perfect an exit option to private industry. For regulators with such professional aspirations, significant financial scandals are an ideal target of opportunity. As the underlying behaviour of regulated firms becomes more multifaceted and complex, regulators and regulatory culture naturally tend to substitute away from (difficult) ex ante pronouncements and towards (easier) ex post litigation.[15]

---

[13] ASX Group, 'Regulatory Framework', available at www.asxgroup.com.au/regulatory-framework.htm.

[14] R. Albergotti and J. Eaglesham, '9 More Banks Subpoenaed Over Libor', *Wall Street Journal*, (25 October 2012), available at http://online.wsj.com/article/SB10001424052970203897404578079413742864842.html.

[15] See eg, Project on Government Oversight (POGO), 'Revolving Regulators: SEC Faces Ethic Challenges with Revolving Door' (Washington DC, Pogo, 2011), available at: www.pogo.org/our-work/reports/2011/fo-fra-20110513.html.

IV   BANKING CULTURE

A final, somewhat more direct source of non-compliance culture was the reporting banks themselves. Although the proposition that banks will manage themselves to maximize profits is hardly a novel one, it gained new traction and urgency by the beginning of the twenty-first century, when their business prospects began to expand as a result the significant loosening of regulatory oversight described above, and their enhanced scope and reach.

Accordingly, two discrete 'phases' of misreporting are described and addressed in the FSA's recent enforcement notices. The first occurred largely before mid-2007, and involved a pattern or practice where a bank would 'shade up' or 'shade down' its reported cost of capital in order to distort resulting Libor to benefit the bank's current derivative positions. For example, if Bank X currently were a net holder of 'floating' positions in Libor-denominated interest-rate swaps, these derivatives' positions would benefit from increases in the posted Libor rate, and the bank could make a profit by 'shading up' its reported cost of debt capital to the BBA/Reuters, likely nudging the average along with it. If, on the other hand, Bank X were a net 'fixed' position holder, it would have an incentive to shade down its position.

In the second phase (which reached maturity around the same time as the *Wall Street Journal* investigation described above) banks are alleged to have systematically reported their cost of debt so as to dampen—somewhat ironically—public media coverage and/or regulatory scrutiny. This latter incentive is thought to have become particularly prominent beginning in late 2007, as banks allegedly began to worry that reporting a high cost of debt capital might induce media, investors, clients and (ultimately) regulators to infer that they were in financial distress, possibly inviting heavy scrutiny or even nationalization.

The first phase of the Libor misreporting scandal described above is notable because it highlights the conflict of interest present within a bank, due to difference in the interests of the fixings submitters versus those of the proprietary trading desk at the bank. The Barclays notice is replete with direct evidence suggesting the deliberate nature of the misreporting. For example, in one email message, a fixings agent wrote, 'I am going 90 altho 91 is what I should be posting,' apparently to satisfy demands from the trading desk.[16] While it is possible the submitters were financially motivated by the belief that profits on Barclays' trading positions would be distributed across the firm, a more plausible theory is that Barclays (and possibly other banks) gave its imprimatur to a culture of back-scratching and support to its highest margin units—particularly its proprietary trading desk. The FSA cites numerous examples of informal entreaties from traders to fixings submitters, such as the following 7 April 2006 missive: 'If it's not too late low 1m and 3m would be nice, but please feel free to say 'no'. . . . Coffees will be coming your way either way, just to say thank you for your help in the past few weeks.'[17]

The Barclays submitters' apparent susceptibility to such pleas may indicate a larger power relationship within the firm, with traders exerting undue influence. For example, it has long been maintained[18] that judgements of traders at large investment banks are given undue confidence due to the magnitude of their decisions, which in turn allows traders to assume and assert their own acumen with little public notice. Looking to a 2003 statement made by former Bear Stern's CEO, Jimmy Cayne, boasting of Bear's achievements, Gladwell

---

[16] Financial Services Authority, *Barclays,* above n1 at 12.

[17] ibid at 13.

[18] See, for example, M Gladwell, 'Cocksure,' *The New Yorker, 27 July 2009* < http://www.newyorker.com/reporting/2009/07/27/090727fa_fact_gladwell>.

writes: 'With the benefit of hindsight, Cayne's words read like the purest hubris. But in 2003 they would have seemed banal. These are the kinds of things that bankers say. . .investment banks are able to borrow billions of dollars and make huge trades because, at the end of the day, their counterparties believe they are capable of making good on their promises.'[19]

To be sure, organizational cultures and incentives almost certainly vary across banks, particularly between investment banks and commercial banks with depository activities. But given the ever-eroding boundaries between the categories, the freewheeling nature of traders has arguably become a more significant factor at all banks. It is notable that some of the very institutions at the centre of the current Libor storm have also recently faced embarrassing lapses in oversight of their trading desks. Consider Kweku Abdoli, a UBS trader notoriously convicted on two counts of fraud after losing $2.3 billion of the bank's capital in 2011. Abdoli was, at the age of 26, handed responsibility over a $50 billion balance sheet. At roughly the same time, Oswald Grübel was appointed CEO of UBS, and soon increased risk limits at the ETF desk where Abdoli worked, despite the continuance of weak punishment for excessive risk-taking. (Though his maximum exposure climbed to $12 billion, Abdoli received only one internal warning about his practices prior to his arrest.)[20] Abdoli's case—including its catastrophic ending—may more than idiosyncratic; it also may be emblematic of widespread interbank culture even at the very same commercial banks who participated in Libor. Relatively inexperienced traders were routinely trusted to manage vast sums of investment capital and were expected to turn quarterly profits on a routine basis. It should not be surprising that such traders would have a natural inclination to turn to others in their networks (both within their banks and without) to assist their efforts.

Although the second phase of the Libor scandal bears a much smaller mark of intrabank conflicts of interest, the first phase almost certainly greased the wheels for a culture of industry-wide misreporting that was easy for banks to leverage. The contacts forged among (and especially between) fixings agents and trading desks–across multiple reporting banks– during the first phase no doubt proved fruitful in the second, where virtually all banks had identical agendas: to avoid public scrutiny.

V   THE UNCERTAIN PATH AHEAD

As suggested above, the underlying root causes of the Libor scandal are likely complex and multifaceted. Some (if not most) are as yet unknown. Consequently, the prudent re-design of Libor may well constitute one of the most vexing international regulatory problems of the next half-decade. At present, there is but one point of general consensus—as noted in the Wheatley Review: robust and reliable benchmark rates are critical to the efficient operation of capital markets, more so now than ever. Indeed, if anything the current push towards mandatory 'clearinghouses' for derivatives redoubles the importance of focal benchmark reference rates.[21] We concur with Wheatley that a core benchmark reference rate is a phenomenon that is here to stay—whether in the guise of Libor or something else.

---

[19] Ibid.

[20] 'The Education of Kweku Abdoli,' *The Economist*, 24 November 2012, available at www.economist.com/news/finance-and-economics/21567134-swiss-bank-also-has-much-learn-education-kweku-adoboli.

[21] AJ Levitin, 'The Tenuous Case for Derivatives Clearinghouses' (2013) 101 *Georgetown Law Journal* 445.

Beyond that, however, countess idiosyncratic proposals have emerged, with little consensus around them. We comment below on some of the principal candidates, offering additional constructive suggestions when appropriate.[22] One set of proposals centres on systemic risk in general, and specifically the reintroduction of regulatory firewalls into large BHCs. The so-called Volcker Rule in the Dodd-Frank Act within the United States, for example, was originally developed to constrain the proprietary trading of commercial banks, and in its final form it may go some distance in addressing the intra-bank agency and influence costs described above, and which plausibly contributed to the crisis. However, these sorts of reforms do little to address many of the other drivers of current crisis in a targeted way—such as the second wave of the crisis (where trading profits were not the driving force), or widespread collaboration that appears to have taken place between reporting banks, not within them. (Moreover, the emerging version of the Volcker Rule now appears to incorporate a plethora of exceptions and variances that arguably have left it toothless.)[23]

The Wheatley Review also proposes retaining the Libor fixings process in a privately administered entity, but subjecting its participants and administrators to the 'sticks' of ex ante regulatory oversight by the FSA and/or others, along with enhanced ex post enforcement oversight.[24] While this proposal has intuitive appeal, it faces at least two serious obstacles as well. First, it places tremendous confidence (and imposes a significant burden) on the same regulators and courts that for the good part of two decades turned a blind eye to a well-known and industry-wide pattern of misreporting. It is not clear whether such regulatory and quasi-regulatory actors will have the motivation and expertise to enforce the new regime effectively.

Second, even if effective regulation/enforcement were credible, the Wheatley proposal imposes both new upfront regulatory compliance costs and new back-end litigation exposure on a group of banks who, as of now, voluntarily participate in the Libor fixings process. The costs the proposal would visit upon reporting banks—costs avoided by non-participant banks or any of the other financial participants who use Libor—seem likely to induce many banks to consider disassociating from Libor. Indeed, over the last month, several significant participants (including Rabobank and BNP Paribas) have fallen into heated disputes with the FSA about their plans to leave the survey,[25] and a number of Euribor (a distant European cousin of Libor) participants have already dissociated. While similar departures from Libor have (for now) been arrested, it is hard to expect the current ceasefire to persist so long as banks are neither (a) required by law to participate, nor (b) remunerated for their participation.

Legal compulsion seems an unlikely long-term solution, since it would put participating banks at a long-term competitive disadvantage to non-participants. Designing financial and regulatory 'carrots' for participation is—in our view—a task that deserves considerably more attention than it has thus far garnered.[26] As a first start, we would propose that along

---

[22]   The discussion below draws on the more technical analysis in E Talley, 'Building a Better LIBOR: Lessons from Mechanism Design' (2013) *UC Berkeley Working Paper.*

[23]   See eg, KD Krawiec, 'Don't "Screw Joe the Plummer": The Sausage-Making of Financial Reform' (2012) (Working Paper), available at scholarship.law.duke.edu/faculty_scholarship/2445.

[24]   HM Treasury, above n8 at 16.

[25]   Enrich, above n9.

[26]   More precisely, the Wheatley Review suggests that banks be required to submit to Libor as a condition for participation in the market, but it ultimately deems compelled participation unnecessary at this stage, see HM Treasury, above n8.

with enhanced exposure to regulatory and legal costs, Libor participants could (and should) be compensated for their submissions, in the form of cash payments, preferred access to central bank capital, or something equivalent. The terms of compensation, moreover, could be designed to fluctuate in an incentive-compatible manner contingent on participants' individual market significance and the deviation in their reports from other metrics (such as market indicatives and others' reports).

In addition, regulators would do well to consider redesigning the way that Libor rates are assembled once reports are received. Currently, Libor and Euribor rates are similarly computed using the arithmetic mean of the individual reports that remain after 'trimming' outliers (a population corresponding roughly to the middle quartiles of survey respondents). To be sure, such an approach has some notable advantages—particularly insofar as it eliminates the marginal incentive of a known outlier reporter to issue an extreme report.[27] By the same token, the current protocols fail in a number of important respects. First, they do not tend to value-weight the reporting entities, and thus even the reports of a principal market participant—if an outlier—would tend to have no effect on announced rates. Second, and relatedly, the current approach of truncating outliers tends to enhance the influence of reporting entities that survive truncation. A promising alternative might be the design of a smoother 'weighted-average' system, where a reporting entity's weight might depend on both its overall market share and its reports' alignment with that of others and/ or calibrating data.[28]

A related approach (and one that could be combined with greater oversight, as described above) would be to marshal more observable market rates from government bonds, swap markets, or commercial paper, as a substitute for—or a partial check on—reported bank borrowing rates.[29] This seems a sensible direction in which to move, given that just such an approach was used by the *Wall Street Journal* that first publicly revealed the discrepancies in Libor reporting as noted above. A key concern for this market-driven approach, however, is that any candidate market indicative of itself may stray from core fundamentals, or may reflect characteristics that go beyond the credit-worthiness of the banks (a factor that may matter significantly to some investors). For example, as the recent financial crisis has demonstrated, swap markets and short-term credit markets are themselves susceptible to systemic liquidity and pricing risks. Moreover, government bonds can also be affected by such systemic risks, as investors flock to the apparent safety of treasuries in times of crisis, driving down treasury yields to artificially low levels. Thus, identifying the reliability and likely biases among various market indicatives—while in generally a laudable idea—is also likely to prove extremely challenging for all but a few tenor/currency combinations. At best, such market measures provide a sensible means to audit and test bank reports; they cannot serve as a reliable substitute for such reports.

Finally, the Wheatley Review recommends 'warehousing' the borrowing costs reported by individual banks away from public view for a defined period after their submission, currently proposed as three months.[30] The evident rationale behind such a proposal is two-fold.

---

[27] For example, an already entity reporting the lowest cost of borrowing in the survey has no incentive to exaggerate its report even further, since its report will be excluded from the reported average.

[28] Both the financial terms of Libor participation as well as the way the index is computed can substitute for some of the otherwise heavy burden that regulatory intervention would otherwise occupy.

[29] HM Treasury, above n8 at 25.

[30] ibid at 38.

First, it will theoretically prevent member banks from strategically engineering their submissions to manipulate the average calculation or exclude themselves from it. Second, it may protect banks truthfully disclosing a high cost of borrowing from the speculations of an overeager press. On the first point, we are sceptical that the warehousing proposal will prevent banks from expending efforts to determine statistically whether and when their reports are likely to influence movements in the index; consequently, the warehousing efforts may be ineffectual. Reporting banks already have access to a wealth of information, including the terms of their own loads to other reporting banks. As for the second point, to the extent that an improved Libor also would cultivate and incorporate observable market rates (such as swap market rates) to benchmark accuracy, significant information will already be available to broader market participants about each bank that, arbitrageurs, the press, regulators, politicians or any other concerned party can use as a proxy.

VI   CONCLUSION

In the end, while this debate is far closer to the starting gate than the finish line, three issues appear clear. First, as noted above, it seems inevitable that Libor in some form (or a close successor) will continue to play a critical role in financial contracting. Financial derivatives markets remain vitally important to the global economy, and their operation turns critically on a credible market benchmark. Second, the imposition of liability exposure and regulatory costs—absent some form of compensation—is unlikely to be a tenable long-term strategy. Finally, whatever long-term solution we craft will likely have to contend with a cascade of civil actions rooted in antitrust, securities fraud, and civil racketeering charges. A prudent regulatory re-design must contend with this significant source of exposure, both for the current scandal and ones down the road—a road whose ultimate destination remains stubbornly opaque.

CHAPTER 8

The Future Role and Power of the Bank of England

Andrew Campbell and Judith Dahlgreen

I   INTRODUCTION

This chapter examines the hugely increased power and extended role given to the Bank of England and its Governor by the Financial Services Act 2012, particularly in relation to prudential supervision of large banks and investment firms and responsibility for controlling systemic risk and creating financial stability in the United Kingdom.[1] The competing objectives and structural complexity inherent in these tasks are contrasted with the relative simplicity of the setting of interest rates by the Monetary Policy Committee of the Bank of England. While we now know what the role of the Bank of England will be in the short-term, the position is less clear on a longer term view. Proposals from the European Commission for a European banking union, coupled with proposals for new EU legislation will inevitably have an impact on the future role of the Bank of England, either directly or indirectly. In addition to the European initiatives, events of a political nature are taking place within the UK that could also have an impact on the future role of the central bank.

The chapter is comprised of five separate sections and a conclusion. The first part considers the historical role of the Bank of England (referred to here as the Bank) as lender to government at the heart of the city of London, monitoring not probity or integrity but creditworthiness so as to protect its own balance sheet. The second part reviews its role as licensor and then supervisor of banks from 1979 and the removal of those responsibilities and addition of monetary policy at the end of the twentieth century. Also addressed is the gradual need to accommodate membership of an area of free movement of financial services and capital: the European Union.

The third part examines the Bank of England's uncertain position under the tripartite structure in the banking crisis of 2007–2009, coupled with the growing recognition, internationally, of the key tasks of maintaining payment systems, securing financial stability and ensuring credit intermediation rather than the sustenance of individual banks as solvent entities.

---

[1] Hereafter 'UK'.

The fourth part analyses the Bank's position under the very different replacement structure of control established by the Financial Services Act 2012. This gives the Bank new and extremely broad responsibilities and huge obligations to coordinate and interact with a wide variety of national, European and international bodies. The Bank must also have regard to proposals to separate retail from investment banking and public and political revulsion at the lack of social utility and excessive personal profitability generated in twenty-first century UK banking. The fifth part considers the influences on the role of the Bank which could have a significant impact on its role in the future. In particular, developments at the EU level are examined as well as some developments closer to home.

There are many other topics which could be discussed in detail. For example, the Bank's roles in relation to Libor, the Basel standards, the provision of emergency liquidity financing[2] and bank insolvency are all critical to the national economy (and are therefore also of political significance) and relevant to the integrity of the UK banking marketplace. Unfortunately, space does not permit these matters to be covered here.

II   LENDER TO GOVERNMENT

From its establishment by Royal Charter in 1694, the Bank of England grew into a formidable institution that gradually developed from being a joint stock bank that was formed to assist in raising finance for a war against France to become the central bank for the United Kingdom, and arguably into the most respected central bank of them all.[3] Beginning as banker, or perhaps lender is a more appropriate term, to the government, it evolved a thriving business of discounting bills and notes and lending on terms to other banks and commercial companies.[4] It was also responsible for a sound currency and the maintenance of reserves to back it up. This happened gradually, but there is no doubt that by the end of the nineteenth century, it was accepted as the central bank of the United Kingdom mainly by virtue of its de facto control of credit lines.[5] It had become a powerful institution and was able to exercise a significant degree of control over the banks operating in the UK. It had no formal powers granted by the state and it operated very much on the basis of expecting banks to act with integrity. 'My word is my bond' was the expectation within the banking system and the Bank of England relied on the expected truthfulness of the words of those who owned and managed banks.[6] Of course, in those earlier, and much less complex, times the banking families did tend to know each other and, to a large extent, move within the same social circles, attend the same schools and so on.[7] That, in itself allowed the Bank of

---

[2]   The Bank's role as lender of last resort is discussed briefly in section 2.

[3]   See ch 2, entitled 'The Bank' in JK Galbraith, *Money: Whence it Came, Where it Went* (London, Penguin, 1976).

[4]   See generally R Roberts and D Kynaston (eds), *The Bank of England: Money, Power and Influence 1694–1994* (Oxford, Oxford University Press, 1995).

[5]   For example, in 1772 the Bank refused generous assistance to the Scottish Ayr Bank which in consequence collapsed into insolvency, taking many of its customers with it.

[6]   It would be naïve to think that there were no liars and cheats within the banking establishment in those simpler times but it does appear to be the case that this approach worked surprisingly well.

[7]   Writing in 1873, Walter Bagehot was generally highly complimentary about the quality of management at the Bank. See ch 8 of W Bagehot *Lombard Street* (London, Henry S King and Co., 1873).

England to automatically have a large amount of intelligence about the commercial and merchant banks and those who controlled them. It also made it easier to exercise influence over how they behaved.[8]

In addition to acting as lender to the Government, central banks perform a number of key functions but this chapter is concerned primarily with the regulation of the banking sector and the emerging responsibility for financial stability. However, a major part of the role of a central bank is to provide 'lender of last resort' financing.[9] This involves the central bank providing liquidity to banks that are experiencing temporary liquidity problems but that are still considered to be solvent. To expect a central bank to provide such financial assistance without having detailed knowledge about the bank receiving financial support would be misguided. Accordingly, one of the reasons[10] why the Bank of England assumed the role of supervising regulator, albeit on the basis of an extremely light touch, is because it provided liquidity financing, where appropriate and initially through discounting bills, to the banks in the United Kingdom.[11] Without having reliable information on any bank seeking assistance, the Bank of England would have been taking a significant, and arguably unjustifiable, risk in providing finance. So this function of the central bank was a major driver in the Bank of England becoming the de facto regulator and supervisor of credit institutions in the UK. It is very interesting that this development took place without any formal powers being granted to the Bank of England by legislation and, as will be seen below, it was not until 1979 that the responsibility for the regulation and supervision of UK banks by the Bank of England was actually set out in statute.[12] By the 1970s, the Bank of England had undoubtedly become the de facto regulator and supervisor of British banks and it is often said that it did this by way of using 'moral suasion'.[13] Prior to the 1970s, it seems that the Bank of England used an extremely light touch in this respect. Banks and other deposit-takers were not subject to a licensing process[14] and no form of deposit insurance was available to those who deposited their money in these institutions. The secondary banking crisis of the early 1970s highlighted the lack of formal supervision of deposit-taking institutions in the UK and there was significant criticism by many of the approach of the Bank of England. Much of this was unfair as the central bank neither had the official power to regulate and supervise, nor did it have resources allocated to it for this purpose. However, the criticisms continued.

---

[8] See generally the discussion in E Hennessy, 'The Governors, Directors and Management of the Bank of England' in R Roberts and D Kynaston, above n4.

[9] Also known as emergency liquidity financing.

[10] This is clearly not the only reason, but for the purposes of this discussion is the one which concerns us.

[11] For a detailed discussion of the theory and practice of the Bank of England's approach to its role as 'lender of last resort,' see Bagehot, above n7. For a more up-to-date account, see A Campbell and R Lastra, 'Revisiting the Lender of Last Resort' (2009) 24(3) *Banking and Finance Law Review* 453.

[12] By the Banking Act 1979. The Bank of England Act 1946 s4(3) contained some provisions which could have been used to direct banks if authorised by the Treasury in certain activities but these do not appear ever to have been used.

[13] See, for example, Hadjiemmanuil who notes that in the UK "banking business was formally unregulated. . . . [U]p through the 1970s governmental control was ensured and practiced through a combination of selective legal restrictions on certain banking activities and the Bank of England's de facto control over the structure and operation of banking markets". C Hadjiemannuil *Banking Regulation and the Bank of England* (Lloyd's Of London Press and Centre for Commercial Legal Studies, Queen Mary, London, 1996) 1.

[14] This was the norm in most developed countries by then. In the United States, for example, banks have been subject to licensing since the Banking Act of 1933.

The situation started to change during the 1970s. The secondary banking crisis led to calls for a more formal approach to supervision and the proposed banking directive from the EEC[15] would inevitably lead to the introduction of legislation which would require the licensing of deposit-taking institutions in the United Kingdom. Change had become unavoidable.

Interestingly, when Shaw's book *The Theory and Principles of Central Banking*[16] was published in 1930, it contained neither the word 'regulation' nor 'supervision'. The regulation and supervision of the banking sector was clearly not considered a function of a central bank at that time, at least in the United Kingdom. Even by the 1950s, according to Capie, 'banking supervision...was distinctly low-key–to the point of invisibility'.[17] Of course, it has to be noted that the financial system in the United Kingdom had experienced a long period of stability, which meant that the issue of bank supervision was not high on the agenda. Perhaps the reason for this was that the Bank of England's approach during this period was a major factor in this stability. That, however, would simply be conjecture on our part. However, Pringle has suggested that the Bank of England had, despite the informal methods used, gained the reputation for being the best banking regulator in the world.[18]

Whether or not this extremely informal approach to supervision was the best approach is a moot point, but this became largely irrelevant in the 1970s because of the two specific developments already referred to briefly; the secondary banking crisis[19] and the proposed European Directive. The problems at the secondary banks led many to question the appropriateness of the Bank of England's approach to supervision, which effectively allowed banks to operate on an unlicensed basis. But this did not really matter as the European developments would make licensing of deposit-taking institutions mandatory in any event. The result of all this was the Banking Act 1979 which came into force before the year was out. For the first time in the UK the supervision of banks had been put on a statutory footing and the responsibility for undertaking this had been given to the Bank of England.

Two extremely significant events for the Bank of England occurred between late 1979 and May 1997 when a new Labour Government was elected. The first of these was the spectacular collapse of the Bank of Commerce and Credit International in July 1991[20] and

---

[15] This eventually became the Council Directive of 17 December 1977 on the coordination of laws, regulations and administrative provisions relating to the taking-up and pursuit of the business of credit institutions, 77/780/EEC known as the First Banking Directive.

[16] WA Shaw, *The Theory and Principles of Central Banking* (London, Pitman, 1930).

[17] F. Capie *The Bank of England: 1950s to 1979* (Cambridge, Cambridge University Press, 2010) 62. Professor Forest Capie was invited to write the history of the Bank of England during this period by the Governor Sir Mervyn King. He was given access to materials which would otherwise not have been available and this allowed him to produce a fascinating and detailed account inter alia of the approach of the officers of the Bank of England to the issue of regulation and supervision. Chapter 12 is entitled 'Banking Supervision' and provides a detailed account of the events of the period between the 1950s and 1979 when the legislation giving the Bank of England the task of supervising banks in the UK came into force.

[18] R Pringle 'The Bank Of England and Central Bank Corporation: 1970–1994' in R Roberts and D Kynaston (eds) above n4.

[19] The Bank of England had to organise a support operation when a number of so-called 'secondary banks' found themselves in financial difficulties in the early 1970s. For further information on this, see A Campbell & P Cartwright, *Banks in Crisis: The Legal Response* (Aldershot, Ashgate, 2002) 4.

[20] See "Report of the Inquiry into the Supervision of the Bank of Credit and Commerce International" (1992) HC 192. Technically BCCI was a Luxembourg bank but in reality its operations were controlled from its London office. The Bank of England's insistence that it was for the Luxembourg authorities to supervise the bank was the

the second was the collapse of Barings Bank in 1995. The Bank of England was severely criticised for its alleged mishandling of both of these. In particular, the scathing criticism from the Monetary Authority of Singapore for its supervision of Barings Bank was very damaging to its reputation as an effective supervisor.[21]

One of the priorities of the new Labour Government was to move responsibility for the supervision of banks to the newly created Financial Services Authority. The Bank of England's formal role as banking supervisor had been relatively short-lived, lasting just over twenty years. This, however, is not the end of the story, as the new regulator and supervisor was considered to be ineffective during the banking crisis of 2008 onwards, and the further reforms that are taking place are discussed in detail below. Once again, the Bank of England will have overall responsibility for the regulation and supervision of banking in the UK.

III AUTHORISOR AND SUPERVISOR

The Banking Act of 1979 provided that no bank could operate as a deposit-taker unless it was a recognised bank[22] or a licensed institution.[23] It was the Bank of England alone that had the power to grant this status and remove it or impose conditions on it if it thought fit. No specific obligation was imposed on the Bank to monitor banks once recognised or licensed.[24] The Act provided a broad procedure for applying for authorisation specifying that the Bank could require whatever information it considered necessary and that the procedure could differ between applicants. The legislation was short and lacking detail compared to today's standards. The primary test was whether the institution enjoyed high standing and repute in the financial community and whether its net assets were commensurate with the nature of its intended scale of operations. The focus on reputation within a tight City of London community is noteworthy. This was an approach that the Bank of England saw as appropriate, allowing it maximum discretion to take account of whatever it thought fit. It was patently not a 'legal' process, but an assessment of credit quality and integrity based on whether others would do business with it. The reliance on information provided by the relevant bank's directors is also significant. This was essentially the beginning of a risk-based approach that placed the onus on the applicant bank to supply appropriate information, in contrast to a more intrusive bank examiner model. The Bank of England was then acting as gatekeeper for entrants to a small London market place which relied on face to face meetings and paper based transactions. In relation to capital adequacy, it was entirely dependent on the honesty of applicant bank directors as to their intended plans for their bank. Interestingly even in 1979, the Act contained 'passporting' type provisions in that the Bank had power to authorise banks whose principal place of business was

subject of much criticism, especially in the United States. The US authorities had become agitated by the lack of action by the Bank of England.

[21] The Monetary Authority of Singapore was strongly critical of the Bank of England's supervision of Barings Bank. See *A New Approach to Regulating and Developing Singapore's Financial Sector* (Singapore, Monetary Authority of Singapore, 1997). See also the Board of Banking Supervision, *Report of the Board of Banking Supervision Inquiry into the Circumstances of the Collapse of Barings* (London, Bank of England, 18 July 1995).

[22] A recognised bank was a larger entity offering a full range of banking services and with a larger capital base.

[23] A more specialised entity with a smaller capital base.

[24] s1(1) Banking Act 1979.

overseas on the basis that it was satisfied with the supervision provided by the overseas regulator. This was discretionary, not mandatory, so at this stage there was a clear opportunity for the Bank to exclude a deposit taker even where it was lawfully undertaking business elsewhere in Europe (or further afield.) Crucially the Bank was given very broad powers to restrict or revoke the authorisation[25] and this power gave it a de facto power of supervision. The obligations on the authorised banks were very scant indeed: making available audited accounts and informing the bank of changes in board composition. There was an appeal to the Chancellor of the Exchequer against any decision of the Bank to repeal, revoke or vary an authorisation and the opportunity for lobbying is obvious. Although the Bank was permitted to give deposit takers directions,[26] this was only in the event that its authorisation had been revoked or was going to be revoked.[27]

The first positive duty to supervise deposit takers in the UK was introduced in the Banking Act in 1986.[28] The objectives to be pursued were not explicit. There was no attempt to define the public interest served in maintaining a competitive, solvent UK banking system and the concept and importance of the UK payment system was not recognised. Payments systems were then regarded as part of the day-to-day business of the clearing banks. As they were then paper-based, or made through BACS Ltd on a three-day cycle,[29] the risks inherent were significantly smaller. It is implicit that the drivers in the legislation were avoiding bank insolvency, the protection of individual depositors and the need to avoid calls on the Deposit Protection Fund.[30] The Act had as its backdrop the first EC Banking Directive.[31] The Bank's power to revoke authorisation was set out in greater detail than previously with specific reference to circumstances where the interests of depositors might be threatened, obligations in relation to liquidity, record keeping, systems and controls and an obligation to maintain sufficient net assets given the particular risks inherent in its operations.[32] The skeleton of its responsibilities was clearly focused on the protection of depositors rather than the financial system as a whole, systemic risk or credit intermediation. The broad heads of supervision are clearly precursors of those set out in the current rulebook but there was, at that stage, a far sparser approach to guidance and discussion papers on how the Bank would approach its tasks, priorities, techniques and resource allocation. Regulation at that stage was distinctly authoritarian in style with little resource devoted to drawing the wider public or the banks themselves into a discussion on aims, methods or objectives.

In being obliged to supervise banks, the relevant committee of the Bank, called the Board of Banking Supervision, had an entirely new task and no precursor UK authority to learn from. There was scepticism about its performance. The report of the Treasury Committee

---

[25] See ss12 and 13 Banking Act 1979 and Schedule 3.

[26] For example, to cease taking deposits.

[27] s19 Banking Act 1979.

[28] This came into force on 1 October 1987. The Banking Act 1987 (Commencement No. 2 Order).

[29] The CHAPS clearing system, to effect payments on the same day, was begun in 1984 but was limited in use initially. For a discussion of electronic funds transfers and banks, see A Hudson, *The Law of Finance* (London, Sweet and Maxwell, 2007) 814.

[30] The statutory framework of the Deposit Protection Fund comprised a good proportion of both the Banking Act 1979 and the Banking Act 1986. They were both relatively short Acts and it is clear that the legislature linked the concepts of deposit insurance and authorisation.

[31] Council Directive of 17 December 1977 on the co-ordination of laws, regulations and administrative provisions relating to the taking-up and pursuit of the business of credit institutions, 77/780/EEC.

[32] See schedule 3 Banking Act 1986.

on the Bank of England in 1993 revealed that in the early 1990s, the concerns then expressed about exactly who should supervise and how aggressive their techniques should be were extremely similar to those being voiced today. The Bank of England gave evidence before the Treasury Committee on its adoption of a more aggressive and intrusive style of supervision, increased technical capacity and knowledge, and an approach that responded to particularly vulnerable or difficult institutions. At that time, key concerns were over the conflict between individual bank supervision and responsibility for monetary policy given the link between inflation, money supply and bank balance sheets.[33] Much press attention rested then, and continues to do so, on the Bank's role in interest rate setting.[34]

In 2012 and 2013, comment on the new Governor Mark Carney has, surprisingly, focused on the Bank's Monetary Policy Committee rather than its extensive and difficult new responsibilities for prudential supervision and financial stability.[35]

The Bank's role in interest-rate setting was one of the most controversial and politically sensitive until the reforms of the Labour Government of 1997.[36] The Bank of England Act 1998, which gave power over monetary policy to an independent committee of the Bank of England called the Monetary Policy Committee, received Royal Assent on 23 April 1998. Prior to this, the discussions between the Bank and the Chancellor on base rate were frequently difficult and attracted unwanted press attention, particularly before general elections. This was largely due to the economic controversy over whether interest rates and employment are directly linked but the newspapers were also happy to make much of the personal relationship between the two key figures. The Bank's desire to increase interest rates to bolster currency or gold reserves, reduce money supply or enhance the capital structure of the Bank frequently collided with the economic and political objectives the Government of the day in reducing inflation, keeping borrowing costs of individuals and businesses to a minimum and securing re-election.[37] The introduction of the Monetary Policy Committee (MPC) in 1998 is viewed almost unanimously as successful. The composition of the MPC and provisions relating to remuneration of members, the appointments process, and quorum for meetings are set out in detail in Schedule 3 of the Bank of England Act 1998. The MPC meets once every month and it has a statutory obligation to publish within six weeks the minutes of each meeting and the vote of each individual member of

---

[33] 93/94 HC 98. Treasury and Civil Service Select Committee. Report on the Bank of England. Volume 1 Part IV paras 88–95.

[34] The decision to grant responsibility for monetary policy to the Bank of England was expected (having been set out in the Labour Party manifesto) but the decision to remove supervisory responsibility to a new regulator and to give debt management to the HM Treasury were not. See commentary in the *Financial Times* and in particular "A Little Old Lady: Robert Chote Looks Within the Bank of England as it Prepares for Radical Change": R Chote, *Financial Times*, 4 August 1997.

[35] See for example the following articles in the *Financial Times*, London editions: C Giles 'Carney pledges to boost UK Recovery' *Financial Times* 8 February 2013, C Jones and A Ross 'Carney's measures to show his mettle' *Financial Times* 13 December 2012: 2, M Wolf 'Welcome to Britain Mr Carney–It Needs You' *Financial Times* 27 November 2012.

[36] See sections 10–12 Bank of England Act 1998. S 10 amends the Bank of England Act 1946 by removing the power of the Treasury to give directions to the bank in relation to monetary policy. S11 is a model of clarity in that it gives the bank a single primary objective, in relation to monetary policy, which is to maintain price stability.

[37] In particular the discussion between Eddie George as Governor of the Bank and Ken Clarke as Chancellor of Exchequer became known as the Ken and Eddie show and attracted a great deal of unwanted publicity. This encouraged the Labour Party's decision to include in its 1997 manifesto a commitment to give the Monetary Policy Committee of the Bank power over interest rates on the basis of a government-set inflation target.

the MPC in relation to any decision.[38] A statement as to the decisions taken must be published as soon as practicable.[39] Membership of the MPC is viewed as prestigious.[40] Press comment is largely well informed and probably improves the quality of the process. The manner of arriving at the interest rate decision and the resources required are lifted out of controversy by the very tight statutory framework and the single objective to be pursued by the MPC. This is in direct contrast to the other new areas of operation, such as supervision and financial stability, which are soon to fall within the Bank's remit where the landscape of objectives, aims and coordinating responsibilities is far less direct.

There is no doubt that the legislature considered the Bank to have been unsuccessful as a bank supervisor when the responsibility for supervision was removed from it in 1998. In part this was prompted by the collapse of BCCI plc and Barings plc, but it was also heavily linked with the desire to put monetary policy with the Bank, thus taking it out of political control, and the view that to link monetary policy with bank supervision presented too many conflicts of interest to be wise. All bank authorisation and supervisory functions were removed from the Bank of England on 1 June 1998.[41] The position of the bank as the monitor of repute and financial standing in the City of London was swept away. The fact that it remained as lender of last resort despite having no patent role in monitoring capital adequacy attracted little comment. The Financial Services Authority assumed the power and obligation to supervise banks and all other authorised financial institutions on 1 June 1998.[42] The common view of its success in that task has been largely driven by the sudden near insolvencies of UK banks such as Northern Rock plc, Royal Bank of Scotland plc and Halifax Bank of Scotland plc and the wide ranging evidence of the lack of integrity and wisdom in the management of a variety of UK-based banks which was not prevented by the Financial Services Authority.[43]

IV   BANKING CRISIS OF 2007–2009

As mentioned above, under the Bank of England Act 1998,[44] the responsibility for bank supervision was transferred to the Financial Services Authority[45] and the Bank of England no longer had a role in relation to authorisation or supervision of banks. Neither did the Bank of England have any explicit statutory role in maintaining financial stability in the UK, monitoring overall levels of bank lending or the strength of bank balance sheets

---

[38] s15 Bank of England Act 1998.

[39] s15 Bank of England Act 1998.

[40] Prominence is given, for example, in the personal web pages, online cv's and autobiographical materials.

[41] Part III Bank of England Act 1998 which came into force on 1 June 1998.

[42] Initially under the Bank of England Act 1998 and then under the Financial Services and Markets Act 2000.

[43] See for example 'Maintaining Financial Stability across the United Kingdom's Banking System : Twelfth Report of session 2009-10 : report, together with formal minutes and oral and written evidence / Public Accounts Committee. House of Commons Papers 2009–2010; 190. Banking crisis: dealing with the failure of the UK banks: seventh report of session 2008–2009: report, together with formal minutes / Treasury Committee. House of Commons papers. 2008–2009; 416.

[44] S21.

[45] See also the general prohibition in s19 and schedule 2 FSMA 2000 and the provisions for authorisation in FSMA 2000 Part III.

or considering the sustainability of payments systems in the UK.[46] A Memorandum of Understanding between HM Treasury, the FSA and the Bank of England had been signed in 1997 and amended in 2006. Its purpose was to allocate roles in relation to the UK's financial system among the three entities, but at the time of real crisis in the late summer of 2007, it did not guide the parties with sufficient clarity and left a yawning gap in the leadership which led to delay and uncertainty.[47] The banking crisis of 2007–2009 first became apparent to the public in the UK with the severe liquidity difficulties experienced by Northern Rock plc and the consequent run on that bank in September 2007. Problems with liquidity and solvency quickly became apparent in a large number of bank and other financial institutions in the UK and other locations. The causes have been discussed at length elsewhere.[48] Obviously, UK bank supervision had not prevented these institutional crises or warned of them with sufficient force to allow remedial or preparatory action to be taken. Lord Turner, Chairman of the FSA, in his very carefully researched and highly regarded review of 2009, strongly recommended a new focus on systemic risk within the financial system as a whole rather than a narrow institution-by-institution approach. He also recommended that a European Union-wide supervisor should be established with a role in monitoring and regulating financial institutions and a mandate to monitor and address macro prudential risks. Here was a very telling message that risk could not now be contained within the UK's borders and therefore that institutions trading in the UK must be subject to Europe-wide regulation and control.[49] Whatever the identity of the UK bank supervisor, it could not do its job without European support and co-operation in an EU wide market for capital and financial services where controls at borders could no longer be exerted.

Much criticism was directed at the then Governor of the Bank of England, Mervyn King, for his failure to act quickly and decisively in the autumn of 2007.[50] However, many prominent academics also pointed to the anomalous position whereby the Bank of England as ultimate provider of emergency funds had no power whatsoever to intervene at all in credit markets or in the affairs of the individual banks or other bank like institutions participating in those credit markets even though it had collective institutional knowledge of the day to day state of such markets.[51] It had no supervisory or directional powers at all. It had certainly lost its position at the heart of the City of London.

---

[46] The financial stability objective was first given to the bank by s238 Banking Act 2009 which amended the Bank of England Act 1998 by inserting new sections 2A-2C . These sections also compelled the establishment of the Financial Stability Committee of the Bank of England and specified its composition.

[47] See the interesting analysis and criticism of it in House of Commons Treasury Select Committee Fifth Report Session 2007–2008 at paragraphs 267–92.

[48] For example: AR Sorkin, *Inside The Battle to Save Wall Street Too Big To Fail* (London, Penguin, 2010), G Tett, *Fool's Gold: How Unrestrained Greed Corrupted a Dream, Shattered Global Markets and Unleashed a Catastrophe* (London, Little Brown, 2009), The Financial Services Authority, *The Turner Review: A Regulatory Response to the Global Banking Crisis*, (London, Financial Services Authority, March 2009).

[49] *The Turner Review* ibid.

[50] For example see the leader article "Portrait of an Old Lady" *The Times*, 26 November 2012.

[51] See for example R Tomasic and F Akinbami 'Towards a New Corporate Governance after the Global Financial Crisis' (2011) 22(8) *International Company and Commercial Law Review* 237–249.

V   FINANCIAL STABILITY AND PRUDENTIAL MONITOR:
THE FINANCIAL SERVICES ACT 2012

Some 14 years after the removal of supervisory responsibilities, the task of prudential supervision of banks in the UK is being passed back to the Bank of England under the Financial Services Act of 2012. Once again the driver for change was a change in government, on this occasion the formation of the Coalition Government in May 2010.[52] Also, the landscape of the new structure is very heavily influenced by membership of the European Union and its drive to create a tighter common platform for supervision of banks, financial institutions and markets.

The new structure of financial services regulation in the UK was prefaced by the Conservative Party's election manifesto in 2010, which promised a disbandment of the FSA and a return of prudential supervision of financial institutions, including banks, to the Bank of England.[53] This twin peaks approach to supervision, with separate regulators for conduct of business and solvency, provides a very clear and narrow focus and fosters the acquisition of knowledge and expertise in capital adequacy and liquidity, free of the day-to-day concerns of the conduct of business regulation.[54] Lord Turner referred to the advantages of giving the central bank the responsibility for prudential supervision as "ensuring an integrated approach to liquidity risk management".[55] It has the major advantage of placing responsibility for prudential supervision in the hands of the UK entity which must decide whether to be, in any case, the lender of last resort and provider of emergency liquidity funding.

The FSA 2012 creates a new regulatory body the Prudential Regulation Authority[56] which is wholly owned by the Bank of England.[57] The PRA is not the prudential regulator of all authorised financial firms in the UK; its remit is a limited group of significant financial institutions[58] and in relation to those, it must focus on their safety and soundness and the prevention of adverse effects on UK financial stability such as discontinuance of payment services.[59] The FSA 2012 created a third Deputy Governor position at the Bank with responsibility for Prudential Regulation. Andrew Bailey takes up this position in April 2013. The first challenge to the Bank is definitional. Secondary legislation will specify what activities a firm must carry out in order to be subject to PRA prudential regulation.[60] All deposit takers, insurers and firms undertaking Lloyds business will fall within this definition and it is then for the PRA itself to designate some other 'investment firms' as falling within its remit on the basis that they are complex, large or have a high degree of interconnectivity

---

[52]   The Conservative Party, having failed to win an overall majority of seats in the UK's Parliament, invited the Liberal Democratic Party to join a coalition government.

[53]   *The Conservative Party Manifesto* 2010, 29.

[54]   P Rawlings, 'Reform of Bank Regulation in the UK: the Opening Salvo' (2010) 25(10) *Journal of International Banking Law and Regulation* 522–28.

[55]   *The Turner Review*, October 2009, 91.

[56]   Hereafter PRA.

[57]   s 6 Financial Services Act 2012 which makes substantial amendments to ss1-18 FSMA 2000 and creates the new regulators: the PRA and the Financial Conduct Authority (which is the Financial Services Authority renamed).

[58]   Approximately 2,000 institutions.

[59]   See s2B "The PRA's General Objective" in ch 2 of part 1A Financial Services and Markets Act 2000 as amended by the Financial Services Act 2012.

[60]   See s22A FSMA 2000 as amended. In October 2012, HM Treasury published a draft of the Financial Services and Markets Act 2000 (PRA-Regulated Activities) Order.

with other PRA-regulated entities. The PRA must be seen to be acting fairly; no doubt firms on the margins of the definition would rather not be PRA-regulated as a greater degree of scrutiny of risk in the balance sheet and liquidity is bound to follow. To be PRA-regulated, the investment firm must trade on its own account and have initial minimum capital of Euro 730,000.[61] Risks within the larger group are also relevant to this decision. Any designation must be agreed to by the other new UK regulator, the Financial Conduct Authority.[62] Clearly an enormous amount of work must be done to allocate investment firms between these two regulators and to ensure that there is no regulatory gap in relation to prudential regulation.[63] In the event of any future failure, this allocation is bound to be scrutinised.[64]

Once the category of PRA-regulated entities is determined, the PRA has power, in relation to those entities, to vary and remove permission to undertake regulated activities, impose directions on certain categories of parent undertakings (even though they themselves are not regulated) and exercise its own initiative powers in response to requests from overseas regulators. Notification of these matters must be given to the European Banking Authority, in relation to credit institutions, and the European Securities and Markets Authority, in relation to investment firms, thus assisting European consolidated supervision of groups and fostering collegiate responsibility in the European Union for very large groups.

The objective of contributing to the protection and enhancement of the stability of the UK financial systems was first given to the Bank of England by the Banking Act 2009 on 1 June 2009 when it was simply mandated to contribute to stability. The objective is now more direct. It is now a specific obligation to protect and enhance the stability of the financial systems of the United Kingdom and this is termed the Financial Stability Objective (FSO).[65] The court of directors of the Bank is obliged to publish its strategy in relation to this objective, having first discussed it with the new Financial Policy Committee of the Bank.[66] Detailed provisions on time limits, publication and updating are included in the new Part 1A of the Bank of England Act 1998.[67] This is a clear and determined attempt to give the Bank of England real responsibility for financial stability within the UK, not simply in relation to forecasting and publishing warnings, but by giving it specific powers to intervene directly in the financial services marketplace by directing the regulators, the PRA and the FCA, to take specific action in relation to specified classes of authorised firms.[68]

Given its multiple new roles, the Bank will be keen to determine as closely as possible the limits of its role. There is every possibility of it being the fall guy for any pitfall which catches

---

[61] So to be PRA-regulated, an investment firm must be one to which Article 9 of Directive 2006/49/EC of the European Parliament and of the Council on the capital adequacy of investment firms and credit institutions applies.

[62] This is the Financial Services Authority renamed.

[63] See for instance the consultation document 'Designation of Investment Firms for Prudential Supervision by the PRA: Consultation on a Draft Policy Statement' October 2012 Bank of England and FSA, London.

[64] A draft order setting out the ambit of the PRA's designation responsibility was published by the Treasury in October 2012 for consultation. The consultation closed on 31 December 2012.

[65] s 2A Bank of England Act 1998 as amended by s2 Financial Services Act 2012 (not yet in force).

[66] The obligation on the Court of Directors of the Bank to establish a new committee called the Financial Policy Committee is set out s4 Financial Services Act 2012 which amends the Bank of England Act 1998.

[67] Inserted by s4 Financial Services Act 2012.

[68] This follows Mervyn King's comments that the Bank repeatedly warned of excessive credit and other structural problems with the UK economy prior to August 2007, but could take no action given its lack of statutory responsibility and power.

the headlines and has a political impact on the government of the day. The Financial Policy Committee of the Bank is mandated to contribute to the achievement by the Bank of the FSO and also to support the economic policy of the government of the day, including its objectives for growth and employment.[69] This is indeed a very powerful new committee and one that has a range of tasks that can put it directly and frequently in the line of controversial economic and political decision-making. On the one hand, it is to be given draconian powers to issue specific directions to the new regulators, the PRA and the FCA, to take regulatory action against very powerful banks and other financial institutions, which are very large employers and taxpayers and aggressive and successful lobbyists in Whitehall and Westminster.[70] On the other hand, it must temper its action by having regard for economic growth and employment. The tensions in its remit are immediately apparent. These difficult balances are usually struck by politicians subject to a democratic mandate and parliamentary discipline and accountability, not by an unelected body such as the Court of Directors of the Bank of England, which is led by the Governor who has an eight year tenure.

In relation to macro prudential supervision, the FPC's role and power reflect very closely the recommendations of the new European Systemic Risk Board (ESRB)[71] which has the task of identifying and controlling systemic risk within the EU in conjunction with the national financial regulators.[72] The ESRB is one part of the new EU-wide supervisory architecture which commenced with the 2009 de Larosiere Report recommending the establishment of an EU-wide system of financial supervision covering banking, insurance, occupational pensions, markets and systemic risk. This architecture[73] is largely ignored by UK politicians, but in fact it provides an overarching level of control and supervision with which all UK legislation must dovetail. The theoretical justification for this is that systemic financial risks are no longer contained within national borders and cannot be controlled by national regulators acting alone. Although unpopular in the UK, this is a sound premise for all banking and financial services regulation, given the speed and freedom with which money, credit and financial services cross national borders. This is as much a function of technological change[74] as it is of legal and economic change such as the removal of exchange controls and legal barriers to the free movement of capital and financial services. Many macro prudential risks within the UK economy will not be controllable by actions of UK regulators. Indeed one can question whether there are likely to be any macro prudential risks which threaten the UK economy alone, given the free market for financial services that exists within the EU and the depth and breadth of the UK's financial services industry's involvement throughout Europe.

The FPC's power to issue directions to regulators to ensure the implementation by firms in the market place of 'macro prudential measures' will be specified more closely

---

[69]   See s9(C) Bank of England Act 1998 as amended by s4 Financial Services Act 2012.

[70]   The banking industry has a strong track record of lobbying in Westminster. See, for example, its success in managing to avoid having a pre-funded deposit guarantee scheme.

[71]   Hereafter ESRB.

[72]   See the website of the European Systemic Risk Board at www.esrb.europa.eu and in particular the latest Systemic Risk Board which attempts to identify potential for macro prudential risk within the European Union. (Last accessed 28/3/13).

[73]   The European Banking Authority, the European Securities and Markets Authority, the European Insurance and Occupational Pensions Authority, the Joint Committee of the European Supervisory Authorities and the European Systemic Risk Board.

[74]   For example, cross-border electronic banking systems started to develop to a much greater degree and the Internet and mobile phone technology have revolutionised how money is transferred.

by delegated legislation. This is the key power that gives real influence on financial stability within the UK but it requires confidence and a clear sense of what lies in the public interest to exercise it. In addition, the FPC is actually prohibited from action that is likely to have a significant adverse effect on the capacity of the financial sector to contribute to the growth of the UK economy in the medium or long term, in other words, an impact on the capacity to lend to UK businesses. This is a significant bar on action by the FPC and depends on a very finely balanced judgement being made by a large committee of individuals on the meaning of 'significant' and 'medium term'. Given the lobbying power and skill of the financial services sector in the UK, it is unlikely that the FPC will have the courage to use the power of direction freely. Given the range and depth of new responsibilities and the potential commercial impact of directions, it will require courage, confidence and political backing to use it. HM Treasury has consulted on the specification of the macro prudential tools that are available to the FPC and a new draft statutory instrument is expected shortly.[75] The Act does not permit a direction to be made in respect of one institution alone. It is obvious that any direction is likely to be controversial and attract much publicity and comment. It is highly likely, therefore, that the FPC will use its power merely to issue recommendations to the new regulators, rather than directions. This will pass the buck to them on when and how to act. The power to direct may never be used, particularly when there may well be the option of a distant faceless European body, the ESRB, taking the decision and its political and economic consequences. The latest proposals are that the macro prudential tools will be: quarterly direction of the level of counter-cyclical buffer for systemically significant institutions pursuant to CRR/D4;[76] power to change firms' capital requirements in relation to exposure to certain sectors such as commercial or residential property;[77] power to specify a binding minimum leverage ratio, but not before such a ratio is implemented through BASEL 3 in the EU.

VI   FUTURE EU AND UK DEVELOPMENTS AND THEIR IMPACT

The European Commission, in September 2012, published a document outlining how it would like to see a European banking union develop.[78] This is the latest of a number of proposals emanating from the Commission which together will have a significant impact

---

[75] See 'The Financial Services Bill: The Financial Policy Committee's Macro-Prudential Tools' Financial Secretary to the Treasury. Cm 8434 September 2012. The consultation on the tools and safeguards closed on 11 December 2012.

[76] In practice, this decision will be taken pursuant to the new EU capital requirements directive (CRD4) which will be implemented in the UK by regulations under s2(2) European Communities Act 1972 rather than under the Financial Services Act 2012. Any direction in relation to this buffer will be subject to significant procedural and reporting requirements and is subject to mandatory reciprocity across the EU up to a certain limit. Therefore any direction compelling increased countercyclical buffers in relation to any class of UK assets would be mirrored across Europe in relation to that class of UK assets held by European banks. An impact on the value of sterling would be almost inevitable.

[77] Once again the consultation paper recognises that such a requirement would impact the cost of capital in the sectors targeted. The political and economic impact is obvious and the countervailing pressures would have to be overt and critical for the FPC to justify this type of measure.

[78] *A Roadmap Towards a Banking Union*, Communication from the Commission to the European Parliament and the Council (Brussels, European Commission, 12. 9. 2012 COM (2012) 510 final).

on virtually all aspects of the regulation and supervision of banks in the EU.[79] It is far from clear at present exactly where all this is likely to lead, but there seems little doubt that the Commission is determined to push forward as quickly as possible with a banking union which would eventually contain a single supervisory mechanism, a single bank resolution procedure, a single supervisory rulebook and a pan-European deposit guarantee scheme funded by all Member States.[80] It is a very ambitious project, which may actually turn out to be too ambitious, but undoubtedly the Europeanisation of all aspects of the regulation and supervision of banking activities will continue to develop and even if the UK decides not to sign up to membership of the banking union,[81] certain aspects of what is being proposed will nonetheless have a significant impact on issues relating to UK banks and, therefore, on at least some aspects of the role of the Bank of England.

Some of what has been published by the Commission relates solely to the Eurozone[82] but other proposals relate to all Member States. This essentially means that whether the UK Government decides not to participate in those proposals which relate only to the Eurozone, it will have no alternative but to institute those parts which are addressed to all Member States. It is clearly beyond the scope of a paper such as this to attempt to study these European proposals in detail and what follows focuses on some issues which are particularly relevant to the future role of the Bank of England.

One thing that becomes very clear from the proposals is the increased role and power that the European Central Bank will enjoy. The Frankfurt-based organisation will be the most powerful financial institution in the European Union. This will bring into focus the relationship between the ECB and the central banks of Member States which are not in the Eurozone. The UK is not member of the Eurozone and the position of the present government is for it to remain that way.

Agreement has now been reached on the introduction of the Single Supervisory Mechanism[83] which means that the ECB will have overall responsibility for the supervision of all banks within the Eurozone.[84] This is likely to happen in mid-2014.[85]

Under this procedure the ECB will have direct responsibility for supervising systemically important banks in the Eurozone while the other banks will continue to be supervised by national supervisors under the overall supervision of the ECB. Of the approximately 6000 banks in the Eurozone only about 150 will be directly supervised by the ECB.[86] However, this relatively small number of banks will account for more than 80% of all the banking

---

[79] In October 2010 the Commission issued its plans for a Union framework for crisis management in the financial sector which "would equip authorities with common and effective tools and powers to tackle bank crises pre-emptively, safeguarding financial stability and minimising taxpayer exposure to losses in insolvency". COM (2010) 579 final.

[80] There have been criticisms from various sources. See, for example, H-W Sinn and H Hau 'The Eurozone's Banking Union is Deeply Flawed', *Financial Times* 12/9/12.

[81] The UK Chancellor, George Osborne, has indicated that the UK will not be joining.

[82] This is the term used to refer to those countries which use the Euro as their currency.

[83] Hereafter 'SMM'.

[84] European Commission–Press Release - Ref: memo/13/251, 19/3/13.

[85] However, there may be further time slippage, especially in view of various political issues and the Cyprus banking crisis of March 2013.

[86] The ECB will have responsibility for directly supervising all banks with assets exceeding €30 billion, and those which are of a size which represents at least 20% of the home country's GDP.

assets in the Eurozone. Accordingly, the ECB will in effect be directly supervising the bulk of banking business in the Eurozone.

Non-Eurozone states can opt in if they wish, but are not required to do so.[87] If a non-Eurozone state does decide to participate it will then be entitled to participate in the newly created Supervisory Board, which will be in charge of planning and executing the supervisory responsibilities to be undertaken by the ECB. This means that any non-Eurozone state which decides not to participate will not have a role to play in policy-making at the Supervisory Board. As the UK government has made it clear that it has no intention of joining the SMM the Bank of England will be excluded from participation in policy-making. This would be a significant development as the Bank of England will continue to have overall responsibility for the regulation and supervision of banks based in London, the leading financial centre in Europe.[88] Many of these banks will be operating throughout the EU and it is difficult to envision the situation where a newly empowered and expanded ECB would wish to see a central bank based in a Member State outside the Eurozone having supervisory responsibility for such banks. It is also difficult to envisage a situation where the ECB would be happy to defer to the Bank of England in supervisory matters. At the least, close cooperation between these two institutions will be vital. But how can this be achieved? This is far from clear.

Another factor which will have a direct impact on the role of the Bank of England is the creation of a single rulebook for all Member States.[89] This makes sense for the Eurozone countries which will have a single regulator and supervisor, but the single rulebook will also apply in the UK and it seems that the Bank of England may only have a peripheral role in the way this rulebook is developed.

Another interesting factor, raised by Matthew Elderfield in a speech made in Brussels in January,[90] is that '. . .it will be important to develop a common supervisory philosophy and risk appetite. Will the SSM under the ECB, be a principles-based supervisor, a rules-based one or some judicious mix of the two?'. It is hard to imagine a powerful ECB with a particular supervisory approach being willing to defer to a different approach by national central banks such as the Bank of England. The ECB will undoubtedly regard itself as the senior partner in the European system of Central Banks.

At a political level it is not only EU developments which may have an impact on the future role of the Bank of England. Constitutional changes within the UK in the not too distant future are now a possibility.[91] The voters of Scotland will have the opportunity in 2014 to decide whether not to remain in the UK. Should the Conservative Party win the next election in 2015, or a UK-wide referendum will be held on whether the UK should remain part of the EU. This Scottish referendum will certainly go ahead, but the UK-wide one is less certain. Clearly a vote to leave the UK by Scotland would lead, at the very least, to

---

[87] The UK government has made it clear that the UK will not be opting in. The position of the other non-Eurozone countries is not quite clear at present.

[88] And, of course, elsewhere in the UK.

[89] This is being developed by the European Banking Authority.

[90] Deputy Governor of the Central Bank of Ireland. Introductory remarks made at the 11th Annual European Financial Services Conference, Brussels, 31 January 2013. At www.bis.org/review/r130201b.pdf. 31/1/13. (Last accessed 28/3/13).

[91] Although not, as yet, a probability.

a potential breakup of the Bank of England.[92] The removal of the UK from the EU would, by the time it were to happen, have a significant impact on the Bank of England. The purpose of mentioning these political and constitutional issues is to draw attention to the fact that times are relatively uncertain.

VII   CONCLUSION

So far as integrity is concerned, one can see that although the Bank's role as gatekeeper to the UK's credit market has not disappeared, its ambit and discretion have been severely limited by the growth in the size of the credit market place, the UK's membership of the European Union and the removal of technical and legal barriers to fast provision of credit across national borders. These factors are all matters which have hugely increased the UK's earnings from the provision of financial services, but have hugely increased the national risk in their provision.

The Bank now has the key task of monitoring financial stability in the UK and has the power to issue recommendations and directions to the new UK regulators to attempt to stave off severe risks that appear on the horizon. Whether it will have the courage and political backing to use these powers remains to be seen. This is particularly so now in an environment where few risks will be limited to the UK and where the ESRB may well be regarded as the entity which is in the best position to monitor and act. On the other hand, this could be a landscape where a new yawning regulatory gap emerges with neither the European nor the UK authorities having the will or confidence to act in the face of the powerful banking lobby.

It seems inevitable that the real power of the Bank of England will be dependent on developments within the EU, especially the continuation of the inexorable growth and importance of the ECB. If the UK remains within the EU but outside the Eurozone, then it becomes inevitable that its influence as a central bank diminishes both within the UK and in the wider European market place. Indeed, should the EU banking union proceed as planned, there will only be one central bank within the EU that will have any real role to play on the international stage and that will be the ECB.

So what about the effect of this on London as one of the world's leading financial centres? It seems unlikely that London would be directly damaged because it acts in an international financial services market place and is an extremely popular place to live and work. Frankfurt does not have the same lure and the prospect of many banks and investment firms relocating to Frankfurt seems remote in the short term, but it also seems quite possible that ECB initiatives in Frankfurt will lead to the growth of that city as a financial centre, perhaps, to the detriment of London.[93]

The UK government has indicated that it will not be participating in the SSM when it comes into force next year, and this means that the Bank of England will continue to have

---

[92] Although the policies proposed by the Scottish Government are designed to avoid the need for this. Interestingly, it is the policy of the Scottish Government to remain part of the EU. However, what is proposed after independence would be a currency union with the rest of the UK with the Bank of England remaining as central bank for the so-called 'Sterlingzone'.

[93] The status of London as one of the world's leading financial centres is a major concern for politicians in the UK. It seems somewhat surprising that UK policymakers are playing very little part in what is going on in Brussels.

supervisory responsibility for all banks based in the UK. If, however, the UK were to decide to join the SSM, the ECB would directly supervise the UK's major banks from its base in Frankfurt. This would obviously have a significant impact on the role and power of the Bank of England and would create the possibility that a regulator based outside the UK could take control of one of the large UK banks, should it be of the opinion that the bank in question is in breach of its regulatory requirements.

All Member States will in due course supervise banks on the basis of a single rulebook, so the Bank of England will be using the same rulebook as the ECB. It is quite likely that their approaches to supervision may be quite different, reflecting different cultural approaches. There is, therefore, scope for tensions to arise. Time will tell how this will work out in practice.

In conclusion, the Financial Services Act 2012 has added considerable complexity to the Bank of England's role. It has a new explicit new focus—UK financial stability—and a new specific responsibility for prudential regulation of systemically important banks, insurance companies and investment firms. Since their creation by the legislature in 1979, supervisory obligations over banks have proved to be a poison pill, first for the Bank and then for the Financial Services Authority. The Bank now also has obligations to coordinate its activities, in a number of ways, with the Financial Conduct Authority and powerful European supervisory authorities. Some of these roles involve it in decisions which are overtly political. It is to be hoped that its budget and management skills are sufficient and that its new Governor Mark Carney enjoys a good relationship with the UK press. Developments in Europe may mean this enormous new role is short lived.

CHAPTER 9

The Sword of Damocles: Deferred Prosecutions and the Search for Accountability

Justin O'Brien*

I INTRODUCTION

The US comprises the most significant export market for Mexican and Columbian drug cartels. Mexican democracy itself has been destabilized by cartel-sponsored corruption. Ongoing political violence, fuelled, in part, by the drug trade, has further weakened social and political capital. When the London-based global bank HSBC uses advertising that claims the importance of knowing when emerging markets have emerged, it most certainly did not have the narcotics industry in mind. Yet this was precisely what occurred as a consequence of systemic compliance failures across the group. From the parent operation in London to affiliated entities in both the United States and Mexico, there was, according to an agreed Statement of Facts tabled in a New York federal court in December 2012, a wanton disregard for the societal implications. When combined with identified inability to control money transfers to North Korea, Burma, Cuba and Sudan in violation of a United States-imposed sanctions regime, the global failure of compliance suggests deep structural problems with HSBC's core business model. Providing local businesses with a global imprimatur without strenuous checks to safeguard reputational capital has been shown to be an exceptionally dangerous strategy.

The $1.92 billion deferred prosecution agreement entered into by HSBC with US regulators contains the largest financial penalty ever imposed on a global bank by prosecutorial authorities in either a civil or criminal matter. The bank is required to disgorge $1.256 billion of profits. It will also pay a total of $665 million in civil penalties to regulatory agencies, including the Office of the Comptroller of the Currency ($500 million) and the Federal Reserve ($165 million). The payment to the Office of the Comptroller of the Currency is a partial, if not complete, vindication of the agency. Given the criticism of its oversight in an

* A version of this chapter appeared in (2012) 63 *Northern Ireland Legal Quarterly* 533 and is reprinted with permission. I acknowledge the financial support of the Australian Research Council for a Future Fellowship evaluating market conduct regulation and two grants associated with financial regulation, The Limits of Disclosure' and 'The Future of Financial Regulation.'

eviscerating report tabled to the United States Congress in July 2012, it is at best an equivocal endorsement of federal priorities.[1] Of even more significance, however, is the requirement that a corporate compliance monitor be appointed to a five-year term, in compliance with a template in operation since at least 2008.[2] Although ostensibly independent, the terms of engagement and accountability structures governing the design and implementation of the monitor's work plan make it abundantly clear that the holder is an agent of the Department of Justice, for which it makes no apology. 'HSBC is being held accountable for stunning failures of oversight—and worse—that led the bank to permit narcotics traffickers and others to launder hundreds of millions of dollars through HSBC subsidiaries, and to facilitate hundreds of millions more in transactions with sanctioned countries', noted the head of the Criminal Division of the Department, Lanny Breuer, in a broadly circulated circular.[3]

In a deferred prosecution, a corporation enters into an effective contract with the prosecutorial authority in which it agrees not to subsequently challenge an agreed narrative and engages in remedial action in exchange for a decision not to proceed with the charges. If there is no repetition of the complained of conduct within an agreed timeframe, the charges are voided. Conversely, a violation allows for a filing of an indictment in which the statement of facts cannot be challenged. It is, therefore, an effective admission of guilt in the event substantive non-compliance with the terms triggers prosecution. It is closely allied to a non-prosecution agreement, which can also contain contractually agreed upon remedial action. In policy terms, the HSBC agreement is one of the most significant uses of the deferred prosecution mechanism since its application to deal with KPMG's development of abusive tax shelters in 2005.[4] The KPMG prosecution had ended with the Department of Justice castigated in the Manhattan Federal Court. Judge Louis Kaplan condemned what he termed its unconstitutional conduct. He voiced grave concern that the prosecutors had 'put a gun to KPMG's head' by forcing it to end legal support for partners whose defence centred on the fact that they were following corporate sanctioned objectives.[5] The Department of Justice, stung by the criticism, retreated largely from forcing change on the financial sector, with the exception of active prosecution of sanctions violations and breaches of the

---

[1] See Senate Permanent Sub Committee on Investigations, *US Vulnerabilities to Money Laundering, Drugs, and Terrorist Financing: HSBC Case History* (US Congress, Washington DC, 17 July 2012) 306 (noting a 2008 examination in which the OCC records 'As the U.S. dollar clearing bank for the Global HSBC network, HBUS maintains numerous relationships with institutions worldwide. . . . The bank does business with numerous customers in both High Intensity Drug Trafficking Area and High Intensity Money Laundering and Related Financial Crime Area locations. HBUS provides pouch services through several business units. Historically, pouch services are vulnerable to money laundering risk).

[2] C Morford, 'Memorandum on Selection and Use of Monitors in Deferred Prosecutions and Non Prosecution Agreements with Corporations' (Department of Justice, Washington, DC, 8 March 2008).

[3] Department of Justice, 'HSBC Holdings Plc. and HSBC Bank USA N.A. Admit to Anti-Money Laundering and Sanctions Violations, Forfeit $1.256 Billion in Deferred Prosecution Agreement', (Press Release, Washington, DC, 11 December 2012).

[4] J O'Brien, *Redesigning Financial Regulation* (Chicester, John Wiley & Sons, 2007) 123–69; for assessment of the Department of Justice's usage, see Government Accountability Office, *Corporate Crime: Preliminary Observations on DOJ's Use and Oversight of Deferred Prosecution Agreements and Non-Prosecution Agreements* (Washington, DC, 25 June 2009).

[5] *United States of America v Jeffrey Stein et al* S1 05 Crim. 0888 (LAK, 26 June 2006) Kaplan further noted 'Those who commit crimes—regardless of whether they wear white or blue collars—must be brought to justice. The government, however, has let its zeal get in the way of its judgment. It has violated the Constitution it is sworn to defend: at 3.' The decision was upheld on appeal in 2008; see *United States v Stein* No. 07-3042 (2d Cir. 28 August 2008).

Foreign Corrupt Practices Act of 1977. With the exception of the settlement with Lloyds Bank TSB, however, it had not imposed an external monitor on a major financial institution for sanctions violations. Instead it had relied on the stated intention of institutions to reform the compliance function.[6] This time, as they say, is different.

The success of the HSBC negotiations, significantly brought not in the Southern District of New York but in neighboring Brooklyn, where HSBC Bank USA holds neither its head office nor conducts major business, served three core purposes. First, it expunged the debilitating error of judgment that informed the prosecution of the KPMG partners. Second, it signaled a determination by the Department to ensure nascent state action, particularly in the sanctions violations space, did not usurp federal leadership in the setting of prosecutorial and regulatory priorities. The settlement came as Standard Chartered, another United Kingdom domiciled bank, agreed an overarching settlement of $327m to draw to a conclusion litigation brought by a range of regulatory agencies, including the Criminal Division.[7] The timing is far from incidental. It follows the success by New York Department of Financial Services in securing a $340m settlement with Standard Chartered in August on broadly similar charges,[8] which were dismissed at the time as the actions of a 'rogue regulator'.[9] The strategic approach adopted by the New York Department of Financial Services followed a playbook made famous by Eliot Spitzer, the former State Attorney General.[10] The decision not to require an independent monitor in the Standard Chartered case is, in part, linked to the fact that the violation amounted to a fraction of what was initially alleged by the New York Department of Financial Services.[11] Third—and most significantly—it repositioned the Department of Justice as a core moderator of regulatory priorities to use threatened prosecution as a catalyst for cultural change,

---

[6] Similar settlements have been reached with a number of banks for sanctions violations involving Cuba and Iran, including—in descending monetary order—ING ($619million), Credit Suisse ($536 million) Lloyds ($350million) and Barclays ($298 million); see C Mollencamp and B Wolf, 'HSBC to Pay Record $1.9 U.S. Billion Fine in Money Laundering Case', *Reuters*, 11 December 2012 www.complinet.com/global/news/news/article.html?ref=160723>; see also S Goff, 'Barclays Fined $298m Over Sanctions Breach', *Financial Times*, 17 August 2010 www.ft.com/intl/cms/s/0/6918f646-a96b-11df-a6f2-00144feabdc0.html#axzz2F4BqZ9tM>. The settlements have prompted judicial skepticism; see, for example, J Eaglesham and J Baer, 'Barclays 'Sweetheart Deal' Under Fire', *Financial Times*, 18 August 2010 <http://www.ft.com/intl/cms/s/0/dece7c62-aa51-11df-9367-00144feabdc0.html#axzz2F4BqZ9tM>.

[7] Department of Justice, 'Standard Chartered Bank Agrees to Forfeit $227 Million for Illegal Transactions with Iran, Sudan, Libya, and Burma' (Press Release, Washington, DC, 10 December 2012).

[8] Department of Financial Services, 'Statement from Benjamin M. Lawsky, Superintendent of Financial Services, Regarding Standard Chartered Bank' (Press Release, New York, 14 August 2012).

[9] K Mahbubani, 'A Lawsky Unto Himself, or Why New York Erred on StanChart' *Financial Times*, 12 August 2012, www.ft.com/intl/cms/s/0/f4c6b142-e2d5-11e1-bf02-00144feab49a.html#axzz24PyoHpnq>.

[10] For discussion of Spitzer's strategy (and the accountability deficit at its heart), see J O'Brien, 'The Politics of Enforcement, Eliot Spitzer, State-Federal Relations and the Redesign of Financial Regulation' (2005) 35 *Publius The Journal of Federalism* 439; see also J Macey, 'Wall Street in Turmoil: State-Federal Relations Post Eliot Spitzer' (2004) 70 *Brooklyn Law Review* 117, 120–22; K Walha and E Filusch, 'Eliot Spitzer: A Crusader Against Corporate Malfeasance or a Politically Ambitions Spotlight Hound? A Case Study of Eliot Spitzer and Marsh & McLennan' (2005) 18 *Georgetown Journal of Legal Ethics* 111, 114–15.

[11] Standard Chartered, 'Standard Chartered Reaches Final Settlement With U.S. Authorities', (Press Release, 12 December 2012). The release notes that the investigation by the Office of Foreign Assets Control found 'that while SCB's omission of information affected approximately 60,000 payments related to Iran totaling $250 billion, the vast majority of those transactions do not appear to have been violations of the Iranian Transactions Regulations". Over the entire period from 2001 to the end of 2007, it found that approximately $24 million of transactions processed on behalf of Iranian parties and a total of $109 million on behalf other sanctioned entities from other countries (Burma, Sudan and Libya) appeared to be in violation of sanctions laws. Over the same period, SCB New York processed $139 trillion in US dollar payments.').

not only within individual entities but also across sectors, at both the national and global level.[12] As such, it signals its return as a pivotal, if unpredictable, force in financial regulation.

The Standard Chartered and HSBC settlements reflect the growing centrality of deferred prosecutions as the preferred prosecutorial tool of choice.[13] The expansion of the measure reflects both its strengths and limitations.[14] On the one hand, it avoids the possibility of broader collateral damage. In the United States, a criminal conviction of a financial services firm would automatically trigger licence revocation. This could have devastating consequences for the individual institution indicted and the livelihoods of those who work for them.[15] Moreover, the licence revocation of a major bank or financial services firm deemed to be of regional or global significance could have an immediate effect on the stability of the global financial system. Indeed, these factors were explicitly noted by the Department of Justice in justifying the decision to delay prosecution. British regulators have gone further. Andrew Bailey, the designate head of the Prudential Regulation Authority, rather plaintively noted that to bring a criminal action against a bank would be a 'very destabilizing issue. Its another version of too big too fail.'[16] The limitation is that absent substantive requirements to change not only compliance practice but also broader risk and corporate governance reporting frameworks, the financial penalties, while substantial, could be and often are written off as part of the cost of doing business.[17]

[12] L Breuer, 'Address to the New York City Bar Association' (Speech delivered to the NYC Bar Association, New York, 13 September 2012).

[13] The use of deferred prosecutions is also under consideration the United Kingdom, with particular references to violations of that jurisdiction's *Bribery Act of 2010*. A consultation process now under review advocated its expansion; see Ministry of Justice, *Deferred Prosecution Agreements* Cm 8348 (2012).

[14] For review, see B Garrett, 'Globalized Corporate Prosecutions' (2011) 97 *Virginia Law Review* 1776. In the United Kingdom there has long been considerable interest in introducing the measure. The government had already signaled its strong support for the introduction of the measure; see C Binham, 'Garnier Eyes US Style Fines and Bargains,' *Financial Times*, 28 September 2011. A consultation process highlighted one critical difference from practice in the United States. There is to be judicial involvement in the initial decision as to deploy the mechanism and the parameters of the proposed terms, see Ministry of Justice, *Deferred Prosecution Agreements* Cm 8348 (2012). On 23 October 2012, the Ministry of Justice announced its introduction; see Ministry of Justice, 'New Tool to Fight Economic Crime' Press Release, London, 23 October 2012, quoting Justice Minister, Damian Green that 'Deferred Prosecution Agreements will give prosecutors an effective new tool to tackle what has become an increasingly complex issue. This will ensure that more unacceptable corporate behaviour is dealt with through substantial penalties, proper reparation to victims, and measures to prevent future wrongdoing.'

[15] See L Thompson, 'Principles of Federal Prosecution of Business Organizations' (Washington DC, US Department of Justice, 20 January 2003), hereinafter *The Thompson Memo*. Following criticism of requirements that organizations under investigation should waive client–attorney privilege and withhold payment of legal fees to individuals prosecuted, most notably in the prosecution of KPMG, these components were subsequently dropped.

[16] H Wilson, 'Banks are to Big to Prosecute Says FSA's Andrew Bailey', *Daily Telegraph*, 14 December 2012 www. telegraph.co.uk/finance/newsbysector/banksandfinance/9743839/Banks-are-too-big-to-prosecute-says-FSAs-Andrew-Bailey.html. Although the introduction of the Deferred Prosecution mechanism is designed primarily for the dealing with corruption, there is no doubt it could be applied by the Serious Fraud Office in relation to the Libor scandal in the event that a criminal prosecution eventuates. On 11 December, British authorities announced that three people had been arrested, see J Traynor, 'Bleak Day for British Banking as Libor Arrests Follow Record HSBC Fine' *The Guardian*, 11 December 2012 www.guardian.co.uk/business/2012/dec/11/banking-libor-fine-hsbc.

[17] This is made manifest in two highly influential if disparate sources, Lex, 'HSBC/StanChart–Rap on the Knuckles', *Financial Times*, 11 December 2012 (noting 'transgressions normally only become public a long time after the fact. Markets seem happy to view these latest as one-off episodes of ancient history.'); see also M Taibi, 'Outrageous HSBC Settlement Proves the Drug War is a Joke', *Rolling Stone*, 11 December 2012 www.rollingstone. com/politics/blogs/taibblog/outrageous-hsbc-settlement-proves-the-drug-war-is-a-joke-20121213.

There is, therefore, a triangulated policy dilemma. If major banks are too big to fail, too big too prosecute and too big to manage, how does one secure substantive warranted commitment to ethical restraint and pro-social rather than anti-social behavior from such entities? One way of offsetting that limitation is to ensure that cultural change is ongoing through the imposition of an external monitor.[18] It is the application of this component of the regulatory toolbox that differentiates the Department of Justice's approach to HSBC. In section 2, the chapter examines the charges themselves, which draw heavily from the damning Senate Permanent Sub-Committee on Investigations report.[19] Section 3 details the remedial action taken by HSBC to date and that mandated by the deferred prosecution agreement. Given this cooperation, Section IV then examines how and why the Department did not to accept remedial action at face value but instead imposed an external monitor with granular terms of reference. Section V of the article assesses the implications of that decision on regulatory design. It argues that the deal represents not the Department's weakness, as broadly reported. Instead it reflects its growing strength. This strength has far-reaching consequences, not just in the United States but internationally. Section VI concludes.

II   A FLAWED BUSINESS MODEL

HSBC was found on 11 December 2012 in the Federal Court in Brooklyn of being responsible for systematic sanctions violations and the facilitation of money laundering on an industrial scale. It was held accountable for threatening national security by providing financing facilities to a Saudi Arabian bank with links to terrorist groups.[20] The four-count charge found that the bank had willfully failed to develop, implement and maintain an effective anti-money laundering program in contravention of the *Bank Secrecy Act of 1970*.[21] The legislation progressively extended in both granularity and geographic scope over the

---

[18] C Ford and D Hess, 'Can Corporate Monitorship's Improve Corporate Compliance' (2009) 34 *Journal of Corporation Law* 679 (noting the danger that these are exercises in symbolism with 'monitors not conducting deep dives into the corporation's culture': at 737); see also V Khanna and T Dickinson, 'The Corporate Monitor: The New Corporate Czar' (2007) 105 *Michigan Law Review* 1713 (noting the de facto creation of a new professional class of advisors and advocating allocation of fiduciary duty to shareholders: at 1727). The critical issue, therefore, pivots on willingness to use nascent power and to whom accountability is owed. There can be no mistaking the potential to gain effective control of corporate strategy. In 2006, for example, the corporate monitor installed at Bristol-Meyer Squibb advocated the sacking of the chief executive officer and the general counsel, recommendations accepted by the board; see B Masters, 'Bristol-Meyers Ousts its Chief at Monitor's Urging', *Washington Post*, 13 September 2006, D1.

[19] *US Vulnerabilities to Money Laundering, Drugs, and Terrorist Financing: HSBC Case History* above, n1; see also C Levin, 'Levin Statement on HSBC Settlement' (Press Release, Washington DC, 11 December 2012), noting 'In an age of international terrorism, drug violence, and organized crime, stopping illicit money flows is a national security imperative. Global banks have global responsibilities to prevent participation in illicit or suspect transactions. The HSBC settlement sends a powerful wakeup call to multinational banks about the consequences of disregarding their anti-money laundering obligations. It also shows the value of congressional oversight in exposing wrongdoing and the ongoing need to hold banks accountable.'

[20] *United States of America v HSBC Bank USA N.A. and HSBC Holdings Inc* 12 Cr 763 (EDNY, 11 December 2012) lib.law.virginia.edu/Garrett/prosecution_agreements/pdf/HSBC.pdf. The online resource contains the charges, the text of the deferred prosecution, an agreed statement of facts and the terms governing the appointment of an external monitor. Hereafter these are referenced as 'United States Charges', 'Deferred Prosecution Terms', 'Attachment A: Statement of Facts' and 'Attachment B: Corporate Compliance Monitor'.

[21] 31 U.S.C. 5311-5332.

years to address an increase in criminal money laundering activities utilizing financial institutions, requires regulated entities to detect and report suspicious activity. Furthermore they are required to maintain records that could be used in criminal, tax or regulatory investigations or court proceedings. The bank's failure to comply with anti-money laundering legislation was not historical. Rather the deficiencies encompassed the period January 2006-December 2010; a period that straddled the Global Financial Crisis. In the same period it was charged that HSBC willfully failed to conduct due diligence on correspondent bank accounts for non-United States persons. Correspondent accounts are set up to make or receive payments from individuals or organizations with which the US-based bank has no direct relationship. Under the terms of the *Bank Secrecy Act*, HSBC Bank USA was required to conduct extensive due diligence on the financial institutions it held these correspondent accounts for. Inexplicably, HSBC Bank USA failed to do so in relation to accounts held by its affiliate in Mexico, notwithstanding the fact that there is no exception for foreign financial institutions within the same holding company. This, the count charged, inhibited the collection of material, which would have reasonably allowed for the detection and reporting of instances of money laundering and other suspicious activity.[22]

The risk posed by initial failure to conduct the due diligence on the establishment of the accounts was magnified by an ongoing failure to monitor wire transfers within and between them. It was further compounded by the absence of anti-money laundering protocols in the HSBC Mexico operation itself. The combination was rendered catastrophic for the parent company by its use of vertical reporting lines. This meant that HSBC Bank USA was not directly informed of growing unease of regulatory, diplomatic and law enforcement agencies on both sides of the Rio Grande about a rapid expansion of money laundering across the Mexican banking sector and in which HSBC Mexico played a pivotal if unwitting role. The money laundering charges were conjoined with two counts dealing with sanctions violation. The third count charged violations of the *International Emergency Economic Powers Act of 1977*.[23] Between 2001–2006, HSBC 'knowingly, intentionally and willfully facilitated prohibited transactions for sanctioned entities in Iran, Libya, Sudan and Burma.' HSBC knowingly and willingly circumvented government safeguards designed to block terrorist funding, allowing, for example, affiliates to shield the fact that thousands of transactions involved links to Iran. The Senate investigation suggested the problem was even more widespread. An independent audit paid for by HSBC found the bank facilitated 25,000 questionable transactions with Iran between 2001 and 2007.[24] The report also detailed that HSBC worked extensively with Saudi Arabia's Al Rajhi Bank, some owners of which have been linked to terrorism financing. HSBC's US affiliate supplied Al Rajhi with nearly $1 billion worth of US banknotes until 2010, and worked with two banks in Bangladesh linked to terrorism financing. The fourth count charged that HSBC had engaged in similar activity in relation to Cuba in violation of the *Trading with the Enemy Act of 1917*.[25]

The reputational damage to HSBC comes primarily, however, from the first two counts, not least because of the immediate cost of the drugs war on American society.[26] Astonishingly, the failure of the compliance policies and procedures is estimated to have

---

[22]   The United States Charges, above n 20, 11.
[23]   50 U.S.C. 1702.
[24]   *U.S. Vulnerabilities to Money Laundering, Drugs and Terrorist Financing: HSBC Case Study*, above n16.
[25]   12 U.S.C. §95a et seq.
[26]   It is this aspect of the case that has dominated media coverage; see for example, Taibi, above n16.

caused at least $881 million in drug proceeds to filter through the United States financial system.[27] This was primarily achieved through the preference of drug cartels for using HSBC Mexico as a conduit for what was termed the 'Black Market Peso Exchange',[28] going as far as designing special containers that fit precisely under the teller windows installed across the bank's branch network. Building on an investigation launched in 2008 by the Department of Homeland Security into how HSBC Bank USA had been compromised, the litigation paints a dismal picture of willful neglect at national and international levels within the bank.[29] When read in conjunction with the detailed Congressional investigation, the Statement of Facts reveals how the cartels operated with apparent impunity.[30] Together, as highlighted above, they point to significant flaws in the entire HSBC business model.

The inability of HSBC, the London-headquartered self-styled world's local bank, to know how its affiliates were operating in critical markets does more than puncture a marketing myth. It also demonstrates the limited power that compliance departments at both national and broader group levels had to influence strategic direction. In operating on a franchise basis, rebranding foreign acquisitions without necessarily changing their culture or integrating them fully into global template, the bank institutionalized a silo approach to corporate governance and risk management. A senior London-based compliance officer noted the risk and likely result in discussions with a counterpart in Mexico as late as 2008,[31]

---

[27] The United States Charges above n 20, 9–12.

[28] 'Attachment A: Statement of Facts', The United States Charges, above n 20 ('In the BMPE, middlemen, often referred to as peso brokers, transform bulk cash from the sale of illegal drugs into revenue from the sale of legitimate goods. In this process, the peso brokers purchase bulk cash in United States dollars from drug cartels at a discounted rate, in return for Colombian pesos that belong to Colombian businessmen. The peso brokers then use the U.S. dollars to purchase legitimate goods from businesses in the United States and other foreign countries, on behalf of the Colombian businessmen. These goods are then sent to the Colombian businessmen, who sell the goods for Colombian pesos to recoup their original investment. In the end, the Colombian businessmen obtain U.S. dollars at a lower exchange rate than otherwise available in Colombia, the Colombian cartel leaders receive Colombian pesos while avoiding the costs associated with depositing U.S. dollars directly into Colombian financial institutions, and the peso brokers receive fees for their services as middlemen' at para. 49).

[29] ibid, para. 50 ('The Department alleges, and HSBC Bank USA and HSBC Holdings do not contest, that, beginning in 2008, an investigation conducted by HSI's El Dorado Task Force, in conjunction with the U.S. Attorney's Office for the Eastern District of New York, identified multiple HSBC Mexico accounts associated with BMPE activity. The investigation further revealed that drug traffickers were depositing hundreds of thousands of dollars in bulk U.S. currency each day into HSBC Mexico accounts. In order to efficiently move this volume of cash through the teller windows at HSBC Mexico branches, drug traffickers designed specially shaped boxes that fit the precise dimensions of the teller windows. The drug traffickers would send numerous boxes filled with cash through the teller windows for deposit into HSBC Mexico accounts. After the cash was deposited in the accounts, peso brokers then wire transferred the U.S. dollars to various exporters located in New York City and other locations throughout the United States to purchase goods for Colombian businesses. The U.S. exporters then sent the goods directly to the businesses in Colombia. . . .The investigation further revealed that, because of its lax AML controls, HSBC Mexico was the preferred financial institution for drug cartels and money launderers. The drug trafficking proceeds (in physical US dollars) deposited at HSBC Mexico as part of the BMPE were sold to HSBC Bank USA through banknotes. In addition, many of the BMPE wire transfers to exporters in the United States passed through HSBC Mexico's correspondent account with HSBC Bank USA.

[30] For analysis of the Congressional investigation and HSBC's response, see J O'Brien, 'Where the Buck Stops' *Australian Financial Review*, 27 July 2012, R1, 14–15.

[31] ibid, (noting that in 'July 2007, a senior compliance officer at HSBC Group told HSBC Mexico's Chief Compliance Officer that '[t]he AML committee just can't keep rubber-stamping unacceptable risks merely because someone on the business side writes a nice letter. It needs to take a firmer stand. It needs some cojones. We have seen this movie before, and it ends badly:' at para. 34).

six years after HSBC's acquisition of Grupo Financiero Bital in 2002, at the time the country's fifth biggest bank, with 1,400 branches and 6 million customers.[32] The catalogue of failure within and between the disparate components of HSBC as outlined in the agreed 'Statement of Facts' is as extensive as it is shocking.

> Specifically, HSBC Bank USA ignored the money laundering risks associated with doing business with certain Mexican customers and failed to implement a BSA/AML program that was adequate to monitor suspicious transactions from Mexico. At the same time, Grupo Financiero HSBC, S.A. de C.V. ("HSBC Mexico"), one of HSBC Bank USA's largest Mexican customers, had its own significant AML problems. As a result of these concurrent AML failures, at least $881 million in drug trafficking proceeds, including proceeds of drug trafficking by the Sinaloa Cartel in Mexico and the Norte del Valle Cartel in Colombia, were laundered through HSBC Bank USA without being detected. HSBC Group was aware of the significant AML compliance problems at HSBC Mexico, yet did not inform HSBC Bank USA of these problems and their potential impact on HSBC Bank USA's AML program.[33]

The identified problems started within the Mexican operation. Despite the fact that the Mexican financial regulatory authority, the Comision Nacional Bancaria y Valores (the 'CNBV'), had flagged its concerns in external reviews, which were, in turn, escalated to the Chief Executive Officer of HSBC Holdings; no integrated approach on how to rank country risk was initiated.[34] Notwithstanding growing national and international concern about the rise of drug trafficking in and through Mexico, HSBC Bank USA maintained a risk ranking of 'standard'. This was the lowest rated risk. It meant that the accounts were given only cursory examination.[35]

Given the critical financial relationship between HSBC Mexico and its counterpart in the United States and awareness in both jurisdictions as well as headquarters in London of how the Mexican financial system was used as a global money laundering gateway, this amounted to a reckless disregard towards risk management. Over $200 trillion in wire transfers passed between HSBC Bank USA and its global affiliates, with $659 billion coming from Mexico alone. The risk was not confined, however, to the retail bank operation. The systemic risk was magnified by the fact that HSBC's global banknotes operation, headquartered in New York, is the largest volume trader of physical currency in the world, controlling sixty per cent of the market.[36] $9.4 billion in physical banknotes were purchased from accounts linked to the Mexican operation in the period July 2006–July 2009 alone. The bank derived its revenue from commissions on the sale or purchase of physical dollars and its transportation and storage at the Federal Reserve. The Statement of Facts notes, however, that the banknotes compliance operation was not only almost ludicrously understaffed.

---

[32] ibid. ('At the time of the acquisition, HSBC Group's Head of Compliance acknowledged there was "no recognizable compliance or money laundering function in Bital at present." HSBC Group Compliance believed it would take one to four years to achieve its required AML standards at HSBC Mexico. However, until at least 2010, HSBC Mexico's AML program was not fully up to HSBC Group's required AML standards for HSBC Group Affiliates: para. 30).

[33] ibid, para 9.

[34] ibid, para 31.

[35] ibid, para 18. (The Statement of Facts further notes that 'from 2006 until May 2009, when HSBC Bank USA raised Mexico's risk rating to high, over 316,000 transactions worth over $670 billion from HSBC Mexico alone were excluded from monitoring in the CAMP system': at para 19).

[36] ibid, para 20.

It also lacked an automated monitoring function.[37] Throughout this period the bank, while aware of the risk, failed to 'provide adequate staffing and other resources to maintain an effective anti-money laundering program'.

The clear inference is that such were the profits deriving from the operation it was not in the interests of HSBC, at any level, to investigate much less close suspicious accounts. According to the Statement of Facts, the problems were addressed only on receipt of a cease and desist order issued by the Federal Reserve and the Office of the Comptroller of the Currency in October 2010.[38] Although the filing of the criminal charges and their subsequent deferral relate only to anti-money-laundering control violations in relation to Mexico, the statement of facts makes clear that the nature of HSBC and its geographic exposure constituted an inherent risk. It sets out that 'HSBC Group Affiliates conducted business in many high-risk international locations, including regions of the world presenting a high vulnerability to the laundering of drug trafficking proceeds'.[39] This speaks directly to the possibility of broader systemic risks. Unstated in the report but clearly inferred is that HSBC's failure in relation to Mexico may well be only the tip of the iceberg.

In this regard, two factors in relation to the HSBC settlement warrant significant attention. First, the scale of the HSBC disgorgement and civil penalties fine sends an unambiguous message that materiality is increasing. As the *Financial Times* has noted, 'a billion here, a billion there and pretty soon you are talking about serious money.'[40] Second, the fine is the least of HSBC's concerns in relation to its ongoing corporate governance and risk evaluation. The imposition of an external monitor sends an unambiguous message that the bank's commitment to reform should not be taken at face value. Before exploring the rationale, terms and implications, it is essential to highlight the extent to which HSBC has already transformed the compliance function.

III   REMEDIAL ACTION

HSBC has done much to improve the quality of its internal governance, including recruiting former heavyweights from the Department of Justice, Treasury and the Department of Homeland Security to pivotal management positions. The newly appointed Chief Legal Officer, Stuart Levey, in particular, was an inspired choice. He was recruited to the bank direct from the US Department of Treasury, where he had developed a formidable reputation as Under Secretary for Terrorism and Financial Intelligence. As HSBC's Chief Legal

---

[37] ibid, para 22.

[38] ibid, para 11. Although the OCC is the recipient of a $500m fine, it is important to note significant unease over its monitoring operations; see *US Vulnerabilities to Money Laundering, Drugs, and Terrorist Financing: HSBC Case History*, n 1 above, 316 (Specifically, the Senate report into the Mexican operation is as critical of the OCC as it is of HSBC itself: 'For more than six years, from July 2004 until April 2010, despite compiling a litany of AML deficiencies, the OCC never cited HBUS for a violation of law, never took a formal or informal enforcement action, and turned down recommendations to issue Cease and Desist Orders targeting particularly egregious AML problems, even though the same problems surfaced again and again. The OCC's failure to compel HBUS to remedy the AML deficiencies repeatedly identified by its examiners over a six-year period indicates that systemic weaknesses in the OCC's AML oversight model require correction').

[39] 'Attachment A: Statement of Facts', above n20, para 12.

[40] Editorial, 'Paying the Price for the Banks' Mistakes', *Financial Times*, 11 December 2012 www.ft.com/intl/cms/s/0/7e97873a-43a1-11e2-a48c-00144feabdc0.html#axzz2F4BqZ9tM.

Officer, Levy flagged many of the remedial actions taken by the bank in an assured performance to the Senate Sub-Committee on Investigations in July.

> While our old model served us well historically, it does not work in an interconnected world where transactions cross borders instantaneously and where weaknesses in one jurisdiction can be quickly exported to others . . ..We have learned that our approach to compliance–and AML in particular–was not adequate to address the risks we face as a global institution. And we have learned that we did not share information effectively enough across our affiliates, with serious consequences. . . . We must implement a global strategy to tackle the root causes of our identified deficiencies.[41]

These deficiencies centered on the fact that at a global level, compliance served an advisory rather than a control function, which had neither the resources or empowerment to provide a monitoring function. Responsibility for ensuring that standards were being implemented was delegated to country level. As the bank now acknowledges, 'this led to inconsistency and in some cases confusion about ownership and escalation responsibility.' In candid testimony to Congress, Levy detailed how he negotiated the job parameters. 'In our conversations, the Chairman of the Board and the new CEO were candid with me about the problems HSBC faced, the reforms they wanted me to help them implement, and the empowerment that I would need and have,' he said. It appears he has now that power.[42] 'Group Compliance is empowered to set standards across the organization and now has the necessary authority to reach down into affiliates and ensure that those standards are being met. . . . The work we have undertaken is ambitious and complicated given our size and our global footprint, but we all recognize that it must be done', he told a receptive audience on Capitol Hill.[43] The work plan centres on the creation of four core business units: global markets and banking, commercial banking, private banking and retail banking and wealth management.

> We gave the heads of each business and function the authority over all personnel in their respective organizations all over the world, thus creating the ability to manage their business or function on a global basis, making it easier to implement consistent policies, standards, and processes,' he said. 'What that means is that the most senior people responsible for managing HSBC globally sit around a table every month, look at our risks, and make decisions. . . . Better global integration makes us better situated today to manage our risk on a global basis, better able to see where risk in one part of HSBC may impact another part, and better able for the first time to ensure that consistent compliance standards and practices are implemented across all of our affiliates.[44]

It is a laudable vision but one that cannot be vouchsafed without external review and validation. The Department of Justice has itself praised the level of cooperation. Significantly, however, in sharp contrast to prior cases involving sanctions violations (or the approach taken by the Securities and Exchange Commission's in its non-prosecution deal with Goldman Sachs to trust the bank to reform), the Department of Justice has not taken HSBC's word for it. It is the fear that symbolism will trump substance that underpins the decision to appoint an external monitor. The terms governing the appointment are

---

[41] S Levey, 'Written Testimony for Senate Permanent Subcommittee on Investigations' (US Congress, Washington, DC, 17 July, 2012).
[42] ibid.
[43] ibid.
[44] ibid.

exceptionally revealing of the level of distrust. It is abundantly clear that the Department of Justice is, at best, sceptical of self-regulation. That scepticism has an explicit extra-territorial dimension and extends beyond the governance of the bank to the global markets in which it operates.

IV   THE IMPOSITION OF AN EXTERNAL MONITOR

In December 2012, two different approaches to embedding restraint began to take shape as London headquartered banks reflect on the exceptional power of the United States Department of Justice to shift cultural mores through the flexing of its prosecutorial discretion. Both provide tangible evidence of the Department's renewed interest in the financial sector. HSBC is in the process of submitting to the Department of Justice a pool of three suitably qualified candidates to the position of Independent Compliance Monitor, a pool that the Department can unilaterally reject.[45] Meanwhile Barclays, which reached a financial settlement in relation to its role in the Libor scandal in August without the imposition of an external monitor is also ruminating over its future. In December 2012, Barclays announced that it had recruited Hector Sants, the former chief executive of the Financial Services Authority as Group Head of Compliance and Government and Regulatory Relations. Given Sants' previous stated interest in and support for the necessity of regulating culture, the appointment serves as a litmus test for both the bank and his own credibility.[46]

The critical but unresolved question for the banks and regulatory authorities on both sides of the Atlantic as well as here in Australia is to what extent the imposition of an external monitor who reports to the regulator rather than the board reflects 'the new normal'—the theme of the March 13 Australian Securities and Investments Commission Annual Forum on international regulatory developments.[47] At its core, this involves an adjudication

---

[45] 'Attachment B: Corporate Compliance Monitor,' n 20 above, para 1.

[46] Barclays Bank, 'Barclays Appoints Sants As Head of Compliance and Government and Regulatory Relations' (Press Release, London, 13 December 2012) http://group.barclays.com/news/news-article/1329927766649. In the period 2009–2010, Sants made three influential speeches on how to design, legitimate and implement regulatory initiatives surrounding the embedding of cultural restraint; see Hector Sants, 'Delivering Intensive Supervision and Credible Deterrence', speech delivered at the Reuters Newsmaker Event, London, 12 March, 2009, 2 noting 'the limitation of a pure principles-based regime have [sic] to be recognized. I continue to believe the majority of market participants are decent people; however a principles-based approach does not work with people who have no principles'; H Sants, 'Annual Lubbock Lecture in Management Studies', speech delivered at Said Business School, University of Oxford, March 12, 2010, noting 'We need to answer the question of whether a regulator has a legitimate focus to intervene on the question of culture. This arguably requires both a view on the right culture and a mechanism for intervention. . . . My personal view is that if we really do wish to learn lessons from the past, we need to change not just the regulatory rules and supervisory approach, but also the culture and attitudes of both society as a whole, and the management of major financial firms. This will not be easy. A cultural trend can be very widespread and resilient–as has been seen by a return to a "business as usual" mentality. Nevertheless, no culture is inevitable'; and H Sants, 'Can Culture Be Regulated', speech delivered at the Ethics and Values in the City Conference, London, 5 October 2010, noting 'The regulator must focus on the actions a firm takes and whether the board has a compelling story to tell about how it ensures it has the right culture that rings true and is consistent with what the firm does.'

[47] In the interests of full disclosure, this author was a keynote speaker (although his address centred on the historical underpinnings of the rationale for intervention).

of what constitutes the appropriate level of external oversight over ongoing corporate practice. As such, it extends far beyond narrow issues of capitalization. It focuses attention
instead on the critical questions of how to ensure warranted trust in the operation of free
markets while balancing more intrusive supervision with requisite levels of both expertise
and accountability.[48] It also underscores the critical importance of evaluating when and on
what basis these decisions are made. Notwithstanding their prevalence, there is a remarkable lack of consistency in the application and use of a deferred prosecution, the size of the
fine and whether an external monitor is imposed. A database compiled by the University of
Virginia Law School reveals that of 258 negotiated prosecutions involving either a deferred
or non-prosecution, 79 have imposed an external monitor: 21 in the case of non-prosecution
deals and 58 in which the prosecution is deferred.[49] Of the total, 56 have involved firms in
the financial sector.[50] Of these, an independent monitor has been imposed 14 times, equally

---

[48] See Morford, above n 2, 5. (The Department of Justice clearly differentiates the role of the monitor, arguing
that the 'monitor is not responsible to the corporation's shareholders. Therefore, from a corporate governance
standpoint, responsibility for designing an ethics and compliance program that will prevent misconduct should
remain with the corporation, subject to the monitor's input, evaluation and recommendations.')

[49] All data sourced from B Garrett and J Ashley, *Federal Organizational Prosecution Agreements*, University of
Virginia School of Law, at lib.law.virginia.edu/Garrett/prosecution_agreements/home.suphp.

[50] Salomon Brothers (jurisdiction not specified; 1/5/92; NPA); John Hancock Mutual Life (Massachusetts;
22/3/94; NPA); Prudential Securities (NY-Southern; 27/10/94; DPA); Lazard Freres (Massachusetts; 26/10/95;
NPA); Arthur Andersen (Connecticut; 17/4/96; DPA); Coopers & Lybrand (jurisdiction not specified;
1/10/96; NPA); Credit Lyonnais (California – Central; 7/6/99; NPA); JB Oxford Holdings, Inc. (California –
Central; 14/2/00; NPA); HSBC (NY–Southern; 1/12/01; NPA); BDO Seidman (Illinois – Southern & USDOJ
Criminal; 12/4/02; DPA); Banco Popular de Puerto Rico (Puerto Rico; 16/1/03 DPA); Bank of New York (NY –
Southern and Eastern; 27/5/03; NPA); PNC Financial (Pennsylvania – Western & USDOJ – Criminal; 1/6/03;
DPA); Merrill Lynch (USDOJ – Enron; 17/10/03; NPA); Canadian Imperial Bank of Commerce (USDOJ –
Enron; 22/12/03; DPA); AmSouth Bancorp (Mississippi – Southern; 12/10/04; DPA); American International
Group (AIG-FP PAGIC Equity Holding Company & AIG Financial Products) (Pennsylvania – Western &
USDOJ – Criminal; 1/11/04; DPA); Edward D Jones (Missouri – Eastern; 1/12/04; DPA); KPMG (NY–Southern;
26/10/05; DPA); HVB (NY–Southern; 1/2/06; DPA); American International Group (USDOJ – Criminal; 7/2/06;
NPA); BankAtlantic (Florida – Southern; 25/4/06; NPA); BAWAG psk (NY–Southern; 2/6/06; NPA); Mellon Bank, NA
(Pennsylvania – Western; 14/8/06; NPA); Prudential Equity Group (Massachusetts; 28/8/06; NPA); Electronic
Clearing House (ECHO) Inc. (NY – Southern; 27/3/07; NPA); Omega Advisors (USDOJ – Criminal Division &
NY Southern; 5/7/07; NPA); United Bank for Africa (NY–Southern; 6/7/07; NPA); NETeller Plc (NY-Southern;
17/7/07; DPA); American Express Bank Intl' (USDOJ – Criminal; 6/8/07; DPA); Union Bank of California
(USDOJ – Criminal; 17/10/07; DPA); Sigue (USDOJ – Criminal; 23/1/08; DPA); Unum Group (California –
Southern; 1/6/08; NPA); Lloyds TSB Bank plc (USDOJ – Criminal; 22/12/08; DPA); UBS AG (Florida – Southern;
18/2/09; DPA); Credit Suisse AG (USDOJ – Criminal; 16/12/09; DPA); General Reinsurance (USDOJ –
Criminal; 18/1/10; NPA); Wachovia (Florida – Southern & USDOJ – Criminal; 16/3/10; DPA); Metropolitan
Life Insurance Company (California – Southern; 15/4/10; NPA); AllianceOne (USDOJ – Criminal; 6/8/10;
DPA); Barclays Bank (USDOJ – Criminal; 16/8/10; DPA); Deutsche Bank AG (NY–Southern and USDOJ –
Tax; 21/12/10; NPA); Baystar Capital Management LLC (California – Northern; 1/3/11; DPA); Community
One Bank (North Carolina – Western and USDOJ – Criminal; 1/5/11; NPA); UBS AG (USDOJ – Antitrust;
4/5/11; NPA); JPMorgan Chase & Co (USDOJ – Criminal; 6/7/11; NPA); Ocean Bank (Florida – Southern;
12/8/11; DPA); Islamic Investment Cos. Of the Gulf (Bahamas) Ltd (USDOJ – Tax; 12/8/11; NPA); Wachovia
Bank NA (USDOJ – Antitrust; 6/12/11; NPA); Aon Corp (USDOJ – Criminal; 20/12/11; NPA); GE Funding
Capital Markets Services Inc (USDOJ – Antitrust; 23/12/11; NPA); Diamondback Capital Management LLC
(NY–Southern; 20/1/12; NPA); Imperial Holdings Inc. (New Hampshire; 30/4/12; NPA); BDO USA LLP (NY –
Southern & USDOJ Tax; 6/6/12; DPA); ING Bank NV (USDOJ – National Security & Criminal Division;
12/6/12; DPA); Barclays Bank (USDOJ – Criminal; 26/6/12; NPA).

split between both non-prosecution[51] and deferred cases.[52] When the decision is made to impose a monitor, however, the terms and conditions follow a generic template.[53] The Department of Justice has also sought to impose consistency in how the monitors operate with the public release of guidance to individual prosecutorial units.[54] The HSBC requirement to subject itself to an external monitor flows precisely those guidelines.

'To the extent that HSBC Holdings' compliance with obligations as set forth below requires it, HSBC Holdings agrees to require that its wholly-owned subsidiaries comply with the requirements and obligations set forth below, to the extent permissible under locally applicable laws and regulations, and the instructions of local regulatory agencies,' runs the opening paragraph of the job description for the position of Corporate Compliance Monitor.[55] The position is a fixed term for five years, at the end of which HSBC must sever ties with the monitor for at least one year. The role is to evaluate the effectiveness of the internal controls, policies and procedures of the holding company and its subsidiaries in relation to both anti-money-laundering legislation and the remedial action taken in response to the identified failures. An initial report is required within 90 calendar days of the appointment, which itself is mandated within 60 days of the agreement. Four additional reviews are to be conducted on an annual basis, unless the agreement is either terminated or rendered moot because a further material breach triggers immediate indictment.

The reports are to be contemporaneously submitted to the Board of Directors of HSBC Holdings and the Chief of the Asset Forfeiture and Anti-Money-Laundering Section of the Criminal Division, the address of which is helpfully provided, as well as to the Federal Reserve and the Financial Services Authority in London. Interestingly, however, the Financial Services Authority is not given any defined right to engage with the Monitor, nor is any of the other parties to the agreement.[56] This is the Department of Justice's show. Although HSBC can identify and propose the candidate, the Department of

---

[51] Coopers & Lybrand (obtaining confidential bid information and lying to grand jury); JB Oxford Holdings, Inc. (securities fraud; failure to disclose activities and beneficial ownership); Bank of New York (money laundering; unlicensed money transfers; no anti-money-laundering program); Merrill Lynch (false statements; aided and abetted Enron); American International Group (misstatements in periodic financial reports; Bank Secrecy Act; failure to maintain effective anti-money-laundering program); Mellon Bank NA (theft of government property; theft of mail matter; conspiracy); Deutsche Bank AG (tax evasion).

[52] The deferred prosecutions requiring an external monitor comprise Prudential Securities (fraud in sale of partnership interests–$330m settlement with SEC; 3 years); Canadian Imperial Bank of Commerce (aided and abetted accounting fraud by Enron–$80m settlement with SEC; 3 years); American International Group (violations of antifraud provisions and aiding and abetting violations of reporting and record keeping–$80 million settlement with Department of Justice); KPMG (tax fraud; conspiracy to defraud IRS; tax evasion – $466 million settlement with Department of Justice ($128m disgorgement of fees; $228 restitution to IRS; $100 fines to IRS; 3 years); NETeller PLC (conspiracy to conduct an illegal gambling business; failure to maintain an anti-money-laundering program–$136 million forfeiture: 2 years); Lloyds TSB Bank Plc (knowing and willful violations of International Emergency Economic Powers Act–$175 million forfeiture to Department of Justice; 2 years); AllianceOne (violation of Foreign corrupt Practices Act–no fine; 3 years).

[53] The requirements and language used to describe those requirements are almost identical to those used in cases against Bionet and Smith & Nephew.

[54] See Morford, above n 2.

[55] 'Attachment B: Corporate Compliance Monitor', above n 20, para 1.

[56] The Financial Services Authority has separately agreed that HSBC should establish an AML/sanctions compliance board level committee, review policies and procedures and notes the employment of an independent monitor who is to communicate to the board and to regulators; see Financial Services Authority, 'FSA Requires Action of the HSBC Group' (Press Release, London, 13 December 2012).

Justice retains a veto over the appointment and the procedures governing the production of her reports. The arms-length terms as they relate to HSBC are explicit. The appointee cannot have had a material association with the bank. They are less clear-cut in relation to the Department of Justice itself. It does not have to justify its preference beyond ensuring that the appointee is regarded as having requisite, if generically explained, expertise.[57] Once appointed, the independent monitor has the capacity to use enormous leverage from the Department of Justice. At stake here, therefore, is not just the credibility of the monitor but also the Department.[58]

The symbiotic nature of the relationship is explicitly spelt out in the terms of the negotiated settlement. The monitor has the right to report any difficulties associated with gaining access to sensitive material, with the Department having the right to make a final determination on what should be disclosed without reference to further external adjudication. Therefore the monitor, although ostensibly independent, is unquestionably an agent of the Department. On an ongoing basis the work plan for conducting the evaluations of policies, procedures and remedial action must be submitted to and approved in advance by the Department. Moreover, 'any disputes between HSBC Holdings and the Monitor with respect to the work plan shall be decided by the Department in its sole discretion.'

Although the monitor is encouraged to work closely with HSBC in the preparation of the reports, the bank itself lacks the discretion on whether to implement any recommendation unless considered 'unduly burdensome, inconsistent with local or other applicable law or regulation, impractical, costly or otherwise inadvisable.' In such an event the bank has to provide reasons for the objections 'and shall propose in writing an alternative policy, procedure or system designed to achieve the same objective or purpose.' The parties are then given 30 days to reach an agreement.

> In the event HSBC Holdings and the Monitor are unable to agree on an acceptable alternative proposal, HSBC Holdings shall promptly consult with the Department, which will make a determination as to whether HSBC Holdings should adopt the Monitor's recommendation or an alternative proposal, and HSBC Holdings shall abide by that determination.[59]

---

[57] Deferred Prosecution Agreement, above n 20, para 9 ('demonstrated expertise with regards to the Bank Secrecy Act; demonstrated expertise in the design and review of corporate compliance policies, procedures and internal controls; the ability to access and deploy resources as necessary to discharge duties and sufficient independence from HSNB Holdings to ensure effective and impartial performance). For examination of how monitors carry out their roles, see Khanna and Dickinson, above n 17, 1725–31 (noting that most tend to be former prosecutors); see also D Hess and C Ford, 'Corporate Corruption and Reform Undertakings: A New Approach to an Old Problem' (2008) 41 *Cornell International Law Journal* 307, 341 (noting the importance of industry experience, the necessity of being 'structurally and psychologically independent from the corporation' and having 'own reputational capital at stake'); see also C Ford, 'Towards a New Model for Securities Law Enforcement' (2005) 57 *Administrative Law Review* 757, 797–802 (noting the emergence of the monitor as an agent of behavioural change).

[58] In December 2012, the American Bar Association announced the formation of a working group to draw up a set of best-practice principles governing how monitorship should operate; see 'ABA Launches Taskforce on Corporate Monitors', *Corporate Crime Monitor*, 5 December 2012 www.corporatecrimereporter.com/news/200/abacorporatemonitortaskforce12052012. The taskforce includes Larry Thompson, the former Deputy Attorney General who rapidly expanded the use of deferred prosecution (see n15) and Mary Jo White, the former District Attorney Southern District of New York who pioneered the extension of the mechanism in the prosecution of Prudential Securities in 1994 (n50). White was subsequently nominated for the chairmanship of the Securities and Exchange Commission and confirmed by the Senate.

[59] 'Attachment B: Corporate Compliance Monitor', above n 20, para 5.

Moreover, the Department is to be informed if—in the course of the Monitor's investigation of the efficacy of internal controls, policies and procedures—improper conduct or a material violation of the law is uncovered, and such activity is to be reported directly to the bank's Chief Legal Officer. This can be bypassed if deemed appropriate by the monitor. The whistle-blowing protection is further embedded in the contractual terms as 'HSBC Holdings shall not take any action to retaliate against the Monitor for any such disclosures or any other reason.'[60] The Department of Justice, recognizing that the information contained in the Compliance Monitors' reports may include 'proprietary, financial, confidential, and business information has agreed, in principle, to keep the reports classified.'[61] Public disclosure 'could discourage cooperation, impede impending or potential government investigations and thus undermine the objectives of the Monitorship.'[62] Even here however, the Department can override the commitment to confidentiality if it 'determines in its sole discretion that disclosure would be in furtherance of the Department's discharge of its duties and responsibilities or is otherwise required by law.'[63]

Taken together, the provisions governing the appointment and ongoing work of the Monitor reflect an unparalleled extension of external oversight. As such, they allay judicial suspicion about limited exercise of discretion.[64] Just as significantly they transfer knowledge directly to the Criminal Division of the Department of Justice, whose remit is governed by very different imperatives than prudential or market conduct regulators. A new cop is on the beat and making its presence felt. Those drinking in the Last Chance Saloon are on notice that Anti-Social Behavior Orders have been written and will be applied in the event of further infractions. It is not before time. The challenge for the Department of Justice, however, is to exercise its enhanced power with restraint and within accountable boundaries. If not, the regulatory cycle will turn once more, with accusations of overreach and unconstitutionality replacing quiescence in the creation of robust external oversight.

---

[60]   ibid, para 8.

[61]   ibid.

[62]   ibid.

[63]   ibid, para 9.

[64]   *SEC v Bank of America* 09 Civ. 6829 (SDNY, 14 September 2009) 8. (Judge Jed Rakoff held 'the proposed settlement in relation to claim that Bank of America had misled investors over the payment of bonuses to executives within Merrill Lynch is described as 'a contrivance designed to provide the SEC with the facade of enforcement and the management of the Bank with a quick resolution of an embarrassing inquiry'). Judge Rakoff reluctantly signed off on the settlement, citing judicial restraint but stating that the settlement was 'half baked justice at best.' See *SEC v Bank of America* 09 Civ. 6829 (SDNY, 22 February 2010) 14. Similar frustration has been voiced by Judge Ellen Segal Huvelle, who refused to endorse a $75million fine agreed upon by Citigroup to settle charges that the bank had misled investors over its sub-prime exposure; see K Scannell, 'Judge Won't Approve Citi-SEC Pact', *Wall Street Journal*, 17 August 2010, B1 ('I look at this and say, "Why would I find this fair and reasonable".... You expect the court to rubber stamp, but we can't'). See generally, B Appelbaum, 'US Judges Sound Off on Bank Settlements' *New York Times*, 23 August 2010, B1 (noting broader opposition to recent settlements proposed with Barclays, Citigroup and Bank of America). In a subsequent case taken against Citigroup, a firm Judge Rakoff described as a 'recidivist' offender, the District Court Judge refused to endorse the agreement. The judgment is currently under appeal, with the Securities and exchange Commission describing it as unwarranted judicial interference on its discretion; see Securities and Exchange Commission, 'Enforcement Director Statement on Citigroup Case' Press Release, Washington DC, 15 December 2011. The United Kingdom intends to ensure that 'a prosecutor is not entering into a "cosy deal" with a commercial organization behind "closed doors" by ensuring judicial oversight of the entire process', Ministry of Justice (above n14), 21.

V THE POLICY IMPLICATIONS

The external monitor at HSBC holds what Lanny Breur describes as a 'Sword of Damocles' over the bank. It also applies to the Department of Justice itself. Future violations will automatically trigger the criminal conviction and could produce the very outcome the settlement is designed to avoid.[65] Equally, the application of external stewardship can have far-reaching consequences. In the aftermath of the settlement, HSBC share price rose marginally, reflecting a degree of closure. If anything, however, the sword is even more delicately poised. As with the global media industry in the aftermath of the Leveson Inquiry in the UK[66] and its facsimile in Australia,[67] however, the banking sector is drinking in the last chance saloon as a consequence of the burgeoning Libor scandal.

Compliance or cultural problems within a single bank, no matter how serious, can be contained by one of three methods. First, the company can adopt voluntary structural reform, an approach initially favored by HSBC's Stuart Levey but ultimately rejected by the Department of Justice. Secondly, as Lanny Breuer of the Department of Justice has advocated, one can use a deferred prosecution to facilitate 'a truly transformative effect on particular companies and, more generally, on corporate culture across the globe.'[68] Thirdly, if necessary, closure is available, an option advanced by Senator Levin. When the identified problems extend to allegations of collusion between banks, however, the entire social construction of the market itself comes under scrutiny. The corruption of core stated values have reached an inflection point with the multi-faceted international investigation now under way into price-fixing within Libor. As the influential United Kingdom Treasury Select Committee reported in August, 'the standards and culture of Barclays, and banking more widely, are in a poor state. Urgent reform, by both regulators and banks, is needed to prevent such misconduct flourishing.'[69]

The now emboldened Department of Justice and, in particular, its Criminal Division under the direction of Lanny Breuer, is playing a pivotal role in these discussions. Its leveraging power in this and other cases is further strengthened by enhanced whistle-blowing legislation in the United States. In particular, the expansion of a bounty system for those willing to report improper, unethical conduct significantly increases the possibility that such conduct will be reported to external agencies.[70] The critical question, then, will not be

---

[65] See Masters, above n17. For review of how individual corporations have fared post corporate prosecution, see G Markoff, 'Arthur Andersen and the Myth of the Corporate Death Penalty: Corporate Criminal Prosecution in the Twenty-First Century' *University of Pennsylvania Journal of Business Law* (2013, *forthcoming*), working paper available at http://ssrn.com/abstract=2132242. The paper notes that no publicly traded corporation convicted in the period 2001–10 has failed, which suggests that corporate prosecutions should be privileged because of its inherently stronger demonstration effect: at 7. He does accept, however, that the deferred prosecution should be used in situations where 'a prosecution might actually threaten a company's survival': at 44. Arguably banks are in this position.

[66] Lord Justice Bran Leveson, *An Inquiry into the Culture, Practices and Ethics of the Press* (The Stationary Office, London 2012) www.official-documents.gov.uk/document/hc1213/hc07/0780/0780.asp.

[67] Justice Raymond Finkelstein, *Independent Inquiry into Media and Media Regulation* (Canberra, The Australian Government, 2 March 2012).

[68] Breur, above n11.

[69] Treasury Select Committee, *Fixing Libor: Some Preliminary Findings*, (HM Parliament, London, 22 August 2012).

[70] *Wall Street Reform and Consumer Protection Act of 2010* (Dodd-Frank), s. 922; see also Securities and Exchange Commission, *Implementation of the Whistleblower Provisions of Section 21F of the Securities Exchange Act of 1934* (Washington, DC, 25 May 2011). Dodd Frank also provides new enforcement tools to deal with fraud and manipulation in the futures, swaps and broader commodities markets by introducing a reckless standard (s. 753), which reduces the scienter threshold from deliberate intent.

the strength of the legal claim but the calculation of whether the conduct complained of can be defended in the court of public opinion.

The reality of complex litigation is that when taking enforcement action, regulatory agencies balance the effect of conviction with the political costs associated with bringing uncertain cases to trial.[71] Beyond the merits of an individual action, wider demonstration effect requires changing both the content and context of the underpinning regulatory regime.[72] First, the preparation of the case and its subsequent staging—including the critical initial presentation of the evidential base—needs to reconfigure media representations of what constitutes acceptable conduct, irrespective of the strength at law of the material claim. Precisely because trial strategies tend to bifurcate between competing (if partially understood) narratives that subsequently gain media traction, it is essential to 'own' the media agenda.[73] Second, the litigation needs to be capable of recalibrating—without credible dissension—the broader policy reform agenda.[74]

This coupling is essential to ensure that neither judicial failure nor premature settlement will translate into an incremental erosion of wider support for the legitimacy of the regulator's operational imperatives.[75] As a consequence of Dodd-Frank, along with public and judicial disquiet at the weakness of settlements, however, the calculation has changed. The agencies most poised to take advantage of looser scienter standards include the Commodity and Futures Trading Commission, which has spearheaded the investigation into Libor scandal. According to its head of enforcement, David Meister, the agency 'is looking to bring high impact cases that influence market behaviour'.[76] The HSBC settlement is arguably, therefore, the most important and likely to be most influential on both regulator and regulated communities alike as a bargaining chip in this complex negotiation. The unresolved question is whether it is an outlier or reflects a determination to ensure ongoing substantive monitoring in order to prevent the fall of what the Assistant Attorney General Breuer terms the 'Sword of Damocles' now hanging over the banking sector.[77]

---

[71] In an interview conducted in the aftermath of the Enron and WorldCom accounting scandals, Steve Cutler, then Director of Enforcement at the Securities and Exchange Commission, noted, the 'reluctance on the part of federal prosecutors to take on complicated accounting fraud cases. These are very difficult cases and require lots of resources, lots of time, [are] difficult to explain to juries and that makes for a less than ideal track record as far as a prosecutor is concerned.' Interview with Steve Cutler, Director of Enforcement, Securities and Exchange Commission (Washington DC, 11 May 2005).

[72] A regulatory regime can be defined as the 'complex of institutional [physical and social] geography, rules, practice and animating ideas that are associated with the regulation of a particular risk or hazard'; see C Hood, H Rothstein and R Baldwin, *The Government of Risk* (Oxford, Oxford University Press, 2001) 8.

[73] See J Malcolm, 'Anatomy of a Murder Trial' *New Yorker*, 3 May 2010, 36. For application to financial crisis, see J Cassidy, 'Scandals' *New Yorker*, 3 May 2010, 21 ('Few things excite the public as much as financial scandals. . . the result is a barrage of news stories that most people do not fully understand but which create a widespread sense that some unprecedented skullduggery has been revealed and that villainous investment bankers will finally be held to account').

[74] J Nash, 'Framing Effects and Regulatory Choice' (2006) 82 *Notre Dame Law Review* 314.

[75] For trenchant critique of the deferred prosecution as an abuse of process, see R Epstein, 'The Deferred Prosecution Racket', *Wall Street Journal*, 28 November 2006, A14 (arguing that the agreed statement of claims 'often read like the confessions of a Stalinist purge trial'.)

[76] S Gittleman, 'US Regulators Caution Financial Firms to Stay Alert for New Priorities, "Game Changers"', *Thomson Reuters Accelus*, 14 December 2012, www.complinet.com/global/news/news/article.html?ref=160823.

[77] D Ruse and J Treaner, 'HSBC's Record $1.9bn Fine Preferable to Prosecution, US Authorities Insist', *The Guardian*, 11 December 2012 www.guardian.co.uk/business/2012/dec/11/hsbc-fine-prosecution-money-laundering>.

VI   CONCLUSION

All too often, in the past banks have made empty promises at congressional hearings before going on to commit further violations, with monetary fines written off as the cost of doing business. In part HSBC's apparent conversion can be traced to narrow self-interest. Senator Carl Levin had warned that regulators must consider the ultimate sanction of bank charter revocation in the US if international banks fail to internally police deviance, the primary reason he endorsed the muscular action taken by the Department of Financial Services in New York.[78] In part, however, the HSBC response also reflects an awareness of custodian and broader gatekeeper obligation that, if monitored effectively, offers a potential model to transform.

The Department of Justice has recognized the value of such an approach but has made it clear that self-regulation can only work effectively if enforced. The uncertainty surrounding self-regulation feeds into a crisis that calls into question as never before both the activities of the banks and their regulators. Globally, the practical and conceptual underpinnings of financial regulation are being questioned as never before. The legitimacy problem is serious, pressing and structural. It is one we ignore at our peril. Following the banking scandals of 2012, it is unsustainable for regulation to be decided and implemented and monitored at a national level. As HSBC has acknowledged, global oversight has become an imperative to reduce the conflicts of interest that may create profitable industries, but not socially beneficial ones. The monitor, as custodian of that purpose, will play an essential validating role. As such, the Department of Justice has taken a first, if uncertain, step towards recognition of globalised agendas. It is an exploration to be welcomed, as much in New York and Washington as in London.

[78] C Levin, 'Levin Statement on Standard Chartered Bank Settlement', (Press Release, Washington, DC, 15 August 2012). Levin argued that the settlement 'showed that holding a bank accountable for past misconduct doesn't need to take years of negotiation over the size of the penalty; it simply requires a regulator with backbone to act. New York's regulatory action sends a strong message that the United States will not tolerate foreign banks giving rogue nations like Iran hidden access to the US financial system.'

CHAPTER 10

Regulating the Legal Profession: A Prototype for Change

Steve Mark and Tahlia Gordon

I   INTRODUCTION

Over the last few decades, increasing concerns have been expressed about the demise of professional practice. This demise, evidenced in the events surrounding the global financial crisis and corporate scandals of late, which have been well documented by the media, have exposed the unethical and immoral advice given and the elaborate schemes developed by bankers, lawyers and accountants. These schemes effectively enabled their clients to hide billions of dollars in debt and inflate profits through off-balance-sheet borrowing.[1] The principal accusation leveraged against these market actors is that they ignored their ethical, moral and professional obligations when they arose in deference to profit.[2] The conduct of such actors has sparked a renewed interest in the concepts of ethical practice, organisational culture and regulatory compliance. As the world attempts to come to terms with the financial meltdown, the philosophical foundations of the current regulatory regimes governing business, the professions and industry are being evaluated and scrutinised at every level. Discussions about ethical conduct, organisational culture and regulatory compliance are today taking place everywhere—amongst governments, regulators, in boardrooms and investor meetings—with calls for answers, solutions and processes to ensure that integrity and morality are prominent considerations in practice. Emerging from these discussions is a general agreement that the current regulatory regime governing professional practice that focuses on top-down compliance is largely ineffective in curbing unethical and immoral behaviour within organisations and that a new approach to regulation is required. In New South Wales, Australia, the Office of the Legal Services Commissioner (OLSC)[3] has developed a model for regulating the culture of the legal profession. It has done so by requiring

---

[1] See generally MC Regan Jr, 'Teaching Enron' (2005) 74 *Fordham Law Review* 1139; SL Schwarcz, 'The Role of Lawyers in the Global Financial Crisis' (2010) 24 *Australian Journal of Corporate Law* 214; WV Rapp, 'The Lawyers and the Meltdown: The Role of Lawyers in the Current Financial Crisis' in S Kim, MD Mckenzie (eds), *International Banking in the New Era: Post-Crisis Challenges and Opportunities* (Bingley, Emerald Publishing Group, 2010).

[2] A Shleifer, 'Does Competition Destroy Ethical Behavior?' (2004) 92 *American Economic Review* 414.

[3] The Office of the Legal Services Commissioner (OLSC) was created by the NSW Government in July 1994 to oversee the investigation and resolution of complaints about lawyers.

law firms to adopt and maintain an 'ethical infrastructure'.[4] The purpose of this chapter is to offer the financial services marketplace such a regulatory model.

It is widely accepted that, like their financial colleagues, lawyers were not immune from complicity in the recent spate of financial scandals experienced over the last decade.[5] Although the role that lawyers played has not been as widely explored as the role played by other professionals,[6] we do know that on many occasions when asked to provide legal advice, some lawyers acted on the instructions of their client where it was unethical or immoral to do so. The disclosure documents prepared by lawyers in applications for mortgage-backed securities that led to the sub-prime mortgage crisis in 2007–2008 provide a clear illustration of this fact.[7] We also know that in some instances lawyers played a far greater role than just preparing the documents. A number of lawyers were directly involved in helping to design and structure financial instruments at the request of their clients and on some occasions mirrored the role of investment bankers.[8] In fact, for one commentator, the role lawyers played in the sub-prime financial crisis was so central that without their involvement the crisis may never have occurred.[9] The conduct of these lawyers vis-à-vis their duties and their clients during this tumultuous period is, however, not unique. Consider, for example, the Australian tobacco litigation case discussed below.

In 2001 a woman by the name of Rolah McCabe brought an action in the Victorian Supreme Court alleging that she had contracted lung cancer as a result of smoking ciga-rettes manufactured by British American Tobacco Australia Services (BATAS).[10] During the discovery phase of the litigation, the solicitors for McCabe sought to discover BATAS docu-ments that they knew had been discovered when another litigant had sued BATAS for a smoking-related illness in 1996. At the time, BATAS in Australia had supplied that litigant's lawyers with 30,000 documents, including documents that related to the known risks of lung cancer and the effects of nicotine. The list of documents used in that matter became public knowledge. When McCabe's lawyers requested the same documents that had been used in 1996, they were informed by the counsel for BATAS that the documents had been destroyed as part of their internal 'document retention policy'.

The trial judge hearing the case struck out the defence, finding that BATAS had failed to comply with an order for discovery and had carried out a policy of systematically destroying

---

[4] The term, 'ethical infrastructure' was coined by Ted Schneyer. See T Schneyer, 'A Tale of Four Systems: Reflections on How Law Influences the "Ethical Infrastructure" of Law Firms' (1998) 39 *South Texas Law Review* 245. It was further developed by Elizabeth Chambliss and David B Wilkins; see E Chambliss and D Wilkins, 'A New Framework for Law Firm Discipline' (2003) 16 *Georgetown Journal of Legal Ethics* 335; E Chambliss and D Wilkins, 'Promoting Effective Ethical Infrastructure in Large Law Firms: A Call for Research and Reporting' (2002) 30 *Hofstra Law Review* 691.

[5] SL Schwarcz, above n 1; CA Hill, 'Who Were the Villains in the Subprime Crisis, and Why It Matters' (2010) 4 *Entrepreneurial Business Law Journal* 323; S. Kellogg, 'Financial Crisis 2008: Where Were the Lawyers?' *DCBAR.* (January 2010) , available at www.dcbar.org/for_lawyers/resources/publications/washington_lawyer/january_2010/financial_crisis.cfm.

[6] CA Hill, above n 5; S Kellogg, above n 5.

[7] Institutions that offer mortgage backed securities commonly retain the services of lawyers to prepare the documents necessary for the applications to be processed. See for example L Browning, 'Small Law Firm's Big Role in Bundling Mortgages' *New York Times* (1 February 2008), available at www.nytimes.com/2008/02/01/business/01legal.html.

[8] See SL Schwarcz, above n 1; CA Hill, above n 5.

[9] WV Rapp, above n 1 at154.

[10] *McCabe v British American Tobacco Australia Ltd* [2002] VSC 73.

documents that were relevant to the litigation. The judge further found that the company's law firm, Clayton Utz, was the principal architect of the advice to destroy the documents and that this was done under the guise of a 'document retention policy' to hide information on BATAS's awareness of the health risks of smoking and a number of other issues. The judge found that BATAS had destroyed thousands of incriminating documents and covered its tracks by asserting innocent motives. The judge further found that Clayton Utz took steps to devise a legal strategy, and did so with the very close assistance of lawyers from the United Kingdom [Lovells] and the USA [Shook Hardy & Bacon] who had performed a similar advisory role for tobacco companies in those countries. With the defence struck out, McCabe became the first successful tobacco litigant in Australia; the jury awarded her damages of $700,000. BATAS, however, successfully appealed.[11] The successful appeal prevented the lawyers involved from being prosecuted. The ramifications of the McCabe litigation were felt beyond Australia. In the United States, for example, the District of Columbia District Court found against BATAS.[12] In doing so, the Court made a number of derogatory findings about tobacco companies' use of information and the conduct of their lawyers.

The allegations of Clayton Utz's conduct in the McCabe litigation are not dissimilar to those raised about the conduct of lawyers in the global financial crisis. In both cases, the lawyers stated that they were acting on the instructions of their clients. To put it bluntly, the lawyers in each scenario did what they were instructed to do. The problem with each scenario is that it appears that upon receiving those instructions, no one within the organisations (or at least those making the final decisions) questioned the efficacy or the moral and ethical implications of acting so. In each of these scenarios, there was little if any evidence that anyone had considered the consequences or the morality of what he or she had been instructed to do so. When questioned about their behaviour Clayton Utz, for example, argued that they acted on the instructions of their clients of which they were obliged to follow and were 'not morally obliged to object.'[13] Although there have been no empirical studies to date examining the role of lawyers in the global financial crisis, it would not be obnoxious to suggest that these lawyers may have stated the same.

The conduct displayed by Clayton Utz, a well-respected top-tier law firm in Australia, and the role lawyers played in the global financial crisis present a number of compelling observations about the way in which some law firms and lawyers view their role vis-à-vis their clients and the courts. Firstly, in both scenarios it appears from the conduct taken that the lawyers involved saw their duty to the client as being penultimate and overriding the traditional obligations of a lawyer's duty to the court and the administration of justice.[14]

---

[11] See C Cameron, 'Hired Guns and Smoking Guns: McCabe v British American Tobacco Australia Ltd' (2002) 25 *University of New South Wales Law Journal* 768; M Harvey and S Le Mire 'Playing for Keeps? Tobacco Litigation, Document Retention, Corporate Culture and Legal Ethics' (2008) 34 *Monash University Law Rreview* 163

[12] *USA v Philip Morris* (2006) WL 2380650.

[13] M Simons, 'Lawyers Not Moral Judges: Clayton Utz Chief' *The Age* (4 August 2002), available at www.theage.com.au/articles/2002/08/03/1028157860572.html.

[14] In Australia a legal practitioner's primary duty is owed to the Court. No other profession shares this duty. As officers of the Court lawyers have a specific ethical and professional obligations that are set out in professional rules and regulations and are supported in common law. Lawyers must not mislead the Court and must act with competence, honesty and courtesy towards other solicitors, parties and witnesses. The duty to the Court also stipulates that lawyers must be independent (free from personal bias), frank in their responses and disclosures to the Court and diligent in their observance of undertakings given to the Court or their opponents. See *Giannarelli v Wraith* (1988) 165 CLR 543; *New South Wales Bar Association v Livesey* [1982] 2 NSWLR 231, 233; *New South Wales Bar Association v Thomas (No 2)*(1989) 18 NSWLR 193, 204; *Wallersteiner v Moir (No 2)* [1975] QB 373, 402.

Secondly the scenarios provide a fascinating example of 'ethical blindness' that is, the failure by actors to 'see' the moral components of their behaviour, not because they are morally uneducated or lack good intentions, but because rationalization processes remove the ethics from view.[15]

Whilst this example of alleged 'ethical blindness' may seem extreme, in the writers experience in regulating the legal profession in New South Wales, it is far from being an isolated event. Nor is it restricted to lawyers practising in the corporate or financial world, despite there being a number of well publicised examples of corporate lawyers acting unethically of late.[16] The writers have experienced many cases where lawyers provide an excuse for unethical behaviour that they were doing no more than "acting on the instructions on their clients." This occurs in relation to family law, criminal law, succession or probate law and virtually every other area of legal practice. What appears to be the common element is that lawyers forget the primacy of their duty to the court when confronted by the pressure from desperate or needy clients or indeed financial opportunity. Inherent in this dichotomy of duties between the client and the court is the tension that exists within a 'profession',[17] which also acts as a 'business.' As many commentators would attest, one of the basic contributors to the global financial crisis was greed and pure self-interest. Regulators of the legal profession must therefore note this tension and focus on reminding lawyers that they are members of a profession and must act accordingly, but not to the exclusion of attaining some profit. In the writers' view, there is no conflict between ethics and profit, but there is between ethics and greed.

This chapter takes as its starting point a discussion of the changes that have taken place in the legal services marketplace over the last few decades. The section begins by considering the impact of globalisation, technology and commercialisation on Australian lawyers and law firms. The section discusses the alleged tensions caused by globalisation and commoditisation and their impact on the lawyer–client relationship. The section notes that the impact of globalisation and commoditisation has forced regulators of the legal profession to reconsider its regulatory framework. Following this, the chapter then discusses the regulatory framework for lawyer regulation in Australia, with a particular focus on NSW, and how the regulator of the legal profession in NSW has responded. This section illustrates the types of processes the legal regulator in NSW has adopted and the effect of these processes on lawyers and legal practice. The chapter then concludes with a recommendation that the

---

[15]   See R Abel, *Lawyers in the Dock: Learning from Attorney Disciplinary Proceedings* (Oxford, Oxford University Press, 2008); MC Regan Jr, *Eat What You Kill: The Fall of a Wall Street Lawyer* (Ann Arbor, University of Michigan Press, 2006) 334–35; R Wasserstrom, 'Roles and Morality' in D Luban (ed), *The Good Lawyer* (New York, Rowman & Littlefield Pub Inc, 1983). See also K Hall and V Holmes, 'The Power of Rationalisation to Influence Lawyers' Decisions to Act Unethically' (2009) 11(2) *Legal Ethics* 137.

[16]   See C Parker and A Evans, *Inside Lawyers' Ethics* (Cambridge, Cambridge University Press, 2007) 212–42.

[17]   The term 'profession' has no commonly accepted definition. As one commentator has eloquently observed, the concept of a 'profession' 'is a slippery one that is not entirely fixed in our conceptual geography.' See JC Callahan, *Ethical Issues in Professional Life* (New York, Oxford University Press, 1999); SF Barker, "What is a Profession?"(1992) 1 *Professional Ethics* 73, 77. Notwithstanding the elusiveness of the term, there is general agreement that the term 'profession' connotes a group of people who adhere to codified ethical standards; who have specialized knowledge or skills; that the community socially acknowledges and accepts; are self-regulated, and who are prepared to apply their knowledge or exercise their skills in the interest of others. See eg, the Australian Council of Professions definition Adopted at the Annual General Meeting of Professions Australia on 26 May 199, see Professions Australia, 'Definition of a Profession', available at www.professions.com.au/defineprofession.html.

prototype developed by the legal regulator could be adopted and implemented by regulators in other markets as an effective way to regulate organisational culture.

II   THE GLOBALISATION AND COMMODITISATION OF LAW

Over the last few decades, we have witnessed a remarkable change in the way legal services have been and continue to be structured and delivered globally. Globalisation and commoditisation has had a profound effect on the practice of law.[18] This section will consider and discuss the structural and behavioural changes that have taken place and continue to take place in the legal services marketplace. Whilst the discussion focuses largely on the Australian legal marketplace, one can infer that similar changes are occurring globally elsewhere.[19] The purpose of the section is to identify and set up the landscape in which regulation is taking place.

The impact of globalisation on legal practice is immense. Globalisation has, for example, seen the expansion of domestic law firms across borders, collaborations with foreign lawyers and the formation of intercontinental mergers, erasing the once traditional boundaries on the geographic scope of the practice of law. In 2012, for example, 96 cross-border mergers were announced around the world.[20] In Australia, the legal services market has seen a variety of mergers and acquisitions between Australian and international corporate law firms.[21]

Globalisation through technology has also permitted law firms to outsource their legal and non-legal work domestically and globally as well as undertake legal and non-legal work outsourced to them.[22] Legal outsourcing, both onshore and offshore, is transforming

---

[18]   The effect of globalisation and commoditisation on the practice of law has been widely documented. See eg, L Terry, 'The Legal World Is Flat: Globalization and Its Effect on Lawyers Practicing in Non-Global Law Firms' (2008) 28 *Northwestern Journal of Interntinal Law and Business* 527; WD Henderson, 'The Globalization of the Legal Profession' (2007) 14 *Indiana Journal of Global Legal Studies* 1; DD Sokol, 'Globalization of Law Firms: A Survey of the Literature and a Research Agenda for Future Study' (2007) 14 *Indiana Journal of Global Legal Studies* 5; S Mark, 'Harmonization or Homoginization?: The Globalization of Law and Legal Ethics: An Australian Viewpoint' (2001) 34 *Vanderbilt Journal of Transnational Law* 1173.

[19]   See eg, MC Regan Jr and PT Heenan, 'Supply Chains and Porous Boundaries: The Disaggregation of Legal Services' (2010) 78 *Fordham Law Review* 2137; R Susskind, *Transforming the Law: Essays on Technology, Justice, and the Legal Marketplace* (Oxford, Oxford University Press, 2000).

[20]   Center for the Study of the Legal Profession and Thompson Reuters Peer Monitor, '2013 Report on the State of the Legal Market' *Georgetown University*, available at www.law.georgetown.edu/continuing-legal-education/executive-education/upload/2013-report.pdf.

[21]   P Redmond, 'Globalisation and the Australian Corporate Law Firm' *Centre for Law, Markets and Regulation*, available at www.clmr.unsw.edu.au/article/compliance/mergers-%26-acquisitions/globalisation-and-australian-corporate-law-firm.

[22]   T Gordon, R Shackel and S Mark, 'Regulation of Legal Services in the E-World: A Need to Short Circuit Hot Spots in Ethics and Novel Practice' (2012) 19 *International Journal of the Legal Profession* 55; C Kenny and T Gordon, 'Outsourcing Issues for Legal Practice' (2012) 50 *Law Society Journal* 72; *Swaab Attorney, Herbert Greer and Lavan Legal*, for example, are known to have outsourced support services: see '2009 In review Key trends: Speaking out about outsourcing' *Lawyers Weekly* (13 December 2009), available at www.lawyersweekly.com.au/blogs/special_reports/archive/2009/12/13/2009-in-review-key-trends-speaking-out-about-outsourcing.aspx; 'Legal Outsourcing Out in the Open' *Lawyers Weekly* (23 July 2009), available at www.lawyersweekly.com.au/blogs/best_practice/archive/2009/07/23/legal-outsourcing-out-in-the-open.aspx; 'Legal Life 2020: Outsourcing Will Remain a Mainstay' *Lawyers Weekly* (17 September 2009), available at www.lawyersweekly.com.au/blogs/special_reports/archive/2009/09/17/legal-life-2020-outsourcing-will-remain-a-mainstay.aspx.

the practice of law as law firms and corporate legal departments seek to minimize costs, increase flexibility and expand their in-house capabilities. Additionally, globalisation has allowed lawyers to operate virtually via the World Wide Web providing an alternative method of practicing law using customised software or standardised web 2.0 tools like Skype and online file management applications that permits flexible work hours and foster a better work/life balance.[23] Social networking is also is changing the way in which lawyers recruit, job hunt, network, locate and discredit witnesses, manage their careers and interact with clients on a global and domestic level.[24]

This change we are witnessing has been facilitated by a fundamental shift in the way the legal services market has been regulated. Traditionally, solicitors in Australia, like many other common law jurisdictions, practiced as sole practitioners, or in partnership with other lawyers, and this remained the dominant legal structure for many years. However, since the 1990s, when competition policy and the liberalisation of trade dominated professional discourse, there has been a notable move away from this structure in Australia toward more innovative alternative business structures (ABS), including incorporated legal practices (ILPs), multidisciplinary practices (MDPs) and publicly listed law firms.[25] The move was sparked by the introduction of legislation in NSW in 2001 permitting incorporation and the public ownership of law firms.[26] The enactment of legislation was driven by a growing perception that the traditional structure of law firms no longer met the needs of both practitioners and clients.[27]

Legislation enabling law firms to change their traditional partnership structure has thus allowed practices the flexibility to create novel structures to suit market needs. In NSW today, for example, there are over twelve hundred ILPs in the legal services marketplace (representing 25 per cent of legal practices).[28] The majority of ILPs are either sole practitioners or firms with three to ten partners. Several of the large national law firms,

---

[23]   T Gordon, R Shackel and S Mark, above n 22; Kimbro, 'Inspired Solo-Stephanie Kimbro the Virtual Law Office', available at www.theinspiredsolo.com/inspired-solo-stephanie-kimbro-the-virtual-law-office/; VirtualLawPractice.org, 'Unbundling Legal Services In a Virtual Law Practice Benefits the Public' (1 December 2008), available at virtuallawpractice.org/2008/12/unbundling-legal-services-in-a-virtual-law-practice-benefits-the-public/.

[24]   T Gordon, R Shackel and S Mark, above n 22; C Kenny and T Gordon, 'Social Media Issues for Legal Practice' (2012) 50 *Law Society Journal* 66; Jordan Furlong, 'Facebook for Law Firms, Law Firm Web Strategy Blog' (29 March 2010), available at www.stemlegal.com/strategyblog/2010/facebook-for-law-firms.

[25]   See eg, S Mark and T Gordon, 'Innovations in Regulation: Responding to a Changing Legal Services Market' (2009) 22 *Georgetown Journal of Legal Ethics* 501.

[26]   In July 2001, legislation came into force in New South Wales enabling providers of legal services to incorporate by registering a company with the Australian Securities & Investment Commission (ASIC), the agency responsible for ensuring compliance with the Federal Corporations Act 2001 (Cth) (Corporations Act). The legislation in NSW provides a legal service provider may incorporate and provide legal services either alone or in conjunction with other legal service providers, who may or may not be legal practitioners. The Legal Profession (Incorporated Legal Practices) Act 2000 (NSW) and the Legal Profession (Incorporated Legal Practices) Regulations 2001 entered into force on 1 July 2001.

[27]   Law Council of Australia, '2010: A Discussion Paper: Challenges for the Legal Profession' (2010) *Law Counil of Australia*, available at www.lawcouncil.asn.au/shadomx/apps/fms/fmsdownload.cfm?file_uuid=0BE36A97-1C23-CACD-2225-CBD6713A3E09&siteName=lca.

[28]   There are a number of reasons why incorporation has become so popular. Firstly, ILPs offer limited liability for their partners (limited to their investment in the practice), as those partners become shareholders. Secondly, there are a number of financial benefits in a corporate structure, including tax advantages, favourable superannuation and redundancy arrangements. Thirdly, the ILP structure provides better options for managing a legal practice. See S Mark, 'Before and After' (2010) 50 *Law Management Magazine* 30–31.

that is, law firms with over thirty partners, have also incorporated in NSW. Incorporation in NSW has taken a number of different forms.[29] These have included multidisciplinary practices, which provide a one-stop-shop for clients, offering, for example, legal, property and financial services, as well as at least one firm that has franchised its practice. Law firms have also used incorporation to attract external funding including through public listing.[30] In addition, the Australian legal services marketplace has seen the emergence of third-party litigation funders and litigation lenders, a number of whom who have listed on the ASX.[31] This diversification of legal practice has had a profound effect. Globalisation and technological advancements have resulted in the commoditisation of law, allowing clients to reap huge efficiencies but at the expense of law firms that fail to adapt to the new models.

The pressure exerted by globalisation and the commoditisation of law has driven an unhealthy competition amongst lawyers to offer greater efficiency but at a heavily reduced price.[32] Technological advancements have levelled the competitive playing field between large and small firms and changed staffing requirements by simplifying tasks that were previously performed by lawyers. Commoditisation is also forcing lawyers to pay much closer attention to the needs and wants of their clients. Clients now expect their law firms to apply technology to bring about efficiencies that would improve service and reduce fees. As one report has recently noted:

'There has been a shift from the seller's market that traditionally dominated the legal industry to a buyer's market that will likely remain the prevailing model for the foreseeable future. What this means is that all of the critical decisions related to the structure and delivery of legal services – including judgments about scheduling, staffing, scope of work, level of effort, pricing, etc. – are now being made primarily by clients and not by their outside lawyers. This represents a fundamental shift in the relationship between lawyers and their clients.

Reflecting the increasing power of clients to define the terms of the attorney/client relationship, this shift has resulted in a new emphasis on efficiency and cost effectiveness in the delivery of legal services. Although obviously not true in all cases, clients increasingly make decisions to hire outside lawyers on the basis of how efficiently, cost effectively, and predictably they can deliver the services the client requires, with quality being taken as a given. As a result, to an extent barely imaginable only a few years ago, firms have found themselves increasingly locked in procurement processes where clients are asking hard questions about schedules, staffing, work process efficiencies, and cost.'[33]

Whilst the developments outlined above have broadened the delivery of legal services and enabled practices to adapt to market forces, they have also brought concern that the

[29] See Law Society of New South Wales, 'Profile Law Society Research Update' (1 February 2013), available at www.lawsociety.com.au/cs/groups/public/documents/internetregistry/685375.pdf.

[30] In May 2007, Slater & Gordon made legal and corporate history when it became the first law firm in the world to list its entire firm on the Australian Securities Exchange (ASX). Two other law firms in Australia, Integrated Legal Holdings (ILH), has since listed on the ASX and in 2013 shine lawyers also listed. A number of other firms have expressed an interest in doing so.

[31] G Barker, 'Third Party Litigation Funding in Australia and Europe' (2011) *Centre for Law and Economics ANU College of Law*, available at law.anu.edu.au/sites/all/files/allfiles/111212_-_cle_working_paper_no_2_2011_barker_george_r.third_part.pdf

[32] See R Susskind, *The End Of Lawyers? Rethinking The Nature Of Legal Services* (Oxford, Oxford University Press, 2010).

[33] Center for the Study of the Legal Profession and Thompson Reuters Peer Monitor, '2013 Report on the State of the Legal Market' *Georgetown University*, available at www.law.georgetown.edu/continuing-legal-education/executive-education/upload/2013-report.pdf.

globalisation and commoditisation of legal practice is diminishing traditional legal practice and bringing the legal profession into disrepute. Critics have argued, for example, that external ownership fundamentally contradicts the principle of a legal practitioner's independence, leads to a lowering of professional standards, and prejudices the standing of all legal practitioners.[34] Critics further argue that commoditisation and globalisation threaten a lawyer's overriding duty to the court and the administration of justice. The most recent articulation of such concerns can be found in the American Bar Association's (ABA) Commission on Ethics 20/20 rejection of the external ownership of law firms in April 2012.[35] For the ABA, permitting alternative business structures into an already saturated legal marketplace in the United States posed too much of a risk of deterioration of traditional standards of the legal profession.

Another significant concern that has been expressed is that commoditisation encourages lawyers to accept and act for clients in circumstances where such instructions may be unethical or immoral, rather than saying no. In doing so, the concern is that lawyers may adopt the persona of the 'zealous advocate'[36] and perhaps not act within the bounds of the law. This is because zealots know no boundaries and are prepared to do whatever is required to advance their (or their client's) cause. For zealots, the end thus always justifies the means. Advocates' zeal can, however, 'blind' lawyers to their professional and ethical obligations and this is where the problem lies. Overzealous lawyers may not thus, for example, honour their duty of candour to courts before which they appear. The problem with such 'ethical blindness' is that it is exacerbated where lawyers practice in large firms.[37] That is, the larger the firm, the more evident the culture of ethical blindness. As Parker et al write:

> '. . .where people work well together in teams, as in many large law firms, they will tend to develop shared ways of seeing their work and the world. This can be an important part of what helps them work well together, but it can also be dysfunctional where shared norms and cultures make people "blind" to alternative world views and degrade their sensitivity and empathy to a range of different

---

[34] Critics argue that nonlawyer ownership would present a serious threat to attorney–client confidentiality: See for exmple, LE Ribstein, 'Want to Own a Law Firm?' *The American* (30 May 2007), available at www.american. com/archive/2007/may-0507/want-to-own-a-law-firm; ES Adams and JH Matheson, 'Law Firms on the Big Board?: A Proposal for Nonlawyer Investment in Law Firms' (1998) 86 1 *California Law Review* 11; JR DeBuse, 'Opening at $25 1/2 is Big Firm U.S.A.: Why America May Eventually Have a Publicly Traded Law Firm, and Why Law Firms Can Succeed Without Going Public' (2008) 34 *Journal of Corporate Law* 317, 336; See also B MacEwan, M Regan and L Ribstein, *Law Firms, Ethics, and Equity Capital: A Conversation* (Georgetown Law, Center for the Study of the Legal Profession, 2007) (unpublished).

[35] The American Bar Associations Commission on Ethics 20/20 was established in 2009 to review the ABA Model Rules of Professional Conduct and the regulation of lawyers in the context of globalisation. The Commission has considered various issues in relation to globalisation and legal practice, including external ownership of law firms by non-lawyers. See ABA Commission on Ethics 20/20 Working Group on Alternative Business Structures, 'Issues Paper Concerning Alternative Business Structures' (2011) available at www.americanbar.org/content/dam/aba/administrative/ethics_2020/abs_issues_paper.authcheckdam.pdf.

[36] The phrase 'zealous advocacy' is frequently invoked to defend unprofessional behavior and a 'Rambo,' or 'win at all costs,' attitude. For a general discussion on the profile of the 'Rambo' lawyer and case examples, see AK Harris, 'The Professionalism Crisis: The "z" Words and Other Rambo Tactics: The Conferences of Chief Justices Solution' (2003) 53 *Supreme Court Law Review* 549; JA George, 'The "Rambo" Problem: Is Mandatory CLE The Way Back To Atticus' (2002) 62 *Louisana Law Review* 467; DR Richmond, 'The Ethics of Zealous Advocacy: Civility, Candour and Parlour Tricks' (2002) 34 *Texas Technical Law Review* 3. RL Felder, 'I'm Paid to Be Rude' *New York Times* (July 1997), A23, cited in CJ Piazzola, 'Ethical Versus Procedural Approaches To Civility: Why Ethics 2000 Should Have Adopted A Civility Rule' (2003) 74 *University of Columbia Law Review* 1197, 1233.

[37] See C Parker, A Evans, L Haller, S Le Mire, R Mortensen, 'The Ethical Infrastructure of Legal Practice in Larger Law Firms: Values, Policy and Behaviour' (2008) 31 *University of New South Wales Law Journal* 158.

perspectives, values and concerns. Lawyers who spend all their time with the same colleagues and clients can begin to see only the interests and values of their clients as significant. This is problematic because, although lawyers' duties to their clients are very important, they are not lawyers' only ethical obligations. In some cases, individual lawyers have felt so strongly aligned with the client and the work team that they no longer identified the ethical problems with conduct that the general public considered an unethical breach of the lawyers' duty to the court, such as devising creative legal strategies to avoid the spirit and intent of the law.'[38]

Moreover 'ethical blindness' can also be exacerbated by a culture that accepts such behaviour.

The consequences of globalisation and the commoditisation of law, discussed above, present a significant challenge to the traditional regulatory frameworks used to regulate the legal profession. Traditionally in Australia the practice of law was self-regulating and was the responsibility of each state and territory to administer its own regime.[39] The regulatory rules were established when practices were localised; few clients had the need to seek legal services in other jurisdictions, and few lawyers had to venture outside their own jurisdiction to do legal work. As this section has demonstrated, this is no longer the status quo. As such, regulators of the legal profession have been forced to reconsider their framework to accommodate the effect of a globalised and commoditised legal world.[40]

The rest of this chapter will discuss the framework for legal regulation and the way regulation has been modified to address such change. The following sections focus on the regulatory framework in Australia generally, but with a particular focus on regulation in NSW. The deliberate focus on NSW is because it is in this jurisdiction where the most innovation in terms of regulation is said to have taken place.[41]

III   THE STRUCTURE OF LEGAL REGULATION IN AUSTRALIA

Regulation of the legal profession in Australia is generally based on a co-regulatory model involving the courts, government and the legal profession.[42] The specifics of regulation and regulatory functions differs in each jurisdiction however according to the jurisdictions own legal, economic and social history and norms.[43] In New South Wales, Victoria and Queensland, for example, regulation of the legal profession is shared amongst law

[38] ibid.

[39] GE Dal Pont, *Lawyers' Professional Responsibility*, 5th edn (Pyrmont, Law Book Co., 2013); D Weisbrot, *Australian Lawyers* (Melbourne, Longman Cheshire, 1990) 193, 199–201.

[40] See LS Terry, S Mark and T Gordon, 'Adopting Regulatory Objectives for the Legal Profession' (2012) 80 *Fordham Law Review* 2685; LS Terry, S Mark and T Gordon, 'Trends and Challenges in Lawyer Regulation: The Impact of Globalisation and Technology' (2012) 80 *Fordham Law Review* 2661.

[41] See for example, T Schneyer, 'On Further Reflection: How "Professional Self-Regulation" Should Promote Compliance with Broad Ethical Duties of Law Firm Management', (2011) 53 *Arizona Law Review* 576.

[42] In the 1970's, serious questions began to be aked about the effectiveness of lawyer self-regulation throughout Australia. In New South Wales the Law Reform Commission, charged with the responsiility of assessing the efficacy of the existing system concluded, 'that a significant number of complaints against lawyers are not dealt with fairly and effectively.' The Commission also noted that problems arising out of matters that concerned the ordinary consumer, including overbilling, neglect of client matters and lack of competence, were not being handled as disciplinary matters. See New South Wales Reform Commission, 'The Legal Profession Discussion Paper No. 2, Complaints, Discipline and Professional Standards–Part 1' (1979), available at www.lawlink.nsw.gov.au/lrc.nsf/pages/dp2out.

[43] For a comprehensive description of the different bodies involved in lawyer regulation in Australia see the website of the Conference of Regulatory Officers, available at www.coro.com.au/

societies[44] and bar associations[45] ('professional associations') and a statutory authority commonly referred to as a 'Commission' or 'Ombudsman.' The statutory authority generally administers the rules: handles complaints, undertakes investigations and resolves consumer disputes. In this model, the professional associations co-regulate in relation to disciplinary matters, usually on referral from the statutory authority, and are also responsible for admission procedures and the like. While statutory authorities and professional associations can and do issue reprimands and impose minor penalties, serious conduct matters are determined by the Courts.

There are many different types of regulatory instruments in Australia. For example, the legal profession is regulated through legislation, such as profession-specific acts, or through or in subordinate legislation such as regulations. In addition, the legal profession in Australia is also regulated by rules of professional conduct[46] and guidelines on issues related to legal practice.

In New South Wales, the legal profession is co-regulated by the OLSC, the Law Society of NSW and the NSW Bar Association (the professional associations) through the *Legal Profession Act 2004 (NSW)*, the *Legal Profession Regulations 2005 (NSW)* and the *Revised Professional Conduct and Practice Rules (Solicitors' Rules) NSW 1995 (Solicitors' Rules)*. The function of the OLSC is to resolve disputes between consumers of legal services and practitioners, and investigate complaints about professional conduct. The OLSC also oversees the investigation about the professional conduct of practitioners where it has referred such a matter to the professional associations for investigation and has the power to review decisions of those bodies. The functions of the OLSC are prescribed in Part 7.3 of the *Legal Profession Act 2004 (NSW)*. These functions include:

(a)   to receive complaints about unsatisfactory professional conduct or professional misconduct of Australian lawyers or Australian-registered foreign lawyers,

(b)   to assist and advise complainants and potential complainants in making and pursuing complaints (including assisting complainants to clarify their complaints and to put their complaints in writing),

(c)   to initiate a complaint against an Australian lawyer or an Australian-registered foreign lawyer,

(d)   to investigate, or take over the investigation of, a complaint if the Commissioner considers it appropriate,

(e)   to refer complaints to the appropriate Council for investigation or mediation in appropriate cases,

(f)   to monitor investigations and give directions and assistance to Councils in connection with the investigation of complaints,

(g)   to review the decisions of Councils to dismiss complaints or to reprimand Australian lawyers or Australian-registered foreign lawyers in connection with complaints,

(h)   to take over investigations or to institute proceedings in the Tribunal against Australian lawyers or Australian-registered foreign lawyers following a review by the Commissioner,

---

[44] Professional associations that represent lawyers.
[45] Professional associations that represent barristers.
[46] See, for example, the *Revised Professional Conduct and Practice Rules (Solicitors' Rules) NSW 1995* (Solicitors' Rules), available at www.lawsociety.com.au/ForSolictors/professionalstandards/Ruleslegislation/Solicitors Rules/index.htm.

(i)   to conduct regular surveys of, and report on, the views and levels of satisfaction of complainants and respondent Australian lawyers with the complaints handling and disciplinary system,

(j)   to monitor the refusal to grant, cancellation and suspension of practising certificates under Part 2.4 on grounds relating to fitness to practise (for example, in connection with acts of bankruptcy, the commission of indictable offences or tax offences or failures to give required notifications),

(k)   functions conferred on the Commissioner under Division 7 of Part 2.4 and Part 4.7 of Chapter 4,

(l)   to review the provisions and operations of Chapter 4 in accordance with section 494 (4),

(m)   to monitor generally the exercise of regulatory functions by the Councils (other than the imposition of conditions on practising certificates),

(n)   to review legal profession rules,

(o)   to assist the Councils to promote community education about the regulation and discipline of the legal profession,

(p)   to assist the Councils in the enhancement of professional ethics and standards, for example, through liaison with legal educators or directly through research, publications or educational seminars,

(q)   to report on the Commissioner's activities under this Act[47]

The OLSC was created by statute in 1994.[48] At the time of its creation, the OLSC was the first regulatory office of its kind and has set the precedent for a co-regulatory model that is now being established and considered in many parts of the world.

The OLSC's purpose (although not enunciated in the *Legal Profession Act 2004* (NSW)) is to reduce complaints against lawyers within a context of consumer protection, protection of the rule of law and increased professionalism. That is, increasing the ethics, integrity, competence and skill of lawyers. Unlike most regulators, the OLSC's purpose is not solely focused on legislative compliance. As a regulator of the legal profession, the OLSC sees its role as more than setting high ethical standards, holding practitioners against these standards and disciplining or removing those that fail. This compliance type of approach is ad hoc and reactive, and triggers only in response to problems that have already occurred. The compliance-based approach is narrow and non-transparent, is incapable of bringing about systematic change and results in practitioners only being disciplined for the specific conduct the subject of a complaint.

The OLSC rejected this 'compliance alone' approach in favour of an approach that focuses on increasing the professionalism of legal practitioners. The rejection of this approach was based on public condemnation of the traditional self-regulatory model.

---

[47]   Legal Profession Act 2004 (NSW) s 688

[48]   Prior to 1994, the the Law Society of New South Wales and the New South Wales Bar Association handled discipline complaints against solicitors and barristers. Their efforts focused primarily on serious misconduct and rarely addressed the more common client complaints like failure to communicate or neglect of client matters. The creation of the OLSC was as a result of consumer dissatisfaction at the perceived bias of the professional associations in relation to complaint handling. This was largely due to the fact that the overwhelming majority of complaints handled resulted in dismissal; see New South Wales Reform Commission, 'The Legal Profession Discussion Paper No. 2, Complaints, Discipline and Professional Standards – Part 1' (1979), available at www.lawlink.nsw.gov.au/lrc.nsf/pages/dp2out; S Mark, 'Complaints Against Lawyers: What Are They About and How Are They Handled' (1995) available at infolink/lawlink/olsc/ll_olsc.nsf/pages/OLSC_may_1995; S Mark, 'Regulation: Putting The Profession In Good Order' (Speech delivered at the 2001 Conference of Regulatory Officers on 28 March 2001), available at infolink/lawlink/olsc/ll_olsc.nsf/pages/OLSC_canberra_2001.

This approach adopted by the OLSC is encapsulated in its mission statement to 'lead in the development of an ethical legal services market which is fairer, more accessible and responsive', and reduce complaints by:

- Developing and maintaining appropriate complaints handling processes;
- Promoting compliance with high ethical standards;
- Encouraging an improved consumer focus in the profession;
- Developing realistic expectations by the community of the legal system.[49]

The OLSC recognises that there are multiple aims to an effective regulatory system.[50] These aims include a consumer dimension, with the consequent need to redress the complaints of dissatisfied users of legal services; a practitioner dimension, ensuring the diligence and competence of individual practitioners; and a profession dimension, maintaining high standards of ethics and practice for the profession generally. The approach taken by the OLSC involves continually building, evaluating and improving it's activities. The philosophy behind this approach is formulated on ensuring that the OLSC will make a lasting and significant contribution to raising standards in the legal services industry—to put the profession in better order so to speak — and ultimately to improve satisfaction with the services delivered to the community by legal practitioners. The OLSC has sought over the years to invoke this approach in three ways; the capture and publication of knowledge, the education of lawyers and would-be lawyers, and the education of consumers and their representatives/agencies.

As an independent regulator, the OLSC sees its clients as complainants, the lawyers who are the subjects of complaints, the community and the profession in general. The OLSC is continuously striving towards improved legal service standards, community expectations of and attitudes towards the profession and promoting a relationship of trust and open communication between the profession and the community. The role of the OLSC is therefore to service both the community and the profession in a way that is responsive to their needs as well challenging them to work towards continuous improvement and mutual understanding. Has this approach been a success?

Since commencing in 1994, the number of complaints against legal practitioners received by the OLSC has remained static at about 3,000 complaints per year.[51] That the number of complaints has remained static over the years is impressive. What is even more impressive, however, is that the complaints have remained static against a rapidly growing legal profession. In the first year of operation, the OLSC received 2,801 written complaints and 6,700 inquiry calls.[52] In 2011–12, the OLSC received 2758 written complaints and 7920 inquiry calls.[53] During that 18-year period, the legal profession has grown from about 12,000 legal practitioners to about 28,000 legal practitioners today.[54]

---

[49] Office of the Legal Services Commissioner, 'About Us', available at infolink/lawlink/olsc/ll_olsc.nsf/pages/OLSC_aboutus

[50] See LS Terry, S Mark & T Gordon, 'Adopting Regulatory Objectives for the Legal Profession'(2012) 80 *Fordham Law Review* 2685

[51] Office of the Legal Services Commissioner, 'Annual Report', 1994–2012, nos 2000–2012 are available at www.olsc.nsw.gov.au/lawlink/olsc/ll_olsc.nsf/pages/OLSC_annualreports

[52] Office of the Legal Services Commissioner, 'Annual Report' (1994).

[53] Office of the Legal Services Commissioner, '2011–2012 Annual Report' , available at www.olsc.nsw.gov.au/lawlink/olsc/ll_olsc.nsf/vwFiles/2011_2012_AnnRep.pdf/$file/2011_2012_AnnRep.pdf

[54] Urbis, '2012 Profile of the Solicitors of NSW Final Report' (2013) *The Law Society of New South Wales*, available at www.lawsociety.com.au/cs/groups/public/documents/internetcontent/687930.pdf

The staticity in complaints is by and large, due to an effective and responsive regulatory regime that creates a framework for instituting ethical behaviour, understanding organizational culture and market dynamics and upholding the professionalism of lawyers. The OLSC has sought to embed this mantra in their regulatory regime since it began operating in 1994. The following section will set out how the OLSC has been able to embed this mantra and ensure that its regulatory framework is relevant to the realities of the legal services marketplace.

IV   RESPONSIVE REGULATION AND ADAPTATION

The foundation of the OLSC's regulatory regime is the 'conversation'. For the OLSC, open communication, honesty and trust between the regulator and the regulatee must underlie the regulatory regime. To this end, the OLSC regularly engages with the profession and consumers of the legal profession to ensure that they are aware of, and understand behaviour and the paradigm within which lawyers practise. So, when the OLSC receives a complaint against a lawyer, unless the complaint involves an obvious and egregious breach of ethics or standards, the OLSC commences an interaction with both the lawyer and the complainant which focuses on determining the nature of the complaint and how the matter can be resolved. This is referred to under the legislation as a 'consumer dispute'.[55]

The legislation which regulates the legal profession in NSW creates a 'protective jurisdiction.' This is so, as it is conceived to 'protect' the public from unscrupulous or unethical lawyers by providing a mechanism for their sanction or even removal from the Roll of Lawyers. Unfortunately, from the affected consumer's perspective, this is of little utility. The process rarely compensates complainants for loss and never for injury. The vast majority of complaints will never reach the standard set by the legislation for unsatisfactory professional conduct and professional misconduct.[56] Traditionally, prior to the establishment of the OLSC, the profession, when engaged in self-regulation, would dismiss all complaints that failed to reach the standard of discipline. At the OLSC, the approach taken has been to attempt to resolve those disputes at the earliest possible stage. This approach is consistent with the OLSC's purpose of reducing complaints.

Where the OLSC receives a complaint alleging serious misconduct as opposed to a consumer dispute, it takes a more formal investigative and potentially disciplinary approach, but notwithstanding this, it's aim is to treat complaints as providing an educational tool for both legal practitioners and complainants. The OLSC's treatment of complaints in this

---

[55] 'Consumer disputes' are disputes between legal practitioners and users of legal services and do not involve misconduct. Examples of consumer disputes are complaints about poor communication, costs, mistakes, delays, handling of documents and poor service. The majority of complaints received by the OLSC are classified as consumer disputes, capable of resolution.

[56] 'Unsatisfactory professional conduct' is defined by the leghal profession legislation in NSW as conduct occurring in connection with the practise of law that falls short of the standard of competence and diligence that a member of the public is entitled to expect of a reasonably competent Australian legal practitioner. 'Professional misconduct' is defined in the legal profession legislation in NSW to include unsatisfactory professional conduct that involves a substantial or consistent failure to reach or maintain a reasonable standard of competence and diligence and conduct, whether occurring in connection with the practice of law or otherwise, which would, if established, justify a finding that the practitioner is not a fit and proper person to engage in legal practice.

manner also enables it to learn from the profession about what actually occurs in practice and understanding the culture within which practitioners act.

The OLSC's role as a regulator is therefore to work with the profession in entrenching an ethical culture and promoting professionalism. The OLSC views this approach as one of 'regulating culture' rather than a simple focus on the professional conduct of individuals. This 'education towards compliance' framework is the dominant paradigm of the OLSC and sits well within its philosophical approach of 'regulating for professionalism.' The OLSC continues to remind lawyers that they are part of a noble profession and as members of a profession, they have both an ethical and statutory obligation to ensure that they do not engage in conduct that diminishes public confidence in the administration of justice or is prejudicial to the administration of justice.

One method of 'conversation' with the profession is through an extensive range of educational programs which focus on, for example, running ethical hypotheticals for lawyers. The focus of these programs is to explore the basis of decision-making within legal practice and particularly the internation between ethics, morality and values. The OLSC's experience in providing hundreds of seminars has shown that many lawyers, be they fresh out of law school or long-term lawyers, readily defer to rules when confronted with ethical dilemmas, often ignoring morality or their personal values. It is often the case that lawyers argue that if there is no rule against a particular type of behaviour, then the behaviour is acceptable. In the Clayton Utz/McCabe litigation discussed at the beginning of this chapter, Clayton Utz could have justified its decision to do so on the basis that at the time of acting there were no professional rules that precluded a lawyer from advising his or her clients that they should destroy documents.[57]

This can obviously result in 'ethical blindness'. The OLSC is concerned that academic legal training coupled with practice in ethically poor cultures has fostered this type of behaviour. It is also apparent that when confronted with ethical connundrums regarding, for example, costs and complaints of overcharging, lawyers tend to structure their justification based on client consent, even where such agreement would otherwise be contrary to sound ethical practice. There seems to be a tendency for lawyers to bow to cost pressure within law firm culture, sometimes at the expense of sound ethical behaviour. This culture of profit over ethics can result in 'ethical blindness' and often client dissatisfaction. The opportunity for lawyers to engage in discussions with the OLSC as the regulator can result in a 'conversation' on ethical behaviour and organizational culture. In addition to providing these programs, the OLSC also publishes a wide range of material for both the profession and the general public about ethical issues and legal practice. The aim of these publications and the educational programs is to enhance and improve the ethical culture within which lawyers practice.

The OLSC's 'conversations' are not just limited to legal practitioners or complainants. The OLSC also engages with a range of organisational stakeholders, including professional associations, legal profession indemnity insurers, and other regulators of the legal profession in Australia and overseas on a regular basis about a wide range of issues, including complaints, discipline, education, policies and procedures. The OLSC has been having these conversations with these organisational stakeholders for many years. These conversations

---

[57] Since the McCabe case, New South Wales and has amended its regulations to include a provision that makes document destruction capable of amounting to professional misconduct. See Regulation 177 of the Legal Profession Regulation 2005 (NSW).

allow the OLSC to better understand the dynamics of the legal services marketplace and to be kept abreast of practice developments and behaviour.

In addition to the conversations with these organizational stakeholders, the OLSC also engages in conversations with other regulators where there is regulatory overlap. Regulatory overlap between different regulatory offices, if not addressed, can cause problems in implementation and practice. For example the OLSC has for some years, maintained a regular conversation with the Migration Agents Registration Authority (MARA) that regulates registered migration agents who may be legal practitioners. The OLSC has met with MARA to discuss regulatory overlap and how it can be addressed. Meetings with MARA have resulted in a Memorandum of Understanding (MOU) between the OLSC and MARA to share information where appropriate. The MOU further states that if either office receives information which it believes to be of relevance to each other, in the discharge of each office's responsibilities each office should liaise with one another and refer matters to the other where appropriate. The MOU also allows each office to conduct joint investigations.

In addition to the MOU with MARA, the OLSC has recently entered into an MOU with the NSW Office of Fair Trading (OFT). The arrangement was forged by the commencement of the *Australia Consumer Law* in January 2011, which applies to all Australian consumers and businesses, including lawyers. The application of this legislation to lawyers creates another level of regulatory overlap for regulators of the legal profession. The OLSC and the OFT have entered into an MOU about their respective roles. Under the MOU, the OLSC and the OFT have agreed to share information and refer matters to each other where appropriate.

The alliances created by these MOUs have been particularly successful. The ability to share information has resulted in a transparent regulatory regime that benefits all parties. The arrangement also prevents unnecessary and costly duplication for all parties involved. The success of these MOUs has prompted the OLSC to pursue arrangements with other regulators, such as the Australian Securities and Investments Commission (ASIC), Australian Prudential Regulatory Authority (APRA) and the Australian Competition and Consumer Commission (ACCC) where there is such an overlap. The OLSC, for example, like ASIC, sees the role of lawyers, and in particular commercial lawyers, as essentially 'gatekeepers' of sound ethical culture.[58]

The OLSC's ability to have 'conversations' has been enhanced by amendments to the legal profession legislation imposing an outcomes-based framework to regulate incorporated legal practices (including multidisciplinary practices). This framework requires incorporated legal practices (ILPs), irrespective of their size, to appoint at least one 'legal practitioner director' who has all of the responsibilities a lawyer has to the Court, all the responsibilities to the corporate regulator (ASIC) and an additional tranche of responsibilities under the legislation.[59] One of those responsibilities is to require the ILP to implement

---

[58] See G Medcraft, 'News From the Regulator' (Speech delivered at the 2011 FOS National Conference), available at www.asic.gov.au/asic/pdflib.nsf/LookupByFileName/News-from-the-regulator-FOS-speech-2-June-2011.pdf/$file/News-from-the-regulator-FOS-speech-2-June-2011.pdf; cf S Mark, 'Walking The Ethical Tightrope: Balancing The Ethical Responsibilities Of In-House Counsel To Key Stakeholders' (Paper delivered to Legalwise Seminar, 12 November 2009), available at www.olsc.nsw.gov.au/lawlink/olsc/ll_olsc.nsf/pages/OLSC_speeches

[59] The primary structural requirement for an incorporated legal practice is that at least one legal practitioner director must be appointed: Section 140(1) of the LPA 2004. A legal practitioner director is defined as a director of an incorporated legal practice who is an Australian legal practitioner holding an unrestricted practicing certificate.

and maintain 'appropriate management systems' to ensure that the ILP complies with the legal profession legislation and the ethical duties of lawyers. Failure to comply with this duty can result in the OLSC taking disciplinary action and even removing from the Roll of Lawyers the legal practitioner director. Should this occur, the ILP has seven days to replace that legal practitioner director or go into involuntary liquidation.

Nowhere in the legislation are 'appropriate management systems' defined. The OLSC, rather than establishing a best-practice management system for law firms, sought to identify what issues a management system should attempt to address to be considered as 'appropriate'. After extensive consultation with the profession and stakeholders, the OLSC identified ten issues that ought to be addressed. These ten issues, which cover principles of sound practice, are based on the most common types of complaints levelled against lawyers. They include as follows:

1. **Negligence** - (providing for competent work practices)
2. **Communication** (providing for effective, timely and courteous communication)
3. **Delay** (providing for timely review, delivery and follow up of legal services)
4. **Liens/file transfers** (providing for timely resolution of document/file transfers)
5. **Cost disclosure/billing practices/termination of retainer** (providing for shared understanding and appropriate documentation on commencement and termination of retainer along with appropriate billing practices during the retainer)
6. **Conflict of interests** (providing for timely identification and resolution of 'conflict of interests', including when acting for both parties or acting against previous clients as well as potential conflicts which may arise in relationships with debt collectors and mercantile agencies, or conducting another business, referral fees and commissions, etc)
7. **Records management** (minimising the likelihood of loss or destruction of correspondence and documents through appropriate document retention, filing, archiving etc and providing for compliance with requirements regarding registers of files, safe custody, financial interests)
8. **Undertakings** (providing for undertakings to be given, monitoring of compliance and timely compliance with notices, orders, rulings, directions or other requirements of regulatory authorities such as the OLSC, courts, costs assessors)
9. **Supervision of practice and staff** (providing for compliance with statutory obligations covering licence and practising certificate conditions, employment of persons and providing for proper quality assurance of work outputs and performance of legal, paralegal and non-legal staff involved in the delivery of legal services)
10. **Trust account regulations** (providing for compliance with Part 3.1 Division 2 of the Legal Profession Act and proper accounting procedures.[60]

The OLSC requires a law firm seeking incorporation to respond to these ten issues by completing a self-assessment form.[61] The assessment must be completed by the legal practitioner director of the ILP. This process is designed to focus the ILP on how to approach the

---

[60] Office of the Legal Services Commissioner, 'Ten Areas to be Addressed to Demonstrate Compliance with "Appropriate Management Systems"', available at www.lawlink.nsw.gov.au/lawlink/olsc/ll_olsc.nsf/pages/OLSC_tenobjectives.

[61] Office of the Legal Services Commissioner, 'Self-Assessment Document: Suggestions Concerning the Elements of "Appropriate Management Systems" for Incorporated Legal Practices in NSW', available at www.lawlink.nsw.gov.au/lawlink/olsc/ll_olsc.nsf/pages/OLSC_ilp.

ten issues and what arguments or evidence they may have to convince the OLSC that their management systems are thereby appropriate.

The purpose of requiring a legal practitioner director to undergo this process is to ensure that they have considered and implemented an organization-wide 'ethical infrastructure' that supports and encourages ethical and client-focused behaviour.[62] From a regulatory perspective, these requirements are intended to preserve the ethics and integrity of law firms, create an ethical culture and increase professionalism.[63] Implementation of such an ethical infrastructure also provides better protection for consumers of legal services. This is because the management systems that ILPs are required to maintain act as educative mechanisms, encouraging practitioners to adopt best practice in order to go beyond simple compliance with the requirements of the legislation and establish an ethical culture.

The framework is supplemented by an audit process, or as the OLSC prefers to refer to them, 'practice reviews' to assist law practices improve their management systems and develop an ethical culture, where lacking.[64] The objectives of an ILP practice review allow the OLSC to evaluate the following factors in relation to the ILP's management systems:

(a) Confirm that appropriate management systems have been implemented and maintained by the ILP, in accordance with section 140(3) of the Legal Profession Act 2004;

(b) Ascertain whether any significant changes in management, organisation, policies, procedures, techniques or technologies are adversely affecting the management systems or welfare of the ILP in general;

(c) Provide relevant guidance, explanations and examples of how similar matters and concerns have been dealt with by other ILPs;

(d) Provide information on suitable and necessary training for staff or the LPD;

(e) Track and analyse ILPs in the self-assessment process;

(f) Improve monitoring of the self-assessment process for ILPs;

(g) Provide further information on relevant elements;

(h) Determine the need for a follow-up audit;

(i) Confirm compliance with obligations under Part 2.6 of the Legal Profession Act 2004; and

(j) Align practice management with concerns following from a complaint history.

---

[62] The term "ethical infrastructure" was first coined by Professor Ted Schneyer more than 20 years ago in his seminal work; T Schneyer, 'Professional Discipline for Law Firms' (1991) 77 *Cornell Law Review* 1. Since that time, the term has provided a framework for scholars and commentators around the world to discuss regulation. See eg, J Chu, 'Ethics Auditing: Should It Be Part of Large Law Firms' Ethical Infrastructure' (2008) 11 *Legal Ethics* 16. Professor Schneyer has described the New South Wales (NSW) framework for regulating ILPs as a prototype for 'proactive, management-based regulation.' See T Schneyer, 'On Further Reflection: How "Professional Self-Regulation" Should Promote Compliance with Broad Ethical Duties of Law Firm Management' (2011) 53 *Arizona Law Review* 576, 584.

[63] See eg, C Parker, 'Law Firms Incorporated: How Incorporation Could and Should Make Firms More Ethically Responsible' (2004) 23 *University of Queensland Law Journal* 347.

[64] The OLSC has, in practice, by agreement with the Law Society, assumed the role of auditing ILPs for compliance with the Legal Profession Act 2004 (NSW). There are two types of audits that can occur under the Act. The first is a general power to audit any law practice regardless of entity status (section 670(1)) – a compliance audit). The second is an audit of an ILP, which is broken into two components – compliance of the ILP with the requirements of Part 2.6 of the LPA 2004 and management of the provision of legal services (section 670(2)(a) & (b) ILP Audit). The OLSC can audit a practice's systems with files and behaviour reflected in a returned self-assessment form.

The initiation of a practice review can occur as a result of a number of events. Adverse media publicity, for example, or a case in which a lawyer has been the subject of a significant number of complaints may trigger a practice review. So too can a referral from a Law Society trust account inspector or a follow-up review which is due as a result of a previous review. Lawyers who have been listed in the NSW Law Society Professional Conduct Committee Reports or practitioners otherwise the subject of information provided by the professional associations or ASIC, for example, may also be subject to a practice review.

Other triggers may include cases in which there is evidence to suggest that the legal practitioner director has misled the Commissioner with respect to appropriate management systems, or where the objectives remain rated less than compliant, or a legal practitioner director or non-legal practitioner director or a solicitor employee is listed in a cost warning or conflict of interest database or the most recent monthly Law Society or NSW Professional Conduct Committee Reports, or the latest Law Society of NSW Inspection Itinerary. Similarly, inclusion in a listing of the ILP in the OLSC's 'Top Thirty' repeat offenders list which is maintained by the OLSC, or being otherwise identified in the OLSC's risk profiling process can also be a trigger. In fact any source that is of concern or any other reason deemed appropriate by the Legal Services Commissioner will trigger a practice review, even if a lawyer has only been the subject of a single complaint, or no complaint at all.

The OLSC has characterised the practice review process as a systematisation of ethical conduct to regulate culture. This approach sits well within the OLSC's general philosophy of regulation in which the regulator educates the profession and consumers of legal services to achieve a culture whereby compliance itself becomes cultural. Once such a culture is achieved, it follows that there will be a reduction in the number of complaints received.

The ethical infrastructure requirement imposed on ILPs has proven to be a great success. The OLSC is, by and large, better and more ethically managed legal practices. The OLSC seeing a fall in the number of complaints. According to the results of a research study we conducted in 2008 together with Dr Christine Parker of the University of Melbourne, the average complaint rate (average number of complaints per practitioner per years) for ILPs after self-assessment dropped by almost two-thirds before self-assessment.[65] This is a huge drop in complaints. The study involved analysing 620 initial self-assessment forms from ILPs. In addition to the complaints data, the study also found that the majority of ILPs assess themselves to be in compliance on all ten objectives from their initial self-assessment (62 per cent). Of the remaining 38 per cent, about half have become compliant within three months of the initial self-assessment. The study further revealed that ILPs have the highest rates of self-assessed compliance with trust accounting obligations and the lowest rates of self-assessed compliance with management systems to ensure good communication and good supervision of practice.

Following this study in 2012, the OLSC participated in a research study with Dr Susan Saab Fortney, Howard Lichtenstein Distinguished Professor of Legal Ethics and Director of the Institute for the Study of Legal Ethics, Hofstra Law School, Hofstra University to evaluate the relationship between the self-assessment process and the ethics norms, systems, conduct, and culture in firms. The study revealed that the framework for regulating ILPs

---

[65] C Parker, T Gordon, S Mark, 'Regulating Law Firm Ethics Management: An Empirical Assessment of the Regulation of Incorporated Legal Practices in NSW' (2010) 37 *Journal of Law and Society Studies* 466.

had the greatest impact on firm management and risk management issues. The study also revealed that regardless of the size of the firm, the imposed regulatory framework assisted in shaping the attitudes of many directors and serves as a valuable learning exercise that enabled firms to improve client service.[*]

The framework instituted for ILPs, as a result of the success, is soon to be expanded to all law practices in NSW. The roll-out will be facilitated by a Portal built by the OLSC to conduct online self-assessments and risk profiling. The Portal will improve the process for regulating and improving ethical behaviour by all legal practices and support the provision of high quality, ethical legal services. The OLSC envisages that this will in turn reduce the number of consumer complaints about the legal profession. The Portal will also enhance the application and technical capacity to address the OLSC's need for complete, timely and accurate information to support decision making, whilst providing the most effective use of OLSC resources. The Portal will further provide an information and educational repository to aid legal practices in improving their management systems, which will support the provision of high quality, ethical legal services by legal practices.

The success of this framework is largely based on the pliability of outcomes-based regulation, which recognises that regulation is not a one size fits all phenomenon. Such pliability has allowed incorporated practices to work together with regulators and design individual management systems that are both flexible and responsive without being onerous.

The authors believe that the approach taken by the OLSC in regulating lawyers is entirely consistent with the needs identified by other authors in this book in relation to the regulation of financial markets. Regulators such as ASIC, APRA and the ACCC could adopt a similar approach for the purpose of moving beyond regulatory compliance to building ethical infrastructure and enabling the regulation of professional culture. The application of ethical infrastructure to corporate law firms, for example, has been raised and supported by others in Australia as a defence against creeping commoditization and commercialisation of law.[66]

V CONCLUSION

Slater & Gordon is a niche national firm that has built up a powerful reputation and profile in the Australian legal market. Slater & Gordon was established in 1935 as a Melbourne law firm providing services to unions and their members, particularly in the area of worker's compensation. Since that time, the firm has established a strong position in the personal injuries and class action litigation market in Australia. Its business strategy has focused on delivering legal services to consumers, rather than to the few corporate and government clients that represent the largest share of total expenditure on legal services in Australia.[67] Furthermore, Slater & Gordon is one of the most recognisable brand names in Australia.[68] In 2001, Slater & Gordon was among the first law firms in Australia to move from being a

---

[*] S.Fortney, T.Gordon, Adopting Law Firm Management systems to survive and thrive. A study of the Australian Approach to management Bad Regulation, (Jan 22, 2013), St.Thomas Law Review.

[66] See C Parker et al, above n 37.

[67] D Bentley, 'Andrew Grech: Leading By Example' *The Law Gazette* (8 February 2012).

[68] A study in July 2010 found that the general brand awareness of the Slater & Gordon name was 87% in Melbourne, 76% in Brisbane, 72% in Perth and 63% in Sydney. There are very few firms in Australia that have built up such a powerful brand. See Slater & Gordon 'Results Presentation', *Annual Report, 2010–11*, available at www.slaterandgordon.com.au/editor_upload/Flash/Flash/SGH_Annual_Report-2011.pdf.

partnership to becoming an incorporated legal practice. Slater & Gordon expanded modestly following incorporation, acquiring six other law firms between 2001 and 2007.[69]

On 21 May 2007, Slater & Gordon made legal and corporate history by listing on the Australian Securities Exchange (ASX), becoming the world's first publicly listed law firm. The firm issued more than 95 million ordinary shares as well as another 12 million non-voting shares. The initial public offering raised $35 million.[70] Around 34 per cent of the firm's shares are held in-house, including as part of the firm's Employee Ownership Plan.[71]

Being publicly listed has allowed Slater & Gordon to undertake a rapid national expansion program through acquisitions, together with organic growth of the existing business. The ability to tap equity markets has allowed Slater & Gordon to access additional funds for acquisitions.[72] Slater & Gordon has increased its share of the Australian personal injury litigation market, which currently stands at 50 per cent.[73] These acquisitions have increased Slater & Gordon's revenue, size and geographical reach.[74] Slater & Gordon has also sought to expand the range of legal services that it offers.[75] In January 2012, Slater & Gordon announced its entry into the United Kingdom by acquiring the mid-sized UK personal injury firm Russell Jones & Walker.[76] The deal was worth £53.8m (around $AUD 80 million), which included the issue of £17.4m in Slater & Gordon shares.[77]

The incorporation and public listing of law firms has created many practical, philosophical and ethical challenges for the legal profession in New South Wales. The public listing of Slater & Gordon in 2007 raised the fundamental concern about the tension between a practitioner's professional duties and the requirements of a company under the Corporations Act 2001 (NSW). It was argued that there is an inherent tension between a solicitor director's duties to a company's shareholders and a solicitor's professional obligations. The

---

[69] Slater & Gordon, 'Expansion into UK Legal Market' presentation (30 January 2012), available at www.asx.com.au/asxpdf/20120130/pdf/4240pb55d5pmm9.pdf.

[70] ibid.

[71] Slater & Gordon, above n 68.

[72] Since the ASX listing, Slater & Gordon has acquired 20 other firms across Australia. These have included McClellands Lawyers (Sydney, Parramatta, Wollongong, ACT) in 2008, D'Arcy's Solicitors in 2008 (Brisbane), and in 2010 Adams Leyland Lawyers (Albury, Dubbo and Gilgandra, NSW), Stewart & Noble Lawyers (Wangaratta, Vic) and the personal injuries practice of Robbins Watson Solicitors (QLD). See Slater & Gordon, above n 69; Slater & Gordon, above n 68.

[73] Slater & Gordon, above n 69.

[74] Since listing in 2007, staff numbers have more than doubled from 418 to 1,102 and office locations increased from 26 to 61. The company's revenue has grown from $79.7 million in 2007–2008 to $182.3 million in 2010–11, equivalent to compound annual growth of 31%. This included revenue growth of 46% in 2010–11, reflecting the acquisition of the Queensland personal injury firm Trilby Misso in August 2010 and NSW firm Keddies in January 2011. Trilby Misso was acquired for $57 million, of which $40 million was raised through share capital. Keddies was also partly funded by share capital and became fully integrated into the Slater & Gordon brand. See Slater & Gordon, above n 69.

[75] In November 2011, Slater & Gordon announced that it would acquire the specialist Queensland conveyancing firm, Conveyancing Works, which would provide a base for expansion into the conveyancing market in Queensland, New South Wales and Victoria. See Slater & Gordon, above n 68.

[76] Russell Jones & Walker has 10 offices, mainly in London, Manchester, Sheffield and Birmingham, with 425 staff. Around 60% of its revenue is from fees for personal injury litigation. The acquisition also includes the claims management brand Claims Direct.

[77] Slater & Gordon, 'Slater & Gordon to enter UK legal market' (ASX announcement, 30 January 2012), available at www.slaterandgordon.com.au/files/editor_upload/File/ark/ASX%20Announcement%20-%20 Slater%20&%20Gordon%20enters%20UK%20Legal%20Market.pdf.

conventional thinking is that a practitioner's professional obligations speak to ethically minded conduct and a paramount duty to the court, which may be antithetical to business objectives.

A major concern of incorporation is related to the perceived conflicts of interest or duties owed by the firm to the court, shareholders and clients. In Australia, a legal practitioner's primary duty is owed to the court. No other profession shares this duty. In stark contrast to the obligations under the Legal Profession Act 2004 (NSW), under the Corporations Act directors have an overriding duty to the company and to the rights and protection of shareholders. The difficulties of this problem were effectively overcome by the Legal Profession (Incorporated Legal Practices) Act 2000 (NSW) and the Legal Profession (Incorporated Legal Practices) Regulation 2001 (NSW). The effect of the relevant provisions is that where there is an inconsistency between the Corporations Act 2001 (Cth) and the Legal Profession Act 2004 (NSW), the latter prevails to the extent of the inconsistency.

In recognition of the possibility of the conflict between the duties owed to the company and shareholders and the duties owed to the court and to clients, the OLSC worked together with Slater & Gordon prior to listing to ensure this issue was dealt with in its prospectus, constituent documents and shareholder agreements. These documents clearly state that for the directors of this publicly listed law firm, their primary duty is to the Court, their secondary duty is to the client and their tertiary duty is to the shareholder. This hierarchy of duties presents a major shift in considering the present dominant paradigm of shareholder value in relation to corporate behaviour. It could be said that now in Australia, there is at least one publicly listed company where the directors' primary duty is to the community (through the duty to the Court). This seems to be entirely consistent with the range of public statements made by political leaders during the global financial crisis that community values and ethics need be incorporated into financial markets, and perhaps to achieve this through regulatory reform.

With the approach taken by the OLSC in regulating lawyers in NSW, Australia may provide a prototype for considering the re-regulation of financial markets through the promotion of ethical infrastructure, increasing professionalism and regulating for an ethical culture.

Part Four

Regulating Culture in the Financial Sector –
Realities and Limitations

CHAPTER 11

The Fiduciary Idea in Financial Services Law

Pamela F Hanrahan

I CULTURE AND THE FIDUCIARY IDEA

This collection is about regulating culture in the financial sector. Poor culture in financial services firms (including investment banks, brokers, financial advisers and investment managers) has been implicated in the Global Financial Crisis (GFC)[1] and the events that have followed; and failure by these firms to put their clients' interests at the ethical centre of their endeavours is often identified as the core cultural deficit. So, can the financial services sector be 'fixed' by using law and law-making to foster (or perhaps force) a culture in which promoting their clients' interests becomes the touchstone in how financial services firms organise themselves, and deal with their clients?[2]

The 'fiduciary idea' is regularly invoked as the proper juridical framework for building such a culture. Command-and-control legal obligations (expressed as broad outcome-based principles or detailed inputs-based rules) based on fiduciary principle and backed by private and public sanctions might force financial services firms to put their clients first. For reform to be effective, both the idea and its implementation need to be right. To that end, this chapter asks a prosaic pair of questions. Just how does the fiduciary idea currently work in the context of the relationship between financial services firms and their clients, at

---

[1] See eg United States Financial Crisis Inquiry Commission, *Financial Crisis Inquiry Report* (New York, Public Affairs, 2011); United Kingdom Financial Services Authority, *The Turner Review: A Regulatory Response to the Global Banking Crisis* (London, Financial Services Authority, 2009); *The High-Level Group on Financial Supervision in the European Union, Report* (Brussels, European Commission, 2009).

[2] For example, in July 2012, Douglas Hodge of PIMCO wrote: 'Good culture within the financial *services* industry should comprise three important elements. First, the culture needs to be centered on its core purpose of serving a legitimate client need. Second, the practice of sound risk management should be an integrated component. Last and most important, the culture within the industry must rest on the foundation of stewardship and a sense of responsibility. The adoption of these principles fortifies trust, which ultimately contributes to positive business results. Once again, the role of finance is to serve broader interests of society. It creates value not for itself, but on behalf of others. Hence, the culture of financial services organizations should reflect this purpose. Internal incentive and reward systems should be aligned to put the interests of the client ahead the firm, and the interests of the firm ahead of individual employees.' (Emphasis in the original.) See www.pimco.com/EN/Insights/Pages/Its-All-About-Culture.aspx.

least under Australian law? And what happens when policymakers try to appropriate the fiduciary idea into the broader project of financial regulation?

The Fiduciary Idea

As Justices Gaudron and McHugh of the High Court of Australia have observed, 'Duty and self-interest, like God and Mammon, make inconsistent calls on the faithful'.[3] Fiduciary principle is an established legal mechanism for resolving this inconsistency. The fiduciary idea recognises in a legal (as distinct from moral or social) sense that some dealings or relationships between people have a special character that demands of one of them unalloyed solicitude for and loyalty to the concerns of the other. This special character arises from what has been described as the 'cardinal aspect' of the fiduciary relationship, that a person 'undertakes to act for, or on behalf, or in the interests of, another person (eg a trustee and cestui que trust) in the exercise of some power or discretion capable of affecting the interests of that other person'.[4]

The accepted categories of fiduciary relationships—including between trustee and beneficiary, agent and principal, solicitor and client, director and company, and partners[5]—all exhibit this special character. But fiduciary relationships can exist outside these accepted categories, including in commercial dealings. While there is 'no generally agreed and unexceptionable definition', a person may be treated in equity as a fiduciary 'when and insofar as that person has undertaken to perform such a function for, or has assumed such a responsibility to, another as would thereby reasonably entitle that other to expect that he or she will act in that other's interest to the exclusion of his or her own or a third party's interest'.[6] This will in many cases describe the relationship between a financial services firm and its client, at least with respect to aspects of their relationship.

In these special situations, equity seeks to foster and promote the proper performance by the fiduciary of its functions and responsibilities by the imposition of two interrelated

---

[3] *Breen v Williams* [1996] HCA 57; (1996) 186 CLR 71 at 108 (*Breen*).

[4] R Meagher and A Maroya, 'Crypto-Fiduciary Duties' (2003) 26 *University of New South Wales Law Journal* 348, paraphrasing Mason J in *Hospital Products Ltd v United States Surgical Corporation* [1984] HCA 64; (1984) 156 CLR 41 at 96-7 (*Hospital Products*). Justice Mason said that a critical feature of the accepted fiduciary relationships was that the fiduciary 'undertakes or agrees to act for or on behalf of or in the interests of another person in the exercise of a power or discretion which will affect the interests of that other person in a legal or practical sense. The relationship between the parties is therefore one which gives the fiduciary a special opportunity to exercise the power or discretion to the detriment of the other person who is accordingly vulnerable to abuse by the fiduciary of his position. The expressions "for", "on behalf of", and "in the interests of" signify that the fiduciary acts in a "representative" character in the exercise of his responsibility'. In *News Limited v Australian Rugby Football League Ltd* (1996) 64 FCR 410 at 541, the Full Federal Court said: 'In the end, an important question—if not the question—is whether, in the words of Professor Finn: "the actual circumstances of a relationship are such that one party is entitled to expect that the other will act in his interests in and for the purposes of the relationship. Ascendancy, influence, vulnerability, trust, confidence or dependence doubtless will be of importance in making this out, but they will be important only to the extent that they evidence a relationship suggesting that entitlement"' [referring to P D Finn, 'The Fiduciary Principle' in T G Youdan (ed), *Equity, Fiduciaries and Trusts* (1989) at 46]'.

[5] *Hospital Products* at CLR 68 (Gibbs CJ) and CLR 96 (per Mason J).

[6] *Grimaldi v Chameleon Mining NL (No 2)* [2012] FCAFC 6; (2012) 200 FCR 296 at [177] (*Grimaldi*), per Finn, Stone and Perram JJ.

proscriptions, known in Australian law as the 'no conflicts rule' and the 'no profits rule'.[7] These rules are directed, in the words of the Full Federal Court, at exacting 'disinterested and undivided loyalty from the fiduciary'; hence their 'focus on conflicts between duty and undisclosed personal interest, conflicts between duty and duty, and misuse of a fiduciary position for personal gain or benefit'.[8]

These proscriptions do not exist in a legal vacuum. They operate alongside, and inform and are informed by, other specific legal duties and obligations that arise for particular relationships and dealings under common law, in equity and by statute. In commercial arrangements for the provision of financial services, these may include contractual and tortious duties of care, equitable duties governing the exercise of discretions, and statutory and regulatory rules such as prohibitions on unconscionable conduct and misleading or deceptive conduct, mandatory disclosure requirements, and prescriptive conduct of business rules.[9]

Post-GFC, policymakers around the world have focused on the role and prospects of the fiduciary idea as a means of improving the performance of financial services firms—both for the protection of clients individually and to strengthen the stability of the financial system generally.

Of particular concern are apparent conflicts of interest in the provision of financial advice, in circumstances where a client (retail or wholesale)[10] retains the firm for its investment expertise, and the financial services firm (or its affiliate) is either the originator or vendor of the financial product acquired by the client, or is remunerated in respect of its services in a way that distorts or skews its advice towards maximising its own return from the relationship.

Various reforms, derived from or referencing the fiduciary idea, have been proposed to address these conflicts in the retail space. In Australia in 2009, the Parliamentary Joint Committee on Corporations and Financial Services (PJC) recommended that the law be amended 'to explicitly include a fiduciary duty for financial advisers operating under an [Australian financial services licence], requiring them to place their clients' interests ahead of their own'.[11] In the United States, Section 913 of Title IX of the Dodd-Frank Wall Street Reform and Consumer Protection Act of 2010 required the Securities and Exchange Commission (SEC) to conduct a study to evaluate the regulation of personalised investment advice and recommendations about securities to retail customers; as a result of the study, SEC Staff recommended that 'the standard of conduct for all brokers, dealers and investment advisers' in these circumstances should be 'to act in the best interest of the customer

---

[7] The fiduciary proscriptions are discussed in detail in section 4 below.

[8] *Grimaldi* at [174].

[9] The specific duties and obligations that attached to the provision of various financial services by licensed entities in Australia are described in section 2 below.

[10] The distinction between retail and wholesale clients is discussed in section 5 below. One (under-developed) aspect of the reform debate post-GFC is whether the provisions of services to retail and wholesale clients should be differently regulated, and if so where the line between the two categories of clients should be drawn.

[11] Commonwealth of Australia *Financial Products and Services in Australia: Report of the Parliamentary Joint Committee on Corporations and Financial Services* (November 2009), [6.29]. The recommendation led to the enactment of new Part 7.7A of the Corporations Act 2001 (Cth) (Corporations Act) which comes into full effect from 1 July 2013, and is discussed in section 5 below.

without regard to the financial or other interest of the broker, dealer or investment adviser providing the advice'.[12]

This renewed focus on the fiduciary idea as a means of improving the performance of financial services firms, and of the reducing the opportunity or incentives for them to engage in conduct that ultimately imperils the stability of the financial system as a whole, requires careful consideration of what the fiduciary idea means in the context of the provision of financial services, and whether (and if so how) it might be adopted, extended or adapted to achieve the twin policy objectives of investor protection and systemic stability identified above.

In that consideration, some broad themes emerge.

First, it is important to understand when the relationship between a financial services firm and its client is already considered fiduciary in nature, under existing principles of equity. This is discussed in section 3 below. Many financial services firms do owe fiduciary duties to their clients, in a range of situations.

Secondly, we need to be clear about the consequences, for the firm, of treating any aspect of its relationship with its client as fiduciary in nature. In particular, it is important to map what the fiduciary proscriptions mean in the context of the provision of financial services, and to understand whether financial services firms that are in a fiduciary relationship with their clients are subject to a positive duty to act in the 'best interests' of the client. This theme is developed in section 4.

Thirdly, we need to decide whether it is desirable for governments to enshrine the fiduciary idea in legislation governing financial services firms. As a policy matter, this involves a series of (political) choices about when the imposition of such a requirement is appropriate—for example whether it should apply to the provision of all types of financial services, and to dealings with both retail and wholesale clients. As a matter of jurisprudence, it involves a series of questions about how such a standard might most effectively be captured in legislation. Recent Australian reforms provide a clear illustration of prevailing approaches to financial sector reform, that focus on prescriptive, input-driven rules rather than clear normative principles based on established legal doctrine. This is the focus of section 5.

II   FINANCIAL SERVICES AND THEIR REGULATION

The fiduciary idea is not and cannot be applied to financial services firms in a legal vacuum. Law is a complex system; understanding the interaction of the various legal rules with each other is as important as understanding the commercial context in which they apply. Financial services firms perform a range of functions: including as product manufacturers,[13] brokers,[14]

---

[12] This standard is referred to in the study as the 'uniform fiduciary standard': United States Securities and Exchange Commission *Study on Investment Advisers and Broker-Dealers* (January 2011) vi. The recommendation, at the time of writing, has not been adopted.

[13] Product manufacture covers the activities of entities such as investment banks that create products (such as securitization interests, structured products and derivatives) and sell them to counterparties. This includes origination in what is sometimes described as the 'shadow banking' sector.

[14] Broking describes the acquisition and disposal of financial products on financial markets on behalf of clients.

financial and corporate advisers,[15] investment managers,[16] market makers and custodians.[17] Individual firms may provide one or more of these services, either directly through their affiliates. In some situations, a firm may combine more than one of these functions—for example by acting as both product manufacturer and adviser, or as broker and adviser. In integrated financial services businesses, the firm or its affiliates may also be a principal (proprietary) trader in markets alongside its clients.

In Australia, the provision of financial services is covered by a unified regulatory regime that came into effect in 2001. The starting point for the modern Australian regulatory regime is that, regardless of the type of financial services they provide or the nature (retail or wholesale) of their clients, all firms that carry on a financial services business in the jurisdiction are required to hold an Australian financial services (AFS) licence, subject only to limited exemptions. AFS licensing is the responsibility of the Australian Securities and Investments Commission (ASIC), the single Commonwealth agency that combines (among others) the functions of companies registrar, corporations and securities regulator, financial services licensing authority, financial markets supervisor, and consumer protection regulator for the financial sector.[18]

The comprehensive coverage of the AFS licensing regime derives in large part from the functional (rather than institutional) approach to defining the key concepts of 'financial product' and 'financial service' adopted in the 2001 legislation.[19] Subject to a (lengthy) list

---

[15] Financial advice may be general or personal. In the author's view, the provision of general financial advice should be regulated under existing laws relating to misleading and deceptive conduct rather than the specialist financial services regime, but in Australia the specialist regime applies. The discussion in this chapter is confined to personal financial advice. The provision of personal financial advice involves making recommendations, relating either to the acquisition or disposal of particular financial products or to more comprehensive financial planning, that are personal to the client. Corporate advisory work, for example of the kind routinely done by investment banks and considered in by Austin J in *Aequitas v Sparad No 100 Ltd (formerly Australian European Finance Corporation Ltd)* [2001] NSWSC 14; (2001) 19 ACLC 1006 (*Aequitas*) and Jacobson J in *Australian Securities and Investments Commission v Citigroup Global Markets Australia Pty Ltd (No 4)* [2007] FCA 963; (2007) 160 FCR 35 (*Citigroup*), is also generally understood to be in the nature of financial services, although such advice is carved-out of the Australian regulatory regime by reg 7.1.29(3)(c) of the Corporations Regulations 2001.

[16] Investment management is used the broad sense to describe arrangements under which the financial services firm exercises its discretion in managing the client's investments, for example in a collective investment scheme (CIS) or superannuation fund or under an individual investment mandate.

[17] Market operators are conceptually separate, and are not treated as financial services firms in this analysis. Market operators and clearing and settlement facilities are separated regulated in Australia under Corporations Act Pt 7.2–7.5.

[18] Under Australia's 'twin peaks' regulatory system established in 1998, ASIC is the conduct, disclosure and consumer protection regulator for the financial sector. Australian authorised deposit-taking institutions (ADIs) (including banks and building societies), insurance companies, and public offer superannuation (that is, pension) funds are subject to additional prudential regulation by the Australian Prudential Regulation Authority (APRA). For a discussion of the 'twin peaks' model, see eg A Jensen and M Kingston 'The Australian "Twin Peaks" Framework of Financial System Regulation: Australia and UK Compared' (2010) 9 *Journal of International Banking and Financial Law* 548.

[19] For a detailed discussion on the philosophy underlying the reforms contained in the Financial Services Reform Act 2001 (Cth) (FSR Act), see R Baxt, A Black and P Hanrahan *Securities and Financial Services Law* (8th ed, LexisNexis, Sydney, 2012) [1.49]–[1.59]. The 2001 legislation introduced what is now Ch 7 of the Corporations Act. Chapter 7, which is entitled 'Financial Services and Markets', has since been amended several times and currently contains 15 parts; these are: 7.1–Preliminary; 7.2–Licensing of financial markets; 7.2A–Supervision of financial markets; 7.3–Licensing of clearing and settlement facilities; 7.4– Limits on involvement with licensees; 7.5–Compensation regime for financial markets; 7.5A–Regulation of derivative transactions and derivative trade

of express inclusions and exclusions, a 'financial product' is defined as 'a facility through which, or through the acquisition of which, a person does one or more of the following: makes a financial investment; manages financial risk; or makes non-cash payments'.[20] It includes securities, derivatives, CIS interests,[21] superannuation interests, insurance products, bank deposits, and government and semi-government securities, but excludes most forms of credit (other than margin lending).

In turn, a 'financial service' involves doing various things in relation to a financial product; these include providing financial product advice (both general and personal); dealing in a financial product; making a market for a financial product, operating a registered CIS; or providing a custodial or depository service.[22] 'Dealing' in this context includes issuing, acquiring, disposing of or varying a financial product or arranging for a person to do any of those things, but excludes dealing undertaken by a person (other than a product issuer) on their own account or the issue by a corporation or government of securities in itself.

The legal framework for the provision of financial services

Financial services firms and their clients operate in a 'law-rich' environment, regardless of whether a fiduciary relationship exists between them. First, there is the contract or other

---

repositories; 7.6–Licensing of providers of financial services; 7.7–Financial services disclosure; 7.7A–Best interests obligation and remuneration; 7.8–Other provisions relating to conduct etc. connected with financial products and financial services, other than financial product disclosure; 7.9–Financial product disclosure and other provision relating to issue, sale and purchase of financial products; 7.10–Market misconduct and other prohibited conduct relating to financial products and financial services; 7.11–Title and transfer; and 7.12–Miscellaneous. The unfair contracts, unconscionable conduct and consumer protection laws that apply to the financial sector, which are also administered by ASIC, are contained in Pt 2, Div 2 of the Australian Securities and Investments Commission Act 2001 (Cth) (ASIC Act).

[20] Corporations Act s 763A(1). While sufficient for our purposes, this greatly understates the complexity of the relevant definitions; see Baxt, Black and Hanrahan, above n 19, Ch 3. The complex, obscure and indeterminate nature of the definitions illuminates the significant pitfalls inherent in the approach taken by the 2001 legislation. In *International Litigation Partners Pty Ltd v Chameleon Mining NL (Receivers and Managers Appointed)* [2012] HCA 45 at [5], the plurality (French CJ, Gummow, Crennan and Bell JJ) observed that, 'The legislative scheme implemented by the [FSR Act] has two significant characteristics. One is over-inclusiveness. Rights and liabilities are drawn in overtly broad terms, on the footing that instances of overreach which become apparent in the administration of the legislation may be remedied by adjustments to the Act made not by remedial legislation but by exercise of powers conferred upon the Executive Government or bodies such as [ASIC]. The second characteristic is the creation by the legislation of rights and liabilities by means of criteria which reflect fluid market and economic usage rather than any ascertainable and stable meaning in the law.' The broad functional coverage of Ch 7 is sometimes viewed as one of the strengths of the Australian regulatory system that contributed to Australia's relatively sound economic performance during the GFC. But it comes at a cost, in both overregulation and imprecision.

[21] In Australia, CIS are known as 'managed investment schemes'. CIS offered to retail customers must be registered with ASIC under Ch 5C of the Corporations Act, and are known as 'registered schemes'. Registered schemes are operated by a 'responsible entity' that must be an Australian public company holding the appropriate form of AFS licence.

[22] Corporations Act s 766A. Each of these concepts is in turn defined in Corporations Act ss 766B – 766E respectively: see Baxt, Black and Hanrahan, above n 19, [13.3]–[13.8]. There are various carveouts and exclusions, including in Corporations Regulations 7.1.29, including in reg 7.1.29(3)(c) for investment banking.

basis upon which the firm agrees to provide the relevant services,[23] the terms of which must be observed.[24] Secondly, the firm will owe to the client a duty of care, arising in contract, tort and (depending on the circumstances) equity. Thirdly, financial intermediaries in all IOSCO member jurisdictions are typically subject to a range of general and specific conduct obligations covering dealings with clients that are imposed by statute or regulatory instrument.[25] In Australia, the statutory requirements and restrictions on AFS licensees' conduct towards their clients are extensive. In addition to the various mandatory disclosure requirements mentioned above,[26] they include:

- general obligations, imposed on all licensees by Corporations Act s 912A(1), including to 'do all things necessary to ensure that the financial services covered by the licence are provided efficiently, honestly and fairly' (Corporations Act s 912A(1)(a)); and to 'have in place adequate arrangements for the management of conflicts of interest that may arise wholly, or partially, in relation to activities undertaken by the licensee or a representative of the licensee in the provision of financial services as part of the financial services business of the licensee or the representative' (Corporations Act s 912A(1)(aa)); and
- prescriptive conduct of business rules for licensees, including rules relating to holding and using client money and property (Corporations Act Pt 7.8, Div 2 and 3); a prohibition on licensees engaging in unconscionable conduct (Corporations Act s 991A); and obligations relating to dealings with non-licensees (Corporations Act s 991E).

Financial services firms, in common with all those who engage in conduct in relation to financial services and financial products, are also subject to general prohibitions on certain types of undesirable conduct in financial markets. These include prohibitions on: market

---

[23] The relationship will usually have a contractual foundation, although a fiduciary relationship can arise in the absence of a contract. In *Beach Petroleum NL v Kennedy* [1999] NSWCA 408; (1999) 48 NSWLR 1 at [192]–[195] (*Beach Petroleum*), the New South Wales Court of Appeal said: 'It is well-established that a person may take upon herself or himself the role of a fiduciary by a less formal arrangement than contract or by self-appointment. . . . Ultimately a fiduciary responsibility is an imposed not an accepted one, one concerned with an imposed standard of behaviour. . . . But whether the relationship derives from retainer, a less formal arrangement or self-appointment, it must be examined to see what duties are thereby imposed on the fiduciary and the scope and ambit of those duties . . . . The existence and scope of the duty may derive from a course of dealing. . . . Moreover a role which was limited when originally assumed may, by reason of conduct in the performance of the role, be expanded so as to extend the duty' (references omitted).

[24] Some contracts for the provision of financial services can be affected by statutory rules for the protection of consumers, relating to unfair contract terms and implied warranties; in Australia, see ASIC Act Pt 2, Div 2, Subdiv BA (unfair contract terms) and Subdiv E (conditions and warranties in consumer transactions). The warranties include that the services will be rendered with due care and skill, and that if the purpose for which the services are acquired are made known to the firm, that the services are reasonably fit for that purpose.

[25] The International Organization of Securities Commissions (IOSCO) is the peak international body for securities regulators: see the IOSCO *Objectives and Principles of Securities Regulation* (Madrid, IOSCO, June 2010) and its *Methodology for Assessing Implementation of the IOSCO Objectives and Principles of Securities Regulation* (Madrid, IOSCO, September 2011) available at www.iosco.org.

[26] An Australian retail client receiving personal financial advice from an AFS licensee gets two mandatory disclosure documents–a Financial Services Guide (FSG) and a Statement of Advice (SoA). The FSG informs the client about the firm and the services being provided, while the SoA records the advice and the basis for arriving at it. A product issuer must give the retail client a Product Disclosure Statement prepared in accordance with Pt 7.9 of the Corporations Act.

manipulation;[27]false trading and market rigging;[28] disseminating information about false trades;[29] making false or misleading statements or representations;[30] fraudulently inducing dealing;[31] dishonest conduct;[32] misleading or deceptive conduct;[33] insider trading;[34] unconscionable conduct;[35] and certain undesirable sales practices such as bait advertising and pyramid selling.[36]

Also, AFS licensees that provide particular financial services are subject to conduct requirements relating to the provision of that specific service; these include:

- conduct of business rules for brokers, including rules requiring licensees to give priority to client orders and relating to the implementation of client instructions to deal through licensed markets, (Corporations Act ss 991B and 991C and Corporations Regulation 7.8.18); the rules contained in the relevant exchange's operating rules; and the market integrity rules made by ASIC pursuant to Corporations Act Pt 7.2A;
- conduct rules that apply to responsible entities of registered managed investment schemes, including the duties in Corporations Act s 601FC(1) to act honestly; to exercise the degree of care and diligence that a reasonable person would exercise if they were in the responsible entity's position; and to act in the best interests of the members and, if there is a conflict between the members' interest and its own interests, give priority to the members' interests;
- conduct rules (in the form of statutory covenants) contained in s 52(2) of the Superannuation Industry (Supervision) Act 1993 (Cth) that apply to trustees of public offer superannuation entities. These include obligations to act honestly; to exercise the same degree of care, skill and diligence as an ordinary prudent person would exercise in dealing with the property of another person for whom the person felt morally bound to provide; and to perform its duties and exercise its powers in the best interests of beneficiaries; and

---

[27] Corporations Act s 1041A.

[28] Corporations Act ss 1041B and 1041C.

[29] Corporations Act s 1041D.

[30] Corporations Act s 1041E and ASIC Act s 12DB.

[31] Corporations Act s 1041F.

[32] Corporations Act s 1041G.

[33] Corporations Act s 1041H, ASIC Act s 12DA and s 18 of the Australian Consumer Law (ACL) proscribe misleading or deceptive conduct in different situations; all are based on the former s 52 of the Trade Practices Act 1974 (Cth) (now the Competition and Consumer Act 2010 (Cth) (CCA)). ACL s 18 may apply (depending on the circumstances) as Commonwealth law or State law or both. These provisions give a person who suffers loss or damage as a result of misleading or deceptive conduct a right to compensation. Notably the misleading or deceptive conduct provisions do not apply to FSGs and SoAs, which have their own liability regime which allow for various defences to liability for errors in or omissions from these documents: see Corporations Act s 1041H(3)(c) and s 1041K; ASIC Act s 12DA(1A)(c); and CCA ss 131 and 131A. Where the general provisions do apply, complex definitions and carveouts determine which of the particular provisions applies to the provision of particular financial services. They are labyrinthine. In *Wingecarribee Shire Council v Lehman Bros Australia Ltd (In Liq)* [2012] FCA 1028 at [948] Rares J asks: 'Why does a court have to waste its time wading through this legislative porridge to work out which one or ones of these provisions apply even though it is likely that the end result will be the same?' Regrettably the answer is that some applicable principles, including relating to apportionment of liability, that apply to claims based in Commonwealth law do not apply if the plaintiff's claim is based on contravention of ACL s 18 applying as State law: see Baxt, Black and Hanrahan, above n 19, [9.30]. It is hard to attribute this inconsistency to anything other than poor legislative design.

[34] Corporations Act Pt 7.10, Div 3.

[35] ASIC Act ss 12CA and 12CB.

[36] ASIC Act ss 12DC – 12DK.

- new rules governing the provision of personal financial advice to retail clients contained in Corporations Act Pt 7.7A.[37] These include the best interest obligation (Pt 7.7A, Div 2), restrictions on charging ongoing fees to clients (Pt 7.7A, Div 3); and restrictions on conflicted remuneration (Pt 7.7A, Div 4) and other banned remuneration (Pt 7.7A, Div 5).

If the relationship between the financial services firm and its client is fiduciary for the reasons explained in section 3 below, then of course the further legal consequences described in section 4 also follow.

III   FINANCIAL SERVICES FIRMS AS FIDUCIARIES

The relationship between a financial services firm (so described) and its client is not one of the accepted fiduciary relationships identified by the High Court in *Hospital Products*, discussed above.[38] So while, for example, the relationship between a solicitor and their client is always acknowledged in equity as fiduciary in character, this is not the case with the relationship between a financial services firm and its client. The question of whether a particular relationship or dealing makes the financial services firm a fiduciary depends on the nature of the service provided, and the circumstances in which it is provided. Often, in the financial services context, the question of whether a fiduciary relationship exists arises when a financial services firm has provided personal financial advice to a client.

It now seems well established in Australian law that, where a financial service firm holds itself out as an expert on financial matters and undertakes to act in the client's interests and not solely in its own interests in the provision of personal advice in relation to those matters, the relationship between the firm and its client is fiduciary with respect to that advice: *Daly v Sydney Stock Exchange Ltd* [1986] HCA 25; (1986) 160 CLR 317 at 377 per Gibbs CJ; at 385 per Brennan J (*Daly*); *Commonwealth Bank of Australia v Smith* (1991) 42 FCR 390 at 319; *Aequitas* at [301], [310]; *Fletcher (as trustee of the Brian Fletcher Family Trust) v St George Bank Ltd (No 2)* [2011] WASC 277 at [116].

In two recent decisions of the Federal Court of Australia arising out of the sale of complex financial products[39] to various local councils prior the GFC, the financial services firms that had dealt with the local councils were found to have been financial advisers to those councils and owed fiduciary duties to them in advising on and recommending the products[40] The applicant councils in both cases were unsophisticated in financial matters, but were nevertheless wholesale clients for the purposes of the Australian regulatory regime.[41]

In *Wingecarribee Shire Council v Lehman Bros Australia Ltd (In Liq)* [2012] FCA 1028 at [733] (*Wingecarribee*), Rares J described financial advisers as one of the 'well recognised

---

[37] These new rules are often referred to as the 'Future of Financial Advice' or 'FoFA' measures.

[38] *Hospital Products* at CLR 68 (per Gibbs CJ) and CLR 96 (per Mason J).

[39] The local councils in each case invested in the financial products on the advice of the relevant financial services firms. The *Bathurst* case involved the rating, sale and purchase of a structured financial product known as a constant proportion debt obligation or CDPO. The *Wingecarribee* case involved synthetic collaterised debt obligations (SCDOs) and other complex financial products.

[40] At the time of writing, both decisions are on appeal.

[41] See the discussion in section 5 below about the distinction between retail and wholesale clients.

categories' of fiduciary agents to which, in the absence of contractual or other modifica-
tions, the fiduciary obligations apply. In *Bathurst Regional Council v Local Government
Financial Services Pty Ltd (No 5)* [2012] FCA 1200 at [2306] (*Bathurst*), Jagot J found that
a financial services firm that had entered into formal agreements to provide investment
advisory services to certain of its clients owed fiduciary duties to those clients because
the firm had 'led [the client] to believe that it would act in their best interests in advising and making recommendations about financial products'. With certain other of its
clients, with which the firm did not have formal investment advisory agreements, the
firm had engaged in a course of conduct over time that her Honour considered took it
beyond being a 'mere salesman' of the financial products in question; it 'knew the context
in which the [clients] functioned and knew that the [clients] perceived [the firm] as acting in their interests and not [the firm's] sole interest'. In so doing the firm 'moved beyond
the role of a mere salesman and acted as an investment adviser and thereby attracted to
itself fiduciary duties': at [2324].

While it is tempting to read the comments of Rares J in *Wingecarribee* as meaning that
anyone described as a 'financial adviser' now falls within a recognised category of fiduciary under Australian law, the position is more nuanced. What matters is the nature of the
undertaking made or given by the adviser and how that undertaking is reasonably understood and acted upon by the client. It is not enough to create a fiduciary relationship
that the firm is a 'mere salesman' of a financial product; nor that it provides information
or opinions or about particular financial products, or general advice about investments,
corporate finance, or financial planning. The advice must be personal to the client; and
the circumstances of the giving and receipt of that advice must be such that the client
would reasonably understand the adviser to be looking out for or motivated by the client's interest (rather than its own or another person's) in arriving at its recommendations.
That said, the advice need not relate to the client's whole financial position or occur in
the context of an ongoing professional relationship between the firm and the client; it
is possible for a fiduciary relationship to arise in respect of particular advice given on a
single occasion.

Despite ASIC's lingering concern (expressed to the PJC in 2009) that the legal position is uncertain,[42] it seems that the provision of personalised financial advice to a client
in Australia will usually give rise to a fiduciary relationship between the adviser and the
client. If a client seeks personal financial advice from a professional financial services firm
in circumstances where the financial services firm has held itself out as having expertise
in such matters and undertaken to advise the client on them, and it is apparent that the
client wants and intends to rely upon the expert recommendations of the adviser (and
not just information or opinions that adviser provides) in taking action that will affect
the financial position of the client, it is unsurprising that a client would expect the firm's
recommendations to be directed at what is in the client's interests, not those of the firm
or some third party. Where that expectation exists, it is likely the relationship between the
client and the firm will be treated as fiduciary. What this means for the firm is discussed
in section 4 below.

For investment managers who control their clients' money for the purposes of investment, the position is simpler. Investment managers are fiduciaries with respect to the

---

[42] Commonwealth of Australia, *Financial Products and Services in Australia*, above n11 [5.70].

carrying out of the relevant trust, scheme or mandate.[43] The manner in which the investment management arrangement is structured may bring the investment manager within the accepted categories of fiduciary, for example as agent or trustee for the client. In any event, an investment management arrangement usually involves the firm undertaking to act 'for or on behalf or in the interests of another person in the exercise of a power or discretion which will affect the interests of that other person in a legal or practical sense'.[44] So, for example, in *Wingecarribee* agreements for the individual management of client (local council) investment portfolios gave rise to a fiduciary relationship between the firm and the client. Custodians, as trustees of assets, are fiduciaries with respect to the handling of those assets.

A stockbroker or futures broker, when acting as the client's agent, clearly is a fiduciary, and therefore fiduciary obligations apply to the execution by the broker of the client's business.[45] A broker is not under an obligation to advise the client,[46] but if it in fact undertakes to give advice to the client in the manner explained above, its fiduciary obligations will extend to the giving of that advice.[47] However, leaving aside investment management arrangements, a product manufacturer or vendor is not, without more, in a fiduciary relationship with the purchaser of that product. Nor is a market maker in a fiduciary relationship with the person with whom it transacts.

Excluding the Fiduciary Relationship by Agreement

Given the restrictions imposed by equity on fiduciaries that are explained in section 4 below, it is unsurprising in commercial (as distinct from altruistic or personal) relationships that the party potentially subject to those restrictions might seek to exclude the existence of a fiduciary relationship by agreement with its client. In *Citigroup*, Jacobson J concluded that this could be done. Where a fiduciary relationship has already arisen between the parties, the informed consent of the client to the disavowal of the fiduciary character of the relationship would be required. Informed consent is discussed in section 4 below. However, where from the outset the relationship was outside the accepted fiduciary categories and was acknowledged and agreed by both parties not to be fiduciary,[48] this will often be effective to exclude it.[49]

---

[43] *In the matter of Idylic Solutions Pty Ltd–Australian Securities and Investments Commission v Hobbs* [2012] NSWSC 1276 at [1497]–[1513] and [2418]–[2431]; *Brisconnections Management Co Ltd v Australian Style Investments Pty Ltd* (2009) 23 VR 253; [2009] VSC 128 at [67]; *Stacks Managed Investments Ltd* [2005] NSWSC 753; (2005) 219 ALR 532 at [56]); *Australian Securities and Investments Commission v ABC Fund Managers Ltd (No 2)* [2001] VSC 383 at [124]. The bases upon which such relationships are fiduciary in character are discussed in P Hanrahan *Funds Management in Australia: Officers' Duties and Liabilities* (Sydney, LexisNexis Butterworths, 2007) [2.11]–[2.16].

[44] *Hospital Products* at CLR 96, per Mason J.

[45] See the discussion about the position of brokers in Baxt, Black and Hanrahan above n19, [14.4]–[14.5]. The position in the United States is different.

[46] *Eric Preston Pty Ltd v Euroz Securities Ltd* [2010] FCA 97; (2010) 77 ACSR 135 at [157]–[168]; aff [2011] FCAFC 11.

[47] *Daly* at CLR 385, per Brennan J.

[48] For example, in *Citigroup*, this was done as a term of the mandate letter pursuant to which the financial services firm agreed to advise the client in relation to a proposed takeover.

[49] *Citigroup* at [768], [809]. For a discussion of the Citigroup decision, see P Hanrahan, '*ASIC v Citigroup*: Investment Banks, Conflicts of Interest and Chinese Walls' in J O'Brien (ed) *Private Equity, Corporate Governance and the Dynamics of Capital Market Regulation* (London, Imperial College Press, 2007) 117–42.

IV   THE CONSEQUENCES OF BEING A FIDUCIARY

Deciding that its relationship with its client is fiduciary in nature is just the beginning of the inquiry as to what that means for the financial services firm. The fiduciary proscriptions (that is, the no-conflicts rule and the no-profits rule) apply to those interactions between the firm and its client that occur in or in connection with the 'fiduciary' part of their relationship. But does it separately indicate, or perhaps require, that the firm must act in the best interests of the client, and if so, what does this mean in the context of the provision of financial services?

The Fiduciary Proscriptions

The first, and uncontroversial, consequence is that as a fiduciary the financial services firm is subject to what the High Court described in *Breen* at CLR 113, as the 'proscriptive fiduciary duties'. The proscriptions preclude the firm from providing the financial service to the client in circumstances where there is a real and sensibility possibility that the firm's personal interests or duty to another person might conflict with its duty to the client, unless it has the client's fully informed consent; and from using the relationship it has with the client (or property, opportunities or information obtained through that relationship) to benefit the firm or another person without the client's fully informed consent.

The effect of the (interrelated) rules is the firm can be made to account to its client for any benefit the firm gains or receives 'in circumstances where there existed a conflict of personal interest and fiduciary duty or a significant possibility of such conflict' or 'by reason of or by use of his fiduciary position or of opportunity or knowledge resulting from it': *Chan v Zacharia* (1984) 154 CLR 178 at 198–99 (*Chan*) per Deane J; see also *Breen* at CLR 113.

In *Wingecarribee* at [732], Rares J succinctly states the rules as follows:

> A fiduciary such as a financial adviser will be under two proscriptive obligations imposed by equity. Those obligations are, unless the fiduciary has the informed consent of the person to whom they are owed, *first*, not to obtain any unauthorised benefit from the relationship and, *secondly*, not to be in a position where the interests or duties of the fiduciary conflict, or there is a real or substantial possibility they may conflict, with the interest of the person to whom the duty is owed: *Pilmer v Duke Group Ltd (In Liq)* (2001) 207 CLR 165 at 197–98 [74], 199 [78]-[79].

Justice Deane, in *Chan* at CLR 198–99, describes the objective of the first rule as being 'to preclude the fiduciary from being swayed by considerations of personal interest'; and of the second as being to 'preclude the fiduciary from actually misusing his position for his personal advantage'. The Full Federal Court in *Grimaldi* at [174] characterised this part of fiduciary law as being:

> concerned with the setting of standards of conduct for persons in fiduciary positions. Its burden, put shortly, is with exacting disinterested and undivided loyalty from a fiduciary—hence, for example, its focus on conflicts between duty and undisclosed personal interest, conflicts between duty and duty and misuse of a fiduciary position for personal gain or benefit.

The fiduciary proscriptions are sometimes described as prophylactic in character – and the description is apt. Viewed this way the normative function of the rules is protect or buttress the integrity of discharge by the firm of its undertaking to the client, by making sure the conditions in which that undertaking is discharged do not tempt the firm to have its eye on anything other than the client's interest.[50] A financial services firm that always conducts its dealings with clients with in circumstances of perfect (personal) disinterest, and with the knowledge that any collateral advantage or benefit it may derive from those dealings belongs in equity to the client, is less likely to be diverted, consciously or unconsciously, from making choices that are directed at or focused on the client's interests.

This is important because the very thing that gives some (but not other) dealings or relationships their fiduciary character is the vulnerability of the person to whom the duties are owed to the choices and actions of the fiduciary. The prophylactic character of the rules has a long genesis in trust law and is why, in *Keech v Sandford* (1726) Sel Cas T King 61; 25 ER 223, the trustee in his personal capacity was the only person in all the world who could not take up a lease, have been refused the opportunity by the landlord to renew it in his capacity as trustee for an infant beneficiary. Of course the rules are also remedial in character, providing the person to whom they are owed with a range of potential remedies in equity for breach.[51]

It is trite to say that in the context of commercial relationships founded in contract the fiduciary duties shape and mould themselves to the agreement between the parties, not the other way around.[52] If a financial services firm has contracted to provide service *x* in circumstances that make it a fiduciary with respect to the provision of service *x*, then its status

---

[50] This idea is encapsulated by the Court of Appeal in New South Wales in *Beach Petroleum* at [199]–[200] in the following terms: 'The law of fiduciary duty with respect to a conflict of duty and interest rests on practical considerations, not morality. In *Breen* (at CLR 108), Gaudron J and McHugh J quoted with approval from the judgment of Lord Herschell in *Bray v Ford* [1896] AC 44 at 51: "human nature being what it is, there is danger, in such circumstances, of the person holding a fiduciary position being swayed by interest rather than by duty, and thus prejudicing those whom he was bound to protect." . . . It was for this reason that equity created what his Lordship described as an 'inflexible rule' that a fiduciary is not allowed to put himself or herself in a position where duty and interest conflict: see also *Warman International Ltd v Dwyer* (1995) 182 CLR 544 at 557–58.' In M Conaglen *Fiduciary Loyalty: Protecting the Due Performance of Non-fiduciary Duties* (Oxford, Hart Publishing, 2010), the author says at p 4: 'the fiduciary concept of 'loyalty' is a convenient encapsulation of a series of legal principles. . .[that] provide a subsidiary and prophylactic form of protection for non-fiduciary duties. The purpose of that protection is to enhance the chance of proper performance of those non-fiduciary duties by seeking to avoid influences or temptations that are likely to distract the fiduciary from providing such proper performance. It is frequently observed that fiduciary doctrine operates in a prophylactic manner, which is undoubtedly the case.'

[51] Remedy for breach of fiduciary duty is a separate topic that ranks, in the field of human endeavour, somewhere alongside brain surgery and rocket science. Australian courts have been busy in this area in 2012, with significant contributions to the jurisprudence in *Grimaldi*, and in *Westpac Banking Corporation v The Bell Group Ltd (In Liq) (No 3)* [2012] WASCA 157; (2012) 270 FLR1; special leave granted [2013] HCATrans 49. The Full Federal Court in *Grimaldi* usefully identifies three possible avenues for recovery by the client in the case of breach of the fiduciary proscriptions, at [183]–[187] (references omitted). '*First*, at the beneficiary's election and subject to considerations of "appropriateness". . .the fiduciary will hold on constructive trust any property or benefit derived in breach of fiduciary duty to the extent that that property or benefit remains extant or can be traced in the fiduciary's hands. . . . *Secondly*, the wrongdoing fiduciary can be held liable in an *in personam* claim to account for profits he or she derived which are attributable to the breach of fiduciary duty. . . . *Thirdly*, a defaulting fiduciary will be liable, at the beneficiary's election, to pay equitable compensation to a beneficiary who has suffered loss thereby, the object of the remedy being to restore the beneficiary to the position in which he or she would have been had there been no breach of fiduciary duty.'

[52] In *Hospital Products* at CLR 97, Mason J says that where contractual and fiduciary relationships co-exist: 'it is the contractual foundation which is all important because it is the contract that regulates the basic rights and liabilities of the parties. The fiduciary relationship, if it is to exist at all, must accommodate itself to the terms of the contract so that it is consistent with, and conforms to, them. The fiduciary relationship cannot be superimposed upon the contract in such a way as to alter the operation which the contract was intended to have according to its true construction.'

as a fiduciary requires it to avoid unauthorised conflicts, and not to make unauthorised profits, in the provision of service *x*. It does not require the firm to provide service *y*. For example, a firm that agrees to provide advice on a certain matter is not required to provide advice on some other matter, or to advise the client generally. Just as a trustee's first duty is to adhere to and carry out the terms of the trust,[53] and solicitor's duty is to carry out his or her retainer and not necessarily to offer advice on the wisdom of the course the client proposes to pursue,[54] the financial services firm is obliged to carry out its undertaking consistent with its obligations as a fiduciary, but not to carry out some other undertaking. The rub, of course, is rightly to identify the nature and scope of the undertaking. This is an inquiry of fact.[55]

Informed consent

The rule in equity is that the fiduciary is not precluded from acting where a conflict of interest and duty, or a conflict of duty and duty, exists so long as it has the informed consent of the person to whom the duty is owed. Similarly, a fiduciary may retain a collateral advantage or benefit it obtains through the relationship provided it has such consent.[56]

Therefore a crucial factor in the application of the fiduciary proscriptions to professional financial services firms is: what amounts to informed consent to the existence of a conflict or the taking of a collateral advantage in these circumstances? In many jurisdictions, including Australia, the regulatory regime requires extensive disclosure of information (including about remuneration and any interests and affiliations that 'might reasonably be expected to be, or have been capable of, influencing' the firm) to retail clients in connection with the

---

[53] *Youyang Pty Ltd v Minter Ellison Morris Fletcher* [2003] HCA 15; (2003) 212 CLR 484 at [32].

[54] In *Beach Petroleum* at [186]–[189], the Court of Appeal says: 'In *Clark Boyce v Mouat* [1994] 1 AC 428 at 437, to which the High Court referred in *Maguire v Makaronis*, Lord Jauncey of Tullichettle, who delivered the judgment of the Privy Council, said: "Their Lordships are accordingly satisfied that Mrs Mouat required of Mr Boyce no more than that he should carry out the necessary conveyancing on her behalf and explain to her the legal implications of the transaction. When a client in full command of his faculties and apparently aware of what he is doing seeks the assistance of a solicitor in the carrying out of a particular transaction, that solicitor is under no duty whether before or after accepting instructions to go beyond those instructions by proffering unsought advice on the wisdom of the transaction." Whether or not there is a duty to advise on the wisdom of a particular transaction depends on the circumstances of the case: see, eg, *Haira v Burbery Mortgage Finance & Savings* [1995] 3 NZLR 396 at 406'.

[55] The precise nature and scope of the undertaking is all-important, even in cases arises out of the accepted categories of (status-based) fiduciary relationship. In *Beach Petroleum* at [188], the Court of Appeal went on to say that: 'Even in the case of a solicitor client relationship, long accepted as a status based fiduciary relationship, the duty is not derived from the status. As in all such cases, the duty is derived from what the solicitor undertakes, or is deemed to have undertaken, to do in the particular circumstances. Not every aspect of a solicitor client relationship is fiduciary. Conduct which may fall within the fiduciary component of the relationship of solicitor and client in one case, may not fall within the fiduciary component in another. The relationship of solicitor and client has at its core an element of confidence and influence which equity will preserve and protect. Nevertheless, the confidence and influence are not always so pervasive as to require equitable intervention in every facet of the relationship'.

[56] As Brennan CJ, Gaudron, McHugh and Gummow JJ point out in *Maguire v Makaronis* [1997] HCA 23; (1997) 188 CLR 449 at 447 (*Maguire*), this is not a duty to obtain consent, rather the existence of an informed consent goes to negate what would otherwise be a breach of duty: see also *Blackmagic Design Pty Ltd v Overliese* (2011) 191 FCR 1; [2011] FCAFC 24 at [105] per Besanko J (Finkelstein and Jacobson JJ agreeing).

provision of financial services to them.[57] Agreements with wholesale clients may similarly contain lengthy disclosures and disclaimers of potential conflicts. Leaving aside very real questions now being raised about the comprehensibility of such disclosure, the likelihood of it actually being read, and its effect if it is read on client decision-making,[58] what effect does it have on the fiduciary proscriptions?

The answer might be—not much. Providing information is not enough on its own to ensure the level of fully informed consent that equity requires. The client must understand the impact of what is being disclosed on its position and its relationship with the financial services firm, and must give its actual consent (express or implied) to the existence of that conflict or collateral advantage.[59] Importantly, the firm has the onus of proving that it obtained the client's fully informed consent to its obtaining any benefit from, or acting when it had a conflict in, that relationship.[60]

In an advisory relationship, where the conflict goes to the heart of the thing that is being advised upon, the burden in equity is high, particularly where the client is unsophisticated. In the solicitor-client cases, it has on occasion required that the client be separately advised in relation to that to which it is being asked to consent. In *Maguire* at CLR 466, Brennan CJ, Gaudron, McHugh and Gummow JJ said:

> What is required for a fully informed consent is a question of fact in all the circumstances of each case and there is no precise formula which will determine in all cases if fully informed consent has been given. The circumstances of the case may include (as they would have here) the importance of obtaining independent and skilled advice from a third party.

The sufficiency of disclosure can depend on the sophistication and intelligence of the persons to whom disclosure must be made; this forms part of the factual inquiry referred

---

[57] Among other (extensive) disclosure, the FSG must include: 'information about the amount of all the remuneration, commission and other benefits that the providing entity (and other persons specified in s942B(2) (e) or 942C(2)(f)) will or reasonably expects to receive in respect of, or that is attributable to, the advice to be provided where this amount can be ascertained at the time the FSG is provided to the client (s942B(2)(e) and 942C(2)(f), regs 7.7.04(3) and 7.7.07(3)); [or] where the providing entity reasonably believes that personal advice will be or is likely to be provided *and* the amount of the remuneration, commission or other benefits cannot be ascertained at the time the FSG is provided—either particulars or general information about the benefit (including ranges or rates of amounts) and a statement that the method of calculating the amount of the benefit will be disclosed at the time the advice is provided or as soon as practicable after that time (regs 7.7.04(4)(c), 7.7.04(4) (d), 7.7.07(4)(c) and 7.7.07(4)(d)); ... [and] details of any associations or relationships that might reasonably be expected to be capable of influencing the providing entity in providing the advice (s942B(2)(f) and 942C(2) (g))': See ASIC Regulatory Guide 175.96(h), (i) and (j). The SoA must include, inter alia: 'information about the remuneration, commission and other benefits that the providing entity (and other persons specified in s947B(2) (d) or 947C(2)(e)) will, or reasonably expects to, receive that might reasonably be expected to be, or have been capable of, influencing the providing entity in providing the advice (s947B(2)(d) and 947C(2)(e), regs 7.7.09BC, 7.7.09BD, 7.7.11 and 7.7.12): see RG 175.168–RG 175.185; information about the remuneration, commissions and other benefits that a person has received or is to receive for referring another person to the AFS licensee or providing entity (regs 7.7.11 and 7.7.12); [and] details of any interests, associations or relationships that might reasonably be expected to be, or to have been capable of, influencing the providing entity in providing the advice (s947B(2)(e) and 947C(2)(f))': ASIC Regulatory Guide 175.157 (f), (g) and (h).

[58] Perversely, clients may not always understand the disclosure of the existence of a conflict as signalling a risk to their interests. Instead they may see such disclosure as making the firm more trustworthy, and therefore be less likely to question its recommendations.

[59] For example, in *Citigroup* at [355], the client's implied actual consent was sufficient.

[60] *Wingecarribee* at [937].

to in *Maguire*: see *Farah Constructions Pty Ltd v Say-Dee Pty Ltd* [2007] HCA 22; (2007) 230 CLR 89 at 138–39 Gleeson CJ, Gummow, Callinan, Heydon and Crennan JJ.

A 'Best Interests' Duty?

We have looked so far at the fiduciary proscriptions—but is there also a prescriptive dimension or consequence to treating financial services firms as fiduciaries? Most people, if asked to describe (rather than define) a fiduciary relationship, would probably say that it involves one person undertaking to do something for another exclusively in the interests of the other person, rather than in their own or another's (inconsistent) interests. This is not to imply, they would say, that person is somehow a 'guarantor' of the other's interests in the sense that if things turn out badly they will have to make it up to them. The obligation goes to what motivates the person's actions, not their outcome. The fiduciary idea is about the object or end to which the person must 'bend their exertions'[61]—that is, whose interests the person must have in mind in making the choices and taking the steps involved in doing the thing the subject of the undertaking.

When Anglo-Australian lawyers talk about whether financial services firms are or ought to be subject to 'fiduciary duties', they mean the fiduciary proscriptions described above.[62] But policymakers and others sometimes invoke the fiduciary idea in this broader descriptive sense. For example, Recommendation 1 made by the PJC in 2009, referred to above, was that the legislation governing financial services firms should be amended to include 'a fiduciary duty for financial advisers ... requiring them to place their clients' interests ahead of their own'.[63] The law is usually reluctant to impose rules that require courts, regulators or others to inquire into people's subjective motives. Hence the prophylactic character of the fiduciary proscriptions—if the fiduciary pursues or makes a profit in circumstances of

---

[61] PD Finn, *Fiduciary Obligations* (Sydney, Law Book Company, 1977) at 27.

[62] The reason is the view expressed in *Breen* at CLR 113, by Gaudron and McHugh JJ, in describing the difference between Canadian and Australian approaches to the duties of fiduciaries. Their Honours said: 'Australian courts only recognise proscriptive fiduciary duties. .... In this country fiduciary obligations arise because a person has come under an obligation to act in another's interests. As a result, equity imposes on the fiduciary proscriptive obligations – not to obtain any unauthorised benefit from the relationship and not to be in a position of conflict. If these obligations are breached, the fiduciary must account for any profits and make good any loss arising from the breach. But the law in this country does not otherwise impose positive legal duties on the fiduciary to act in the interests of the person to whom the duty is owed'. In *Aequitas* at [284], Austin J concluded on this basis that, 'Obligations to act in the interests of another, or to act prudently, are not fiduciary obligations'. The difference between the proscriptive and prescriptive duties is discussed at length in P Hanrahan 'The Responsible Entity as Trustee' in I Ramsay (ed) *Key Developments in Corporate Law and Trusts Law* (Sydney, LexisNexis Butterworths, 2002), 227–70.

[63] See above n1. In accepting the PJC's recommendation, the (then) Minister for Financial Services, Superannuation and Corporate Law indicated the Government's intention to introduce a 'statutory fiduciary duty for financial advisers requiring them to act in the best interests of their clients and to place the interests of their clients ahead of their own when providing personal advice to retail clients': see Office of the Hon Chris Bowen MP, Minister for Human Services, Minister for Financial Services, Superannuation and Corporate Law, 'The Future of Financial Advice: Information Pack Monday 26 April 2010', 2. The final form of the legislation and related materials (including the Explanatory Memorandum to the Corporations Amendment (Further Future of Financial Advice Measures) Bill 2010 and the Second Reading Speech by the Hon Bill Shorten MP on 24 November 2011) move away from describing the new statutory duty as a 'fiduciary duty' and instead describe it as a 'best interest' duty. The new statutory duty is discussed in section 5 below.

conflict, then there is no need to inquire into their actual motives for acting and they are simply held to account; Mason J makes this point in *Hospital Products* at CLR 94.[64]

So aside from any statutory provision to that effect,[65] are fiduciaries subject at general law to some prescriptive duty in the form of a positive legal obligation to act in the interests of the other person? The question may appear circular, in that the relationship will not be fiduciary in the first place unless the firm has somehow undertaken to act 'for or on behalf or in the interests of another person in the exercise of a power or discretion which will affect the interests of that other person in a legal or practical sense'.[66] The fiduciary relationship may indicate (but not necessarily be the source of) some overarching obligation to act in the interests of the client, arising in contract or tort,[67] or otherwise in equity – an obligation described by the authors of *Jacob's Law of Trusts in Australia* as the 'equitable obligation proper'.[68] Wherever it comes from, it is not appropriate to describe this obligation as fiduciary in a strict sense.[69]

When the best interest concept is used in fiduciary law, it is used as a description, rather than a prescription—that is, it describes a cluster of obligations that otherwise exist between the parties. There are three ways to understand what it describes. The first (and narrowest) possibility is that the best interest concept and the proscriptions are two sides of the one coin—a person is obliged to act in the interests of another *in that* they are subject to the no conflicts and no profits rules in the discharge of their undertaking. This view is too narrow.

The second is that the best interest concept may be an omnibus description of the other equitable principles defining the relationship between the parties. These are what the Full Federal Court in *Grimaldi* at [174], describes as the 'other part' of modern Australian fiduciary law, concerned with the exercise of the powers and discretions given to the fiduciary to be exercised for the benefit of another person. The Court describes this aspect of fiduciary law in these terms:

> Its essential concern is with judicial review of the exercise of powers, duties and discretions given to a fiduciary to be exercised in the interests of another ("the beneficiary") where the beneficiary does

---

[64] Taking an integrative approach to the fiduciary proscriptions, his Honour says, 'Accordingly, the fiduciary's duty may be ... expressed by saying that he is under an obligation not to promote his personal interest by making or pursuing a gain in circumstances in which there is a conflict or a real or substantial possibility of a conflict between his personal interests and those of the persons whom he is bound to protect' (*Aberdeen Railway Co. v. Blaikie Brothers* (1854) 1 Macq 461, at p 471). By linking the obligation not to make a profit or take a benefit to a situation of conflict or possible conflict of interest the proposition, in accordance with the authorities, (a) **excludes the relevance of an inquiry into the actual motives of the fiduciary**; and (b) excludes restitutionary relief when the interest of the fiduciary is remote or insubstantial . See *Boulting v. Association of Cinematograph, Television and Allied Technicians* (1963) 2 QB 606, at pp 637–38; *Phelan v. Middle States Oil Corporation* [1955] USCA2 324; (1955) 220 F 2d 593, at pp 602–603' (emphasis added).

[65] Many AFS licensees are subject to statutory 'best interest' obligations, including responsible entities of registered schemes; RSE licensees that are trustees of public offer superannuation funds, and (from 1 July 2013) financial advisers who provide personal advice to retail clients. These are discussed in Section V below.

[66] *Hospital Products* at CLR 96 (per Mason J). In *C-Shirt Pty Ltd v Barnett Marketing and Management Pty Ltd* (1996) 37 IPR 315 at 336 Lehane J said that the 'fundamental question' for determining whether a relationship is fiduciary in nature is 'for what purpose, and for the promotion of whose interests, are powers held?'

[67] See R Austin "Moulding the Content of Fiduciary Duties" in A J Oakley (ed) *Trends in Contemporary Trust Law* (Oxford, Clarendon Press, 1996) at 153, 160-1. Austin J returned to this theme in *Aequitas*, above at [282].

[68] R Meagher and W Gummow *Jacob's Law of Trusts in Australia* (6th ed, Sydney, LexisNexis Butterworths, 1997) [110].

[69] See above n62. *Aequitas* at [284], per Austin J.

not have the right to dictate or to veto how the power, discretion, etc is exercised by the fiduciary. Here the law channels and directs how "fiduciary discretions" are exercised. Unsurprisingly, there is quite some similarity between the grounds of judicial review of the decisions and actions of fiduciaries entrusted with such powers etc–for example, trustees, company directors and executors – and the grounds of judicial review of administrative action.

Elsewhere I have described these grounds for judicial review or intervention (in relation to investment managers) as encompassing overlapping elements of good faith, genuine consideration, and proper purpose.[70] These elements go to the manner in which the fiduciary arrives at its decisions, not the outcome of those decisions; it does not involve a hindsight review of the merits of the decision. Courts have always been unwilling to engage in second-guessing decisions of fiduciaries that, while properly arrived out, turned out badly. As the authors of *Jacob's Law of Trusts in Australia* say in relation to review of the exercise by trustees of their discretions, 'it is irrelevant whether or not the decision proves beneficial or prudent, and equally irrelevant whether the court would exercise the power in the same way'.[71]

The third view is that the best interest concept picks up all of the special rules or constraints arising out of or connected to the undertaking, including the firm's contractual and tortious duties and the various statutory rules that apply. In *Fiduciary Loyalty*, Conaglen makes this interesting observation: 'the concept of acting in good faith in the interests of the principal indicates to the fiduciary "to what end he must bend his exertions" [referring to Finn, *Fiduciary Obligations*, at 27], but it can be understood as **a composite of the duties to act in good faith, with the requisite degree of care, and only for proper purposes'** (emphasis added).[72] This third view accommodates what can be described as the 'positive' elements of the adviser's duties described by Brennan J in *Daly* at CLR 385:

> The duty of an investment adviser who is approached by a client for advice and undertakes to give it, and who proposes to offer the client an investment in which the adviser has a financial interest, is a heavy one. His duty is to furnish the client with all the relevant knowledge which the adviser possesses, concealing nothing that might reasonably be regarded as relevant to the making of the investment decision including the identity of the buyer or seller of the investment when that identity is relevant, to give the best advice which the adviser could give if he did not have, but a third party did have, a financial interest in the investment to be offered, to reveal fully the adviser's financial interest, and to obtain for the client the best terms which the client would obtain from a third party if the adviser were to exercise due diligence on behalf of his client in such a transaction. Such a duty has been established by authority: see *Haywood v Roadknight* [1927] VLR 512 and the

---

[70] See Hanrahan, 'The Responsible Entity as Trustee', above n 62, 236–39. Good faith involves, at least, subjective honesty—that is, a subjective belief on the part of the fiduciary that the decision or action is in the interests of the person to whom the obligation is owed. Genuine consideration requires the fiduciary to give due consideration to the matter, and not act capriciously or wantonly. Proper purpose means the power or discretion must be exercised for the purpose for which it was given, and not for some ulterior motive (such as benefiting the fiduciary or another person). Put simply, if someone is given the power to make a decision or take an action for the purpose of protecting or advancing the interests of another, then it must be used for that purpose and not any other (otherwise it is akin to a fraud on the power).

[71] Meagher and Gummow, above n68, [1610]. Thus, as Lord Eldon famously observed in *Carlen v Drury* (1812) 1 V & B 154; 35 ER 61 in relation to review of the exercise of directors' discretions: "This court is not to be required on every occasion to take the management of every playhouse and brewhouse in the Kingdom".

[72] M Conaglen, *Fiduciary Loyalty*, above n30 at 56.

cases therein referred to at p 521, especially *Gibson v Jeyes* [1801] 6 Ves Jun 266 at 271, 278; 31 ER 1044 at 1046–7, 1050 and *McPherson v Watt* [1877] 3 App Cas 254 at 266.

On this view, it would capture the duties described by Meagher and Maroya in 2003 as 'crypto-fiduciary'.[73]

V   LEGISLATING FOR 'FIDUCIARY TYPE' DUTIES

In the aftermath of the GFC, policymakers internationally have returned to the question of whether the kind of loyalty expected of fiduciaries ought to be demanded of financial services firms towards their clients, and if so whether this needs to be achieved through legislation.

Extending the fiduciary idea further into the realm of financial services, or limiting the capacity of parties to exclude or contract around the fiduciary proscriptions, is not a decision to be arrived at lightly. Australian courts have often cautioned against too freely extending fiduciary relationships into the commercial sphere, although they have been willing to do so. I have argued elsewhere that the real policy question is whether a conceptual model that is built around 'loyalty, confidence and good faith' (the core concerns of equity), rather than one emphasising 'honest, careful conduct and keeping one's promises' (the concern of the common law) is the right one.[74] The proper basis for arriving at an answer to that question has, in the post-GFC debate, often seemed elusive. The extent to which a financial services firm should have to subordinate its interests to those of their clients is, ultimately, a political decision.

If the imposition of a fiduciary standard is settled upon as a desirable public policy goal, there are a number of reasons why legislation might be needed to achieve it. First, while the effect of fiduciary law on a financial services firm's dealing with its clients within accepted categories of fiduciary relationship (for example, agent or trustee) is probably well understood, what the fiduciary idea means in other contexts might be more difficult to identify. Reasons for this might include that the firm is unsure whether it is a fiduciary; it is unsure what the fiduciary law requires of it; or it is unsure which aspects of its relationship are fiduciary (and which are not). Legislation may have a role to play in clarifying and directing attention to existing obligations.

Secondly, where a fiduciary obligation already exists, there might be reasons to do with the overall operation of the financial system, rather than the interests of individual (legally and morally autonomous) clients, that suggest some modification of existing doctrine: for example modifying that the rule that fiduciary relationships can be excluded by agreement; or that the effect of fiduciary proscriptions can be navigated around by 'disclose and consent' practices. This would limit the individual freedom of parties to allow conflicts of interests and collateral advantage, either because of recognition that 'informed consent' for many clients in this context can be illusory, or in the broader interests of the financial system

---

[73] Meagher and Mayora, above n4.

[74] See P Hanrahan 'Fiduciary Duty and the Market: Private Law and the Public Good', paper presented at Obligations IV, Singapore 23 July 2008, quoting Lord Millett's Foreword to J McGhee *Snell's Equity* 30th edn (London, Sweet & Maxwell, 2000). The paper is available at http:/ssrn.com/abstract+1184443.

generally (for example, because allowing conflicts even with informed consent undermine the confidence of others in the integrity of the market for financial services).

A third reason may be that the risk of private claims by individual clients is insufficient to ensure all firms will comply with fiduciary law (that is, to deter non-compliance) and that therefore some kind of regulation reinforced by public sanctions, in addition to private relief for breach, is needed. Public enforcement may provide for more effective general deterrence, and help maintain public confidence in the financial sector.

A fourth may be that the fiduciary idea should apply to more financial services firms, or to financial services firms in respect of more of their activities, that is the case under exiting equitable doctrine. This would involve extending the reach of the rules by enactment. These all provide potential justifications for legislating for the fiduciary idea, rather than leaving it to equity.

The Australian Experience

Australian financial services legislation contains several provisions that are intended to apply (aspects of) the fiduciary idea to financial services firms. These include Corporations Act s 912A(1)(aa), which imposes an obligation on AFS licensees to have in place adequate arrangements for the management of conflicts of interest; s 601FC, which makes a responsible entity of a registered scheme trustee of the property of that scheme and imposes an explicit best interest duty and elements of the no profit rule on it; and Pt 7.7A, which applies (from 1 July 2103) to AFS licensees providing personal financial advice to retail clients, and contains a 'best interest' obligation and restricts certain types of conflicted remuneration.

None of these statutory duties excludes the existing equitable principles where they would otherwise apply; instead these principles continue to operate alongside (but not coextensively with) the statutory provisions. That is, the Australian provisions do not purport to codify the law. In each case the rules and restrictions applied by the statute are narrower than those that arise in equity if the financial services firm is a fiduciary. What distinguishes them from the equitable principles, though, are the limited extent to which they can be modified or excluded by agreement between the parties, and the regulatory sanctions that apply for their breach.

As with other parts of the law (such as statutory directors' duties) that pick up or reference elements of fiduciary obligation, the statutory duties imposed on financial services firms raise a number of avowedly 'legal' issues – related to the way the provisions are formulated and how they are to be interpreted and enforced. Some are specific to the particular drafting of the relevant provision, but others are more thematic. The thematic issues include: (i) how (if at all) they apply to financial services firms that are not fiduciaries; (ii) whether their content is the same as the relevant elements of fiduciary law; (iii) if not, how their application to financial services firms that are fiduciaries impacts on the obligations of those firms arising at general law; and (iv) how elements of the duties are to be framed in actions to enforce them, and their relationship with other potential causes of action arising on the same facts.

A measure of the quality of legislation in this area is how easily it allows for the resolution of these issues, and how closely the position so resolved conforms to the stated policy intention. Where the reach or meaning of a statute is obscure or difficult to discern; where its relationship with and impact on the general law or other statutory regimes is uncertain;

or where its elements cannot be pleaded effectively in proceedings, the impact of reform is reduced.[75] It is lost entirely if, in the eventual (judicial) resolution of these issues, the legislative outcome is not what was intended as a matter of policy.

Part 7.7A of the Corporations Act

One of the more high profile post-GFC reforms in Australia has been the enactment of Corporations Act Pt 7.7A, which comes into full effect from 1 July 2013. Part 7.7A applies to AFS licensees that provide financial advice to retail clients (as defined).[76] Of particular relevance are Div 2, which is entitled 'best interest obligations', and Div 4, dealing with conflicted remuneration.[77]

Because of the breadth of the definition of 'financial product advice' in the Corporations Act, the new law applies to some financial services firms that are not fiduciaries with respect to the giving of that advice at general law. However, because of the narrow definition of retail client, many financial advisers who are fiduciaries (for example, the advisers in *Wingecarribee* and *Bathurst*) are not subject to the new law.

The key 'best interest' provisions, which apply only to the provision of personal financial advice to retail clients, are: Corporations Act s 961B(1), which says that the provider of the advice 'must act in the best interests of the client in relation to the advice'; Corporations Act s 961B(2), which says that a provider 'satisfies the duty in subsection (1) if the provider

---

[75] These problems are common to many contemporary regulatory statutes, including the Corporations Act. Recent judicial comment of Ch 7 of the Corporations Act is set out in n 20, 34 and 77. If it is impossible to know with certainty to whom, and in what situations, a rule applies; what the rule requires of the person; what its relationship with other legal rules is; or how alleged contraventions of can be established to the satisfaction of a Court, that rule is unlikely to do much beyond creating moral hazard and adding to compliance burdens.

[76] Australian law draws a distinction between retail and wholesale clients for the purposes of financial services regulation. Firms dealing with retail and wholesale clients are both regulated by ASIC, but some rules apply only to dealings with retail clients. These include: dispute resolution arrangements (Corporations Act s 912A(1)(g) and (2)); compensation arrangements (s 912B); FSGs (Pt 7.7, Div 2); SoAs (Pt 7.7, Div 3); general advice warnings (s 949A); best interest obligation (Pt 7.7A, Div 2); and restrictions on certain remuneration (Pt 7.7A, Div 3, 4 and 5). Broadly, for investment-related transactions, a person is treated as a retail client unless he or she: invests more than $500,000; a large business; is a high net worth individual; is considered (and certified) by the financial services firm to be an experienced investor; or is a professional investor (such as an AFS licensee or APRA regulated entity): see Corporations Act ss 761G and 761GA and Corporations Regulations reg 7.1.11–7.1.28 and 7.6.02AB–7.6.02AF. As the *Wingecarribee* and *Bathurst* decisions illustrate, and as the Madoff experience in the United States reinforces, wholesale clients can include people entrusted with the investment of funds held by bodies such as local councils, charities, endowments, not-for-profit organisations and self-managed superannuation funds who are not 'sophisticated' in financial matters and whose lack of sophistication exposes the people who should have the benefit of those funds to loss. Serious consideration needs to be given to amending the law to treat these entities as retail clients.

[77] Part 7.7A contains the usual array of definitions, qualifications, carveouts and explanatory notes that, regrettably, have become the defining feature of Australia's financial services law. Chapter 7 of the Corporations Act is frequently criticised for this reason. In *International Litigation Partners Pty Ltd v Chameleon Mining NL* [2011] NSWCA 50; (2011) 276 ALR 138, Young JA says at [152]–[153]: 'It might be remarked at this initial stage that Ch 7 of the Corporations Act is drafted in the most obscure and convoluted manner. . . I know it is our job to make plain that which is obscure, and I know that commercial lawyers are thought by the legislation to be so able to find loopholes that every possible eventuality must be thought of and covered. However the main aim is to protect the investing public and the investing public gain little comfort from obscure legislation'.

proves that the provider has done' the things set out in that subsection;[78] and Corporations Act s 961J(1), which says that if the adviser 'knows, or reasonably ought to know, that there is a conflict between the interests of the client and the interests of [the provider and various people connected to it], the provider must give priority to the client's interests when giving the advice'. Corporations Act s 961G goes on to say that the provider 'must only provide the advice to the client if it would be reasonable to conclude that the advice is appropriate to the client, had the provider satisfied the duty under Corporations Act s 961B to act in the best interests of the client'. Section 961G replaces the old (and more onerous) suitability rule, formerly contained in s 945A of the Corporations Act.[79]

The conflicted remuneration provisions are Corporations Act ss 963E–963K; they prohibit various people giving or receiving 'conflicted remuneration'. Conflicted remuneration is defined in Corporations Act s 963A to mean 'any benefit, whether monetary or non-monetary, given to a financial services licensee, or a representative of a financial services licensee, who provides financial product advice to persons as retail clients that, because of the nature of the benefit or the circumstances in which it is given: (a) could reasonably be expected to influence the choice of financial product recommended by the licensee or representative to retail clients; or (b) could reasonably be expected to influence the financial product advice given to retail clients by the licensee or representative'. Certain volume-based benefits are deemed by Corporations Act s 963L to be conflicted remuneration unless the contrary is proved; and certain monetary and non-monetary benefits are carved out of the definition by ss 963B and 963C.

The consequences of breach of Pt 7.7A, Div 2 include civil remedies[80] and civil penalties,[81] and for breach of Div 4, civil penalties.[82] Breach of the financial services laws is a breach of s 912A(1)(c), and therefore triggers ASIC's licensing and other administrative powers.

The policy intention behind the new 'best interests' obligation in Pt 7.7A, Div 2 is clear. In 2009, following its inquiry into regulation of financial products and services, the PJC's first recommendation was that the law should be amended 'to explicitly include a fiduciary

---

[78] Paragraphs 961B(2)(a)–(f) set out various 'steps' that a provider should take in arriving at its advice that are essentially related to the exercise of appropriate care, skill and diligence by the provider (although are not as broad as its overall duty of care). Paragraph 961B(2)(g) goes on to require that the provider, in order to satisfy the best interest obligation in s 961B(1), show that it has 'taken any other step that, at the time the advice is provided, would reasonably be regarded as being in the best interests of the client, given the client's relevant circumstances'. A note to the subsection says that it 'anticipates that a client may seek scaled advice and that the inquiries made by the provider will be tailored to the advice sought'. Sections 961C, 961D and 961E define certain concepts used in s 961B(2), including 'reasonably apparent', 'reasonable investigation', and when it is reasonable to regard the taking of a particular steps as being in the best interests of the client (to wit, when 'a person with a reasonable level of expertise in the subject matter of the advice that has been sought by the client, exercising care and objectively assessing the client's relevant circumstances, would regard it as in the best interest of the client, given the client's relevant circumstances, to take that step').

[79] Section 945A(1) said that 'The providing entity must only provide the advice to the client if: (a) the providing entity: (i) determines the relevant personal circumstances in relation to giving the advice; and (ii) makes reasonable inquiries in relation to those personal circumstances; and (b) having regard to information obtained from the client in relation to those personal circumstances, the providing entity has given such consideration to, and conducted such investigation of, the subject matter of the advice as is reasonable in all of the circumstances; and (iii) the advice is appropriate to the client, having regard to that consideration and investigation.'

[80] Corporations Act s 961M.

[81] Corporations Act s 961K, 961L, 961Q and 1317E.

[82] Corporations Act s 1317E.

duty for financial advisers operating under an [AFS licence], requiring them to place their clients' interests ahead of their own'.[83] The Australian government agreed with that recommendation, and in April 2010 proposed a 'statutory fiduciary duty for financial advisers requiring them to act in the best interests of clients and to place the interests of their clients ahead of their own when providing personal advice to retail clients'.[84] In November 2011 the then responsible Minister moved away from characterising the duty as fiduciary, describing it as a 'statutory best interest duty…[requiring] financial advisers to act in the best interests of their clients, and to put their client's interests ahead of their own'.[85]

The new duty, 'to act in the best interests of their clients, and to put their client's interests ahead of their own', took the Minister in his Second Reading Speech less than twenty words to express. In contrast, Pt 7.7A, Div 2 runs to 2,762 words. Even without the headings and the enforcement provisions, it is 1,736 words.

As the foregoing discussion indicates, elements of the 'best interest' concept are spread across three operative provisions. The first says that a person providing personal advice to a retail client 'must act in the best interests of the client in relation to the advice', but that providers are taken to satisfy that duty if they can prove that they took certain specified steps in the preparation of the advice. The second says that if the provider 'knows, or reasonably ought to know, that there is a conflict between the interests of the client and the interests of [the adviser and various people connected to it], the provider must give priority to the client's interests when giving the advice'. The third is that the provider 'must only provide the advice to the client if it would be reasonable to conclude that the advice is appropriate to the client, had the provider satisfied [their statutory duty] to act in the best interests of the client'.

The first—the list of steps the provider has to prove it took to satisfy the best interest duty—runs to 259 words. The notes and definitions explaining those steps are an additional 305 words; they include definitions of things like 'reasonably apparent' and 'reasonable investigation'. Among the list of steps that must be taken is 'any other step that, at the time the advice is provided, would reasonably be regarded as being in the best interests of the client, given the client's relevant circumstances'.[86] The Act then allows for additional steps to be mandated by regulation.

It is worth contrasting this approach to legislative drafting with s 601FC, which was enacted in 1998. It imposes a statutory duty on the responsible entity of a registered scheme, in exercising its powers and carrying out its duties, to 'act in the best interests of the members and, if there is a conflict between the members' interests and its own interests, give priority to the members' interests'. That duty is encapsulated in 28 operative words. The corresponding duty on company directors, to 'exercise their powers

---

[83] See above n63.

[84] See Information Pack, above n63.

[85] House of Representatives *Hansard*, Thursday 24 November 2011, 13751 (Shorten, Bill, MP).

[86] The law goes on to specify that 'it would reasonably be regarded as in the best interests of the client to take a step, if a person with a reasonable level of expertise in the subject matter of the advice that has been sought by the client, exercising care and objectively assessing the client's relevant circumstances, would regard it as in the best interests of the client, given the client's relevant circumstances, to take that step'.

and discharge their duties in good faith in the best interests of the corporation' takes 17 words.[87]

It is tempting to see the immediate challenge as being to understand whether the 2,762 words that make up the best-interest duty mean the same thing as the 19 words the Minister used to describe the obligation in his Second Reading Speech in November 2011. Currently, this is where the commentary is focused. Because of the way Pt 7.7A, Div 2 is drafted, the thematic legal issues identified above are very much to the fore. In particular, the complex interplay between the statutory language and the equitable principles from which that statutory language may (or may not) be derived will need to be addressed.[88]

As it stands, the statutory best interest provision appears a long way from what equity understands the 'best interest' concept to mean, on even the narrowest view of that understanding explained above. The statutory best interest obligation is expressed as a series of steps to be taken, not as an obligation to prefer the client's interests over the firm's or to avoid the situations of conflict or collateral advantage that fiduciary law proscribes. Although the statute is not expressed to oust fiduciary principles where they apply, it is possible that these more diffuse statutory obligations might operate to limit existing fiduciary duties of financial advisers of the kind recognised by the High Court in *Daly*, apparently contrary to the intention of the post-GFC reforms.[89]

---

[87] Corporations Act s 181(1) requires that company officers 'exercise their powers and discharge their duties: (a) in good faith in the best interests of the corporation; and (b) for a proper purpose'. For a discussion of the directors' duty to act in the best interests of the company, see R Austin and I Ramsay *Ford's Principles of Corporations Law* (LexisNexis Butterworths, online) [8.070]–[8.160]. The company director cases are often concerned with situations where a director has misconceived or mischaracterised what is meant by 'the company' for the purposes of the discharge of his or her duties, and has instead looked to the interests of another (such as a majority shareholder or the corporate group) or failed appropriately to take into account the interests of creditors when the company is in 'the zone of insolvency'. That said, the cases are evolving. Directors are frequently found to have contravened s 181(1)(a) in cases involving breaches of their other duties (such as their duty of care or duty not to misuse their position), even where this kind of mischaracterisation (and therefore misdirection) has not occurred. These cases lend support to the proposition that s 181(1)(a) involves concepts of impropriety.

[88] In *Esso Australia Resources Ltd v Federal Commissioner of Taxation* (1999) 201 CLR 49; [1999] HCA 67 at [18] (*Esso*), Gleeson CJ, Gaudron and Gummow JJ remarked that the interrelation and interaction between the common law and statute may trigger 'varied and complex questions'. One is a question of statutory construction: do the words used in the statute mean what they mean in the general law? In *Vines v Australian Securities and Investments Commission* (2007) 62 ACSR 1: [2007] NSWCA 75 at [136], Spigelman CJ (interpreting the directors' statutory duty of care) said, 'It is clearly the case that the Parliament did have reference to the existence of a duty at common law for purposes of enacting the statutory standard. Nevertheless, when a common law formulation is incorporated as a provision in a statute, its legal nature is altered. The words must now be interpreted as statutory language, albeit having regard, in an appropriate way, to the origins of the statutory formulation. The whole of the law of statutory interpretation must be applied including, relevantly, the statutory context which provides for a structure of sanctions for breach of the statutory standard.' Legislating for the general duties of companies directors in the United Kingdom, s 170 of Companies Act 2006 (UK) expressly provides as follows: (3) The general duties are based on certain common law rules and equitable principles as they apply in relation to directors and have effect in place of those rules and principles as regards the duties owed to a company by a director. (4) The general duties shall be interpreted and applied in the same way as common law rules or equitable principles, and regard shall be had to the corresponding common law rules and equitable principles in interpreting and applying the general duties.

[89] A separate question raised by the interplay between the common law and statute is whether the statute might provide an analogy for the purpose of developing the common law: see *Esso* at [19]–[20]; *Andrews v Australia and New Zealand Banking Group Ltd* (2012) 290 ALR 595; [2012] HCA 30 at [5].

VI   CONCLUSION

The 'fiduciary idea' is a powerful one in Anglo-Australian law. Although the relationship between a financial services firm and its client is not one of the accepted (status-based) categories of fiduciary relationship, it is clear in the financial services context that financial and corporate advisers, brokers, investment managers and custodians can (and in the circumstances explained above, will) owe fiduciary obligations to their clients unless those obligations are effectively excluded by the parties.

The fiduciary character of these relationships means that the firm cannot provide the relevant service to its client where there is a real sensible possibility that the firm's personal interest (or duty to another person) may conflict with its duty to act in the interests of the client, without the client's fully informed consent. Nor cannot it retain any profit or advantage it derives from the relationship without the client's fully informed consent. Its duty to act in the interests of the client comprises the mosaic of good faith, due care and proper purpose obligations that attach to that relationship at common law and in equity and under the legislative regime governing financial services providers, which is particular to the nature of the undertaking from which the fiduciary obligation springs.

Post-GFC, significant attention has focused on whether self-interested conduct on the part of financial services firms caused or contributed to the crisis. This has led to calls in a number of jurisdictions to legislate for fiduciary-type duties, particularly in relation to the provision of personal financial advice to retail clients. The fact that many financial services firms were already subject to fiduciary duties that did not prevent them from engaging in self-interested conduct should sharpen our focus on why and how legislating to encapsulate or impose those duties will make a difference. Australia has gone down the legislative path, with the enactment of Pt 7.7A of the Corporations Act. The United States and others may yet follow suit.

If the Australian experience is anything to go by, the path is a rocky one. It provides a forceful illustration of the real difficulties faced in achieving meaningful and effective regulatory reform. Contemporary approaches to financial regulation have been criticised as favouring 'complexity over simplicity; rules over discretion; codes of compliance over individual and corporate responsibility'.[90] It is hard to think of a clearer example of this than the 'best interests' provisions in Pt 7.7A. Many financial services firms already owe proscriptive fiduciary duties and positive 'best interest' duties to their clients. Therefore such duties already have established application and content in this context arising in equity, as the recent *Wingecarribee* and *Bathurst* decisions demonstrate. However despite the clear intention of the government to capture those 'fiduciary-type' duties in legislation, Pt 7.7A does not do so. Rather than adopting the direct drafting used in, for example, Corporations Act s 181 (directors' duties) or s 601FC (responsible entities' duties), the new legislation for financial advisers qualifies, defines, hedges, explains and carves-out, and in so doing hollows out the hortatory potential of the reform and runs directly into the thematic legal

---

[90] N Ferguson *The Great Degeneration* (London, Allen Lane, 2012) 58. The comment was made in Ferguson's 2012 Reith Lectures for the BBC. Ferguson goes on to say: 'I believe this approach is based on a flawed understanding of how financial markets work. It puts me in mind of the great Viennese satirist Karl Kraus's famous quip about psychoanalysis that it was the disease of which it pretended to be the cure. I believe excessively complex regulation is the disease of which it pretends to be the cure'.

difficulties identified above. It is an example of a prevailing approach to regulation that focuses on prescribing compliance steps or processes that has helped to create an 'industry of compliance' but which recent experience suggests may be incapable of doing much else.

Making a policy decision that certain norms ought to apply to particular relationships and dealings in the financial sector is just the beginning of any effective reform discussion. If a decision is made to force the adoption of those norms through legislation, these thematic legal issues must be addressed. Law reform processes that ignore or work against the resolution of those issues represent structural and institutional impediments to effective reform. If they result in laws in which the legal principles are so adulterated that they no longer truly encapsulate the intended policy, the illusion of reform can be more dangerous than no action at all. This is the broader challenge.

CHAPTER 12

Class Actions and Regulating Culture in Financial Organisations: Observations from a Comparison of US and Australian Bank Class Actions

Michael Legg

I INTRODUCTION

Class actions have a long history in the United States of being employed in relation to securities law contraventions and have been regularly employed by shareholders in Australia since at least 2005.[1] Shareholder class actions are usually advocated on the basis that they deter misconduct by allowing for the enforcement of statutory requirements for disclosure and prohibitions on misleading conduct as an adjunct to actions by regulators such as the Securities and Exchange Commission (SEC) and the Australian Securities and Investments Commission (ASIC).[2] Further, being able to commence legal proceedings allows for compensation to those who have suffered loss or damage as a result of misconduct.[3] However, both the deterrence and compensation rationales for class actions have been subject to

---

[1] In the United States, rule 23 of the Federal Rules of Civil Procedure have set out the requirements of the modern class action since 1966. Securities class actions have been begun in the US since the 1960s: J Tidmarsh and R Trangsrud, *Modern Complex Litigation* (Foundation Press, 2d edn 2010) 447. In Australia, class actions were introduced at the federal level through Pt IVA of the *Federal Court of Australia Act 1976* (Cth) in 1992. Similar procedures were introduced in the State of Victoria through Part 4A of the *Supreme Court Act 1986* (Vic) and in the State of New South Wales in Part 10 of the Civil Procedure Act 2005 (NSW). Australia's first shareholder class action was commenced in 1999: *King v GIO Australia Holdings Ltd* (2000) 100 FCR 209, but since 2005 the number of shareholder class actions has steadily increased. For a comparison of US and Australian class action procedure, see M Legg and L Travers, 'Necessity is the Mother of Invention: The Adoption of Third Party Litigation Funding and the Closed Class in Australian Class Actions' (2009) 38(3) *Common Law World Review* 245.

[2] *Bateman Eichler, Hill Richards Inc v Berner* 472 US 299, 310 (1985), *J I Case Co v Borack* 377 US 426, 432 (1964), *Kirby v Centro Properties Limited* [2008] FCA 1505, [8].

[3] *Deposit Guaranty Bank v Roper* 445 US 326, 339 (1980); J Cox, 'The Social Meaning of Shareholder Suits' (1999) 65 *Brooklyn Law Review* 3, 8–9.

criticism.[4] This chapter examines whether another rationale for class actions commenced by shareholders against financial organisations can be advanced, namely the regulation of culture.

Culture has many meanings depending on its context, but is considered here as a component of corporate governance. Corporate governance 'describes the framework of rules, relationships, systems and processes within and by which authority is exercised and controlled in corporations. Understood in this way, the expression "corporate governance" embraces not only the models or systems themselves but also the practices by which that exercise and control of authority is in fact effected'.[5] Corporate culture is the link between documented rules and policies and how they are actually implemented.[6] Where that culture is permissive of unethical conduct, corrupt or rises to the level of 'administrative evil', the pursuit of profit or personal gain can inflict substantial harm such as corporate scandals and collapses.[7]

In financial organisations, culture has a direct link with risk appetite and management.[8] Many banks in the lead-up to the global financial crisis developed a culture of risk-taking that saw risk management policies and practices be ignored, incorrectly applied or circumvented.[9] The risk management department was seen as an obstruction or hindrance in consummating money-making (at the time) transactions.[10] Whether a bank sees itself as an institution operating for the public good (providing deposit-taking, liquidity production, credit and security) or trying to make the greatest profit possible so as to fuel executives' incomes and competitiveness is influenced by culture.[11] However, both culture and risk can be influenced by economic incentives. A central concern arising from the global financial crisis was whether remuneration structures, including bonuses, could thwart corporate

---

[4] J Coffee, 'Reforming the Securities Class Action: An Essay on Deterrence and Its Implementation' (2006) 106 *Columbia Law Review* 1534, 1536–38, A Rose, 'Reforming Securities Litigation Reform: Restructuring the Relationship Between Public and Private Enforcement of Rule 10B-5' (2008) 108 *Columbia Law Review* 1301, 1312–14; M Legg, 'Shareholder Class Actions in Australia—The Perfect Storm?' (2008) 31 (3) *UNSWLJ* 669, 709.

[5] HIH Royal Commission, *The Failure of HIH Insurance, Volume 1: A Corporate Collapse and Its Lessons*, Commonwealth of Australia, April 2003 xxxiii.

[6] ibid page xvii ('By "corporate culture" I mean the charism or personality—sometimes overt but often unstated—that guides the decision-making process at all levels of an organisation.') and J Cohan, '"I Didn't Know" and "I Was Only Doing My Job": Has Corporate Governance Careened Out of Control? A Case Study of Enron's Information Myopia' (2002) 40 *Journal of Business Ethics* 275, 287–88. See also Australian Securities Exchange Corporate Governance Council, *Corporate Governance Principles and Recommendations with 2010 Amendments* (2007)13.

[7] P Zimbardo, *The Lucifer Effect: Understanding How Good People Turn Evil* (Random House 2008) ch 15 and T Leap, *Dishonest Dollars: The Dynamics of White-Collar Crime* (Ithaca, Cornell University Press 2007) 42–43.

[8] Above n5 at xvii, xxi and KPMG LLP, *The Audit Committee Journey: Charting Gains, Gaps and Oversight Priorities: 2007–2008 Public Company Audit Committee Member Survey* (2008) 6 (reporting that one of the key risks that audit committees were concerned about was 'the culture, tone and incentives underlying the risk environment').

[9] M Baily, R Litan and M Johnson, *The Origins of the Financial Crisis* (Washington, DC, Brookings Institute, November 2008) 42; UBS; *Shareholder Report on UBS's Write Downs* (Zurich, UBS, 2008) 34, D Ladipo, S Nestor and D Risser, *Board Profile, Structure and Practice in Large European Banks: A Comparative Corporate Governance Study* (London, Nestor Advisors, 2008) 45.

[10] G Kirkpatrick, *The Corporate Governance Lessons from the Financial Crisis* (Paris, OECD, 2009) 12 and 'Confessions of a Risk Manager', *The Economist*, 9 August 2008, 72–73.

governance requirements.[12] However, economic incentives can also promote corporate governance, whether provided by the organisation internally or through externally imposed enforcement sanctions.[13]

In the US, the link between changing corporate culture and enforcement has received growing recognition. The Federal Sentencing Guidelines provide that in considering whether corporations took reasonable steps to prevent and detect criminal conduct they are required to have an ethics and compliance program that must 'promote an organizational culture that encourages ethical conduct and a commitment to compliance with the law.'[14] Likewise, the Department of Justice views corporate culture as an important component of compliance programs, having commented that '[a] strong ethical culture directly supports a strong compliance program'.[15]

The significance of culture and the prospect that external sanctions can influence culture in a positive manner suggests that an examination of the relationship between class actions and culture in financial organisations may be fruitful. This chapter examines the relationship through the lens of the Bank of America Corporation class action arising from the acquisition of Merrill Lynch & Co in the United States and the National Australia Bank Limited class action arising from the increase in provisions for losses from its portfolio of collateralised debt obligations (CDOs) in Australia. The prospect of influencing culture is explored by examining the following questions: who sues? who gets sued? what are the causes of action? and what are the outcomes?

II   BANK OF AMERICA CLASS ACTION

The Bank of America Corporation (Bank of America) securities class action arises from the global financial crisis in 2008 that decimated American investment banks. On 16 March 2008, JP Morgan Chase acquired Bear Stearns for US$2.00 per share, later raised to US$10.00 per share. On 15 September 2008, Lehman Bros announced it would file for bankruptcy. On 22 September 2008, Goldman Sachs and Morgan Stanley were approved by the Federal Reserve to become bank holding companies.[16]

The relevant facts[17] for the Bank of America securities class action commenced on 13 September 2008 with the CEO of Merrill Lynch & Co (Merrill), John Thain having witnessed the demise of Bear Stearns and believing that Lehman Bros would soon file for

---

[11]   C Morris, *The Trillion Dollar Meltdown* (New York, Public Affairs, 2008) 152–55.

[12]   A Blundell-Wignall, P Atkinson and S Hoon Lee, *The Current Financial Crisis: Causes and Policy Issues* (Paris, OECD, 2008) 15–16 and G Kirkpatrick, above n10, 17.

[13]   See eg A Shleifer and R Vishny, 'A Survey of Corporate Governance' (1997) 52(2) *The Journal of Finance* 737, 744–45, R Thompson and H Sale, 'Securities Fraud as Corporate Governance: Reflections Upon Federalism' (2003) 56 *Vanderbilt Law Review* 859.

[14]   *U.S. Sentencing Guidelines Manual* § 8B2.1(a)(2).

[15]   Department of Justice, *A Resource Guide to the U.S. Foreign Corrupt Practices Act* (Washington, DC, Department of Justice, November 2012) 57.

[16]   M Legg and J Harris, 'How the American Dream Became a Global Nightmare: An Analysis of the Causes of the Global Financial Crisis' (2009) 32 *UNSW Law Journal* 350, 357–58.

[17]   The factual background is drawn from the judgment on the first set of strike-out motions *In re Bank of Am. Corp. Sec., Derivative & Emp. Ret. Income Sec. Act (ERISA) Litig.*, 757 F Supp 2d 260 (SDNY 2010). See also A R Sorkin, *Too Big to Fail*, (New York, Penguin Books, 2010) and W Cohan, 'The Final Days of Merrill Lynch', *The Atlantic*, September 2009.

bankruptcy, which could also render Merrill insolvent. Thain contacted the CEO of the Bank of America, Kenneth Lewis, in the hope of saving Merrill. On Sunday, 14 September 2008, Lewis agreed that Bank of America would buy Merrill for US$50 billion, which valued Merrill stock at US$29.00 per share, which was a 70 per cent premium over Merrill's US$17.00 NYSE closing price the day before. The acquisition was memorialised in a merger agreement that was signed in the early morning of Monday, 15 September 2008. One of the main negotiating points in the acquisition of Merrill was the payment of Merrill's bonus pool. Merrill wanted to pay its officers and employees US$5.8 billion in bonuses. It also wanted to pay those bonuses on an accelerated basis and prior to the transaction closing, even though the timing was contrary to its past practice. Bank of America agreed to all of these requirements. For Bank of America to be able to finance the acquisition, it conducted a secondary offering of common stock in which it sold 455 million shares at US$22.00 per share to obtain proceeds of US$9.9 billion.

In October and November 2008, Merrill incurred significant losses exceeding US$15 billion. There was discussion amongst the Bank of America's executives and board of directors as to whether the losses should be disclosed to shareholders who were required to approve the transaction or whether the material adverse condition clause in the Merger Agreement should be invoked to terminate the acquisition. The terms of the merger were set out in a Joint Proxy Statement dated 31 October 2008 (Joint Proxy) which was filed with the SEC and mailed to shareholders on 3 November 2008. In the Joint Proxy, the Bank of America directors solicited proxies to vote on the acquisition at a special meeting to be held on 5 December 2008. The Joint Proxy explained to shareholders the terms and conditions of, and the basis of the board's recommendations for, the acquisition. The Joint Proxy did not disclose Merrill's fourth quarter of 2008 losses or the bonuses that were to be paid to Merrill personnel prior to the transaction closing. On 5 December 2008, the shareholders of Bank of America and Merrill voted to approve the transaction.

Merrill continued to suffer losses, which caused Lewis to again consider exercising the right to terminate the transaction prior to closing. Lewis communicated this to Treasury Secretary Paulson. Paulson instructed Lewis to meet with him and Chairman of the Federal Reserve Board, Ben Bernanke. After further discussions among the three men, Lewis advised that the Bank of America board had determined that going through with the transaction would jeopardise Bank of America's existence as a going concern and that the transaction should be terminated. Paulson told Lewis that if the transaction was not completed, he would remove the Bank of America's directors and management from their positions. This was conveyed to the Bank of America's board of directors and it was agreed to complete the transaction.

Interestingly, Lewis feared that the consummation of the transaction could subject Bank of America to shareholder suits and he approached Federal officials to request measures to protect Bank of America from potential liability. No measures were provided. However, the Bank of America did receive a US$138 billion taxpayer bailout which consisted of a US$20 billion capital infusion and a US$118 billion guarantee against losses on certain risky assets acquired from Merrill. No written agreement was entered into because Bank of America did not wish to publicly disclose the government loans prior to the closing of the transaction.

Bank of America's acquisition of Merrill closed on 1 January 2009. On 16 January 2009, Bank of America disclosed the previous quarter's performances of both Bank of America and Merrill. It also disclosed the Federal funding. Merrill's after-tax loss for the fourth quarter of 2008 totalled US$15.31 billion, or more than US$21 billion before taxes. On 21 January 2009, news broke of Merrill's bonus arrangement. The securities class action was commenced in the Southern District of New York in relation to the non-disclosure of the bonuses to be paid to Merrill officers and employees, the fourth quarter losses sustained by Merrill and the financial assistance from the Federal government. As these facts became known, the price of Bank of America common stock plummeted from US$12.99 per share to a low of US$5.10 per share, causing a market capitalization loss of approximately US$50 billion.

III   NATIONAL BANK OF AUSTRALIA (NAB) CLASS ACTION

As part of its securitisation business, nabCapital (a division of the NAB Group) purchased A $1.2 billion of CDOs through the provision of liquidity lines to conduit financing vehicles. These CDOs comprised residential mortgage-backed securities, including exposure to US subprime assets. The purchase of CDOs was part of nabCapital providing access to international debt markets for its customers. NAB's difficulties with its CDO portfolio grew out of the problems in the US subprime debt market that led to the global financial crisis.[18]

On 9 May 2008, NAB's 2008 Half-Year Results were published on the Australian Securities Exchange (ASX) website. The 2008 Results contained the following statement:[19]

nabCapital has approximately US$1.1 billion ($1.2 billion) of CDOs in nabCapital sponsored conduits whose assets have been downgraded by rating agencies. These conduits contain exposures to US sub-prime assets of $360 million. While all assets are performing at 31 March 2008, we have established a collective provision of $181 million against the liquidity facilities extended to this asset class.

At that time, 9 May 2008, NAB told investors that the US$181 million provision was the result of 'a forensic deep dive' into the portfolio and represented 'a strong provisioning position that protects our balance sheet against whatever may come out of these in a credit sense in the future'.[20]

On 25 July 2008, NAB announced:[21]

an additional provision of $830 million to its portfolio of 10 Collateralised Debt Obligations of Asset Backed Securities (ABS CDOs). ... The amount announced today is in addition to the $181 million charge taken in the Group's half year results to 31 March 2008. The portfolio is now provisioned to a level of nearly 90%.

Consequently, with a total provision of over US$1 billion for its portfolio of CDOs, the price of NAB shares fell 13.5 per cent. Subsequently, US$880 million of the US$1 billion provision was written off.[22] As a result, a group proceeding under Pt 4A of the Supreme Court Act 1986 (Vic) alleged that NAB knew, or should have known, that it would suffer material losses on its CDO portfolio by at least as early as 1 January 2008.[23] The quantum of the claim was estimated to be A$450 million.[24]

---

[18] Legg & Harris, above n16, 351–354.

[19] National Australia Bank Ltd, *2008 Half Year Results* p 68.

[20] Amended Statement of Claim, 28 August 2012 para 37.

[21] National Australia Bank Ltd, *ASX Announcement–NAB Makes Provision in Response to Unprecedented Global Credit Conditions*, 25 July 2008.

[22] National Australia Bank Ltd, *2008 Annual Financial Report* p 69.

[23] *National Australia Bank Ltd v Pathway Investments Pty Ltd* [2012] VSCA 168.

[24] *Pathway Investments Pty Ltd v National Australia Bank Limited* [2012] VSC 97 at [47].

IV   WHO SUES?

The entity that acts as the lead plaintiff or representative party that commences the proceedings is important because it represents the group members' interests, give instructions to the lawyers on litigation strategy and decides whether to make or accept a settlement offer. US Courts traditionally appointed the lead plaintiff and the lead counsel on a 'first come, first serve' basis.[25] This meant that the need to choose among multiple class actions was resolved in favour of whoever won the race to the courthouse. This approach created considerable concern because it produced largely lawyer-driven litigation,[26] the clients were often 'professional plaintiffs' who lacked the incentive to monitor the lawyers effectively,[27] and it gave rise to 'strike suits' (litigation commenced in the hope that a corporate defendant would settle because it was cheaper than defending the matter).[28]

The US Congress responded to the above concerns by enacting the Private Securities Litigation Reform Act of 1995 (PSLRA) that sets out mandatory procedures for the appointment of a lead plaintiff in securities class actions. The procedure, in brief, builds on the class action requirement in Rule 23 of the *Federal Rules of Civil Procedure* (FRCP) of an adequate representative party by requiring the court to consider the losses allegedly suffered by the various plaintiffs that seek to serve as the lead plaintiff and select the 'presumptively most adequate plaintiff' being the 'person or group of persons that . . . has the largest financial interest' in the suit.[29] The lead plaintiff has the responsibility, subject to the approval of the court, of selecting and retaining counsel.[30]

In short, the PSLRA addressed the concerns about lawyer control and unmeritorious litigation through the appointment of a group member with a large financial stake. As the lead plaintiff had significant funds at stake and was a sophisticated user of legal services they would, and could, actively monitor the conduct of a securities class action so as to reduce the litigation agency costs that may arise when lead counsel's interests diverged from the interests of group members.[31]

---

[25] E Weiss and J Beckerman, 'Let the Money Do the Monitoring: How Institutional Investors Can Reduce Agency Costs in Securities Class Actions' (1995) 104 *Yale Law Journal* 2053, 2062; *In re Cendant Corp Litig.* 264 F 3d 201, 255 (3d Cir 2001); and *In re Cavanaugh* 306 F 3d 726, 729 (9th Cir 2002).

[26] See *In re Enron Corp Securities Litigation* 206 FRD 427, 441–442 (SD Tex 2002) ('Congress was reacting to significant evidence of abusive practices and manipulation by class action lawyers of their clients in private securities lawsuits . . . . Because class counsel's fees and expenses sometimes amount to one-third or more of the recovery, class counsel frequently has a significantly greater interest in the litigation than any individual member of the class').

[27] R. C Heck, 'Conflict and Aggregation: Appointing Institutional Investors as Sole Lead Plaintiffs Under the PSLRA' (1999) 66 *University of Chicago Law Review* 1199, 1202. The indictment of law firm Milberg Weiss reveals that the 'professional plaintiffs' were often paid kickbacks in exchange for serving as lead plaintiff on class actions devised by the law firm. See J McDonald, 'Milberg's Monopoly: Restoring Honesty and Competition to the Plaintiffs' Bar' (2008) 58 *Duke Law Journal* 507.

[28] See *Blue Chip Stamps v Manor Drug Stores* 421 US 723, 740–743 (1975) and J Cooper Alexander, 'Do the Merits Matter? A Study of Settlements in Securities Class Actions' (1991) 43 *Stanford Law Review* 497, 548–50.

[29] 15 USC §78u-4(a)(3)(B)(iii)(I)(bb). The presumption can be rebutted if the proposed lead plaintiff would not fairly and adequately protect the interests of the class, or was subject to unique defences that made the plaintiff incapable of adequately representing the class. The operation of the presumption and attempts to rebut it are dealt with in *In re Cendant Corporation Litigation* 264 F3d 201 (3d Cir 2001).

[30] 15 USC §78u-4(a)(3)(B)(v). See also Federal Judicial Centre, *Manual for Complex Litigation* (4th edn 2004) 538–39.

[31] See Weiss & Beckerman, above n25

The success of the PSLRA has been demonstrated through an empirical study of securities class actions from 1996 to 2005 which found that institutional investors out perform individual investors in terms of the proceedings surviving motions to dismiss, achieving larger settlements and obtaining greater corporate governance reform.[32] However, while pension funds for public and union employees[33] have actively offered themselves as lead plaintiffs, private institutional investors[34] have stepped forward far less. The PriceWaterhouseCoopers 2011 Securities litigation study found that pension funds appeared as a lead plaintiff in twice as many cases as other institutional investors did in cases filed during 2011, and accounted for $2.7 billion, or 79 per cent, of total settlements during 2011.[35] This is reflective of a continuing trend since at least 2007 as shown by figure 1.

In the Bank of America class action the lead plaintiffs were The State Teachers Retirement System of Ohio, The Ohio Public Employees Retirement System, The Teacher Retirement System of Texas, the Netherlands pension fund, Stichting Pensioenfonds Zorg en Welzijn, represented by PGGM Vermogensbeheer B.V., and the Swedish pension fund Fjärde AP-Fonden.

In Australia there are no additional requirements for being the representative party in a shareholder class action compared to any other class action. The choice of representative

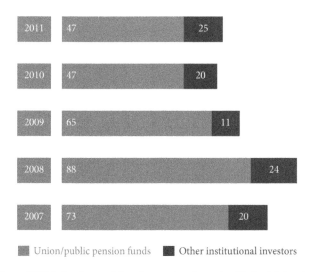

■ Union/public pension funds   ■ Other institutional investors

Figure 1.   Number of US federal securities class action lawsuits filed with institutional investors as lead plaintiff, 2007–2011 [†]
[†]Final 2011 data is not available to date; the full year projections are based upon filings through June 30, 2011
Source: PriceWaterhouseCoopers, 2011 Securities litigation study (April 2012)

---

[32] A Cheng, H He Huang, Y Li and G Lobo, 'Institutional Monitoring Through Shareholder Litigation' (2010) 95 *Journal of Financial Economics* 356.
[33] For example, California Public Employees' Retirement System, the New York State Common Retirement Fund, the New York City Pension Funds, Teachers Retirement System of Oklahoma, Electrical Workers Local 357 Pension Fund, and City of Fort Myers Police Officers' Retirement System.
[34] For example, banks, mutual funds, hedge funds and insurance companies.
[35] PriceWaterhouseCoopers, *2011 Securities litigation study* (April 2012) 27–29.

party is left to the lawyers and litigation funders running the litigation, provided the requirements in the legislation are complied with.[36] While participation in shareholder class actions has not been empirically examined, anecdotal evidence suggests that industry and private superannuation funds participate, as do institutional investors and individuals.[37] However, superannuation funds and institutions have avoided being the representative party. This is likely to result from a preference for the relative anonymity that accompanies group member status, being free of litigation responsibilities such as providing discovery and because they are paying a significant percentage of any recovery to a litigation funder to devise a litigation strategy and manage the litigation process, including the lawyers.[38] This scenario was borne out in the NAB class action where Pathway Investments Pty Ltd and Doystoy Pty Ltd were the co-representative parties, both being small investors, but the group was 'wholly or mainly' institutional investors.[39]

The entity that sues, the lead plaintiff or representative party, has the capacity to influence the direction and outcome of a class action, including causes of action relied on, entities that are named as defendants and the remedy, such as the quantum accepted in a settlement. These decisions carry with them the ability to influence culture. Whether this capacity to make decisions is exercised will depend on the influence wielded by the lawyers, and in Australia, the litigation funders.

The proliferation of pension funds as lead plaintiffs in the US has been linked to their activist ideology, limited relationships with corporate management and concerns with corporate governance but also class action lawyer's contributions to public sector fund trustees and union-related political action committees to encourage the pension fund to seek to be lead plaintiff and retain the lawyers as lead counsel.[40] The latter explanation is the so-called 'pay-to-play' arrangements which have caused concern because they undermine the aims of the PSLRA by creating conflicts of interest and allowing for the lawyers to retain control of the proceedings. Even without 'pay-to-play' arrangements, it must still be recognised that the lawyers will exercise considerable influence over the proceedings due to their expertise and desire for a fee. Without in-depth consideration of the lawyer-client relationship in class actions, the pension fund as a repeat player in shareholder class actions still has significant incentives to promote its interests (and its members) as a long-term shareholder in numerous corporations, including the one that is the defendant.

Pension funds, individuals or smaller corporate investors are able to bring to bear an outsider's view on corporate culture that may align more generally with society's expectations of banks and other financial organisations. This is likely to be more risk adverse and have greater concern for shareholder or consumer interests than if another institutional investor

---

[36] Supreme Court Act 1986 (Vic) ss 33C and 33D which effectively require the representative party to have a 'sufficient interest' to commence a proceeding on their own behalf and that they have a claim against the defendant which is in respect of, or arises out of 'the same, similar or related circumstances' and gives rise to 'a substantial common question of law or fact' as other claimants.

[37] A Hepworth, 'Big Funds in Class Act', The Australian Financial Review, 28 July 2006, 1, M Dunckley, 'Bid to Separate Centro Actions', The Australian Financial Review, 25 August 2008 57 and A Boxsell, 'Mum and Dad Take to Class Action', The Weekend Australian Financial Review, 11–12 July 2009 37–39.

[38] M Legg, 'Institutional Investors and Shareholder Class Actions: The Law and Economics of Participation' (2007) 81 Australian Law Journal 478.

[39] National Australia Bank Ltd v Pathway Investments Pty Ltd [2012] VSCA 168, [7].

[40] C Silver and S Dinkin, 'Incentivizing Institutional Investors to Serve as Lead Plaintiffs in Securities Fraud Class Actions' (2008) 57 DePaul Law Review 471, 482–87.

such as a bank or insurance company, which may have a similar culture or at least a concern at supporting cultural change through class actions, was the lead plaintiff. The different requirements and experiences between the US and Australian class actions also raise for consideration whether the pension fund or the small corporate investor is to be preferred from the perspective of cultural change. The greater resources and longer term perspective of the pension fund suggest that it may have greater inclination to pursue corporate governance and cultural change than the small corporate investor. Further, the pension fund is more capable of exercising independent discretion from its lawyers than the small investor, should it wish to do so.

V   CAUSES OF ACTION – ARE MORALITY OR ETHICS IMPLICATED?

Securities class actions are principally brought pursuant to section 10(b) of the Securities Exchange Act of 1934 (the Exchange Act), 15 U.S.C. § 78j(b) and rule 10b-5.[41] This cause of action was implicated in the Bank of America class action along with section 14(a) of the Exchange Act, 15 U.S.C. § 78n(a) and rule 14a-9 due to the issue of the Joint Proxy and sections 11, 12 and 15 of the Securities Act of 1933 (the Securities Act), 15 U.S.C. §§ 77k, 77l(a)(2), 77o due to the secondary offering.

Rule 10b-5, the implementing rule to section 10(b), states among other things that '[i]t shall be unlawful for any person, directly or indirectly. . .(b) to make any untrue statement of material fact or omit to state a material fact necessary in order to make the statements. . .not misleading'. Although section 10(b) does not provide for a private right of action, US courts have been implying a private right of action for over 30 years.[42] The elements of a section 10(b) claim are: (1) a material misrepresentation (or omission); (2) scienter; (3) a connection with the purchase or sale of a security; (4) reliance, or transaction causation; (5) economic loss; and (6) loss causation.[43] Of main concern here is the requirement for scienter. The US Supreme Court in *Ernst & Ernst v Hochfelder* (1976) 425 US 185 held that negligence was insufficient for civil liability under section 10(b); instead scienter required a showing of specific intent to defraud.[44] However, courts have also allowed deliberate or gross recklessness to suffice in certain circumstances.[45] The Second Circuit has held that 'scienter can be established by alleging facts to show either (1) that defendants had motive and opportunity to commit fraud, or (2) strong circumstantial evidence of conscious misbehavior or recklessness'.[46]

---

[41]   W Rubenstein, A Conte, H Newberg (eds), *Newberg on Class Actions* (4th ed New York, Westlaw, 2010) §22.1 and C Harris, *Securities Class Actions: An Australia and United States Comparative Analysis* (2011) PhD Thesis, Queen Mary, University of London 55.

[42]   See *Blue Chip Stamps v Manor Drug Stores* 421 US 723 (1975).

[43]   *Dura Pharms, Inc v Broudo* 544 US 336, 341 (2005).

[44]   *Ernst & Ernst v Hochfelder* 425 US 185, 193 n 12 (1976).

[45]   *Matrixx Initiatives, Inc v Siracusano* 131 S Ct 1309, 1323–24 (2011) ('We have not decided whether recklessness suffices to fulfill the scienter requirement. Because Matrixx does not challenge the Court of Appeals' holding that the scienter requirement may be satisfied by a showing of "deliberate recklessness," we assume, without deciding, that the standard applied by the Court of Appeals is sufficient to establish scienter.' (internal citations omitted)) and William Kuehnle, 'On Scienter, Knowledge, and Recklessness Under the Federal Securities Laws' (1997) 34 *Houston Law Review* 121, 179. ('For the scienter element, most courts have concluded that recklessness is sufficient.')

[46]   *ECA, Local 134 IBEW Joint Pension Trust of Chi. v. JP Morgan Chase Co.*, 553 F 3d 187, 198 (2d Cir.2009).

Rule 14a-9 prohibits the solicitation of any proxy with a statement that is misleading or omits material facts. In *JI Case Co v Borak* 377 US 426 (1964), the US Supreme Court implied a private right of action and observed that '[t]he purpose of § 14(a) is to prevent management or others from obtaining authorization for corporate action by means of deceptive or inadequate disclosure in proxy solicitation'.[47] Section 14(a) may be satisfied by pleading negligence. The plaintiffs do not need to allege 'highly unreasonable' conduct, an 'extreme departure' from the ordinary of care, or 'strong evidence' of recklessness. Rather, an allegation of awareness of material deficiencies in a proxy statement is sufficient.[48]

Sections 11 and 12 create express private causes of action for material misstatements or omissions. Section 11 applies to registration statements, and § 12(a)(2) applies to prospectuses and oral communications. Specified persons may be sued—such as the issuer, directors, auditor, underwriters and lawyers. Section 15 creates liability for individuals or entities that control any person liable under §§ 11 or 12. Thus, the success of a claim under § 15 relies, in part, on a plaintiff's ability to demonstrate primary liability under §§ 11 and 12.[49]

Issuers are subject to virtually absolute liability under § 11, while the remaining potential defendants under §§ 11 and 12(a)(2) may be held liable for mere negligence. Moreover, unlike securities fraud claims pursuant to § 10(b) of the Exchange Act, plaintiffs bringing claims under §§ 11 and 12(a)(2) need not allege scienter, reliance, or loss causation.[50]

The causes of action and allegations that sufficiently pleaded the required state of mind to avoid being struck out in the Bank of America class action are set out in figure 2.

The US causes of action can be usefully contrasted with the law in Australia. The Australian causes of action invoked in shareholder class actions generally, and in relation to NAB specifically, contain no state of mind requirement. The Corporations Act 2001 (Cth) section 1041H prohibits persons from engaging in conduct in relation to a financial product or a financial service that is misleading and deceptive. The ASIC Act 2001 (Cth) section 12DA is in similar terms to section 1041H but it only relates to 'financial services'. Both are based on the consumer protection provision, section 52 of the Trade Practices Act 1974 (Cth) (now section 18 of the Australian Consumer Law which is schedule 2 to the Competition and Consumer Act 2010 (Cth)). The Corporations Act 2001 (Cth) section 1041I and ASIC Act 2001 (Cth) section 12GF(1) provide that a person who suffers loss or damage by conduct in contravention of section 1041H or section 12DA respectively, may recover the amount of loss or damage by action against the person contravening the section or against any person involved in the contravention. These provisions are based on section 82 of the Trade Practices Act 1974 (Cth) (now section 82 of the Competition and Consumer Act 2010 (Cth)).

---

[47] *JI Case Co v Borak* 377 US 426, 431 (1964). See also *United Paperworkers Int'l Union v Int'l Paper Co* 985 F 2d 1190, 1197–98 (2d Cir.1993). (The SEC 'promulgated Rule 14a–9 with the goal of preserving for all shareholders who are entitled to vote, not just for those who sponsor proposals, the right to make decisions based on information that is not false or misleading'.)

[48] See *Kalnit v Eichler* 264 F 3d 131, 142–44 (2d Cir 2001) and *Wilson v Great Am. Inds. Inc* 855 F 2d 987, 995 (2d Cir 1988)

[49] *Lindsay v Morgan Stanley* 592 F 3d 347, 358–59 (2d Cir 2010).

[50] *Herman & MacLean v Huddleston* 459 US 375, 382 (1983), *Lindsay v Morgan Stanley* 592 F 3d 347, 359 (2d Cir 2010).

	Section 10(b) and Rule 10b-5–scienter	Section 14(a) and Rule 14a-9–negligence	Sections 11, 12 and 15–negligence
Merrill bonuses	Yes–Bank of America, Merrill, Lewis, Thain [51]	Yes–Bank of America, Merrill, Lewis, Thain, Bank of America's directors[52]	n/a
Merrill 4th quarter losses	Yes–Lewis, Price[53]	Yes–Lewis, Price, Cotty, Thain, Bank of America's directors [54]	n/a
Federal financial support	No[55]	n/a	n/a
Secondary offering	n/a	n/a	Yes[56] Bank of America (issuer), Lewis, Price, Cotty, BofA's board of directors, Banc of America Securities LLC (underwriter) and Merrill Lynch, Pierce, Fenner & Smith Incorporated (underwriter)

Figure 2.   State of mind and strike-out motions in the Bank of America class action

There is no requirement to show intent in relation to the prohibitions on misleading or deceptive conduct.[57] The provisions are drafted so as to be concerned with consequences

---

[51] *In re Bank of Am. Corp. Sec., Derivative & Emp. Ret. Income Sec. Act (ERISA) Litig.*, 757 F Supp 2d 260, 322–24 (SDNY 2010).

[52] *In re Bank of Am. Corp. Sec., Derivative & Emp. Ret. Income Sec. Act (ERISA) Litig.*, 757 F Supp 2d 260, 322–24 (SDNY 2010).

[53] This cause of action was initially struck out: *In re Bank of Am. Corp. Sec., Derivative & Emp. Ret. Income Sec. Act (ERISA) Litig.*, 757 F Supp 2d 260, 325–26 (SDNY 2010) but an amended complaint survived a further strike out motion: *In re Bank of Am. Corp. Sec., Derivative & Emp. Ret. Income Sec. Act (ERISA) Litig.*, 2011 WL 3211472, *5–*10 (SDNY 2010).

[54] *In re Bank of Am. Corp. Sec., Derivative & Emp. Ret. Income Sec. Act (ERISA) Litig.*, 757 F Supp 2d 260, 326 (SDNY 2010).

[55] *In re Bank of Am. Corp. Sec., Derivative & Emp. Ret. Income Sec. Act (ERISA) Litig.*, 757 F Supp 2d 260, 327–28 (SDNY 2010) and again *In re Bank of Am. Corp. Sec., Derivative & Emp. Ret. Income Sec. Act (ERISA) Litig.*, 2011 WL 3211472, *10–*11 (SDNY 2010).

[56] *In re Bank of Am. Corp. Sec., Derivative & Emp. Ret. Income Sec. Act (ERISA) Litig.*, 757 F Supp 2d 260, 332–34 (SDNY 2010).

[57] *Google Inc v Australian Competition and Consumer Commission* [2013] HCA 1, [9], [97], *Hornsby Building Information Centre Pty Ltd v Sydney Building Information Centre Ltd* (1978) 140 CLR 216, 228, 234, *Brown v Jam Factory Pty Ltd* (1981) 35 ALR 79, 86 and *ASIC v Online Investors Advantage Inc* (2006) (2005) 194 FLR 449, [138] ('Intention is irrelevant to determining whether conduct is deceptive or misleading or likely to be so.'), *ASIC v Stone Assets Management Pty Ltd* [2012] FCA 630, [33] ('Section 1041H deals with misleading or deceptive conduct. It does not require proof of a mental element.').

not the contravener's state of mind.[58] In relation to the original misleading and deceptive provision, section 52 of the Trade Practices Act 1974 (Cth), the High Court of Australia has observed that conduct not intended to mislead or deceive and which was engaged in 'honestly and reasonably' might nevertheless contravene section 52.[59]

In relation to the section 82 of the Trade Practices Act 1974 (Cth), the High Court has held that loss or damages may be recovered:[60]

> in cases in which the contravener's conduct is intentional or even directed at harming the person who suffers loss and damage. It can be engaged in cases, . . . , in which the contravener can be said to have fallen short of a standard of reasonable care as well as contravene the Act, and in cases in which there was neither want of care nor intention to harm, but still a contravention of the Act.

Chapter 6CA of the Corporations Act 2001 (Cth) gives the ASX Listing Rules legislative backing, by requiring listed disclosing entities to notify the ASX of information required to be disclosed by Listing rule 3.1 where that information is not generally available and is information that a reasonable person would expect, if it were generally available, to have a material effect on the price or value of the securities of the entity.[61] Originally a claim for damages was required to at least prove negligence.[62] Since the Financial Services Reform Act 2001 (Cth), which took effect from 11 March 2002, intent or fault has been irrelevant.[63]

The state of mind or standard of misconduct is important in achieving cultural change because it sends a message to financial organisations and the broader community of the view the law takes of the conduct. The alleged perpetrators are 'tarred' with the disapproval that accompanies labels such as fraudulent, reckless or negligent. Importantly this means that others working in the industry witness that condemnation. Fraud reflects more serious or objectionable conduct compared to negligence. Fraud has been described as 'among the most serious, costly, stigmatizing, and punitive forms of liability imposed on actors in modern corporations and financial markets'.[64] Further, '[f]raud is in the business of condemnation and punishment, not just compensation'.[65] The link between fraud and morality means that it creates a direct link to unethical behaviour which a financial organisation would wish to distance itself from or avoid.[66] There is a strong incentive to avoid being tarred as a

---

[58] *Hornsby Building Information Centre Pty Ltd v Sydney Building Information Centre Ltd* (1978) 140 CLR 216, 228 ('As I read section 52 (1). . .it is concerned with consequences as giving to particular conduct a particular colour. If the consequence is deception, that suffices to make the conduct deceptive').

[59] *Google Inc v Australian Competition and Consumer Commission* [2013] HCA 1, [9], *Parkdale Custom Built Furniture Pty Ltd v Puxu Pty Ltd* (1982) 149 CLR 191, 197 and *Yorke v Lucas* (1985) 158 CLR 661, 666.

[60] *I & L Securities Pty Ltd v HTW Valuers (Brisbane) Pty Ltd* (2002) 210 CLR 109, [42].

[61] Corporations Act 2001 (Cth) s 674 deals with listed disclosing entities and s 675 deals with other disclosing entities. When information is generally available is defined in s 676, and the material effect on price or value is defined in s 677.

[62] See Corporations Law s 1005, *Riley v Jubilee Mines NL* (2006) 59 ACSR 252 and *Australian Securities and Investments Commission v Chemeq Limited* (2006) 58 ACSR 169, [31].

[63] See Revised Explanatory Memorandum for the Financial Services Reform Act, [18.3] and *Australian Securities and Investments Commission v Chemeq Limited* (2006) 58 ACSR 169, [46].

[64] S Buell, 'What is Securities Fraud?' (2011) 61 *Duke Law Journal* 511, 521 and J Karpoff, D. Scott Lee and G Martin, *The Legal Penalties for Financial Misrepresentation* 8 (2 May 2007) (unpublished manuscript), available at http://ssrn.com/abstract=933333.

[65] Buell, ibid.

[66] J Park, 'Rules, Principles and the Competition to Enforce Securities Laws' (2012)100 *California Law Review* 115, 169. ('Prohibitions against fraud, breaches of duty by fiduciaries, and theft are not just part of securities regulation but reflect common social norms that are reflected in the common law.').

fraudster. The rule 10b-5 requirement of scienter has been criticised because something less than clear fraudulent behaviour, namely recklessness, is sufficient for a contravention thus diluting the moral turpitude associated with a particular activity.[67] Nonetheless, if a specified state of mind or standard of behaviour such as recklessness or negligence is required then the perpetrators cannot be heard to say that it was an innocent mistake or inadvertence. Their actions still deserve blame and financial organisations receive direction as to the conduct they should prevent.

The focus in Australia is consumer protection and fostering an informed market—utilitarian rather than moralising.[68] While rule 10b-5 may be criticised for being a 'legal Swiss army knife' that has multiple purposes including shaming, regulating and compensating so that one is uncertain as to the character of the underlying conduct,[69] the Australian misleading conduct prohibitions and continuous disclosure provisions are limited to the latter two objectives so there is never any occasion to allege, let alone prove conduct that has the colour of fraud. The Australian provisions lack the degree of culpability that is found in the US provisions and consequently do not seek to demonstrate moral turpitude. The lack of a fault element means that the stigma which can be associated with a successful claim, or even allegation, is significantly lower, if non-existent compared to the US causes of action. It is therefore suggested that the US causes of action have a greater ability to promote cultural change than the Australian provisions. But this is likely to be mediated by how class action suits are perceived by financial organisations and the public, as well as whether claims are actually proven or simply result in settlements. These factors are explored further below.

VI   WHO GETS SUED?

A further issue in examining whether shareholder class actions are effective at achieving cultural change is whether such change is best transmitted through suits that are brought against the financial organisation and/or against individuals, such as directors and officers of that organisation.

In the United States, shareholder class actions are brought against the company but also frequently name a number of individuals such as the Chief Executive Officer and directors. In Bank of America the claims that survived strike out motions resulted in the following entities and individuals being sued:

- Bank of America
- Kenneth Lewis (Bank of America CEO, President and Chairman)
- Joe Price (Bank of America CFO)
- Neil Cotty (Bank of America Chief Accounting Officer)
- Fifteen Bank of America directors
- Merrill
- Thain (Merrill CEO and Chairman)
- Banc of America and MLPFS (underwriters)

---

[67]   Buell, above n64, 552.

[68]   *Sons of Gwalia v Margaretic* (2007) 231 CLR 160; [2007] HCA 1, [18], [122]; *Jubilee Mines NL v Riley* (2009) 226 FLR 201; [2009] WASCA 62, [87]; *National Australia Bank Ltd v Pathway Investments Pty Ltd* [2012] VSCA 168, [61].

[69]   Buell, n.64 above, 540–541.

Not all persons or entities were the subject of each cause of action. Figure 2 shows which causes of action were brought against each person or entity. The prevalence of claims against individuals, more generally, is demonstrated by figure 3 which shows the percentage of class actions that named particular officers between 2007 and 2011.

It should also be noted that in the US there is no aiding and abetting liability in relation to the main provision relied on for private securities actions, Rule 10b-5.[70] Consequently individuals must personally contravene rule 10b-5 rather than assist the corporation in a contravention.

In Australia, shareholder class actions are usually brought against the corporation only, as was the case in relation to NAB. This is the case even though the provisions imposing liability for a breach of the continuous disclosure regime or misleading conduct do allow for claims of aiding and abetting, otherwise known as accessorial liability.[71] Individuals such as directors are usually only joined to proceedings when the corporation lacks the financial resources to pay a judgment or settlement and the plaintiff wants to be able to access the director's insurance policy.[72] The other exception has been where directors are the subject of a cross-claim by either the corporation or another defendant, such as an adviser.[73]

From a cultural change perspective, one school of thought is that directors and officers need to be held responsible because it is those individuals who create and give effect to culture. Ethical behaviour by directors can promote ethical behaviour by the organisation.[74] This approach is exemplified by the 'tone at the top' approach to corporate governance which has been adopted by a number of influential US corporate governance codes or recommendations, including Business Roundtable (an association of CEOs of leading US corporations), The Conference Board Commission on Public Trust and Private Enterprise and Teachers Insurance and Annuity Association–College Retirement Equities Fund

Title	2007	2008	2009	2010	2011
CEO	90%	74%	79%	86%	86%
CFO	79%	65%	61%	63%	69%
Chairman	66%	50%	46%	66%	59%
President	56%	53%	62%	71%	57%
Director	51%	35%	42%	58%	64%

Figure 3.   Percentage of US federal securities class action lawsuits naming particular officers, 2007–2011
Titles are based on those named in the complaint
Source: PriceWaterhouseCoopers, 2011 Securities Litigation Study (April 2012)

---

[70] *Central Bank of Denver NA v First Interstate Bank of Denver NA* 511 US 164, 177 (1994); *Stoneridge Inv. Partners, LLC v Scientific-Atlanta, Inc* 552 US 148, 158 (2008).

[71] Corporations Act 2001 (Cth) ss 79, 674(2A), 675(2A), 1041I and *ASIC Act 2001* (Cth) s 12GF(1).

[72] See eg, *Guglielmin v Trescowthick (No 2)* (2005) 220 ALR 515; Matthew Drummond, 'Scarfe Action Settled' *The Australian Financial Review*, 13 October 2006 16.

[73] N Lenaghan, 'Alarm as Centro Moves to Sue Its Auditor', *The Australian Financial Review*, 27 May 2009 50; N Lenaghan, 'Auditor Fights Back with Counter-Attack', *The Australian Financial Review*, 15 July 2009 56.

[74] J J du Plessis, A Hargovan and M Bagaric, *Principles of Contemporary Corporate Governance* 2nd edn (Cambridge, Cambridge University Press, 2011) 125.

(a private pension fund that is the largest US pension fund, public or private).[75] Moreover the National Association of Corporate Directors' *Key Agreed Principles to Strengthen Corporate Governance for U.S. Publicly Traded Companies* specifically provides that 'it is the board that is charged with … setting the "tone at the top"'.[76] Further, in the context of enforcement the DOJ has observed that 'Within a business organization, compliance begins with the board of directors and senior executives setting the proper tone for the rest of the company'.[77] If directors and officers are responsible for corporate culture, then holding them accountable for failures of that culture is a sensible approach.

However, the effectiveness of claims against directors and officers must take account of two factors. First, if those individuals are insured and the claims settle so that no wrongdoing is found, then it is not the individuals who pay but an insurer. In the US, the insurance policy covers directors provided they act in good faith and in the best interests of the corporation. Settlement prevents any findings that would show a director to have acted contrary to these requirements.[78] Similar requirements exist in Australia.[79] Second, a settlement may be paid in full by the organisation so that the individuals, once again, do not pay. In the US, the corporate entity may favour settlement so as to not compromise its insurance which may exclude claims based on fraud, which can be an element of US causes of action.[80] In the Bank of America class action settlement, the organisation paid the entire settlement with no contribution from any individual.[81] In Australia, the fear of fraudulent conduct does not arise due to the nature of the contraventions. While personal liability may be seen as a way in which to encourage a positive corporate culture, the incentives in insurance may undermine personal liability as a practical solution.

Another approach is to see culture as something greater than any particular individual. Corporate culture is more than the sum of its directors and officers; it has historical, economic and sociological aspects. The corporation as a separate legal entity may be conceived of as also having a separate culture or ethos from the individuals who compose it. The financial organisation may be conceived of as a 'group' that through situational forces causes individuals to act differently compared to when they are alone.[82] If it is organisational cultural change that is sought, then it is the organisation that must be found to have contravened the law.[83] A focus on individuals allows the organisation to avoid responsibility

---

[75] Weil, Gotshal & Manges LLP, *Comparison of Corporate Governance Guidelines and Codes of Best Practice: United States* (December 2012) 5, 7, 58.

[76] National Association of Corporate Directors, *Key Agreed Principles to Strengthen Corporate Governance for U.S. Publicly Traded Companies* (2008) 5.

[77] Department of Justice, *A Resource Guide to the U.S. Foreign Corrupt Practices Act* (November 2012) 57.

[78] M Klausner, 'Personal Liability of Officers in US Securities Class Actions' (2009) 9(2) *Journal of Corporate Law Studies* 349, 355.

[79] P Mann, 'Directors' & Officers' Insurance in the Regulatory Litigation Context' in M Legg (ed), *Regulation, Litigation and Enforcement* (Sydney, Thomson Reuters, 2011) 73–74, 76.

[80] Klausner, above n78.

[81] A Frankel, 'How BofA Was Forced to Settle $2.43bln Merrill Class Action' *Thomson Reuters News & Insight*, 28 September 2012.

[82] See eg, N K Katyal, 'Conspiracy Theory' (2003) 112 *Yale Law Journal* 1307, 1316–24, 1355–58 and Zimbardo, above n7, ch 12.

[83] See Memorandum from Larry Thompson, Deputy Attorney General, US Department of Justice, to Heads of Department Components, US Department of Justice (Washington DC, Department of Justice 20 January 2003) ('Indicting corporations for wrongdoing enables the government to address and be a force for positive change of corporate culture, alter corporate behavior, and prevent, discover, and punish white collar crime.').

and point at the 'bad apple,' the individual who is responsible. To put the argument another way, contraventions of the law that arise because of the organisational culture rather than the misdeeds of certain individuals require the organisation to be held to account.[84]

The organisational or enterprise liability approach has been subject to criticism in terms of both deterrence and compensation in the area of securities law because payments by the institution for wrongdoing, whether fines or damages, are effectively payments made with shareholder funds and that punishes the shareholders, rather than management which is responsible for the contravention.[85] Further, it is the directors, not the shareholders, who determine how to deter misconduct within the organisation, yet they may be the ones engaged in misconduct.[86] The debate as to whether organisational liability or individual liability is more effective in achieving compensation or deterrence is likely to continue. The addition of a new objective in terms of cultural change provides a further perspective on that debate.

VII   OUTCOMES

In the United States, a trial by jury is a constitutional right in common law suits where the value in controversy exceeds $20.[87] The jury was 'an important element in the emergence of democratic-egalitarian values in Anglo-American society' due to its 'populist, lay quality'.[88] Moreover, juries allow for social judgments as to what is fair and equitable.[89] The jury as the ultimate finder of fact and in rendering the verdict can provide societies with input on what is acceptable conduct in financial organisations. A class action with trial by jury could allow for society to pass judgment on Bank of America's conduct. The Australian legal system places far less reliance on jury trials than the United States, but they are available, subject to the court's discretion, for class actions in Victoria.[90] However, the merits of the jury trial, or a reasoned and public judicial determination, do not require further assessment as almost all class actions settle.

The prospect of a public trial with evidence in which financial organisations are called to account is very remote. In the US, from the passage of the PSLRA in late 1995 until the end of 2011, there had been only 29 securities class action trials, as compared to a total of over 3,800 filings. Of those 29 trials, 6 settled prior to a verdict being reached.[91] In Australia, no

---

[84] See S Buell, "The Blaming Function of Entity Criminal Liability" (2006) 81 *Indiana Law Journal* 473 (examining the rationale for criminal institutional liability).

[85] J Arlen and W Carney, 'Vicarious Liability for Fraud on Securities Markets: Theory and Evidence' (1992) *University of Illinois Law Review* 691, 719; J Coffee, 'Reforming the Securities Class Action: An Essay on Deterrence and Its Implementation' (2006) 106 *Columbia Law Review* 1534, 1556–57; *SEC v Bank of America Corp* 653 F Supp 2d 507, 509 (SDNY 2009) (finding a consent judgment involving the corporate entity paying a fine of US$33 million as unfair as 'it does not comport with the most elementary notions of justice and morality, in that it proposes that the shareholders who were the victims of the Bank's alleged misconduct now pay the penalty for that misconduct') and *SEC v Bank of America Corp* 2010 US Dist Lexis 15460, *15–16 (SDNY Feb 22 2010).

[86] Arlen and Carney, *ibid*, 711–712. The derivative suit provides an avenue whereby shareholders may pursue corporate claims against directors for misconduct.

[87] US Constitution, Seventh Amendment.

[88] J Friedenthal, M K Kane and A Miller, *Civil Procedure* 4th edn (New York, Westlaw, 2005) 508–509.

[89] ibid, 510.

[90] *Matthews v SPI Electricity Pty Ltd (Ruling No 8)* [2012] VSC 318 (motion for jury trial by representative party in class action arising from bush fire denied).

[91] J Milev, R Patton, S Starykh, and J Montgomery, *Recent Trends in Securities Class Action Litigation: 2011 Year-End Review* (New York, NERA Economic Consulting, 14 December 2011) 12–14.

shareholder class action, whether against financial organisations or other listed corporations, have resulted in a judgment. The Centro, Australian Wheat Board, GPT Group and Aristocrat shareholder class actions went to trial but settled at various points prior to judgment.[92]

Neither the Bank of America or NAB class actions went to trial. Bank of America agreed to pay US$2.43 billion and continue a series of corporate governance measures that the SEC had obtained through its enforcement action. The lawyers were awarded legal fees of US$153 million and litigation expenses of US$8 million.[93] NAB has agreed to pay A$115 million in settlement of the proceedings, including interest and legal costs of A$11.8 million.[94]

Settlement rather than trial can reduce the force of a class action in communicating what is acceptable conduct because no violation is found.[95] However, settlement does not completely deprive the community of an examination of the alleged illegal conduct as in both the US and Australia the settlement of a class action requires court approval.[96] In the US, the court may approve a settlement only after a hearing and on finding that it is 'fair, reasonable, and adequate'.[97] The Federal and Victorian Courts in Australia have adopted practice notes that specify:[98]

> When applying for Court approval of a settlement, the parties will usually need to persuade the Court that: (a) the proposed settlement is fair and reasonable having regard to the claims made on behalf of the group members who will be bound by the settlement; and (b) the proposed settlement has been undertaken in the interests of group members, as well as those of the Plaintiff, and not just in the interests of the Plaintiff and the Defendant/s.

Court approval of the settlement usually requires evidence from the parties as to why the settlement should be approved which includes opinions on prospects of success, allows for group members to object to the settlement, provides an opportunity for the media to bring the settlement to the public's attention and results in a judgment setting out the key terms of the settlement, such as the amount paid.[99]

---

[92] Multi-party financial product proceedings brought by 'customers' against banks have displayed a different trend with two proceedings, one involving synthetic collateralised debt obligations (SCDOs) against Lehman Bros Australia Ltd and another constant proportion debt obligations (CPDOs) against Local Government Financial Services Pty Limited, ABN AMRO Bank NV and Standard & Poor's, all being tried and judgments being delivered: *Wingecarribee Shire Council v Lehman Brothers Australia Ltd (in liq)* [2012] FCA 1028 and *Bathurst Regional Council v Local Government Financial Services Pty Ltd (No 5)* [2012] FCA 1200.

[93] *In re Bank of Am. Corp. Sec., Derivative & Emp. Ret. Income Sec. Act (ERISA) Litig.*, Order Awarding Attorneys' Fees and Expenses (SDNY Castel J, 8 April 2013) [4], [10].

[94] *Pathway Investments Pty Ltd v National Australia Bank Ltd* [2012] VSC 625, [13], [15].

[95] R Frankel, "The Disappearing Opt-Out Right in Punitive-Damages Class Actions" (2011) *Wisconsin Law Review* 563, 608. ("A settlement is little more than a truce between the parties, that is, an agreement to resolve a dispute rather than any statement about the defendant's wrongdoing.").

[96] *Federal Rules of Civil Procedure* (US) r 23(e), *Federal Court of Australia Act 1976* (Cth) s 33V and *Supreme Court Act 1986* (Vic) s 33V.

[97] *Federal Rules of Civil Procedure* (US) r 23(e)(2).

[98] Federal Court of Australia, Practice Note CM17, *Representative Proceedings Commenced under Part IVA of the Federal Court of Australia Act 1976*, 1 August 2011 at [11.1] and Supreme Court of Victoria, Practice Note No 9 of 2010, *Conduct of Group Proceedings*, 29 November 2010 at [11.1].

[99] M Legg, 'Role of the Judge in the Settlement of Representative Proceedings: Lessons from the United States' Class Action Experience' (2004) 78 *Australian Law Journal* 58.

[100] Park above n66, 160.

The amount of a settlement can send a signal about the nature of the violation. A significant settlement can indicate that there is merit to an allegation and the law has been violated.[100] The Bank of America settlement of US$2.43 billion is the eighth largest securities class action lawsuit settlement in US history and the fourth largest settlement funded by a single defendant for violations of the federal securities laws.[101] The NAB settlement makes it the third largest shareholder class action settlement in Australian history, behind the Centro settlement of A$200 million (although PriceWaterhouseCoopers contributed an estimated A$67 million) and the Aristocrat Leisure settlement of A$144.5m and just ahead of the Multiplex settlement of A$110 million.

Both class actions result in large monetary settlements relative to other class action settlements for similar causes of action. However, the meaning of those amounts in terms of wrongdoing must factor in that losses as a result of Bank of America's and NAB's alleged misconduct was estimated to be US$50 billion and A$450 million, respectively. When the settlements are looked at from the perspective of a percentage of losses, Bank of America's settlement is 4.8 per cent of the losses (excluding legal fees) and NAB's settlement is 23 per cent of losses (excluding legal fees).

Further, like most securities class action settlements, the Bank of America settlement does not come with any admission of liability; indeed, the bank asserted in a statement that it was done 'to eliminate the uncertainties, burden and expense of further protracted litigation.'[102] Similarly, the NAB's announcement to the ASX stated that 'The settlement has been reached on a commercial basis and there is no admission of liability by NAB'.[103] Yet, in contrast, the plaintiff's lawyer in the NAB proceedings told reporters: [104]

> It's the biggest company in Australian history to pay a class action settlement of this size: over $100 million…In that sense, we think it sends a message to all Australian companies, no matter how big they are, that they do have an obligation to keep their shareholders informed of important material information, and that shareholders are willing and able to seek compensation where something goes wrong.

There is a clear contrast between the defendant's position of settlement being a cost-benefit analysis and the plaintiff's view that large payments send a message to organisations about the need to comply with legal requirements. The effectiveness of financial payouts, especially when the size of the settlement is compared to the losses caused, is questionable. A US$2 billion payment is serious money but does that headline figure assist in changing culture when the losses caused are many multiples of that amount? More generally, it has been reported that in the US the median ratio of settlements to investor losses has declined from 7 percent in 1996 to 1.8 percent in 2012.[105]

---

[101] The ten largest securities class action settlements are recorded on the Stanford Securities Class Action Clearinghouse website: http://securities.stanford.edu/top_ten_list.html   The three largest single-defendant securities class action settlements are Tyco's $2.975 billion settlement in 2007; Cendant's 1998 settlement ($2.83 billion); and Citigroup's $2.65 billion contribution to the WorldCom case settlement. The total amount paid in settlement in each of these cases was larger than these amounts due to the contributions of other defendants.

[102] P Henning and S Davidoff, 'For Bank of America, More Trouble From Merrill Lynch Merger', *The New York Times – DealBook*, 28 September 2012.

[103] National Australia Bank, ASX Announcement – Class action Settlement, 9 November 2012.

[104] 'NAB Class Action Settled for $115million', 9 News Finance, 9 November 2012 available at http://finance. ninemsn.com.au/newsbusiness/aap/8561824/nab-settles-class-action-for-85m.

[105] R Comolli, S Klein, R Miller and S Starykh, *Recent Trends in Securities Class Action Litigation: 2012 Full-Year Review* (New York, NERA Economic Consulting, 29 January 2013) 33.

The combination of low percentage recoveries, lucrative fees for lawyers and the view that it is one set of shareholders compensating another has resulted in US class actions being referred to as 'legalized blackmail', 'litigation monsters' and 'litigation that enriches lawyers without providing any real benefit to society'.[106] The US Chamber of Commerce has stated that 'securities class actions are costly and burdensome, do not serve the goals of compensating injured investors or deterring wrongful conduct, and enrich lawyers at the expense of the average shareholder'.[107] The prospect of cultural change driven by either a desire to avoid monetary payments or adverse reputational effects is limited if class actions lack legitimacy.

However, before dismissing settlement payments as too low, it is necessary to consider the alternative—regulator action.[108] In both of the class actions under study, the actions of regulators were implicated. Bank of America had previously paid a US$150 million penalty in 2010 in a case filed by the SEC over the proxy disclosure.[109] In relation to NAB, there have been no reported fines or penalties but the Australian Prudential Regulation Authority (APRA) had been communicating with NAB over its portfolio of CDOs during the relevant period. The plaintiffs sought to subpoena documents from APRA relating to meetings between it and NAB but the subpoena was set aside as the court found that section 56 of the Australian Prudential Regulation Authority Act 1998 (Cth) prevented disclosure.[110] There was also no public action taken by the securities regulator, ASIC. Without the class action shareholders in NAB would most likely have recovered no compensation. From a regulatory approach perspective a regulator may choose not to impose fines or pursue litigation because the circumstances may be such that compliance can be better achieved through cooperation.[111] However an effective compliance outcome for the regulator may be cold comfort for an out-of-pocket shareholder.

Class actions can also include corporate governance reforms as part of a settlement, although this is rare in the US and unheard of in Australia. The settlement agreement with Bank of America requires that the bank will institute and/or continue certain corporate governance enhancements until January 1, 2015, including those relating to majority voting in director elections, annual disclosure of noncompliance with stock ownership guidelines, policies for a board committee regarding future acquisitions, the independence of the board's compensation committee and its compensation consultants, and conducting

---

[106] A Bloom, 'From Justice to Global Peace: A (Brief) Genealogy of the Class Action Crisis' (2006) 39 *Loyola of Los Angeles Law Review* 719, 720; N Scott, 'Don't Forget Me! The Client in a Class Action Lawsuit' (2002) 15 *Georgetown Journal of Legal Ethics* 561.

[107] US Chamber of Commerce's Institute for Legal Reform, *Securities Class Action Litigation: The Problem, Its Impact, and the Path To Reform* (July 2008) 1.

[108] Another alternative would be individual suits but the lack of economies of scale and collective action problems make this less likely.

[109] See *SEC v Bank of America Corp* 2010 US Dist Lexis 15460 (SDNY Feb 22 2010). An earlier settlement of US$33 million had been rejected. See *SEC v. Bank of America Corporation* 653 F Supp 2d 507 (SDNY 2009).

[110] *Pathway Investments Pty Ltd v National Australia Bank Ltd* [2012] VSC 429.

[111] This approach is consistent with the influential responsive regulation and enforcement pyramid approach set out in I Ayres and J Braithwaite, *Responsive Regulation* (Oxford, Oxford University Press 1992). However J Braithwaite, *Regulatory Capitalism* (Cheltenham, Edward Elgar 2008) 76 has suggested that private enforcement should be included in a tri-partite responsive regulation.

[112] Bank of America, Media Release - Bank of America Reaches Settlement in Merrill Lynch Acquisition-Related Class Action Litigation, 28 September 2012.

an annual 'say-on-pay' vote by shareholders.[112] Corporate governance reforms whereby the corporation agrees to improve its governance in specific areas and to retain, at its own expense, an independent third-party to oversee and report on the corporation's implementation of that program can achieve more far-reaching and longstanding cultural change than the payment of compensation.[113] These types of reforms have usually been the province of regulatory agencies or derivative suits, but if used more frequently in class actions, they could reverse the lack of legitimacy referred to above. This is because they address governance directly for the benefit of continuing shareholders and without any gain to lawyers or litigation funders. Further, governance reforms can be specific and intrusive as shown by Bank of America's refusal to accept some of the suggested changes put forward by Judge Rakoff in relation to the proposed consent judgment agreed with the SEC.[114] If a defendant agrees to specific governance reforms as part of a settlement, then this may signal that past policies were problematic and that change is needed. Further, settlement negotiations over governance reforms require the parties to consider the scope of the reform and what it will achieve. This process may facilitate cultural change through the representative party articulating existing shortcomings and the defendant either agreeing or defending the current position. However, governance reforms are not a panacea as they could be window dressing rather than real reform, but in a class action that must receive court approval the prospect of a judge, like Judge Rakoff, giving the reforms close attention would provide some protection.

VIII   CONCLUSION

This chapter has sought to examine whether class actions can be used to regulate culture in financial organisations. To address that topic the following questions were posed and considered: Who sues? Who gets sued? What are the causes of action and what are the outcomes? The analysis suggests that corporate culture may be influenced indirectly through class actions creating an incentive for the organisation to takes steps to prevent future contraventions and the associated reputational harm and need to pay compensation. In many ways the analysis of class actions promoting deterrence applies to class actions and cultural change. This includes a number of factors which both hamper deterrence and the likelihood of class actions being successful in achieving cultural change. In particular, the combination of most class actions settling, the settlement amount being a small percentage of actual losses and the corporate view that class actions lack legitimacy may undermine the prospects of cultural change. All three of these factors were present in Bank of America and NAB, with both defendants settling without any admission of liability and citing the settlement as being entered into to minimise corporate costs. It is difficult to see how a class action can be a harbinger of change when its meaning is so readily contestable. In the Australian context, the class action is further undermined by the lack of a moral or fault element in the substantive causes of action.

---

[113]   D Hess and C Ford, 'Corporate Corruption and Reform Undertakings: A New Approach to an Old Problem' (2008) 41 *Cornell International Law Journal* 307.

[114]   *SEC v Bank of America Corp* 2010 US Dist Lexis 15460, *14–15 (SDNY Feb 22 2010) (suggesting that a compensation consultant be chosen jointly by the bank, the SEC and the Court).

However, this gloomy portrait must be balanced against a number of positives. The class action, especially with a pension fund but also an individual investor as the representative party, offers an external monitor of corporate conduct that has a different culture to the defendant corporation and may be more in tune with broader social expectations of financial organisations. The class action can also draw attention to alleged corporate misbehaviour that regulators either do not take action on, in the case of NAB, or resolve for small sums of money, as was the case with Bank of America. Subject to the limitations discussed above, the class action can impact reputations and the bottom line. Class actions can also include corporate governance changes that may promote cultural change through altering and monitoring corporate policies. The inclusion of corporate governance reforms may also respond to the arguments that class actions lack legitimacy. The role and effectiveness of class actions in the US and Australia are highly contested. As a result, the ability of the class action to regulate culture is not clear cut with both opportunities and hindrances to achieving culture change within financial organisations.

CHAPTER 13

Corporate Criminal Liability: The Influence of Corporate Culture

Olivia Dixon

I INTRODUCTION

Most countries agree that corporations can be sanctioned under civil and administrative laws. However, whether the corporation, as a legal entity, should be charged as a criminal defendant has historically been, and continues to be, a complex and contentious subject.[1] Theoretical difficulties[2] arise because the criminal law was developed to apply to individuals with a physical and moral existence, to seek to deter and punish their misconduct.[3] Critics argue that criminal liability should not extend to corporations based on the maxim *societas delinquere non potest*[4] and on the belief that civil and administrative sanctions are superior forms of liability. In contrast, proponents believe that the stigma associated with criminal conviction is the only effective deterrent to corporate misconduct.[5] Doctrinal debate

---

[1] This chapter does not express any opinion about the appropriateness of corporate criminal liability. For discussion of this issue, see, for example, DR Fischel and AO Sykes, 'Corporate Crime' (1996) 25 *Journal of Legal Studies* 319; L Friedman, 'In Defense of Corporate Criminal Liability' (2000) 23 *Harvard Journal of Law and Public Policy* 833; VS Khanna, 'Corporate Criminal Liability: What Purpose Does It Serve?' (1996) 109 *Harvard Law Review* 1477; J Coffee, 'No Soul to Damn: No Body to Kick: An Unscandalized Inquiry into the Problem of Corporate Punishment' (1981) 79 *Michigan Law Review* 386; C Wells, *Corporations and Criminal Responsibility* (Oxford, Oxford University Press, 2001); J FC Di Mento, G Geis and JM Gelfand, 'Corporate Criminal Liability: A Bibliography' (2000) 28 *Western State University Law Review* 2; P Grabosky and A Sutton (eds) *Stains on a White Collar: Fourteen Studies in Corporate Crime or Corporate Harm* (Sydney, Century Hutchinson, 1989).

[2] Theoretical difficulties include how corporate criminal liability might be determined; what sanctions are likely to be most effective against corporations; how mainstream criminal law offences interact with offences under discreet legislation; and in what circumstances, if any, individuals associated with the corporation ought to be criminally liable. K Wheelwright, 'Goodbye Directing Mind and Will, Hello Management Failure: A Brief Critique of Some New Models of Corporate Criminal Liability' (2006) 19 *Australian Journal of Corporate Law* 287, 288.

[3] Australian Law Reform Commission 'Principles Regulation: Civil and Administrative Penalties in Australian Federal Regulation' (2002) Report 95, [7.7]; M Wilkinson, 'Corporate Criminal Liability: The Move Towards Recognising Genuine Corporate Fault' (2003) 9 *Canterbury Law Journal* 142, 142.

[4] Which translates to 'a legal entity cannot be blameworthy.' EB Diskant, 'Comparative Corporate Criminal Liability: Exploring the Uniquely American Doctrine through Comparative Criminal Procedure' (2008) 118 *Yale Law Journal* 126, 129.

[5] See, eg, J Coffee, 'Does "Unlawful" Mean "Criminal"?: Reflections on the Disappearing Tort/Crime Distinction in American Law' (1991) 71 *Boston University Law Review* 193, 235–38.

aside, the realities of corporate misconduct cannot be ignored. A new wave of transnational financial-services sector scandals have demonstrated the power and capacity of the corporation to commit large-scale social and economic harm,[6] fuelling public demands to deter or minimise such harm by criminally prosecuting and punishing the reckless or negligent corporation.[7]

This chapter investigates corporate criminal liability in Australia, where the law has been reformed at the Commonwealth level under Australia's *Criminal Code Act 1995* (Cth) (Criminal Code), but has yet to be substantively implemented by most states and territories. Described as 'arguably the most sophisticated model of corporate criminal liability in the world',[8] the Criminal Code addresses the fault elements of an offence through notions of organisational blameworthiness, taking into account such factors as the corporation's culture, systems and operating policies.[9] Consideration of corporate culture at the liability stage extends the breadth of Australia's corporate liability regime far beyond any other jurisdiction. In doing so, it incentivises corporate self-monitoring and the development of a general culture of compliance, as a failure to do so increases the risk of prosecution. However, theoretical promise has yet to translate into practice. The provisions have not been tested in a criminal prosecution, although, as in the United States, corporate culture has often been referred to in regulatory offences[10] as a factor in sentencing.[11]

The purpose of this chapter is to identify the conceptual and practical issues that may have driven prosecutorial reticence in relying upon the corporate culture provisions of the Criminal Code as a basis of liability. Part II traces the theoretical development of corporate criminal liability under the common law, from derivative to holistic models. Part III considers the operation of the corporate criminal liability provisions under the Criminal Code and the extent to which the provisions address the limitations of the traditional models. Part IV identifies issues that are potentially acting as roadblocks to prosecution based on corporate culture. Part V concludes.

II COMMON LAW THEORIES OF CORPORATE CRIMINAL LIABILITY

The extent to which models of corporate criminal liability vary between jurisdictions can be traced to the relationship between conflicting views of the proper place or individual to

---

[6] For example, in 2012 alone, the systematic manipulation of the London Interbank Offer Rate (LIBOR); the anti-money-laundering failures at HSBC and Standard Chartered and, more locally, the foreign bribery allegations surrounding subsidiaries of the Reserve Bank of Australia, Securency International and Note Printing Australia. See also M Schmidt, 'The Principles That Apply to the Sentencing of Corporate Offenders: The $17 Million Speeding Offence' (National Judicial College Sentencing Conference 2010: ANU).

[7] Wheelwright, above n 2, 288.

[8] J Clough and C Mulhern, *The Prosecution of Corporations* (Melbourne, Oxford University Press, 2002) 138.

[9] *Criminal Code Act 1995* (Cth), Part 2.5, cl 12.1–12.6.

[10] Regulatory offences commonly involve minor breaches of the criminal law (eg, breach of licence requirements), while corporate misconduct incurring criminal liability is generally regarded as more serious (eg, fraud). Whether corporate criminal misconduct is considered regulatory or conventionally criminal in nature is 'usually determined by reference to the administrative process that attends its detection and punishment.' New South Wales Law Reform Commission (2003) 'Sentencing: Corporate Offenders' Report 102 [1.7] citing S Simpson, *Corporate Crime, Law and Social Control* (New York, Cambridge University Press, 2002), 7.

[11] See, eg, *ACCC v Rural Press Ltd* [2001] ATPR ¶41-833; *ACCC v Nissan Motor Company (Australia) Pty Ltd* [1998] FCA 1048; *TPC v CSR Ltd* [1991] ATPR ¶41-076; *ASIC v Chemeq Ltd* [2006] FCA 936.

locate the mens rea of the offence and the theories of the firm.[12] Traditional or 'nominalist' approaches[13] transfer civil law principles into the criminal law and rely upon on the view that every group is, in principle, definable in terms of the behavior of its individual members. Under this view, the idea that a corporation can act in its own capacity is fictitious.[14] The common law applies either principles of vicarious liability or the 'identification theory' to determine when a corporation should be held criminally liable for the acts and omissions of its agents and employees.[15] The primary difference between the models is the range of individuals from whom liability may be imputed to the corporation. The 'alter ago' or 'identification theory' attaches liability to the corporation for the acts of a narrow group of individual agents who make up the corporation's directing 'mind or will'. Through vicarious liability, adopted from *respondeat superior* in the law of torts,[16] a corporation may be held accountable for the acts of any individual agent within the corporation if the agent commits the crime within the scope of their employment with the purpose of benefiting the corporation.

In recent years, there has been a conceptual paradigm shift in identifying and proving corporate criminal responsibility. Contemporary approaches,[17] referred to by *Wells (2001)* as 'holistic' models,[18] dispense with any necessary connection between corporate and individual liability. Each corporation is viewed as having a distinct and identifiable personality independent of specific individuals who control or are employed by the corporation, which 'reveals the collective will of the company'.[19] Holistic approaches have been justified on the basis that 'harm from corporate crime may have, in many situations, less to do with misconduct by or incompetence of individuals and more to do with systems that fail to address problems of risk.'[20] These approaches have been advanced in a variety of forms, ranging from a corporation's failure to react appropriately to misconduct or implement adequate internal controls to original offenses relying upon a defective corporate culture. However, while many view derivative forms of liability as no longer reflecting the realities of multinational corporate structuring, there is little consensus on the most appropriate alternative.

Derivative Approach: Individual Liability

i   Identification Theory

Identification theory, also called the alter ego theory, was developed by English law through importing the concept from the civil liability of tort[21] and is the traditional method

---

[12] For a summary of the debate in the Australian context, see J Hill and R Harmer, 'Criminal Liability of Corporations–Australia' in H Doelder and K Tiedermann (eds), *Criminal Liability of Corporations* (The Hague, Kluwer Law International, 1996) 75–77.

[13] Traditional theories are often associated with the 'nexus of contracts' theory of the firm and reflect concern as to how concepts of moral culpability can be attributed to juristic persons. See, eg, E Colvin, 'Corporate Personality and Criminal Liability' (1995) 6(1) *Criminal Law Forum* 1, 2.

[14] ibid.

[15] Wilkinson above n3, 149.

[16] J Gobert and M Punch, *Rethinking Corporate Crime* (Cambridge, Cambridge University Press, 2003) 55.

[17] Contemporary theories are linked to the entity theory of the firm, which views a corporation as something more than the sum of the individuals within it.

[18] Wells above n1, 156–57.

[19] New South Wales Law Reform Commission, 'Sentencing: Corporate Offenders' (2003) Report 201, [2.21].

[20] ibid, [2.23].

[21] G Stessens, 'Corporate Criminal Liability: A Comparative Perspective' (1994) 43 *International and Comparative Law Quarterly* 493, 494.

by which companies are held liable in most countries, including Australia, under the principles of the common law.[22] As with vicarious liability, the identification theory relies upon an individual to attribute liability to a corporation. Under this anthropomorphic theory, a sufficiently high-ranking individual agent is assumed to be acting as the corporation and not for the corporation. Corporate intent is effectively found by merging the individual within the corporation with the corporation itself. In *Tesco Supermarkets Ltd. v. Nattrass*,[23] the leading authority, the House of Lords, referred to a metaphor used by Lord Denning in an earlier case:

> A company may in many ways be likened to a human body. It has a brain and a nerve centre which controls what it does. It also has hands which hold the tools and act in accordance with directions from the centre. Some of the people in the company are mere servants and agents who are nothing more than hands to do the work and cannot be said to represent the directing mind and will of the company, and control what it does. The state of mind of these managers is the state of mind of the company and is treated by the law as such.[24]

The *Tesco* criterion is still the most frequently used for determining which individual can be identified as the embodiment of the corporation itself, and was approved by the High Court of Australia in *Hamilton v Whitehead*.[25] The guilty mind or 'brain' of the corporation must be a 'vital' organ of the corporation, an individual who is sufficiently senior within the corporate structure to represent, metaphorically, the mind of the corporation. Although the array of personnel whose acts can be imputed to the corporation varies from jurisdiction to jurisdiction,[26] in a general sense, the guilty mind can be identified with 'the board of directors, the managing director and perhaps other superior officers of a company that carry out the functions of management and speak and act as the company.'[27]

ii   Vicarious Liability (*Respondeat Superior*)

An alternative approach, adopted predominantly in the United States, is the *respondeat superior* model which 'represents the implementation of the principles governing vicarious liability: the actus reus and the mens rea of the individuals who act on behalf of a corporation are automatically attributed to the corporation.'[28] Under this theory, corporations are considered to be purely juristic persons, without the capacity to possess intent. The only means by which to impute intent to a corporation is to consider the intent of the individuals.

---

[22]   See, e.g. *Tesco Supermarket v. Nattrass* [1971] 2 WLR 1166 (England); *Hamilton v. Whitehead* (1988) 166 CLR 121 (Australia); *Canadian Dredge Dock Co Ltd v. The Queen* (1985) 19 DLR (4th) 314 (Canada); *Nordik Industries Ltd v. Regional Controller of Internal Revenue* (1976) 1 NZLR. 194 (New Zealand).

[23]   *Tesco Supermarket v. Nattrass* above n22.

[24]   ibid, 1177, citing L J Denning in *H L Bolton (Engineering) Co Ltd v T J Graham & Sons Ltd* [1957] 1 QB 159, 172.

[25]   (1988) 166 CLR 121.

[26]   For example, in England the standard is strictly followed, yet shaped differently in each situation. See *Meridian Global Fund Management Asia Ltd v Securities Commission* [1995] 2 AC 500 PC; G Ross, 'Corporate Knowledge: Identification or Attribution' (1996) 59 *Modern Law Review* 733. Canada has widened the set of personnel that can be identified with the corporation. See *R v Canadian Dredge & Dock Ltd* (1985) 10 CCC (3d) 1 (SCC).

[27]   *Tesco Supermarket v. Nattrass* above n22, 172.

[28]   C De Maglie, 'Models of Corporate Criminal Liability in Comparative Law' (2005) 4 *Washington University Global Studies Law Review* 547, 553.

Under the prevailing legal rule in United States federal court[29] and in most states, a corporation will be held vicariously liable for the acts of any[30] of its individual agents if the agent commits a crime while acting within the scope of their employment with the intent to benefit the corporation.[31] The potential scope of the rule is therefore prohibitively broad. If any individual's conduct is contrary to the corporation's compliance policy and directives, the corporation may still be found liable.[32] Further, the existence of an effective compliance policy is not a defence to criminal liability; it is a mitigating factor used by courts in assessing a corporation's culpability for the purposes of sentencing.[33] For these reasons, in other jurisdictions, *respondeat superior* is generally restrictively applied for strict liability offenses and for crimes for which the law expressly or impliedly provides for indirect liability.[34]

iii   Aggregation Theory

Some United States federal court decisions[35] have held that for the purposes of calculating corporate criminal liability, the states of mind and culpability of individuals should be 'aggregated.' Aggregation theory provides that where no individual had sufficient information necessary to meet the required mens rea of the offense, if multiple individuals within the organisation possess the elements of such knowledge collectively, their aggregate knowledge can be attributed to the corporation.[36] In *Bank of New England*,[37] the court explained that:

> Corporations compartmentalize knowledge, subdividing the elements of specific duties and operations into smaller components. The aggregate of those components constitutes the corporation's knowledge of a particular operation. It is irrelevant whether employees administering one component of an operation knew the specific activities of employees administering another aspect of the operation.[38]

The idea of aggregation has been largely rejected by other common law jurisdictions,[39] although Australia has permitted the aggregation of negligence.[40] The rationale being that 'a series of minor failures by relevant officers of the company might add to a gross breach by the company of its duty of care'[41] but that 'two innocent states of mind cannot be added

---

[29] In the federal system, this rule derives from a sole Supreme Court case, *New York Central & Hudson River R.R. v. US*, 212 U.S. 481 (1909), as there is no generally applicable criminal statute embodying this standard.

[30] *US v Gold*, 734 F.2d 800 (5th Cir. 1984); *US v. Automatic Medical Laboratories, Inc.*, 770 F.2d 399 (4th Cir. 1985). See also, De Maglie, above n28, 553–54.

[31] EM Wise, 'Criminal Liability of Corporations–US' in H Doelder and K Tiedermann (eds), *Criminal Liability of Corporations* (The Hague, Kluwer Law International, 1996), 75–77.

[32] See *US v Automatic Medical Laboratories, Inc.*, above n30, 407.

[33] *United States Federal Sentencing Guidelines Manual*, §8B2.1.

[34] See, eg, *Allen v Whitehead* [1930] 1 KB 211 (England).

[35] See *United States v. Bank of New England*, 821 F. 2d 844 (1st Cir. 1987), cert. denied, 484 US 943.

[36] ibid.

[37] ibid.

[38] ibid, 856.

[39] See, eg, *Kent & Sussex Contractors Ltd* [1944] KB 146 (England); *R v HM Coroner for East Kent* 88 Crim App 10, 16 (England); *R v Australian Films Ltd* (1921) 29 CLR 195 (Australia).

[40] Criminal Code, §12.4(2)(b) provides if 'no individual employee, agent or officer of the body corporate has that fault element; that fault element may exist on the part of the body corporate if the body corporate's conduct is negligent when viewed as a whole (that is, by aggregating the conduct of any number of its employees, agents or officers).'

[41] Colvin above n13, 23.

together to produce a guilty state of mind. Any such doctrine could have no application in offenses requiring knowledge, intention or recklessness.'[42]

iv   Criticism of Derivative Models

The flaws in these derivative theories are axiomatic. In each case, corporate fault is found through linking back to an individual or a group of individuals, rather than through identifying original, discrete elements of organisational fault. The complexity and diffusion of power and responsibility in the large, modern corporation makes it extremely difficult to identify the individual whose intention could be attributed to the corporation, creating challenges for the imposition of corporate criminal liability based on individualistic approaches.

The identification theory has been largely criticised 'on a number of levels, both practical and theoretical'.[43] The limited number of individuals who are identified with the corporation substantially constrains the applicability of the criminal law. The theory can only function for corporations with a rigid hierarchical corporate structure, where high-level managers are involved in the decision-making process.[44] However, in practice, many corporations have 'flatter structures with greater delegation being given to relatively junior officers.'[45] The theory is therefore counterproductive as in large corporations, the separation between high-level managers and middle- or low-level employees can result in the 'mind or will' being sheltered from liability.[46] Such displacement of responsibility by high-level managers effectively results in mid-level managers becoming 'the potential fall guys when things go wrong'.[47] Further, as Fisse and Braithwaite (1993) note, 'to prove fault on the part of one managerial representative of the company is not to show that the company was at fault but merely that one representative was at fault.'[48]

The justification for vicarious liability, that it extends corporate liability for individual misconduct down to mid- and low-level employees, is similarly flawed. It is criticised as being both too broad and too narrow in its scope. Like the identification theory, it is too narrow in that fault must first be present in an individual. It is too broad because if individual liability attaches, corporate liability automatically attaches, even in the absence of evidence of organisational fault. In practical terms, in a large multinational corporation it may be difficult to adequately supervise an extraordinary number of low-level employees. Further, even if the corporation derives no benefit from an isolated act of misconduct of a low-level employee and has expressly prohibited employees from committing the act of misconduct in question, the corporation may still be criminally liable.[49]

Aggregation represents a partial solution to the limitations of the identification and vicarious liability approaches by taking into account the multilevel decision making structure of many corporations. However, aggregating the mens rea of one individual with the

---

[42]   JC Smith and B Hogan, *Criminal Law*, 7th edn (London, Butterworths, 1992) 184.

[43]   Hill and Harmer above n12, 81.

[44]   See B Fisse, *Howard's Criminal Law*, 5th edn (Sydney, Law Book Company Limited, 1990) 603; B Fisse and J Braithwaite, *Corporations, Crime and Accountability* (Sydney, Cambridge University Press, 1993) 47.

[45]   Criminal Law Officers Committee of the Standing Committee of Attorneys General, *Model Criminal Code: Chapter 2: General Principles of Criminal Responsibility* (Final Report, 1992) 501.

[46]   See C Wells, 'Corporate Liability and Consumer Protection: Tesco v Natrass Revisited', 57 *Modern Law Review* 817, note 36.

[47]   R Jackall, *Moral Mazes* (New York, Oxford University Press, 1988) 20–21.

[48]   Fisse and Braithwaite above n44.

[49]   J Gobert, 'Corporate Criminality: Four Models of Fault' (1994) 14 *Legal Studies* 393, 398.

actus reus of another individual is conceptually artificial. Individualism is still present in the application of aggregation theory. Aggregated mens rea equates to corporate or group fault, not true organisational fault. The expansion of corporate criminal liability is more appropriately theoretically justified through holistic approaches to organisational liability.

Holistic Approach: Organisational Liability

i   Reactive Fault

Under the reactive fault model,[50] first proposed by Fisse (1988),[51] following an act of misconduct by or on behalf of a corporation, a court should be empowered to order the corporation to undertake an internal investigation. To comply with the order, the corporation should investigate the offense, enforce disciplinary measures against the individual or division of the corporation responsible and return a detailed compliance report to the court.

Fisse and Braithwaite (1988) broadly define reactive fault as 'unreasonable corporate failure to devise and undertake satisfactory preventive or corrective measures in response to the commission of the actus reus of an offense by personnel acting on behalf of the organisation.'[52] Under this model, the culpability of the corporation is therefore not assessed at the time of the act of criminal misconduct. Rather, the liability of the corporation will be attributed when it fails to react appropriately to the misconduct or when it fails to responds satisfactorily to the commission of the actus reus of an offence, such as where no action is taken to rectify the misconduct.[53] While the corporation would be vicariously liable for the actus reus of the offense committed by its employee, the mens rea of the offense would be evidenced through a culture of non-compliance or a failure to take reasonable precautions and to exercise due diligence.[54]

ii   Preventative Fault

The 'preventative fault' model attaches liability when a corporation fails to insert and implement adequate internal controls to prevent the commission of a criminal offense. The model is most notably found in the United States Federal Sentencing Guidelines (US Guidelines), where the implementation of an 'effective' compliance and ethics program 'requires that the organization has exercised due diligence to prevent the crime' and it has fostered 'an organizational culture that encourages ethical conduct and commitment to compliance with the law.'[55] Corporate culture acts as both a mitigating and aggravating factor. If a crime is committed and the corporation can show that it occurred despite having an effective compliance and ethics program in place, the fine can be reduced by as much

---

[50] For criticisms of this model, see GR Sullivan, 'The Attribution of Culpability to Limited Corporations' (1996) 55 *Cambridge Law Journal* 515, 526–27; WS Laufer, *Corporate Bodies and Guilty Minds: The Failure of Corporate Criminal Liability* (Chicago, University of Chicago Press, 2008) 672.

[51] B Fisse, 'Restructuring Corporate Law: Deterrence, Retribution, Fault and Sanctions (1983) 56 *Southern California Law Review* 1141. See also B Fisse and J Braithwaite, 'The Allocation of Responsibility for Corporate Crime: Individualism, Collectivism and Accountability' (1988) 11 *Sydney Law Review* 469.

[52] Fisse and Braithwaite above n51, 505.

[53] B Fisse, 'Recent Developments in Corporate Criminal Law and Corporate Liability to Monetary Penalties' (1990) 13 *UNSW Law Journal* 1, 14.

[54] B Fisse, 'The Attribution of Criminal Liability to Corporations: A Statutory Model' (1991) 13 *Sydney Law Review* 277, 279.

[55] *United States Federal Sentencing Guidelines Manual*, §8B2.1(b).

as ninety-five percent and probation avoided.[56] However, if it is found that no compliance program is in place, or it is ineffective, then heavy fines and penalties apply.[57]

This model is applied in Australia in the sentencing of regulatory offences, particularly under the former *Trade Practices Act 1974* (Cth) (now the *Competition and Consumer Act 2010*). For example, Justice French in *Trade Practices Commission v CSR Ltd* imposed close to the maximum penalty on CSR, despite the fact that CSR had a compliance program in place. His Honour looked at the substance of the program and found it lacking, noting that there was 'little convincing evidence of a corporate culture seriously committed to the need to comply with the requirements of the Act' and that the compliance program was 'desultory and in need of reinforcement'.[58] Elements of the preventative fault model are also contained in the Criminal Code. Where corporate liability is based on a derivative approach, it is a defense if the corporation can show that it exercised due diligence to prevent the conduct, the authorisation or the permission.[59]

iii   Corporate 'Ethos'

The 'corporate ethos' model, developed by *Bucy (1991)*, is potentially the most practical of the holistic approaches and 'results from the dynamic of many individuals working together towards corporate goals.'[60] Corporate ethos is defined as 'the abstract, and intangible, character of a corporation separate from the substance of what it actually does, whether manufacturing, retailing, finance or other activity.'[61] Although Bucy notes that the term is not equivalent to corporate culture or corporate personality,[62] the corporate ethos standard can be placed in the same category as holistic theories based on the idea of corporate culture, assuming that each corporate entity has a distinct and identifiable 'ethos' that can be translated into mens rea.

Like the organisational approaches under the Criminal Code, this standard imposes liability on the corporation only if it proves that the corporate structure encouraged the individual to commit the criminal act and that the criminal act was committed by an agent of the corporation. However, Bucy notes that it is not necessary to ascertain the overall and complete ethos of an organisation, only the ethos that is relevant to the criminal behavior in question.[63]

iv   Critique of Holistic Models

Both the preventative fault and the reactive fault models 'all but abandon the requirement for finding a mens rea, or a mental state associated with corporate acts,'[64] and instead rely upon negligence. Under the preventative fault model, corporations are liable when they fail to make reasonable efforts to implement policies and procedures that prevent the criminal act. The same basis of attributing liability to corporations is proposed by the reactive fault model; however, preventative fault is assessed as fault prior to the commission of the offense and reactive fault is assessed after the commission of the offense.

---

[56] ibid, §8C2.5(f). See also, C de Maglie, above n28, at 565.

[57] ibid, §§8C2.4; 8C2.5.

[58] (1991) ATPR ¶41-076 at 52,155.

[59] Criminal Code, §12.3(3). See also Section III(A), below.

[60] PH Bucy, 'Corporate Ethos: A Standard for Imposing Corporate Liability' (1991) 75 *Minnesota Law Review* 1095, 1099.

[61] ibid, 1123.

[62] ibid, 1121 n98.

[63] ibid, at 1127.

[64] Laufer above n50, 699.

Under the reactive fault model, the liability of the corporation is determined on the basis of a failure to react and not on the basis of an act. That is, when a corporation commits a crime, liability is not determined by that act of misconduct. Liability is only imputed if the corporation fails to accept and implement corrective measures after the crime. While this model has practical utility, whether it is theoretically grounded is questionable. A failure to react cannot form the requisite mens rea in relation to the original act of misconduct.[65] It can only serve as evidence of intention, recklessness or negligence in relation to any subsequent act of misconduct.[66] One of the cornerstones of criminal law is punishment, and the reactive fault model leaves the original criminal act of misconduct unpunished.

While the corporate ethos model advocates that the mens rea of an offense can be found in the corporation itself, defines corporate culture and justifies why it is an appropriate place to identify corporate intent, its primary failing is that it lacks specificity. It fails to differentiate between varying degrees of culpability such as knowledge, recklessness and negligence, and does not offer suggestions as to the process one would undertake to determine the ethos that is relevant to the criminal act in question. However, while not flawless, the model deepens our understanding of corporate culture, which currently 'presents one of the strongest cases for holding companies liable as accessories to the crimes of their workforce.'[67]

III   CORPORATE CRIMINAL LIABILITY IN AUSTRALIA

Under the Criminal Code, the traditional elements of actus reus and mens rea are displaced by 'physical elements' and 'fault elements'. The Criminal Code is structurally unique in that it applies each of the identification doctrine,[68] vicarious liability,[69] aggregation[70] and organisational fault[71] as tests of corporate criminal responsibility. First, it uses principles of vicarious liability and aggregation to attribute the physical elements of the offense from the acts of individuals acting within the scope of their authority or employment. Next, it divides the attribution of fault elements between those requiring negligence and those that require the higher subjective mental states of intention, knowledge and recklessness. For actions based on negligence, a corporation may be held criminally liable if 'the body corporate's conduct is negligent when viewed as a whole (that is, by aggregating the conduct of any number of its employees, agents or officers).'[72] Corporate negligence may be evidenced by the fact that the prohibited conduct was substantially attributable to a 'failure to provide adequate systems for conveying relevant information to relevant persons in the body corporate.'[73] Where

---

[65] See WS Laufer and A Strudler, 'Corporate Intentionality, Desert, and Variants of Vicarious Liability' (2000) 37 *American Criminal Law Review* 1285.

[66] A M Boisvert, 'Corporate Criminal Liability–A Discussion Paper' (Uniform Law Conference of Canada: 2000 Victoria BC Annual Meeting).

[67] Gobert and Punch above n16, 74.

[68] Criminal Code, §12.3(2)(a) and (b).

[69] Criminal Code, §12.2.

[70] Criminal Code, §12.4(2).

[71] Criminal Code, §12.3(2)(c) and (d). See also §12.3(6).

[72] Criminal Code, §12.4(2)(b).

[73] Criminal Code, §12.4(3)(b).

the action requires a higher level of subjective intent, the Criminal Code provides several alternatives upon which to base corporate liability.

Derivative Liability

The first two methods parallel the common law *Tesco* principle, through proof that 'the body corporate's board of directors intentionally, knowingly or recklessly engaged in the relevant conduct, or expressly tacitly or impliedly authorised or permitted the commission of the offence'[74] or 'a high managerial agent of the body corporate intentionally, knowingly or recklessly engaged in the relevant conduct, or expressly, tacitly or impliedly authorised or permitted the commission of the offense'[75] and the corporation did not 'exercise due diligence to prevent the conduct or the authorisation or permission'.[76] The due diligence defence is designed to protect the corporation from being held liable for the misconduct or authorisation of misconduct by a high managerial agent when the board of directors has actively taken steps to prevent the misconduct at issue. A failure to exercise due diligence may be evidenced by the fact that the misconduct was substantially attributable to 'inadequate corporate management, control or supervision of the conduct of one or more of its employees, agents or officers'[77] or 'failure to provide adequate systems for conveying relevant information to relevant persons in the body corporate.'[78]

Organisational Liability

The last two means by which authorisation or permission can be established are unique to Australia, and extend far beyond the principles enunciated in *Tesco*. When these provisions apply, 'the fault of any agent in the corporation, no matter how minor or peripheral their role, can be attributed to the corporation.'[79] The corporation will be taken to have authorised or permitted the commission of an offence if it is proved that 'a corporate culture existed within the body corporate that directed, encouraged, tolerated or led to non-compliance'[80]; or 'the body corporate failed to create and maintain a corporate culture that required compliance.'[81] The Criminal Code 'treats proof of absence of a culture of compliance and proof of the existence of a culture of non-compliance as equivalent grounds for the conclusion that the corporation gave its authorisation or permission for the offence.'[82] The expression 'corporate culture' is defined to mean 'an attitude, policy, rule, course of conduct or practice existing within the body corporate generally or in the part of the body

---

[74] Criminal Code, §12.3(2)(a).
[75] Criminal Code, §12.3(2)(b).
[76] Criminal Code, §12.3(3).
[77] Criminal Code, §12.5(2)(a).
[78] Criminal Code, §12.5(2)(b).
[79] I Leader-Elliott, 'The Commonwealth Criminal Code: A Guide for Practitioners', (March 2002) 319.
[80] Criminal Code, §12.3(2)(c).
[81] Criminal Code, §12.3(2)(d).
[82] Leader-Elliott above n79, 321.

corporate in which the relevant activities take place,'[83] meaning that the corporation can be subdivided for the purposes of identifying corporate culture.

Factors relevant to whether a culture of non-compliance existed includes 'whether authority to commit an offence of the same or a similar character had been given by a high managerial agent of the body corporate'[84] and 'whether the employee, agent or officer of the body corporate who committed the offence believed on reasonable grounds, or entertained a reasonable expectation, that a high managerial agent of the body corporate would have authorised or permitted the commission of the offence.'[85] As noted by Leader-Elliott , it is likely that any corporate policy of non-compliance will be tacit or implied, rather than overt.[86] Prosecution of the corporation based on corporate culture will therefore be contingent on evidence of management's attitude to compliance from the individual accused of the misconduct. Objectively, reasonableness 'will turn upon the real manner in which the corporation operates. Whilst it would be reasonable for an employee of a company which merely paid lip service to compliance to draw the inference that his illegal conduct would be permitted by senior officers, it would certainly be less reasonable for an employee to hold such a belief where the company had in place a genuine, efficient compliance system'.[87] However, due to the heterogeneous nature of corporations, the elements of an 'effective' compliance system or program are elusive.[88] At the most basic level, a written compliance plan in and of itself is not enough:

> Compliance policies and procedures will not be effective unless there is, within the corporation, a degree of awareness and sensitivity to the need to consider regulatory obligations as a routine incident of corporate decision-making. This kind of general sensitivity to the issues underpins what is sometimes called a 'culture of compliance.'[89]

Guidance for preparation of a compliance plan is set out in Australian Standard 3806-2006 (AS 3806)[90] under four broad sets of principles: commitment, implementation, monitoring and measuring, and continual improvement. To demonstrate 'commitment', there must be: commitment by the governing body and top management to effective compliance that permeates the whole organisation; the compliance policy is aligned to the organisation's strategy and business objectives and is endorsed by the governing body; appropriate resources are allocated to develop, implement, maintain and improve the compliance program; the objectives and strategies of the compliance program are endorsed by the governing body and top management; and compliance obligations are identified and assessed. To demonstrate 'implementation', the program must show that responsibility for compliant outcomes is clearly articulated and assigned; competence and training

---

[83]   Criminal Code, §12.3(6).

[84]   Criminal Code, §12.3(4)(a).

[85]   Criminal Code, §12.3(4)(b).

[86]   Leader-Elliott, above n79.

[87]   T Woolf, 'The Criminal Code Act 1995 (Cth)–Towards a Realist Vision of Corporate Criminal Liability' (1997) 21 *Criminal Law Journal* 257, 263.

[88]   See, eg, C Parker, 'Is There a Reliable Way to Evaluate Organisational Compliance Programs' (Paper presented at the Current Issues In Regulation: Enforcement and Compliance Conference convened by the Australian Institute of Criminology, Melbourne, 2–3 September 2002).

[89]   *ASIC v Chemeq Ltd* above n11, §86.

[90]   For background to the introduction of AS 3806 and the limitations of its predecessor, AS 3806-1998, see, eg, C Parker, 'The Emergence of the Australian Compliance Industry: Trends and Accomplishments' (1999) 27 *Australian Business Law Review* 178; P Carroll and M McGregor-Lowndes, 'A Standard for Regulatory Compliance? Industry Self-Regulation, the Courts and AS3806-1998' (2001) 60 *Australian Journal of Public Administration* 80.

needs are identified and addressed to enable employees to fulfill their compliance obligations; behaviours that create and support compliance are encouraged and behaviours that compromise compliance are not tolerated; and controls are in place to manage the identified compliance obligations and achieve desired behaviours. However if implementation is insufficient, there must also be continuous oversight. The performance of the compliance program must be monitored, measured and reported, and the organisation must be able to demonstrate its compliance program through both documentation and practice. Further, the compliance program must be regularly reviewed and continually improved.

While there is an absence of judicial interpretation of AS 3806 from a criminal perspective, there is a body of precedent based on regulatory offenses under the former *Trade Practices Act 1974*, where corporate culture is often a factor considered during sentencing. In *ACCC v Rural Press Ltd*, the court noted that AS 3806 is a guide only, has no statutory recognition and cautioned against the assumption that AS 3806 is necessarily superior to a tailored compliance program prepared by an independent expert for a particular entity.[91] In *ACCC v Real Estate Institute of Western Australia*, an alleged price fixing action was resolved by agreement between the parties and a consent order was placed before the court for approval. It included a requirement that the Real Estate Institute of Western Australia institute a trade practices compliance program complying with AS 3808. Justice French stated:

> Once an undertaking is accepted by the Court or a consent order made, their breach is enforceable by proceedings for contempt. The undertakings and orders must therefore be formulated with precision so that they are capable of being readily obeyed. Undertakings or orders which are likely to involve vague evaluative judgments or significant debates on their interpretation are not likely to be given the Court's sanction. Similarly, undertakings or orders which are likely to require the Court to be concerned with the ongoing supervision of the conduct of the parties to them will also raise serious questions as to their appropriateness. So in this case the requirement of compliance with the Australian Accounting Standards standard for compliance programs imposes standards which are aspirational in their expression and not readily measured in application.[92]

For these reasons, Australian courts are reluctant to order the implementation of a compliance plan and ratify AS 3806 as a best-practices benchmark for an 'effective' compliance plan. In *ACCC v Wizard Mortgage Corporation Limited*, Justice Merkel was of the view that 'the injunctive orders…are a sufficient inducement to Wizard to establish an appropriate compliance program based on the legal advice it receives.'[93] Similarly, in *ACCC v Gary Peer & Associates Pty Ltd*, Justice Sundberg declined to make an order requested by the ACCC requiring a compliance program, noting that:

> the institution of the proceeding, its conduct, its outcome, including the findings of contravention, the making of the declaration and the costs order, will in my view sufficiently concentrate the minds of the respondent and its officers on the need in the future to avoid contravening conduct to make it unnecessary for a compliance program to be imposed on them.[94]

While a genuine, efficient compliance program may negate the 'reasonableness' of an individual's testimony, these cases highlight that the essential elements of an effective compliance program remain opaque.

---

[91]   *ACCC v. Rural Press Ltd* above n11, 43, 293–94.
[92]   *ACCC v Real Estate Institute of Western Australia* above n11, 606–607.
[93]   *ACCC v Wizard Mortgage Corporation Limited* above n11.
[94]   *ACCC v Gary Peer & Associates Pty Ltd* above n11.

Like AS 3806, the US Guidelines identify a framework of seven core elements which are minimally necessary to ensure that the organisation has met its core obligations to 'exercise due diligence to prevent and detect criminal conduct and otherwise promote an organizational culture that encourages ethical conduct and a commitment to compliance with the law.'[95] Those seven elements include: adequate compliance standards and procedures; effective compliance oversight by specific high-level personnel; careful delegation and due care in hiring and screening employees; effective training and education for employees and agents on their roles and responsibilities; active steps to ensure compliance, such as monitoring, auditing and hotlines; enforcement for violations; and, after an offense is detected, appropriate corrective action. As the US Guidelines have been extensively judicially tested, they may provide a useful supplementary benchmark to Australian corporations in drafting a compliance plan.

However, a written compliance plan in and of itself is insufficient; it must also be 'lived' by the corporation. To assess if a compliance plan is embedded in the corporation's culture necessitates first identifying that culture. Bucy sets out seven indicators that should be considered when determining the corporate culture of a corporation charged with a criminal offense: corporate hierarchy, corporate goals, education of employees, monitoring of employees, the facts considered under the *respondeat superior* and Model Penal Code standards, how the corporation reacted to past violations, and the compensation policies of the corporation.[96] Yet, as noted below,[97] identifying and finding evidence of corporate culture is a significant roadblock to the practicality of the corporate culture provisions.

IV   PROSECUTING BASED ON CORPORATE CULTURE

Clough and Mulhern have described the corporate culture provisions as 'displaying more academic purity than practical utility'[98] and, to date, prosecutors faced with the burden of proving corporate culture under the Criminal Code have formed the same view. The uncertainty as to the elements of a written 'effective compliance plan' and the difficulties inherent in identifying the corporate culture associated with the physical act, have likely facilitated prosecutorial reticence in pursuing actions based on corporate culture. However, there are a number of other conceptual and practical roadblocks that suggest that, without amendment, these provisions may continue to have limited practical application.

Limited Scope of Application

The Criminal Code applies to all offenses under Commonwealth law unless expressly excluded. Prominent exclusions include the *Corporations Act 2001 (Cth)*,[99] chapter 7, relating

---

[95] ibid.
[96] Bucy above n60, 1147.
[97] See Section IV, below.
[98] Clough and Mulhern above n8, 148.
[99] *Corporations Act 2001* (Cth), §1308A.

to 'Financial Services and Markets,'[100] consumer protection offenses in the *Trade Practices Act 1974 (Cth)* and taxation offences in the *Taxation Administration Act 1953 (Cth)*.[101]

However, despite applying to all Commonwealth offences, the organisational liability provisions are limited in scope. The majority of Australia's criminal law is state-based law. The major offences covered by the Criminal Code include (i) offenses to protect the security of the Commonwealth;[102] (ii) offenses to ensure the proper administration of the Commonwealth government;[103] (iii) offenses against humanity;[104] and (iv) offenses related to threats to the community.[105] Other major categories of offenses include money laundering,[106] postal offences,[107] telecommunications offences,[108] computer offences,[109] financial information offences,[110] and, more recently, the bribery of foreign officials, inserted into the Criminal Code through the *Criminal Code Amendment (Bribery of Foreign Public Officials) Act* 1999 (Cth). While the harmonisation of criminal law throughout Australia via a model criminal code has been actively encouraged by the Law Council for over ten years, to date only the Commonwealth, Australian Capital Territory and Northern Territory have enacted parts of the model code. The other states, some of which are common-law-based and some of which are code-based, have made little progress and show no signs of making progress.[111]

A Non-Compliant Corporate Culture is Not a Stand-Alone Offense

Perhaps the greatest misunderstanding regarding the corporate culture provisions is that having a non-compliant corporate culture is not an offence in itself. The Criminal Code provides that if an offence requires fault to be proved, 'that fault element must be attributed to a body corporate that expressly, tacitly or impliedly authorised or permitted the

---

[100] *Corporations Act 2001* (Cth), §769A. Corporate criminal liability in relation to ch 7 is covered by principles of vicarious liability under section 769B of the Corporations Act, which is a much wider scope of attributing criminal liability than that provided under the Criminal Code.

[101] See S Bottomley, 'Book Review: The Prosecution of Corporations by Jonathan Clough and Carmel Mulhern', (2003) 27(2) *Melbourne University Law Review* 627.

[102] Treason and sedition (Part 5.1); espionage (Part 5.2); terrorism (Part 5.3); harm to Australians (Part 5.4).

[103] Property offences (Part 7.2); fraud against the Commonwealth (Part 7.3); bribery (Part 7.6); forgery (Part 7.7); causing harm to, and impersonation and obstruction of Commonwealth officials (Part 7.8).

[104] Genocide and war crimes (Division 268); slavery and sexual servitude (Division 270); people trafficking (Division 271).

[105] Serious drug offences (Part 9.1); dangerous weapons (Part 9.4).

[106] Part 10.2.

[107] Part 10.5.

[108] Part 10.6.

[109] Part 10.7.

[110] Part 10.8.

[111] See, for example, Law Council of Australia, 'Letter to Mr Roger Wilkins AO, Secretary, Attorney-General's Department: Review of Chapter 2 of the Model Criminal Code' (18 December 2009); Australian Attorney General's Department, 'Letter from Mr Ian Govey, Acting Secretary, Attorney-General's Department: Review of Chapter 2 of the Model Criminal Code' (15 January 2010); T Dick, 'Uniform Criminal Code Urged for States' *The Sydney Morning Herald* (9 January 2007); For background to drafting of the Model Criminal Code, see M R Goode, 'Constructing Criminal Law Reform and the Model Criminal Code' (15th International Conference of the International Society for the Reform of Criminal Law, Canberra, Australia, 26–30 August 2001).

commission of the offense.'[112] This interpretation is patently highlighted by the 2006 final report of the Cole Inquiry into the UN Oil-for-Food Programme, which stated that the Australian Wheat Board (AWB) had:

> a closed culture of superiority and impregnability, of dominance and self-importance. Legislation cannot destroy such a culture or create a satisfactory one. That is the task of boards and the management of companies. The starting point is an ethical base. At AWB the Board and management failed to create, instill or maintain a culture of ethical dealing.[113]

Such a corporate culture was in direct conflict with AWB's Code of Conduct which stated that 'AWB does not approve' of illegal payments and that employees should avoid payments that are unethical or likely to 'cause embarrassment to the Company.'[114] Despite these findings, AWB was not criminally prosecuted because corporate culture is relevant to determining whether that corporation has committed a fault offense, and AWB's 'approach and conduct did not constitute a breach of any Commonwealth, State or Territory law.'[115]

A textual reading supports the same interpretation, the corporate culture provisions requiring 'proof of intention, knowledge or recklessness on the part of some human agent if fault is to be attributed to the corporation.'[116] Individual culpability therefore is a condition precedent to organisational culpability, inevitably due to evidentiary constraints. It would be incredibly difficult to establish that a particular criminal corporate culture existed beyond a reasonable doubt. Even though the corporation is divisible for the purposes of determining culture, inevitably the larger the corporation, the more difficult it will be to identify the corporate culture. If the corporation is small, the more likely it will be that corporate decision making is centralised with high managerial agents and that any prosecution would be based upon the derivative liability rather than the corporate culture provisions of the Criminal Code.

Inadequate Sentencing Guidelines

Although Australia has enacted sophisticated corporate criminal liability legislation, the accompanying sentencing guidelines are grossly inadequate, consisting predominantly of fines. General sentencing principles are specified in the *Crimes Act 1914* (Cth)[117] but they do not deal specifically with corporations.[118] Under the Criminal Code, if a corporation is found guilty of an offense carrying a term of imprisonment,[119] section 4B of the *Crimes Act 1914* converts that period of incarceration into a purely pecuniary penalty, expressed as a

---

[112] Criminal Code, §12.3(1).
[113] 'Report of the Inquiry into Certain Australian Companies in Relation to the UN Oil-For-Food Programme', *Volume 1: Summary, Recommendations and Background* (November 2006), xii.
[114] AWB Code of Conduct, Exhibit 0022.
[115] n.113 above 243.
[116] Leader Elliot above n79, 319.
[117] §16A.
[118] §21B permits the making of reparation orders and §20AB provides some other alternatives, but the recommendations made by the ALRC have not been taken up.
[119] Criminal Code, §12.1(2).

number of penalty units.[120] However, when the maximum available penalties under criminal law are compared to the gravity of the offense, they could be viewed by some corporations as a 'mere cost of doing business.'[121] While punishment, in the form of fines, must be an element of any law on corporate criminal liability, legislatures must focus on alternate ways of remedying corporate misconduct and to incentives to avoid criminal conduct from the outset. Sentencing is an area where, as in the United States, special provisions for corporations should be considered, including remedial measures, publication of convictions, and adjustment of punishment to reflect the responsiveness of the corporation in efforts to avoid future misconduct.

Corporate sentencing reform has been considered at both the state and federal level. In 2003, the NSW Law Reform Commission made a number of recommendations for the amendment of the *Crimes (Sentencing Procedure) Act* 1999 to make express provision for the sentencing of corporate offenders.[122] These included the addition of a number of aggravating or mitigating factors and the adoption of alternatives to the imposition of a fine, such as incapacitation order, correction orders, community service orders, publicity orders, orders in relation to the dissolution of a company, as well as disqualification orders preventing corporations from engaging in commercial activities, revoking or suspending licences held, disqualifying the corporation from entering certain contracts and denying the use of profits for a specified period. In 2006, the Australian Law Reform Commission produced its report on the sentencing of federal offenders,[123] which included recommendations to include options such as orders disqualifying a corporation from undertaking commercial activities, that the corporation undertake internal corrective action, community service, and publication of the offending conduct and orders dissolving the corporation. In both cases, these measures have largely not been acted upon.

The US Guidelines,[124] published by the US Sentencing Commission and applied to corporations when they are sentenced for federal criminal offences, incorporate many of the elements proposed by the NSW and federal law reform commissions and have been extensively judicially tested. *In re Caremark*, the Delaware Court of Chancery credited the guidelines with providing 'powerful incentives for corporations today to have in place compliance programs to detect violations of the law, promptly to report violations to appropriate public officials when discovered, and to make prompt, voluntary remedial efforts.'[125] The guidelines for sentencing organisations start with a base 'culpability score' of five points. The court then add points for aggravating factors, such as if the organisation's management was knowingly involved in, condoned or was tolerant of, the criminal act; if the organisation has a history of prior breaches; if it violated a court order or if it had obstructed justice. Points are then deducted for mitigating factors such as if the organisation cooperated with authorities and accepted responsibility for its conduct; and if the offence occurred even

---

[120] For an individual, the formula is the term of imprisonment expressed in months multiplied by five. In the case of a corporation, the maximum penalty is five times that that could be imposed on an individual (Crimes Act 1914, §4B(3)). A term of imprisonment of twelve months would convert to a pecuniary penalty of $51,000 for a corporation.

[121] See NSW Sentencing, [6.7], [7.23] and [6.3].

[122] NSW Law Reform Commission, *Sentencing: Corporate Offenders*, Report No 102 (2003).

[123] Australian Law Reform Commission, *Same Crime, Same Time: Sentencing of Federal Offenders*, Report 103 (2006).

[124] See *US Federal Sentencing Guidelines Manual*, §8B2.

[125] *Re Caremark International Inc. Derivative Litigation* (1996) 698 A.2d 959, 969.

though the organisation had in place at the time of the offence an effective compliance and ethics program. However, the deduction does not apply if, after becoming aware of an offense, the organisation unreasonably delayed reporting the offence to appropriate governmental authorities or if certain high-level personnel participated in, condoned, or were willfully ignorant of the offence.

Finding Evidence of Corporate Culture

A more fundamental roadblock relates to the 'practical difficulties of basing a corporate prosecution on such a nebulous concept.'[126] Prosecuting based on corporate culture involves the onerous task of proving that culture. One of the primary difficulties of this task is that the culture must relate to the physical act and be evidenced at the point in time that the physical act took place.

Objectively, the primary source of evidence as to a corporation's culture is likely to be written corporate policy as 'the policies, standing orders, regulations and institutionalised practices of corporations are evidence of corporate aims, intentions and knowledge of individuals within the corporation.'[127] However, it is unlikely that any corporate policy would disclose anything but a mandate to act in compliance with the law. As noted above, prosecution will therefore depend upon subjective evidence from individuals from within the corporation who are familiar with the corporation's culture and operations. The issues raised by leading with subjective evidence are manifold. The limited[128] public and private whistleblower protection in Australia is a disincentive for an individual to proactively come forward and, if an individual is mandated to provide evidence, 'factors of loyalty, secrecy, or selective memory loss within the organisation may also hamper the investigation and prosecution.'[129] Further, there are presently no guidelines for how to reconcile objective, formal policies and procedures with subjective testimony as to informal policies and procedures. The threshold of a non-compliant corporate culture is also open to debate. How will courts differentiate between a less than satisfactory culture of compliance with one that is worthy of criminal prosecution? With judicial reluctance to interpret the elements of an 'effective' compliance plan, it is likely that any reasoning will be ad hoc.

V   CONCLUSION

While the theoretical grounding for the corporate culture approach to organisational liability is sound, there are fundamental conceptual and practical issues that have led to prosecutorial reticence. Prosecution based on corporate culture is presently not a stand-alone offense. It is a ground for implied authorisation of the physical act, which must be

---

[126] Clough and Mulhern above n8, 144.

[127] Model Criminal Code Officers Committee, *General Principles of Criminal Responsibility,* 113.

[128] See, eg, AJ Brown, 'Everyone Backs Whistleblowing Laws. So Why Are We Still Waiting For Them?' *The Sydney Morning Herald* (2 October 2012); M Rout, 'UN Urges Whistleblower Laws' *The Australian* (10 July 2012).

[129] A Cowan, 'Scarlet Letters for Corporations? Punishment by Publicity Under the New Sentencing Guidelines' (1992) 65 *Southern California Law Review* 2387, 2392.

connected to an individual. Although corporate culture is currently the most compelling approach to attach corporate criminal liability, it suffers from evidential burdens too high to meet with any practical certainty. Successful prosecution will inevitably rely upon the 'reasonableness' of the testimony of the individual accused of the physical act as to whether or not a culture of non-compliance exists. While the 'reasonableness' of the testimony is rebuttable by the corporation through evidence of a culture of compliance, judicial reluctance to ratify AS 3806 as an appropriate benchmark, or provide reasoning as to what constitutes an 'effective' compliance plan raises significant evidentiary concerns. For the corporate culture provisions to successfully transition from 'academic purity' to 'practical utility', legislative reform is desirable. Harmonisation of Australia's Commonwealth and State-based criminal laws is imperative to expand the limited scope of offenses. Guidance on interpreting fundamental aspects of the provisions, including how to prove a corporation's culture will be required. Arguably, however, corporate culture is most practical as part of robust sentencing guidelines that extend beyond mere pecuniary penalties. As the US Guidelines have demonstrated, consideration of corporate culture as part of a sentencing decision will have the same deterrent effect as an original basis for liability: to incentivise corporate self-monitoring and the creation of a general culture of compliance.

Conclusion

Cultures of Redemptive Finance

John Braithwaite

I STORYTELLING AND CULTURAL REDEMPTION

The editors' Introduction catalogues well the significance of each chapter to the aims of this book. In this chapter I draw selectively from all the chapters to paint the ambition of the book in even more ambitious terms than we authors commenced this journey. This book ponders the integration of purposes, principles, rules and trust into a framework for transforming harmful corporate cultures of finance. It can be an apt jibe that resort to culture as explanation happens when scholars are despairing and desperate to explain. Yet I see this book in the tradition of seeking to understand how institutions enable actions which enact cultures that reproduce institutions. Such a framework is not necessarily platitudinous. It can make distinctions. Consider trust as something that on the one hand can reduce transaction and agency costs and on the other invites abuse, actively constituting the opportunity structure of financial crime. This is a book about how to institutionalize distrust and enculture trust. How can institutions create spaces for dialogue to allow trust to build between Wall Street and Main Street, among regulators, regulatees and critics of both? At the same time, how do we institutionalize distrust, for example, by rules against abuse of power that are enforceable?

The book establishes a good case for regulating finance through culture. Its chapters are convincing that the culture of banking has globalised as one of greed that is widely oblivious to legal and ethical obligations. This is clear in the breadth, depth and routinised nature of fraud in the Libor allegations that have been growing since 2012 as discussed in the chapters by George Gilligan,[1] Andrew Campbell and Judith Dahlgreen,[2] Eric Talley and

---

[1] G Gilligan, "Bad" Behaviour in International Financial Markets: National and Multi-Lateral Perspectives', this volume.

[2] A Campbell and J Dahlgreen, 'The Future Role of the Bank of England: Role and Power of the Bank of England from 2013', this volume.

Samantha Strimling,[3] and in the sheer magnitude of the Libor fraud that Seumus Miller's chapter[4] argues was worsened by global interdependence. The problem of the culture of finance was clear in diagnoses of the root causes of the crash of 2008, in the run of scandals of 2001 than included Enron in the US and HIH in Australia, in the BCCI and Barings scandals of the 1990s, in the Savings and Loans scandals across America in the 1980s and the 'greed is good' scandals on Wall Street of that time. Institutionally, the book shows that we learnt little from each wave of scandal. This when in historical terms they occurred in relatively quick succession.

How appalling that we only seem able to brace ourselves for the next catastrophe. The authors of this book are to be commended for sticking with analysis of the fundamentals of the problem. Those of us who sought since the 1980s to build interdisciplinary communities of regulatory scholars to confront what we saw as the analytic errors of myopic legalism and economism have also failed as an interdisciplinary scholarly community to tackle these fundamentals until now. We failed to persuade governments, the dominant professions, regulatory institutions that a new compact for transformative change is needed to secure our future. The same is true of the failure of the interdisciplinary regulatory academy to champion solutions that are implemented and that work to confront climate change and wider environmental challenges. Many settled for getting behind the economists' advocacy of emissions trading schemes as the potentially most helpful train leaving the station. This when we well know that this is not nearly enough. We also know that its trading rules will be gamed as a result of the same cultural problems that caused the financial crises that are the focus of this book.

I was among those who hoped, with the election of President Obama, that widespread recognition of these two massive crises could deliver a Green New Deal.[5] When the sheer audacity of the Enron fraud became public, President Bush gave speeches on how terrible his former friends, the bad apples, were. He did not give speeches like those of FDR quoted by Justin O'Brien,[6] that championed the New Deal as root and branch cultural transformation of business. Rather we saw a suite of piecemeal reforms in both 2001 and 2008 instead of a new social compact with business. President Roosevelt's speeches went to the need for a fundamental cultural change in the way business values are seen in government, by regulators, in the courts, in the community and in business itself.

An argument of this chapter is that banking culture and financial regulatory culture is not a rulebook, but a storybook.[7] President Roosevelt was reading his speeches in the 1930s from a different kind of storybook than Presidents Bush or Obama in the 2000s. President

---

[3] E Talley and S Strimling, 'The World's Most Important Number: How a Web of Skewed Incentives, Broken Hierarchies and Compliance Cultures Conspired to Undermine Libor', this volume.

[4] S Miller, 'The Libor Scandal: Culture, Corruption and Collective Action Problems in the Global Banking Sector', this volume.

[5] Green New Deal Group, *A Green New Deal: Joined-up Policies to Solve the Triple Crunch of the Credit Crisis, Climate Change and High Oil Prices*, (London, Green New Deal Group, 2008); E Barbier, *A Global Green New Deal: Rethinking the Economic Recovery*, (Cambridge, Cambridge University Press, 2010); K Tienhaara 'A Tale of Two Crises: What the Global Financial Crisis Means for the Global Environmental Crisis' (2010) 20 *Environmental Policy and Governance* 197.

[6] J. O'Brien, 'Back to the Future: James M Landis, Regulatory Purpose and the Rationale for Intervention in Capital Markets', this volume.

[7] C Shearing and RV Ericson 'Towards a Configurative Conception of Action' (1991) 42 *British Journal of Sociology*, 481–506.

Obama put insiders in charge from the business, economic and legal elites whose techno-cratic style was a root cause of the problem. Their storybook came to dominate the culture of the Obama White House and continued to rule across the executive branch.

Technocratically capable Presidents who work into the night understanding the details of new legislative rules, like Jimmy Carter, tend not to be those who change the course of history. His successor, Ronald Reagan, was not as technocratically competent, did not work as hard, yet had a paradigmatic impact because he changed the stories America told about itself. Abraham Lincoln could be seen as an incompetent President who failed to steer his country away from a bloodbath of a civil war. Once war started, Lincoln managed to choose generals who lost battles against a foe with inferior human resources and industrial might. Lincoln's greatness was that in his final months he could restory what it meant to be an American. Whether North or South, black or white, to be an American after his Gettysburg address was to be a victim of a terrible institution, slavery, to be part of a nation whose iden-tity is tied to the struggle to overcome the legacy of that institution.[8] Just as Nelson Mandela restoried South African identity, black or white, in terms of transcending apartheid as an institution.

Not only is Presidential leadership important to restorying business culture, so is the storytelling of business leaders, regulatory leaders, leaders of professions, educational lead-ers, leaders of families. Ideological leaders like Ayn Rand,[9] who had a significant influence on the mentality of US Federal Reserve chairman Alan Greenspan,[10] and religious leaders like Dullah Omar and Osama Bin Laden, also accomplished potent restorying of the work of the institutions of finance and Islam respectively. This storytelling power is not mediated by persuading a majority of business executives to become libertarians or a majority of Muslims to become salafist jihadists. The story can execute a power to transform the world in the hands of but a tiny minority. Part of the power of the story is that the precept of a libertarian script can be enacted by a young trader who is illiterate in libertarian theory. A teenager who cannot read the Holy Quran can follow the script of strapping himself into a suicide vest to enter paradise.

Cultures of mainstream storytelling must fight back against destructive minority stories. Storytelling can convince Muslims of the shamefulness of suicide bombing, business people of the shamefulness of greed and exploitation. The fight back is also best through stories because lectures and writings of political theory or theology miss these marks. The criminal law does not do the job of evocative storytelling with financial crime as well as it does with murder because the technical complexity of the conduct can be hard to narrate and trials usually do not occur until the years of national soul searching have moved on in the media attention cycle. Sometimes trials occur after the nation has ceased feeling sorry for the sins of its last affairs with greed as it embraces the seductive allure of the next boom. In that cli-mate, one of the worries political leaders have about convictions of their old business cro-nies is that they will dampen the 'business confidence' that is finally lifting the economy and the electorate. They are right that 'business confidence' does lift the economy. The problem

---

[8] R Meister, 'Forgiving and Forgetting: Lincoln and the Politics of National Recovery.' In C. Hesse and R. Post (eds), *Human Rights in Political Transitions: Gettysburg to Bosnia* (New York, Zone Books, 1999.)

[9] M Bustillos 'When Alyn Met Ayn: "Atlas Shrugged" and our Tanked Economy,' www.theawl.com/2011/04/when-alan-met-ayn-atlas-shrugged-and-our-tanked-economy (Tuesday, April 12th, 2011).

[10] ibid.

is that hope, humility and history never rhyme on Wall Street.[11] Yet legal processes that draw out stories in a timely fashion to reset society's compass before it is seduced by the next wave of 'business confidence' is vital to preventing, delaying, ameliorating the next crisis.

Restorative justice is a more narrative style of justice, and a speedier form, that can be fit for this purpose. The empirical criminology of Shadd Maruna found that serious Liverpool criminals were more likely to 'make good', turning away from a life of crime, when they adopted a 'redemption script'.[12] Such a redemption script can be about the bad influences, the domination the offender once suffered, but how she has now found a positive path to be a contributor to society rather than a destroyer of it. A society like Indonesia, which has been successful in reducing Islamist terrorism, which once had the highest incidence of terrorist bombings of any country, has quite a high density of former terrorists with a public profile in which they denounce violent jihad.[13] There is a shortage of former white-collar criminals who narrate stories of redemption with a high western profile. Convicted Watergate criminal Charles Colson, who died in 2012, was one. Though he was not a financial criminal, he was a white-collar offender who worked through his redemption script in prison to found Prison Fellowship International, which has become one of the global leaders of advocacy for restorative justice. It is actually hard to think of financial crime redemption narratives that have a high narrative profile. Bill Gates pouring his stupendous wealth into solving root causes of poverty and disease is inspiring; but it is no redemption narrative of redeeming monopolistic practices of his Microsoft Corporation. There is no redemption narrative in Rockefeller, Carnegie and Ford in establishing their great foundations. Nor is the founding of Bond University in Australia a redemption narrative! The Michael Douglas character in the two Wall Street movies after the 1987 and 2008 crashes supplies the best known narrative, hardly a redemption script. The Michael Douglas character was loosely based on Michael Milkin, inventor of the junk bond, arguably the greatest genius of Wall Street in the 1980s, and Ivan Beosky, the convicted insider trader who made famous the expression 'greed is good'. I horrified my consumer movement colleague Ralph Nader at the time when I argued that the prosecutor should take Michael Milkin into a restorative justice process to pick up his proposal that an alternative to prison could be for Milkin to work on his ideas to resolve the Third World debt crisis of that time. Part of my ethical reasoning was about broadening our conception of justice beyond punitive justice to 'justice as a better future'.[14] Another was enabling high profile redemption narratives on Wall Street that might have restoried finance capitalism.

Redemption narratives have a special power over peoples' ethical imaginations because they involve the humility of wrongdoers shaming their own past. This has more persuasive power than Main Street stigmatizing Wall Street, Wall Street denying their crimes,[15]

---

[11] This is because finance is cyclical, with booms always sowing seeds of the next bust. The expression 'when hope and history rhyme' comes from Seumus Heaney, see S Heaney, *The Cure at Troy* (London, Faber & Faber, 1990).

[12] S Maruna, *Making Good: How Ex-Convicts Reshape and Rebuild their Lives* (Washington, DC, American Psychological Association, 2000).

[13] J Braithwaite, V Braithwaite, M Cookson, and L Dunn, *Anomie and Violence: Non-Truth and Reconciliation in Indonesia* (Canberra, ANU E Press, 2010) Chapter 1.

[14] J Froestad and C Shearing 'Practicing Justice-The Zwelethemba Model of Conflict Resolution', in Slakmond et al (eds), *Justicia Restaurativa, Brasilia*, (Brasilia, Ministerio da Justica do Brasil, 2005).

[15] This is not just a matter of individual and corporate denial. As Gilligan above n1 points out in relation to the Savings and Loans scandal, and as is now apparent from the content of this book for the 2008–2012 scandals,

condemning sermonizing on Main Street as naïve and unhelpful to moving forward, political elites agreeing that responses like the occupy movement are 'unhelpful', and ultimately Main Street capitulating to this hegemony once 'business confidence' returns and their pension accounts, house valuations and job opportunities start to lift. Finance capitalism suffers a redemption bypass in comparison say with military culture, which exposes us frequently enough to retired generals, even former US Defence Secretaries, who condemn the criminality of the wars they fought and through that redemptive cultural work lay a foundation for peace on the ashes of war. Perhaps a Truth and Reconciliation Commission might have been established on Wall Street in 2008. There would have been Wall Street equivalents to Archbishop Desmond Tutu and Nelson Mandela who might have elicited redemptive narratives. Hope, humility and history might have rhymed at that moment because it was so clearly true, whether one worked for Lehman Brothers, owned a home in Peoria, or had investments in a pension fund, almost all were victims of American banking institutions.

Even when criminal law lacks the redemptiveness of restorative justice, it still has a limited role in delivering a spoonful of deterrence to resist the shovelfuls of sugar gorged by criminal traders. In addition, as Ferguson's chapter[16] concludes, reputational stock price impacts of a conviction can be nine times the size of fines imposed, at least when misconduct directly affects parties who trade with the firm such as customers and investors.[17] More importantly, criminal law still has a role in signifying, in the most solemn way our culture allows, that this behavior was shameful. Shaming is more powerful when it is reintegrative and redemptive. But even when redemption is bypassed, it is better for the society to signify the shame of crimes to those who deny them than for the state to be complicit in denial. It follows that while institutionalized storytelling that drives cultural reform after a crisis is crucial, law reform is also important even as it fails to connect to a cultural politics of redemption.

II   BACK TO LAW REFORM

Many of the law reforms that the Europeans and President Obama's finance technocrats put in place were needed. Hanrahan's chapter argues arrestingly that fiduciary law reform in the aftermath of the crisis in Australia shows the risks of complexity displacing simplicity, of a compliance industry that profits from codes and rules without catalyzing individual and corporate responsibility.[18] While some law reforms will prove counterproductive, as argued in other chapters of this book, of course a good debate was needed in the aftermath of crisis on how the nuts and bolts of rules needed to change. This did happen. It would be wrong to say that none of the changes were major. This book shows that what did not change was our reform mentality. That continued to be that we make use of a crisis to render the rules more

---

in the early post-crisis years there was a problem of hegemonic denial in which the media, academia, political and business leaders joined to suggest that the problems were about negligence and mismanagement rather than criminality. In contrast, Gilligan suggests the literature now finds fraud as a central factor in 70 to 80 percent of the Savings and Loans failures of the 1980s.

[16] B Ferguson, 'Sanctions, Incentives and Better Behaved Banks', this volume.

[17] J Armour, C Mayer and A Polo, 'Regulatory Sanctions and Reputational Damage in Financial Markets' Oxford Legal Studies Research Paper No. 62/2010 3 (2012) available at ssrn.com/abstract=1678028.

[18] P Hanrahan, 'The Fiduciary Idea in Financial Services Law', this volume.

serviceable for the large challenges of financial regulation. Then later in the reform cycle, the conservatives, sometimes rightly, get the upper hand in the public debate by arguing that the law reform went too far, is too much of a burden on firms as they seek to recover. So law reform grinds to snail pace–until the next crisis. Yet again, the big change that we fail to put in place is to render the law more continuously responsive–a law constantly adapting to the gaming of the law by finance capitalism. Grand post-crisis regulatory reform projects that bog down before they become genuinely grand are part of the problem. Regulatory scholars like myself have contributed to that problem by putting too much emphasis on the strategy of having reform blueprints in the top drawer waiting for the moment of the next crisis. Peter Drahos and I called this the 'model monger' strategy that links up to the strategies of 'model missionaries' in constituencies like reform NGOs and 'model mercenaries' like new compliance professions and the mainstream professions of law and accounting.[19] It is energising to be a reform romantic, but how romantic were we with our Green New Deal hopes? No FDR arrived on a shimmering stallion to crack the whip on Wall Street.

From this perspective, one of the disappointing ways the British debate post-crisis, as opposed to the Australian, American and other national debates, has run, concerns hand-wringing over whether there was error in moving from a more rule-based to a more principle-based regulation. This is a topic helpfully addressed in Campbell and Loughrey's chapter.[20] As I have argued elsewhere,[21] it is a mistake to have either a fundamentally rule-based regulation or an overwhelmingly principle-based regulation. Any regulatory regime has little hope of effectiveness without many rules[22] that allow specificity of enforcement where certain bright lines can and should be drawn. And it has little hope without a well crafted set of principles that save regulation from collapse in the face of gaming and other problems of criss-crossing bright lines. That writing makes the point simply by reference to the game of tennis. The foot-fault rule is a good one, quintessentially bright line. It is never grossly or intentionally violated. Infrequently, it is unintentionally breached by millimeters. When this happens the probability of sanction is high. Enforcing bright line rules is generally the best way to get compliance when a regulated phenomenon is not overly complex, not subject to flux or gaming.

Yet tennis has not always had an ethical culture. The 1970s and 80s saw the rise of a type of tennis player who sought to unsettle the ethical majority who still embibed the gentlemanly and ladylike culture of the pre-1970 game by calculated tantrums, racket smashing, abuse of umpires and line officials, or just standing their ground refusing to continue. Obviously it was easy to execute this gamesmanship in the face of any new rule against, for example, 'racket abuse'. Tennis, like all professional sports, must complement its suite of rules with principles of broad reach concerning 'unsporting conduct', 'conduct that brings the game into disrepute', 'physical abuse', 'umpire abuse', 'verbal abuse' that vary in name from sport to sport. Most professional sports have enforced such broad principles very effectively in response to periods and players where this problem has reeled out of hand.

---

[19] J Braithwaite and P Drahos, *Global Business Regulation* (Cambridge, Cambridge University Press, 2000).

[20] D Campbell and J Loughrey,' The Regulation of Self-interest in Financial Markets', in this volume.

[21] J Braithwaite, 'Rules and Principles: A Theory of Legal Certainty' (2002) 27 *Australian Journal of Legal Philosophy*; J Braithwaite, *Markets in Vice, Markets in Virtue* (Sydney, Federation Press, 2005).

[22] Rules and principles are defined here simply in the way chosen by Joseph Raz: 'Rules prescribe relatively specific acts; principles prescribe highly unspecific actions,' see J Raz 'Legal Principles and the Limits of the Law' (1972) 81 *Yale Law Journal,* 823. Safe driving in light of road conditions is a principle; a proscription of speed over 80 km per hour is a rule.

The complexity and dynamism of banking of course means that it needs both rules and principles that cover each others' weaknesses even more than tennis.

In tennis, both foot-faults and tantrums are fairly consistently sanctioned. The thing about rules and principles in banking is that they are not, either formally by the courts or informally through the culture. Of course a move to principles is not going to work with a particular regulatory challenge if we rely on courts[23] to enforce them and if judges are more comfortable with rules and reluctant to enforce principles. This chapter's analysis goes to six ways in which our response to financial crises may have been insufficiently transformative:

1. A transformation of transnational judicial culture is needed toward accepting a regulatory approach that requires rules to be interpreted in the light of overarching principles when those rules are gamed. This is a shift from extant judicial culture where rules are seen as trumping principles.

2. A transformation of judicial, rulemaking, drafting cultures is needed to become continuously, dynamically responsive to new forms of gaming, new kinds of financial products, new kinds of business entities and business environments. More nimble legal institutions must strike down old rules that no longer work and rely on judicial enforcement of principles to fill the gap while better, newer rules are continuously redrafted for new realities.

3. Increased reliance on the more holistic justice of restorative justice is needed for front-line enforcement. However well it is reformed, the formal law of finance will continue to deliver impunity to most offenders and will continue to allow individuals and entities who are not the largest villains to be scapegoated in attempts to make the rule of law appear to work. The key move of restorative justice is to displace proportionate punishment as a cardinal virtue with a more plural lens for seeing the multidimensionality of justice, so that some kind of enforcement and some kind of justice, holistically conceived, is possible in response to any and all crimes of finance. This involves a sacrifice of proportionality to end impunity.

4. A restorative justice approach is also needed to jump start ethical deliberation among professional stakeholders, such as lawyers, accountants and compliance professionals who mostly have lower levels of culpability than the principals who directly stuff the cash in their pockets. Formal law tends to let the lawyers off, almost always.

5. The most fatal flaw of any approach like that in points 1–4 above is that it fails to come to grips with the problem that the regulatory state can be as corrupted, as afflicted with the diagnosed pathologies, as banks themselves. Because public enforcement is regularly captured by the ethics and the hegemony of finance capitalism, a radical privatization, rather a radical hybridity, of enforcement is needed as a check on public enforcement.

6. It is wrong to conclude that because regulatory bureaucracies, enforcement staffs, and cases investigated have grown progressively across the histories of most countries that increased investment in regulatory infrastructure is irrelevant to solving the problem. Yes they have grown, but they have not grown in proportion to growth in the number of transactions banks make, to the variety of financial instruments and organizational forms and to the sophistication of the financial rocket scientists who launch their

---

[23] Campbell and Loughrey's above n 20 discussion of the British struggle to enforce principles which only reached fruition after the FSA adopted its policy of credible deterrence in 2008 is instructive on this.

rockets. Regulatory growth and innovation must be continuous and must be responsive to business growth and innovation.

Let us now consider in turn these six reforms as suggestions for a new way of layering the ideas in this book, starting with the first two grouped together.

1 and 2. Rules should not trump principles; both rules and principles must become continuously responsive.

A transformation of the judicial culture of finance transnationally is needed toward accepting a regulatory approach that requires rules to be interpreted in the light of overarching principles when those rules are gamed. Most national judicial cultures hold that if specified rules exist, those rules will be found to trump principles. Better to craft rules as instantiations of principles. So there must be legal principles set down in statutes that guide the design of financial products and finance organizations. Then there can be detailed rules that define what you can and cannot do if you call yourself a bank and/or are licensed as a bank, other rules for when you are licensed as a credit union, others for a partnership of financial advisors. The important thing is that all financial organizations and all financial products follow rules that the law justifies in terms of general principles. This means it is no longer possible to create unregulated financial products or financial organizations of a form that the law has never conceived. If your new financial organization does not fit the rules a bank or a credit union must follow, whatever kind of entity it is, it must follow the principles regulating all financial organizations. Even though it does not have a positive licence as a bank or a credit union, a regulator can take it before a judge, argue that its unethical conduct fails to meet the principles that regulate all financial organizations, and request that the judge negatively licence it (close it), nationalize it, or order its reorganization under the supervision of the regulator in compliance with the principles of the law.

Likewise, such an approach would have made the concept of 'unregulated derivatives' impossible. Any financial product would be regulated by the principles that justify the rules that apply to all financial products. New kinds of derivatives will be traded without rules to guide that trade, but are always vulnerable to being struck down by the courts for non-compliance with the principles of financial law. When particular kinds of derivatives become popular enough, it becomes economically efficient for the state to invest in rule adaptation to give the law specificity of content in relation to those newly common derivatives. Why is this important? It gives less innovative players who are not financial engineers, who cannot afford a sophisticated legal adviser, a path to trading this new product that lowers their transaction costs and increases certainty for them through a law that in effect lays down an acceptable recipe for a particular kind of product and a legal way of trading it.

Conceptually, this is not particularly radical in financial law. Many national tax laws in recent decades have acquired General Anti-Avoidance Rules. These are mis-named 'rules' because they are actually principles. Their legal formulation varies from nation to nation and varies in breadth, being quite narrow in the range of tax behavior touched in US law, for example, compared to Australian, New Zealand or Canadian law. When the US Treasury initiated a discussion in 1999 on the need for a general anti-avoidance principle, which in the US literature is called a General Anti-Abuse Rule (GAAR), its conception of an abusive tax shelter was similar to the Australian conception of 'aggressive tax planning'. A shelter that would be caught by the GAAR involved attempting to 'obtain a tax benefit in a tax avoidance transaction' where a 'tax avoidance transaction' is any transaction (i) 'in which reasonably anticipated pre-tax profit . . . is insignificant relative to the reasonably expected tax benefits', or (ii) 'that inappropriately eliminates or significantly reduces tax on economic income'.[24] In Australia, aggressive tax planning can mean engineering transactions that generate tax losses, excluding income from taxation, deferring recognition of income into a later year, or converting income into a different, lower-taxed form. Contrivance is used to 'shelter' income, wealth or capital gain from being taxed, for example by artificially valuing intellectual property rights that are moved to tax havens. Most aggressive tax planning involves the asymmetric treatment of losses and profits across two or more taxable entities. Funds are shuffled among entities so that the losses will be held where they generate a maximum tax loss and the profits flow to where they are untaxed (or less taxed). Because aggressive tax planning is characterized by innovation in finding new ways of getting around the intended effects of tax rules, legal definitions with too much specificity and insufficient adaptability risk capturing known tax shelters without netting newly emerging tax products. I have argued for a broad definition of aggressive tax planning as ' a scheme or arrangement put in place with the dominant purpose of avoiding tax'.[25] In terms of Australian law, this conceives of any tax planning that the courts find to be a breach of Part IVA of the Income Tax Assessment Act 1936 (Cth), Australia's general anti-avoidance provision, as aggressive tax planning. Michael Graetz in a more light-hearted, but more communicative vein, characterizes shelters as deals 'done by very smart people that, absent tax considerations, would be very stupid'.[26]

Some readers may think this heads on a tangent from this book. They would be in error in two ways. The most important proximate cause of the Global Financial Crisis up to 2008 was flaws in the financial regulation of banks. In 2012 and early 2013 that is no longer the proximate reason the crisis continues, why most of the west continues to be in recession. Fiscal crisis driven by aggressive tax planning is now a more important proximate cause. All western economies now face a situation where many of the most profitable companies that operate on their shores pay no company tax or almost none. This is not a problem China faces. A company that makes profits in China but fails to leave a reasonably proportionate tax payment behind knows they risk being sent packing. This is one reason authoritarian capitalist societies like China[27] are building formidable competitive advantages over liberal capitalist economies in contemporary conditions of financial engineering. In the west, this new proximate cause of national insolvency is driven by corporate cultures and professional cultures of greed akin to those that caused the banking crisis, and permitted by the same overly narrow rulishness of financial law. Ruthless competition between lawyers, accountants and financial advisers in the tax advice market, just as in the market for advice on financial products, is also a shared root cause, as explained by one distinguished New York tax lawyer interviewed in 2001:

In Arcadia, tax lawyers would discuss with each other what was a fair interpretation confident that the IRS would be looking for that fair interpretation and that the courts would be looking for it as well. The worm in the apple was progressively more ruthless competition for tax business that was

[24] E Kleinbard 'Corporate Tax Shelters and Corporate Tax Management' (1999) 51 *Tax Executive* 235.
[25] Braithwaite, above n21, 16.
[26] M Graetz quoted in Department of the Treasury, *The Problem of Corporate Tax Shelters: Discussion, Analysis and Legislative Proposals* (Washington, D.C., Department of Treasury, 1999) v.
[27] The term authoritarian capitalism comes from W Thornton and S Thornton, *Toward a Geopolitics of Hope* (Thousand Oaks, Calif., Sage Publications, 2012).

not under the control of any single set of professional norms, certainly not those of tax lawyers alone. Accounting firms, investment banks, financial advisers, all with in-house lawyers compete with law firms for advice.[28]

With tax law, as with banking law, it is important for the law to be sufficiently principle-based to support many spaces for ethical deliberation about the purposes of the law, deliberation that is ultimately refereed by legislatures and courts that enforce and resettle principles which dynamically adapt. In both tax and banking law it is vital to reap the benefits of rules–clear guidance to taxpayers, investors, depositors in common situations–while judicially enforcing principles informed by ethical deliberation in business to regulate the pathologies of rules discussed in chapters such as that of Campbell and Loughrey.[29] One is reminded of the lessons Joseph Rees[30] and the Kemeny Commission[31] drew from the Three Mile Island near nuclear meltdown as one reads this book. The problem they found was that operatives and managers of the plant had become rule-following automatons in response to an excessively rulish regime. Consequently, when a massive systemic crisis in the engineering environment arose, they had lost the art of thinking systemically about their own safety system. How can one but compare this to our editors' discussion of the conclusion of the British Treasury Select Committee in 2012 that 'The FSA has concentrated too much on ensuring narrow rule-based compliance, often leading to the collection of data of little value and to box ticking, and too little on making judgments about what will cause serious problems for consumers and the financial system.'[32]

It has been demonstrated to a degree in some tax jurisdictions that it is possible for tax law to list rules for transactions that are common, leaving judicial enforcement of principles, and in particular a general anti-avoidance principle, to mop up when unusual transactions or entities, such as those engineered to be unusual, are in contest. In the list of suggestions below, I attempt to be specific with the tax example about how a transformation of transnational legal culture could be accomplished that would create a space for continuous dialogue about an ethical legal and financial culture:[33]

(a)   Define the overarching principles and make them binding on taxpayers.
(b)   Make one of those overarching principles a general anti-avoidance principle which states that schemes are illegal when their dominant purpose is a tax advantage, even if the scheme "works" as a shelter from detailed tax rules.
(c)   Define a set of rules to cover each complex area of tax law.
(d)   Urge the legislature to lay down, perhaps through an Acts Interpretation Act,[34] that in a contest between a rule and an overarching principle, it will not be the rule that is binding.

---

[28] Braithwaite, above n21, 197.

[29] Campbell and Loughrey above n20; Braithwaite, above n21, also summarizes some of these pathologies, 145–149.

[30] J V Rees, *Hostages of Each Other: The Transformation of Nuclear Safety Since Three Mile Island* (Chicago, University of Chicago Press, 1994).

[31] JG Kemeny (Chairman, *President's Commission: The Need For Change: The Legacy Of TMI* (Washington DC, 1979).

[32] House of Commons Treasury Committee, *Fixing LIBOR: Some Preliminary Findings* (London, HM Government, 18 August 2012) 112.

[33] This list is only a slightly revised version of the list that appears in Braithwaite, above n21, Chapter 10.

[34] Other elements of the legislative history of specific statutes can also be mobilized to this end, for example explanatory memoranda and second reading speeches in the Australian parliamentary context. Both New Zealand and Australia revised their Acts Interpretation Acts to complement their General Anti-Avoidance provisions. See Sections 15AA and 15AB, Acts Interpretation Act 1901 (Cth); Section 6-6B, Tax Administration Act 1994 (NZ).

That is, the principle is not merely used to assist in interpreting the rule. Rather it is the principle that is binding, with the rules used to assist in applying the principle.

(e)   In a complex field of tax, write specific sets of rules for the most commonly used types of transactions or business arrangements. This might involve a dozen different sets of rules to regulate concrete arrangements. Such rules actually merely specify examples of how the principles apply.

(f)   Follow each of the dozen sets of illustrative rules with the explanation that the reason for the rules being this way in this concrete situation is to honour specified overarching principles. This is a way for the legislature to make it clear to judges that it is the principles that are the binding feature of the law. Hence when a legal entrepreneur reengineers concrete financial product number 11 as an 11A, or corporate structure number 9 as a 9A, to get around the law, judges must go back to the principles to decide what to do.

(g)   When judges fail to do this, reverting to old habits of privileging rules, enact a simple statute that says the 11A shelter violates named principles in the tax law and should be disallowed in future. Its effect is simply to strike down the court's precedent in the 11A case and to engage the judiciary in an ethical conversation with the legislature on the clarity of its intention to have principle-driven tax rules.[35]

(h)   Foster educative dialogue with judges, company directors and the community about the principles in the tax law in the hope that conversations among judges and tax practitioners, around the Boardroom table and around the table of dinner parties will develop shared sensibilities and corporate cultures oriented to those principles.

A transformation of judicial, rulemaking and drafting cultures to become continuously, dynamically responsive to new forms of gaming, new financial products and business environments can be pursued through this roadmap for more nimble legal institutions.

3 and 4. Increased reliance on more holistic justice that creates spaces for deliberation of ethical cultures.

However well it is reformed, the formal law of finance will continue to deliver impunity to most offenders. It will continue to allow individuals and entities who are not the largest villains to be scapegoated to create the false appearance that the rule of law works. This is a long established empirical finding about corporate crime enforcement in finance and beyond.[36] The US pharmaceutical industry in the 1970s even had 'Vice Presidnts Responsible for Going to Jail'; lines of accountability were structured so that they would take the rap if top management broke the law. After a period of faithful service as the Vice President Responsible for Going to Jail they were promoted sideways to a safe vice presidency.[37] Experience with restorative justice in corporate regulation, such as with enforceable undertakings at the Australian Competition and Consumer Commission of the 1990s,[38] shows that a regulator

---

[35]   I am indebted to conversations with Daniel Shaviro of New York University and Ernst Willheim of ANU for this thought.

[36]   B Fisse and J Braithwaite, *Corporations, Crime and Accountability* (Cambridge: Cambridge University Press, 1993).

[37]   J Braithwaite, *Corporate Crime in the Pharmaceutical Industry* (London, Routledge, 1984).

[38]   For a discussion of this program as it operated in the 1990s see C Parker, 'Restorative Justice in Business Regulation? The Australian Competition and Consumer Commission's Use of Enforceable Undertakings' (2004) 67 *Modern Law Review*, 209.

can initiate a large number of restorative justice conferences to repair the harm of many different offences at a lower cost than a single criminal or civil case in the courts.

The key move of restorative justice in response to the scapegoating challenge is to displace proportionate punishment as a cardinal virtue with a more plural lens for seeing the multidimensionality of justice. This allows for the possibility of 'emotionally intelligent justice'[39] based on high profile rituals of apology and leadership toward 'justice as a better future'.[40] It allows for corporations to requite their criminality by taking compliance up through a new ceiling for their industry, combined with formal undertakings to measure the performance of competitors to evaluate whether they follow the reformed bank up through that ethical ceiling.[41] It allows for organizational renewal by replacing culpable leaders with more ethical ones as a just remedy, combined with cultural retaining for middle and lower-level people. It allows for victim compensation, for environmental clean-up, for consumer education initiatives toward the prevention of future victimization. It allows for a program of corporate cultural transformation. Indeed it allows for, but of course cannot guarantee, whatever it is that stakeholders in an injustice say would allow them to believe that just repair has occurred. Of course there must be upper limits placed on unjust excess in demands, but under those limits, restorative justice does not pre-judge what proportional justice means. That is something for stakeholders to settle in a conversational contest of what justice should mean.

Of course formal law also allows these things. Indeed we saw in Chapter 9 (O'Brien)[42] that deferred prosecution agreements (also discussed in Ferguson's chapter)[43] can create a space for a more restorative form of justice that allows many of them. Generally they have not done so in the past, with only 79 of the 258 negotiated prosecutions in the University of Virginia database cited by O'Brien involving an external monitor.[44] Even when there are external monitors, they can approach their task as a purely technocratic one of compliance system reform rather than as catalysing culture change. O'Brien finds culture change to be a hopeful prospect in monitor cases like HSBC. Monitors can emulate the light John J. McCloy put on the hill as an external monitor of the Gulf Oil Corporation in the 1970s.[45] McCloy challenged, cajoled, coaxed and caressed the ethical core of Gulf. He engaged with their corporate culture and invited external audiences to join in a conversation with that corporate culture to transform it.

The idea of deferred prosecutions is an evidence-based one. Criminological data on common crime shows that prosecution is more greatly feared before it happens, but once felons have been prosecuted they mostly conclude it is not the end of the world; thenceforth the prospect of future prosecution no longer holds an imponderable fear in their imaginations. Interestingly, in the randomized controlled trials of restorative justice in Canberra, a restorative justice conference increased the fear of a future prosecution, sharpening the

---

[39] L Sherman 'Reason for Emotion: Reinventing Justice with Theories, Innovations and Research' (2002) 41 *The American Society of Criminology.*

[40] Froestad and Chearing, above n14.

[41] This was one of the things Solomons Carpets did in one of the Australian consumer protection cases; see Parker above n38.

[42] J O'Brien 'The Sword of Damocles: Deferred Prosecution and the Search for Accountability', this volume

[43] Ferguson, above n16.

[44] B Garrett and J Ashley, *Federal Organizational Prosecution Agreements*, University of Virginia School of Law, at lib.law.virginia.edu/Garrett/prosecution_agreements/home.suphp.

[45] J McCloy, *The Great Oil Spill* (New York, Chelsea House, 1976).

Sword of Damocles.[46] There is also strong evidence from the United States that when a full-time resident inspector is located at a coal mine with a corner-cutting safety culture, the best of these resident inspectors work with unions and local communities to challenge that safety culture in a way not dissimilar to the corporate cultural work of McCloy at Gulf. Mines selected for having an unusually high risk profile in the US were put into the resident inspector program; these mines finished with accident and fatality rates that were well below the national average.[47] For the same reason that restorative justice is an evidence-based idea for improving regulatory outcomes,[48] the reform we have seen in South Korea, Australia and beyond since the Asian Financial Crisis of tax authorities like the Australian Taxation Office and securities regulators like ASIC basing a resident supervisor in the corporate headquarters of many firms is also a good idea. In practice, however, these 'key client managers' routinely succumb to a client service mentality and eschew the challenge of being the irritant to the corporate culture that McCloy was at Gulf. Or worse, they can become merely a post-box from regulatory HQ, delivering advice on new rules and policies.

One check on this risk of capture can be bounty programs for whistleblowers, a prospect that Justin O'Brien also signals.[49] Empowered whistleblowers pose the danger to a resident financial supervisor who is overly comfortable with an abusive corporate culture, the danger of revealing something the supervisor failed to expose. More variegated checks and balances as a way of thinking about the separation of powers is the key idea here, where separated private powers can be just as useful as separated public powers.[50] There are many ways of doing this. For example, there is a current strategic policy conversation in Canberra about experimenting with private contracting of tax audit combined with contracting to a different firm measurement of the effectiveness of different private auditors and their outcomes compared with those achieved by state auditors. One advantage of such a privatization could be that it would provide a more independent check on ATO key client managers who were slothful or captured. Yet another option is a corporate policy, perhaps mandated by law, that any individual who observes a breach of any corporate ethics policy must not only report it to their supervisor. If they do not receive a written report back from their supervisor that either concludes that no breach occurred or indicates what has been done to fix it, the employee is then in breach of the ethics policy if she does not report both the original alleged breach *and the failure to hear back* on its resolution to the Board Audit Committee.[51] Given that Board Audit Committees in most countries mandate outsiders whose job it is to challenge the ethics of the corporate culture, a policy that forces a free route to the top prevents middle managers protecting top management from the taint of knowledge of illegality.

---

[46] For a discussion of this aspect of the Canberra Restorative Justice experiments led by Lawrence Sherman and Heather Strang and for a wider discussion of the criminological literature on the Sword of Damocles, see J Braithwaite, *Restorative Justice and Responsive Regulation*, (Oxford, Oxford University Press, 2002) 117–122.

[47] J Braithwaite, *To Punish or Persuade: Enforcement of Coal Mine Safety* (Albany, State University of New York Press, 1985) 82–83.

[48] J Latimer, C Dowden and D Muise, *The Effectiveness of Restorative Justice Practices: A Meta-Anlysis (Ottawa: Department of Justice, Canada, 2001)*; Braithwaite above n46; L. Sherman and H. Strang, *Restorative Justice, The Evidence* (The Smith Institute, 2007).

[49] O'Brien above n42.

[50] J Braithwaite 'On Speaking Softly and Carrying Big Sticks: Neglected Dimensions of a Republican Separation of Powers' (1997) 47 *University of Toronto Law Journal* 305.

[51] The Exxon corporation had and probably still have a policy to this effect. Interviews with the Controller, General Counsel and Auditor-General of Exxon Corporation, New York.

What formal western law lacks when it applies techniques such as deferred prosecution is a philosophy of why allowing justice as repair and redemption should be the mainline response even when doing so involves a breach of the principle of proportional punishment. A restorative justice philosophy allows us to accept that if a victim wishes to forgive in return for some other dimension of justice beyond proportional sanctioning, after discussing the option with other stakeholders, this can be just. Again, there is nothing new or radical in this approach. Islamic law and most forms of indigenous law across the world allow victims to forgive even murder after a ritual of healing and exchange of gifts if that is the justice their family wants. It is western criminal law jurisprudence that sees forgiveness as selling justice short. Western legal traditionalists obsessed with proportionality of punishment must now confront the recent criminological evidence that forgiveness can greatly reduce the suffering of victims,[52] can reduce crime and violence,[53] including financial crime.[54]

We need the greater frequency of formal criminal enforcement of financial crime that would be allowed by reforms 1 and 2. Restorative deliberation might also be considered because it is quicker and cheaper, being based on consensual deliberation among the stakeholders in a breach of law *or ethics*. This also means it can be deployed on a wide front compared with costly litigation, and for early intervention, as soon as any stakeholder asserts a credible challenge to the ethics of a corporate culture. Because it is cheaper, preventative and open to non-zero-sum solutions that leave both the corporation and its victims better off, restorative justice can improve the performance of an economy. We need a restorative justice that creates more participatory (and reconciliatory) spaces where many players of the banking game can engage in ethical deliberation about something that allegedly went wrong and how stakeholders can be actively responsible for a future that prevents recurrence. This contrasts with the western legal tradition's approach of holding wrongdoers passively responsible for the past, as traversed elegantly in Dixon's discussion of the alternatives of reactive fault, preventive fault and corporate ethos in Chapter 13.[55]

---

[52]   C Coyle and R Enright, 'Forgiveness Intervention with Post-Abortion Men' (1997) 65 *Journal of Consulting and Clinical Psychology* 1042; S Freedman and R Enright, 'Forgiveness as an Intervention Goal with Incest Survivors' (1996) 64 *Journal of Consulting and Clinical Psychology* 983; M McCullough, E Worthington and K Rachal, 'Interpersonal Forgiving in Close Relationships' (1997) 19 *Journal of Personality and Social Psychology*, 43; C Witvliet, T Ludwig and K Vander Laan, 'Granting Forgiveness or Harboring Grudges: Implications for Emotion, Physiology and Health' (2001) 12 *Psychological Science* 117; E Worthington and M Scherer, 'Forgiveness is an Emotion-Focused Coping Strategy that can Reduce Health Risks and Promote Health Resilience: Theory, Review, and Hypotheses' (2004) 19 *Psychology and Health,* 385; H Wallace, J Exline and R Baumeister, 'Interpersonal Consequences of Forgiveness: Does Forgiveness Deter or Encourage Repeat Offences' (2008) 44 *Journal of Experimental Social Psychology* 453; C Struthers, J Eaton, N Shirvani, M Georghiou and E Edell, 'The Effect of Preemptive Forgiveness and a Transgressor's Responsibility on Shame, Motivation to Reconcile and Repentance' (2008) 30 *Basic and Applied Social Psychology* 130; BR Kelln and JH Ellard, 'An Equity Theory Analysis of the Impact of Forgiveness and Retribution on transgressor Compliance' (1999) 25 *Personality and Social Psychology Bulletin* 864.

[53]   E Ahmed and J Braithwaite 'Forgiveness, Shaming, Shame and Bullying' (2013) 38 *Australian and New Zealand Journal of Criminology* 298; E Ahmed and V Braithwaite, 'Forgiveness, Reconcilation and Shame: Three Key Variables in Reducing School Bullying' (2006) 62 *Journal of Social Issues* 347.

[54]   K Murphy and I Helmer 'Testing the Importance of Forgiveness for Reducing Repeat Offending' (2013) 46 *Australian and New Zealand Journal of Criminology* 142.

[55]   O Dixon, 'Corporate Criminal Liability: The Influence of Corporate Culture' in this volume also discusses helpfully both the potential for catalyzing ethical deliberation and the legal limits of the guidance for preparation of a compliance plan set out in Australian Standard 3806–2006 (AS 3806) under four broad sets of principles: commitment; implementation; monitoring and measuring; and continual improvement.

Courtroom deliberation and backroom deals with prosecutors in contrast are thin on participatory ethical conversation and settle for passive responsibility for past wrongs. Michael Legg's chapter suggests that this is also true of the frequent failure of class actions to catalyse culture change.[56] Critical conversations with outsiders are important because, as David Westbrook points out,[57] people and organizations who chase money are not always good at knowing thyself: 'the financial world is necessarily somewhat blind to itself.' From the perspective of a restorative justice philosophy, this is the problem with the way deferred prosecution agreements and Corporate Integrity Agreements in the US have been negotiated in practice as backroom deals. The negotiation of enforceable undertakings in Australia has been more restorative at times, but far from consistently so.[58]

Restorative justice can help overcome formal law's scapegoating of those incompetent enough to leave themselves vulnerable to conviction beyond reasonable doubt. Scapegoating happens in corporate criminal law because senior individuals who share culpability for the crime are granted immunity in return for testimony against the selected scapegoat. When the defendant attempts to accuse them of the greater culpability, the court reminds her that it is she who is on trial. No such discipline applies in the restorative justice circle of course, in which those who turn against a scapegoat can find their culpability greatly exposed.[59] This book also shows that with a bank which is too big to fail it is important to protect a criminal corporation from a conviction that will disqualify it from a banking licence.[60] So the criminal corporation will agree to a civil penalty in return for testimony from it that turns on the criminalized individual scapegoat (while whitewashing its corporate culture in collusion with the prosecutor). So the restorative justice philosopher argues that corporate criminal law willfully creates a fiction of proportionality in a legal ritual designed to comfort the citizenry that the rule of law is not always asleep at the wheel of the justice machine.

Consider the bank, law firm or accounting firm that has made a corporate cultural contribution to financial crime and seeks to finger a fall guy to throw to baying media. The restorative justice philosopher has an interesting response. It is to praise the bank or the gatekeeping firm for its diligence in turning over the rocks to reveal culpability within its organization. The regulator invites the 'rogue partner' of the law firm who is about to be thrown to the media to a restorative justice circle with all the partners in attendance. The 'rogue partner' is encouraged to bring along supporters that would usually include their family, friends from the office and older mentors who are now retired. The latter can be robust participants in a conversation in which it is argued that the ethics of the firm have changed, that this 'rogue partner' is a scapegoat who was actually enacting the corporate culture of the firm in a way he and his supervisors have done in prior cases. Such testimony is not ruled out of order under the holistic justice norms of restorative justice.[61]

A restorative justice approach is therefore useful for jump starting ethical deliberation among professional stakeholders, such as lawyers, accountants and compliance professionals, who mostly have lower levels of culpability than the principals who stuff the cash in

---

[56] M Legg 'Class Actions and Regulating Culture in Financial Organisations: Observations from a Comparison of US and Australian Bank Class Actions', this volume.

[57] D Westbrook 'The Culture of Financial Institutions: The Influence of Political Economy' in this volume.

[58] Parker above n38.

[59] For a case study of this happening and a discussion of this issue, see Braithwaite above n46, 47–49.

[60] See O'Brien above n42.

[61] Braithwaite above n46, Chapter 8.

their pockets. More commonly, their failing is what Steve Mark and Tahlia Gordon call 'ethical blindness'.[62]   Formal law tends to let the lawyers off, almost always. As Seumus Miller's chapter argues,[63] gatekeepers have preventive leverage. Sadly though, the potential of that gatekeeping leverage is frequently missing in the most devastating cases of financial malfeasance. Even so, the situation would be even worse if gatekeepers did not exist. As we have seen, competition between professions in the advice markets of booms can become an ethical race to the bottom.[64] A more participatory, deliberative form of professional regula-tion over the long haul is illustrated by the beginning New South Wales has made to driving down ethics complaints against lawyers with conversational management-based regulation mediated by 'legal practitioner directors' and self-assessment that seeks to catalyse culture change, as discussed in the chapter by Mark and Gordon.[65]

5. Privatised enforcement as a check on corrupted and captured regulatory states.

This book argues that the most fatal flaw of any approach akin to points 1–4 above is that they fail to solve the problem that the regulatory state can be as corrupted and as afflicted with diagnosed pathologies as banks themselves. Seumus Miller's chapter characterises this as 'who guards the guardians'.[66] Because public enforcement is regularly captured by the ethics and the hegemony of finance capitalism, a radical privatization of enforcement is one possible check on public enforcement. This is an example of a more general approach to the dilemma of what to do when public guardians are ordered in a hierarchy and each new guardian we appoint to guard guardians below is itself corrupted. A solution is to abandon arraying guardians in a hierarchy. Instead, we can array guardians in a circle where every guardian is accountable to every other guardian (as much as possible). Then the guardian-ship fish is not vulnerable to rotting from the head down. The guardianship of one rotten guardian can be cross-checked by the lateral guardianship of many other guardians who are all guarding one another. This is part of the idea of guardianship in a restorative justice circle. It can make a police officer vulnerable to the guardianship of a mother in the circle who accosts the police about excessive force in the arrest of her son. If she speaks up in an attempt to do this in a courtroom, she will be silenced. This is because it is the job of someone else in the police and Ombudsman hierarchy to hold the police to account for heavy-handedness.

After Rudolf Guiliani's prosecutions on Wall Street quarter of a century ago, there was reason to be hopeful that public prosecution was on an upward trajectory of enforcement against the powerful. Some of Guiliani's techniques were crude but effective. His team would come across evidence of the crime of some comparatively minor malefactor within a target corporation. They would sit him down, say gotcha, promise immunity if he can provide testimony against a bigger fish; then that bigger fish still would turn on an even bigger fish who would be turned against a bigger fish still. This approach led Guiliani's team up to Donald Levine and Michael Milkin. We glimpse a remarkable failure to follow this approach in the documentary feature film *Inside Story.* The madam of a Wall Street brothel disclosed that she had credit cards from major Wall Street firms on which she was authorised to record prostitution services as 'payments to compliance consultants'! Then

---

[62] S Mark and T Gordon, 'Regulating the Legal Profession: A Prototype for Change', this volume.
[63] Miller above n4.
[64] Braithwaite above n21.
[65] Mark and Gordon above n62.
[66] Miller above n4.

she reveals that no law enforcement authorities had asked to examine these credit card records. If US law enforcement were serious about putting Wall Street Criminals behind bars it would have used the Guiliani strategy. A comparatively minor credit card fraud of this kind is ideal for sitting someone down to say you will be going to jail for the fraud and you will suffer the shame of your family knowing your lurid motivation for the fraud unless you give me the evidence of more major fraud against a bigger fish in your organization. Then hopefully moving up from that fish to something genuinely major.

Why would prosecutors in 2008 fail to follow the same simple approach that worked so well after 1987? Perhaps they feared criticism for pursuing a minor case in a brothel when there were so many massive frauds. Perhaps they felt the Guiliani approach was crude and speculative about whether there would be a return, that a more synoptic approach that diagnosed who the big fish were would work. Perhaps they were simply less aggressive than Guiliani. After some public backlash against President Reagan's deregulatory politics there was a niche for a Republican presidential hopeful like Guiliani to get tough on Wall Street.

Whatever the reason for prosecutorial timidity in this case, we can agree that prosecutorial aggression is consistently missing around the globe when it comes to targeting the big end of town. The most simple general reason is that it does not look good for prosecutors to lose a lot and if they run cases targeting the big end of town they can lose big and often. The main reason that defendants get off in major corporate crime cases is that the defence has better access to inside information than the prosecution.[67] The False Claims Act 1986 became the reform that has been most effectively used by prosecutors to win major corporate fraud cases because it draws out whistleblowers with the inducement of large payouts if they take a fraud case to a False Claims Act law firm and persuade them to underwrite private enforcement action to get a share of the whistleblower payout. Hence, it was a reform that simultaneously dissolved the two biggest obstacles–access to insider knowledge of crime and public prosecutor timidity that was resolved by private prosecutors stepping in where public prosecutors feared to tread.

It is not the purpose of this paper to retrace the pros and cons, the best ways to design this privatization of law enforcement to protect rights and prevent vexatious litigation.[68] Suffice it to say that the genius of the dual plaintiff design of the False Claims Act reforms is that law firms mostly walk away from their client if the Justice Department declines to take over their case; they almost always do so if Justice delivers a credible retort to the law firm that theirs is a vexatious litigant and that Justice intends to go before the judge to argue that the reason the it declined to join this case was the belief that the case was vexatious. The False Claims Act reforms of 1986 were limited to fraud against the government, excluding tax fraud.

The extension of its bounty concept to crimes of finance, first in tax fraud and more recently for certain securities offences, has unfortunately been much more timid than the original, jettisoning the key ingredient of the dual plaintiff design. The IRS and SEC successfully lobbied the Obama administration to forbid private prosecutions for tax and securities fraud bounties in cases where the state chose not to take on the prosecution. In this, the IRS and SEC and their political masters showed that their prime interest was in avoiding egg

---

[67] P Bucy, 'Private Justice' (2002) 76 *Southern California Law Review* 1; P Bucy, 'Information as a Commodity in the Regulatory World' (2002) 39 *Houston. Law Review.* 905; P Bucy, 'Games and Stories: Game Theory and the Civil False Claims Act' (2004) 31 *Florida State University Law Review* 603; P Bucy, 'Game Theory and the Civil False Claims Act: Iterated Games and Close-Knit Groups' (2004) 35 *Loyola University of Chicago Law Journal* 1021.

[68] See Bucy's papers ibid for a rich treatment of these issues.

on their faces from rebuffing a corporate crime case that a private prosecutor then proved. They were less interested in increasing enforcement effectiveness against financial crime.

As a general proposition, the best way to fight the capture and corruption of public prosecutors and regulators is with hybrid public-private enforcement where the private regulator is a check on the capture or corruption of the public regulator.[69] One reason for regulators like the SEC and IRS to resist the dual plaintiff False Claims Act design is that they lack the litigation budget for all these cases. They also worry about privatized litigation causing systemic risk in an attack on a key bank, though they can manage this by taking over the litigation. These problems are best managed by offering restorative justice to most securities offenders who beat the whistleblower to confess to the SEC. Indeed, this policy would motivate an avalanche of confession from firms willing to foil their whistleblower by contritely confronting the deficits of their compliance culture with the SEC.[70]

6. Responsive regulation implies growing investment in regulation.
Should we conclude that because regulatory bureaucracies, enforcement staffs, and cases investigated have grown, increased investment in regulatory infrastructure is irrelevant to solving financial problems? Regulators and their powers have not grown in proportion to growth in the number of bank transactions, to the variety of financial instruments and organizational forms and to the sophistication of the financial engineering. Regulatory growth and innovation must be responsive to business growth and innovation. In eras when financial engineering becomes more complex, growth in derivatives accelerates, regulators cannot begin to understand what is happening without investing in more and better people, better management, better information technology.

This is not to say that investing more in regulation will work if the wrong kind of investment is made, for example an investment that is purely technocratic and oblivious to culture and ethical renewal. It is to say that it is difficult to regulate an industry that is bigger, more complex and cleverer at contriving complexity without a regulator that is bigger and cleverer. This is a necessary but not a sufficient condition for crisis prevention.

III   CONCLUSION

David Campbell and Joan Loughrey[71] argue that we should not be so radical in what we ask of business as to aim for markets that are not driven by enlightened self-interest. One of Campbell and Loughrey's lessons from Adam Smith is that the interest in making profits is a great driver of invention and efficiency. Therefore this is a driver we should want to strengthen rather than weaken. It is also something we should want to steer, for example, to compliance with the Financial Stability Board's Principles and Standards on Sound Compensation so that bonuses are deferred for three years and coupled with clawback provisions to steer self-interest to long-term profitability, as discussed in Ferguson's chapter.[72] Adam Smith was also

---

[69] See I Ayres and J Braithwaite, *Responsive Regulation: Transcending the De-regulation Debate* (New York, Oxford, 1992) Chapters 3 and Conclusion.

[70] See the discussion of this issue in J Braithwaite, *Regulatory Capitalism: How it Works, Ideas for Making it Work Better* (Cheltenham, Edward Elgar, 2008) Chapter 3.

[71] Campbell and Loughrey above n20.

[72] Ferguson above n16.

wise, Campbell and Loughrey conclude, about moral sentiments as things we should want to strengthen. This chapter has argued for stronger regulatory institutions that form stronger moral sentiments, which are more imperative when markets become stronger. We can be better off when the creativity and energy of markets is harnessed to solve a wider range of problems. Markets in technologies of carbon emission reduction are a good example. But if some things in life are ethically good and others ethically bad, however good and bad are defined, greater vibrancy of markets will engender both the more efficient and innovative production of goods and the more efficient and innovative production of bads.[73] So the progressively more vibrant market economy leaders want demands stronger regulation. At least it does if we wish to reap the benefits of markets in virtue while curbing the excesses of markets in vice.

This book helps us to see in a more complex way how to do this. It does not necessarily mean proportionate growth in the number of rules and the severity and frequency of punishment for regulatory infractions. It can mean regulators who are cleverer at harnessing and nurturing the moral sentiments in corporate cultures, regulators who dispense more emotionally intelligent justice, regulators who engender rich business engagement over the moral and legal principles that should animate financial law.

The additional take in this concluding chapter is that smart regulation[74] will:

(a) constantly grow in a way that is responsive to flux in business realities; continually writing new rules when old ones become obsolete or are gamed;
(b) responsively refine principles that justify those rules, cover their gaps and contradictions;
(c) continuously create new spaces where ethical conversation around those principles can be engaged through means like deferred prosecutions that lead to external monitors, resident inspectors, privatized auditors, who are assessed according to how meaningfully they challenge unethical corporate cultures and engage outside audiences with that contestation;
(d) deliver variegated forms of justice that are meaningful to victims of financial exploitation through restorative justice in circumstances where punishment proportionate to the harm is impossible;
(e) displace passive with active responsibility[75] and thereby constitute cultures of ethical commitment where the combination of ethical contestation of principles and restorative dialogue among business, gatekeepers and citizens can be made to work;
(f) contest capture of regulators by third parties in civil society, the professions and government, including privatized law enforcers.

All these options are richly opened up in this book as checks that might be layered to deliver greater redundancy to the pursuit of the good and the checking of the bad in corporate cultures. Most fundamentally, we need a democracy with more robust and relevant contestation of what is good and bad about corporate cultures.[76]

---

[73] This is the argument first laid out in the introduction and then more deeply explored in the rest of the book, J. Braithwaite, above n21. As Gilligan's chapter above n1 also implies, regulatory competition can also be either competition in regulatory goods or in regulatory bads.

[74] A term adopted from Gunningham and Grabosky's book of that name because I hope the ambition here complements the ambition of that book, see N Gunningham and P Grabosky, *Smart Regulation: Designing Environmental Policy* (Oxford Clarendon Press, 1998).

[75] Braithwaite above n46, 129-130, 132-134.

[76] See the development of the republican ideal of a contestatory democracy that maximizes freedom as non-domination in P Pettit, *Republicanism* (Oxford, Oxford University Press, 1997).